TIMES SQUARE
BROADWAY

THE
HANDY
NEW YORK
CITY
ANSWER
BOOK

Chris Barsanti

VISIBLE
INK
PRESS

Detroit

THE HANDY NEW YORK CITY ANSWER BOOK

Visible Ink Press®
43311 Joy Rd., #414
Canton, MI 48187–2075

Visible Ink Press is a registered trademark of Visible Ink Press LLC.

Most Visible Ink Press books are available at special quantity discounts when purchased in bulk by corporations, organizations, or groups. Customized printings, special imprints, messages, and excerpts can be produced to meet your needs. For more information, contact Special Markets Director, Visible Ink Press, www.visibleink.com, or 734–667–3211.

Managing Editor: Kevin S. Hile
Art Director: Mary Claire Krzewinski
Typesetting: Marco DiVita
Proofreaders: Larry Baker and Janet Hile
Indexer: Shoshana Hurwitz

Cover images: Thule symbol by NsMn (Wikicommons), Rosy Cross of the Golden Dawn (public domain); all others, Shutterstock.

Library of Congress Cataloging–in–Publication Data

Names: Barsanti, Chris, author.
Title: The handy New York City answer book / Chris Barsanti.
Description: Detroit, MI : Visible Ink Press, 2017. | Series: Handy answers series
Identifiers: LCCN 2016058321| ISBN 9781578595860 (paperback) | ISBN 9781578596553 (epub) | ISBN 9781578596546 (pdf)
Subjects: LCSH: New York (N.Y.)–Miscellanea. | New York (N.Y.)–History–Miscellanea. | BISAC: HISTORY / United States / State & Local / Middle Atlantic (DC, DE, MD, NJ, NY, PA). | HISTORY / United States / State & Local / General. | HISTORY / United States / General. | EDUCATION / History.
Classification: LCC F128.3 .B37 2017 | DDC 974.7/1–dc23
LC record available at https://lccn.loc.gov/2016058321

Printed in the United States of America

10 9 8 7 6 5 4 3 2 1

About the Author

Chris Barsanti is the author of *Where New York City: Eat!, Filmology: A Movie-a-Day Guide to the Movies You Need to Know, The Sci-Fi Movie Guide*, and the *Eyes Wide Open* film guide series. He is co-author of *Monty Python FAQ,* and he has written for a variety of publications, including *PopMatters,* the *Chicago Tribune, Playboy, The Millions,* the *Virginia Quarterly Review, Publishers Weekly,* and *Where New York*. He earned a master's degree in journalism from Northwestern University, and he resides in New York City.

ALSO FROM VISIBLE INK PRESS

The Handy Math Answer Book,
   2nd edition
by Patricia Barnes-Svarney and Thomas
   E. Svarney
ISBN: 978-1-57859-373-6

The Handy Military History Answer
   Book
by Samuel Willard Crompton
ISBN: 978-1-57859-509-9

The Handy Mythology Answer Book,
by David A. Leeming, Ph.D.
ISBN: 978-1-57859-475-7

The Handy New York City Answer Book
by Chris Barsanti
ISBN: 978-1-57859-586-0

The Handy Nutrition Answer Book
by Patricia Barnes-Svarney and Thomas
   E. Svarney
ISBN: 978-1-57859-484-9

The Handy Ocean Answer Book
by Patricia Barnes-Svarney and Thomas
   E. Svarney
ISBN: 978-1-57859-063-6

The Handy Personal Finance Answer
   Book
by Paul A. Tucci
ISBN: 978-1-57859-322-4

The Handy Philosophy Answer Book
by Naomi Zack
ISBN: 978-1-57859-226-5

The Handy Physics Answer Book,
   2nd edition
By Paul W. Zitzewitz, Ph.D.
ISBN: 978-1-57859-305-7

The Handy Politics Answer Book
by Gina Misiroglu
ISBN: 978-1-57859-139-8

The Handy Presidents Answer Book,
   2nd edition
by David L. Hudson
ISB N: 978-1-57859-317-0

The Handy Psychology Answer Book,
   2nd edition
by Lisa J. Cohen
ISBN: 978-1-57859-508-2

The Handy Religion Answer Book,
   2nd edition
by John Renard
ISBN: 978-1-57859-379-8

The Handy Science Answer Book,
   4th edition
by The Carnegie Library of Pittsburgh
ISBN: 978-1-57859-321-7

The Handy State-by-State Answer Book
by Samuel Willard Crompton
ISBN: 978-1-57859-565-5

The Handy Supreme Court Answer
   Book
by David L Hudson, Jr.
ISBN: 978-1-57859-196-1

The Handy Technology Answer Book
by Naomi Bobick and James Balaban
ISBN: 978-1-57859-563-1

The Handy Weather Answer Book,
   2nd edition
by Kevin S. Hile
ISBN: 978-1-57859-221-0

PLEASE VISIT THE "HANDY ANSWERS" SERIES
WEBSITE AT WWW.HANDYANSWERS.COM.

Acknowledgments

I would like to gratefully acknowledge the assistance of the estimable Barry Moreno, whose invaluable help got me started in the right direction, the staff of the New York Public Library for providing the needed resources without which this book would never have been completed, Roger Jänecke for giving me the opportunity to take on such a fascinating project, and of course my friends and family for all their patience and support.

Table of Contents

ACKNOWLEDGMENTS *vi*

PHOTO SOURCES *ix*

TIMELINE *xi*

INTRODUCTION *xvii*

THE BASICS ... 1

Climate, Flora, and Fauna (3) ... People (10) ... Government and Politics (15) ... Business and the Economy (21) ... Transportation (27)

PRE-COLONIAL TIMES THROUGH THE REVOLUTIONARY ERA ... 33

Pre-Colonial New York (33) ... The Dutch and British Colonial Years (36) ... The Revolutionary War (55) ... After Independence (66)

THE CIVIL WAR ERA THROUGH THE GILDED AGE ... 91

Slavery and the Civil War (91) ... Industrialization and Immigration (97) ... The Gilded Age (116)

THE GREAT DEPRESSION TO A NEW CENTURY ... 137

World War II and the Postwar Era (146) ... The Sixties to 9/11 (155) ... Rebuilding and Moving Forward (182)

MANHATTAN ... 191

Financial District/Battery Park/Civic Center (192) ... Chinatown/Little Italy/Lower East Side/Tribeca/SoHo (206) ... Greenwich Village/East Village (211) ... Union Square/Flatiron/Madison Square/Gramercy (218) ... Chelsea/Garment District/Hudson Yards (225) ... Times Square/Midtown West/Hell's Kitchen (231) ... Midtown East (236) ... Central Park (244) ... Lincoln Square/Upper West Side (247) ... Upper East Side (250) ... Morningside Heights/Harlem (255) ... Upper Manhattan (261)

THE BRONX, BROOKLYN, QUEENS, AND STATEN ISLAND ... 267

The Bronx (267) ... Brooklyn (273) ... Queens (286) ... Staten Island (291)

SPORTS AND NIGHT LIFE ... 305

Sports (305) ... Food and Dining (316) ... Bars and Nightlife (330)

THE ARTS ... 339

Theater (339) ... Music (347) ... Film and TV (354) ... Art (359) ... Writing (363)

MAYORS OF NEW YORK CITY ... 399
IDIOMS, SLANG, AND EXPRESSIONS ... 403
FOR FURTHER RESEARCH ... 407
INDEX ... 409

Photo Sources

Acme Newspictures: p. 149.

Alextrevelian 006 (Wikicommons): p. 208.

Keith Allison: p. 312.

Arad (Wikicommons): p. 252.

Aude (Wikicommons): p. 16.

Jessie Tarbox Beals: p. 393 (top).

Beyond My Ken (Wikicommons): p. 222.

Bibliothèque Nationale de France: p. 102.

Bjoertvedt (Wikicommons): p. 282.

Blacren (Wikicommons): p. 175.

Bloomberg Philanthropies: p. 184.

Brooklyn4083 (Wikicommons): p. 259.

Byron Company: p. 117.

Carol M. Highsmith Archive, Library of Congress: p. 163.

Kevin Case: p. 186.

Cflm008 (Wikicommons): p. 181.

Chensiyuan (Wikicommons): pp. 206, 219.

Cowles Communications, Inc.: p. 307.

Rob C. Croes: p. 170.

Francesco Dazzi: p. 17.

Ramon de la Fuente: p. 231.

Dmadeo (Wikicommons): p. 318.

Drivemaster King (Wikicommons): p. 62.

Pawel Drozd: p. 264.

Dutch National Archives, The Hague, Fotocollectie Algemeen Nederlands Persbureau: p. 381.

Farragutful (Wikicommons): p. 199.

George Grantham Bain Collection, Library of Congress: pp. 115, 129, 269.

Gryffindor (Wikicommons): p. 193.

Karl Gildemeister: p. 85.

Thomas Gimbrede: p. 45.

Gotanero (Wikicommons): p. 348.

Gottscho-Schleisner, Inc.: p. 68.

H. B. Hall: p. 56.

Jim Henderson: pp. 243, 254, 262, 298, 346 (right).

Heritage Auction Gallery: p. 372.

Oscar Hinrichs: p. 245.

Hybirdd (Wikicommons): p. 4.

Alex Israel: p. 355.

Joi Ito: p. 18.

JoeyJoJo86 (Wikicommons): p. 159.

JonathanRe (Wikicommons): p. 290, 314.

Library of Congress: p. 112.

Alex Lozupone: p. 344.

Matteo X (Wikicommons): p. 161.

Metropolitan Transportation Authority of the State of New York: pp. 8, 30.

Craig Michaud: p. 177.

Midtownguy2012 (Wikicommons): p. 133.

Rich Mitchell: p. 229.

MrPanyGoff (Wikicommons): p. 210.

NASA: p. 203.

National Archives and Records Administration: pp. 105, 118, 140, 364.

Timeline

Date	Event
1300	First evidence of agriculture by Lenape Indians in the New York area
1524	Giovanni di Verrazano the first European to sail into New York Harbor
1609	British explorer-for-hire Henry Hudson sails into New York Harbor, effectively claiming it for the Dutch
1624	Arrival of first group of settlers with the Dutch West India Company
1626	Manhattan "purchased" by the Dutch from local Indians for 60 guilders
1641	Kieft's War breaks out between the Dutch and Indians
1647	"Lord General" Peter Stuyvesant takes control of New Amsterdam
1655	Hundreds of Indians attack New Amsterdam at the start of the Peach War
1664	British army takes New Netherlands, renaming it New York
1665	Thomas Willet appointed first mayor of New York
1679	Slavery of Indians outlawed
1689	Peter Delanoy becomes New York's first elected mayor
1701	New York's best known pirate, William Kidd, is hanged in London
1712	The city's first slave uprising is swiftly and violently put down
1725	Publication of the city's first newspaper, the *New-York Gazette*
1736	New York's first fire house opens on Broad Street
1741	Mysterious fires stoke fears of a phantom Catholic-led slave rebellion, leading to preemptive tortures and executions
1754	King's College (later, Columbia University) is chartered
1756	French and Indian War breaks out
1765	New York hosts first Colonial Congress
1771	One-third of the population of Brooklyn are slaves

Date	Event
1776	The Continental Army is driven out of New York by British and Hessian troops
1776–83	British occupy New York
1785	The all-white New York Manumission Society founded, starting the city's abolitionist movement
1785–90	New York is the first capital of the United States of America
1788	Founding of Society of St. Tammany, later Tammany Hall
1789	George Washington inaugurated at City Hall, now Federal Hall, on Wall Street
1792	New York Stock Exchange established
1800	Population recorded at 79,216
1804	Former Treasury Secretary Alexander Hamilton shot dead in a duel with Vice President Aaron Burr just across the Hudson River in New Jersey
1809	Washington Irving's *A History of New York* is published
1811	Release of the Commissioner's Plan, a radical street grid that will dramatically reconfigure New York for the future
1825	Erie Canal completed, connecting New York's markets to the American heartland
1827	Slavery abolished in New York state
1829	First hotel opened at Coney Island
1831	New York University built near Greenwich Village
1835	The Great Fire burns down a quarter of the city
	The New York Herald, the city's first popular tabloid, starts publication
1839	U.S. Navy seizes the slave ship *Amistad* off Long Island; its prisoners had revolted two months before and killed all crew members except for the navigator
1841	P.T. Barnum opens the American Museum on Broadway
	Charles Dickens visits New York
1845	Creation of New York Municipal Police Force
1850	Population reaches 696,115
1852	German-Jewish merchants, blocked from joining private clubs, form their own: the Harmonie Club
1853	Crystal Palace opens in Manhattan
1855	Walt Whitman publishes first edition of *Leaves of Grass*
1857	First true global financial crisis decimates New York economy, leaving thousands unemployed
1859	First sections of Central Park open to the public
1860	Presidential candidate Abraham Lincoln's speech at Cooper Union electrifies crowd and cements his status in the race
1861	Mayor Fernando Wood proposes that New York secede from Union
	Civil War breaks out

Date	Event
1863	The Draft Riots, the largest civic disturbance in the nation's history, convulse the city for a week
1865	160,000 New Yorkers take part in Abraham Lincoln's funeral procession through city
	Metropolitan Fire Department created
1870	Alfred Ely Beach opens the city's first subway
1871	After years of crippling graft, New York's most powerful political boss, William Tweed, is driven from power
	Protestant-Catholic Irish strife breaks out in the Orange Riot
1881	Department of Street Cleaning created to pick up all the garbage that the street-roaming pigs aren't ingesting
1882	Thomas Edison opens Pearl Street power station
1883	Brooklyn Bridge opens
1886	Completed Statue of Liberty revealed to public for the first time
1887	Passage of the Small Parks Act leads to many parks being built in crowded, lower-class neighborhoods
1888	New York's first skyscraper, the Tower Building, opens on Broadway
1889	Opening of Brooklyn Children's Museum, the world's first such institution
1890	Jacob Riis publishes *How the Other Half Lives*
1892	Ellis Island receives first immigrant
1896	First motion picture footage of New York captured on Herald Square
1898	Consolidation unites all five boroughs into a larger New York City
1900	Population hits 3,437,202
	Lower East Side becomes the world's most densely populated neighborhood
1902	Macy's moves uptown to Herald Square
1904	The *General Slocum* catches fire and sinks in the East River
	Interborough Rapid Transit underground railway begins operation
1905	Lombardi's opens, arguably invents American-style pizza
	The 5,200-seat Hippodrome, the largest theater in the world, opens on Sixth Avenue and 43rd Street
1907	Immigrants processed through Ellis Island peaks at 1.2 million in one year
1910	Pennsylvania Station, the largest in the nation, opens for business
1911	The Triangle Shirtwaist Factory Fire kills 145 workers, mostly young immigrant women
1913	First trains roll out of new Grand Central Terminal
	Completion of the 60-story Woolworth Building, the tallest building in the world
1916	Two million pounds of munitions stored on the Black Tom peninsula near Jersey City detonate in an explosion that kills seven and is later blamed on German saboteurs

Date	Event
1917	United States enters World War I
	Nation's first civil rights march, the Silent Parade, held on Fifth Avenue
1920	Anarchist bombs the Wall Street headquarters of J. P. Morgan
	Prohibition begins
1921	Black vaudeville revue *Shuffle Along* opens on Broadway, launching careers of Paul Robeson and Josephine Baker
1925	F. Scott Fitzgerald publishes *The Great Gatsby*
	First issue of *The New Yorker* hits the streets
1927	267 shows produced on Broadway in one year
1928	Al Smith, born on the Lower East Side, becomes first Catholic presidential nominee
1929	Panic on Wall Street as stock market collapses; the Great Depression begins
1929–31	Castellammarese War rages between two powerful Mafia factions
1930	Empire State Building opens for business
1931	City's "Five Families" of organized crime form "The Commission" to settle differences in a more businesslike fashion
1932	Corruption-plagued Mayor Jimmy Walker steps down from office while on European vacation
	More than 1.5 million New Yorkers on public relief
	Mayor Jimmy Walker leads a 100,000-strong "Beer Parade" on Fifth Avenue, calling for an end to Prohibition
1933	Prohibition ends
	Fiorello LaGuardia wins the first of an unprecedented three mayoral elections
1934	Robert Moses consolidates control of region's parks and bridges, launching a transformative, decades-long infrastructure project
	The Bloody Mary enters circulation at the St. Regis's King Cole Bar
1938	"The Long Island Express" hurricane cuts a swath of devastation across the city, killing 17 on Long Island and ten in New York
1939	New York World's Fair opens in an infamous Queens trash dump rehabilitated into a park
1942	German spies captured on Long Island
1943	Race riot erupts in Harlem after a black soldier is shot by police; days of looting and rioting follow
	Oklahoma! premieres on Broadway; its innovative style in which the songs actually advance the story became the model for American musicals that followed
1945	B-25 bomber crashes into the Empire State Building, killing 13
1950	Population reaches 7,891,984
1952	Construction begins on Robert Moses's Cross-Bronx Expressway, eventually displacing 250,000 people

Date	Event
1956	*West Side Story* opens
1957	Brooklyn's Benjamin Eisenstadt invents the first successful artificial sweetener, Sweet 'N Low®
	Brooklyn Dodgers move to Los Angeles; New York Giants move to San Francisco
1962	Andy Warhol's first one-man show
1965	Brooklyn Heights city's first historic district
1970	First Christopher Street Gay Liberation Day march—later, the Pride Parade—commemorates previous year's uprising at the Stonewall bar
1970	On April 22, the first Earth Day was celebrated by millions around the nation. In New York, all cars and trucks were banned for two hours from much of Manhattan.
1972	The Knapp Commission releases its blockbuster 264-page report detailing the extensive network of corruption infecting the city's police department
1973	Completion of second tower of the World Trade Center
1975	New York narrowly avoids bankruptcy
1977	A 25-hour blackout leads to widespread looting and chaos; some neighborhoods never recover
1980	Donald Trump's first high-profile project, the Grand Hyatt, opens
1982	One million people march in Central Park to call for an end to the nuclear arms race
1984	Crack epidemic hits New York
1987	Tom Wolfe publishes *The Bonfire of the Vanities*
1989	David Dinkins elected New York's first black mayor, defeating three-term incumbent Ed Koch
	Spike Lee's *Do the Right Thing* premieres
1990	New York records highest-ever number of murders in one year: 2,245
1994	New police commissioner Bill Bratton overhauls NYPD strategies; already-dropping crime rates start to plummet
1998	HBO premieres *Sex and the City*, a romantic comedy series based on the *New York Observer* column by Candace Bushnell parts of America reconsider their hatred of New York
2000	Population reaches 8,008,278
2001	Terrorists connected to the al-Qaeda network fly hijacked airliners into the World Trade Center, destroying both towers and killing thousands in the worst terrorist attack in American history
2003	New York's new 311 hotline for non-emergency questions opens
2006	Legendary punk club CBGB's closes with a final set by Patti Smith

Date	Event
2008	Lehman Brothers, founded in 1850, goes bankrupt in the collapse of the housing market
2009	After spending a record $102 million on his campaign, or about $175 a vote, "Mayor Mike" Bloomberg wins a third term
	The New York Yankees win their twenty-seventh World Series
2010	Plans to build a 13-story Islamic community center downtown are derailed after protesters term it the "Ground Zero Mosque"
2011	Protest group Occupy Wall Street takes over downtown park
2012	Hurricane Sandy hits the city, killing dozens
2014	Promising to narrow the gap between poor and wealthy, former city advocate Bill de Blasio elected mayor
2015	*Hamilton* premieres on Broadway
2016	After decrying rival Republican candidate Donald Trump's "New York values," Texas senator Ted Cruz is crushed in the New York primary

Introduction

New York is a sort of anthology of urban civilization.

—R. L. Duffus

Here I was in New York, city of prose and fantasy, of capitalist automation, its streets a triumph of cubism … more than any other city, it is the fullest expression of our modern age.

—Leon Trotsky

In New York, you can be a new man.

—Lin-Manuel Miranda, *Hamilton*

He had the true New Yorker's secret belief that people living anywhere else had to be, in some sense, kidding.

—John Updike, *Bech Is Back*

What is New York? One way to answer that question would be to ask Walt Whitman. After all, his inability to modulate his expressiveness is about on par with the average New Yorker's inability to stay silent if they overhear somebody being given wrong (to their mind, at least) directions. How would Whitman define the city? Per Brooklyn's poet laureate, in 1842 he called it "the great place of the western continent, the heart, the brain, the focus, the main spring, the pinnacle, the extremity, the no more beyond, of the New World."

Not everything stays the same, of course. Lingo shifts and mutates with the warp and woof of the times. This is particularly true of New York. But even though New Yorkers don't "take the papers," some will still go out to their corner deli to "get the papers." That's because no other city in America hosts as many voices clamoring to be heard, as many bullhorns for them to be heard, and as many things for them to talk about.

Why is that?

At the risk of indulging in superlatives about a place that naturally lends itself to such things, New York is the true capital of America. Like America, it was born in conflict and commerce and lives in a mix of prose and poetry.

When the first Europeans settled at the southern tip of a wooded and marshy island called Mannahatta, they marveled at its beauty. But they also knew a good thing when they saw it: sheltered and with a deep harbor, there was rich farmland, plentiful beaver for trading, and no rival European settlers. It wasn't long before the Lenape tribespeople who lived quietly in a few scattered villages here would be pushed out. Slaves were imported by the thousands. A remorseless street grid leveled and smoothed out Manhattan's irregularities, turning most of the island into right angles. Beautiful buildings are erected, reveled in, and then smashed down just a few decades later. Since signing their first trading agreement under a tree on Wall Street in 1792, the financial captains of downtown are treated as heroes when flooding the city with money in flush years, and villains when the markets turn south. But they are never asked to stop. Not much in New York is ever allowed to stand in the way of progress. And progress just about always means commerce.

But while the American way of work, with its long hours and skimpy vacations, is alive and well in New York, this is also the rare American city that takes its leisure time seriously. For centuries, this has been the beating heart of national creativity. Almost every American play of note originated on Broadway or on off-Broadway stages. No other city boasts as many writers or bookstores. Every major American musical genre of the twentieth century—from jazz to disco and punk—was either born or perfected here. And the city's collection of well-appointed museums is truly an embarrassment of riches. Just as importantly, the city has always been flush with the nation's richest collection of restaurants, cafés, clubs, and bars for its creative spirits to congregate in.

Curiously for such a fast-paced city, New York took its time getting started. Boston and Philadelphia were quicker out the gate in the early colonial years, with more families of note and a semblance of culture. Until the conclusion of the Revolutionary War, New York was still mostly a hodgepodge of randomly assorted buildings below Wall Street. There were only a few thousand inhabitants and not much culture to speak of.

But once the city got going, particularly after the opening of the Erie Canal in 1825 kicked its economy into overdrive, it was nearly impossible to stop. Not long after that came the first wave of immigrants. Other American cities like Chicago and Miami have been changed by large influxes of immigrants, but no other city has welcomed them in such large numbers and for so long a time. Whether one is talking about the Irish, Jews, and Italians of the late-nineteenth and early twentieth centuries, or the Pakistanis, Mexicans, Chinese, and Dominicans of more recent years, each group has been changed by the city, and changed it in return.

Nothing stays still in New York for long. The woman who told *New York* magazine in 2012 that she felt like she'd moved "when all I did was stay at home" expressed the feelings of just about anybody who has spent more than a couple decades here. Because of that constant churn of new people, new trends, new buildings, and new everything, New York is a city that crackles with the excitement of the new. Most of the older things that have survived have managed to do so for a reason: they had to *fight* to keep their place.

The churn can be exhausting. Everywhere in America you can find New York expats who gave up on the hustle and decamped for calmer, quieter surroundings. (Not that real New Yorkers can ever quite change, though. New Yorkers who leave the city, even temporarily, tend never to be impressed with anything, or anybody.)

It can also make New York a lonely place, an emotion that Stephen Sondheim (1930–) put music and lyrics to in his 1970 musical, *Company*: "It's a city of strangers / Some come to work, some to play." Decades earlier, Mark Twain (1835–1910) called it "a domed and steepled solitude, where the stranger is lonely in the midst of a million of his race."

But excitement and change is the coin of the realm in New York. It's part and parcel of what makes the city so vital to America.

Much of what will follow may seem inordinately tilted towards eruptions of violence and discontent. Riots, shootings, discontent, mobs, controversy, mayhem, corruption, protests, and yet more riots. There's a reason for this. It's not to show New York as some caricature of the teeming entrepôt where anything goes. New York is, in the title of Joanne Reitano's splendid short history of urban discontent, "The Restless City."

It's a restlessness that isn't just born of discontent, though. New York is a city that's always bursting with invention, ideas, and transition. It would be impossible, after all, to throw this many races, languages, faiths, beliefs, and theories into such a crowded archipelago of islands and not expect strife and change on a great scale.

More surprisingly is how well the city works, given all the headwinds against it. All of those chaotic elements have created the most unique city in America. No other urban area can boast as wide a variety of moods and places, from the fairytale splendor of Central Park to the clamor of Midtown's skyscraper canyons, the quiet, brownstone-lined streets of Brooklyn to the crowds on a hot summer's day at Coney Island. It's a city of small and peaceful enclaves, and massive high-rises, brought together in the forced intimacy of the subway.

New York is also the city where nearly all the strands woven together into American history can be found. The first great battle of the Revolutionary War was fought here. Slaves were brought to safety here by way of the Underground Railroad, while free blacks were kidnapped and sent into slavery. Socialists marched in the streets by the thousands. Robber barons and hedge fund kings created fortunes that could have purchased small nations. Innovations were pioneered here in everything from medicine and atomic science to abstruse financial trading instruments. Immigrants turned clusters of crowded buildings into ersatz recreations of their old villages, with traditions, languages, and cuisines little known elsewhere in America. Skyscrapers pierce the clouds while the streets below throng with people from all corners of the world speaking hundreds of languages and dancing the complicated minuet of New York sidewalks.

So what is New York? It's everything that comes to mind when you think of a city.

In *The Handy New York City Answer Book*, you will find out why.

THE BASICS

Where is New York?

New York City is centered around one of the world's great natural harbors, situated at the mouth of the Hudson River on the eastern seaboard of the United States. It is the only major American city located almost entirely on an archipelago of islands. The city is divided into five "boroughs," which were all once their own independent cities, and only one of them (the Bronx) is located on the mainland of the continental United States.

What is New York's landscape like?

The islands that make up the New York City area were mostly rearranged into their present shape after the end of the Wisconsin Glacial Stage roughly 18,000 years ago. When that massive sheet of ice, which covered almost the entire area except the lower part of Long Island, began to retreat, it left not only massive piles and ridges of rock but also dug out the channels like the East River and Spuyten Duyvil Creek into which the Atlantic Ocean flowed. The collection of deep and secure bays with hundreds of miles of coastline and rich oyster beds first made the New York area an attractive habitation for Indian tribes and again later for European colonists.

What are the five "boroughs" of New York?

- Bronx
- Brooklyn
- Manhattan
- Queens
- Staten Island

How large are each of the boroughs?

- Bronx—44 square miles (114 square kilometers)
- Brooklyn—81.8 square miles (211.9 square kilometers)
- Manhattan—23.7 square miles (61.4 square kilometers)
- Queens—112.2 square miles (290.6 square kilometers)
- Staten Island—60.2 square miles (155.9 square kilometers)

Why is New York called "The Big Apple"?

Of all New York's nicknames, the Big Apple is both the most familiar and the least understood. Even though it's graced the names of any number of establishments and T-shirts for decades, the average person couldn't tell you where the name came from. The

The five boroughs of New York City are Manhattan, Brooklyn, the Bronx, Queens, and Staten Island.

etymology is somewhat tangled. The term "big apple" was apparently used in the nineteenth century to denote a big or important thing or place. In addition, starting in the 1870s, newly bred, large, delicious red apples were highly desired items.

Also, in the early twentieth century the phrase was a popular betting term, meaning a sure thing. One theory has it that a racetrack columnist for the New York *Morning Telegraph* in the early 1920s began using the term in his columns after he overhead a New Orleans stablehand leaving for New York's racetracks say he was going to "the big apple." Not long after, the city's jazz musicians started using "the big apple" when referring to New York. The term truly hit the mainstream in the 1970s, when it was revived for use in a tourism campaign.

What is on the official seal of the city of New York?

The city's seal was first created around 1654. Like many designs of this kind, it's a semi-successful attempt to jam as many historically and culturally significant images into a small space in a way that is both evocative and authoritative. The centerpiece speaks heavily of the colony's early years: a windmill for the Dutch, barrels of flour for the city's export monopoly in the early years, and two beavers, whose furry pelts fueled the trade that was the economic lifeblood of the young city. Around those items are arrayed an Indian with a bow, an English sailor dropping a sounding line, an eagle, and the year "1625."

There have been modifications over the years. The eagle replaced a royal crown in 1784. The seal was originally dated 1686, the year that the city was given a charter from the king, then 1664 for the year that the English took possession of the city from the Dutch, and eventually 1625; the latter change was due in large part to the 1970s' lobbying of Paul O'Dwyer (1907–98), an Irish-born politician from Staten Island who didn't appreciate the attention being paid to England.

CLIMATE, FLORA, AND FAUNA

What is New York's weather like?

You would never know it to hear the population expostulate about the supposedly searing summers and icebox winters, but New York has one of the most moderated temperate climates of any major city in the United States. Boasting four distinct seasons, the city has a mild range of temperatures. The average low in January, the coldest month, is 26°F (–3°C) and the average high in July, the hottest month, is 83°F (28°C). Muggy August has traditionally been the month that everybody with the means to get out of the city for as long as possible, does.

The city gets about 54 inches (137 centimeters) of precipitation annually, spread pretty evenly throughout the year. Snow and rainfalls are measured by what's fallen in Central

3

Park, but as New Yorkers can tell you, the results can vary widely from there to the far ends of Staten Island and Queens. Snow falls are generally mild, though occasional winter storms have been known to blast through, like the great blizzard of March 1888, which dumped over 20 inches of snow on the city and killed upwards of 200 people.

Are there a lot of big storms?

Given its proximity to the Atlantic Ocean and the Jet Stream, New York is hit by more hurricanes than the nearest big cities like Boston (too far north) and Washington, D.C. (too far from the coast). Large hurricanes arrive every few decades on average—1938's Long Island Express

Hurricane Sandy caused a large power outage in New York City in 2012.

and 2012's Hurricane Sandy being among the most destructive recent examples—just about far enough apart for everybody to get a little too relaxed about preparing for the next one.

How many trees are there in New York?

According to the United States Forest Service, there are about 5.2 million trees in the metropolitan area. Their canopies shade about one-quarter of the city's surface. About 40 percent of them can be found in Queens, but the borough with the densest tree coverage per mile of sidewalk is Manhattan.

What is the most common tree in New York?

At last count, 168 species of trees were identified in New York, with ten of them accounting for three-fourths of the city's trees. The London planetree is the most commonly found, making up fifteen percent of the tree population. Originally created as a hybrid in London in 1645, the planetree is a popular choice for cities as it's a sturdy shade-giving tree with strong limbs and a proven ability to weather dirty air and drought. The next most common trees are the Norway maple (14%) and the Callery pear (11%).

Where is the oldest tree in New York?

There is of course no way to definitively answer this one way or the other. But after Peter Stuyvesant's (1610-1672) pear tree in the East Village was knocked down after standing at the same spot for over two centuries, the newest claimant to being the oldest tree in New York is widely believed to be the so-called Queens Giant. A 134-foot- (41-meter-) tall tulip tree, it is believed to be around 450 years old, thus predating the first European explorers to arrive in the area, making it not only the oldest tree but the oldest living thing in the city.

You can find it in one of the city's few old-growth forests along one of the trails in Queens' Alley Pond Park, a long narrow park near Douglas Plaza Mall bisected by the Long Island, Grand Central, and Cross Island highways. Oddly the Queens Giant, which has a hollowed-out interior large enough for people to step inside, isn't at this time marked off or protected in any way.

What are some of the animals that used to live on Manhattan?

- Beavers: Pushed out by the early nineteenth century, started to return in the 2000s.
- Black bears: One was killed in the area that became Maiden Lane in downtown Manhattan in 1630.
- Wolves: Cleared from Inwood in the 1720s.

Why is there a statue of a coyote in the Bronx?

On a grassy corner of Van Cortlandt Park in the Bronx, visitors might think they see a dog perched on top of a rock. In fact, that is a bronze statue of a coyote peering eagerly south towards the rest of New York. Named "Major," the 1998 statue was inspired by a surprise occurrence in 1995 when two coyotes were found dead in the Bronx, one on the Major Deegan Expressway. The plaque notes that this was the first time coyotes had been spotted in the city since 1946, though there had also been at least one sighting the year before in the Bronx's Woodlawn Cemetery.

Do coyotes live in New York?

Yes. Eastern coyotes have been around New York state since the 1920s. This species, sometimes called "coydogs" by upstate New York residents, is believed by some to be a cross between either dogs and wolves or dogs and western coyotes. They travel and live alone, in pairs, or sometimes in small packs of three to four. After the Bronx sightings in the mid-1990s, coyotes were occasionally spotted everywhere from Riverside Park to Central Park, Queens, and even in the middle of the street in Battery Park City. They are believed to travel between the city's islands via train tunnels. Due to the coyotes' mostly nocturnal habits and natural wariness, they are often well established in an area before humans ever see one.

What animal was once a common sight on New York streets?

The preponderance of pigs in New York dates back to the early days of New Amsterdam, where pigs were allowed to wander at will. This infuriated Stuyvesant, who wrote a vituperative letter to city leaders in 1653 complaining about how pigs were damaging the new palisades thrown up to offer the colony some measure of protection. The ubiquity of pigs on the street continued into the nineteenth century, when Charles Dickens (1812-1870), in *American Notes*, made sarcastic note of their odd presence on otherwise civilized thoroughfares. By 1820, it was estimated that there were about twenty thousand pigs in the city, or about one for every five people.

5

Not exactly universally appreciated, pigs did serve a purpose in the urban ecosystem. In a time when the city's garbage removal system was still essentially nonexistent, voracious and omnivorous pigs at least did their part to clean up the streets. Young boys also loved riding on their backs for sport. At the same time, though, the often boisterous pigs also dug up the unpaved streets, tore up sidewalks, and tended to knock more petite city dwellers into the gutter.

What happened to all the pigs?

Starting in the early 1800s, city disquiet over the pig problem spiked. In 1816, after the Common Council considered banning all free-roaming pigs, the issue exploded, with anti-pig forces raining down attacks that ranged from classist to racist (it was often assumed that only poor downtown Irish and blacks owned pigs). Pig owners pushed back against the proposed fines and in at least one case rioted when the city's pig catchers tried to enforce new regulations.

The drive to get pigs off the streets continued in fits and starts over the following decades. The swine were driven progressively further uptown, along with their attendant industries, the "piggeries," offal-boiling sites, and their attendant working-class shanties. Harlem's 125th Street was so thick with these necessary but unwelcome businesses that it was known as Pig Alley, while the particularly redolent blocks in the Fifties between Sixth and Seventh avenues were called simply Hogtown. Manhattan didn't manage to become mostly pig-free until the 1880s.

How about the dogs?

In addition to fears of cholera and other diseases supposedly spread by pigs, nineteenth-century New York was frequently convulsed by rabies scares. There were plenty of dogs to be concerned about, as they happily rooted about in the city's garbage-strewn streets. Eventually, concerns over rabid dogs became too much to ignore.

In 1811, the Common Council passed the "Law Concerning Dogs," which allowed any New Yorker to kill any dog they found outside a very restricted downtown area. Very quickly, people took advantage of the bounty. In the summer of 1811, over 2,600 dogs were killed. Just as with attempts to crack down on pigs (and even more so, given peoples' stronger emotional attachments to dogs), the city's occasional dog decimation campaigns met with outbreaks of violent public resistance. By the end of the nineteenth century, with the growth of animal-protection societies and a greater antipathy toward such widespread cruelty, the city ended its dog-bounty program. These days, New York is a much kinder place for its four-legged residents, epitomized more by the canine waste law that mandates all dog owners to clean up their dog's leavings.

How many different bird species are there in New York?

Since New York is situated right along the Atlantic flyway, a kind of major avian traffic artery, the city has become a popular stopping-off point for migrating birds. Over 200

> ## How many pets do New Yorkers own?
>
> As of 2012, there were about 1.1 million pets in New York, or about one per three households. Most of them were dogs (600,000) or cats (500,000). The percentage of ownership is lower than the United States as a whole, where six in ten households have at least one pet. Areas with the highest concentration of pets include Staten Island, the Upper East and West sides, Williamsburg, and Astoria. The Bronx has among the lowest pet ownership rates in the city.

species, roughly one-third of those living in the entire United States, migrate through New York (Manhattan, in particular) at some point. They are particularly prominent in the heavily forested Central Park, where over 280 species have been observed. This density and richness of the bird population has made Central Park one of the world's most beloved spots for birding. There is a great diversity of birds in the New York area, ranging from beautiful great egrets to chestnut-side mallards, warblers, finches, orioles, kestrels, and the endangered nesting piping plovers found on sandy beaches in Queens and Long Island.

Why are there so many pigeons in New York?

Like many things associated with New York, the pigeons one sees strutting calmly about looking for scraps or fluttering up to the sky in giant numbers originally hail from somewhere else. Also known as rock doves, pigeons were most likely first introduced to America by Europeans sometime in the 1600s. They were actually one of the first animals to be domesticated, possibly as long as ten thousand years ago in the Middle East. People raised pigeons for both their guano, which was highly prized as fertilizer, and for their meat. Pigeons were also widely utilized for delivering messages during both world wars, and the military operated a pigeon breeding and training center at Fort Monmouth not far down the Jersey Shore from 1917 to 1957. Eventually, pigeon and squab (young, domestically raised pigeons that haven't flown yet) became less frequently seen on menus.

During the twentieth century, most of the people still raising pigeons in New York were doing so not for food but hobby or sport. For decades, New Yorkers have raised pigeons in rooftop coops as pets and also occasionally racing them. Nobody truly knows why New York has so many wild pigeons; they are thought to number at least one million. (Some cities have it worse: Venice reportedly has three pigeons for every one human.) One theory has it that pigeons thrive in any city where there are lots of public spaces such as parks with benches and people who like to sit on those benches and feed pigeons. Controlling the city's pigeons, whose massive production of guano is a constant eyesore and destructive presence on the city's buildings and statuary, has become more difficult since 2000, when avicide (poisoning birds) was made illegal.

Are there falcons in New York?

The peregrine falcon (*Falco peregrinus*) is an awe-inspiring, slate-grey-colored bird of prey about the size of a crow and is known to have reached speeds of 180 mph (290 kph) while diving for its prey. These falcons are found around the world from North and South America to Eurasia, Africa, and even Australia. During the 1970s they were placed on the endangered species list because of the effects of certain pesticides.

In recent years the species has made a strong recovery with the help of scientists who carefully monitored falcons they reintroduced into the wild. But falcons are also urban creatures. In 1983, two pairs of falcons were moved to New York. Falcons prefer to nest high off the ground, and these were no different. One pair nested on the Verrazano Narrows Bridge, the other on the Throgs' Neck Bridge. Since then they have made their homes all over the city, including the Financial District skyscraper at 55 Water Street, the MetLife building, Riverside Church, the Brooklyn Bridge, and even the Empire State Building. An urban environment like New York would not seem to be ideal hunting grounds for wild animals; as many as half of the young do not survive.

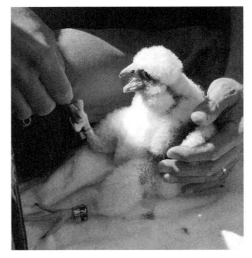

Metropolitan Transit Authority staff have worked with the NYC Department of Environmental Protection to help falcons survive in the city, such as this bird that was found living under the Throgs Neck Bridge.

What do falcons like about New York?

New York offers at least one strong draw (besides the plethora of high places mostly unreachable by humans) for falcons, whose primary prey is other birds. In other words, watch out, pigeons. A falcon can kill one or two pigeons each day. There are now dozens of falcon pairs living in New York, one of the highest concentrations in any urban area. Falcons were taken off the endangered species list in 1999. But their survival in New York is largely still dependent on human help. Currently, city workers and volunteers monitor the known falcon nesting sites, going so far as place trays on ledges to secure falcon eggs.

What other birds of prey live or can be seen in New York?

- Bald eagles: Earlier in the twentieth century, the bald eagle was threatened, as were many other bird species, by hunting, habitat destruction, and the usage of chemicals like DDT. By 1976 there was only one nesting pair left in New York state. However, programs launched by New York and New Jersey states (along with the outlawing of DDT) slowly but surely helped to reintroduce healthy bald eagles to the area. In recent years, bald eagles nesting along the Hudson River could be seen by commuters on the George Washington Bridge. In 2015, a pair of bald eagles built a nest on the south shore of Staten Island, the first time for one of their species in over a century. That same year, a bald eagle was spotted in Central Park.

- Red-tailed hawks: Falcons share the sky with and are sometimes confused with the smaller, red-tailed hawks that nest in Central Park and the occasional Upper East Side co-op. When a Fifth Avenue building tried to remove the nest of a red-tailed hawk known as Pale Male in 2004, the case became a cause célèbre for lovers of hunting birds. They can be spotted around the city, hunting squirrels, rats, and even sometimes pigeons.

Why were oysters so important to New York?

The beaver is featured prominently on the New York seal, and was a crucial component of the city's early economy. It pales in comparison, however, to the prominence that the oyster once had in New York. In *The Big Oyster*, Mark Kurlansky (1948–) wrote: "Before the 20th century, when people thought of New York, they thought of oysters." The massive mounds of oyster shells (middens) that have been dug up over the years shows that the Lenape also feasted regularly on great heaps of the succulent bivalves. Easy access to such a rich food supply may in fact have been one of the factors that attracted the Lenape to the region. At one point, the lower Hudson estuary held something like 350 square miles (around 900 square kilometers) of oyster beds, making it one of the richest supplies in the world. It has been estimated that New York Harbor held half of the world's entire supply of oysters. Oyster shells even helped build the city, being used to pave Pearl Street and being ground into mortar paste for building construction.

Before pollution, landfill, and overfishing decimated the oyster fields, cheap and plentiful oysters were one of the city's most popular and distinctive foods. Oyster cellars could be found all over the city, as well as street carts selling oysters. Ice-packed wagons delivered oysters to the New York-style oyster bars that opened in Midwestern cities.

What does Shakespeare have to do with all the starlings around?

In 1890, a drug manufacturer named Eugene Schieffelin (1827–1906) entered Central Park with a purpose. A group that the enthusiast birder was a member of, the American Acclimatization Society, had decided that it would be a perfectly swell idea to introduce all sixty-four species of birds mentioned in the plays of Shakespeare to the Americas. A number of the species, like skylarks and nightingales, didn't take to their new environment. But the hundred skylarks (mentioned in *Henry IV, Part I* by Hotspur: "Nay, I'll have a starling shall be taught to speak nothing but 'Mortimer'") that Schieffelin and the society released between 1890 and 1891 did just fine. Those hundred have by now multiplied past Central Park to Mexico and Canada, numbering about two hundred million these days, and many of them can be found thronging the sidewalks and skies of New York.

Are there ever shark attacks in the waters around New York?

Not often, but every few years there is certainly a scare involving sharks in the water. Some are more serious than others. One of the most infamous shark attacks took place in the summer of 1916 along the Jersey Shore. On July 1, twenty-five-year-old Charles Vansant was swimming near Beach Haven when he was bitten by a shark and bled to death soon afterward. Several days afterward, twenty-seven-year-old Charles Bruder was killed by a great white in the waters near Spring Lake about fifty miles (eighty kilometers) north. While these attacks were rare, the one that followed was even stranger. A shark apparently swam upstream along New Jersey's Matawan Creek—which empties into Raritan Bay just across from the south shore of Staten Island—and on July 12 attacked eleven-year-old Lester Stillwell, who was playing in the creek sixteen miles (twenty-six kilometers) inland. Both Stillwell and Watson Stanley Fisher, who was trying to save Stillwell, died in the attack. Many seaside communities gave bounties to fishermen for every shark head they brought. The shark was ultimately caught, killed, and put on display in New York. Rumor has often claimed that these attacks were what inspired Peter Benchley (1940–2006) to write the 1974 novel *Jaws*. Benchley denied that.

In 1860, about twelve million oysters were sold in New York markets. The last of the oyster beds was shut down in 1927. The Oyster Bar in Grand Central still serves over two dozen varieties of oysters, but they don't come from New York Harbor anymore.

PEOPLE

What is the population of New York?

According to the 2010 Census, the total population of New York was about 8.175 million; this is nearly half the population of New York state and about 2.5 percent of the nation. New York remains the largest city in the United States, with over double the population of the second largest, Los Angeles, which has a population of 3.8 million. If broken out by themselves, some of New York's boroughs would rank in the nation's top ten largest cities: Brooklyn and Queens are about equal to third-place Chicago's 2.7 million, while Manhattan's 1.59 million is roughly comparable to fourth-place Houston's 2.1 million, and the Bronx's 1.39 million lines up with sixth-place Phoenix's 1.45 million.

Who were the first New Yorkers?

Native Americans of the Lenape tribe first settled on Manhattan island, which they called Lenapehoking ("where the Lenapes dwell"), thousands of years ago. The Lenape were an Algonquin-speaking grouping of tribes also known as the Lennai Lenape or Delaware who were spread along the Atlantic coast from the Hudson River down to the Delaware. By the mid-sixteenth century, around 15,000 Lenape lived on the heavily forested island of Manhattan.

How many Native Americans still live in New York?

According to the U.S. Census Bureau, as of 2010, there were just over 110,000 Native American residents of New York. This might be a very small percentage of the population, but it means there are far more Native Americans living in New York than any other American city. The next largest urban Indian population can be found in Los Angeles, numbering around 54,000.

Is it true that many ironworkers in New York have traditionally been Indians?

Building the bridges and skyscrapers of New York has always required men and women who didn't mind perching themselves hundreds of feet in the air on steel beams. It's daring and nerve-wracking work. For many decades one group heavily represented in the ironworker trade has been Mohawk Indians, many of them hailing from a small reservation outside of Montreal, Canada. The number of Mohawk Indians in New York peaked in the 1950s at about five hundred. One popular legend had it that Mohawks were so well-suited for the work because they had no fear of heights. That is actually not true, and a Mohawk ironworker was quoted in the Smithsonian's National Museum exhibit on the subject: "We have as much fear as the next guy. The difference is that we deal with it better."

Who were the first European New Yorkers?

When New Amsterdam was first established by the Dutch West India Company, most of its European residents were Dutch and Walloons. However, there was great diversity, at least of Europeans, at the colony's beginning, with many French-speaking Huguenots, Germans, and British in the mix.

How many people live in each of the boroughs?

The metropolitan area's population is spread fairly evenly over the four largest boroughs. Staten Island is the exception for obvious reasons, being both far smaller than any other borough and the most isolated. That being said, the population of Staten Island grew faster than any other borough between the 2000 and 2010 censuses.

- Bronx—1.39 million
- Brooklyn—2.5 million
- Manhattan—1.59 million
- Queens—2.23 million
- Staten Island—0.47 million

Is New York the biggest city in America by population?

Yes. According to the 2010 U.S. Census, there were over 8.1 million people living in New York. The next closest city in population was Los Angeles, with less than half the population at 3.7 million, followed by Chicago (2.6 million), Houston (2 million), and Philadelphia (1.5 million). Boston, which was outpaced by New York centuries ago and is now its rather permanently embittered rival, ranks twenty-fourth in the nation (0.6 million), behind Jacksonville and Indianapolis.

How has the city's population changed over the years?

Like many older American cities in the Northeast and Midwest, New York gained population steadily through the middle of the twentieth century, hit a period of decline in the postwar years, and then saw another growth spurt in the early twenty-first century. New York's population grew explosively through the nineteenth century, with 60,515 residents in 1800, 515,547 in 1850, and 3.4 million in 1900. (Note that the last census period saw exceptionally large growth, more than doubling the 1890 number of 1.5 million, in part because of large immigration numbers but mostly because of the 1898 consolidation of all five boroughs into one city.)

Immigration and economic prosperity kept the city growing after consolidation, with its population hitting 7.5 million just before World War II. The postwar economy remained strong and new residents continued to arrive in large numbers (particularly from the American South and Puerto Rico). But net population growth leveled off sharply, due primarily to the growth of suburbs both nearby and in the Sunbelt. The shift of population from urban to suburban areas actually hit New York less than other municipalities, because the city boundaries had been drawn so generously that many suburban neighborhoods in outlying areas are still counted as part of New York.

What is the current ethnic makeup of New York?

The ethnic diversity of New York has always been a study in fluctuations, both because of the dynamic and ever-shifting nature of the city's economy, which both draws in and pushes out different populations, and its traditional place as the immigration hub of America. Currently, whites account for about a third of the total population, with Hispanics roughly another third, blacks around one-quarter, and Asians approximately one-seventh.

- White—33%
- Hispanic—29%

When did New York actually lose population?

The number of city residents peaked in 1970 at 7.89 million, then declined for the two census periods (the only time in the city's history), only to hit a new peak in 2000 of eight million and continue growing thereafter. It's estimated by the Census Bureau that New York gained nearly 316,000 residents between 2010 and 2014, an increase of about 4 percent. Of the five boroughs, Brooklyn had the largest increase in population (4.7%) and Staten Island had the least (1%).

- Black—23%
- Asian—13%
- Native American, Pacific Islander, and other—2%

How many New Yorkers are foreign-born?

In short, a lot. New York has traditionally been the primary entry point to America for immigrants looking to make a life in the country. Going back to the 1850s, the percentage of New York residents born in another country has varied but is normally somewhere between one-third and one-fourth. Here are some representative numbers:

Year	Total Population	Foreign-Born Population
1850	515,547	235,733
1900	3,437,202	1,270,080
1950	7,891,957	1,784,206
2000	8,008,278	2,871,032

Where do most of the immigrants in New York currently hail from?

The percentage of New Yorkers who were born in a foreign country was particularly high in the early twentieth century and then saw a decline in later decades. Due in large part to the sweeping changes in immigration quotas in 1965, the numbers of foreign-born New Yorkers increased substantially in the last few decades of the twentieth century. According to the city's 2013 report "The Newest New Yorkers," about three million New Yorkers were born in a foreign country. In 1970, over sixty percent of immigrants hailed from Europe. As of 2011, these are the most common countries of origin:

- Dominican Republic: 12.4%
- China: 11.4%
- Mexico: 6.1%
- Jamaica: 5.5%
- Guyana: 4.6%
- Ecuador: 4.5%
- Haiti: 3.1%
- Trinidad and Tobago: 2.9%
- India: 2.5%
- Russia: 2.5%
- Bangladesh: 2.4%

How different is immigration to New York from America in general?

Patterns of immigration to New York remain somewhat different from the country as a whole. Similar to other parts of the nation, many foreign-born Americans in New York hail from Mexico, but other groups that are heavily represented in New York—such as immigrants from the Caribbean and Africa—are found in much smaller numbers elsewhere in the country.

Where do most immigrants settle in New York?

At one time, lower Manhattan—in particular the tenements of the Lower East Side—was the traditional first stop for immigrants to New York. These days, with the expansion of more affordable housing into the boroughs and the extension of public transportation to those areas, not to mention the transitioning of the Lower East Side into multi-million-dollar condominiums, the immigrant influx has moved to the boroughs.

About two-thirds of foreign-born New Yorkers settle today in Brooklyn (particularly Bensonhurst and Sunset Park, following the N subway) or Queens (especially Jackson Heights, Elmhurst, and Flushing along the 7 subway line), with the other third divided about evenly between Manhattan (the far northwestern neighborhood of Morningside Heights most heavily) and the Bronx.

How many languages are spoken in New York?

As many as eight hundred languages are spoken by the residents of New York. Just over half of New Yorkers speak only English at home. For the other forty-nine percent, about half speak primarily Spanish or Spanish Creole. The next most common non-English language is Chinese (primarily Cantonese, but increasingly Mandarin), with large blocs of Russian, French Creole, Hebrew, Arabic, and French speakers as well.

What are some of the less common languages?

Because New York contains such a diversity of immigrant groups, it also serves as a kind of laboratory for linguists who study languages that are disappearing in their native lands. Among the rare languages spoken by pockets of immigrants in New York, most commonly Queens, are:

- Aramaic (Syria)
- Bukhari (Uzbekistan / Tajikistan)
- Garifuna (Central America)
- Judeo-Kashani (Iran)
- Ormuri (Afghanistan / Pakistan)
- Pennsylvania Dutch
- Rhaeto-Romanic (Switzerland)
- Vlashki (Croatia)

How religious are New Yorkers?

This is, of course, a question that is open to many interpretations. There are some parts of the country that would assume that New York, as the country's self-identified capital for over-educated smarty-pants, would be a particularly secular zone where the religious dare not tread. However, according to data put together in 2008 by *Gotham* magazine, over eighty percent of New Yorkers self-identify as being religiously observant. That number had declined somewhat in recent years, but it remains a higher percentage than most of America outside of the Bible Belt. The city is thick with places of worship, from storefront revival churches and modest masjids to grand cathedrals. In 1855, the city recorded 465 Protestant churches, 53 Catholic parishes, and 11 synagogues. Not for nothing was Brooklyn known as the "City of Churches."

Has New York always been religiously diverse?

What sets New York apart is *what* religious beliefs they follow, perhaps a result of the city's long-standing diversity of faiths, from Baha'i to Baptists, Orthodox Jews to Catholics, Hindus to Jehovah's Witnesses, the Church of Jesus Christ of Latter-day Saints to the Nation of Islam. This multiplicity of faiths dates to the early colonial days. Even after the British takeover in 1664, when the colony became officially Anglican, New Yorkers included people of many faiths who were less than welcome elsewhere in Europe or the other colonies, from Quakers to Catholics, Anabaptists, German Lutherans, Baptists, French Calvinists, and America's first Jewish community. In 1678, Governor Edmund Andros commented that there were "religions of all sorts" in the colony, including "Independents most numerous."

What are New York's religious demographics today?

The city is far more Catholic and Jewish, and substantially less Protestant, than America as a whole. The largest single bloc of religious New Yorkers are Catholics, who make up about a third of the population. About a quarter of the population is Protestant: evangelical (9%), mainline (8%), and historically black Protestant (6%).

The next largest segment of religious New Yorkers are Jews, who make up about 8 percent of the population and are in fact more numerous in the city than anywhere in the world outside of Israel. The remaining significant faiths are Muslim (3%), Hindu (3%), and Buddhist (1%). Among religious New Yorkers, Muslims are one of the fastest growing populations, while the percentage of Jews identifying as Orthodox has grown substantially in recent years. Roughly a quarter of New Yorkers identify as either atheist, agnostic, or unaffiliated.

GOVERNMENT AND POLITICS

How is New York governed?

Administration of the city of New York is divided between executive, legislative, and judicial branches. The mayor is popularly elected to a four-year term, with no more than three consecutive terms allowed, and is responsible for the budget, which was approximately $78 billion in 2015. The mayor is the chief legislator, his or her power held in check by other centers of power: the fifty-one elected members of the City Council (who

New York's City Hall is located at City Hall Park between Broadway and Park Row. The building was completed in 1811 and has a French Renaissance Revival architectural style.

represent all five boroughs) and the state government in Albany, the latter of which has traditionally held as tight a reign as possible on the city government. There are seven Congressional districts mostly or entirely within the city, giving it an unusually large representation in the U.S. House of Representatives.

Why are there so many boroughs?

It may seem to some as though four of the boroughs are merely suburbs to the central borough of Manhattan. But New York is actually more like a federation of individual cities than a single, unified urban area. The five boroughs operated as their own independent entities from the establishment of the first Dutch colony in 1626. That changed in 1898, when consolidation transformed them all into one unified city. Given the size of the city, and its constituent bodies' independent leanings, the boroughs were each allowed to keep some form of self-government, even if it was primarily symbolic.

How many people work for the city?

The city of New York is the urban area's largest single employer. According to a 2013 Government Workforce report, at the time there were over 327,000 people working (full-

and part-time) for the city of New York. They are mostly union workers (93%), and more of them are minorities than are white (sixty-three percent minority versus thirty-nine percent white), and female to male (fifty-seven percent female). Four out of ten city workers are employed by the Department of Education, with police (15%) and health workers (12%) comprising the next two largest groups. The departments with the fewest workers are Cultural Affairs and Records and Information Services, which each have fewer than sixty workers.

When did the police department start?

Policing in New York dates back to the early days of the Dutch colony, when Governor Peter Stuyvesant instituted an eight-man nighttime patrol responsible for everything from corralling drunken sailors to keeping an eye peeled for Indian raids. Policing was a pretty haphazard and understaffed affair well into the nineteenth century, when a tiny band of leather-helmeted constables known as "leatherheads" patrolled the city. The New York Municipal Police Force, created in 1845, was the city's first true law enforcement body and progenitor of the modern New York Police Department (NYPD).

How large is the police department?

Currently, the NYPD has over 17,000 civilian employees and about 34,500 uniformed officers. The number of uniformed officers is expected to grow by over a thousand in 2016, with about a third of them being assigned to the counterterrorism unit. Budget issues had trimmed the force to about 28,000 officers during the late 1970s and early '80s before steadily rising and then peaking in October 2000 at 40,800. About fifty percent of the officers are white, roughly twenty-five percent Hispanic, and sixteen percent black.

Which cops handle what?

Today, the NYPD's civilian staff handles office and management duties. Uniformed officers do the work that people associate them with: enforcing the law on the street. All officers are assigned to one of the seventy-eight precincts that divide up law enforcement responsibility in the five boroughs. Given New York's unique status as the nation's densest city, its varied coastlines, the dense lattice of bridges and tunnels connecting everything, and being the unofficial headquarters of America's financial and media businesses, the NYPD's remit spreads far wider than that of the average police department. In addition to its uniformed patrol officers—split between

One Police Plaza, the current headquarters for the NYPD, was built in 1973 and inaugurated in 1979.

17

precinct, transit, and housing—the NYPD has about 300 specialized units, ranging from the detective bureau and the K-9 unit to mounted units, the harbor and aviation patrols, and organized crime.

What about counterterrorism?

Given New York's position as the likeliest terrorist target in the country, an entire subset of the NYPD is organized in a counterterrorism unit. Every day, about a thousand officers are on counterterror duty in the city. Also, the NYPD stations intelligence liaison officers in numerous cities overseas at any given time. The occasionally militaristic profile of the NYPD's counterterrorism capabilities, which reportedly include everything from submarine drones to anti-aircraft weaponry, led Mayor Michael Bloomberg to boast in 2011 that "I have my own army in the NYPD."

Who were the first firefighters?

As with the police force, the city's early firefighting apparatus was for many years an ad-hoc and not wholly efficient operation. By the time of the Revolutionary War, the city had about 170 volunteer firefighters using eight hand-pumped firefighting engines. There was an explosive growth of volunteer fire companies, loosely controlled by the city, in the early part of the nineteenth century, encouraged both by the city's rapid growth and the city's decision in 1816 to exempt some firefighters from jury and militia duty.

The Manhattan Ladder Company 8 building was used in the movies *Ghostbusters* and *Ghostbusters 2* as the heroes' headquarters.

The chaotic rise of often rival fire companies, which seemed at times to be more political patronage operations with opportunities for carousing and theft than actual firefighting units, led to surreal moments in which different companies would compete to fight fires. It was in fact the Black Joke Engine Company that started the fire at a conscription office on July 13, 1863, that helped kick off the Draft Riots. The Metropolitan Fire Department, forebearer of today's Fire Department of the City of New York (FDNY), was established in 1865 in part to streamline these overlapping and not always very effective companies. It was organized along military lines by General Alexander T. Shaler (1827–1911).

What is the FDNY like today?

The FDNY grew with the city and the times, shifting from horse-drawn to motorized fire engines in the early twentieth century and admitting its first female firefighters in 1982. The department is still the city's least diverse (over three-fourths of its employees are white). The 2013 graduating class was the most diverse in FDNY history, with over half of that year's probationary firefighters being minorities.

How many fire houses are manned by the FDNY?

The FDNY is the largest such department in the country. Responsible for protecting over 300 square miles (777 square kilometers) of densely populated land from fire, the FDNY operates 218 fire houses and 37 Emergency Medical Services (EMS) stations in the five boroughs, staffed by over 10,000 uniformed fire personnel, more than 3,700 uniformed EMS personnel, and about 1,800 civilian personnel.

How many calls do they answer each year?

In a typical year, using statistics compiled in 2014, the FDNY responded to roughly half a million incidents, including over 26,000 structural fires and nearly a quarter-million medical emergencies. They saved or rescued some 50,000 civilians in those calls, including 300 saved in building fires and almost 40,000 trapped in elevators.

When did schooling begin in New York?

As in the rest of colonial America, the idea of public education was hardly a given. The first schools were nearly all aligned with churches and charged some form of tuition. Starting with the founding of the Free School Society in 1805, however, and with the urging of Mayor DeWitt Clinton, the city began to recognize the necessity of educating all of its young citizens. Since then, schooling has been one of the greatest, most controversial, expensive, and prideful responsibilities of the municipal government.

How many schools does New York operate?

Today, the New York City Department of Education is a massive operation, with an annual operating budget of nearly $22 billion. The country's largest school district, it operates roughly 1,800 schools, including 496 public high schools, and is responsible for educating about 1.1 million children. Of those students, over 171,000 are classified as English Language Learners and about 141,000 special education students. Some 180 different languages are spoken by the students, with the school system being required to provide translation assistance for those speaking the nine most common: Arabic, Bengali, Chinese, French, Haitian Creole, Korean, Russian, Spanish, and Urdu.

The New York school system also includes nearly 200 public charter schools. Between 2002 and 2012, the number of students at these institutions increased by roughly 65,000. About twenty percent of the city's K-12 student body attends private schools. Traditionally these have been primarily Roman Catholic, but in recent years, Jewish schools have overtaken them in number.

What is New York like, politically?

Despite being a world financial capital and a frequently old-fashioned place when it comes to social mores, New York has enjoyed a reputation in the United States as being one of the country's most politically radical cities. As Woody Allen joked in *Annie Hall*: "The rest of the country looks upon New York like we're left-wing, communist, Jewish, homosexual pornographers. *I* think of us that way sometimes and I live here."

So is New York a liberal city?

Yes, and no. New York has a long history of radical leftist movements, from the early twentieth-century anarchism of Emma Goldman to the Yippies in the 1960s and more recently Occupy Wall Street. Following the Bolshevik Revolution, communists were briefly a force to be reckoned with, publishing two competing daily newspapers—one in Yiddish. In 1927, the Communist Party USA (CPUSA) established its headquarters just below Union Square, the site of frequent labor demonstrations. The party had strong labor support and drew on a strong socialist tradition among many intellectuals and immigrant workers before sharply dwindling in power in the 1940s. The much-reduced CPUSA is actually still headquartered in New York, on 23rd Street across from the Hotel Chelsea.

Interestingly, because so much of the nation's intellectual and financial power is centered here, New York has also served as headquarters of sorts to many iterations of the modern conservative movement. William F. Buckley's (1925–2008) influential magazine, *National Review* (which famously planned to "[stand] athwart history, yelling Stop"), was founded in 1955 and remains based in New York, as is *Commentary*, which dates back to 1945. On a ground level, the negative reaction by some white ethnic groups in the 1960s and 1970s against progressive policies and racial integration was as potent in New York as it was in more ostensibly conservative parts of the country.

Even after many years of Republican mayors (Giuliani, Bloomberg), sending Donald Trump to the White House, and the city's long embrace of muscular capitalism, the stereotype lives on. Just witness Senator Ted Cruz's scornful reference to "New York values" in the 2016 Republican primary. This label is not entirely undeserved, as the city has gone through several waves of progressive leaders and vociferous social movements, even as the stock markets and real estate deals kept humming along.

However, New York's progressive spirit has not always been channeled along heavily organized channels, more often waxing and waning with the influxes of various immigrant groups or various economic and political factors. The city also features such a mix of populations and interests that it can accommodate (not always quietly) the mixture of, say, outer-borough Republicans with genteel Park Slope and Upper West Side lefties, as well as a mass of generally socially liberal, middle-of-the-road voters primarily concerned with keeping crime low and the streets quickly plowed after a blizzard.

BUSINESS AND THE ECONOMY

What was the early business of New York?

In these times of high-frequency trading, $50 million Wall Street bonuses, $5 million apartment boxes that wouldn't rate a second glance anywhere else in America, and glittering philanthropic balls, it is worth remembering that New Amsterdam was founded as a convenient port that the Dutch could use to ship beaver pelts back home. It wasn't long before the beavers were hunted out. But the harbor was still the best on the Eastern Seaboard, with the Hudson River as a convenient waterway into the Northeast's interior. Cities like Boston and Philadelphia were early leaders in the role of being America's chief urban centers. But by the late 1720s, exports from New York outstripped both of those cities.

Throughout the seventeenth and eighteenth centuries, New York consolidated its position as a center of business, trade, and shipping—in part because of the ability of well-organized local merchants to bend civic polity to their needs. Later eras would see the growth in the city of everything from manufacturing to service industries. But the buying, selling, and transportation of commodities have always been the lifeblood of the city's economy.

Is New York a business-friendly city?

New York has long been particularly engaged in the business of organizing business in ways that improve efficiencies and advocate for better conditions and infrastructure from the government. Alexander Hamilton promulgated his theories of a central federalized bank and financial system in New York. The city's stockbrokers organized early, setting up the so-called Buttonwood Agreement for more regulated stock trading in 1792. Years before, in 1768, twenty New York merchants organized the New York Cham-

21

ber of Commerce and Industry in order to better promote the "General Interest of the Colony and the Commerce of this City in particular." This was the first commercial organization of its kind in the country, if not the world. Like today, the first Chamber of Commerce was interested in improving conditions for merchants and other business-people. Unlike today's button-down and abstemious gatherings in generic conference rooms, in those days, merchants conducted business at Fraunces Tavern and smoked long-stemmed, clay Dutch pipes around the fireplace.

This focus on the business of business filled municipal coffers and individual wallets but was also seen by some to give the city a reputation for fiercely relentless mercantilism at the expense of all else. Allen Ginsberg would lyrically rue what he saw as New York's transformation into a veritable soulless "Moloch" of "electricity and banks." A more even-handed perspective comes from historian Steven H. Jaffe, who points out that unlike some other parts of the colonies, New York was "[f]ounded not as a refuge for embattled religions but as a base for commercial exchange."

What role did early warfare play in the city's business affairs?

Starting in 1689, the British Empire tangled in war after war with France and Spain. As a result of this, colonial ports like New York became the headquarters for squadrons of privateers who sallied forth to attack boats sailing under enemy flags for Queen and Country … and profit. The privateers would then sail back into New York Harbor towing their captured ships, whose cargo would then be sold in the city's markets. Benjamin Fletcher (1640–1703), appointed governor of New York in 1692, was all too happy to let this business go on, as well as the blatantly illegal business of smuggling and trad-

---

How important was New York to the early American economy?

At the dawn of the nineteenth century, New York was not just the largest city in the country by population, it was also responsible for one-third of all federal tax revenue collected by the fledgling government. Since then, other cities from Chicago to Los Angeles and even Houston have occasionally appeared to challenge its dominance. There has not, however, been a single decade in which New York was not America's business clearinghouse. That remained true even after the defection of many businesses in the twentieth century's postwar years. In part this was simply due to tradition; when a company became big enough it always needed to open a New York office, if not move its headquarters there completely. But it had more to do with the economies of scale that came with Manhattan's dense networks of financial and legal specialists to advise on and attend to a growing company's every need. Like it or not, New York (in this case, meaning Manhattan) has by and large remained where one goes to get deals done and to be taken seriously in business.

ing with Britain's enemies, as long as he was cut in on the deal. Piracy and smuggling were both leading factors in pushing New York's economic development in the decades leading up to the Revolutionary War, as well as more legitimate means of doing business like loaning money to the wartime government and supplying Britain's occupying army.

How did Wall Street help fight America's wars?

New York's financial sector had been a thriving business prior to the War of 1812. But it was during that conflict when the city's bankers, brokers, and insurers starting to cluster around the East River side of Wall Street began to play a crucial role in America's military establishment. In part, that was because in 1811 Congress had allowed the First Bank of the United States' charter to expire, allowing the country to enter the war without any dedicated line to emergency credit. New York bankers, and some from Philadelphia, stepped into the gap, underwriting a large part of the country's war debt. As a result, already wealthy men like John Jacob Astor (1763-1848) made a great deal of profit, Wall Street was established as Washington's go-to place for war financing, and suspicion was fueled in some quarters (repeated with each new conflict) that the city's bankers were little more than war profiteers.

Why was New York so economically well-advantaged?

Put most simply, geography. As is repeated elsewhere in this book, New York is the best deep-water harbor on the Eastern seaboard. For the first two-plus centuries of the city's history, shipping was the single most economical way to ship goods from one location to another. But New York didn't just have a superbly situated and protected harbor, it was also located at the mouth of the Hudson River, which in early American history reached deep into the fur-rich colonial hinterland. This meant that Indians in what would become upstate New York were more easily able to trade beaver fur for wampum and/or manufactured goods with Dutch and coast-dwelling Algonquin Indians, who could then sell the furs to the European market.

At the same time as the fur trade boomed, European colonists who acquired great estates north of New Amsterdam began farming, which created a booming trade in agricultural goods that flowed out of the harbor. Boston and Philadelphia were also great centers for importing and exporting. But their harbors were shallower and more prone to ice than New York's, which ultimately helped situate it as Eastern America's trading nexus. Also, those cities' more homogeneous and religious straight-laced traditions couldn't compete with New Amsterdam and later New York's more gung-ho mercantilist ambitions.

What were New York's most important early industries?

Eventually, the beaver ran out and there was only so much money to be made from agricultural products. Trade boomed, particularly between New York and the Caribbean. This led to a large infrastructure of shipping-related businesses and an ever-growing necklace of docks encircling lower Manhattan. In around 1720, about one in four New

York adult men worked as sailors. The Revolutionary War probably worked in the city's favor economically, as it was the British headquarters for almost all of the hostilities and thus the recipient of military largesse. After the Revolution, the country's neutrality in the Napoleonic wars between Britain and France helped New York expand on its business lead and make crucial trade linkages between Europe and the farms and plantations of the Midwest and South. In the mid-nineteenth century, a third of America's exports and half its imports flowed through New York.

What businesses prospered in the nineteenth century?

According to a paper by Harvard economics professor Edward L. Glaeser, when New York transitioned to a manufacturing powerhouse in the nineteenth century, it was dominated by three industries: garments, publishing, and sugar refining. The latter is the most surprising, since little evidence remains of that industry except for the Havemeyer family's giant old Domino Sugar Refinery complex on the Williamsburg waterfront. Sugar refining was one crucial part of the "triangle trade" with the West Indies, meaning that sugar cut there by slaves was brought into New York on ships that returned with raw materials.

New York's Garment District was a hub of activity back when this photo was taken in 1955. The city is still important for the fashion industry, though the actual manufacturing of clothes is done elsewhere.

Buoyed by the rise of the ready-to-wear industry, a manufacturing process that required relatively little room on a space-starved island, and an influx of eager-to-work immigrants, the garment industry soon employed tens of thousands of New Yorkers. In 1860, 30 percent of manufacturing jobs were garment-related. For its part, publishing never employed all that many people, but the ones it did were generally well-paid relative to other workers. Also publishing and media's importance to the local economy, not to mention the (surprisingly important) intangibles provided by just having so many creative workers around, helped cement New York's long-standing reputation as an idea factory.

Is clothing still crucial to New York business?

Yes, though not necessarily as vital as it was a few decades ago. From the 1920s until well after World War II, the jam-packed manufacturing center of the Garment District brought incalculable wealth and even prestige to the city. In 1960, the area comprised over 8 million square feet (7.4 million square meters) of workspace where upwards of a hundred thousand workers produced 95 percent of clothing bought by Americans. A *Life* magazine article from that year reported that the Garment District's 4,500 women's clothing firms made women's garments "the principal industry in the city, with an annual dollar volume of $4.4 billion."

Offshoring of labor and mass-produced factory clothing shrunk the industry every year after that. Currently, a much reduced cadre of some 24,000 clothing workers is still employed in the area. The garment business still brings in about $2 billion annually. The Garment District now makes around three percent of the nation's clothing, focusing primarily on high-end fashion.

Why did manufacturing decline so dramatically in New York?

For the same reasons that it did in many other American cities. A confluence of factors made the city less attractive to manufacturers after World War II. The new highway system, and the attendant increased ease and reduced costs for trucking goods around the country, erased many of the efficiency advantages gained by dense urban areas like New York in terms of transportation and infrastructure.

What took the place of manufacturing?

For a time, that was the question everybody wanted to know: What next for New York? The answer was something that New York has always been well-versed in: finance. From the early days when stocks were traded in downtown coffee houses to all the ancillary businesses that the city's booming port required, New York had an edge in the business of trading on information that it has never quite relinquished. Even when the city began to lose its status as critical port after the introduction of container shipping in the late 1950s, finance and related businesses grew. This was particularly pronounced even during the comparative economic decline of the 1970s. In that decade, the workers in the city employed by either finance, insurance, or real estate firms jumped from over 7 percent to 12 percent.

What is a bodega?

Aparticularly New York kind of business that has traditionally flourished in nearly every kind of neighborhood, the bodega has long been considered the first stop for New Yorkers looking to find any of the staples of modern urban life: coffee, newspapers, devotional candles, lottery tickets, batteries, beer, cigarettes, aspirin, sandwiches, detergent, and even flowers. In some neighborhoods, the owners will even extend credit to their more frequent customers. The term comes from the Spanish *la bodega* (grocery store), though they're often also just called corner stores.

While bodegas were traditionally situated primarily in Spanish-speaking, particularly Puerto Rican areas, they can be found in pretty much any neighborhood, particularly in the boroughs or the northern reaches of Manhattan, located further away from major retailers. Somewhat confusingly for non-New Yorkers, plenty of the small stores and delis that would be called corner stores elsewhere and run not just by Latinos but Koreans—and an increasingly large number of Yemenis—are also generically referred to by locals as bodegas. Seemingly a small business, bodegas employ around 65,000 people and take in about $7 billion in sales every year.

Who are the biggest employers in New York today?

New York is historically a monument to free enterprise, embodied in its early and continued history as a world trading center and its current status as world capital of finance and banking. However, measured by the sheer number of employees, the greatest single employer in the five boroughs isn't private industry but the city itself. In 2014, the two entities employing the most people in New York were City Hall (over 150,000 workers) and the Department of Education (over 119,000). The next three biggest employers were the federal government, New York state government, and the Metropolitan Transit Authority.

How many tourists come to New York each year?

Tourism is massive business in New York and is becoming ever more so in the twenty-first century. Around fifty four million tourists arrive annually, spending nearly $40 billion a year in the city and helping to support a vast infrastructure of restaurants and hotels and arts and entertainment venues, as well as the nearly 360,000 employees who work there. In an average year, nearly forty-three million Americans visit New York, as well as more than eleven million foreign tourists. Here is where most foreign visitors hail from (as of 2013):

- United Kingdom: 1.1 million
- Canada: 1.1 million
- Brazil: 895,000
- France: 697,000
- China: 646,000

TRANSPORTATION

How do New Yorkers get around?

There are plenty of cars and trucks in New York. Just look down any Midtown intersection at pretty much any time of day. But the honking, cursing tide of vehicular traffic is deceptively dense. If New Yorkers drove as often as the average American, each street would be gridlocked, forever. Only about twenty-three out of every one hundred New Yorkers owns a car, as compared to about seventy-eight per one hundred people elsewhere in the country. That translates to about 4.5 million fewer cars overall. However, the average New Yorker still travels about 14 miles (22.5 kilometers) every day. So how do they get around? As we discuss elsewhere, many people travel by commuter rail, subway, and bus, as well as bicycle or just plain old walking. When none of those options will work, then New Yorkers try to hail a yellow cab.

What's a yellow cab?

When people refer to "yellow cabs," they generally are referring to the dark lemon-hued taxi cabs whose ubiquity in certain parts of the city can make some streets look as though they've been repainted yellow. The original cabs were the horse-drawn "hackney" carriages, whose name survives in the habit of calling cab drivers "hacks." The first gas-powered cab company to operate in New York was the Chicago-based Yellow Cab Company, which was started by John Hertz (as in Hertz rental cars) in 1907 and whose cars sported a distinctive yellow color that was picked up by rivals and quickly became standardized. (The city actually made it the law for all cabs to be painted yellow in 1967.)

From 1952 to 1986, the standard model was the A8/Marathon, the so-called "Checker cab" with its distinctive yellow color and horizontal black-and-white checkerboard strips. The Checkers began to be discontinued once they couldn't keep up with the city's more stringent air pollution standards; the last was retired in 1999. In the 1990s, Chevy Caprices and later the low-slung and roomy Crown Victorias took over. The city has been trying for years to make the new boxy Nissan NV200 the new standard yellow cab, but various legal disputes have delayed that adoption.

How much does a taxi medallion cost?

After decades of chaotic competition, the taxi industry began to be regulated in New York in 1937, with the passage of the Haas Act. This law allowed for only a certain number of taxicab licenses, or medallions, to be operating in the city at any given time. In 1937, the first medallions were sold for $10. By 1950, their value had already increased to $5,000. The city limited the number of medallions it would sell each year, because if there were too few cabs on the street then nobody could get a ride, and if there were too many, drivers couldn't make a living. Eventually, the cost soared well beyond the ability of the average individual to afford, resulting in some deep-pocketed fleet owners purchasing the medallions and leasing them to drivers.

What's a livery car?

Also known as car services, livery cars come in many different forms and are run by many different operators. Unlike cabs, you cannot hail them on the street. Also unlike cabs, there is no meter; riders pay a flat fee, plus tip and tolls. Because they can be summoned to any location and their flat fares are usually competitively priced against cabs, livery cabs are particularly useful and popular in borough neighborhoods without good public transit. There are about 25,000 of them operating in the city at any given time in a wide variety of vehicles: anything from old retired cab Crown Victorias to Lincoln Towncars and brand-new Lexuses.

The cost of a single medallion peaked in 2014, when a city auction of 368 medallions saw them go for a staggering $1.2 million apiece. (By comparison, medallion sales in Chicago peaked in 2013 at around $360,000.) Quickly afterward, though, the entire industry was upended by the arrival of online ride-on-demand services like Uber, which starting taking business away from traditional hired-car rides. As a result, in June 2015, just a year after their peak, medallions were selling for about $760,000, with every indication that the price would continue to drop.

What are black cars?

There is another differentiation of cars-for-hire: black cars. These cars operate pretty much the same as livery cars (most New Yorkers couldn't tell you the difference) but their fares are paid as part of a prearranged contract with a client. Because they mostly serve corporate clients, these cars are frequently nicer and larger. They are the gleaming black Suburbans and BMWs you see gliding up to the curb at JFK while you're waiting behind twenty-five people in the dispatch line for a cab.

What is a green cab?

The relatively new green cabs are a hybrid category acting like both a livery car and yellow cab for outer-borough residents who have a hard time coaxing drivers out of the tourist- and businessperson-heavy Midtown and downtown Manhattan districts where ninety percent of all cab pickups take place. These generally smaller, green-colored cabs can operate anywhere in the New York area except Manhattan below 110th Street on the west and 96th Street on the east.

Where do most cab drivers hail from?

The flexibility of schedule for cab drivers, as well as the punishing hours and not particularly great pay (not to mention the tendency to be robbed, which resulted in the city mandating partitions between driver and passenger in 1968), has made it both an unwelcome job for most New Yorkers and consequently a popular avenue of employment for successive waves of immigrant groups. In the industry's earlier years, the population of drivers drew heavily from white ethnics like Jews, Italians, and the Irish.

Over the years, this ethnic makeup has transitioned along with changing patterns of immigration. Currently, about ninety percent of cab drivers are immigrants. The largest single ethnic group represented in the taxi industry is Bangladeshis, who constitute over a third of all drivers, with Pakistan and India following closely behind as the country of origin of the largest group of cab drivers. Curiously, even though less than two percent of cab drivers are from the Dominican Republic, they comprise about a fifth of all livery-cab drivers. Nearly half of all cabbies live in Queens, and almost a quarter in Brooklyn.

How many bridges are there in New York?

Given that traveling from one borough to the next always involves (unless traveling between Brooklyn and Queens) either going over water or under it, bridge-traffic is a big part of getting around in the city. The metropolitan area features some 1,445 bridges. Of those, over a thousand were recently categorized as "functionally obsolete" by the State Department of Transportation. Queens has the most bridges, with 486. Staten Island has the fewest, with 156.

Are there people in New York who still drive?

Due in large part to the density of its network of subways and bus lines (not to mention the impossibility of finding a good parking spot), New York has less than half as many car owners per capita as the American average. Manhattan, which also has the greatest density of trains and buses, has the fewest number of car-owning households in the city, at just 23 percent.

How big is the New York transit system?

The Metropolitan Transit Authority (MTA) is a massive, city-spanning public transportation system, by far the most expansive and most frequently used in the country. Its 469 stations were mostly built in a great burst of construction between 1904 and 1940. The MTA has approximately 6,300 train cars and 5,600 buses, plus the Staten Island Ferry.

Laid end to end, the MTA's train tracks, both elevated and subterranean, would stretch all the way to Chicago. If you take the A train from 207th Street in uptown Manhattan to Far Rockaway, Queens, you'll have traveled over thirty-one miles (fifty kilometers) for the price of a single fare. Unlike most other transit systems, the majority of the MTA's lines operate twenty-four hours a day. Its subway trains traveled 361 million miles (581 million kilometers) in 2015.

How many people use the MTA?

Peak MTA ridership was in 1946, with 2.07 billion passengers. In 2015, the MTA carried around 1.76 billion passengers a year, 20 million on the Staten Island Ferry alone. This

The elaborate New York subway system carries billions of passengers each year throughout the boroughs.

ranks New York as city number seven in annual subway ridership, just behind Guangzhou (2.4 billion) and just ahead of Hong Kong (1.71 billion); it is the only American city to break the top ten.

What are the busiest subway stations?

Station	Annual Ridership
Times Sq-42 St	66.4 million
Grand Central-42 St	46.7 million
34 St-Herald Sq	39.5 million
14 St-Union Sq	35.3 million
34 St-Penn Station	28.3 million

How much does it cost to ride the subway?

Originally, riders on the New York subway system needed to purchase tickets. That was the system until 1920, when coin-operated turnstiles were installed. The fare was a nickel per ride for decades, only increasing to a dime in 1948. A few years afterward the city wanted to make the fare fifteen cents. The lack of a fifteen-cent coin necessitated the introduction of the coin-like metal token stamped "Good for one fare." Tokens started to be phased out in the late–1990s as the MTA retrofitted the whole system to accept the electronic MetroCard.

Tokens were phased out in 2003, since they were expensive, and sometimes easy to counterfeit—the Transit Museum in downtown Brooklyn even has a display of the frequently hand-made fake tokens, called slugs. Today, a single subway or local bus ride costs $2.75 for people who already have a MetroCard; to encourage recycling of old cards, there's a $1 new-card fee for those who don't. Many New Yorkers commute using thirty-day unlimited MetroCards purchased via their employer.

Where does all the art in the subway come from?

As part of the city's attempt to rehabilitate the crumbling subway, the MTA began its Arts for Transit program in 1985. In the decades since, the program has worked with over 200 established and emerging artists to produce site-specific works for stations all over the five boroughs. Many of them work in durable media like the Beaux Arts mosaics which were incorporated into many of the original stations when they were first built in the early twentieth century, but the styles and media cover a broad range. Some of them you need to keep an eye peeled for, but others are right in your face. Here are some notable examples:

A Gathering (Canal Street)—These 180 bronze birds by Walter Martin (1953–) and Paloma Muñoz (1965–) can be seen in high spots all around this station.

Life Underground (14th Street–8th Avenue)—One of the subway's most distinctive installations is Tom Otterness's (1952–) adorable gaggle of tiny bronze cartoon figures who can be spotted all over the station working on construction or just waiting for a train.

31

Masstransiscope (Myrtle Avenue, now closed, but visible from Manhattan-bound express trains after they pass DeKalb)—Bill Brand's (1949–) installation consists of 228 panels that, when seen through the columns on a passing train, create a zoetrope effect that turns them into a mini-movie.

Times Square Mural (42nd Street-Times Square)—One of several pieces in this massive station, this is a comic-strip mural donated by the estate of Roy Lichtenstein (1923–1997).

What is the Pizza Connection?

That is the widely believed but not exactly proven theory that the price of the average slice of pizza is commensurate with subway and bus fares. When one goes up, in theory, so does the other.

PRE-COLONIAL TIMES THROUGH THE REVOLUTIONARY ERA

PRE–COLONIAL NEW YORK

What created New York?

It should be clear to everybody reading this that New York is really, as the song says, a state of mind. But geologically speaking, it exists as it does today because of water and ice. For hundreds of millions of years, the area that would become New York was frequently under water. Around 18,000 years ago, a massive glacier called the Laurentide ice sheet covered most of modern-day Canada as well as part of the American Upper Midwest (forming the Great Lakes) and Northeast.

One section of glacier, called the Wisconsin Ice Sheet, spread down from eastern Canada roughly 1.5 million years ago, after the end of the Pleistocene Era. It covered most of the New York metropolitan area with a thousand feet of ice. The mark of its southern border can be seen in modern-day Brooklyn, where the higher elevations of northern, once ice-covered Brooklyn give way to the uncovered flatlands of Canarsie and Flatbush.

As the glacier began to pull back, it left behind a line of glacial moraine that essentially created the backbone of Long Island, which would otherwise today sit below the ocean's surface. The long ridge of glacier deposit that arcs through Brooklyn and Queens is notable for the greenspaces like Prospect Park and Forest Park or cemeteries like Greenwood and Cypress Hills placed there due to the rocky moraine making for poor farmland. The glacier's long retreat left hills and piles of rocky debris everywhere, carved out valleys and grooves, and deepened existing water channels like the Hudson River Valley (the southernmost glacial fjord in the Americas) or created entirely new ones like the East River.

Who were the earliest human settlers of New York?

The people who lived in the New York area before the arrival of European colonists were mostly semi-nomadic groups who started populating the region anywhere between five to ten thousand years ago; though evidence of at least temporary human habitation dates from thousands of years earlier. Mostly hunter-gatherers, they also engaged in agriculture. These groups kept small plots of cropland and rotated between numerous semi-permanent dwellings on the various islands. Pottery shards and arrowheads have

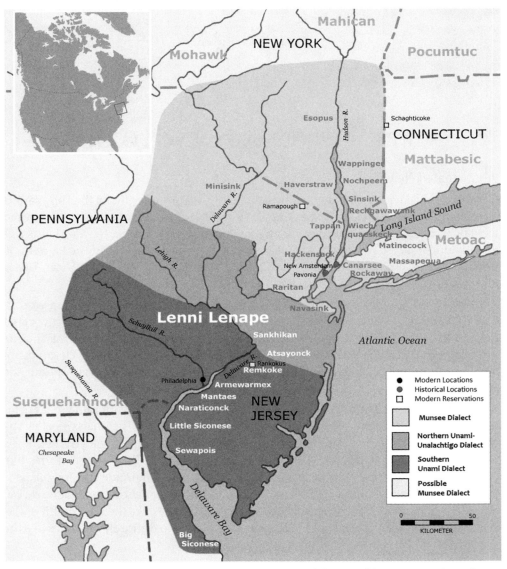

A map showing regions where the Lenape language was spoken around the time of the New Amsterdam colony.

been uncovered over the years, usually by accident when some new building is being constructed. But there isn't a strong archaeological record of pre-European human settlement in the area.

Most of the area that became New York state was populated by Iroquois Indians who had formed the Five Nations confederacy in the fifteenth century. They were generally aligned against the Algonquin tribes, which included the Mahicans, who lived along the Hudson River. The residents of the future New York city were the Lenape.

Who were the Lenape?

Known as "the people" or "the Ancient Ones," the Lenape Indians settled on the island later called Manhattan hundreds of years before the first Europeans arrived. They were mainly hunter-gatherers, but they began farming crops like corn, beans, and squash starting around 1300 C.E. The Lenape were part of the Northeast Algonquin, their reach extending from modern-day Connecticut to Delaware; they would, in fact, later be known as the Delaware. Manhattan was probably never inhabited by more than a thousand Lenape at any given time in the three dwelling clusters, and even then most likely not for the entire year. It is believed the Lenape stuck to more sheltered places on the mainland during the winter months. On Manhattan, they lived in dome-shaped houses whose skeletons were made of saplings that were covered first in bark and then animal skins. Today, Delaware communities are located in New Jersey and Oklahoma and in Ontario, Canada.

The Indians who lived on Long Island were believed by the Europeans to have been divided into thirteen tribes organized in a confederacy by a Montauk chief. But later scholarship has indicated that the Lenape were more loosely organized groups and only started creating tribal structures as a defensive reaction to the influx of European settlers.

What are some of the other Indian groups who lived in the New York area?

Some of the tribes include:

- Canarsie—Also "Canarsee." Lived mostly in the marshy area around Jamaica Bay in southern Brooklyn, where the soil was particularly rich. Like many of the Indian tribes in the region, they roamed all over. They sold Cripplebush, the area that became Williamsburg, to the Dutch in 1638.

- Hackensack—A Lenape tribe also called the Achkenheshacky. Made their home in the Hackensack river valley in New Jersey. In 1641, some Hackensacks were accused of killing a couple of Dutch farmers whose cows trampled the Indians' corn fields. Governor Willem Kieft (1597–1647) offered bounties for Hackensack scalps.

- Montauk—Several of the Indian groups who lived on the eastern half of Long Island were later known collectively as the Montauk Indians for their similar linguistic heritage.

- Raritan—A band who lived in the swampy area around where the Raritan River flows into the Lower Bay just west of Staten Island. In 1641, after a surprise raid by Dutch troops on one of their villages the previous year left several dead, the Raritans raided a Staten Island farm, escalating the Indian-Dutch guerrilla conflict known as Kieft's War.

- Rockaway—Likely related to the Canarsie Indians, the Rockaway Indians, also known as Reckouwacky or "the place of our own people," lived around the Rockaway Islands. Much of what was "known" about them, like with many long-gone Indian tribes from Long Island, is buried in myth and legend. There is a curious seven-foot- (2.1-meter-) tall stone monument in the Five Towns part of Long Island—just north of the Rockaways and east of JFK Airport—dedicated to Cullullo Telawana, "the last of the Rockaway," who supposedly passed away in 1818.

What happened to the Indian tribes of the New York area?

As European settlements spread across the North American seaboard during the mid-to-late seventeenth century, pressures increased between the European settlers and the New York region's original inhabitants. Even though the area had never been densely populated, once the Dutch started buying all the land they could from the Indians, it started to severely limit the amount of land the Indians could use for living and farming. There were some instances of Indians being forced into slavery, although that was abolished in New York in 1679.

By the mid-1600s, several eruptions of violence between the Dutch and Indians resulted in large losses of life (proportional to the relatively small populations), particularly civilians, on both sides. The Dutch traded with but ultimately had very little respect for the Indians, whom they called *wilden* ("savages"). These often brutal skirmishes, and the even more devastating rampages of smallpox that the Europeans brought with them, took a harsh toll. By the eighteenth century, most Indians had removed themselves to the mainland, further away from European settlement.

THE DUTCH AND BRITISH COLONIAL YEARS

Who was the first European to enter New York Harbor?

Giovanni di Verrazzano (1485–1528) was an Italian explorer who, like so many others, crossed the Atlantic to the New World in order to find new trade routes to China. The dream of finding the so-called "Northwest Passage" led Verrazzano and other explorers to traverse the Atlantic coastline looking for waterways through the continent.

Verrazzano, who had been sent to claim new territories for France, sailed into New York Harbor in his ship *Dauphine* on April 17, 1524, and cast anchor in the Lower Bay between Staten Island and Brooklyn. In a letter to Francis I, Verrazzano described how "we found a very agreeable place between two small but prominent hills, in the midst of which flowed to the sea a very great river."

What happened then?

The sight of the *Dauphine* sent some thirty canoes of Indians congregating around the vessel. Initially, Verrazzano dispatched a boat into the Upper Bay between Staten Island and Manhattan. But when a storm threatened to rise, Verrazzano pulled up anchor and sailed off up the coast towards what became known as Martha's Vineyard and Rhode Island before giving up hope of finding the Northwest Passage. Another expeditionary voyage of Verrazzano's in 1528 turned out even worse for him, when he and some crewmen were reportedly killed and eaten by cannibals on an island somewhere south of Jamaica.

Which European explorer followed Verrazzano into New York Harbor?

One year after Verrazzano's expedition to New York Harbor, King Charles I of Spain (1500–58) sent a black Portuguese navigator named Esteban Gomez (1483–1538) to explore the area. He sailed into the harbor on January 17, 1526. It being St. Anthony's feast day, he named the river flowing down the western shore of Manhattan island the San Antonio. He departed soon thereafter.

That was the extent of Gomez's contribution to New York history, which has mostly forgotten him, but for this bit of deathless rhyme published in the 1917 anthology *The Book of New York Verse*:

The Portugee came in from sea,
Sir Estevan de Gomez;
"I smell," said he, "no spicery …"

Where did the Hudson River get its name?

When English sailor Henry Hudson (1565–1611) sailed into New York Harbor in 1609, he didn't have a good record. He had twice attempted what it seems every other great European mariner of his day had already tried: To discover the fabled Northwest Passage to Asia and the (it was thought) limitless trading riches of China. Both missions failed when he ran into Greenland.

In 1609 Hudson was sailing under the auspices of the Dutch West India Company, which had a very strong business interest in finding the Northwest Passage. His ship, the *Halve Maene* (*Half Moon*), was a relatively small eighty-tonner with two sails and a crew of just twenty. After almost going the wrong way north again, Hudson's crew steered him in the right direction toward the New World. He sailed into New York Harbor on September 2, 1609.

How long did Henry Hudson and his crew stay?

According to the journal kept by Hudson's first mate Robert Juet (?–1611), "We came to three great rivers." Hudson stayed for several days in what was probably the Lower Bay. During that time, Indians rowed out to the *Half Moon*, eager to see the newcomers. Juet noted that "they are very glad of our coming … they desire clothes and are very civil."

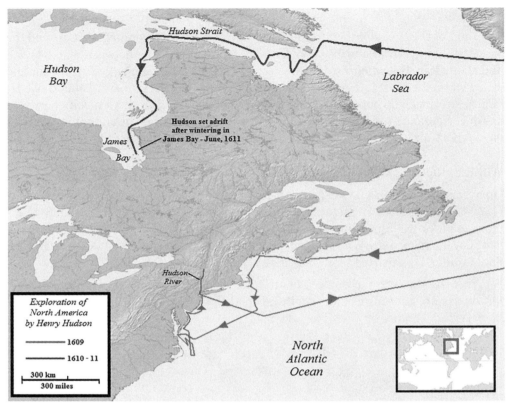

A map showing the routes taken by English explorer Henry Hudson, after whom the New York river and the bay in Canada are named.

On September 11, Hudson sailed through the Narrows between Staten Island and Brooklyn, under where the Verrazano Narrows Bridge (the official name of the bridge is misspelled, an error locals are trying to correct) would soar centuries later. He started sailing north up the river that he most likely did not know had been named the San Antonio, which would later be called the Hudson River.

What were early relationships like between the Europeans and Indians?

The two groups had vastly different cultures but realized that they had mutually beneficial economic trading interests. In other words, the Indians and the new arrivals dealt with each other in order to trade what the Europeans wanted (foodstuffs, particularly in the lean early years, and access to land) and what the Indians wanted (manufactured goods and tools). Except when they didn't. The relationship was marked by cooperation but also tension and flare-ups of violent disagreement brought about by bad communication and cultural misunderstanding.

A few days after crewman John Colman was killed by an arrow in his neck, Hudson's crew had two other violent run-ins with Indians (perhaps caused in part by the fact that he had taken two of them against their will back to Europe as exotic specimens). One involved about a hundred Lenape attacking the *Half Moon* and being bloodily repulsed by cannon fire. In the decades that followed, conflict continually flared up as colonists pushed ever further into Indian territory and responded with often overwhelming violence to even the slightest provocation.

Who was the first non-Indian resident of Manhattan?

In 1613, the trading vessel *Jonge Tobias* sailed into New York Harbor. On board was Juan Rodriguez, a native of Santo Domingo in the Dominican Republic. When the *Jonge Tobias* returned to its home of the Netherlands, Rodriguez stayed behind, apparently threatening to jump overboard otherwise. He was left with 80 hatchets and other tools and may have used them in the running of a small trading post.

Not much is known about Rodriguez, except that he was probably of African descent (the ship's crew referred to him as a "Spaniard" and "mulatto"), he lived in the area for at least a year, and may have taken an Indian wife. But in his honor, in 2013 the city renamed a long stretch of uptown Broadway—from 159th Street in Washington Heights to 218th Street in Inwood—Juan Rodriguez Way.

What was the Dutch West India Company?

The Dutch West India Company was a public-private trading company that was founded in 1621 as a way of expanding the Netherlands' dominance in the Americas and Africa by both economic and military means. It was viewed in Calvinist Amsterdam as another way to combat their sworn enemies, the Catholic Spanish Empire, against whom the Dutch had just relaunched a war. Supposedly a private business, the firm also maintained land- and sea-based military forces operating under the remit of the Dutch government, which encouraged it to plunder everything it could from Spanish holdings. Wherever it was believed necessary, the company also used its soldiers and warships to subdue and decimate native populations.

After being given a monopoly by its government on trading in the Western Hemisphere and Africa, the Dutch West India Company established a massive network of colonies from the west coast of Africa to the Caribbean to New Amsterdam. The colonies were primarily expected to export raw materials back home, trade with each other where expedient, and import finished goods from the Netherlands. Mike Wallace, co-author of the historical tome *Gotham*, has likened the firm's business model to being "Exxon with guns." This company was ultimately less successful than its more storied Pacific-monopoly counterpart, the Dutch East India Company, and was ultimately dissolved in 1794.

What was New Netherland?

New Netherland was the name of the territory that the government of Holland granted to the Dutch West India Company in 1621. Its boundaries reached from the island of Manhattan north up the shores of the Hudson River all the way to the colony of Fort Orange (established in 1624), which would later become the settlement of Albany.

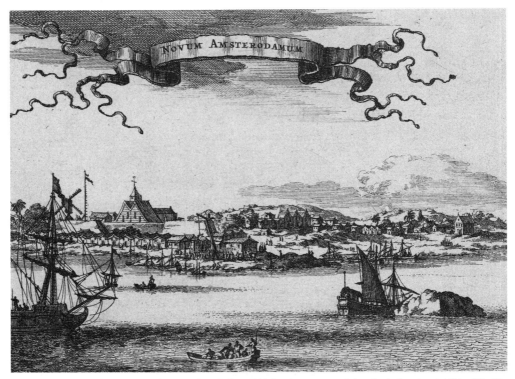

The Dutch colony of New Amsterdam was founded in 1624, but it was several decades before it established itself as a viable and growing settlement.

New Netherland was expanded in 1655 along the Delaware River—which runs between the states of Delaware, New Jersey, and Pennsylvania—when a detachment of Dutch troops led by Peter Stuyvesant overwhelmed the garrison of the Swedish fort at the current site of Wilmington, Delaware, ending the short-lived history of the New Sweden colony.

When was New Amsterdam founded?

In May 1624, the Dutch West India Company vessel *Nieu Nederlandt* sailed into New York Harbor carrying some thirty families, comprising over a hundred settlers (mostly Protestant French-speaking Walloons fleeing religious persecution). It deposited several men on the lower tip of Manhattan island where they built Fort Amsterdam. Some families were left also on Nut Island (Governor's Island), though that settlement would quickly fold up and relocate to Manhattan, and the base of Fort Orange was built far up the Hudson River at what would become the state capital of Albany. A handful of traders also set up on the far, or Brooklyn, side of the East River in Wallabout Bay. But the settlers' living quarters and trading business—which again was their stated purpose for traveling across the Atlantic—coalesced around the lower Manhattan settlement of New Amsterdam.

How fast did New Amsterdam grow?

The colony took some time to truly establish itself. It was initially a rude collection of buildings huddling near the (mostly ungarrisoned) fort. In 1626, a stronger fortification was constructed, along with thirty houses. By 1643, the colony only numbered seven hundred. However, what New Amsterdam didn't have in size, it made up for in diversity. That same year, the French Jesuit missionary Isaac Jogues (1607–1646) disapprovingly noted hearing eighteen different languages spoken in the small trading colony that was already bustling with representatives from nearly every European ethnic group from Norwegians to Italians, Irish to Bohemians.

What was New Amsterdam like in the early days?

From its founding until around the time of the Revolutionary War, New Amsterdam was little more than a typical raw colonial seaport hacked out of the surrounding forest. Its few hundred houses, workshops, and taverns were built out of local wood and some brick hauled over from Europe as ballast on ships. The streets were established in fairly random manner, based on where people happened to set up their buildings. Some old Lenape pathways were widened into streets and later avenues like Broadway and Bowery. Many homes were surrounded by orchards and gardens. Being a Dutch colony, there was a canal (later filled in and called Broad Street), and the occasional windmill.

The earliest detailed map of New Amsterdam, dating from 1660, shows houses clustered on the East River side, with a protective wall running along today's Wall Street. North of there, most of Manhattan was still swamps and forest. But bit by bit the wealthier Dutch were buying up sections of central and northern Manhattan from Indians and turning them into *bouwerijs* ("farms"). Perhaps because it was seen at first as more of a trading center than future metropolis, there wasn't much in the way of urban planning. Urban historian Gerard Koeppel notes that New York started off like Philadelphia, also set between rivers and settled first by the Lenape before the Dutch and the English. But unlike Philadelphia's "lovely grid of varied densities, broad central streets, and open squares," early New York was laid out almost by whim and chance.

How did the early Dutch settlement support itself?

The early history of Europeans in New York is one of a people finding a wonderful place and spending years trying to figure out what to do with it. New York Harbor might have been one of the finest in the world, but it didn't immediately lend itself to mercantile purposes. Remember that the reason for early explorers coming to the region was a quest for the fabled Northwest Passage. The early economic impetus for the tiny colony barely hanging on at the southern tip of Manhattan during those first few difficult years was in fact the beaver fur trade. Beaver fur was highly desired in the Netherlands for the making of fur coats, hats, and other stylish cold-weather clothing.

Trying to avoid the duties placed on beaver fur imported from Russia, Dutch merchants discovered a more lucrative source: trading for furs with Indians to the north.

The Dutch West India Company was founded essentially to exploit this lucrative natural resource. Once they discovered the European appetite for beaver fur, Indians eager to trade for goods like knives and glassware began bringing pelts to Dutch traders. Between 1626 and 1632, over 50,000 beaver pelts were shipped back to Europe. Beavers were considered important enough to be given a place of pride on the city's official seal.

Did the Dutch bring windmills to New York?

Given its Dutch provenance, it's no surprise that the earliest Manhattan skyline, such as it was, featured a windmill. It may have been located just north of Fort Amsterdam, near where the Customs House now faces the northeast corner of Battery Park; the winds always blow stronger on the Hudson River side. In 1638 there were four windmills in the city. Seen today as decorative elements in the Dutch landscape, at that time they were used to power sawmills and deliver storm warnings for ships on the East River.

Was Manhattan actually bought for $24?

In 1626, when New Amsterdam was just five years old, it already had a representative in the Dutch parliament back in Amsterdam: Peter Schagen (1589–1638). In November of that year, Schagen sent a momentous letter to parliament after debriefing the crew of the ship *Arms of Amsterdam*, which had sailed from the New World in September. Among other more mundane matters, such as the number of beaver (7,246) and muskrat (34) skins included in the cargo, his letter contained a rather momentous announcement.

A 1909 painting by Alfred Frederick depicts the purchase of Manhattan Island by the Dutch in 1626.

After noting that "our people are in good spirit and live in peace" and that "the women also have borne some children there," he recorded that "They have purchased the island Manhattes from the Indians for the value of 60 guilders. It is 11,000 morgens (about 22,000 acres) in size."

How did the purchase actually happen?

Although there is a historical plaque commemorating the purchase all the way up on the north side of Manhattan in Inwood Hill Park, the deal actually took place in May 1626 on Bowling Green. It was one of the first official acts of the colony's newly appointed director general, Peter Minuit (c. 1580–1638). Since 60 guilders worked out to about $24, this purchase was later trumpeted as the greatest real estate deal in history. The ship's other cargo was computed to be worth about 45,000 guilders.

This transaction was viewed later as among the first of many deceitful deals that swindled Indians—who often moved with the hunting and growing seasons and so didn't have the same fixed view of property as the Europeans—out of land they didn't even permanently live on and didn't realize they were agreeing to give up in perpetuity. In any case, Minuit was lionized in later years as the man whose shrewd skills secured Manhattan at a cheap price.

What happened to Indians in the area after Manhattan was sold?

As happened up and down the Eastern Seaboard, wherever there were large concentrations of European settlers, Indian tribes were eventually relocated, either willingly or by force. New Amsterdam was no different. The autocratic Willem Kieft, named autocratic director-general (or governor) of New Netherland in 1638, used a heavy hand to reign, whether it was stamping out illicit smuggling or fighting off colonial rivals like the English. Kieft's approach to resolving conflict with nearby Indians was generally military, as compared to the more conciliatory nature of earlier governors like Peter Minuit. His determination to increase taxes, even levying a fee on the Lenape for protection against other Indian tribes, didn't make him any more popular.

When did Kieft's War begin?

In 1641, Raritan Indians burned a Staten Island plantation and killed four farmers in apparent revenge for the Dutch burning down one of their villages the year before. Later that same year a Weckquaesgeek Indian from north of Manhattan—whose uncle had been murdered in 1626 by settlers who stole the beaverskins he had been hoping to trade—killed a Dutchman at his farm, also in apparent revenge. A military expedition convinced the Indian's tribe to hand him over for punishment. The cycle of vengeful guerrilla conflict called Kieft's War sputtered on for several years.

Who were the Twelve Men?

The first semblance of any kind of representational government in New York occured in 1641 after Kieft asked the colony's leading families to select twelve men to form a com-

What was the "Year of the Blood"?

In 1643, which came to be known as the "Year of the Blood," Iroquois armed with Dutch muskets drove their rivals the Algonquins south. In what became known as the Pavonia Massacre, Kieft ordered his soldiers to attack the mostly defenseless Algonquins. After slaughtering eighty Algonquins, Kieft's soldiers marched into New Amsterdam bearing the severed heads of their victims. Another forty defenseless Indian refugees were massacred at Corlears Hook in what became the Lower East Side.

Eleven Algonquin tribes then started raiding Dutch territory in retaliation, burning homes, killing farmers, and taking women and children into captivity. This caused the Dutch to build a defensive palisade across Manhattan along what became known as Wall Street. The Dutch assaulted an Indian stronghold in modern-day Connecticut and killed nearly all of its inhabitants—over five hundred men, women, and children. In 1645, a ceasefire concluded the fighting for several years.

mittee that would advise him on relations with the Indians the colony was currently warring with. The so-called Twelve Men were a short-lived experiment in democracy, though. In less than a year, Kieft had dissolved the committee and made unauthorized public meetings illegal.

Kieft then organized *another* council of eight in 1643. When they disagreed with his plan to import mercenaries to defend New Amsterdam (and tax the people to pay for them), Kieft simply ignored them. A petition sent by the Eight Men back to Amsterdam listed their criticisms of the rash Kieft—including the Pavonia Massacre and his autocratic stubbornness, which led him to spurn a peace offering by Indian sachems in 1643 that could have stopped years of fighting. This set the wheels in motion for Kieft's recall and the appointment of a poor-tempered, peg-legged, religiously intolerant replacement who would prove even less popular.

Who was "Peg Leg Peter"?

The last director general of the New Netherlands was also its most memorable, in many ways. Peter Stuyvesant was an ambitious, religious, tough, highly prejudiced, nearly dictatorial leader who ultimately surrendered his colony to the British without firing a single shot and has as strong a claim as any to being the true father of New York. Born in the Netherlands in 1610 to a minister, Stuyvesant went to work for the Dutch West India Company at a young age. In 1644, he was leading the company's naval assault on a Spanish fort on the Caribbean island of Saint Martin when a cannonball hit his lower right leg. It was replaced by a wooden peg.

Stuyvesant arrived in New York in 1647 as the new director general. Almost immediately, he began instituting changes that established his reputation for bullheaded intolerance. Besides restricting the sale of alcohol on Sunday, he tried to stop Quakers and Jews from entering the colony and banned the observance of any religion except the Dutch Reformed Church. He also tried to quash discontent about the previous director's culpability in provoking the last Indian war, put the colony on a stronger economic footing, and infuriated many with his anti-democratic leadership style.

What started the Peach War?

In his *History of New York*, Washington Irving's (1783–1859) euphemistic take on Indian-European relationships was that "the good understanding between our ancestors and their savage neighbors was liable to occasional interruptions." One of those "interruptions" took place in September 1655, when a Dutch farmer, seeing an Indian woman stealing peaches from his farm just south of Trinity Church, shot

Peter Stuyvesant was the Dutch director-general of New Amsterdam from 1647 to 1664, when the colony was taken over by the British and renamed New York.

her dead. Hundreds of infuriated Indians entered the city, which was nearly defenseless because Stuyvesant and his soldiers were out of town, fighting to wrest control of the Delaware Valley from the Swedes. When the short, sharp Peach War ended three days later, over a hundred settlers had been killed, and much of New Jersey and Staten Island put to the torch. Another peace was eventually negotiated.

What was the Flushing Remonstrance?

In 1657, among the heavily English Protestant communities of Queens, opposition was growing to Stuyvesant's banning the practice of all religions except for the Dutch Reformed Church. The governor had even announced a fine for anybody who housed or transported Quakers. In response, in December thirty settlers from the farming community of Flushing wrote a letter to Stuyvesant denouncing his religious bigotry. "We are bound by the law to do good unto all men, especially to those of the household of faith," they wrote, adding that this included even "Jews, Turks and Egyptians, as they are considered sons of Adam." The governor responded by putting two of the letter's signers in jail and replacing the leaders of Flushing. By 1663, Stuyvesant was forced to open up religious freedom.

The Flushing Remonstrance, as the letter is known, has been called a forerunner to the first amendment of the Constitution of the United States. Even though the Remonstrance is one of Queens's most important historical documents, its remaining fragment is held at the state archives in Albany.

How were the poor looked after in colonial New York?

In keeping with then-common European practice, New Amsterdam had no public-welfare system for taking care of its poor, sick, and indigent citizens. An almshouse (also known as "poor house") for the poor opened in 1653 and was later replaced by church-operated "deacons' houses." In 1736, the city opened an almshouse where City Hall is today. Like many almshouses, it was something of a one-size-fits-all place, with a workhouse for those able to work, correctional facility for criminals, small hospital, and the city's first community garden.

When did the first Jewish colonists arrive in New Amsterdam?

In 1654, a group of twenty-three Sephardic Jews landed in New Amsterdam. They had traveled from Recife, Brazil, which the Netherlands had just lost to the Portuguese, who came loaded with the threat of the Inquisition. Governor Peter Stuyvesant immediately petitioned the directors of the Dutch West Indies Company to bar any Jews (whom he referred to as a "deceitful race" and "hateful enemies") from settling in the colony. His petition was denied by the directors, who noted that "this would be somewhat unreasonable and unfair."

The new arrivals established the oldest North American Jewish congregation, Shearith Israel ("Remnant of Israel"), the year of their arrival. The continent's first Rosh Hashanah service was held—in private, as the only legal public services were those of the Dutch Reformed Church—on September 12, 1654. Shearith Israel didn't build a synagogue until 1730 (on South William Street), using funds solicited from other congregations in Europe and the West Indies. It was New York's only Jewish congregation until 1825. Since 1897 they have met in a synagogue on 70th Street and Central Park West designed by Louis Comfort Tiffany (1848–1933).

How were Jews initially received in New Amsterdam?

The prejudice of leaders like Stuyvesant was hardly unique in New Amsterdam. But Jewish immigrants still found the colony to be a generally more hospitable home than elsewhere in the colonies. There was actually more overt discrimination against religious groups like Catholics, particularly under later British rule when "freedom of conscience" was given to Jews and non-Anglican Protestants, but not Catholics. However, the price that many Jews in New Amsterdam and early New York had to pay was not inconsiderable. For years, the legislature rejected applications to build a synagogue, and the Dutch also didn't allow Jews to work in retail or the craft trades.

Jews in New Amsterdam faced considerable pressure to culturally assimilate and not openly broadcast their religious faith. Intermarriage was common, particularly among the Sephardic Jews. There were some cases of Christians converting to Judaism. The Jews were given more freedom under British rule, with some acquiring large estates and gaining full citizenship. It wasn't until 1777 that Jews were given full suffrage by the Revolutionary constitution.

How did New Amsterdam become New York?

In 1664, the colony of New Amsterdam was growing more successful but not necessarily more content. That made it both a plum target for other colonial powers and a relatively easy one to take. In March of that year, England's King Charles II (1630–1685) granted his brother James Stuart, Duke of York (1633–1701), a great stretch of land in the New World that included Maine, Long Island, and everything between the Connecticut and Delaware rivers. The fact that this grant included the Dutch settlement of New Amsterdam meant that Charles II's deed was a soft announcement of hostilities, and the undeclared start of the Second Anglo–Dutch War.

On August 26, 1664, four British frigates carrying 450 soldiers dropped anchor in Gravesend Bay east of Coney Island. The British demanded the colony's surrender and drew up a twenty-three-point Articles of Capitulation that included

King Charles II granted his brother James Stuart, Duke of York (who later became King James II of England), pictured here, land that included Long Island and areas already settled by the Dutch.

guarantees for everything from freedom of religion to the continued operation of bars. Stuyvesant haughtily shredded the paper, even though the colony's defenses were in deplorable state and he had less than two hundred soldiers at his command. A group of city leaders reconstructed the letter and convinced Stuyvesant of the implausibility of putting up a fight. To the relief of New Amsterdam's 1,500 inhabitants, their stubborn director general agreed.

Was it a dramatic invasion?

The British occupied New Amsterdam without firing a shot, and promptly renamed it New York in honor of the Duke of York. This changeover meant that the city would forever after be an English-speaking port. But very little else seemed to change on the ground. The colony's new rulers promised their subjects, in the name of the king, "free and peaceable possession of their property, unobstructed and trade and navigation, not only to the King's dominions, but also to the Netherlands with their own ships and people."

The British, seeing a prospering trading post whose generally tolerant people preferred to get on with the business of business, probably decided to not to mess with a promising new profit center. Ironically, it was only after the possession of New York passed from the Dutch West India Company's private hands to the British government that it would start to become a business success.

How did the Dutch lose New York ... again?

The British were happy to have gained possession of a major colony in the New World. They did not, however, prove adept at safeguarding it. Only a few years after New Amsterdam had been renamed New York, a Dutch fleet that had been wreaking havoc on British possessions and ships all the way up the Atlantic coast, showed up in New York Harbor in August 1673. British forces, outnumbered and with some of their cannons spiked by pro-Dutch citizens, surrendered in a matter of days. The Dutch renamed their old colony New Orange, for the Prince of Orange.

However, their success would be short-lived. In 1674, the Treaty of Westminster, which brought an end to hostilities between England and the Netherlands signed over rights to Dutch North American possessions to the British. Later that year, New Orange became New York again. It would stay under British control, except for a brief occupation by rebel forces at the start of the American Revolution, until 1783.

Who was New York's first mayor?

Born to English Puritans and raised in Holland, Thomas Willett (1605–1674) arrived in America on the *Mayflower* in 1629 and quickly became active in politics and business. Being fluent in both Dutch and English was a great asset for Willett, who became a very successful trader with his own fleet of ships. Willett was also a colonial administrator for the British and helped negotiate Stuyvesant's surrender of New Amsterdam in 1664.

The new colony's governor, Richard Nicoll (1624–1672), appointed Willett the first mayor of New York in 1665. It was not a necessarily auspicious appointment, as the city was still just a tiny settlement of about 1,500 people comprising just a few lanes south of Wall Street, a few hundred cottages, and the occasional windmill. Also, the city's mayor was in many ways a powerless position, as most authority over the city resided in the hands of the governor in Albany, who retained the right to appoint the mayor. That situation would remain largely unchanged for centuries. Willett was also the chief magistrate of the Mayor's court and established the city's jury trial system.

Why did the Bolting Act matter?

New York has been blessed with everything from good weather to one of the world's greatest harbors. But the city's industry has had more than a few winds at its back. One of the earliest of those grants to New York's fortune was the Bolting Act of 1680. Governor Edmund Andros (1637–1714) had already given the city such improvements as the first street lamps and a large commercial dock at the terminus on Whitehall Street and having New York declared the entire colony's only port of entry for imports.

The Bolting Act decreed that all grain being exported from New York state had to be ground in New York City. This monopoly not only necessitated the construction of windmills (which then earned a prominent place on the city's seal) to help in the flour-grinding labor, but helped triple the city's population and wealth in just a couple decades.

When did New York become a city?

The answer to that question could vary, depending on criteria like population. But one simple measure of New York's transformation from colony to city can be dated from April 27, 1686. That was the year that Thomas Dongan (1634–1715), governor of the New York province, signed the Charter of 1686—an earlier charter in 1665 had set up a municipal government with a mayor and aldermen—officially establishing New York as a city and defining its boundaries (which included "all the waste, vacant, un-patented and unappropriated lands lyeing and being within the said City of New York and on Manhattan's Island aforesaid, extending and reaching to the lower water mark").

Thomas Dongan, 2nd Earl of Limerick, was the governor who signed the Charter of 1686.

Dongan also divided the city into a half-dozen wards. Each ward elected an alderman and assistant alderman to serve on the city's new Common Council, its first true example of legislative democracy. Like other city institutions such as the mayor, the Common Council's powers were strictly limited by the governor, who could veto its rulings at any time. The Common Council was eventually renamed the City Council. Currently it has one member each from fifty-one council districts and is the city's sole legislative body.

Who was New York's first elected mayor?

As a foreshadowing of the city's history of fractious politics, its first mayoral election took place during a tumultuous time and the results didn't last too long. In 1689, civil war back in England and a popular uprising in New York (see below) threw the colonial government into chaos. That year, a provincial convention endorsed the electing of aldermen, councilmen, and the mayor. Peter Delanoy (1650–1696), a Dutch businessman, was elected the city's eighteenth mayor. He served just two years until the British reestablished control over the colony. Delanoy would be the only elected mayor of the city until Cornelius Van Wyck Lawrence (1791–1861) won at the ballot box in 1834.

What was the Leisler Rebellion?

In 1688, England's "Glorious Rebellion" of Protestants had thrown the Catholic King James II from the throne and installed the Dutch William of Orange (1650–1702) on the throne. The ensuing chaos created a power vacuum in the colonies, due in part to a lack of clear communication from England about the new rulers and lines of authority. War broke out between France and England, sewing further confusion and fright in the colonies, where it wasn't clear who would be responsible for defense. The local militia stepped into the vacuum in 1689, seizing Fort James and preparing for a possible invasion by the French or attacks by disloyal Catholic colonists. Militia captain Jacob Leisler (1640–1691) was made the colony's military commander. The vehemently anti-Catholic Leisler became increasingly power-hungry. He ignored royal communications, named himself lieutenant governor, briefly planned to invade Canada, and started arresting "Papists" at will.

In 1691, newly appointed lieutenant governor Richard Ingoldsbody (1617–1685) landed in New York with a small force and demanded access to Fort James. In a comical twist, Ingoldsbody's official letters from the British throne were on another ship, the *Archangel*, that hadn't arrived yet. This gave Leisler an excuse to ignore the request. That delay led to a weeks-long city-wide battle between the city's pro- and anti-Leisler factions. After the *Archangel* landed with the new royal governor Henry Sloughter (d. 1691), Leisler and his men surrendered. Leisler and his son-in-law were convicted of treason. Sloughter was reluctant to go ahead with the execution until he heard back from London about the defendants' appeal. But he was apparently plied with drink by anti-Leislerians and eventually agreed to execute the men by hanging.

Why did New York become a pirate haven?

In the 1690s, Governor Benjamin Fletcher (1640–1703) had a widely acknowledged appetite for graft. That included being business partners with pirates. For a modest price, Fletcher made the city's port a safe place for pirates looking to fence their ill-gotten gains; most ports were not nearly so accommodating. Several local financiers and pirate captains became quite wealthy in the ensuing trade, which helped boost the city's economy considerably.

Who was New York's best-known pirate?

One of the pirates who did particularly well by New York was William Kidd (1645–1701). Born in Scotland in 1645, Kidd spent years as a privateer operating under a "letter of marque" from the British throne that allowed him to essentially operate like a licensed pirate, boarding and plundering ships belonging to enemies of the empire. By the time he first landed in New York in 1691, Kidd was one of England's most storied privateers. He even assisted imperial forces sent to put down Leisler's uprising. Once established in New York, Kidd married a wealthy widow and settled himself into city life. He owned many properties downtown, including a luxurious waterfront family home at Hanover and Pearl streets.

Within a few years, though, Kidd left his newly respectable life behind. In 1695 he sailed back to London and secured another commission as a privateer, this time to hunt down pirates attacking British East India Company ships in the Indian Ocean. Back in

"Captain Kidd in New York Harbor" is a circa 1920 painting by Jean Leon Gerome Ferris. William Kidd found success and popularity working for the English government before turning into the very type of pirate he once hunted down. The decision led to his execution.

New York, Kidd outfitted a thirty-four-gun galley named *Adventure*, and set off to restore justice to the far side of the world. Within a short time, though, Kidd had exceeded his remit and become a pirate himself. He was eventually arrested and executed by hanging. Many treasure-seekers are convinced that Kidd buried some of his loot, perhaps on or near the (still privately owned) Gardiners Island off the east coast of Long Island, or near Sandy Hook in New Jersey.

What was New York like under the British in the early 1700s?

Following the British transformation of New Amsterdam into New York, the city continued and even accelerated its growth. An etching from 1717 shows the city from the East River, which is filled with ships. At the time, the population was around seven thousand, making it the third-largest city in the American colonies after Boston and Philadelphia. About 225 ships came into the port annually, usually arriving with West Indian sugar and leaving with supplies to operate the islands' slave plantations. Shipbuilding and other maritime businesses boomed at this time.

As New York continued its transformation from colonial outpost to city, the burgeoning trade sector saw an ancillary increase in businesses like law firms and insurance companies that would soon become a cornerstone of the local economy. The early eighteenth century also saw more urban attractions like a racetrack and the turning of lower Broadway into a tree-shaded promenade popular with strolling couples in powdered wigs and hoopskirts.

What prompted the formation of the city's first fire company?

For more than a century after the founding of New Amsterdam, firefighters were more a loose patrol of volunteer watchmen who would run the bucket brigades of citizens. That changed in 1731, the year that the Common Council imported a pair of hand-pumped fire engines from London. They were housed in the city's first firehouse, which opened on Broad Street in 1736. The "pumpers" needed crews, and so a more organized volunteer company was established to operate them. In 1737, legislation was passed to allow the formation of a volunteer fire company of up to forty two men. By the end of the eighteenth century, multiple fire engine houses and companies had been set up. In 1795, each engine house was equipped with poles that the firemen could use to carry up to a dozen buckets of water on. This development hurried the demise of the citizen fire brigade and symbolized the turn toward a more disciplined and organized fire-fighting apparatus.

Did early New York have any hospitals?

Like the rest of the American colonies, for many years that answer was simply no. Until well into the eighteenth century there was no centralized healthcare institution in all of New York. The first hospital of any kind was the six-bed Almshouse Hospital, which opened in 1736 where City Hall is today. In 1816, the city opened up a new almshouse on a site between Second Avenue and the East River above 23rd Street that was named the Bellevue Establishment.

Today the word "Bellevue" is primarily associated with mental illness, and the hospital was long associated with serving just the mentally challenged and indigent. But it was actually America's first hospital. Later in the century, Bellevue became one of the nation's most pioneering medical institutions. A maternity ward and medical college, as well as America's first ambulance service (horse-and-buggy), were added on later.

When were the first slaves brought to New York?

New York is now seen as one of America's most deeply northern cities, as culturally distinct from the South as it is from Alaska. But both regions share at least one deep similarity: A long history of slavery. The first slaves brought to North America most likely landed in the Jamestown colony in 1617. They were followed by eleven slaves brought to New Amsterdam around 1627. This began a long and insalubrious period in the city's history.

Curiously, given the important role it would later play in the abolitionist movement, New York's economy was unusually and heavily dependent on slave labor for a northern city. In 1771, one-third of the population of Brooklyn was enslaved. When the Revolutionary War began, there were about 20,000 slaves in the New York area, the densest concentration of slaves in the north and more than any other colonial city except for Charleston, South Carolina. When the United States of America became a free country, one-fifth of New York's population was black, both free and enslaved.

How many slaves were there in early New York?

Many more than is commonly thought. In the early 1700s, over fourteen percent of the population of New York was enslaved. A 1738 census showed that an incredible one in four people in Kings County (Queens and Brooklyn) were slaves. As everywhere else in the Western Hemisphere, they lived in deplorable conditions (some of the female skeletons found in the African Burial Ground showed collapsed skulls, possibly from having been forced to repeatedly carry massive weights on their heads) and treated as subhuman under the law. Prior to 1686 it hadn't even been illegal to injure or murder a slave. However, unlike in the South, where they were frequently spread out in isolated and closely guarded plantations, slaves in New York often lived and worked in very close quarters to whites and free blacks. This may have made for more accessible lines of communication that led to the city's first slave uprising.

How did New York's first slave uprising start?

After midnight on April 6, 1712, a group of armed slaves gathered on Maiden Lane. They set fire to a house and then attacked the white townspeople who came to see what was happening, killing nine. After an alarm was sounded, soldiers and militia quickly rushed to the scene and broke the insurrection, capturing nearly all of the rebels. Six of the slaves killed themselves rather than be put back in chains.

The response was swift and brutal. Twenty-one slaves were executed, several after medieval tortures that included two being burned alive and another suspended in chains for ten days until dying from lack of food or water. A pregnant slave was kept alive until she gave birth, and then executed. Afterwards, a series of punitive laws were passed, including ordinances that forbade more than three black slaves from gathering at one time and broad allowances for owners to punish their slaves in whatever way they felt necessary.

When did the next slave rebellion take place?

By 1741, two thousand of New York's ten thousand inhabitants were slaves. Nearly half the households in the city owned a slave. In the aftermath of the 1712 rebellion, white slave owners fearful of other uprisings restricted the rights of slaves to gather or even visit members of their family. In March 1741, mysterious fires burned down Fort George and several other structures over the course of several weeks. Regardless of the likelihood that there had ever been a slave arson plot, suspicion grew in an increasingly hysterical city. The common cry was "The Negroes are rising!" White colonists whispered about a "Great Negro Plot."

How did the city respond to the fires of 1741?

An investigating judge, Daniel Horsmanden (1691–1778), laid blame on a "hellish conspiracy" of slaves and whites, also decrying for good measure the supposed influence of "rampant popery" (Catholicism). Just half a century after the 1692 Salem Witch Trials, the city instituted its own just as ferocious but mostly forgotten terrorizing show trials for a never-proven crime. Horsmanden threw over 150 slaves and several whites into the City Hall dungeon. Mary Burton, a white indentured servant arrested for theft, was happy to oblige the judge with fantastical claims in exchange for freedom and 100 pounds. She named several slaves who she claimed met regularly to plan a massacre of the city's white population. Fires continued to break out. After one such fire in Hackensack, New Jersey, two blacks were burned at the stake for arson.

Over a dozen blacks were burned at the stake and more were hung after slaves were blamed for the 1741 fires that burned New York.

That level of savagery was soon repeated in New York proper. Two slaves were burned at the stake near where the city and county courthouses now stand near the Brooklyn Bridge; before they died, they named more supposed accomplices. The conflagration grew from March through August, with demented fantasies about devilish Catholic plots and murderous slaves spreading following the brutal executions. By the time the hysteria was over, at least four whites and thirty blacks had been hung or even burned alive. Burton's flood of accusations finally stopped gaining an audience once she began implicating more whites than blacks.

What is the oldest college in New York?

In 1754, King George II (1683–1760) chartered the state of New York's first institution of higher learning, King's College. An Anglican college, King's was founded as a response to schools started by other Protestant denominations, like Boston's Harvard and New Haven, Connecticut's Yale (both Congregationalist) and the Presbyterian College of New Jersey (later Princeton University). King's College started with just eight students and for years lagged behind its rivals in enrollment. One of its most famous early students was one Alexander Hamilton (c. 1755–1804), who enrolled in 1773. King's College was renamed Columbia College when it reopened after the Revolutionary War—during the war its building had been used as a hospital—and then Columbia University in 1912.

How did the French and Indian War affect New York?

Even though the so-called French and Indian War (1756–1763) was a sprawling conflict that embroiled most of the American colonies to some extent, it was really just one remote campaign in the world-spanning Seven Years' War between the French and British empires. In his *History of the English-Speaking Peoples*, Winston Churchill called it the first world war. New York was never directly threatened during the fighting. Still, the city was close enough to French-held Canada to remain acutely aware of the conflict. Several battles around the porous and ill-defined border took place in upstate New York. French raiding parties struck down the Hudson Valley as far south as Albany and French privateers waited nearby to pounce on unwary ships leaving the city's harbor.

Agitation over the fighting, however, didn't keep astute New York merchants from finding an angle to exploit. All through the war, many of them kept up trading with the French in Canada. The dozens of privateers operating out of New York also made fortunes capturing French merchant ships. Up to a thousand New York men were working on privateer vessels during the height of the war. At the same time, massive quantities of goods like lumber and sugar were being shipped through New York to a hungry England. The result was an economic boom for the city. Another opportunity for money-making was the large contingents of British troops disembarking in the city on their way to the front that had to be quartered and provisioned. The British Empire poured men and materiel into protecting and enlarging their sphere of influence in the Americas. But the subjects they were ostensibly protecting—and indirectly making wealthy, in the case of many New York merchants—would soon come to resent all that expenditure, which would indirectly help spark the Revolution.

THE REVOLUTIONARY WAR

What was New York like on the verge of the Revolutionary War?

In the 1760s and early 1770s, New York was still primarily a place of business, not culture. Like everywhere else in America at the time, the arts were still in their infancy, though live theater had been percolating in the city ever since the first performances by professional actors began in the 1750s. Most public life was conducted in the city's many taverns. In 1772, when the city's population stood at 22,000, there was one tavern for every fifty-five residents. They had a lot to talk about over their grog, as the past several years had seen an increased interest in democratic reforms and anti-royalist agitation, particularly after the passage of the Stamp Act in 1765.

How did a tax on playing cards precipitate the American Revolution?

After the conclusion of the long and expensive French and Indian War in 1763, the British government was deep in debt. Thinking that their colonists in the New World needed to bear some of the financial burden for their past and future defense, Parliament passed the first direct tax of the colonies in March 1765. The Stamp Act declared that every printed document needed to have an official embossed revenue stamp. This included everything from legal documents and licenses to newspapers and even playing cards. While the actual fees involved were generally nominal, the reaction was intense and fiery. This was partially due to the passage, during the past year, of two new taxes, the Sugar Act and the Currency Act, as well as the Quartering Act, which forced colonists to give lodging and food to British soldiers. The Stamp Act's critics decried it as "taxation without representation." Unlike citizens in England, British colonists had no representatives to advocate for their rights in Parliament.

Adding another grievance to colonists' charges of incipient "despotism," violations of the Stamp Act were adjudicated in courts without a jury. Over the following months, protests erupted in cities up and down the Atlantic Coast. In the fall of 1765, the Stamp Act Congress convened in New York's City Hall to draw up their list of grievances. It was the first coordinated response to British power between all thirteen colonies and would provide the template for later gatherings, including the Continental Congress.

What did New Yorkers think of the Stamp Act?

Being the colonies' largest port and center of business, any overarching change like the Stamp Act that would add to the cost and clerical work involved in commerce was bound to be unpopular. In the fall of 1765, a group of radical underground seditionists who called themselves the Sons of Liberty—led by Alexander McDougall (1731–1786) and Isaac Sears (1730–1786), a couple of ex-privateers—began organizing in New York to stop the Stamp Act from being put into effect. In October, a similar group known as the Liberty Boys said it would riot if a British ship was allowed to unload its cargo of official stamps; the cargo was eventually locked up under guard at the fort. A pamphlet was spread throughout New York with a warning: "Pro Patria. The first man that either distributes or makes use of stamped paper, let him take care of his house, person, and effects. *Vox Populi*. We dare."

Meanwhile, the Stamp Act Congress helped crystallize the city's frustration over their perceived powerlessness. Nevertheless, the events of November 1, 1765, took many by surprise. On that day, the Stamp Act was to take effect. Led in part by the Sons of Liberty, thousands of agitated people began gathering in the Commons. They hung and burned Governor Cadwallader Colden in effigy and threatened that he would "die a Martyr to your own Villainy" if any troops fired on the mob. Colden fled the city while business ground to a halt in protest. On November 13, the new governor, Sir Henry Moore (1713–1769), arrived in New York and suspended enforcement of the Stamp Act.

How did the British react to the anti-Stamp Act fervor?

The Stamp Act was repealed in 1766. But by then, the damage had already been done. Populist agitation against the Stamp Act became so heated that British military

Alexander McDougall (shown here) and Isaac Sears led the Sons of Liberty in protest against the Stamp Act.

leaders took note of the heated rebellious rhetoric. In 1763, most British forces had been stationed on the northern verge of the colonies to protect against invasion from French territories in Canada. By 1775, however, the bulk of British armed forces had been relocated to garrisons in American cities like Boston and New York.

Who rebelled against the British first, New York or Boston?

With its Freedom Trail and restored old taverns that summon the spirit of ale-quaffing Sons of Liberty—not to mention the fact that it remained free for much of the war— Boston has long been more evocative of the American Revolution than New York. But while the symbolic beginning of the rebellion is more often linked to the Boston Massacre of 1770 or the Boston Tea Party of 1773, rebellious agitation was clearly afoot in both cities years earlier.

New York followed the Boston Tea Party of December 16, 1773, with its own protest four months later, in which eighteen boxes of tea were tossed into the harbor to protest the British East Indian Company's tea monopoly. Responding to the British Parliament's passage of the so-called Intolerable Acts that tightened imperial control over the increasingly restive colonies, in May 1774, the Committee of 51 was formed in New York. One of the city's first democratic organizations, the Committee was responsible for sending delegates to a new Congress that would meet in Philadelphia to discuss ways of resolving colonials' ever-worsening relationship with mother England.

What was a "liberty pole"?

Oddly enough, the curious chain of events that led to the liberty pole phenomenon was not unlike the way in which a meme might spread in today's Internet culture. In the 1760s, one of the thorns in the side of the British leadership was Radical Whig John Wilkes (1725– 1797). At a time when rising food prices and poor harvests had resulted in food riots and thousands of tenant farmers leaving Scotland and England for the American colonies, Wilkes led a passionate drive for government reform, becoming an odd hero to American agitators. A 1763 caricature by William Hogarth (1697–1764) showed a sneering and villainous Wilkes holding a staff topped by a cap that reads "Liberty." Hogarth's print inadvertently furthered Wilkes' celebrity in America, where Patriots started raising so-called "liberty poles" as protests against the Stamp Act and other inequities of British rule. They became symbols of anti-royalist anger; tax collectors would sometimes be hung in effigy from them.

The first New York liberty pole probably went up in the Commons (City Hall Park today) in 1766 to celebrate the repeal of the Stamp Act. British soldiers from a nearby garrison cut it down almost immediately. Local Patriot groups like the Sons of Liberty put up another pole, further annoying the soldiers, who took it for the anti-royalist insult that it was. This action-reaction occurred several times over the following years.

What started the Battle of Golden Hill?

In January 1770, British soldiers tried to blow up the fourth liberty pole with gunpowder. But since the pole had been fortified with iron bands, the sabotage failed. The soldiers attacked again, the Sons of Liberty gathered in response, and a week of intermittent street fighting between the two groups resulted. Another assault by the Redcoats was successful, allowing them to cut the pole down and saw it into pieces. A crowd of three thousand Patriots gathered in fury, wielding rocks and clubs against the soldiers' bayonets and swords.

An 1880 illustration depicting the 1770 Battle of Golden Hill, a skirmish in New York City that was a precursor to the Revolutionary War.

The sprawling riot, later dubbed the Battle of Golden Hill (for the rise at the epicenter of the fighting where wheat was once grown), resulted in no casualties but the erection of a fifth liberty pole on the Commons. It would stand until it was pulled down by British occupiers in 1776. Three months later, British soldiers opened fire on protestors in Boston, killing five and infuriating colonists up and down the Atlantic Seaboard. The Boston Massacre is obviously far more famous. That hasn't stopped some proud New Yorkers from insisting that they brought the fight to the British months earlier at the Battle of Golden Hill.

How was George Washington almost assassinated in New York?

In the early days of the Revolutionary War, General George Washington (1732–1799) ordered that a select group of soldiers be organized as his personal bodyguard unit, who became known as the "General's Guard" or "Life Guards." Not long after the unit was formed in 1776, a conspiracy was discovered wherein several of Washington's bodyguards were charged with plotting to assassinate him while encamped with the army in Manhattan. Sergeant Thomas Hickey, a British army deserter, was charged with sedition and mutiny. Hickey was hanged on June 28, 1776, in front of thousands of spectators, making him the first American soldier executed after a court martial.

There were many rumors of other plots in the heavily royalist city to kidnap or assassinate Washington, including one rather incredible claim that a plate of poisoned peas (Washington's favorite food) were served to the general at Fraunces Tavern. After Washington passed on the peas—one story had it that Washington's housekeeper Phoebe Fraunces, who was also Hickey's lover, informed the general of his bodyguard's intentions—they were thrown outside to feed some chickens, who later died.

How was a statue of King George III used against his own troops?

One of the more vivid examples of early New Yorkers' eagerness to be rid of the British crown once and for all took place in 1776. Back in 1766, some New Yorkers had been so grateful to King George III (1738–1820) for his repealing of the Stamp Act that they erected a statue in his honor in Bowling Green. Ten years later, though, the king's favorability ratings in the city had plummeted. On July 9, 1776, Washington ordered the brand-new Declaration of Independence read aloud in front of City Hall. The audience's reaction was so enthusiastic that they poured south and pulled the king's statue to the ground. Washington was displeased with this display of mob behavior, but not so upset that he turned down the tens of thousands of bullets molded from the statue's melted-down lead and given to the Continental Army as one of the war's more ironic weapons.

Why did the Continental Army come to New York?

After the Continental Army lost its first major engagement with the British at the Battle of Bunker Hill in June 1775, they continued the fight under a new leader: General George Washington. After the months-long Siege of Boston, in March 1776, Washington's men seized a key piece of high ground in the city, forcing the British to withdraw. The Americans knew that the next target for the British would be New York, due to the strategic significance of its harbor and command of the Hudson River. John Adams (1767–1848) had written to Washington in January 1776 explaining the "vast importance" of New York, which he considered "a kind of key to the whole continent … no effort to secure it ought to be omitted."

Washington moved 19,000 men south to defend the city. Certain that the British would strike but uncertain as to where it would happen, he built a chain of forts around the city, from Brooklyn Heights to northern Manhattan, and waited for the attack. Thousands of residents boarded up their homes and businesses and fled the city. Agitation against pro-British New Yorkers rose during this time, with instances of mob violence against suspected Tories.

When did the British invade New York?

When the British finally arrived in late June, they clearly intended to crush the rebellion with overwhelming force. Their fleet of 400 ships carrying 32,000 troops (including royal marines, veteran Scottish Highlanders, and thousands of German mercenaries called Hessians) was the largest naval expeditionary force ever launched by a European power, eclipsing even the Spanish Armada. Under the capable command of General William Howe (1729–1814), the British initially landed on Staten Island. They were still there in July 1776 when the Continental Congress officially declared the new nation's independence.

What was the first battle of the Revolutionary War fought in New York?

The state of American coastal defenses can be judged by British captain Archibald Roberts's comment that they only encountered ineffective musket fire in response to the landing: "Lucky for us the Rebels had no cannon here or we must have suffered a great deal." Howe sent two flags of truce to Washington, who rejected both, even though his army was outnumbered, inexperienced, and woefully undersupplied. Instead of assaulting the main body of Washington's troops on Manhattan, Howe sent 20,000 men to make an amphibious landing at Gravesend Bay near modern-day Coney Island. Washington sent reinforcements to bolster his lines as the British advanced north through Brooklyn and skirmishers clashed.

On August 26, British soldiers took watermelons from a patch near a tavern in modern-day Sunset Park and were engaged by Continental soldiers. Thus did the Battle of Brooklyn (or Battle of Long Island), the first great battle of the Revolutionary War, begin very inauspiciously.

How did Washington lose the Battle of Brooklyn?

There were a few reasons. Washington's forces were made up in large part of relatively green militia. They were outnumbered, with no naval support to speak of. The British and Hessians had more veterans in their ranks, one of the world's top navies at their beck and call, not to mention better equipment, more experienced officers, and all the accoutrements of an imperial military that had years of experience in subduing rebel upstarts like the Americans in colonies all over the world. There was also a spectacular strategic blunder on the part of Washington and his staff, who failed to ensure that their men guarding the ridge of hills bisecting central Brooklyn adequately guarded all of the passes.

On the morning of August 27, the main British force of 15,000 marched through the practically undefended Jamaica Pass (where Flatbush Avenue runs through today) and broke the American front line. Some three hundred surrounded Continental soldiers tried

What was "America's Dunkirk"?

After the disastrous retreat to Brooklyn Heights, Washington realized that he had no choice but to evacuate. Taking advantage of two days of strong winds that kept the British fleet at bay, and Howe's reluctance to make a full-frontal assault on the American fortifications, Washington stealthily assembled a motley fleet for a last-ditch escape. On the night of August 29, while the British prepared their final assault, all 9,300 Continental soldiers rowed across the East River, their oars muffled with rags. According to legend, Washington was on the last boat to leave Brooklyn.

Like the Dunkirk evacuation, the operation kept a resounding tactical defeat from becoming a strategic disaster. Had Howe pressed his advantage and cornered the Americans in Brooklyn Heights, the entire course of the war would have been dramatically altered. Historian David McCullough (1933–) noted that "if the wind had been blowing in a different direction that day, we'd all be sipping tea and singing 'God Save the Queen.'" Instead, the Americans' great blunder at Jamaica Pass was matched by Howe's woeful inability to detect their final retreat. Washington's army survived to face the next confrontation with the British on the island of Manhattan.

to surrender and were massacred with bayonets. A small Maryland unit's brave and costly delaying action at a stone farmhouse (a reconstruction of which stands in Park Slope) allowed their fellow soldiers to retreat across the Gowanus Canal to the relative safety of fortified Brooklyn Heights. At this point, defeat for the demoralized Americans was inevitable.

When did the British invade Manhattan?

Having lost the Battle of Brooklyn, the Continental Army was badly in need of a victory. Howe even met with representatives from the Continental Congress (including Ben Franklin and John Adams) to discuss terms of surrender; but the Americans rejected his offer to simply lay down their arms and hope to be well-treated.

On September 15, British naval cannon fire raked American forces at Kip's Bay on the East River. When British troops landed, they easily routed a unit of Connecticut militia. Washington wrote to Congress of what he called the unit's "disgraceful and dastardly conduct." Supposedly, Howe and his staff had reached a point in the hilly nearby estate, around where East 37th Street and Park Avenue are today, of Robert Murray (1721–1786)—who inspired the neighborhood's current name of Murray Hill—when they were invited for tea by Murray's wife. It was long believed by many that the good Mrs. Murray's tea delayed the British advance long enough to give the Americans time to regroup to the north. While that story is most likely false, the day was a close-run thing for the Americans. About five thousand American soldiers raced up the west side of Manhattan while the British advanced south on the east side. The Americans then regrouped in the hilly northern district called Harlem Heights for what would be their last stand in New York.

Who won the Battle of Harlem Heights?

The Continental Army won, finally. On September 16, Washington was encamped with his army near what is now the Columbia University campus, around 120th Street and Broadway. That morning, Washington ordered a brigade to engage the British directly while sending another force, including 150 rangers, around the British flank. The Continentals' mixture of cunning tactics, surprise, and superior knowledge of the land ultimately forced the British to withdraw.

The battle wasn't decisive. Nevertheless, it gave Washington and his battered forces a greatly needed respite that they used to affect their final escape from Manhattan. Pamphleteer and young Continental army officer Alexander Hamilton (1755–1804) fought in this battle, later building his estate, the Grange, not far to the north. There is a superbly heroic memorial plaque for the battle engraved by James Edward Kelly on a wall along the western verge of the Columbia campus along Broadway above 116th Street.

Why was the *Turtle* historically important but militarily insignificant?

The first underwater attack by a submarine in history took place in New York Harbor on September 7, 1776. David Bushnell (1742–1824) was an inventor who had started working on underwater mines while studying at Yale. He came up with a plan for a submersible vessel to plant his mines. Washington built a one-man hand-powered submarine out of oak timbers that was bound with iron bands and tarred to keep it watertight. Some compared its appearance to two turtle shells sealed together, garnering it the nickname of "Bushnell's Turtle."

On September 7, the *Turtle* was maneuvered into position near the HMS *Eagle*, a sixty-four-gun warship whose crew remained unaware of the threat. However, the *Turtle*'s tools failed to attach the mine to the *Eagle*. The *Turtle* was sent into action several more times but never made a successful attack. Even though his vessel's poor performance in action caused Bushnell some ridicule, Washington

A replica of the *Turtle* at the U.S. Navy Submarine Force Museum and Library in Groton, Connecticut, shows how small the submersible was.

thought highly enough of the inventor, who later became known as the father of the submarine, to make him an Army engineer later in the war.

Who tried to burn down New York in 1776?

On the night of September 21, 1776, while Washington was still holding some ground in upper Manhattan, a devastating fire broke out in the city's more densely populated south. Starting in a tavern called the Fighting Cocks near Whitehall Slip and fanned by a brisk southward wind, the fire spread quickly through the congested city. By the next morning, a quarter of the city (about five hundred houses) was burned. The damage was particularly heavy between Broadway and the Hudson River. The city's most important structure, Trinity Church, was lost. But an assistant minister at Trinity gathered a volunteer bucket brigade to keep the fire from consuming St. Paul's Chapel to the north. (In 2010, a leather fire bucket marked "1768" was found in the bell tower of St. Paul's.) One witness later wrote that the fire burned so bright that for hours the deck of his ship in the harbor "was lighted as at noon-day."

Did George Washington set the blaze?

No, but he wanted to. The fire of 1776 might have been devastating for the people still living in the city, but it was a boon for the rebels. During the summer just past, after losing the Battle of Brooklyn, Washington had worried that the city would provide "warm and comfortable barracks" for the British in the winter to come. He wrote to the Continental Congress asking for permission to put the city to the torch. Congress refused.

Some Tories later claimed that rebels had stolen bells from church towers and cut holes in the bottoms of fire buckets, and Washington later wrote, "Providence—or some good honest Fellow, has done more for us than we were disposed to do for ourselves." There was never any proof to show that the Americans had in fact deliberately burned the city. That didn't stop the British from immediately trying to find patriots who may have started the blaze.

Who was Nathan Hale?

In the immediate aftermath of the Great Fire of 1776, with a good portion of the city's population living in tents, the out-

One of the most memorable figures of the American Revolution was Nathan Hale, who was captured and hung by the British for being a spy.

raged British occupiers rounded up over one hundred suspects. Among those they captured was Captain Nathan Hale (1755–1776). A Yale graduate and former teacher in Connecticut, Hale had joined the Continental Army after the Battle of Lexington and Concord. During the Battle of Harlem Heights, Washington asked for a volunteer to reconnoiter behind enemy lines. The twenty-four-year-old Hale, pretending to be a schoolmaster looking for work, started his mission on September 10. He was captured on September 21 in Huntington, Long Island, possibly after being betrayed by his Loyalist cousin Samuel Hale. After Hale admitted to being a spy, British General Howe ordered him to be executed. Before his hanging, Hale is reported to have said, "I only regret that I have but one life to lose for my country." A statue of Hale currently stands in front of City Hall.

When did the Continental Army leave New York?

Following the Battle of Harlem Heights, Washington and his men continued to hold part of upper Manhattan. They were headquartered at Fort Washington, on the cliffs above the Hudson near the George Washington Bridge and the highest point on the island. Additional landings of British forces in the Bronx and Westchester County forced the outnumbered Washington to move forces north to keep his position from being surrounded. At the Battle of White Plains on October 28, 1776, the rebels were defeated by a larger British force, setting the stage for the Americans' retreat. Washington ultimately retreated into New Jersey with several thousand troops. On November 16, about eight thousand Redcoats and Hessians lay siege to Fort Washington, which surrendered before nightfall. Thousands of soldiers and rebel civilians were taken prisoner. The British would occupy New York for nearly seven years.

What was the Ethiopian Regiment?

Some free blacks joined up early on with the Continental Army, though Washington cut off all new recruitment of blacks in July 1775. Up to 12,000 runaway slaves gathered in New York during its British occupation, eventually making up almost half the city's population. When the newly free blacks mingled in Manhattan with white British at so-called "Ethiopian balls," the interracial socializing scandalized white colonists. Accordingly, the British sought to turn this to their military advantage. In Virginia, black soldiers fighting for the British formed the "Ethiopian Regiment." Their uniforms read "Liberty to Slaves." As the battle for New York was still raging in August 1776, the Ethiopian Regiment was billeted on Staten Island, where the British had already head-quartered the Black Brigade, a unit of roughly 800 free black soldiers led by escaped slave Colonel Tye (1753–1780), who led guerrilla-style raids on patriot-allied areas in New Jersey.

How did New York fare under British occupation?

During the occupation, the city's population boomed with Tories and British troops, providing ample opportunities for sharp-eyed New York merchants to do well in supplying food, shelter, and other goods. Once again, sanctioned piracy boosted the city's coffers, with privateers sailing forth almost daily to hunt for rebel ships to capture. Theoretically, General Henry Clinton (1730–1795) meant to use a light hand while occupying New York during the Revolutionary War. Nevertheless, much of the island of Manhattan suffered under his command. Some believe this animus derived from fury over the Great Fire of 1776, which the occupiers believed to have been deliberated arson on the part of the Americans.

But the suffering of New York during the war was caused in part by Clinton having given his soldiers (as his aide-de-camp wrote) "free liberty … to ravage at will." The area around the city became a burned-over war zone, fought over by competing bands of marauders. On Manhattan, one account noted that most churches and other public buildings were turned over to the British and left in a state of complete disrepair.

What was New York like when Washington returned?

On his victory march south through Manhattan in 1783, Washington noted with dismay that the island had been "totally stripped of trees." Numerous fires during the occupation devastated the city's housing, leaving thousands living in befouled tent cities. Many homeowners hoping to return to their abandoned dwellings found instead just fire-blackened ruins. Historian Edward Ellis wrote that New York "was occupied longer and suffered more than any other great American city." Not surprisingly, given the occupation's grim conditions, Tories found themselves unwelcome in New York after the cessation of hostilities. Many left for Canada.

What and when was Evacuation Day?

The Treaty of Paris that ended the Revolutionary War was signed on September 3, 1783. The last British troops did not depart until that November 25. The last post they evacuated from was New York. British soldiers finally left that afternoon, just as American soldiers were finishing up their victorious march to the city. A column of Continental soldiers marched behind Washington, south along the trail of Broadway, following much the same path along which they had retreated back in 1776.

The reception to Washington's march grew increasingly heated the further south they marched, from the Bull's Head Tavern on the Bowery to Fort George on Battery Park. There, even as British troops still floated in the harbor, the Union Jack was taken down—with some difficulty, as the stubborn British had nailed the flag to the staff, which had itself been smeared with grease—and the American flag raised in its place. A British officer who witnessed the ultimately peaceful evacuation joked that "these Americans are a curious original people … they know how to govern themselves, but nobody else can govern them." Eventually some 29,000 civilians evacuated, including 3,000 black Royalists. Many of the latter settled in British-controlled Nova Scotia and then later moved again, to Sierra Leone, where some American abolitionists had already moved.

How was Evacuation Day celebrated?

For years after 1783, November 25 was an official New York city holiday and a particularly exuberant one. Evacuation Day was marked by parades of soldiers and enough patriotic pomp and circumstance to rival July 4. Children got the day off school. A well-known

This circa 1838 lithograph by Ludwig Restein is titled "'Evacuation Day' and Washington's Triumphal Entry in New York City, November 25, 1783."

rhyme went, "It's Evacuation Day, when the British ran away, / Please, dear Mister, give us holiday!" One of the day's popular contests was pole-climbing, in honor of the limber sailor who, legend had it, was finally able to shimmy up the greased pole at Fort George and haul down the Union Jack. The size of the day's spectacles seemed curious to outsiders. In 1834 a Maine newspaper asked "Why the New Yorkers celebrate this evacuation day.... Isn't it as well to forget that an enemy once had possession of your city?"

Celebrations of Evacuation Day peaked with the 1883 centennial, which featured a four-hour parade of some twenty thousand marchers, massive banquets, and festivities attended by over a half-million people. The popularity of the holiday waned afterward, at around the same time that Thanksgiving became the more widely celebrated national history. The last known Evacuation Day was celebrated in 1916, when sixty veterans gathered for a flag raising at the Battery.

What role did Fraunces Tavern play in the liberation of New York?

This historic and still-operating tavern is notable for, in a way, hosting the closing ceremony of the entire Revolutionary War. On Evacuation Day, after raising the American flag over Fort George, a dinner was hosted at the tavern by Governor Clinton. As part of the festivities, thirteen toasts were proffered, among them toasts to "the fleet and armies of France, which have served in America" and "May America be an asylum to the persecuted of the Earth." The celebrations went on for days, concluding on December 4 when Washington hosted a farewell gathering for his officers, also at Fraunces Tavern. One officer wrote later of this emotional farewell: "Such a scene of sorrow and weeping I had never before witnessed and fondly hope I may never be called to witness again."

AFTER INDEPENDENCE

Was New York's longest serving governor also its first to be elected?

Yes. A consummate leader, George Clinton (1739–1812) distinguished himself first by his service in the French and Indian War and later as a member of the Continental Congress. He fought in the Continental Army as a brigadier general. In 1777, Clinton became the first elected governor of New York state. Later known as the "Father of New York State," he stayed in office until 1795, making him the longest serving governor in the state's history. In 1804, Clinton achieved another landmark by becoming America's first elected vice president, a position he held in the administrations of both Presidents Thomas Jefferson and James Madison.

Why did medical students start a riot in 1788?

During the 1780s, medical students at Columbia College and New York Hospital, needing raw material for their studies, resorted to a practice handled at the time in the British Isles by the so-called Resurrection Men. At night, the students would steal into cemeteries and dig up the corpses they needed to dissect in order to study human anatomy. Some of the first aggrieved people were local blacks, who petitioned the City Council in February 1788 to have the practice stopped after it was discovered that the African Burial Ground was a frequent target of the students. Nothing was done to address their grievance. In April, it was discovered that the students were also digging up dead white bodies. A story, possibly apocryphal, has it that a student at New York Hospital waved a corpse's arm out the window at a group of boys, yelling "this is your mother's arm!" One of the boys, whose mother had recently died, ran to tell his father, who discovered that his wife's body had in fact been removed from its grave. He and an angry mob stormed the hospital and hauled body parts out into the street in a fury; several doctors had to be put in jail overnight for their safety.

The following day, a mob numbering in the thousands swarmed the hospital and jail. The militia opened fire and killed several rioters. Alexander Hamilton, John Jay (1745–1829), and Governor George Clinton, who had all tried earlier to calm the rioters, were all injured in the chaos that ultimately last several days during which doctors and medical students all around the city were afraid to leave their homes. In 1789 a law was passed that allowed for the dissection of criminals condemned to death.

What was the capital of the United States before Washington, D.C.?

The United States had several capitals before Congress finally convened in the purpose-built District of Columbia in November 1800. Starting with the first Continental Congress in 1774, the nascent American government convened in state houses, court houses, and taverns in Philadelphia, Baltimore, Lancaster, Princeton, Annapolis, and Trenton. Between January 1785 and August 1790, Congress—first under the Articles of Confederation and then the Constitution—convened at New York's City Hall, Federal Hall, and even Fraunces Tavern. The decision to relocate the capital to Washington, D.C., was made at a dinner party in June 1790 hosted by Thomas Jefferson. At the party, Jefferson had brought together Secretary of the Treasury Alexander Hamilton and Virginia Representative James Madison, who had been embroiled for months in a political dispute (Hamilton favored the federal government taking on the states' war debts; Madison was opposed).

The account of the party came from Jefferson and was later described as somewhat self-serving—the actual compromise was more likely worked out over the course of many meetings instead of just one evening. However it came about, the result was critical to the future of the nation. Madison agreed that his southern coalition would stop blocking Hamilton's plan in exchange for permanently relocating the capital to the south in Maryland. In the meantime, the government would meet in Philadelphia. Abigail Adams (1744–1818) famously said that she would try to make the best of things in the new capital, but sighed that "When all is done, it will not be Broadway."

What was the Buttonwood Agreement?

Prior to May 17, 1792, New York had a deeply rooted and thriving financial community. Nevertheless, it took the meeting of two dozen merchants and stockbrokers on that day under a sycamore (also known as a button-wood) tree that stood at 68 Wall Street to help establish a more regulated way of doing business. Perhaps not coincidentally, earlier that year saw the country's first true financial panic, a crash caused at least in part by a speculation scheme centered on the Bank of New York. It was adroitly managed by Treasury Secretary Alexander Hamilton. Another event that may have spurred the meeting was Hamilton's issuing of $80 million in government bonds, which increased the brokers' business.

A 1945 depiction of traders meeting under a button-wood (sycamore) tree in 1792 to discuss what would eventually become the New York Stock Exchange.

The Buttonwood Agreement held all the signees to fix commission rates and to give preferential treatment in their dealings to fellow signees. This single-page document was claimed by some to be the basis for what became the New York Stock Exchange (also known as the "Big Board") in 1817. The traders held their meetings and did their business in the taverns and coffeehouses that crowded downtown, particularly the Tontine Coffee House at Wall and Water streets which later became the headquarters of the New York Insurance Company. The exchange didn't move into its own building until 1865, the same year that a storm took down the original buttonwood tree.

What did Aaron Burr and Alexander Hamilton have against each other?

Aaron Burr (1756–1836) and Hamilton, as leaders who had both served with distinction in the Revolutionary War and settled in New York after the war with an eye towards political advancement, would seem to have had a lot in common. They were both leading men in the nascent American establishment who seemed bound for marble-bust status even while they were still relatively young. But Burr, a Republican, and Hamilton, a Federalist, had been at each other's throats for years.

Hamilton never trusted Burr's glad-handing, politically expedient style. So he wrote to and told everybody he could that the dashingly charming Burr was in fact an immoral opportunist. Burr, who came from a line of respected clergymen, resented the criticisms of a striver like Hamilton, who had been born in the West Indies to unmarried parents and was never allowed to forget it by many in the early country's establishment. (John Adams called Hamilton the "bastard brat of a Scottish peddler," a critique that only endeared Hamilton to generations of New Yorkers, who claimed the self-made immigrant as one of their own.)

The two men even ran rival banks. The Bank of the Manhattan Company, established as part of Burr's Manhattan water utility company and which later prospered as JPMorgan Chase, made political loans to Republicans, while the Hamilton-created Bank

Why did the Aaron Burr–Alexander Hamilton duel take place in New Jersey?

While dueling was illegal in both New York and New Jersey, the law wasn't as aggressively enforced across the Hudson River. After their years of rivalry finally boiled over in 1804, a furious Burr challenged Hamilton to a duel that the starchy Hamilton (who had been involved in a few almost-duels before, including one over an affair he had with a married woman, and another, three years earlier, when he had lost his son to a duel) did not feel he could avoid for political reasons. The two men met in Weehawken, New Jersey, early on the morning of July 11, 1804, a confrontation that seems impossible to contemplate, given that the duelers were two of the most famous and important citizens of their time. Burr was Thomas Jefferson's vice president at the time and Hamilton had been the nation's first Secretary of the Treasury. Both fired with .56 caliber dueling pistols. Hamilton missed; Burr did not. Hamilton died the following day; Burr's political career died as well.

of New York loaned to Federalists. Things came to a head in 1804, when Hamilton courted Federalists not to support Burr's run for governor. Burr fumed when he lost, convinced that Hamilton's behind-the-scenes maneuvering had cost him the election. Burr was further incensed was Hamilton's "despicable opinion" of him was made public in an Albany newspaper.

What were early schools like in New York?

At the start of the nineteenth century, most adult New Yorkers, who themselves had received little or no organized schooling, simply assumed that their children would receive none, either. Schooling for New York children was still primarily a haphazard thing, mostly confined to small private and church (also known as charity) schools. The schools run by the Dutch Reformed, Catholic, and other churches, generally spent as much time on religious training as they did on fundamentals like reading and writing.

One exception to this was the African Free School, established in 1787 for the general education of the children of slaves and former slaves. By 1823, its schools (there were eventually seven) had some nine hundred students, about half the school-age black children in the city. Since blacks were generally not hired for anything more than manual labor, the school included practical training, like navigation for sailors.

When did public schooling start?

In 1805, Mayor DeWitt Clinton (1769–1828) helped gather a group of prominent citizens who were concerned about a city whose future generations were dangerously uncultivated. The group importuned Albany to rectify this problem: "The rich having ample means of educating their offspring, it must be apparent that the laboring poor—a class of citizens so evidently useful—have a superior claim to the public support." The combination of private organization and philanthropy and public funding would help create the basis for free and (theoretically) nonsectarian public education in New York.

When it opened its doors in 1806, the Free School Society was open to poor white children whose parents couldn't afford a private school. Even more unusual, the school was nondenominational. At the time, many church schools still received public funding. The Free School Society, which still allowed Protestant proselytizing in its classrooms, successfully fought to repeal that allowance in 1824—which caused them to be castigated by Catholic Bishop John Hughes (1797–1864), who had led the effort to create the growing network of parish schools that attempted to provide a complete, not just religious, education—and then changed its name to the Public School Society. By the time it merged with the Board of Education in 1853, the Public School Society claimed to have educated over a half million children.

Where did the first steamboat travel?

The Pennsylvania-born inventor Robert Fulton (1765–1815) started off as a painter but switched to engineering once his artistic ambitions were not fondly received in London. In 1797, he tried to interest the French government in his proposal for a submarine that could be used in its war with Britain. When that didn't work, he shopped the same idea to the British, who were disappointed with the combat results of his inventions. Failing in the weapons business, Fulton moved to New York and started finalizing a design for a steam-powered boat that he had been working on with Robert Livingston (1746–1813), who held a monopoly for steamboat navigation in New York state (granted, interestingly, before the invention had been proven to work). In August 1807, Fulton's 150-foot- (46-meter-) long steamboat *Clermont* took thirty-two hours to travel up the Hudson River from New York City to Albany and back. It was an impressive feat, given that ships usually took four days to traverse the same distance. Fulton's boat began commercial operations the following month, inaugurating the age of steam-powered travel.

Why are Manhattan's streets laid out in a grid?

At the start of the nineteenth century, New York didn't extend much above its unofficial northern boundary of Houston Street (still called North Street then). But the demographics of a growing population and a narrow island were producing pressure for more real estate. Numerous fires and outbreaks of disease—like the 1798 yellow fever epidemic that killed about 2,000 people (out of a total population of 60,000)—also convinced city leaders that straight, broad streets were better for public health and safety, not to mention a more generally organized city.

Up to this point, the city's streets had generally been laid out almost at random as houses and other buildings went up, with little thought for ease of use. Ironically, given how the grid was later lionized and emulated in cities from Chicago to Los Angeles, it was

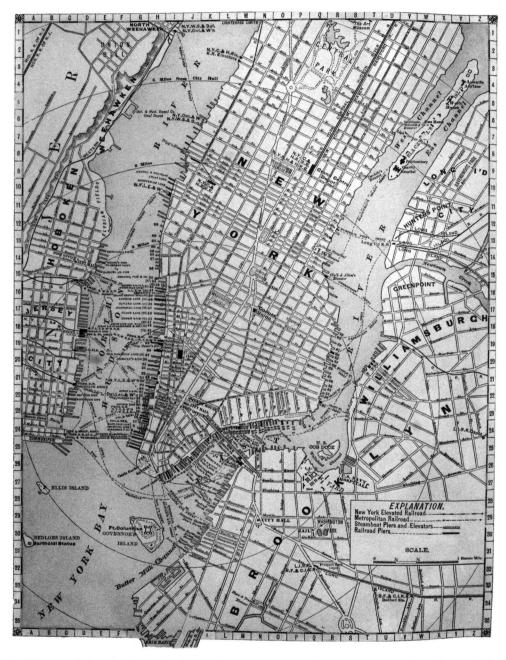

An 1889 map of Manhattan shows how the streets were arranged in a straightforward grid, just as they are today.

actually thrown together in a somewhat ad-hoc manner. The grid plan's three commissioners—Gouverneur Morris (1752–1816), Simeon DeWitt (1756–1834), and John Rutherfurd (1760–1840)—all lived outside Manhattan, didn't care for its density, and were given near-total authority to translate their not always well-considered plans into reality.

When did the street plan go into effect?

In 1807, the city council was authorized by the state legislature—which the city had brought in to referee the contentious reaction to the plan—to lay out Manhattan's future streets in a way that emphasized "health, convenience, and beauty." The ambitious Commissioners' Plan released on March 22, 1811, established the Manhattan that we recognize today. It called for a rectangular grid of 12 north-south avenues and 155 east-west streets comprising some two thousand blocks marching inexorably some thirteen miles (twenty-one kilometers) all the way up the forested island to 155th Street. The commissioners decided not to bother plotting anything out north of 155th because, as Morris opined, "it is improbable that (for centuries to come) the grounds north of Harlem Flat will be covered with houses."

About the only exceptions to this dense lattice of imaginary streets were Broadway, still allowed to meander diagonally up the island, and Greenwich Village, the only spot on the island north of North Street with a previously established street plan. One rather crucial element that the commissioners failed to account for was parks. The thinking at the time was that all of Manhattan's waterfront would provide enough vistas and open air. These were added later in great numbers. After Central Park was carved out of the grid's midsection in the 1860s, some concessions were also made to the plan in uptown quadrants that allowed roads like Riverside and Morningside drives and St. Nicholas Terrace to curve and undulate in a pleasingly non-grid manner.

How did the grid transform Manhattan?

The surveyors quickly started denoting future intersections with hundreds of short white marble markers or, in rougher terrain, iron bolts (one of which can still be seen poking up from a rock in Central Park). In short order, engineers were laying out streets according to the grid. Enduring heated abuse and the occasional lawsuit along the way, they leveled most of the many hills, emptied the marshes and ponds, and (having been given near-total authority of eminent domain by the 1807 law) moved or razed the hundreds of scattered houses that were in their way. They also demolished any previously laid out streets that didn't adhere to the plan's canted perspective. (An exception can be found in the East Village, where old Stuyvesant Street exists as the last vestige of Peter Stuyvesant's pre–1811 Bowery Village grid, laid out on a truly north-south axis.) Given the explosion in immigration numbers and the subsequent pressure for more housing in the mid-nineteenth century, the grid appears to have been plotted out just in time.

As the once-imaginary blocks swiftly filled, land speculation became rampant. John Jacob Astor (1763–1848) made himself the wealthiest man in America simply by putting his fur-trading wealth into buying up land north of the city that hadn't been built on yet.

Year after year, the old up-island estates and *bouweijs* with their rolling hills, ponds, and orchards disappeared under the uniform grid at a faster and faster pace. Designed for convenience, the grid—with its lack of diagonals and intrablock service alleys—later proved poorly suited to large amounts of horse-drawn cart and then automobile traffic. The grid's effect on vehicular traffic ultimately inspired the term "gridlock," first used during the 1980 transit strike, and now used interchangeably for heavy traffic in almost any major city.

How successful was the grid plan?

The Manhattan street grid, with its 11,000 acres of uniformity, came in for its share of criticism then and now: Lewis Mumford (1895–1990) called it a "straight jacket" for the city, and Jean-Paul Sartre (1905–1980)

Famed author Washington Irving wrote stories that helped to make "Knickerbocker" a word referring to New Yorkers and "Gotham" to refer to New York City.

wrote that the grid left "nothing to focus on but the vanishing point." There were also those who thought it a perfect solution to the city's pressing space problems. (In fact, the grid was so popular with some that on more than one occasion it was suggested in complete seriousness that the city should just fill in the East River and extend the grid

---

Who came up with the name "Knickerbocker"?

"**K**nickerbocker" has come to mean New Yorker, but the term dates back to the Dutch settlers and the baggy pants they wore, called knickerbockers. Later, the word evolved to mean New Yorkers of Dutch descent, and then just to New Yorkers as a whole. This was reinforced by the writings of author Washington Irving (1783–1859). In 1809, the first edition of a soon-to-be bestseller was published that would redefine New York's view of itself, in ways intended and not. Written by the New York-born Irving, *A History of New York from the Beginning of the World to the End of the Dutch Dynasty, by Diedrich Knickerbocker* was a semi-fantastical mock epic about the early days of the colony that mixed up real and imagined history for partially satirical means. Irving also had a more serious purpose for his book: to create a recorded Dutch American past for a city that had lost so many historical structures and documents during the fire of 1776. His fictional narrator Diedrich Knickerbocker later inspired a cartoon character, Father Knickerbocker, who became something of an unofficial mascot for the city.

east over all the new landfill.) But whether people liked it or not, the grid proved remarkably resilient and survives to this day almost completely intact.

How did the name "Gotham" come about?

That nickname for New York can be traced back to Washington Irving as well. Unlike Knickerbocker (a name Irving simply borrowed from an upstate New York family), Gotham has a foggier history. There are English stories about a village in Nottinghamshire called Gotham ("Goat's Town" in Anglo-Saxon) whose residents pretended to be insane so that King John would not want to come through (madness was thought to be contagious) and possibly take any of their property. The legend gave rise to the saying "There are more fools pass through Gotham than remain in it." Irving always referred to New York as "Gotham" in the magazine *Salmagundi Papers* that he and some friends published in the early 1800s. It was first used as the name for Batman's home city in 1940 after a writer for the comic was flipping through a phone book and saw the listing for Gotham Jewelers.

How did New York react to the War of 1812?

New York had allowed its defenses to atrophy since the Revolution, with the old Battery fort having been turned into a park. When war broke out, the harbor was hurriedly refortified. New redoubts were thrown up on Liberty Island and Mill Rock, as well as in the mid-Manhattan hinterlands that would later become Central Park. Castle Clinton was constructed just off the Battery and connected to it by a drawbridge. Cannon-bristling forts bracketed the Narrows between Staten Island and Brooklyn, and their potentially deadly crossfire was planned to deter any British naval forces from daring to enter the harbor. The northern water approach by Hell's Gate was less fortified, under the assumption that its churning waters and dangerous rocks would deter enemy ships. By 1814, the city was defended by 25,000 troops and 900 cannon. At the same time, the British blockade was decimating the American economy, a series of defeats at sea had crippled the U.S. Navy, and British troops (some fresh from Europe following the abdication of Napoleon) sacked Washington. That July, a British naval squadron appeared off Sandy Hook but never took action against the city.

What did the Erie Canal have to do with New York?

Governor DeWitt Clinton (1769–1828), son of the state's longest-serving governor, George Clinton, was one of the most vocal proponents of the long-gestating plan to build a waterway that would connect the Great Lakes with the Hudson River. Under his relentless and exacting stewardship, construction of the Erie Canal was finally begun in 1817. The forty-foot-wide and seven-foot-deep (12-meter-wide by 2-meter-deep) canal disparagingly nicknamed "Clinton's Ditch" stretched for 363 miles (584 kilometers) through rocky and forested wilderness from the city of Buffalo on Lake Erie to the town of Troy on the Hudson River. After just eight years of construction, one of the engineering marvels of the nineteenth century opened for business on October 26, 1825, under budget and three years ahead of schedule. Its inaugural vessel, a boat named *Seneca Chief*, left Buffalo carrying three ceremonial kegs of water that Clinton poured into the Atlantic eight days later in New York.

How did the Erie Canal affect New York?

This first linkage of the American interior with the Eastern seaboard was revolutionary for commerce and transportation for the country in general and New York in particular. Getting freight from Buffalo to New York cost $100 per ton when shipped by road. But once the Erie Canal opened, merchants could ship freight on it for only $10 per ton. The effect on New York and the surrounding area was extraordinary. Trade exploded.

Two years after the canal opened, 3,640 bushels of wheat were shipped down from Buffalo to New York; by 1841, that figure had hit one million. By the 1830s, the city was practically surrounded by sails; over a thousand ships could be counted at New York docks and in its surrounding waters at any given time. Clinton's belief that the canal would turn New York into "the granary of the world, the emporium of commerce, the seat of manufactures, the focus of great moneyed operations," soon became a reality.

When did the first great expansion of suffrage in New York happen?

The Revolution might have brought democracy to New York, but it was a limited form of democracy. Only white men were allowed to vote, and even then there were property restrictions. One of the greatest expansions to the right to vote in elections came in 1821, when New York state ratified its second constitution. White men could no longer be barred from voting due to owning no property. However, "men of color" had to prove at least one year of owning land with a value over $250. Women would not be given the vote in New York until 1917.

What was Tammany Hall?

Originally just another benevolent society, Tammany Hall would become one of the longest-lasting and most powerful forces in politics that the country ever witnessed. An Irish immigrant named William Mooney founded the Society of St. Tammany on May 13, 1788. Also known as the Columbian Order, Tammany was originally an antiroyalist fraternal order with a constitution whose stated goals included perpetuating "the name of liberty … the love freedom or the political advantage of the country." Their earliest meetings were held in bars.

The society's popularity quickly grew, in part because its wide-open membership policy was particularly generous compared to most of the city's clubs. Despite Mooney's national ambitions, within a few decades, it was clear that the Society of St. Tammany, or Tammany Hall as it would later be called, would be first and foremost a New York institution. After just a few years, Tammany Hall had been transformed into a vote-getting and patronage-disbursing political machine, particularly after Aaron Burr used it to help elect Thomas Jefferson president in 1800. By the 1820s and '30s, Tammany Hall had es-

The Tammany Hall building (shown here in 1914) was razed in 1927 to make way for new construction.

sentially become the beating heart of the Democratic Party in New York, a status it would keep for more than a century.

How did Tammany Hall stay so powerful?

By a combination of the oldest forces in politics: Tribal loyalties and the lubricant of graft. The bosses of Tammany Hall would become most famous for the latter, ensuring that every outstretched hand near a new public works project would end up with cash in it and a not-so-gentle reminder of which vote-needing political party it came from. They were even more adept, though, at engineering the former. This was put to practice as the number of new immigrants to the city began to swell, giving them a rising tide of new, often discriminated voters whose vulnerabilities and resentments they could harness to battle the old establishment. Street gangs, the corner saloon, and volunteer firefighting companies were important recruiting tools, as was the great vote-getting machine known as patronage. Helping Tammany Hall make its case was the blatantly anti-immigrant viewpoint of the city's upper class and its news outlets like the *New York Tribune* and the *New York Times*.

Tammany Hall couldn't exactly be described as the upright democratic champion of the working class, though, what with its habits of hiring so-called "shoulder hitters" to either stuff or guard ballot boxes and doling out jobs and housing to new immigrants in exchange for loyal votes. But given the somewhat Hobbesian nature of urban democracy in America at the time, Tammany Hall also represented one of the city's most powerful voices for the lower classes and immigrants. It represented the classic conundrum of machine politics: The machine stayed in power by ensuring that their voices would be heard and paying attention to its constituents' needs with an eye to personal attention that seems shocking in the electronic age. But at the same time, the machine's insatiable appetite for graft siphoned off funds that could have improved its constituents' lives.

Who was the second elected mayor of New York?

Almost a century and a half elapsed between the time of Peter Delanoy, New York's first elected mayor in 1689, and the 1834 election for the second. Previously, mayors had been either appointed by governors or selected by the Common Council. In 1834, the Flushing-born Cornelius Van Wyck Lawrence (1791–1861; a New York representative known both for crying in Congress and his disinclination to turn down money) stood as a Democrat with Andrew Jackson-like anti-bank attitudes against Whig merchant, politician, and banker Gulian Verplanck (1751–1799). Lawrence won, but only after days of rioting and by fewer than 200 votes.

What was the election of 1834 like?

The closest analogy would be the protests surrounding the 1968 Democratic convention in Chicago, only far more chaotic and weaponized, and with an actual election in the bal-

Why did the election of 1834 turn into a riot?

Like many elections in nineteenth century urban America, the New York mayoral election of 1834 was a particularly heated one. There were sharp divisions between the competing parties, the populist Jacksonian Democrats who were pushing for expanded democratic rights (for white men, at least) and the establishment Whigs who cautioned about the downside of what they considered mob rule. An incredibly impassioned debate also raged over the very existence of the Bank of the United States, which the Democrats opposed and the Whigs supported. These divisions were only exacerbated by the national debates raging between the polarized sides. Three days were set aside for voting in April to accommodate the 35,000-plus voters (out of an estimated city population of over 200,000) who would have to crowd into the packed voting centers, of which there was just one per ward. The mood was tense, with neither party willing to let mere democracy choose the winner of the election. In the Eleventh Ward, the Jacksonians took no chances, operating two private doors at the voting center for their supporters, while their thugs kept potential Whig voters from entering via the public door.

ance. On the first day of voting, April 8, rioting broke out in the Sixth Ward, the densely populated immigrant neighborhood north of City Hall that encompassed the heavily Irish Five Points. Accounts vary as to what started the violence. But conflict was inevitable, particularly after a thousands-strong Whig parade marched into the Democratic Sixth Ward. A gang of club- and knife-wielding Democrats destroyed a Whig committee room. Whether it was Democrats' attacks on Whigs or Whigs shouting "to keep those damned Irishmen in order!," fierce street fighting broke out in the Sixth Ward, with masses of men battling in the streets.

On April 9, many shopkeepers closed, possibly so that the owners could send their workers out to keep the Irish from voting for the Democrats. The Whigs dispatched hundreds of armed men to clear access to polls and federal troops were deployed. April 10, the last day of voting, saw some of the worst violence. Rival mobs met in front of Masonic Hall on Broadway near Duane Street where the Whigs were meeting. A pitched battle ensued, an unintentionally comic side note being that it was all set off because of a fight over a miniature model of the *Constitution* borne by the Whigs. A police captain died in the fighting, which only came to a close after detachments of federal cavalry rode down Broadway and dispersed the mobs. After all was said and done, Lawrence won the mayorship by fewer than two hundred votes, and the Whigs controlled the Common Council. Both sides were able to claim victory.

What did the Whigs and their allies have against the Irish?

In the 1830s and '40s, the power structure in New York was still mostly as it had always been. Almost exclusively Protestant and heavily Anglo and Dutch, they generally backed the Whig party and preferred a top-down hierarchy, as opposed to the bottom-up approach to politics favored by the surging Jacksonians. The Whigs also tended to be suspicious of the large numbers of non-Protestant immigrants who began entering New York in the early to mid-nineteenth century, particularly the Irish. While the Irish had been coming to New York for decades—and some, like Mayor James Duane (1733–1797) and Mayor and Governor DeWitt Clinton, had been accepted by the establishment—they had generally been Protestants. But the Irish who started showing up in the early 1800s were mostly Catholics. This was an unwelcome development to many New Yorkers, already nervous about a weakening economy in the 1830s.

The virulently anti-immigrant Aaron Clark (1787–1861) was elected to the mayor's office in 1837. As the Whig party weakened in the 1840s and '50s, some supporters started defecting to more strictly anti-immigrant nativist groups like the "Know Nothing" movement, which started in New York in 1843. In a refrain that would be echoed throughout the century, many native-born Protestants questioned the mostly Catholic immigrants' loyalty to America, suggesting that they constituted a veritable fifth column whose allegiances were more to the pope in Vatican than the Constitution of their newly adopted country. In response, the Irish swelled the ranks of the more welcoming Democratic Party, whose get-out-the-vote apparatus helped return the favor in the form of municipal jobs.

Why were there so many Irish policemen?

The stereotype of the Irish New York cop, with his mustache and brogue, began in the mid-nineteenth century, when the police force was still a relatively recent innovation. When New York's Democratic political machine dispensed jobs to new Irish immigrants, they were most often with the police force. In 1855, over a quarter of New York's police officers had been

Ads such as this one in the *New York Times*, which plainly discriminated against the Irish, were common in the 1800s.

born in Ireland. Their disproportionate representation on the force is shown by the fact that in 1869, thirty-two police captains were Ireland-born, while none were born in Germany, even though Germans were the city's next-biggest immigrant group after the Irish. Even today, when the department is far more ethnically diverse (about half the police force is Hispanic, Asian, or black), many of the department's traditions, particularly the ceremonial bagpipe and drum marching band, can be traced to its heavily Irish roots.

Where there actually signs in New York that read "No Irish Need Apply"?

By 1840, the Irish accounted for half of all new immigrants to America. Large numbers of them settled in Northeastern cities like New York. Once arrived, the Irish settled into neighborhoods like Five Points in Manhattan and Vinegar Hill in Brooklyn and took on many of the city's menial jobs. By the 1850s, the Irish made up eighty percent of the city's domestic servants. Discrimination was widespread, particularly once the devastating Great Famine that began in 1845 sent 1.5 million Irish to American shores over the following decade. The *New York Sun* ran fifteen job ads in 1842 alone that included the caveat "No Irish Need Apply." Some newspaper ads of the time even specified that applicants should be "Protestant" or "American."

How pervasive was such discrimination in antebellum New York?

While blatantly discriminating against religion and ethnicity is shocking by today's standards, it should be remembered that anti-Irish and -Catholic sentiment was common in primarily Protestant New York, which was undergoing radical demographic changes starting in the 1830s. In 1806 only one in seven New Yorkers was Catholic; by the end of the Civil War, Catholics were almost half of the city's population. Conspiracy theories abounded, abetted by lurid pamphlets.

Former mayor George Templeton Strong (1820–1875) displayed an attitude typical of many worried nativists when he wrote in his diary that "the gorilla is superior to the Celtic in muscle and hardly their inferior in a moral sense" and that "Our Celtic fellow citizens are almost as remote from us in temperament … as the Chinese." Walt Whitman (1819–1892), normally a celebrator of New York in all its vibrancy, worried about the influence of an "unshaven, filthy, Irish rabble" and their priests ("foreign filth") on the city's political infrastructure. Similar worries would be voiced later against groups ranging from Italians, Jews, and Chinese to blacks and Puerto Ricans, often by descendants of the very same newcomers who had once been at the bottom of the ladder.

Who did the riots of 1844 target?

The targets were Catholics, which, in New York at the time, generally meant the Irish; while a great number of new German immigrants were also Catholic, they were less frequently the targets of discrimination. When the Maclay Bill, which outlawed religious instruction in public schools (and was seen as protecting Catholic children from common attempts at indoctrination by Protestant teachers), passed in 1842, nativist mobs threatened Catholic churches. (Partly as a result of this reaction, the Catholic diocese began establishing a network of parish-affiliated schools, as well as post-secondary institutions like Fordham University.)

In the summer of 1844, anti-Catholic riots in Philadelphia targeted the Irish community, killing thirteen, and threatened to spread to nearby New York. The city's bishop, "Dagger" John Hughes (1797–1864), organized an armed Catholic militia to defend their places of worship. In a famous piece of invective, Hughes informed the mayor that if any church was attacked, the city would be turned into a "second Moscow" (referring to how the Russians burned Moscow to the ground instead of allowing Napoleon to occupy it in 1812).

Why did the Five Points attract so much negative attention?

Also known as the Sixth Ward, the Five Points neighborhood comprises most of what is known as Little Italy and Chinatown today. It was bordered roughly on the south by Chatham and Pearl Streets (just above the modern-day cluster of government and court buildings near City Hall), on the north by Canal Street, to the west by Centre Street and the east by Bowery. Inside its boundaries were a crowded, swampy warren of tangled streets (the 1811 grid never penetrated here) and dangerously rickety and fire-prone buildings packed with workshops, groggeries, and apartments overflowing with people. Inhabited mostly by Germans (Jewish and Christian), blacks, and Irish, the neighborhood became most known for its concentration of the last two groups.

By the mid-nineteenth century, the Five Points was as synonymous with vice and crime as any of London's most notorious slums, which it was in fact compared to by Charles Dickens (1812–1870) when he visited in 1841. Besides the many bordellos with their often under-aged prostitutes and its hundreds of drinking establishments (forty-six on Mulberry Street alone), the Five Points was also famous for its vivacious entertainments such as plays at the Bowery Theater and (scandalously race-mixed) dance halls—where black dance and the Irish jig and reels combined to create tap dance. Just as the city's swells would later go "slumming" in Harlem or the Village, during the nineteenth century there was no better place in the city for vicarious thrills, or at least easily obtainable drink and prostitution. Needless to say, the Five Points was very popular with the city's sporting men, some of whom translated their love of action into volunteering for the neighborhood's many volunteer fire companies who spent almost more time fighting each other than fires.

Who were the "Bowery Boys"?

In the 1840s, an increasingly crowded lower Manhattan started offering a greater density of attractions for its new residents. Theaters, saloons, gambling parlors, brothels, and thoroughfares like the Bowery were thronged with a new subset of dandified toughs called "sporting men" or, more specifically, "Bowery B'hoys." Like London's Teddy Boys in the next century, they mixed rarified attire with guttersnipe grit. Sporting a uniform of black silk hats, black frock coats, silk vests, "soaplocked" hair, and heavy fighting boots with cigars clenched in their teeth, the Bowery B'hoys mixed their gambling, boozing, and occasional political-faction rioting with promenading around with their female auxiliaries, the Bowery G'hals. Stories about the fightin', drinkin', hard-workin' B'hoys were in vogue in the late 1840s and '50s after George Foster's wildly popular series of plays about a B'hoy volunteer firefighter character named Mose who loved to fight (his tag line: "If I don't have a muss soon, I'll spile").

The popular perception of the B'hoys—or just plain "Bowery Boys" as they would later be known—as good-natured rascals wasn't entirely inaccurate. But their rowdy attitudes were also deeply embedded with darker strains of nativism and political corruption. In the years leading up to the Civil War, the Bowery Boys were frequently enlisted for ballot-stuffing duties for the anti-immigrant Know-Nothings when they weren't making life miserable for the Irish and other foreign-born New Yorkers.

What was the most destructive event in New York history?

There have been storms and riots aplenty over the years in New York, not to mention terrorist attacks, gang wars, and even one actual war. But no event destroyed more property in the city than the Great Fire of 1835. On the night of December 16, a watchman discovered a fire in a warehouse at Pearl and Exchange streets. Strong winds and below-zero temperatures hampered the firefighters, whose hoses froze solid. The conflagration raced through the crowded downtown district, sending flames high enough into the sky that they could be seen from Philadelphia. The furnace-like temperatures caused the copper roofs and iron shutters to melt and pour in hissing streams into the street. Within a matter of hours, one-fourth of the city was incinerated. Incredibly, only two lives were lost. The material damage was immense, with the Post Office, Delmonico's, and the Stock Exchange among hundreds of buildings destroyed. Former mayor Philip Hone (1780–1851) called it "the most awful calamity which has ever visited these United States."

What were some of the after-effects of the Great Fire of 1835?

After the Great Fire had reduced some twenty square blocks of downtown Manhattan to ash, the tally was sobering: $20 million in losses (over $400 million by today's reckoning); twenty-three of the city's twenty-six insurance companies forced into bankruptcy; 4,000 unemployed. One abolitionist businessman was able to collect on his policy be-

The Great Fire of December 16, 1835, burned about twenty square blocks and cost the equivalent of $400 million in today's dollars.

cause he was insured by a Boston company; New York firms didn't insure abolitionists. One of the city's more piratical Wall Street financiers, Jeremiah Hamilton (1806–1875)—also known as the "Prince of Darkness," which was probably at least partly a racial slur, he being the city's only black millionaire—was said to have taken advantage of some fire victims' losses and gained a profit of (in today's dollars) $5 million.

The combination of massive infrastructure damage, crippling unemployment, and a terrible harvest combined the following year to create one of the worst food crises in the city's history. Flour shortages and rumor-mongering helped spark the so-called "Flour Riot" in February 1837 that was only quelled by the National Guard. However, the most devastating day in the city's history prior to September 11, 2001, also had some positive results. Incredibly, within a year, most of downtown Manhattan had already been rebuilt, with straighter and wider roads, stronger zoning regulations, and a reorganized fire department, not to mention a stronger demand for a more reliable municipal water supply.

How did cholera give birth to the Croton Aqueduct?

New York residents might brag today about their water supply, but no such bragging rights existed before the Croton Aqueduct. Jill Lepore writes in *New York Burning*, "By the middle of the eighteenth century, Manhattan's water was already infamous: there was too little of it and what little there was tasted terrible." Alcohol was generally safer to drink (and tea, being boiled first, *always* safer) than the brackish water from public wells (often polluted, sometimes by seepage from privies). The limited system that delivered water to a small number of houses via hollowed-out tree trunks, introduced in 1801 by Aaron Burr, or the expensive carting of barrels of water from upstate by horse-drawn wagon, was not sufficient for the city's clean-water needs. The political inertia that typified some aspects of city polity through much of its history kept anything from changing. Then, in 1832, a cholera epidemic swept through the city, killing over 3,500 New Yorkers—one out of every sixty residents. This was just the latest in a series of cholera outbreaks that convinced the city leadership that a better water supply was needed.

When did New York decide to start doing something about its water supply?

In 1835, the city approved a plan by which the Croton River, forty miles (64 kilometers) north of the city in Dutchess County, would be dammed and its fresh water sent via an awe-inspiring series of conduits. The dam created a four-hundred-acre lake, five miles (eight kilometers) long. Designed in part on principles learned from ancient Roman aqueducts, the Croton's water ran mostly along a gravity-fed iron-lined masonry tube that dropped thirteen inches every mile. It delivered water first to the Receiving Reservoir, a fortress-like structure that sat where Central Park's Great Lawn is now (the beautiful Belvedere Castle once overlooked its southwest corner). The water was sent on to the Croton Reservoir, a beautiful twenty-million-gallon tank with walls designed like an Egyptian temple situated where the main branch of the Public Library is now on 42nd Street; at the time this was still one mile north of the city limits.

One of the greatest and most ambitious public works in the city's history, the Croton Aqueduct began delivering water to New York in 1842. Civic celebrations at City Hall, where an aqueduct-fed fountain shot water fifty feet in the air, even featured a song written for the occasion: "Croton Ode." Designed to last one hundred years, the Aqueduct was built just as the city's immigrant population began to explode and soon it was barely keeping pace. In order to keep up with demand, the New Croton Aqueduct, a thirty-three-mile long, thirteen-foot- (four-meter-) diameter brick-lined gravity tunnel, was constructed in 1890 to deliver water to the Jerome Park Reservoir in the Bronx.

Why are there massive water barrels on top of many larger New York buildings?

When the Croton Aqueduct was first built, it delivered water to the city by means of simple gravity. Then and today, the pressure in the city's water supply system can send water up to buildings' sixth floors. In order to get water to floors seven and above, it has to be pumped up to large tanks on their roofs and then piped down by gravity. The water tanks—of which there are anywhere between 12,000 and 17,000 today—started to sprout across the city skyline starting later in the nineteenth century as more buildings breached the old six-story limit. While climbing up the ladders affixed to the tanks'

Why did the Croton Reservoir look like an Egyptian temple?

Primarily to camouflage the fact to passers-by that there was an immense reservoir standing in what eventually would become the heart of Manhattan. As a key link in the ambitious Croton Aqueduct project, the reservoir was opened in 1842 on Fifth Avenue between 40th and 42nd streets. It was designed to deliver twenty-four gallons of water to 600,000 people every day. The thick, slanted, fortress-like walls were made of granite and gneiss and made to suggest the lower part of an Egyptian pyramid. The views from the top of the walls were apparently splendid, making them a popular spot for couples out for a stroll. Eventually, the reservoir's usefulness was surpassed by the increasing density of underground water mains. It was demolished in 1900. A few pieces of its foundation were used in the construction of the New York Public Library's main branch on the same site. Otherwise, it only lives on in the name of the Croton Reservoir Tavern on 40th Street.

side and going swimming in them on hot summer days has been a long-running activity for more adventurous apartment dwellers, it's not an advisable hobby to pick up.

Where could New Yorkers get a free college degree?

In 1847, a city referendum established the Free Academy of the City of New York to provide free education to the poor, with admission determined by academic merit alone. This economically democratic stance alone set it apart from other city schools like Columbia University (originally King's College) and New York University (founded in 1832), which were aiming for a more Ivy League class of student body. Renamed the City College of New York in 1866, it established a reputation not just for its high academic prowess, but not discriminating against Jews, who were denied access at many other institutions of higher learning.

In 1907, City College moved to a striking new neo-Gothic campus (now landmarked) of Manhattan schist and terra-cotta in Harlem designed by George Post (1837–1913), who also designed the Stock Exchange and the Brooklyn Historical Society. In the early twentieth century, City College became a mecca for Jewish intellectuals denied access to other colleges, earning its sobriquet "Harvard of the Proletariat." City College was incorporated into the City University of New York system when it was established in 1961. Its alumni range from Upton Sinclair and Ira Gershwin to Ed Koch and Colin Powell.

Who was the Rosa Parks of New York?

Despite the presence of a strong abolitionist community, in the mid-nineteenth century New York was starkly segregated, with the boundaries between the races strictly enforced. In 1854, Elizabeth Jennings (1826–1901), a black schoolteacher, and a friend were running late for a service at a church on the Bowery where she was the organist. To save time, she didn't wait for a blacks-allowed streetcar and just hailed the first one she saw. The conductor tried to throw Jennings off, but she held on tightly, only being dislodged when a policeman intervened. Jennings pressed a legal case, with the help of her father, a well-known abolitionist, publicity in the *New York Tribune*, and a young white lawyer named Chester Arthur (1829–1886) who became president in 1881. *Jennings v. Third Avenue Railroad* (1855) helped force the integration of public transportation in New York. Forty years later, Jennings founded the city's first kindergarten for black children.

Where was America's first world fair held?

One of the few examples of New York following London, the Crystal Palace was inspired by that city's 1851 Great Exhibition, which took place in a massive glass-covered building. Some New York businessmen looking for ways to boost the city's profile formed a consortium to replicate the success of London's Crystal Palace in Manhattan. In 1853, a massive building made of a cast-iron frame and thousands of windows opened in what is now Bryant Park, with the Croton Reservoir to the east and Sixth Avenue to the west. Shaped like a Greek cross, it was built around a Moorish-styled dome and believed to be utterly fireproof.

The Crystal Palace's Exhibition of the Industry of All Nations was the nation's first world fair, featuring four thousand exhibitors from around the world showing off the newest advances in technology and industry. It also included the greatest collection of

The New York Crystal Palace, which opened in 1853, was inspired by a similar building in London that debuted two years earlier.

art that Americans had ever seen in one place. Elisha Otis (1811–1861) introduced his new invention in dramatic fashion: He raised himself in an elevator a hundred feet off the Crystal Palace's floor and ordered an assistant to cut the elevator cables with a sword. The audience screamed, but the plummeting elevator was safely stopped from disaster by Otis's new braking mechanism, which would help make his company's elevators ubiquitous in the skyscrapers that would start springing up around the city in just a few years. Like so many other grand nineteenth-century structures, the Crystal Palace eventually succumbed to fire, burning to the ground in a mere fifteen minutes in 1858.

Who was the first president born in New York?

Some might find it fitting that the first U.S. president who was born in New York was a temperamental loudmouth with a rebellious streak who looked out for the little guy and was known as an independent thinker. Theodore Roosevelt (1858–1919) was born in a brownstone on West 20th Street. The sickly young Roosevelt lived there until the family moved in 1872. The house was torn down in 1916, seven years after his death, but reconstructed in 1923 based on how Roosevelt described it in his autobiography. The multi-talented Roosevelt left a broad legacy in the city and state, ranging from spearheading the construction of the Museum of Natural History to serving as a reformist police commissioner and writing a history of the city whose conclusion included this paean to the city's character: "the average New Yorker yet possesses courage, energy, business capacity, much generosity of a practical sort, and shrewd, humorous common sense."

What was the Greensward Plan?

In 1857, the city announced a competition to turn its newly cleared acquisition into a thing of beauty. Ultimately, Frederick Law Olmsted (1822–1903), a college dropout who

---

How long did it take to build Central Park?

Ironically, one of the greatest public works projects in the history of New York was the construction of its most famous "natural" space. Around 20,000 primarily Irish and German laborers working ten-hour days for no more than $1.50 per day moved three million cubic yards of soil, planted over 270,000 trees and shrubs, and availed themselves of more gunpowder than was used at the Battle of Gettysburg to blast ridges into shapes that matched Olmsted and Vaux's vision. They cut four transverse roads for crosstown traffic that ran below the surface of the park to minimize traffic disturbance, and built three dozen arches and bridges, multiple ponds, and a network of artfully staged bucolic vistas. Incredibly, the first sections of the park began opening to the public in the winter of 1859, when visitors skated on frozen ponds. In the 1870s, two of the park's major attractions would open: Central Park Zoo and the Metropolitan Museum of Art.

became something of a landscaping hobbyist, and Calvert Vaux (1824–1895), an English architect who shared many of Olmsted's ideas, agreed to co-design the park according to a so-called "Greensward Plan." This design, both revolutionary and Arcadian, would reconfigure the park's rough-and-tumble terrain into a landscaped garden that, beautiful as it was, had almost as little to do with the natural world as the regimented urban blocks growing ever more crowded around its borders. They planned a series of vignettes and vistas that visitors would experience almost as though they were in a grand outdoor art gallery. The plan also included an interlacing network of winding pathways and roadways designed to keep pedestrians and visitors in carriages from interfering with the other. The 843-acre greenspace would become America's first major landscaped park.

What was the effect of Central Park on New York?

Like any other human endeavor, there were critics of Central Park. Granted, they mostly voiced concerns about the *way* it was operated instead of its actual existence. In less than a decade, the park was seeing over seven million visitors a year. The incredible idea that a person could walk into a park so large and well-tended that they could forget for a time that they were in the heart of a sprawling metropolis was soon considered more of a right than a privilege. Central Park was soon seen as an essential component to the urban fabric that needed to be nurtured, protected, and improved over the years to follow, and never questioned. Historian and novelist Caleb Carr accurately described the park's importance when he observed that New York is "not a practical proposition" without it.

What was the city's first true police force?

Since the city of New York, in the mid-nineteenth century, was still yoked to Albany, it wasn't until the state legislature gave its approval in 1844 that the metropolitan area was authorized to field a true police force. (Prior to then, the city had been mostly watched over by amateur watchmen or constables elected from the various wards that they watched over.) The idea was for the city to begin organizing a proper uniformed constabulary, but bickering over patronage and local control kept the force decentralized.

But Mayor James Harper (1795–1869) was determined to move ahead and so quickly appointed two hundred officers, who became known as "Harper's police." The system was reorganized under the New York Municipal Police Force, which was established in 1845 with a force of nine hundred men. The city's new policemen differed from the old constable system in that they were salaried, uniformed professionals instead of amateurs. While this was a step forward in keeping the city safe, the establishment of a new city department also provided Tammany Hall with a new source from which to dole out patronage jobs.

Why did New York briefly have two police departments?

In the 1850s, the ever-smoldering conflict between New York city and Albany burst, as it is still wont to do, into open war. The ambitious reformist mayor of New York, Fernando Wood (1812–1881), a wealthy shipping merchant and former Democratic representative who had been elected in 1854, had set out an ambitious slate of proposed changes, including hiring the unemployed to work on public projects, cracking down on gangs and prostitution, improving city services, and centralizing command of the police. However, Wood ran afoul of the upstate government, which didn't appreciate either his bid for greater autonomy or his popularity with the city's surging immigrant population.

In response, in 1857 Albany passed a series of bills to undercut the mayor's power, restricted liquor sales (a direct and intended affront to the city's German and Irish immigrants), and most controversially created a new Albany-directed Metropolitan Police force operating independently of City Hall. After Wood rejected Albany's authority in the matter, the city briefly had two police forces, the Metropolitan and the Municipal; the former was staffed mostly with native-borns, and the latter's ranks were heavily weighted toward Wood-supporting immigrants. It was a recipe ripe for conflict and a general breakdown in law and order, with criminals often finding themselves arrested by one police force only to be let go by the other.

How did the Metropolitan and Municipal police resolve their differences?

In the same manner that many disputes were resolved (or not) in nineteenth century New York: a good old-fashioned street riot. In June 1857, the Metropolitans tried to serve an arrest warrant on Wood at City Hall. They were driven away by a force of Municipals and an auxiliary of pro-Wood civilians. The bloody street fighting was only broken up after the Seventh Regiment cleared the streets and arrested Wood. He ultimately relented and disbanded his Municipals on July 3. Tensions were already high on Independence Day, which was when the new liquor law was supposed to take effect. The Irish Dead Rabbits gang started a fight with the Metropolitans and their nativist allies, the Bowery Boys. The result was a raging melee on Bayard Street between barricades on Mulberry and Elizabeth streets that sucked in thousands of combatants and resulted in

An illustration of a run on Seamen's Savings Bank in New York during the Panic of 1857, when the market underwent a bad crash, though not as severe as the 1929 crash by any means.

twelve deaths. Order was eventually restored, but it left the city in a precariously nervous condition right before it was due to be hit with its next great crisis.

How bad was the Panic of 1857?

In strictly financial terms, the market collapse of August 24, 1857, was probably not quite as damaging as the previous crashes. But its place in New York market history looms large for a couple of reasons. First, it was the first truly global financial crisis, with the conflagration spreading quickly from New York to London, Paris, and even Vienna; it would not be the last time that such a panic would ripple outward from the city. Also, if considered in terms of what today is called "optics," the crash appeared catastrophic. Once banks, with their specie reserves (gold and silver) threatened—particularly after a ship carrying millions of dollars in gold from the San Francisco Mint sank in mid-September—started restricting transactions, panic spread like a brushfire. Rumors of collapse amplified and proliferated, assisted in part by the speed of that new-fangled telegraph, leading to mass withdrawals, runs on numerous institutions, and then the actual collapse of many banks. The frenzy reached such a pitch that at one point, revivalist prayer meetings in lower Manhattan were attracting thousands of panicked people. Thousands of businesses across the city went bankrupt.

Later in the year, the newly unemployed were milling angrily in New York's streets, many of them convinced they knew who to blame: Wall Street, speculators and banks in particular. In early November, thousands of people marched to Wall Street, and then a few days later, to City Hall, demanding that banks and other institutions start loaning money so that workers could be re-hired. Mayor Fernando Wood couldn't convince the City Council to provide aid to the unemployed. But he was able to employ thousands of workers on public works projects, denting somewhat the effects of the recession that followed.

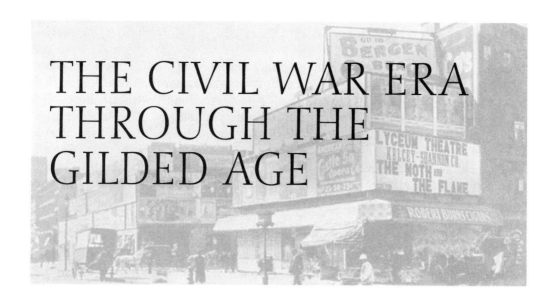

THE CIVIL WAR ERA THROUGH THE GILDED AGE

SLAVERY AND THE CIVIL WAR

When was slavery outlawed in New York and New Jersey?

Early in the colony's history, both blacks and Indians were enslaved, though enslavement of the latter was officially outlawed in 1690 as a way of keeping peace with local tribes. Gradual emancipation laws for black slaves were passed in 1799 and 1817, stipulating that children born to slaves after July 4, 1799, would be free after a number of years. Slavery wasn't officially abolished in New York until July 4, 1827. The neighboring state of New Jersey was even slower in this process. New Jersey also passed gradual emancipation laws prior to the Civil War (1861–1865) and passed a law in 1846 that technically emancipated slaves with the exception of several blacks held as "apprentices for life." Complete emancipation didn't occur in New Jersey until the end of the Civil War.

Did New York play a role in the Underground Railroad?

Yes. The issue of slaves who escaped to free states but could still be legally brought back to their owners by force helped galvanize the abolitionist movement throughout the north, especially in New York. As early as 1793 Congress had passed a law that made it possible for a slave's owner or the owner's agent to bring a fugitive slave before a judge anywhere in the country to get back possession of their "property." This meant that even after a slave had undergone the frequently grueling and terrifying process of escaping from the slave-owning part of the country, they could still be legally kidnapped by private citizens and returned to bondage (and frequently harsh punishment) at any time. The Fugitive Slave Law of 1850 gave slave-owners and their agents even more impunity.

The Underground Railroad, the informal name for a loosely organized network of white (often Quaker) and black abolitionists that started operating in the early 1830s, had two missions: to help fugitive slaves escape; and to keep them from being recaptured

91

once they were in the north. Even though it was a bastion of pro-Southern sentiment, New York served as one of the most important way stations for the Underground Railroad in the mid-Atlantic region. With the city's many land- and sea-based transit points and its secretive network of abolitionists and other anti-slavery activists and sympathizers, it was well-positioned to provide assistance for fugitives who were heading elsewhere. Many slaves, in fact, passed through New York on their way north to Canada, where they would be safe from slavers' kidnappers. Historian Eric Foner estimates that three to four thousand fugitive slaves were assisted while transiting through New York between 1835 and 1860.

Who were the "Know-Nothings," and how did they get their name?

The Know-Nothings were originally a virulently racist and nativist segment of the Whigs. As anti-immigrant rhetoric was ratcheted up in the decades before the Civil War, they splintered from the mainstream Whigs and formed the short-lived American Party. Their nickname came from members' strict instructions to say "I know nothing" when asked about the group. Ostensibly a political party, the Know-Nothings' penchant for rioting and close ties with the Bowery Boys and the infamous likes of Bill the Butcher (1821–1855) gave them the patina of a proto-fascist (and ultimately unsuccessful) street mob.

How big was New York before the Civil War?

According to the U.S. Census Bureau, the population of New York in 1860 was 813,669, the largest in the nation. Counting the population of Brooklyn (number 3 with 266,661), the metropolitan area was over twice the size of not just the next largest city, Philadelphia (565,529), but also double what its own population had been just ten years earlier.

Was "Bill the Butcher" actually a butcher?

Yes, not only as his job but it was something of a hobby as well when it came to the brawling he enjoyed so much. William Poole (1821–1855) ran a butcher shop in Washington Market near the Hudson River docks. He stood over six feet tall, dressed like a dandy, liked using knives at work and at play, hated foreigners, and was by all accounts an extremely imposing and effective street fighter—though there is unfortunately no evidence that he sported a glass eye with an American flag as portrayed in Martin Scorsese's vivid but historically loose film *Gangs of New York*. He died, predictably, after a bar fight one night in 1855. No matter that it seems too melodramatic to be true, history still records Poole's dying words as "Good-bye boys, I die a true American"; it was quickly worked into an applause line for downtown theatrical productions. His funeral procession included half a dozen brass bands, five thousand marchers, and a boat that ferried his corpse to Brooklyn's Green-Wood Cemetery.

When the Civil War began, New York was not just the largest city in the nation, but its economic and cultural capital as well, where well-to-do Southerners came to be entertained and to do business.

What were New Yorkers' attitude towards the Civil War?

Given the amount of revenue that the slave trade and all its ancillary businesses like cotton generated, some New Yorkers were reluctant to engage in any conflict with the slave-holding South. Theodore Roosevelt's mother, Martha "Mittie" Bulloch (1835-1884), remained a die-hard Southerner even after moving to New York, entrancing young Teddy with stories of his Confederate soldier uncles' heroic feats. Many New York natives were pro-Confederacy, or at least anti-war. An acceptance of slavery, or at least an attitude that it was best ignored for the sake of national unity or business, was deeply baked into the Democratic Party. At the same time that some New Yorkers led in the abolition movement, they were countered by a strong anti-abolitionist sentiment that found support everywhere from the financial community to immigrant workers (many of whom were afraid that freed blacks would compete with them for jobs). These fears were further stoked by anti-Lincoln newspapers like the *New York Herald* and *New York Daily News*, the latter of which warned that if Lincoln became president, the city would find "negroes among us thicker than blackberries."

Did New York almost secede from the Union?

It's been something of a joke among New Yorkers that since the city stands so apart from the rest of the United States anyway, it might as well secede. Curiously, that came closest to happening on the eve of the Civil War. Mayor Fernando Wood was no enemy of the South. As tensions grew during the 1850s, he urged compromise instead of war. Wood's message sent to the Common Council on January 7, 1861, was nevertheless shocking. He proposed that New York (meaning Manhattan) should declare itself a "free city" in order to not disrupt "friendly relations and a common sympathy" with "our aggrieved brethren of the Slave States."

Wood hoped to keep the city's lucrative position in the international cotton trade. He also promised that without needing to pay federal duty on imports (which comprised over three-fourths of federal revenue), "we could live free from taxes, and have cheap goods nearly duty free." Wood certainly had support in the heavily Democratic city. Some of the city's top businessmen even plotted to seize the federal government's military facilities in New York.

Could it have actually happened?

It is impossible to know exactly how far Mayor Fernando Wood's plan would have gone, because on April 12, Confederate forces fired on Fort Sumter, turning the majority of the city's population into enthusiastic supporters of the Union cause. Wood and some of his Democratic allies kept fighting for accommodation with the South. In July, the pro-Lincoln *New York Tribune* coined the term "Copperhead" to describe anti-war northern Democrats. After the failure of the secession plan, it would be two years before opposition to the war came to a head in New York.

How did the Civil War affect New York?

As in most wars, New York's robust manufacturing base and work-hungry immigrant population were ideally suited to supplying the needs of a country at war. Everything from wagons to pharmaceuticals and uniforms poured out of the city's factories and workshops. Also, as in just about every other American conflict, the outbreak of the Civil War found New York unprepared to defend itself. The one exception was a pair of comparatively new forts bracketing the Narrows. Rebel privateers were skulking around the harbor and the Confederate navy was planning to send its new ironclad gunship *Merrimack* north to destroy New

New York's Mayor Fernando Wood was anti-war and urged a compromise with the South.

York Harbor (a plan foiled after the New York-built Union ironclad *Monitor* sailed south and sank the *Merrimack*). A vigorous fortification plan was put into place. However, little thought was given to defending the city from a land-borne assault, a nightmare that became a very real possibility in the summer of 1863. Prior to that point, the city's experience of the war was primarily felt in the newspaper lists of the dead and wounded.

In April 1861, 150,000 people rallied for the Union cause at Union Square in what was then the largest public gathering ever seen in the Western Hemisphere. Even after the initial surge of patriotism was tempered by the rout of Union troops at the First Battle of Bull Run, New Yorkers kept signing up, particularly for the city's many ethnic-based units like the Italian Garibaldi Guard, the German 20th, the Irish 69th, and the 39th with its eleven companies divided up by national heritage (German, Hungarian, French, and so on). At least 100,000 New Yorkers ultimately fought in the war. But the city's sometimes ambivalent attitude about the war and the mounting casualty count generated increasing discontent. At the Second Battle of Bull Run in 1862, in just ten minutes of fighting, the 5th New York Regiment lost 124 soldiers; more fatalities than any regiment suffered in any battle throughout the war. After several years, the city had wearied of war, and in 1864 New York again voted resoundingly against Abraham Lincoln (1809–1865) in the presidential election.

What was the origin of the Draft Riots?

The Draft Riots of 1863, one of the most devastating events in New York history, occurred in part because of a tragic confluence of economic and racial pressures, which resulted in a horrific pogrom unlike anything the country had ever seen. In the mid-nineteenth century, New York's black community remained small, totaling only about 13,000 people in 1860. At the same time, the city contained about 200,000 Irish residents, many of whom were desperate to get a grip on the economic ladder's lowest rung and determined to keep out blacks, their greatest competition for low-wage jobs. Tensions were exacerbated by Wood's claim that Republicans believed blacks to be "superior to the poor white." This contributed to Irish trade unions banning blacks from membership.

Democratic leaders whipped up fears with racist propaganda. Irish attacks on blacks in the street apparently became common enough that bricks came to be known as "Irish confetti." Thousands of Irish, many practically right off the boat from the auld sod, had proudly signed up for military service. The 69th "Irish Brigade" was blessed by Archbishop John Hughes at St. Patrick's Cathedral in April 1861 before going off to war. Most believed they were fighting to preserve the Union and not to free an enslaved race. The combination of Lincoln's issuance of first the Emancipation Proclamation and then the Conscription Act in 1863 served as proof to some of a Republican conspiracy to value Southern blacks over northern working-class immigrant whites.

How did the Draft Riots start?

After all the racist fear-mongering indulged in by New York's Democratic politicians and media, the Conscription Act passed in March 1863 made it easier to paint Lincoln as a tool of the Republican elite. Copperheads denounced the law for being both unconstitutional and an assault on the working class; wealthier draftees had the option of hiring substitutes for $300. New York governor Horatio Seymour (1810–1886) got into the demagoguery business, proclaiming on July 4 that "the bloody and treasonable and revolutionary doctrine of public necessity can be proclaimed by a mob as well as by a government."

The city's draft lottery began on July 11. The city's quota was 24,000 men. On Monday the 13th, hundreds of protestors in front of the draft office on 46th Street and Third Avenue were spurred into action after the Black Joke Engine Company—strongly linked, as most volunteer fire companies were, to the Democratic party machine, and angry about not being given draft exemptions—started throwing stones through the windows. Soon the draft office was burning. Soldiers of the U.S. Army's Invalid Corps, some of the only troops left in the city, were sent to restore order. But they were overwhelmed by the mob and lost several men. The riots had begun.

Who was targeted in the Draft Riots?

By Monday afternoon, tens of thousands of mostly white immigrant rioters were pouring through the city, killing and burning and looting armories for weapons. Whole blocks burned; among those called to fight the fire were the very same Black Joke Engine Company who helped spark the conflagration. Wealthy men who could pay their way out of the draft, the so-called "$300 men," were often set upon by angry crowds. The mansions and stores of the wealthy were also attacked and looted. In a reversal of the religious riots of the 1840s, Catholics went after Protestant churches.

The primary focus of the rioters' rage, though, would be the city's black population, targeted for everything from the war to economic hardship (a strike that spring by Irish longshoremen which had failed after a shipping company brought in black strikebreakers). As the rioting spread, blacks were hunted down with vicious dedication. The homes of many blacks were burnt to the ground, as was the Colored Orphan Asylum on 44th Street, where the superintendent snuck his 237 wards out the back door while the enraged crowd smashed the doors with axes. One young girl who had been left behind was discovered by the mob and beaten to death. Blacks were murdered in the streets and lynched from lampposts, their bodies often burned, mutilated, and dragged through the streets. White women who had married black men were the focus of the mob's rage as well.

In July 1863 one of the largest civil insurrections in American history occurred in New York City when people rioted in protest against men being drafted to fight in the Civil War.

How did the Draft Riots end?

The riot only began to subside on Thursday, July 16, after five regiments of troops arrived. Fresh from smashing Robert E. Lee's army at Gettysburg, the Union soldiers (including many New Yorkers) did not look kindly on the rampaging crowds of draft resisters. The troops used flesh-shredding grapeshot to clear the streets, tore down the rioters' barricades, and used bayonets for close-quarter combat. By Friday, the riot was over. The official body count was 105, but estimates have ranged as high as 500 dead. The reaction of much of the North could be summed up by a *Harper's Weekly* cartoon showing a club-wielding mob attacking a kneeling and unarmed black man and child, with the scathing caption: "How to Escape the Draft."

What was New York's reaction to the death of Abraham Lincoln?

Even though his speech at New York's Cooper Union in 1860 had helped him secure the presidency, Abraham Lincoln had never lacked for enemies in the city. He lost both elections there and was often denounced by the city's Democrats for what they called his dictatorial actions. Nevertheless, after his assassination in April 1865, New Yorkers mourned along with the rest of the nation. Walt Whitman wrote that on the day after Lincoln's death, "All Broadway is black with mourning … the horror, fever, uncertainty, alarm in the public." Angry crowds had to be stopped from attacking Wall Street firms who were thought to be Confederate sympathizers.

On April 26, Lincoln's funeral train stopped in New York on its way to his home of Springfield, Illinois. The hearse was drawn by six horses draped in black and escorted through the jam-packed city streets by the 7th Regiment and a procession of 160,000 people, whose last group was two hundred black men carrying a banner that read "Abraham Lincoln—Our Emancipator."

Why was the New York Fire Department created?

Since the 1830s, companies of firefighters had been growing in size, number, and political clout. Their smart uniforms, shown off in dramatic parade-like rushes through teeming streets to the next fire, made for dramatic city theater. More than a few commentators in the mid-nineteenth century noted that the volunteer companies seemed more like political clubs than actual fire-prevention units. At the start of the Civil War, firefighters formed the 11th New York Regiment and, like several other units in the war, adopted the fancifully colorful so-called "Zouave" attire inspired by French Algerian soldiers' uniforms. Having multiple fire companies appear at the same place and brawl with each other instead of fighting the fire (the nascent police force sometimes had to separate battling firefighters) was a less than optimal situation.

The Metropolitan Fire Department, later the Fire Department of the City of New York (FDNY), was created by the state legislature in 1865. Engine Company Number 1, the city's first professional firefighting unit, started operating on July 31, 1865, from a station on Centre Street in downtown Manhattan. From this point on, firefighters were no longer volunteers—though some volunteers would continue to fight fires in outlying areas until the 1930s—but full-time, paid, public employees who had to pass a physical examination and take firefighting instruction. Innovations like horse-drawn steam engines (the old pumpers had to be pulled by hand) and high-pressure pumping stations helped the FDNY keep up with the rapidly growing and fire-prone city.

INDUSTRIALIZATION AND IMMIGRATION

Where was the first elevated railway in New York?

The idea for an elevated train line that would take some of the pressure off the ever-more crowded city's streets was first mooted as early as 1825. After many plans and starts and stops, the world's first commercial passenger cable railway opened for business on July 4, 1868. Cars were pulled along by cables on a high track that ran up Greenwich Street and Ninth Avenue between Dey and 29th streets. The New York Elevated Railroad Company replaced the slow and problem-plagued cable line with steam locomotives in 1871, which dramatically increased ridership. The line was steadily extended northward and other elevated lines began to be stitched across the city's streetscape, their massive steel frames throwing many avenues into deep and soot-covered shadow.

The trains' regularity and insulation from the vicissitudes of street traffic made them immediately popular and helped open up distant parts of the city, from Harlem to Queens, to residential development. However, the trains were still susceptible to weather delays, such as the one that occurred during the blizzard of 1888, when about 15,000 commuters were trapped by snowdrifts in elevated cars. Some entrepreneurial New Yorkers charged a dollar a head to hoist ladders up to the trains and help the stranded passengers clamber down. Starting in the early twentieth century, elevated train lines in Manhattan were torn down one by one as their routes were replaced by the more efficient subway trains. About seventy miles' (113 kilometers') worth of elevated lines remain in operation out in the boroughs.

What were "sweatshops"?

In the mid-to-late nineteenth century, as New York convulsed with the energies and creative destruction of the Industrial Revolution, advances in machinery and trade combined with the influx of new immigrants to create a new (for America, at least) type of factory: the sweatshop. Essentially a miniature factory, instead of being a standalone purpose-built structure with hundreds of laborers at work, the sweatshop occupied anywhere from a couple floors of a building to a tenement apartment. While looking no different from the outside, inside the sweatshop would be packed with workers doing piece work—almost always as part of the garment industry—for terrible pay in generally horrendous conditions. The term is thought by some to refer to the sweaty conditions created by generally unventilated spaces with people and machinery in close quarters. More likely the term originates from as far back as 1830 and referred to the middlemen (or "sweater"). These people subcontracted much of the work done in the garment trade and tended to make their money by aggressively underpricing the competition and, as a consequence, underpaying and mistreating their workers, who were generally seen as easily replaceable cogs.

How much money did Boss Tweed steal from the city?

For several years, it would have been difficult to find a single person in New York who had more power than William M. "Boss" Tweed (1823–1878). It would also have been impossible to find anyone who made such a good living as a public servant. The barrel-chested and garrulous Tweed started out in the late 1840s run-

A political cartoon by Thomas Nast, published in 1871, depicts Boss William Tweed surrounded by the rubble of Tammany Hall.

ning a politically influential firefighting company. He worked his way up through the Democratic machine, serving as a congressman before being made grand sachem of Tammany Hall in 1863. In that post, as well as being the head of several key committees, Tweed had the ability to appoint officials to key posts and to steer city business to his various companies.

This was all of a piece with previous Tammany bosses. But where Tweed and his grasping confederates, known as the Tweed Ring—building on the previous high-water mark for civic corruption, the infamous "Forty Thieves" of the Common Council in the 1850s—exceeded their forbears was their efficiency at milking appointments and the assigning of contracts for every dollar they were worth. Over the few short years of Tweed's reign, he was estimated to have defrauded the city out of up to $200 million (over $2 billion in modern currency). One of the city's biggest landowners, he lived lavishly in a Fifth Avenue mansion and could be spotted by the large diamond stud on his shirtfront. At the same time as Tweed and his cronies made millions, the city's debt and taxes spiked and services suffered under the weight of patronage. The Tweed Ring played its working-class and heavily immigrant supporters adroitly, spreading around just enough jobs and public works to keep people from asking too many questions.

Who or what finally drove Boss Tweed from power?

The decision of two mighty media entities to turn their attentions to Boss Tweed's octopus-like control over so much of New York's finances and day-to-day governance, not to mention the lazy extravagance of his corruption, finally managed to bring Tweed down in 1871. From 1869, *Harper's Weekly* cartoons by Thomas Nast (1840–1902) had been painting a vivid portrait of Tweed as the grasping symbol of big-city corruption that so many anti-urbanists and anti-populists had been warning about with the advent of modern cities and democracy. A strident reformer, Nast was disgusted by the greed of Tammany Hall in general and Tweed in particular. A frequent target of the city's newspapers, Tweed saw the threat in the vituperative illustrated lampooning from Nast—an immigrant himself (from Germany) who didn't mind playing off anti-immigrant and anti-Rome sentiment when attacking the heavily Irish Catholic political machine. The boss of Tammany Hall supposedly demanded to know what could be done to "stop them damn pictures!" After all, he had once declared, "I don't care a straw for your newspaper articles; my constituents don't know how to read, but they can't help seeing them damned pictures!" Tweed's cohorts even tried to pay Nast to take a European vacation in order to stop his cartoons.

Closing the circle with Nast's vivid caricatures, in July 1871 the *New York Times*, building on document leaks from disgruntled Tammany Hall members, ran its first blockbuster investigation: a series of articles describing in vivid detail the machine's rampant corruption. Tammany Hall's power was further eroded by its glaring inability to control its constituents during the Orange Riot. The 1871 elections saw many disgraced Tammany officials go down in defeat. Tweed was ultimately indicted on multiple counts of fraud, grand larceny, and a variety of misdemeanors. Convicted to twelve years

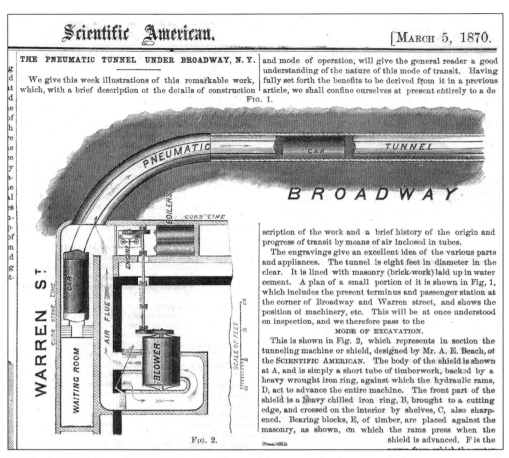

Scientific American. [MARCH 5, 1870.

THE PNEUMATIC TUNNEL UNDER BROADWAY, N. Y.

We give this week illustrations of this remarkable work, which, with a brief description of the details of construction

FIG. 1.

and mode of operation, will give the general reader a good understanding of the nature of this mode of transit. Having fully set forth the benefits to be derived from it in a previous article, we shall confine ourselves at present entirely to a description of the work and a brief history of the origin and progress of transit by means of air inclosed in tubes.

The engravings give an excellent idea of the various parts and appliances. The tunnel is eight feet in diameter in the clear. It is lined with masonry (brick-work) laid up in water cement. A plan of a small portion of it is shown in Fig, 1, which includes the present terminus and passenger station at the corner of Broadway and Warren street, and shows the position of machinery, etc. This will be at once understood on inspection, and we therefore pass to the

MODE OF EXCAVATION.

This is shown in Fig. 2, which represents in section the tunneling machine or shield, designed by Mr. A. E. Beach, of the SCIENTIFIC AMERICAN. The body of the shield is shown at A, and is simply a short tube of timberwork, backed by a heavy wrought iron ring, against which the hydraulic rams, D, act to advance the entire machine. The front part of the shield is a heavy chilled iron ring, B, brought to a cutting edge, and crossed on the interior by shelves, C, also sharpened. Bearing blocks, E, of timber, are placed against the masonry, as shown, on which the rams press when the shield is advanced. F is the

The March 5, 1870, issue of *Scientific American* discussed the pneumatic tube-powered subway system proposed by inventor Alfred Ely Beach.

in prison, Tweed later escaped to Cuba and eventually Spain. He was caught in Spain, by police who allegedly recognized Tweed because of Nast's cartoons, and extradited to New York. Tweed died in prison of pneumonia in 1878.

What was the first New York subway?

As with so many things in New York during the reign of the Tweed Ring, the subway system would have been finished much earlier had Boss Tweed not been involved. A railroad operator from Michigan tried to build one in the 1860s, but it was opposed by Tweed, who controlled other transit lines and didn't want competition.

In 1870, inventor Alfred Ely Beach (1826–1896) opened the city's first subway line. More of a novelty than a commuter transit system, the beautifully appointed station and ingenious pneumatic tube-powered subway car took passengers for a one-block ride under Broadway between Warren and Murray streets. Several hundred thousand people rode the train in its first year of operation. When Beach applied to the state legislature for permission to extend the subway line five miles (eight kilometers) north to Central Park, even though the bill was passed, the Tweed-backed governor vetoed it. Beach's tunnel was bricked up and forgotten until it was excavated in 1912 by workers digging a new transit tunnel.

How is it possible to have a "walking riot"?

The riot occurred in 1879, when Daniel O'Leary faced Charles Rowell in New York for the prize of the Astley Belt: a prize for, yes, competitive walking. At the time, people came from far and wide to watch men walk hundreds of miles with only short breaks, for days at a time, in epic contests of sheer endurance. Giving the 1879 match extra frisson was the fact that O'Leary was an Irish immigrant and Rowell was British. The ethnic antagonisms were already ratcheting up as crowds gathered before the start of the six-day match at Gilmore's Garden at Madison Avenue and 26th Street late on the night of Sunday, March 9, 1879. The excitement inside built to a fever pitch.

Meanwhile, a crowd of thousands outside, enraged by the slow pace of entry, started rushing the gates. Police captain Alexander "Clubber" Williams (1839–1917)—a notoriously corrupt official who gave the vice-ridden nightlife district its old nickname of the "Tenderloin" when on being told of his transfer to the bribe-rich precinct, he reportedly said, "I have had chuck for a long time, and now I am going to eat tenderloin"—told his men to clear the Garden's lobby. Soon the clubs were swinging. There, the altercation turned into a full-blown riot, possibly the worst the city had seen since the Draft Riots sixteen years earlier. Six days and some 500 miles (800 kilometers) later, Rowell won the race and the Astley Belt.

Who created "The Greatest Show on Earth"?

Phineas Taylor Barnum (1810–1891), the city's most famous and swashbuckling entertainer during the nineteenth century. The Connecticut-born Barnum had been running sideshows in Manhattan since 1835, when he exhibited Joice Heth, an old black woman he advertised as being George Washington's 160-year-old nurse, at a theater on Broadway and Prince. After that came the American Museum, a five-story building across Broadway from St. Paul's Chapel that Barnum stuffed with every kind of attraction that would bring in the "suckers": misfits, a flea circus, exotic animals, fortune tellers, and supposedly ancient artifacts. There was even a band of purposefully horrible musicians whose caterwauling Barnum hoped would drive customers inside.

After the American Museum burned down a couple times, Barnum opened his Hippodrome—the latest of several exhibition halls in the city by that name—near Madison Square in 1873 as a permanent place to showcase his touring circus, which he billed as "The Greatest Show on Earth" when it had first opened in Brooklyn two years before. The space under the massive big top was half menagerie of wild and tamed animals from all corners of the earth and half circus performances; a mix that proved wildly successful. Years later, the show merged with a British circus to become the Barnum & Bailey Greatest Show on Earth, which by the 1890s was touring with 28 rail cars and over 1,000 people. In 1919, twenty-eight years after Barnum's death (reportedly his dying words were asking what the day's receipts had been at Madison Square Garden), the circus merged with its greatest rivals to become the better-known mouthful Ringling Bros. and Barnum & Bailey Combined Shows, the Greatest Show on Earth.

Whose idea was the Statue of Liberty?

In 1865, French political theorist Édouard de Laboulaye (1811–1883) came up with the idea for France to present the United States with the gift of a massive monument symbolizing not just freedom and

French jurist, author, and anti-slavery activist Édouard de Laboulaye was the first to suggest a monumental gift to the United States: the Statue of Liberty.

liberty but the two nations' enduring connection. As an ardent abolitionist who pushed for the eradication of slavery everywhere, Laboulaye thought that this "Statue of Liberty" would further the cause of democracy around the world. In 1875, sculptor Auguste Bartholdi (1834–1904) and Laboulaye presented their proposal for a 111-foot-tall (33.8-meter-tall) statue of copper sheets representing the Roman goddess of liberty; Bartholdi had originally wanted to plant a statue of a woman at the opening of the Suez Canal, but that plan fell through. The plan was for France to build the statue and America to fund the nearly 200-foot (61-meter) stone pedestal she was to stand on. As fundraising and construction began, Laboulaye petitioned President Ulysses S. Grant (1822–1885) for the right to use Bedloe's Island for their grand new symbol.

When was the Statue of Liberty first assembled?

It almost didn't happen. First, in 1879, Bartholdi's engineer on the statue died. Six years later, the statue was ready to be shipped from Paris, but the U.S.-based Franco-American Union hadn't hit its fundraising goals. At the last minute, publisher Joseph Pulitzer (1847–1911) saved the day with a last-minute campaign that raised $100,000. By the time the statue—broken into 350 pieces and packed in 214 crates—arrived in New York Harbor on June 17, Bedloe's Island wasn't ready, so she was put into storage. The pedestal wasn't finished until the following year, and the statue took some four months to assemble; the last stage of it finished under a highly theatrical mask covering her face. The Statue of Liberty herself was not fully revealed until October 28, 1886, when one million people showed up for the city's first ticker-tape parade.

Why was the Statue of Liberty so important to many new immigrants?

When Ellis Island opened nearby in 1892, the sight of the grand figure of liberation became one of the first impressions many new immigrants had of the United States. Entire books could be filled with nothing but the glowing memories of immigrants first gazing upon the copper-sheathed statue gleaming in the New World sun.

The statue became so associated with immigration, in fact, that the sonnet by Emma Lazarus (1849–1887), "The New Colossus," was inscribed on a bronze plaque and attached to the statue's base in 1903. The poem's soaring idealism—"Give me your tired, your poor, / Your huddled masses yearning to breathe free, / The wretched refuse of your teeming shore"— would later be threaded into many New Yorkers' vision of their city as a welcoming gateway for immigrants seeking better lives. But initially the poem was ignored.

Many immigrants from Europe were greeted by the Statue of Liberty as they approached Ellis Island. The statue stood as a beacon of hope for a new, better life.

In 1901, seventeen years after Lazarus died, a friend of hers found the poem in a bookshop and led the successful effort to bring it to the public's attention.

When was the first Labor Day parade held?

Along with the many other strides that the nascent labor movement was making in the late nineteenth century was the push for a holiday to honor workers. Carpenter and cofounder of the American Federation of Labor Peter J. McGuire (1852–1906) came up with the idea, believing it was right to celebrate and honor those workers "who from rude nature have delved and carved all the grandeur we behold." The first Labor Day parade was held on September 5, 1882. Around ten thousand male workers marched on Fifth Avenue singing songs and presenting banners with messages like "To the Workers Should Belong the Wealth," "Don't Smoke Cigars Without the Union Label," and "Party Hacks to the Rear." The parade ended with a picnic that featured bands and a beer garden. President Grover Cleveland (1837–1908) made Labor Day a federal holiday in 1894 after a massive railroad strike led to riots that left more than a dozen workers dead. The tradition of parading on Labor Day eventually declined as the holiday became more of an extra day off for families to spend together at the end of the summer.

When was New York electrified?

In the 1870s, Thomas Edison (1847–1931) was the nation's, and the world's, foremost inventor. He secured hundreds of patents on everything from new telegraphy systems to light bulbs, movie cameras, and a stencil pen that was later modified for use as a tattoo gun. Besides being one of the century's most ambitious men, he was also one of its most competitive. The crusade that occupied much of Edison's time in the late nineteenth century was showing the superiority of his incandescent lighting system. In the 1870s and 1880s, cities like Paris and New York were intermittently illuminated by carbon arc lights, which cast a broader light than flickering gas lamps but also had an uncomfortably harsh glare. In order to illustrate the incandescent lighting system, Edison went into business as the city's first real electric utility: Edison Electric Illuminating Company of New York (now Consolidated Edison, or more commonly "ConEd," the city's main utility).

On September 4, 1882, a massive power plant on Pearl Street with six 27-ton steam-powered dynamos was switched on, allowing downtown businesses and residents to purchase electricity at rates competitive to gas lighting. The *New York Times*, whose building was lit by electricity for the first time, reported that "the light was soft, mellow, and grateful to the eye." Following the success of the Pearl Street grid, similar utilities opened up in urban areas around the country. By the turn of the century there were over thirty electric utilities competing with Edison in the New York area alone.

Who were the "Four Hundred" of New York society?

The Civil War and the industrial growth that followed created a new class of wealthy individuals in New York. With all that new money and those new millionaires flowing through the city, different metrics were used to determine membership in the city's ruling class. In 1880, the most crucial gatherings of New York society, for those who were keeping track of such things, were those held at the ballroom of Caroline Schermerhorn Astor (1830–1908), which according to legend held only 400, though later reports had it that Mrs. Astor's list topped out at 304.

Before the Brooklyn Bridge, how did people get on and off Manhattan?

For people arriving from the north, there were a few bridges that connected Manhattan to the mainland. The King's Bridge, the city's first, was built in 1693 across Spuyten Duyvil Creek between Manhattan and the Bronx. A second, nearby bridge was built in 1759 to avoid the high tolls charged on the first. Other spans like the High Bridge, built in 1848 and the city's oldest standing bridge, also linked ground transportation to Manhattan's north. For people trying to get to and from New Jersey or Long Island (including Brooklyn and Queens), ferries were the only option for well over two centuries. In the city's early history these were powered by oar, sail, and paddlewheel. But in the early nineteenth century, there were several larger operations making regular runs of commuters and market items across the East River (though some farmers brought their goods over on their own private boats) in boats powered by several horses driving a water wheel.

Steamboat ferry service between Hoboken and Manhattan started in 1811, with Robert Fulton's more famed steamboat ferry service between lower Manhattan and Brooklyn Heights beginning operations in 1814. The city's growing population led to a proliferation of rival ferry services that vigorously competed for monopolistic control. Cornelius Vanderbilt (1794–1877), whose Dutch farming family hauled their wares from Staten Island to Manhattan for sale, made his first fortune in the early nineteenth-century ferry business by undercutting his rivals and also securing a lucrative government contract during the War of 1812. By 1840 Vanderbilt's ferry service included 100 steamships carrying passengers as far as Philadelphia and Connecticut and made him the largest employer in America. By the start of the Civil War, about 100,000 people were utilizing the great armada of East River boats to cross to and from Manhattan each day. Walt Whitman sang the glories of the waterborne ballet on the crowded East River, and its bringing together of all the city's differentiated peoples, in one of his most beloved poems, "Crossing Brooklyn Ferry."

Where did the idea to build the Brooklyn Bridge originate?

The idea of a bridge across the ever-more ferry-clogged East River had been frequently mooted by prominent Brooklynites, who met resistance from their equals in Manhattan who, according to historian Edward Ellis, complained that such a project would drain the city's resources "in order to fertilize the sandy wastes of Long Island." But the final factor that convinced the city of the ultimate impracticality of ferries was illustrated by the effects of harsh winters. In 1821, the East River froze solid enough that taverns were opened up midriver to warm up the hardy commuters braving the traverse. The winter of 1866–1867 was even more brutally cold; in January the river froze again, and for long enough that stores in Manhattan started running out of goods. Later that year, the state legislature incorporated the New York Bridge Company to build a span across the East River at its narrowest point. After a reported $60,000 in incentives to city aldermen and a large chunk of the company's private stock to Boss Tweed, John Augustus Roebling (1806–1869) was named chief engineer and planning for the massive undertaking began.

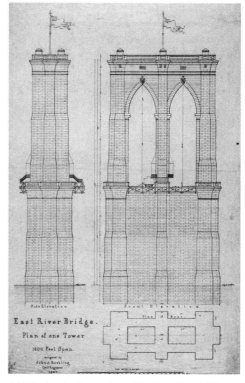

A 1867 plan for Tower One of the Brooklyn Bridge.

Why was the construction of the Brooklyn Bridge so deadly?

The Brooklyn Bridge was one of the most audacious engineering projects ever attempted in a city where such feats became almost commonplace. At 3,460 feet, it was the longest suspension bridge yet to be built, and it was also the first bridge of its kind to use steel cable to hold up its roadways and the first to use giant compressed-air underwater boxes called caissons to sink its anchors into the riverbed. Construction hadn't even begun in 1869 when designer and chief engineer John Roebling had his foot crushed in an accident. After a quick amputation, complications set in and he died seventeen days later from lockjaw.

In 1870, workers started painstakingly blasting out the foundations of the bridge's Brooklyn-side tower. Many would die in horrific ways from the rapid changes in pressure that came with their worksite: It wasn't until years later that the deadly phenomenon known at that time as "caisson's disease" and later as "the bends" would be understood. John Roebling's son Washington (1837–1926), who took over the project from his father, was himself crippled by it in 1872, and spent the remainder of the bridge's construction surveying it from the window of a nearby Brooklyn Heights apartment; his wife Emily Roebling (1843–1903) would relay instructions to the project managers.

Who was the first person to officially cross the Brooklyn Bridge?

The New York or East River bridge—it wasn't officially named the Brooklyn Bridge until 1915—opened to traffic on May 24, 1883, after fourteen years, at least twenty deaths, many stoppages and cost overruns, and tens of thousands of dollars in bribes from Tweed. The ceremonies featured a seventy-piece band, a twenty-two-man drum corps, thousands of onlookers (the borough of Brooklyn was essentially closed for the day), a massive salute of cannon fire from naval vessels and nearby fortifications, President Chester A. Arthur, Governor Grover Cleveland, and (according to the *Times*) "other more or less distinguished guests."

Emily Roebling was given the honor of crossing the bridge before the other dignitaries. The bridge was not opened to general foot traffic until May 30, when a mistaken rumor that it was about to collapse caused a terrifying stampede that killed a dozen people. Future mayor Alfred "Al" Smith (1873–1944) was ten years old and playing under the bridge that day with some friends. He would recall later the rain of coats and hats discarded by the panicked crowds above.

What kind of discrimination did Jews face in New York/?

During the first half of the nineteenth century, the majority of Jewish immigrants to America were German speakers from Central Europe. There were Jewish communities scattered around the country; at the start of the Revolutionary War, Charleston, South Carolina, actually had a larger Jewish population than New York. But as the century wore on, New York increasingly became a nexus for Jewish-American life. In 1850, the city had fifteen synagogues, several Jewish newspapers, and was home to about a third of America's 50,000 Jews.

Despite New York's reputation for cosmopolitanism, Jews still faced discrimination in an overwhelmingly Protestant society that still saw even fellow Christians like Catholics as irredeemably exotic. Even the city's wealthy German-Jewish merchants, who sometimes went to great lengths to fit into Gentile society and not call attention to their differences, were blackballed from several exclusive private clubs in the mid-nineteenth century. In response, several German-Jewish merchants formed the Harmonie Club in 1852; it was notable for having German as its official language and a portrait of the Kaiser prominently displayed for many years.

When did Jewish immigration start to increase?

Starting around 1880, the nature of Jewish immigration began to change dramatically. First, the numbers sharply increased. In 1880 there were about 300,000 Jews in America. Between 1881 and 1915, a staggering 1.4 million arrived. Much as the rapid influx of Irish during and after the Potato Famine irrevocably changed the city's texture and the nature of its political structure, the new Jewish New Yorkers would help to greatly transform the city.

Unlike the more assimilationist German Jews already established in the city, the new Jewish immigrants were generally Russian and/or Yiddish speakers from the Pale of Settlement in eastern Europe. They were for the most part less educated and hailed from more rural backgrounds than earlier Jewish immigrants. Also, while many (though not all) of their predecessors had come to America seeking economic opportunities, the newcomers were also fleeing the frequent pogroms that had been steadily devastating their shtetls. About two-thirds of them settled into the Lower East Side, which by 1900 became the most densely populated neighborhood in the world, with over a quarter-million people per square mile. Small synagogues opened by the dozens, as did Jewish businesses, some of which were helped along by Gentile customers, by dint of remaining open on Sunday.

How did the new Jewish immigration transform New York?

New York's largely Reform German-Jewish elite were often uncomfortable with the newcomers' more conservative, and foreign-seeming, Orthodox habits. Nevertheless, the generally uptown-dwelling elites formed a network of aid societies to swiftly acculturate the newer downtown Jewish immigrants to American society, as well as find them housing and employment. By the turn of the century, Eastern European Jews—the majority of whom were skilled laborers—both owned and worked in the hundreds of small factories and sweatshops, creating a booming garment industry. The profusion of kosher butchers also bolstered the city's meatpacking business, while kosher dietary staples from seltzer to pickles and knishes became a part of the city's culinary language. On a more intangible level, the community's density of thinkers and writers who were aflame with everything from Zionism and Marxism to anarchism helped to establish the city as the nation's capital of intellectual and political discourse.

After the turn of the century, Jews had become critical enough to the city's political establishment that Tammany Hall began courting their votes and in 1901 even supported a Jewish candidate to represent the Lower East Side in Congress. Anti-Semitism continued in New York in the late nineteenth and early twentieth centuries, part of another nativist backlash against how new immigrants were changing the face of New York. In an ironic but predictable example of how a previous era's victims of discrimination can become its progenitors, in 1902 a funeral procession for a rabbi was attacked by Irish workers throwing debris; when the (heavily Irish) police turned up, they began clubbing outraged Jews instead of their attackers.

When did Italian immigration to New York peak?

While Italians have been part of New York since the very beginning—Venetian craftsman Peter Caesar Alberti moved to Brooklyn in 1635—for over two centuries they comprised a very small proportion of the city's population, numbering only around 20,000 in 1880. At the same time that more Jewish immigrants from Russia and Poland began arriving at Ellis Island, the numbers of Italian immigrants spiked as well. By the turn of the century, there were a quarter million Italians living in New York. Many at first were landless male farmers working for the *padrones* who contracted laboring jobs.

Like the Irish wave that had preceded them, the Italian newcomers quickly took a commanding position in the city's day laborer trades. The Italians clustered in the Lower East Side around the Five Points' infamous Mulberry Bend, Greenwich Village, and East Harlem. The Italians were initially more likely than other immigrant groups to settle into enclaves based on their places of origin (Neapolitans on one block, Sicilians on another). Those differences mostly smoothed out not long after their arrival.

What was New York's first skyscraper?

Since the term "skyscraper" is not a precisely defined architectural term—even its etymology is murky, though some point to its inspiration being the topmost sail of the clipper ships that once crowded New York Harbor—the status of the city's first such building has always been somewhat in debate. Generally, though, a skyscraper is determined less by its height than whether it has a steel skeleton holding it up. With the growth of urban populations and the need for more efficient maximizing of limited real estate, the mid-to-late-nineteenth century saw a surge of innovative ideas, such as elevators, for building taller structures.

The title of world's first skyscraper is likely held by the ten-story Home Insurance Building, erected in Chicago in 1884. Architect William Le Baron Jenney's (1832–1907) usage of a relatively thin internal steel frame instead of thick masonry walls meant that much more of a building's interior could be given over to office or residential space instead of structural support. Four years later, architect Bradford Lee Gilbert's (1853–1911) eleven-story Tower Building went up at Broadway near Exchange Place, a pinched intersection that only allowed for a building a little over twenty feet wide. Gilbert's innovative internal structure was given a permit, despite protests from public officials, engineers, and the general public, who termed the project "The Idiotic Building." At least one nearby tenant moved away out of fear that the new building would simply fall over.

Why were so many people hanging around the Tower Building on a windy day?

People were so convinced of the Tower Building's likelihood of collapse that when the city was lashed by hurricane winds one day in 1889, crowds gathered to watch Gilbert's seemingly impossibly tall and thin tower fall over. They were disappointed. The Tower Building never collapsed. It was soon eclipsed by the rash of skyscrapers that followed, and it was torn down in 1914, a particularly short lifespan for a building of such notoriety, even in New York.

What was the first New York building taller than Trinity Church?

The first skyscraper in New York City was the eleven-story Tower Building, completed in 1888.

In 1890, Joseph Pulitzer's (1847–1911) *New York World* opened its new sixteen-story headquarters just across Park Row from City Hall. The 309-foot (94-meter) structure was covered in red sandstone and terra-cotta, and topped by a bright gilded dome and lantern. It was the first structure in New York to exceed Trinity Church's 284 feet (86.5 meters) in height. Pulitzer's new headquarters was a not-so-subtle message to all his nearby competitors, whose buildings he could now literally look down upon. It was torn down in 1955 to make way for an on-ramp to the Brooklyn Bridge.

Where did the term "the other half" come from?

He most likely did not invent it, but reformer Jacob Riis (1849–1914) certainly mainstreamed the term with his 1890 *cri de coeur, How the Other Half Lives*. Unlike many reformers of the time, Riis actually had personal experience of New York's seamier side. Born in Denmark in 1849, Riis immigrated to the city in 1870. He couldn't find work and resorted to sleeping in police lodging houses—police stations started offering overnight lodging as an emergency measure once the homeless population began exploding in the 1870s—and begging for sustenance on the street. Riis eventually landed a job as police reporter for the *New York Tribune*. He started taking a camera along on his assignments in the poorest, most crime-ridden city precincts. Those photographs, some of the first such documents of the American underclass, along with Riis's vivid and emotional descriptions of the squalor suffered by the city's lower classes collected in his writings, brought the issue to the attention of the wider society in a way that had never happened before.

How the Other Half Lives was an instant success, with its distressing accounts of filthy, crowded tenements that bred hunger, disease, and crime. Riis included powerful accounts of the limited circumstances faced by the city poor, including one vivid story about schoolchildren who lived just a five-minute walk from the Brooklyn Bridge who had never seen it. The book included among its many fans police commissioner Theodore Roosevelt, who called Riis the city's "most useful citizen."

What were "settlement houses"?

Starting in the late nineteenth century, as part of the so-called settlement house movement, social reformers (generally from the upper classes) began moving into poorer neighborhoods to directly engage with the people whose lives they were aiming to improve. Starting in 1886, similar efforts were made in New York to help the growing number of often destitute immigrants who were crowding into the city's more poverty-stricken districts. Different houses focused on different groups, from Christodora House in the East Village (established in 1897 to help young women immigrants, particularly Russian, Polish, and Ukrainians), Henry Street Settlement on the Lower East Side (1893; nursing care), and Madison House in Chinatown (established by German Jews in 1898 to help the influx of newer Jewish immigrants).

When did New York stop being quite so famous for its trash?

In 1881 a Department of Street Cleaning was created to introduce humans to the chore of garbage reduction. But the horribly inefficient department didn't manage to clean up much until 1895. That was the year reformist Mayor William Strong (1808–1895) appointed Civil

Why was New York so famously filthy?

Like many large metropolises, New York has always been associated with garbage and grime. That reputation these days has generally outlived its reality and is based mostly on outdated memories from various garbage strikes over the years that briefly allowed trash to pile up on the sidewalk and stink up the town instead of being sent where it belonged: to a landfill in Staten Island.

For much of the nineteenth century, though, the city's only concession to trash collection was to allow pigs to roam loose in the streets, eating as much of it as possible. But even thousands of pigs couldn't dispose of the mounds of odiferous waste (everything from discarded food to animal corpses and piles of manure), which posed obvious difficulties for a city trying to stand side by side with Paris and London.

War veteran and sanitation engineer George Waring (1833–1898) to clean things up. Waring dressed his workers in white to associate them with cleanliness and hygiene.

By the time Waring left in 1898, the city's sanitation workers, known as "white wings," had made remarkable strides in not just cleaning up the city streets but establishing an organized method for sorting and disposing of its tons of garbage. Riis wrote, "It was Colonel Waring's broom that first let light into the slum."

Which future president prowled New York slums at night as part of his job?

Theodore Roosevelt didn't start his career in politics in the swashbuckling manner one might imagine. He served as civil service commissioner from 1889 to 1895, before getting a job that more suited his temperament. That year, he was named police commissioner by fellow reform Republican Mayor Strong and immediately set about trying to transform the department, and a vice-loving city, from top to bottom. He went after multiple powerful constituencies, facing down corrupt police officers who essentially did nothing and collected copious bribes for the privilege and enforced the city's (laxly enforced) ban on Sunday liquor sales. He instituted pistol marksmanship training for officers and severely punished those who treated civilians brutally.

Roosevelt loved to employ dramatic gestures, such as assigning a squad of Jewish policemen to provide security for an anti-Semitic preacher from Germany. Roosevelt later recalled that "it was an object-lesson to our people, whose greatest need it is to learn that there must be no division by class hatred." The dramatic impact of Roosevelt's hard-charging style garnered reams of favorable press coverage. Particularly colorful were his nighttime trawls through the city's most unsavory quarters, led by his guide to the underworld, Jacob Riis. One of Roosevelt's most popular innovations was to creep up on loafing police officers in the middle of the night and shame them into doing their duty. Roosevelt left the position in 1897 after being appointed assistant secretary of the navy.

When did playgrounds become legally mandated?

As the immigrant influx in the late 1800s pushed overcrowding to heretofore unseen levels in downtown New York, charity organizations began opening playgrounds (known as "sand gardens") in poor neighborhoods so that children would have some opportunity for recreation. In 1895, New York state passed a law stating that no schools could be built in the city "without an open-air playground attached to or used in connection with the same." By 1915, the city boasted seventy playgrounds equipped with swings, slides, and the like.

Who were the "Street Arabs"?

"Street Arabs" was the somewhat colorful name given to the swarms of homeless children, many of whom stayed alive by hawking newspapers, who were common sights on New York streets in the late nineteenth century. The 1898 Thomas Edison short film *A Street Arab* shows a young New York "street urchin" going through a number of acrobatic moves (including handsprings and spinning on his head), which he likely performed on a regular basis for money. The term was popularized by Riis in *How the Other Half Lives*. He writes first in vivid terms about the children themselves, and the industry to which they were particularly drawn: "Vagabond that [the Street Arab] is, acknowledging no authority and owing no allegiance to anybody or anything, with his grimy fist raised against society whenever it tries to coerce him, he is as bright and sharp as the weasel, which, among all the predatory beasts, he most resembles."

Like the good Victorian reformer that he was, Riis went on to describe the functioning of the Newsboys' Lodging-house and how it provided beds and food every night for many of those boys, and his belief that with the right kind of education, the problem of homeless children could be eradicated in the city. Riis was eventually proven right, though not precisely in the way he would have preferred. Visitors to today's New York are no longer likely to see clusters of "Street Arabs" (as described in the 1892 book *Darkness and Daylight: A Woman's Story of Gospel, Temperance, Mission, and Rescue Work*) "hugging some warm corner or huddled into some dark passage, waiting for the moment when the papers shall be ready for distribution." However, in 2014 over 40,000 children spent at least one night in a New York homeless shelter.

When did Ellis Island open?

The federal government took control of Ellis Island in 1890 and set about transforming the island from a small harbor fort and naval arsenal to a new immigration station that

A 1902 photo of immigrants arriving on Ellis Island.

would supplant Castle Garden in Battery Park, which had been processing immigrants since 1855. Landfill, some from the ballast of incoming ships, was used to almost double the island's size to six acres. A receiving station built of Georgia pine opened in 1892. It burned to the ground in 1897. The station's new Main Building, a grand brick-faced Beaux-Arts structure that serves today as the National Park Service museum and visitor's center, opened in 1900. Eventually some thirty structures, including everything from staff housing and recreation centers to quarantine and psychiatric wards, would be built over the three connected islands.

Who was the first immigrant to land at Ellis Island?

The seventeen-year-old Annie Moore (1874–1924) didn't know when she embarked with her two younger brothers from Queenstown in Ireland on December 20, 1891, just how historic her trip would become. When she was processed through the station at Ellis Island on January 1, 1892 (during which a man supposedly shouted "Ladies first"), Moore was memorialized as the legendary station's first immigrant. Described by a newspaper as a "rosy-cheeked Irish girl" from County Cork, Moore was presented with a $10 gold coin by the superintendent of immigration and soon afterward she and her brothers were reunited with their parents, already living in New York.

As with most immigrants of modest birth, the details of Moore's life were difficult to piece together afterwards. A particularly popular strand of urban myth had it that she moved out west, married a descendant of the great Irish liberator Daniel O'Connell, and died after being hit by a streetcar in Texas in 1923. Later research revealed that Moore actually settled in Manhattan, had eleven children, and by the time she died in 1924 had lived almost all of her American life within a few blocks of the Lower East Side. There are statues of Moore by the same artist at the Ellis Island museum and also in Cobh, Ireland.

What was it like to arrive at Ellis Island?

There are some popular ideas about what happened to immigrants when they arrived at Ellis Island that are not quite true. For instance, the idea that when immigration officials couldn't understand somebody's name they would just write down the closest English approximation they could come up with has turned out to be more of an urban legend. That being said, the general impression of arrival at Ellis Island—heterogeneous crowds speaking a Babel of languages from Serbo-Croatian to Arabic and Yiddish shuffling forward in long lines like a supersized DMV—is pretty close to the truth. Ships docked elsewhere, usually Manhattan, and their passengers boarded ferries for Ellis Island.

Once at the island, the prospective immigrants entered the Main Building and walked up a staircase into the Great Hall's registry room where the inspection began. (In reality, the inspection had already started, as medical personnel kept an eye on those who had a hard time navigating the stairs as potential medical risks.) The immigrants were checked out by staff members looking to answer two basic questions: Is this person disabled or carrying a contagious disease? Will this person be able to support themselves or be supported by somebody else so that they won't become a ward of the state? Those suspected of carrying disease were marked by inspectors for further examination (a chalk-mark of "H" on the immigrant's clothing, for example, meant that doctors should look for heart problems). Young women were given particularly intense scrutiny, over fears that they would end up as prostitutes.

What precipitated Chinese immigration to New York?

Due to New York's status as North America's entrepôt, the constant influx of merchant vessels meant that there had long been a small transient population of Chinese merchant marines and traders. The city's Chinese population, primarily Cantonese, grew steadily after the Civil War (1861–1865). The 1890 census counted about 2,000 Chinese in New York, but the real number is widely believed to be at least four times that. Some made their way to New York from California after race riots and discriminatory laws made that state no longer a viable place to live. Others came by way of Cuba, where sugar plantations had imported Chinese laborers only to pay them so horrendously that they left.

New York's small but closely tied Chinese community (comprised almost entirely of men until after the turn of the century) began to congregate in a corner of Five Points along Mott Street that became known as Chinatown. Many worked as small merchants or cigar vendors. Starting in the late 1870s, Chinese New Yorkers seized on a burgeoning industry with low startup costs and an exponential demand. Within a decade there were 2,000 Chinese-operated hand laundries in Manhattan.

Was the real Chinatown anything like how it was later depicted?

The popular image of nineteenth- and early twentieth-century Chinatown has long been that of mysterious clans and secret societies engaging in secret warfare amid the warren of tangled streets surrounded by teeming tenements packed with dormitory-style housing and sweatshops above and lantern-lit restaurants and smoky dens of iniquity down below. As with so much else written about ethnic enclaves in New York at this time, it remains difficult to separate fact from fantasy.

What is certain is that Chinatown, by dint of the extreme prejudice exhibited against Chinese everywhere else in the city, would become increasingly crowded as more and more immigrants were slotted into a narrow slice of lower Manhattan. It is also true that clan-like mutual aid societies called *fang* ("house") gave the overwhelmingly male population a kind of surrogate kin and socializing outlet and that the growing number of gambling and opium dens were operated by secret societies called *tongs* that sometimes went to war with each other.

When did the first "tong wars" begin?

Like many things with Chinatown, stories of the skirmishes between different tongs far exceeded the reality. But nevertheless, just as gangs like the Five Pointers were active in the nearby Italian neighborhood, tongs held some sway in Chinatown and frequently fought over territory starting in the late nineteenth century. In September 1897, the *New York Times* reported on an internecine struggle in the relatively new Hip Sing tong. A man accused of corruption had been ejected from Hip Sing and attacked the tong's president twice, the second time "with a cleaver and a snicker-snee [a kind of fighting knife]." The newspaper said the fight "will probably cause trouble" because the Hip Sings were preparing an anti-vice "crusade against the gamblers and the opium joints."

This circa 1915 photo of the Hell's Kitchen neighborhood shows a mission, where poor people often went for help and some shelter.

Who were the Gophers?

Much of the remembered history of Hell's Kitchen—a rapidly gentrifying tenement-thick area between the Theater District and the Hudson—involves crime, decay, poverty, and rioting. True to the neighborhood's name, it was New York's most fertile breeding ground for vividly depraved gangs outside of the Five Points. Starting in the late nineteenth century, many of the Irish street gangs in the neighborhood either coalesced into or were allied with the Gophers, whose name came from their habit of meeting in basements. A battalion of toughs many hundreds strong, the Gophers' numbers, organizational skills, and ferocity made them one of the most feared criminal enterprises in the city. Under the leadership of figures like "One Lung" Curran, "Mallet" Murphy, and Owney Madden (who later became a bootlegger and opened the Cotton Club in Harlem, in addition to being Mae West's boyfriend), the Gophers headquartered in Battle Row saloons.

Besides the usual extortion rackets, the Gophers made a habit of attacking trains of the New York Central Railroad that came through the neighborhood, forcing the rail company to hire special companies of guards to fight them off. The Gophers even had a female auxiliary, the Battle Row Ladies' Social and Athletic Club, more popularly known as the Lady Gophers. Led by the feared "Battle Annie"—according to Herbert Asbury, "she was partial to mayhem" like her "illustrious predecessors" Sadie the Goat and Hell Cat Maggie—the Lady Gophers were reputed to be just as vicious as their male counterparts, even hiring themselves out for street combat in labor actions involving female-centric unions.

What was "The Mistake of '98"?

That would be the decision in 1898—the same year, by the way, that America annexed Guam, Hawaii, the Philippines, and Puerto Rico at the conclusion of the Spanish-American War—to consolidate all five heretofore distinct boroughs of New York under what Pete Hamill (1935–) once described as "the benevolent dictatorship of Manhattan." There aren't any old-timers left to still grouse about it, but there were plenty of hurt feelings for years afterward at the loss of self-determination, particularly in boroughs like Brooklyn (the fourth-largest city in America at the time) that had long prized their independence and unique identities. That pre-1898 independence was always something of an illusion, of course.

What the consolidation of 1898 truly did, as it was primarily driven by the city's business elite who were looking to increase efficiencies in the city's scattered power structures, was codify the orientation of Greater New York around the power and lucre of Manhattan. All one has to do is look at any subway map to see how most of the lines are constructed in order to best facilitate travel from the outer boroughs into Manhattan, not, say, between Queens and Brooklyn.

Who was the first auto fatality in America?

In 1899, automobiles were becoming a more common sight on New York streets. Pedestrians were frequently injured by street cars and horse-drawn wagons. But automobiles' speed and weight, along with the lack of traffic lights (the first wouldn't be installed until 1916) made them a dangerous mix with city residents who were still not quite used to the scurrying machines. On September 13, a realtor named Henry Bliss stepped off a trolley car at Central Park West and 74th Street and turned to help a woman down. He was hit by a motorized taxi, the impact crushing his skull and chest. Bliss died the following day. The driver, Arthur Smith, was charged with homicide, unlike today when drivers in accidents like this are most often let go with a warning. On the centenary of Bliss's death, a pedestrian safety group installed a historical plaque at the intersection, which was known even back in 1899 as the "Dangerous Stretch" and is still one of the city's riskier street crossings.

THE GILDED AGE

When did Times Square become *Times Square*?

Best known today for camera-wielding tourists, chain restaurants, and people dressed up in giant Sesame Street suits, Midtown's Times Square wasn't always the face the city put forward to its visitors. The city's beating pulse was generally located further south, the buzz of power that swirled around City Hall and the newspapers headquartered nearby on Park Row, the mercantile hustle of Wall Street, or the nightlife of the Bowery. In the mid-to-late 1800s, what would become known as Times Square was still called Longacre Square. The land had been bought up by John Jacob Astor in the 1830s and for years afterward it was a relatively exclusive neighborhood. Later on, it became known for the manufacture of horse carriages and harnesses. Also, fitting the neighborhood's later reputation for sin and entertainment, it was the site of many "silk hat brothels" that catered to a higher-income customer and were prized for their discretion, as well as theaters and vaudeville.

Its transformation began on April 5, 1904, when Longacre Square was officially renamed Times Square in honor of the *New York Times*, which was relocating from its old offices on Park Row to the new One Times Square tower on Broadway and 42nd Street. (Not long before, in 1895, its rival, the *New York Herald,* had moved into new offices a few blocks to the south and had Herald Square named for it.) A few months afterward, the beautiful eleven-story Beaux Arts Hotel Astor opened on Broadway, between 44th and 45th streets. At the same time, the city's new subway system was opening several stations along 42nd Street, and cabarets and lavish eateries like the briefly fashionable "lobster palaces" were dotting the blocks around Broadway and 42nd. By the time the first giant ball dropped from the top of One Times Square on New Year's Eve, Times Square was already transforming into the gaudy showcase recognizable today.

An 1898 photo taken at the corner of Broadway and 42nd Street, when the area was still known as Longacre Square and not Times Square.

When did the Williamsburg Bridge open?

In just a few years after it opened for business, the Brooklyn Bridge became overwhelmed. The city planned another bridge situated just to the north that would provide another connection between the boroughs by stretching between the Lower East Side's Delancey Street and Williamsburg's Marcy Avenue. When the 1,600-foot- (488-meter-) long Williamsburg Bridge opened in 1903 after a mere seven years, it was the longest suspension bridge in the world and the first built with all-steel towers. One unexpected result was that the bridge encouraged many Jews from the teeming Lower East Side to move across the East River to the roomier and less crowded Williamsburg.

What is the story behind the last voyage of the SS *General Slocum*?

On the morning of June 15, 1904, the paddle boat SS *General Slocum* set off from the East Third Street pier and sailed up the East River. It was filled with over 1,350 passengers, mostly women and children, from St. Mark's Evangelical Lutheran Church on 6th Street, which had chartered the boat for their annual picnic on Long Island's north shore. Just before 10:00 A.M., fire was discovered below deck. The *Slocum* had been found by a fire inspector just the month before to be in fine shape. Almost everything that happened would prove that assessment to have been a lie. The crew, which hadn't been trained in fire drills, tried putting the blaze out with fire hoses that turned out to be rotten and unusable. The rotted life preservers were also useless.

When Captain William Van Schaick finally became aware of the fire, the rocks and powerful currents of Hell Gate made it impossible (he believed) to make it to a dock. As fire consumed the ship, Van Schaick attempted what he thought was their only hope: Beaching the *Slocum* on North Brother Island. Meanwhile, passengers faced a horrific choice: Jump overboard and likely drown as most could not swim, or stay aboard and probably burn to death. By the time the *Slocum* ran aground off the island, it was a blazing inferno. Bodies washed ashore for days afterward.

The SS *General Slocum* was launched in 1891 and had several accidents, including groundings, ending in a fire and sinking in 1904.

How many people died on the *General Slocum*?

The staggering loss of life totaled 1,021 people, mostly women and children. It was the worst tragedy that New York suffered until 9/11. After more than a week's worth of funerals, the emptiness of the old German Lower East Side neighborhood of Kleindeutschland (Little Germany) weighed on the residents. Not long after the *Slocum* disaster, most of the area's German inhabitants had dispersed across the city, some clustering in Yorkville on the Upper East Side. A memorial fountain commemorating the victims was erected in Tompkins Square Park in 1906.

What was the first subway line to carry New York commuters?

As frustrations built through the second half of the nineteenth century due to overcrowding and the inefficiency of the limited elevated train system, a consensus developed by the end of the century that an ambitious new system was necessary. While business leaders like J. P. Morgan (1837–1913) were in favor of private ownership, and the city wanted the system to be run by the municipality, both sides compromised with a publically owned and privately run train system.

The New York subway system as we know it today opened for business on October 27, 1904, the first day of operation for the Interborough Rapid Transit underground railway (IRT). In just four years, nearly eight thousand workers had carved twenty miles (thirty-two kilometers) of tunnels beneath Manhattan. Even though today New York is tightly linked in many people's minds to underground transit, the city actually came late to it. The IRT was beaten to the punch by both the London Underground (1863) and, almost more gallingly, Boston's subway (1897).

Where did the subway run in its first years?

The IRT's first line ran from City Hall to Grand Central, then over to Times Square and up the west side to 145th Street. Amazingly, the whole nine-mile and twenty-eight-station system only took four years to build. Mayor George McClellan (1826–1885) was given the honor of ceremonially starting the first car, but he insisted on driving all the way to the line's end in Harlem. Between the official opening to the public that night and the following morning, an incredible 110,000 people rode the subway.

The IRT expanded to the Bronx the following year, Brooklyn in 1908, and Queens in 1915. In order to accommodate the city's desire to push the system out into the boroughs as quickly as possible, the Brooklyn-Manhattan Transit Co. (BMT) operated as a dual system with the IRT; they merged in the 1920s. The pace of construction was blistering in the system's first few decades. By the time the country entered World War II, the subway system included over 400 stations, connecting more than 700 miles (1,126 kilometers) of track.

When did immigration to New York hit its peak?

In 1907, 1.2 million immigrants entered America through New York, about twice the number that immigrated in 1882. Ellis Island's single busiest day was April 17, 1907, when an incredible 11,747 immigrants were processed. This massive influx left the island scrambling to build enough facilities to handle everybody who wanted to become an American. It also caused more consternation among some elements of the American public, distressed by how the previous two decades had seen the percentage of immigrants from northern European countries decline precipitously, to be replaced by those hailing from southern and eastern Europe.

Which skyscraper held the record as world's tallest building for just eighteen months?

In 1908, the Singer Sewing Machine Corporation finished an awe-inspiring addition to the red brick and stone Singer Building, which had been constructed at 149 Broadway in 1896. A new Beaux Arts tower now soared over 600 feet (183 meters) in the air, making it the tallest inhabited building in the world. Only the Eiffel Tower was taller. The Singer Building's slenderness was not just an aesthetic decision, but a marketing statement, given that its size limited the amount of rentable space available and thus turned the building into more of a symbolic structure. Its lobby featured a forest of marble columns trimmed with bronze beading.

But the city's skyward rush wasn't delayed for long. In 1908, the 700-foot- (213-meter-) tall Metropolitan Life Tower, a sleeker classical building modeled on the San Marco bell tower in Venice, opened on the east side of Madison Square and claimed the mantle of world's tallest building for a whole five years before being in turn toppled from that perch by the Woolworth Building. Of these three towers, the Singer is the only one that didn't survive. It was taken down in 1967, the tallest building to be demolished until the collapse of the World Trade Center in 2001.

What convinced the Vanderbilts to build Grand Central Station?

A hard-to-resist combination of rivalry, public outrage, and threats of government action. The original Grand Central Depot had opened in 1871 at 4th Avenue and 42nd Street to handle the ever-increasing influx of trains pouring into the city. It was all a Cor-

Giuseppe "Joe" Petrosino (1860–1909) was a Sicilian-born immigrant whose command of multiple Italian dialects made him useful as an informant to the NYPD, which he joined in 1883. For years he was a rarity on the still Irish-dominated force. In 1904, even though Italians were roughly ten percent of the city population, just seventeen out of more than 8,100 police officers were Italian. Still, the department quickly recognized his abilities. Police Commissioner Theodore Roosevelt put Petrosino in charge of the homicide division in 1895. Six years later he correctly warned that President William McKinley's life was in danger from anarchists.

After Petrosino helped establish the department's bomb and canine squads (the nation's first), he was put in charge of the clandestine Italian Squad. His secret group of officers with the politically incorrect name went after two of the biggest threats seen in the Italian community: anarchists and organized criminal groups like the Camorra and the Black Hand. The Italian Squad was soon arresting thousands and ultimately put five hundred behind bars. On February 20, 1909, the New York *Sun* reported that the indefatigable Petrosino would be conducting a no-longer secret investigation in Sicily. Petrosino was gunned down by two Black Hand assassins outside his hotel in Palermo on March 12. The crime was never solved. Petrosino remains the only NYPD officer killed in the line of duty outside the United States.

nelius Vanderbilt operation; at the time his New York Central Railroad held a monopoly on train traffic in and out of New York.

By the turn of the century, the whole area had become an eyesore—inconvenient, thick with noise and smoke, impossible to get around, and highly dangerous because of all the trains running down Park Avenue and other thoroughfares at street level. After a train crash in 1902 killed fifteen people, the resulting uproar proved that the entire neighborhood had become untenable. The city mandated that within a few years all trains operating in the city had to be electric. Rather than an imposition, this mandated change proved to be a boon to the New York Central, because non-polluting electrics could be safely directed underground, under their smoke-belching forebears. At the same time, the New York Central's dread rival, the Pennsylvania Railroad, was digging tunnels under the Hudson River to connect their massive station in Jersey City with a grand new edifice, Pennsylvania Station, between 7th and 8th avenues in the low 30s.

How long did Grand Central Station take to build?

Ten years. The New York Central Railroad's chief engineer, William Wilgus (1865–1949), conceived the concept to bury all the tracks around the old Grand Central underground, lay streets on top of them, and top it off with a temple-like terminal built in a luxuriantly classical style. But his innovative plan ran into an old problem: money. The whole undertaking would eventually cost about $2 billion in today's money and far exceeded the finances of even a very successful company like Vanderbilt's local monopoly.

To pay for it, Wilgus came up with another far-seeing innovation: After burying the sooty spiderweb of tracks, the company sold what came to be called "air rights" (literally what it sounds like) to developers who wanted to build on the newly created blocks around the station. Wilgus's operation was one of the greatest the city has ever seen, digging over 40 feet (12 meters) down, removing over 3 million cubic yards (2.29 million cubic meters) of earth, installing some 1,500 columns to hold up the street-level deck, and doing all of this without disrupting daily train operations. After all, people still needed to get into work and back out to Tuckahoe each day. Within a day of the terminal's opening on February 2, 1913, some 150,000 people had poured through what Tom Wolfe called "the grandest, most glorious of all" big city railroad stations.

If Grand Central Terminal is a railway station, where are all the trains?

Hidden away underground, as they should be in any crowded metropolitan area. Grand Central certainly looks big when facing the gorgeous 42nd street façade with its mon-

Grand Central Station at Park Avenue and 42nd Street is not only a hub for train transportation, but it is also a beautiful example of nineteenth-century architecture, as well as a spot any tourist to Manhattan would like to visit.

umental mythological statues, where it imposingly occupies an entire block (three blocks if you include the MetLife Building complex that it's attached to on the north side). But in terms of real estate, it's dwarfed by the size of what you don't see. But the multiple layers of sixty seven tracks and forty four platforms buried underneath sprawls over forty eight acres from 42nd all the way up to St. Bartholomew's Church on Park Avenue and 51st.

Tourists coming into the soaring Beaux Arts terminal may look down from the grand entrance staircases at the marbled floor and up to the Main Concourse's constellation-covered 125-foot- (38-meter-) high vaulted ceiling and sun-pouring arched windows and wonder why all the commuters dashing to catch the next Harlem Line train to Scarsdale on the hidden lower levels are in such a hurry. Shouldn't they want to sit a spell and soak in the church-like contemplative beauty of New York's single most astounding sight?

How did New York's first "Murder of the Century" happen?

On June 25, 1906, highly unstable Pittsburgh millionaire Harry Thaw (1847–1947) and his wife Evelyn Nesbit (1884–1967) were getting ready for a trip to Europe. A onetime chorus girl, Nesbit ran into her former lover, famed architect Stanford White (1853–1906), on the street. This news sparked Thaw's anger, as Nesbit had told him the married White had once raped her. That night, Nesbit, Thaw, and White all happened to be at a performance of the musical comedy *Mamzelle Champagne* in the rooftop garden of the second Madison Square Garden, a fantastical structure that White had designed. During the climax of the show, Thaw walked up to White and shot him three times, once in the eye, killing him. He surrendered calmly after firing several more times into

---

What are some of the secrets of Grand Central Terminal?

- If you quietly whisper something near an arch just outside of the downstairs Oyster Bar, somebody standing by an arch on the other side of the gallery can hear you perfectly, no matter how noisy it is.

- The walls in the Main Concourse look like French limestone, but they're actually made of a lighter artificial material that was easier to mold and didn't put so much strain on the building's frame.

- That mural of the October zodiac on the ceiling of the Main Concourse? It was painted on backwards.

- An in-depth restoration in the 1990s cleaned up decades of cigarette soot from the Main Concourse ceiling. However, one patch of blackened ick was left in the northwest corner near Pisces, supposedly as a visual reminder of just how grimy it had been.

the air. Thaw said "I did it because he ruined my wife." The combination of celebrity, wealth, and location grabbed the public's attention. Thomas Edison even cranked out a movie, *Rooftop Murder*, that hit nickelodeons just a week after the killing.

The trial was a media sensation that was reported on around the world and was almost instantly dubbed the "Murder of the Century." There were so many reporters in the courtroom that none of the public could fit in. Readers were scandalized by tales of White's womanizing, particularly his Tenderloin seduction pad's four-poster bed with mirrored headboard and canopy, and the red velvet swing he loved to have teenage showgirls swing on. Thaw's lawyers' rather incredible defense was that he had a disorder they termed "dementia Americana," which they claimed caused American men to become violent upon learning their wives or daughters had been victimized by another man. Thaw was found not guilty by reason of insanity and stayed in a mental institution until 1915.

Who was "Typhoid Mary"?

Mary Mallon (1869–1938) immigrated to America from Ireland in 1883. Over the intervening years, she worked as a servant, mostly a cook, for several families, mostly in the New York area. What took years to uncover was that she was an asymptomatic carrier of typhoid, an incredibly deadly bacterial disease usually passed along by way of contaminated food or water. This wasn't known at the time, however. Most previous outbreaks of typhoid in New York had been assumed to arise from general contamination such as "sewer gases."

Regardless of how off-base the contemporary science was, the turn of the century saw an increased public concern and awareness about sanitary conditions. In response to those worries, in 1906 Congress had passed the groundbreaking Pure Food and Drug Act. That same year, a city sanitary engineer was hired by the wealthy owners of a home in Oyster Bay to investigate why six people in the house had come down with typhoid. Mallon was cooking at the house at the time, but she wasn't linked to the typhoid cluster until the following year, when after another outbreak happened in a Manhattan house where Mallon was working. Ultimately some twenty-two cases of typhoid around the metropolitan area were linked to Mallon.

What happened to Mary Mallon?

Mallon was confined by health officials from 1907 to 1910. She was first called "Typhoid Mary" in a 1909 article in the *New York American* which labeled her "Most Harmless and Yet the Most Dangerous Woman in America." After her initial release from isolation, she disappeared. Mallon was soon linked to outbreaks of typhoid at hospitals in New York and New

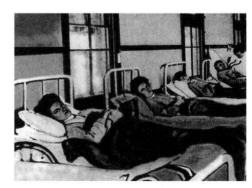

Mary Mallon (a.k.a. Typhoid Mary) is shown here (foreground) in 1907, when she was forced into confinement at a New York hospital.

Jersey where she (without any other means of sustaining herself) worked as a cook under a false name; some two hundred more people were infected. Mallon was apprehended again in 1915 and quarantined on North Brother Island in the East River until her death in 1938.

Has any New York mayor been assassinated while in office?

On August 9, 1910, New York mayor William Jay Gaynor (1849–1913) was in Hoboken, New Jersey, boarding the liner *Kaiser Wilhelm der Grosse* for a month-long vacation to Europe. While posing for photographs and talking on deck with family members, Gaynor was approached by John J. Gallagher. An Irish immigrant who had been fired a few weeks earlier from his job as a night watchman for the city's docks department, Gallagher claimed to have been the victim of a conspiracy. All of his letters to Gaynor's office had never been answered and his attempt to talk to Gaynor in person had failed. Gallagher approached Gaynor and fired several shots from a .38 revolver, hitting Gaynor in the throat and his sanitation commissioner, William H. Edwards, in the arm.

The bullet did not kill Gaynor immediately, but it remained lodged in his throat. Because Gaynor apparently recovered from the shooting, Gallagher was only sentenced to twelve years in prison. However, Gaynor was weakened by the attack and became gradually frailer as the years passed. That did not stop him from continuing his assault on corruption while running for mayor in 1913 (a campaign that lost him the support of Tammany Hall). Gaynor eventually died of a heart attack on September 10, 1913, ironically while on a steamship heading to Europe for another vacation.

What landmark opened in 1910?

In the first decade of the twentieth century, railroads were the ultimate expression of American capitalist might, combining technological and engineering prowess and the consolidation of vast wealth into one nation-spanning enterprise. At the same time that the Vanderbilts' New York Central Railroad was building its Grand Central terminal on the east side, the Pennsylvania Railroad was building its own temple to transit in a recently (and secretly) purchased swath of the Tenderloin between 7th and 8th avenues, from 31st to 33rd streets. In order to link its dense network of rail lines just across the Hudson River to New York, the Pennsylvania Railroad (then the largest in the nation) dug some sixteen miles (twenty-six kilometers) of underground tunnels and connected them to the Long Island Rail Road in a beautiful new station on Manhattan's west side.

When the station opened in September 1910 after just four years of construction, a crowd of 100,000 were overwhelmed by what they saw. Designed by Charles McKim (1847–1909) as a grand, sprawling symphony of classicism, drawing both from the Roman Baths of Caracalla and Berlin's Brandenburg Gate, Pennsylvania Station was the fourth largest building in the world and among its most beautiful. The eastern side of the building was lined with massive Tuscan columns while the central waiting room was a soaring, grand space with 150-foot (46-meter) ceilings. Within just a few years, some eighteen million passengers came through the station each year. Architecture critic Paul Goldberger said that it "was a symbol not only of the greatness and power of the railroad, but also of the greatness and power of the city."

What prompted New York to outlaw handguns?

On January 23, 1911, popular novelist and star muckraking journalist David Graham Phillips (1867–1911) had just left his apartment near Gramercy Park when he was approached outside the Princeton Club by Fitzhugh Coyle Goldsborough (1879–1911), a somewhat unhinged aristocrat who thought that Phillips' 1909 satire *The Fashionable Adventures of Joshua Craig* had been based on and slandered his family. Shouting, "Here you go!," Goldsborough fired six shots from his .32 caliber handgun into Phillips, who died the next day. Goldsborough shot himself dead on the spot.

Not surprisingly, the shocking society shooting made for many bold-faced headlines. But the brazen nature of it, as well as the growing number of gun-related homicides, spurred Tammany Hall official George LeBrun to agitate against the easy availability of handguns in the city. He enlisted state senator Tim "Big Feller" Sullivan, who represented the Lower East Side, to push through the legislation that became known as Sullivan's Law. On May 10, 1911, the easy passage of the bill made the carrying of concealed weapons a felony and required any New Yorker who wanted to carry a revolver to obtain a license from the police. The Sullivan Law later became a model for gun-control legislation around the country and remains in effect in New York today.

How did the Triangle Shirtwaist Fire start?

To this day, nobody knows. What is known is that on the afternoon of March 25, 1911, a fire broke out in a room filled with scraps of clothing material on the eighth floor of the Triangle Shirtwaist Factory, located in the Asch Building on the eastern side of Washington Square Park. Given the amount of flammable material packed into the crowded factory (which had been touted as fireproof), the conflagration spread with demonic speed. The panicked workers, mostly young Jewish and Italian immigrant women, tried to escape but most were trapped because the doors had been locked by managers who wanted to prevent their staff from taking unauthorized breaks.

While smoke billowed out of the factory windows, crowds gathered below. When firefighters arrived, neither their

The deaths of 146 people at the 1911 Triangle Shirtwaist fire resulted in the passage of regulations aimed at preventing such massive loss of life in building fires again.

hoses nor ladders could reach any of the affected floors. New York University students in higher adjacent buildings saved some workers by lowering ladders onto the Asch Building's roof. But after the poorly constructed fire escape tore away from the side of the building, sending several people to their deaths, the trapped workers in the burning factory were left with little choice. Eyewitness accounts of the young women who leaped to their deaths, some holding hands as they jumped, to avoid being burned to death, are some of the most horrifying stories in New York history. The sidewalks surrounding the factory were soon littered with the crumpled bodies of those who jumped. A total of 146 people, all but 23 of them young women, lost their lives in the fire.

What were the aftereffects of the Triangle Shirtwaist Fire?

Making the tragedy even harder to bear was the fact that the accident occurred only two years after the factory's workers had led an industry-wide strike for better pay, a union, and safer working conditions. The factory's owners agreed to some changes but stubbornly held the line at a union, even hiring off-duty policemen to assault the strikers. Once the strike was over, though, most of the changes requested by the factory's workers, including better ventilation and unlocked doors, were never implemented.

The outrage that the devastating fire caused in the city and nation was immediate and palpable. A state legislative committee swiftly established sweeping new rules requiring new protections like fire sprinklers and limiting the work week to fifty-four hours. One of the witnesses to the fire was Frances Perkins. Scarred by the memory of that horrible day, she went on to push through more worker protections as the first female secretary of labor. Today, the Asch Building is known as the Brown Building. Thoroughly renovated, it now houses science facilities for NYU. Every year on the anniversary of the Triangle Shirtwaist Fire, a remembrance ceremony is held in front of the building.

What was the Great Migration?

After the end of World War I, black life in New York irrevocably changed. The return of soldiers from overseas meant the arrival of a large group who had seen a larger world where institutionalized racism wasn't taken as a given. At the same time, the "Great Migration" of some six million blacks from the Jim Crow South to the cities of the north and west was in full swing. New York's black population, which had declined after the Draft Riots of 1863, grew from 60,000 in 1900 to about 327,000 in 1930. A great number of them moved to Harlem, by then the center of black life in the city and one of the only neighborhoods open to blacks.

When did the New York Police Department hire its first black officer?

Samuel Jesse Battle (1883–1966) was born to former slaves in North Carolina. He later moved north to New York, settling in Harlem and working in a hotel and as a Red Cap baggage handler at Grand Central Terminal (a service, incidentally, no longer offered at that station). After an initial rejection in 1910, on June 28, 1911, Battle became the first black New York police officer at a time when blacks were roughly three percent of the city's population. A sturdy presence at 6' 3" and almost 300 pounds (136 kilograms), Battle was first assigned to Harlem, where the mere sight of a black cop made him an instant sensation.

According to Arthur Browne's book *One Righteous Man*, Battle was even a tourist attraction for a time, with sightseeing buses announcing "Here's New York's first colored policeman." His first arrest was complicated by the fact that the white male arrestee refused to believe that Battle was actually an officer. During a race riot in 1919, Battle was credited with saving the life of a white police officer at 135th Street and Lenox Avenue. That corner was later named Samuel J. Battle Plaza. Langston Hughes (1902–1967) worked with Battle on a biography that was never published.

Who was the "Boy Mayor"?

The Bronx-born John Purroy Mitchel (1879–1918) gained attention in city politics as an anti-Tammany reformer. He was elected mayor in 1913 at the age of thirty-four, mak-

---

Why did Black Tom Island explode?

During World War I, well before the United States directly entered the conflict, New York was the primary shipping point for millions of dollars' worth of munitions and other materiel being sent across the Atlantic to French, British, and Russian ports. Much of that incendiary cargo was stored at the freight depot on Black Tom Island, connected by a rail line to the New Jersey shore west of Ellis Island. Late at night on July 30, 1916, some guards on the island noticed some small fires. Most fled, knowing that the island was currently storing about a thousand tons (907 metric tons) of ammunition and 50 tons (45 metric tons) of TNT. A little after 2:00 A.M., the island erupted in the greatest explosion the city has ever seen. All of those explosives detonating nearly at once was the equivalent of an earthquake measuring 5.5 on the Richter scale. The force of the blast hurled people from their beds in Jersey City and Manhattan and shattered windows for miles. Shrapnel and debris hit the Statue of Liberty and Ellis Island, which had to be evacuated. At least four people died. Black Tom was essentially no more, and today has been subsumed by landfill into Liberty State Park.

At first, authorities blamed the explosion on negligence by the railroad operating the depot. President Woodrow Wilson (1856–1924) actually thought it was impossible that Germans would have done such a thing. But German saboteur rings were operating in New York, trying to disrupt shipments of armaments to their enemies. Agents using small, delayed-release "pencil bombs" sank many cargo ships that left New York Harbor. In 1939, it was determined that German agents had set the detonators that caused the massive explosion. Germany was declared to owe the United States $50 million in damages, which it finished paying off in 1979.

ing him still the youngest person ever to hold the office. Mitchel lost his re-election campaign and enlisted in the Army aviation corps in 1918. He died during a training flight in Louisiana a few months later. There is a beautiful granite and bronze monument to Mitchel at the Engineers' Gate entrance to the Reservoir at Fifth Avenue and 90th Street, whose opening he presided over at 1917.

Why did the Boy Mayor draw his revolver?

One of the most dramatic episodes of his time in office happened on April 17, 1914, when Mitchel and several other city officials were fired upon by seventy-one-year-old Irish immigrant Michael P. Mahoney as they were getting into a car in front of City Hall. The bullet pierced the jaw of city's corporation counsel Frank Polk, shattering his jawbone and knocking out two of his teeth. According to a *New York Times* account, Polk "received back his extracted teeth from the chauffeur … and said he would have them mounted in gold." While police officers swarmed Mahoney, Mitchel leaped up in the car, brandishing his revolver but not firing. Mahoney was taken into custody without any more shots being fired. Even though the Sullivan Law had banned the carrying of concealed weapons three years earlier, Mitchel was one of the roughly eight thousand New Yorkers to have concealed-carry permits. He was said to have been carrying a revolver since Mayor Gaynor's death from the wounds suffered in the 1910 assassination attempt.

Why did New York streets get (a little) brighter after 1916?

In the early twentieth century, New York City began considering the negative as well as the positive impact that all of its soaring new skyscrapers were having on the city. Previously, the city's density had been defined only by how close it could pack its structures together, or how far up and outside of Manhattan Island they could spread. Once skyscrapers came into the picture, a third dimension was added to the already considerable debate raging over just how crowded the city could become and remain livable. Singer Building architect Ernest Flagg articulated many people's concerns about how much darkness was being thrown over the city by all of these behemoths (he had tried to do his part by keeping the Singer Building as narrow as possible). Bringing this discontent to a hard boil was the erection in 1915 of the monstrous Equitable Building at 120 Broadway. The city's first true office block, its forty-story structure held 1.2 million square feet (111,500 square meters) of office space on one acre and threw a shadow seven acres large.

The following year, New York enacted the Zoning Resolution of 1916, a sweeping urban planning document that (rather incredibly) spelled out a maximum population of fifty-five million and a host of building regulations. The most impactful of these dictated that a skyscraper could be any height, as long as it didn't take up more than 25 percent of its lot; any more than that and the building would have to have "setbacks" that would keep the building from soaring straight up into the air and cutting off more light. Those setbacks are why so many buildings from the pre-World War II years have a tiered, wedding cake-look to them at their higher levels. Further tweaks to the zoning laws in the postwar years resulted in many new office towers in Midtown being surrounded by arcades and courtyards that were supposed to provide breathing room but only increased the sense of sterility.

What precipitated the city's first civil rights march?

In 1917, a series of devastating race riots swept the country. One of the most horrific took place on July 2 in East St. Louis, Illinois, where whites lynched and burned their way through a black neighborhood, leaving mass casualties in their wake. After nearly a week of rioting, dozens were dead and thousands of blacks fled the city. Sympathetic outrage swept through New York's black community.

In what became known as the "Silent Parade," on July 28, around eight thousand blacks dressed in white marched down Fifth Avenue in quiet protest against the riots elsewhere and segregation and discrimination in New York. A banner that showed a black woman kneeling before Wilson and pleading for democracy at home was pulled down after police objected. It was not only the first civil rights march in the city's history but also possibly the first mass protest by blacks anywhere in America.

Who was Marcus Garvey?

Marcus Garvey (1887–1940) was a Jamaican printer, journalist, activist, and black separatist with an early bent towards Pan-Africanism (the promotion of increasing ties between Africans of all nationalities) decades before it became *au courant* in certain circles. He also had a desire and genius for self-promotion. Garvey settled in Harlem in 1917. A few years later he started up the American chapter of his Universal Negro Improvement Association (UNIA), whose stated purpose was to unite the African diaspora and start a country of their own. Until that dream could be achieved, Garvey focused on promoting racial pride. UNIA meetings mixed the impassioned rhetoric of a revival meeting (Garvey having learned his craft from seeing preacher Billy Sunday) with a quasi-military discipline (UNIA members wore impressive uniforms and attracted admiring or frightened stares when they marched in formation through the city). At its height, the UNIA had hundreds of thousands of members in dozens of chapters around America and the world.

Garvey was later charged with mail fraud and ultimately deported to Jamaica. The chief cause of his downfall? A young

Journalist, businessman, and activist Marcus Garvey was founder of the Universal Negro Improvement Association and African Communities League and promoted Pan-Africanism.

Justice Department attorney named J. Edgar Hoover (1895–1972) who was fixated on the supposed danger that Garvey posed for America, whom he called the "Negro Moses"—coincidentally the same term Hoover would use while the Federal Bureau of Investigation waged guerrilla warfare on the Black Panthers decades later.

Who were the Harlem Hellfighters?

The 369th Infantry Regiment, a.k.a. the Harlem Hellfighters, was the first black American infantry unit to see combat in World War I. Originally comprised of white and black soldiers as the 15th New York National Guard Infantry, the unit was redesignated as a black-only U.S. Army regiment in 1917 as part of the 93rd Division. Arriving in France that December, they were put under French command and received French training. Being in the French, as opposed to the American, chain of command meant that the soldiers saw much less discrimination and were regularly given commendations for bravery in combat. In fact, the 369th's soldiers became the first Americans to receive the Croix de Guerre medal for extraordinary valor.

It could be argued that in addition to defending France, the 369th also left behind the gift of music: According to legend, their regimental band gave the French their first taste of jazz. The unit actually received its nickname of the "Harlem Hellfighters" from the German soldiers they faced in vicious fighting at Chateau-Thierry and Belleau Wood. The Hellfighters served nearly two hundred days in combat and came home one of the nation's most decorated units. On February 18, 1919, three thousand Hellfighters paraded up Fifth Avenue to the heart of Harlem (which about two-thirds of the men called home) at 145th Street and Lenox Avenue. An enthusiastic crowd of hundreds of thousands lined the parade route. The *New York Tribune* described the march of the "ebony warriors" in rhapsodic terms: "Up the wide avenue they swung. Their smiles outshone the golden sunlight. In every line proud chests expanded beneath the medals valor had won."

When did Prohibition begin in New York?

Technically, not until 1920 with the passage of the Eighteenth Amendment. But the winds of sobriety began to blow years before, specifically in 1874 with the founding of the Women's Christian Temperance Union. In 1877, the Moderation Society was founded specifically to encourage people on the Lower East Side to drink water instead of alcohol. To facilitate sobriety, wealthy San Franciscan temperance activist Henry D. Cogswell (1820–1900) constructed a "temperance fountain" in Tompkins Square Park, a thirteen-foot- (four-meter-) high neoclassical stone kiosk over a drinking fountain that still stands today. Temperance received a true shot in the arm when Carry Nation (1846–1911) first came to town. The imposing, deeply religious six-foot- (two-meter-) tall Kentuckian, whose first husband drank himself to death, had become disgusted with alcohol's effect on society. Calling herself "a bulldog running along at the feet of Jesus, barking at what he doesn't like," she took to greeting saloon-owners with "Good morning, destroyer of men's souls!" and later smashing up saloons in Kansas with a hatchet.

Nation brought her crusade to New York in 1901, whereupon she promptly destroyed a Coney Island cigar shop (she didn't like tobacco, either). In subsequent years, the woman later called "Prohibition's Avenging Angel" assaulted dozens of saloons, calling out "smash, ladies, smash!" to her followers. Nation made for great copy. Still, it was groups like the well-organized WCTU and the Anti-Saloon League, with their many religious and suffragette supporters, who were ultimately able to get the Eighteenth Amendment to pass. It went into effect at midnight on January 18, 1920. A madam named Polly Walker foretold the future when she joked, "They might as well try to dry up the Atlantic with a post office blotter."

What was the effect of Prohibition on New York?

Not surprisingly, New York did not go willingly into Prohibition. The Eighteenth Amendment was viewed by many as not just a religious and moral crusade to save families from the ravages of drunkenness (William Jennings Bryan said in a speech that "King Alcohol has slain more children than Herod ever did"), but as a two-pronged assault on the nature of the city itself. The temperance movement received a good deal of its support from nativist rural Protestants suspicious of cities like New York, with their large non-Protestant immigrant populations supposedly given to excessive drink and general bad behavior. One leader of the Anti-Saloon League went so far as to call New York "Satan's Seat."

Given this undercurrent to much of the temperance movement's rhetoric, not to mention the city's long history of friendliness to King Alcohol—a common theme in reports from leaders of the early Dutch colony were complaints about the citizenry's drunkenness—Prohibition's rules were quickly and broadly flouted, all the way from Lower East Side tenements to penthouses on Park Avenue. Illegally produced liquor was available in such quantity that in 1928, sixty people died of wood-alcohol poisoning. In 1929, the mayor of Berlin, Gustav Boess, was being given a tour of New York by Mayor James Walker (1881–1946). At one point, Boess turned to ask Walker, "When does the Prohibition law go into effect?" It was apparently not obvious to him that the notice had *already* been the law for nine years. In the political battles that divided the country into "Wet" and "Dry" factions, New York would be resolutely wet.

How did New Yorkers get liquor during Prohibition?

Given that New York was a major port and also close to the Canadian border, it never suffered much for supplies of alcohol during Prohibition. Also, because the Eighteenth Amendment included a provision that made it legal to drink alcohol legally procured before the law went into effect, and gave everybody a year between passage and enforcement, many people simply stockpiled. Famously, New York's Yale Club had piled up a large enough stock before January 17, 1920, that kept them from ever going dry. News reports describe a rush on wheelbarrows and baby carriages for people to haul home as much legal liquor as possible before the stroke of midnight. With such a steady supply on hand, there were seemingly speakeasies on every corner. At one point, New York's police commissioner estimated that there were about 32,000 of the establishments in the city, a remarkable number even if you allow for hyperbole.

What was a speakeasy?

The origins of "speakeasy" aren't clear. H. L. Mencken and some others point to it being Irish-American slang about keeping quiet when the cops are afoot. One source points to it having originated in late-nineteenth-century Philadelphia, where a saloon-keeper who refused to pay for a liquor license and operated illegally would implore her sometimes rowdy customers to keep it down and "speak easy, boys." Once Prohibition came into effect, the term translated easily to the secretive drinking establishments that began popping up almost immediately around New York. By 1925 there were thousands of speakeasies in New York. Unlike the shuttered saloons that littered the cities, speakeasies couldn't openly advertise themselves, with the exception of the bigger restaurants like "21" and jazz joints like the Cotton Club that got away with serving alcohol in fairly brazen fashion.

What were the other effects of Prohibition on New York?

As in most other major metropolitan areas in America, Prohibition saw a dramatic increase in crime in New York. Gangs, which had heretofore been mostly neighborhood mobs based around small-scale rackets, discovered a lucrative new source of income that resulted in a great expansion of their power. With all that new-found revenue and the promise of more came not only the impetus but the means by which to fight with each other. More prosaically, the state's finances were hard hit. At the start of Prohibition, about three-fourths of the New York state budget was funded through liquor taxes. One of the least-discussed aftereffects of Prohibition was that by the time it was repealed, the government (both on a state and federal level) had gotten used to funding themselves with income taxes.

Who started the Thanksgiving Day Parade?

Probably the first Thanksgiving parade to be sponsored by a department store took place in Philadelphia in 1920, sponsored by Gimbel Brothers. Four years later, Macy's department store—which had just expanded that year to sprawl over a whole city block in Herald Square—held its first parade on Thanksgiving morning. Being that Macy's was trying to draw attention to its new flagship location, which it called the "World's Largest Store," and wanted to remind consumers that the Christmas shopping season was now officially underway, the store at first called it the "Macy's Christmas Parade." It started at 145th Street in Harlem and culminated at Herald Square. The first parade included floats featuring fairy tale characters, marching bands, and animals from the Central Park Zoo.

The parade became an annual institution that only grew as the years went by. Giant balloons of characters like Felix the Cat were introduced in 1927 and became one of the parade's most notable attractions. The size of the balloons, along with sometimes unpredictable late November weather, occasionally caused problems, as in 1999 when a giant

The Macy's Thanksgiving Day Parade has become a famous part of the holidays. People look forward to the huge balloons, the giant turkey, and, at the end of the parade, Santa arriving on his huge sleigh.

M&M balloon was punctured and injured two spectators as it collapsed. The parade route has been shortened from six miles to about two and a half (ten to four kilometers), and the event is now generally referred to as the "Macy's Day Parade." But the crowds, if anything, have only grown over the years. Millions around the country tune in to watch the parade on television, with local stations even covering the workers inflating the giant balloons.

When did New York's immigration boom end?

The immigration boom ended rather abruptly, with the 1921 passage of the Emergency Quota Act, which established quotas and restricted the total, annual number of immigrants to 357,000. Immigration dropped further in 1924 with the National Origins Act, which cut the annual number to 150,000 and enacted more stringent quotas specifically designed to restrict immigration from southern and eastern Europe and eliminate it from Asia entirely. The new laws, the result of nativist fears about an increasingly urban and foreign-born population and the post-World War I tilt towards isolationism, made for a drastic shift, considering that between 1909 and 1919 alone, over six million immigrants had entered the country.

The quotas had a dramatic effect on New York's population, to say the least. In 1920, about one of every three New Yorkers had been born in another country; by 1950, that number was down to less than one in five. The effect was also visible after 1921 on Ellis Island, which ended up housing large numbers of hopeful immigrants waiting to see if

133

they would be expelled or not. As the numbers dropped, Ellis Island transitioned from being an immigrant processing station to more of a center for detaining and deporting foreigners. Later, during World War II and the Red Scare, the island also housed foreigners suspected of enemy or radical behavior.

How did the Ku Klux Klan almost ruin Memorial Day?

The Ku Klux Klan had made inroads in upstate New York and the southern reaches of New Jersey during the 1920s following its brief nationwide resurgence following D.W. Griffith's 1915 pro-Klan propaganda film, *The Birth of a Nation*. But it failed to gain much traction in New York, due at least in part to the Klan's anti-Catholic and pro-Prohibition stance. In 1923 the NYPD, acting on the orders of Mayor John Hylan (1868–1936), discovered that there were at least 800 Klan members in the city (about thirty of whom were actually police officers) and broke up meetings of the Klan in Brooklyn.

On June 1, 1927, the *New York Times* reported that the police commissioner wanted fewer "extraneous" parades for "this, that and the other thing" on Memorial Day because it stretched the NYPD too thin. The driving impulse behind this announcement appeared to be a pair of violent incidents on Memorial Day. According to the paper, two Italian Fascisti (supporters of Benito Mussolini) "were killed on their way to join a detachment of black shirts in the Manhattan parade." On the same day, a thousand Klan members battled with a hundred cops as well as anti-Klan protestors during a march in Jamaica, Queens. Seven men were arrested as part of the riot. The arrestees included Fred Trump (1905–1999), who became a real estate magnate and father to another real estate magnate (as well as celebrity gadfly and U.S. president) Donald Trump (1946–). Following the arrest, handbills apparently distributed by the Klan in Jamaica exclaimed, "Americans Assaulted by Roman Catholic Police of New York City!"

Why was Mayor Jimmy Walker so popular?

Even in a city like New York, which has seen its share of politicians with personality to spare, Mayor Jimmy Walker (1881–1946) stood apart. A Greenwich Village-raised son of Irish Catholic immigrants, Walker graduated from New York Law School in 1904 but didn't waste much time practicing the law. A denizen of the city's nightlife, he married a singer and had a career of sorts as a Tin Pan Alley songwriter; his biggest hit was "Will You Love Me in December (As You Do in May)?"

Walker entered politics under the mentorship of Governor Alfred E. Smith (1873–1944), another larger-than-life Irish charmer, and was elected to the state Senate in 1914. There, Walker was known more for his dashing sense of fashion and ability to carry out Smith's orders than political acumen. Still, he was elected mayor of New York in 1925 with a massive margin of victory. Walker was in some ways the perfect mayor of the city for the Jazz Age (*The Great Gatsby* was in fact published the same year as his election). Dashing, dressed to the nines, always cavorting at the city's hottest nightclub or hobnobbing with celebrities at a Broadway premiere, he embodied the era's brash materialism and hunger for entertainment. Walker dated chorus girls and conducted most business (or at least spent most of his time at) the Casino nightclub in Central Park. Many of his constituents loved him for such extravagant style, even gathering on the piers to send him off on one of his many vacations; he spent about five months of his first two years in office on holiday. Nevertheless, the hard-playing and barely working Walker easily won re-election in 1929.

What was Walker's downfall?

The rot that lay beneath the Jazz Age's champagne-slicked surface caught up with Walker not long after the period's exuberance collapsed in the Great Depression. In 1931, an investigation was opened into the corruption rumored to be flourishing under Walker's leadership. When pulled out into the open, the resulting scandal was shocking even by New York standards.

Charismatic mayor Jimmy Walker led the city from 1926 to 1932, but he was forced out of office when it was discovered he took over a million dollars in bribes.

In the Walker administration, pay-to-play was the custom. Vice-squad cops had blackmailed hundreds of innocent women as prostitutes and sent them to jail if they didn't pay up. Judgeships were for sale. And this wasn't just corruption that the mayor had benignly presided over; he dove right in. Walker himself turned out to have received over $1 million in "beneficences" from companies that had contracts with the city. On September 1, 1932, with Governor Franklin D. Roosevelt on the verge of removing Walker from office, the mayor made the decision to resign while out of town on another of his European tours.

THE GREAT DEPRESSION TO A NEW CENTURY

Where and how did the stock market crash of 1929 begin?

Like every market bubble that preceded and followed it, the Great Crash of 1929 was easily predicted and yet nobody making quick fortunes off of it was the least bit interested in stopping the party. Between 1924 and 1929, the Dow Jones Industrial Average quadrupled in value. By the end of the decade, America and New York in particular was in a frenzy of get-rich-quick investing schemes. The bubble had an intoxicatingly democratic spirit about it, with everybody swapping hot tips, from the shoeshine boys to actors, one of whom turned her Park Avenue apartment into a stock-trading office. Nevertheless, the market's precariousness increased as more people flooded into it, buying stocks on margin (meaning people borrowed money from their broker).

What happened on Black Thursday?

The peak was hit on September 3, 1929. Warning signs were everywhere, with the failure of several banks and steel production down. But few paid heed, even as prices began to drop. The true panic hit on October 24, Black Thursday. On that day, thirteen million shares traded hands. October 28, Black Monday, removed all cause for hope, as the value of even blue-chip stocks like General Electric and American Telephone and Telegraph were decimated. Reportedly the opening bell at the New York Stock Exchange on October 29 couldn't be heard over the din of "Sell! Sell!" As margin calls flooded in, all those investors who had borrowed money, cashed in their life savings, or mortgaged their homes, were financially ruined in moments. Rumors spread about stock brokers leaping to their deaths. Even though these stories were mostly later shown to be false, they quickly calcified into grim truths that only fed the panic. The market eventually bottomed out in November. About $319 billion in modern-day wealth was erased from the ledger books, roughly the same amount America spent on World War I (1914–1918).

How severely did the Great Depression hit New York?

Within a year of the stock market crash, the streets of New York were already crowded with apple-sellers, traditionally the last resort of the city's destitute. Foreclosures mounted, with many families fighting attempts at eviction. The homeless were everywhere. The city's budget was savaged as businesses shuttered in great waves, each throwing more people out of work, reducing tax revenues at the same time that the need for relief increased. Many businesses that stayed open cut their workers' hours, pay, or both. Within a few months, dozens of bread lines were operating just on the Lower East Side.

By 1932, New York was in desperate shape. About a third of the city's manufacturing plants had closed. Over a million and a half New Yorkers were on public relief. That summer, the Dow Jones Industrial Average had roughly a tenth the value it held in 1929. The city was so desperate for revenue that laying off 11,000 teachers didn't even make a dent in the problem. The streets were filled with scenes of desperation, from families scavenging in garbage dumps to the soup kitchens set up in army trucks in Times Square to the "Hooverville" shantytown that sprawled behind the Metropolitan Museum of Art to the thousands of homeless men who showed up every single day at the Municipal Lodging Houses looking for food and shelter. Immigration to New York dropped precipitously during the Depression, with only about a half million new arrivals during the entire 1930s. For the first few years, even the construction of new buildings ground mostly to a halt.

What was done to help New York?

After President Franklin Delano Roosevelt (1882–1945) entered office in 1932, the influx of funding from the Civil Works Administration (CWA) and the later Works Progress Administration (WPA) and the attendant jobs had an immediate impact on the city. In early 1933, an incredible 6,000 projects put about 200,000 people to work. Slum clearance and the construction of public housing followed soon after, helping not only to improve the conditions of many New Yorkers but also filling the jobs gap left by the downturn in construction. Funding was provided for other kinds of employment as well, putting even writers, actors, and mural painters to work.

In addition, the indomitable, if combative, team of Mayor Fiorello LaGuardia (1882–1947) and parks commissioner Robert Moses (1888–1981) were able to not just funnel massive amounts of federal funding into the city but leveraged it to knit together an awe-inspiring legacy of parks, highways, tunnels, bridges, and other public works that forever changed the face of the city.

How did Prohibition help the Mafia?

Italian criminal organizations like the Black Hand had been operating in New York for years before Prohibition. Even so, it was the profits enabled by that era's underground economy of liquor that truly created the modern American Mafia. All that money meant lots of rivalries, which meant shootings and stabbings that attracted attention and drove down profit margins. A 1929 summit between Italian gangsters and leaders of rival Jewish and Irish gangs attempted to divide up New York and the rest of the country into clearly delineated territories.

The peace soon collapsed, when a war broke out between factions led by Sicilian-born Salvatore Maranzano (1886–1931)—one of the old-country gangsters familiarly known as "Moustache Petes"—and mainland Italian Joe Masseria (1886–1931). Masseria was killed in April 1931. Maranzano's reign as *capo di tutti capi* (boss of all the bosses) was short-lived; he was executed that September, and most of his associates were wiped out soon after.

Who were the "Five Families" of New York crime?

In an attempt to consolidate control, Charles "Lucky" Luciano (1896–1962), a younger Sicilian-born bootlegger who despised all the infighting, had helped orchestrate, with Meyer Lansky (1902–1983) and Murder, Inc., the killings that brought the war to an end. Afterward, Luciano took control of the Genovese crime family. He also organized what would become known as "The Commission." Under Luciano's plan, the famous "Five Families" of the Commission—which controlled New York, the only city with more than one major Mafia family—would meet on a regular basis to arrange deals and keep conflicts from erupting into open warfare again. It didn't always work, as wars continued to occasionally break out between and inside families.

The Commission's members included the Gambino, Genovese, Lucchese, Bonanno, and Colombo organized-crime "families." Each had a clearly delineated leadership structure, from the boss at the top, to the *caporegimes* (lieutenants) and "soldiers" beneath. The families' hundreds of associates ran schemes like loan-sharking, protection rackets, gambling, and extortion, which netted vast profits for decades after Prohibition came to an end.

Which New York mayor lasted only a year in office?

After Walker took himself out of City Hall in 1932, Tammany Hall was left without a mayor. They turned to John O'Brien (1873–1953), a judge and lawyer. He handily won the special election but would later be known mostly for being unremembered. O'Brien's legacy as a consummate tool of Tammany Hall was cemented when

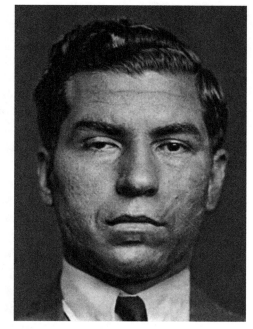

Charles "Lucky" Luciano is considered by some to have been the father of the modern Mafia in the United States.

Mayor LaGuardia (left) is seen here in 1938 with President Franklin D. Roosevelt.

his response to a reporter's question about who his police commissioner would be was, "I don't know. They haven't told me yet." During his time in office, Tammany appointees continued to drain the city coffers, including federal relief meant to help the destitute suffering the effects of the Great Depression.

Who was the first New York mayor to serve three consecutive terms?

Fiorello Henry LaGuardia. Born on Sullivan Street to an Italian father and Jewish mother, LaGuardia spent his years of civic service fighting tenaciously for the people of New York. LaGuardia grew up far from the city's ethnic mosaic that he embodied and loved. An army brat, he attended high school in Arizona. As a teenager he moved to his mother's hometown in Trieste and later worked at American consulates in Budapest and Fiume (then part of Austria-Hungary, now Croatia).

Back in America, LaGuardia studied law at New York University while using his knowledge of Yiddish, German, French, and Italian (he also had some Hungarian and knew a few Croatian dialects) in his job as an interpreter at Ellis Island. An evaluation of LaGuardia by Ellis Island's comissioner concluded that he was "energetic [and] intelligent ... inclined to be peppery ... inclined to be argumentative." All those qualities were well represented in the diminutive (5' 2") and fiery crusader who served several terms as a progressive Republican congressman before winning the mayor's office for the first time in 1933. He was reelected twice, stepping down in 1946.

What did the "Little Flower" accomplish during his time in office?

LaGuardia's nickname "Little Flower," from the Italian translation of his first name, was an ironic counterpart to his muscular governing style. He entered office as an anti-graft reform candidate and on Inauguration Day he reportedly shouted, *"E finita la cuccagna!"* ("No more free lunch!"). LaGuardia, who once quipped that "Every time the city built a school, a politician went into the real estate business," arguably did more than any previous politician to fight corruption and break Tammany Hall's lock on municipal power. He reorganized government with a new City Charter, built the city's first municipal airport, and unified the previously fragmented transit system. Nominally a Republican, LaGuardia's progressive ideals and eagerness to showcase the positive effects of good government marked him a firebrand New Dealer.

LaGuardia's rare mixture of high ideology and gritty pragmatism was best reflected in his close relationship with President Roosevelt. Their relationship was a rare combination of pragmatism and a true personal connection that yielded great dividends for the city. The mayor's strong partnership with Roosevelt, who shared LaGuardia's deep-seated desire to improve the lives of working-class and poor Americans, netted the city copious funding for a broad swath of public works, ranging from public housing to hospitals and schools. Among the projects that the WPA helped build in New York are many of the city's most visible landmarks, such as the Grand Concourse in the Bronx, LaGuardia Airport (originally Idlewild), the Central Park Zoo, the Coney Island boardwalk, and the Lincoln and Holland tunnels.

What were some of LaGuardia's many crusades?

Like many Italian-American New Yorkers in the early twentieth century, LaGuardia resented the many stereotypes that came with his ethnicity. This streak of pride shaded with defensiveness influenced some of his more notable campaigns while in office. At one point, LaGuardia banned organ grinders from the city streets, ostensibly because

Why did LaGuardia read the funnies to New York children?

The indefatigable LaGuardia was also a showman par excellence, rushing to fires, picking fights with Hitler, delivering speeches in whatever language necessary, and making sure there were cameras present when he vigorously took a sledgehammer to a pile of Mafia-operated slot machines. During a 1945 newspaper strike, the mayor, known for his high and squeaky voice, took to WNYC's airwaves to read the Sunday funnies out loud. He believed that children "should not be deprived of [the comics] due to a squabble among the adults."

they interfered with traffic but by some accounts because he had been mocked as an organ grinder by bullies when he was younger. LaGuardia had a bigger chip on his shoulder when it came to the Mafia, not just because they perpetuated the stereotype of the Italian gangster, or "stiletto man," but because they gummed up the works and kept the city from running smoothly.

To that end, LaGuardia launched a crusade against slot machines, a racket that was mostly Mafia-run. (This also made for fantastic newsreel footage of the diminutive mayor enthusiastically taking a sledgehammer to a heap of slot machines, which were then dumped into Long Island Sound.) The mayor also went after many gangsters themselves, getting "Lucky" Luciano convicted in 1936.

Who did LaGuardia bring in to reinvigorate the city's parks system?

In 1934, seeking to provide more recreational and greenspaces to the working classes of New York, LaGuardia turned to one of Albany's most respected and feared operators: Robert Moses (1888–1981). A hard-charging, onetime municipal reformer who had tried to streamline the city's bloated bureaucracy years earlier, only to get sidelined by his enemies, Moses later became Al Smith's right-hand man in Albany. Once there, the infamously aggressive Moses pushed to build public works that he believed would transform the city, not to mention put his name down in history. After taking charge of the Long Island State Park Commission, his mastery of budgeting wizardry and state legal minutiae quickly showed. Wherever Moses desired to build a park or the new roadways through the Long Island countryside (which he ingeniously defined as his prerogative by placing them inside "ribbon parks"), he could. Moses's carefully cultivated network of allies in city and state government, the business community, reform groups, and the press could be counted on to support just about any proposal that he put forward. When

What did LaGuardia have against artichokes?

LaGuardia was willing to use just about any tool at hand to bring down Italian-American gangsters, no matter how unorthodox. One of his targets was Ciro "The Artichoke King" Terranova (1888–1938). A rackets boss from East Harlem whose legacy dated back to the days of the Black Hand, Terranova's control of artichoke sales in the city was a $1 million a year business. On a cold morning in December 1935, LaGuardia appeared at the Bronx Terminal Market, a Terranova stronghold, and announced a ban on selling and displaying so-called "small" artichokes, the kind favored by Italian immigrants and supplied mostly by California importers controlled by Terranova. LaGuardia promised that going forward "no thugs, racketeers or punks" would be strong-arming vendors. The ban lasted a mere three days, but the Artichoke King's power was shattered nonetheless.

Moses endorsed LaGuardia in the 1933 mayoral election, it helped the Republican win in the traditionally Democratic town.

On a personal level, the avuncular downtown populist LaGuardia (who was proud of his Italian-Jewish heritage) couldn't stand Moses, an acerbic Yale-educated elitist (though born to German-Jewish parents he frequently denied his heritage and once threatened to sue the publisher of a Jewish encyclopedia for libel if it included his biography) who referred to LaGuardia as "dago" or "wop." But personal animus aside, LaGuardia respected Moses's control of the levers of power and saw that it could assist his desire to build great things for the people of New York. By the time LaGuardia took office, Moses was already possibly the most powerful person in the state. Once LaGuardia unified the five boroughs' park departments and made Moses commissioner in 1934, the change was nearly immediate.

Urban planner Robert Moses has been called the master builder of twentieth-century New York City.

What was Moses able to build?

Moses leveraged the federal funds available as part of WPA to radically transform the city parks. The unprecedented whirlwind of activity saw 70,000 Parks Department relief workers leap into action with some 1,700 projects that expanded and rebuilt parks all over the city. It was just the start of a massive construction binge unlike anything the city or America witnessed before or since. Over the next three-plus decades of Moses's nearly unchallenged power, he cannily deployed public funds and eminent domain to build 658 playgrounds, 150,000 housing units, 416 miles (670 kilometers) of parkway, and 13 bridges, including the massive Triborough Bridge complex (now the Robert F. Kennedy Bridge) that links Manhattan to the Bronx and Queens.

In the process, Moses studded the city with monuments from the beloved to the despised, devastated neighborhoods that got in the way of his highways, and displaced a quarter-million people. His decades-long campaign to recast the city as a car-friendly business and cultural center for commuters was radical enough to eventually galvanize an opposition, led in the postwar slum-clearing years by activist Jane Jacobs (1916–2006), that gave birth to the urban renewal and preservation movement.

What was the first public housing complex built in New York?

Part of LaGuardia's campaign to uplift the people of New York was his desire to expand access to decent and affordable housing. The first fruits of that campaign was First Houses, a complex of eight four- and five-story buildings on 3rd Street and Avenue A,

What kind of a gang was Murder, Inc.?

Murder, Inc., was somewhat unique in the annals of American organized crime. Founded in the 1930s by a network based in Brooklyn's Brownsville neighborhood, this gang was not interested in bootlegging, drug dealing, extortion, gambling, prostitution, or any of the other traditional pursuits of an organized gang at the time. Instead, it acted as more of an actual business, a business with one very specific product to offer: contract killings. In a relatively short number of years, Murder, Inc.—which counted among its members "Lucky" Luciano, Meyer Lansky, and Frank Costello—carried out hundreds of gangland executions. The group came to a fairly abrupt end in 1941, after member Abe "Kid Twist" Reles (1906–1941) exposed its inner workings and testified against its leaders, such as Albert "Chief Executioner" Anastasia (1902–1957), who Reles said was responsible for sixty-three murders. That November, Reles mysteriously "fell" to his death from the Coney Island hotel room where he was being guarded by police night and day.

constituting the first municipal public housing complex in the nation. Instead of the mass slum-clearance projects that would later mar New York and many other cities, the plan for First Houses involved partial demolition and reconstruction and renovation to reduce density. The 122 apartments in the squat, solid brick structures around an airy courtyard were dedicated at a ceremony on December 3, 1935, attended by Eleanor Roosevelt (1884–1962), an ebullient LaGuardia, and thousands of spectators. First Houses was made a landmark building in 1974 and still stands today, part of New York's tradition (different from most other American municipalities) of rehabilitating instead of demolishing old structures.

What was the Long Island Express?

Hurricanes in America are more associated with cities like Miami, but New York has been battered by a few of them over the years, with at least three large storms recorded in the nineteenth century. One of the most devastating, however, was the Great New England Hurricane of 1938, nicknamed the Long Island Express (or sometimes the Yankee Clipper) in New York. The storm started near Cape Verde on September 9 and moved steadily across the Atlantic towards Miami. It then made a surprise sharp turn, moving north so fast that there was no time to issue warnings. The storm made landfall on Long Island and southern Connecticut on the afternoon of September 21 as a Category 3 storm with sustained winds of 121 mph (195 kph) gusting up to 183 mph (295 kph). Dozens were killed as homes were swept off their moorings by 15-foot (4.5-meter) surges. In the city itself there were power outages, the East River flooded, and the Empire State Building supposedly swayed more than 4 inches under the force of the winds. The devastation was ultimately worse throughout New England, but fifty people died in the storm on Long Island and ten in the city.

What was Café Society?

The writing, and in some ways the life, of Minnesota-born F. Scott Fitzgerald (1896–1940) helped capture not just one particular generation of New York, but an entire way of thinking about and living it. Fitzgerald moved to New York in 1919 and over the next six years published three novels—*This Side of Paradise* (1920), *The Beautiful and the Damned* (1920), and *The Great Gatsby* (1925)—whose reckless and high living characters epitomized the seductive charm of Jazz Age New York.

Fitzgerald didn't just write about this life, he lived it, with his high-strung wife, Zelda. The city's nightlife boom was powered by a multitude of factors, from the illicit appeal of the speakeasy, the surprising erasing of once-impregnable social barriers, and the sudden ubiquity of a radical and raucous new form of music: jazz. At the same time that the city was partying, it was also coming to life intellectually, with a heady swirl of writers and radicals who infused the new atmosphere with a kind of social significance that wouldn't

Who was the "Mad Bomber"?

George Metesky (1903–1994) was one of America's most prolific terrorists, remaining on the run roughly as long as Ted Kaczynski (1942–). One great difference between Metesky (aka "The Mad Bomber") and Kaczynski (aka "The Unabomber"), though, was that the former wasn't hiding out in the remote western wilderness; he was resident all the while in New York. The son of Lithuanian immigrants, Metesky was working for ConEd in 1931 when a boiler accident severely injured him. He was later fired and his claims for compensation denied. Like many disgruntled workers, he nurtured a grievance against the company he believed had wronged him. Unlike almost every other disgruntled worker, he waged a sixteen-year bombing campaign in the interest of (according to a letter he wrote to the police) bringing "Con Edison to justice" and making it "pay for their dastardly deeds." Between 1940 and 1956, he wrote angry letters to newspapers signed "F.P." (for "Fair Play") and planted over thirty homemade bombs all around the city. The bombs targeted landmarks from Grand Central and Penn Station to Radio City Music Hall and the New York Public Library.

In all, some fifteen people were injured by Metesky's campaign, even though he often planted his bombs in places that he believed would cause minimal harm, and later said "I used to pray no one would be hurt by my bombs, especially on Sunday." Eventually ConEd was able to provide police with personnel information matching a profile created by a psychiatrist who had worked in military counter-intelligence. In 1957 Metesky was tracked down to his Connecticut house. Declared incompetent to stand trial by reason of insanity, Metesky spent seventeen years in asylums. Today, his house in Connecticut serves as a group home for the mentally ill.

be seen in America until the 1960s. The traveling party of bright young things was collectively called the "Café Society" by some. They were defined by historian James Sanders as having given new life to the nightlife scene "by patronizing a series of 'smart' nightclubs, where debutantes danced with racketeers, and chorus girls with foreign dignitaries, as once-strict demarcations of class and social background broke down." Like many of his contemporaries, including Dashiell Hammett, Clifford Odets, and Damon Runyon, Fitzgerald eventually heeded the call of Hollywood and moved west, once the Great Crash killed the party for Café Society and just about everybody else.

WORLD WAR II AND THE POSTWAR ERA

How did New York's different ethnic groups react to World War II?

Even before World War II (1939–1945) began, the drumbeat of conflict from across the ocean was evident in tensions between the city's often factional ethnic groups. Japan's 1931 invasion of Manchuria infuriated the city's Chinese population, though there were few Japanese residents to take their anger out on. Causing more friction was Italy's 1935 invasion of Ethiopia. Many Italian-Americans in the city, frustrated by years of discrimination and obnoxious stereotypes, had thrilled with pride at the rise to power of Benito Mussolini (1883–1945) in the 1920s. When he declared war on Ethiopia in 1935, New York reverberated with aftershocks. Bands of black and Italian kids battled with sawed-off pool cues at a Brooklyn school, while groups of blacks in Harlem waved the Ethiopian flag and called to run Italians out of the neighborhood. James Baldwin (1924–1987) later wrote that he "remembered the Italian priests and bishops blessing Italian boys who were on their way to [fight in] Ethiopia."

Given the antagonism targeted at them during World War I, German-Americans in New York were much more reticent to support the new Nazi regime. However, the German-American Bund (founded in 1937) held a 20,000-strong pro-Nazi rally at Madison Square Garden in 1939, operated Hitler Youth-like camps, called for boycotts of Jewish businesses in New York, and engaged in street fights with Jewish veterans of World War I.

Did the Nazis plant spies in New York?

Yes, but for a variety of reasons they never got up to any mischief as substantial as the previous war's Black Tom explosion. That doesn't mean they were not active. Even in 1935, four years before the United States and Germany were in a state of open war, agents of the Abwehr (military intelli-

The flag of the German-American Bund, a group that had tens of thousands of members in the United States during the 1930s.

gence) bureau were embedded in New York, particularly in the Upper East Side German-American neighborhood of Yorkville. Elaborate sabotage plans were concocted and efforts made to steal plans for the top-secret Norden bombsight. American counterespionage efforts were hampered by rivalry between the NYPD and the FBI, who had little experience with spy operations; Soviet agents supposedly joked that you could walk down Broadway with a sign identifying yourself as a spy and still avoid arrest. But the German spies were generally so ineffective that little damage was done.

In 1941, dozens of Abwehr spies were exposed by a German-American double agent. More embarrassing for the Third Reich's intelligence efforts was the night of June 13, 1942, when four German agents disembarked from a U-Boat and landed on a beach near Amagansett, Long Island. They carried massive amounts of explosives and primers for an extended sabotage campaign targeting the American defense industry. They were spotted by a suspicious coast guardsman, whom they tried to bribe to stay quiet. He reported them anyway, and they were all captured within a week.

What did Hitler have against LaGuardia?

Fiorello LaGuardia was, to put it mildly, no fan of Adolf Hitler's. In 1937, the mayor gave a speech to the women's division of the American Jewish Congress in New York in which he said that the Chamber of Horrors in the forthcoming World's Fair should include a wax figure of Hitler. He also referred to the "three madmen running the world" (Hitler, Mussolini, and Joseph Stalin), saying in Yiddish *Ich kehn die drie menshen—die schald zoi zei nehmen* ("I know the three men—the devil take them"). The German government was outraged and made formal complaints to Washington, precipitating official apologies from Secretary of State Cordell Hull. LaGuardia also called Hitler a "perverted maniac."

The Nazi propaganda machine, dismayed by the mayor's pointed attacks (dismissed by most New York newspapers as nothing more than a cheap bid for Jewish votes), made much of LaGuardia's Italian-Jewish mother. Meanwhile, Hermann Goering drew up plans for an air assault on New York to "stop somewhat the mouths of the arrogant people over there." A map of the plan had a bull's eye drawn at the corner of Bowery and Delancey. The Nazi high command claimed in 1944 that a V-3 rocket with intercontinental capabilities was about to be ready to launch on New York. Needless to say, that threat never materialized.

Were there actually U-boats prowling off Long Island?

In the film *Radio Days* by Woody Allen (1935–), a young boy at Coney Island sees a German U-boat offshore just for a minute before it slips beneath the waves again. The scene is played as something that could have just been a war-fevered boy's dream, but it could have actually happened. In January 1942, just over a month after war was declared, *U-123* sailed down Long Island past the blazing lights of Coney Island's Wonder Wheel and right into New York Harbor. The crew, listening to music broadcast on New York's public radio station WNYC, was surprised to see the city lit up as though America wasn't actually at war. The submarine's captain, Reinhard Hardegan (1913–), found this blasé attitude toward defense "incomprehensible." Hardegan didn't spy a target worth wasting a torpedo on in the crowded and undefended harbor. Later that night, *U-123* sank the oil tanker *Coimbra* off the eastern end of Long Island, killing thirty-six of her crew.

U-boats continued to skulk in America's coastal waters throughout the war, sinking eighty-seven ships in the first four months of 1942 alone. But after *U-123*'s jaunt into New York Harbor, the city became more serious about its defenses. Air raid wardens enforced blackout rules, an antisubmarine net was stretched between the Narrows, and an enthusiastic group of volunteers formed a rag-tag but somewhat effective civilian naval patrol officially called the Corsair Fleet but known to its members (a mix of wealthy yachters, fishermen, boat enthusiasts, and ex-Prohibition rum runners) as the Hooligan Navy.

Prior to 9/11, had any New York buildings been hit by a plane?

On July 28, 1945, a twin-engine, ten-ton Army Air Corps B-25 bomber was on a routine flight mission from Massachusetts to LaGuardia Airport. The bomber's pilot, decorated combat veteran William F. Smith, was having difficulty seeing anything in the dense morning fog. Smith dropped his B-25 below the recommended minimum altitude of 1,500 feet (457 meters), flying dangerously low into Manhattan. In the confusion that followed, Smith frantically tried to navigate his way out of the maze of skyscrapers, but it was ultimately for naught.

The bomber crashed into the north side of the Empire State Building that faced onto 34th Street, ripping a massive gash through the 78th and 79th floors. The plane's

---

What is rent control?

One of those quirks of real estate found only in a very few cities, rent control keeps rents in certain designated apartments from rising at an unsustainable rate for their inhabitants. While New York had some rent regulation laws in place during the early twentieth century, it wasn't until World War II that the federal government established a nationwide system of rent controls to stop exorbitant rent hikes. There were also concerns about housing shortages, with relatively few buildings being constructed and large numbers of returning soldiers needing affordable places to live. Over a million apartments in the city had their rents frozen from 1943 until 1947, after which some increases were allowed. The number of rent-controlled apartments fell steadily in the postwar decades, as the legislature weakened regulations and landlords shifted more rental apartments to co-op and condo units. In 2016, the city had only about 27,000 rent-controlled units, and many of their residents aren't going anywhere, as rent control laws were specifically written to protect long-term tenants from rent increases. Also, their median rent as of 2014 was just $900 a month.

fuel tanks erupted through the impacted floors, sending flames shooting up to the observatory almost ten stories above. The kinetic impact was incredible, with a propeller embedding itself in a wall and one of the engines smashing through the skyscraper completely, landing on the roof of a twelve-story office building on 33rd Street and destroying a penthouse owned by a man who was out playing golf at the time. The Empire State Building remained structurally sound despite the severe damage. Smith and his two passengers were killed, along with eleven occupants of the building. There would have been far more casualties if the crash hadn't taken place on a Saturday. One of the most long-lasting effects of the crash was its role in the passage, the following year, of the Federal Tort Claims Act, which for the first time made it possible for citizens to sue the fed-

Remains of the B-25 bomber are wedged into the side of the Empire State Building in this 1945 photograph.

eral government. The following year, a less-remembered accident happened when an army transport plane crashed into the 58th floor of the skyscraper at 40 Wall Street, killing all four on board but nobody in the building.

When did ridership on the subway system peak?

New York's population didn't register its first drop until the period between the 1950 and 1960 censuses. One sign of the impending decline occurred in 1946. That year, the subway system hit its peak of 2.1 billion riders. The number of subway riders later entered a period of general decline that lasted into the 1970s. At this time, the subway's vast network was seeing a decline in maintenance and a need for expensive maintenance that the IRT and BMT networks were increasingly unable to keep up. In 1953, the state formed the New York City Transit Authority to take over operation of both the subway and bus systems. The fare, set at an inflation-lagging nickel for decades—Mayor Hylan won reelection in 1921 in part due to his holding off a fare rise—and then a dime in 1948, was raised to 15 cents, which necessitated the introduction of the token. The current Metropolitan Transit Authority (MTA) was given control of the systems in 1967.

Why did Mayor O'Dwyer get an ambassadorship to Mexico?

William "Bill-O" O'Dwyer (1890–1964) was another of New York's avuncular and generally beloved mayors whose charm obscured (albeit imperfectly) other misdeeds. An Irish immigrant who worked his way up as construction worker and police officer,   **149**

O'Dwyer made a name for himself fighting organized crime gangs like Murder, Inc. while he was a Brooklyn district attorney. O'Dwyer easily won the mayoral campaign in 1945. Due to his personal popularity, his helping to secure the United Nations headquarters in New York, and reputation for strong leadership in a troubled time for the city (housing shortages and general municipal chaos), he was reelected for a second term.

1950 saw the eruption of a long-brewing scandal in which flamboyant Brooklyn gambling boss Harry Gross was accused of keeping hundreds of police officers on a payroll to keep his city-wide network of betting parlors and numbers joints free from raids. At around the same time that policemen were resigning in droves, O'Dwyer also resigned, just eight months into his second term—ostensibly to accept President Truman's appointment of him as the new ambassador to Mexico. Historians have speculated that the timing wasn't precisely a coincidence, though O'Dwyer reportedly at least spoke Spanish, unlike most mayors. In 1951, O'Dwyer briefly returned to the States to testify before Senator Estes Kefauver's organized crime committee. He couldn't quite explain his close connections with shadowy figures like Frank "Prime Minister of the Underworld" Costello (1891–1973). O'Dwyer didn't move back to New York until 1960 and lived a quiet life until passing away four years later.

Was New York a target during the Cold War?

Many American cities take pride in their having been seen as important enough to have been targeted by Soviet ICBMs (intercontinental ballistic missiles) and bombers during the Cold War. New York is perhaps an exception to this rule. Not because the city wasn't a target. As the nexus of American finance and commerce, not to mention a major transportation and shipping hub, it most certainly was. But for the most part, New Yorkers wouldn't feel the need to brag about it. They would assume that everybody would understand the critical role that New York played in a fully functioning United States of America.

How was New York guarded from the "Soviet menace"?

Starting in 1954, New York was ringed by a system of nineteen Nike missile defense sites. Connected by radar and operated by the U.S. Army Air Defense Command, the Nike missile batteries were on twenty-four-hour duty. Their mission was to guard the region from long-range Soviet Bear bombers, which the missiles were designed to intercept and destroy while still miles from their target. The missile sites were situated everywhere from Hart Island (the city's potter's field) to Fort Tilden on Rockaway Island and Fort Hancock on the Sandy Hook peninsula that juts north from New Jersey's Atlantic Highlands. They were all dismantled in 1974 as part of the Strategic Arms Limitation Treaty (SALT), which the United States signed with the Soviet Union.

What caused the great influx of Puerto Rican immigrants to New York in the 1950s?

Inhabitants of Puerto Rico, which became an American territory after the Spanish–American War in 1898, had been U.S. citizens since 1917. But for the first half of the twentieth century, relatively few moved to the mainland. That changed after World War II, when poor economic conditions on the island and the advent of cheaper air travel resulted in a spike in Puerto Rican emigration. Many of the islanders who came to the mainland during the "Great Migration" settled in New York. In 1945, there were about 13,000 Puerto Ricans in the city; by the mid-1960s, that number was over a million. One great difference between the new Puerto Ricans and earlier-arriving ethnic groups was the close ties that many were able to keep to their homeland. What with the relatively short distance and comparative ease of travel, it wasn't uncommon for extended families to have residences in both the city and on the island.) It wasn't until 2014 that another group (Dominicans) surpassed Puerto Ricans as the largest Hispanic group in the city.

Like many other large influxes of immigrants, Puerto Ricans were initially clustered in poorer Manhattan neighborhoods. They experienced job discrimination and were frequently blamed for the visible rise (among just about all groups) of ethnic-allied teenage gangs in the 1950s. One of the first attempts to create a sense of ethnic pride was the creation of the Puerto Rican Day Parade in 1958. These days, the parade is a mega-sized Fifth Avenue event with about two million spectators, many of whom are draped in or waving Puerto Rican flags.

Who fought in the Battle of Central Park?

Neither redcoats nor colonial soldiers fought in this bloodless skirmish that pitted a platoon of well-organized mothers who lived on and around Central Park West against Parks commissioner Robert Moses. In 1956, Moses wanted to accommodate the expected new business for the park's Tavern on the Green restaurant from the New York Coliseum convention center, set to open nearby at Columbus Circle, by building a new parking lot that obliterated a small glen beloved by children and their mothers. Normally this kind of destruction would have escaped scrutiny. But a few things were different this time. First, Moses wasn't upsetting mothers in Harlem or the Bronx, these were well-financed mothers with high-placed connections to lawyers and media. Second, he wasn't knocking down trees in a faraway park that most New Yorkers weren't familiar with, this was Central Park. As Robert Caro (1935–) wrote: "Central Park was "the symbol of beauty, open space, peace, fun … the holy of holies—a thing that must be preserved."

The media-savvy campaign to save the trees was waged in the daily papers and on the nightly news, with blaring headlines ("Moms vs. Moses" shouted the *Daily News*) and dramatic photographs highlighting the stand of determined mothers and their children in strollers against a cruel-seeming Moses and his bulldozers. Moses thought he won the battle by sending in his men to knock the trees down in the middle of the night. But in

An 1881 illustration of one of New York's opium dens, which were fairly common in the late-nineteenth and early twentieth centuries.

fact he lost the war. After the Battle of Central Park and its city-wide outpouring of anger and grief, the imperious parks commissioner—"I don't have time to argue about taking down six trees!" the tone-deaf Moses insisted—who had cowed the local media into unquestioning acquiescence, became mortal.

When did the last New York opium den close?

There may not have been a joss stick-scented opium den down every Mott Street hallway, as depicted in popular entertainment from *The Knick* to *Once Upon a Time in America*. But in the early twentieth century, hip non-Chinese New Yorkers often ventured down to Chinatown to "kick the gong around," as the Cab Calloway (1907–1994) song had it. It has even been theorized that the etymology of "hip" derived from the classic opium-smoking position of lying on one's side. Opium-den culture fell out of favor once drug prohibition laws started sweeping the country and other derivatives like morphine and heroin grew in popularity. The last known opium den in New York was a rather modest affair in an apartment at 295 Broome Street that was shut down by the police in 1957.

How true to life was *West Side Story*?

Pauline Kael mocked some of her fellow critics when they described the film adaptation of *West Side Story* as having a realistic take on New York street gangs. While she certainly had a point about the small likelihood of most film critics having even a passing knowledge of the sociology of street criminals, the 1957 musical—which turned *Romeo and Juliet* into a New York-based tragic love story set within a war between a Puerto Rican and white gang—did spring to some degree out of the heated gang warfare crackling around New York during that decade. Some of the set pieces from the musical, where the Jets and the Sharks negotiate over turf and plan skirmishes like warring armies, come straight from the gangs' elaborate rituals governing combat and governance—only without the jazzy Leonard Bernstein music and all the dancing.

The musical was actually first conceived by Jerome Robbins (1918–1988) in 1949 as *East Side Story*, with a story about a star-crossed Catholic boy and Jewish girl whose communities didn't approve of their relationship. But by the mid-1950s, with up to 100 teen gangs chopping their crowded city up into spiky little fiefdoms of ethnically concentrated tenements—Italians battling blacks battling Puerto Ricans battling Irish—it made sense for the musical's central conflict to be updated.

When did the city's postwar decline set in?

New York's period of deepest and most publicly acknowledged malaise came in the 1970s. However, the sense that things were going wrong began years earlier. A case in point was the article by Nathan Glazer (1923–), "Is New York City Ungovernable?," a shot across the municipal bow from the September 1, 1961, *Commentary*. While Glazer's piece wasn't nearly as apocalyptic as the title suggested, he pointed out several creeping tendrils of decay that would sprout more malignantly in the following decade. His primary concern was the growth of ever-bigger and ever more sclerotic bureaucracies.

According to Glazer's research, the city's Board of Education taught 1.06 million schoolchildren in 1940 with about 37,600 teachers and support personnel; twenty years later it took more workers (45,700) to educate fewer students (980,000) less adequately. Similarly, between 1946 and 1961, the police department expanded its payroll by thirty five percent (20,171 employees to 27,239), while the city's population grew only about four percent, crime worsened, *and* public respect for officers declined. (Glazer believed that this last change was due at least in part to the police focusing on "vindictive hounding of Greenwich Village coffee houses and bookstores" and the "entrapment of prostitutes and homosexuals" instead of public safety.)

What was the first building to bear the Trump name?

Fred Trump had started his own construction company while still a teenager and by the late 1920s was building single-family homes in Queens. Aggressive and penny-pinching, he became one of the most important developers in postwar New York, building over 27,000, often government-funded, apartments and houses in a swath of working- and middle-class neighborhoods across Queens and Brooklyn. In 1964, he opened the first building to bear his family name: Trump Village is a complex of seven twenty-three-story brick towers in Coney Island packed with thousands of sturdy, unpretentious units. As typical as it is of Fred Trump's housing preferences, Trump Village couldn't be more

Who are the Shmira?

After World War II, many members of the ultra-conservative Jewish sect the Lubavitchers began moving into the Brooklyn neighborhood of Crown Heights. In response to fears about crime in the neighborhood, in 1964, they formed a neighborhood watch. Initially known as the Crown Heights Maccabees (for the fierce Old Testament warriors of Israel) and later splitting into two rival groups, the Shmira and Shomrim, the watch became a kind of unarmed auxiliary police force, complete with their own uniforms, dispatch system, and patrol cars. Controversy in the form of charges of race-based vigilantism and corruption has followed both groups over the years. Still, the city in general and NYPD in specific has adopted a generally hands-off approach.

different in style from the glitzy condo towers and hotels his son Donald would later become famous for. Eventually, the unassuming developer (known to worry enough about costs that he would pick up unused nails at his construction sights and later return them to his workers) amassed a fortune of over $250 million and a network of political connections, both of which played a key role in Donald Trump's rise to power.

Who was Kitty Genovese?

Late on a March evening in 1964, a twenty-eight-year-old barmaid named Kitty Genovese was walking to her apartment building in Kew Gardens, Queens, when she was viciously raped and stabbed to death. The story that grew up around the attack, promulgated initially by the *New York Times*'s zealous metro editor A.M. Rosenthal and then closely tracked by the *Times*-following local media, was that Genovese's screams for help went on for a half hour and were ignored by the thirty-eight people who listened and did nothing.

The worldwide horror over this apparent sign of criminal apathy helped create the 911 emergency response system. Genovese's story turned from scorching headline outrage to outraged books (Rosenthal's *38 Witnesses* among them) and case studies in sociology and psychology texts, which began talking of concepts like "the bystander effect" that kept normally conscientious people from acting morally in groups. The narrative of apathy expressed the fears of a nation then rapidly deurbanizing—in the city, nobody hears you scream, and even if they do, they don't give a damn. Later mostly debunked— at least two neighbors actually tried to help, and most of the "witnesses" couldn't see anything—the Genovese story remains one of those parables of the alienation of urban life that will probably outlive anybody's living memory.

Why were tens of thousands of girls screaming at Shea Stadium on August 15, 1965?

That would be because the Beatles were playing there. It was the pinnacle of their barnstorming American tour and the first concert at the nearly brand-new ballpark (acts from Bruce Springsteen to Stevie Wonder would later play there). The concert was so successful that the Beatles returned the following August for yet more pandemonium. That was actually the term the *New York Times* used to describe the reaction of the largely teen and pre-teen female audience: "Their immature lungs produced a sound so staggering, so massive, so shrill and sustained that it quickly crossed the line from enthusiasm into hysteria ... the classic Greek meaning of the word pandemonium—the region of all demons." The crowd's noise was so deafening, the writer noted, that it was nearly impossible for anybody to hear the band they had all paid $5.10 to see play for just a half hour.

Pope Paul VI was the first leader of the Catholic Church to visit New York City, which he did in 1965.

Who was the first pope to visit New York?

Pope Paul VI (1897–1978) was the first head of the Catholic Church to visit the Western Hemisphere. He arrived in New York on October 4, 1965, and spent just over half a day in the city. Perhaps because of the attenuated duration of his visit, the pent-up desire to get a glimpse of the pontiff was even higher-pitched. Millions lined the streets, jostling with some 18,000 police officers fighting to hold back the crowds along the twenty-five-mile route of his procession through the city. Security precautions included bartenders asked to report customers expressing extreme anti-Catholicism, and religious-supply stores requested to inform the police about anybody making unusual cassock purchases. At the United Nations, the pope delivered a passionate plea for nuclear disarmament. He also stopped into St. Patrick's Cathedral, met with President Lyndon Johnson (1908–1973) at the Waldorf Astoria, and celebrated mass with 90,000 people at Yankee Stadium; hot dogs were on sale at the stadium, but no beer.

THE SIXTIES TO 9/11

How did a police raid on a gay bar lead to the Stonewall Uprising?

In the 1960s, police raids on gay bars were commonplace. Arrests were frequently based on flimsy evidence of "lewd conduct" or an 1845 law against "masquerading" that specifically targeted gay men in drag or lesbians in supposedly male-only clothing. The constant threats of imprisonment and public humiliation at a time of extreme prejudice against gay people resulted in a build-up of resentment that, combined with the decade's anti-police sentiment, was bound to explode at some point.

On the night of June 28, 1969, a small number of officers tried to raid the Stonewall Inn, a Mafia-operated bar in the heart of the Village's gay district at 57 Christopher Street. Several things were different that night. First, there were more patrons on hand, since for some reason the police hadn't followed their usual practice of tipping off the owners and raiding during less-busy times. The combination of pent-up rage against police harassment, a hot Saturday night, and larger crowds culminated in an explosive reaction against the arresting officers. In short order, the police were forced to barricade themselves inside the Stonewall while hundreds and possibly thousands of mostly gay protestors raged outside. Eventually the NYPD's Tactical Patrol Force, armed with riot shields and nightclubs, arrived on the scene. The result was a pitched battle of smashed windows, trash-can fires, numerous arrests, and bloodied protestors that went on for several nights.

What was the result of the Stonewall Uprising?

More than one participant in the Stonewall protests referred to it as the gay rights movement's "Rosa Parks moment," after which nothing would be the same. Though seen today as a civil rights watershed moment, at the time the protests were happening they received little news attention. A headline in the *New York Daily News* gives an idea of the mainstream press's dismissive coverage: "Homo Nest Raided, Queen Bees Are Stinging Mad." Prior to Stonewall, the gay rights movement was mostly composed of "homophile" groups like the Mattachine Society, which advocated slow and steady progress.

The day after the first night of rioting, a leaflet distributed by the "Homophile Youth Movement" was a call to "Get the Mafia and the Cops Out of Gay Bars" and demanded that Mayor John Lindsay take action "to correct this intolerable situation." The most visible result of the Stonewall Uprising occurred on June 28, 1970, when the Christopher Street Liberation Day march from the Village to Central Park celebrated its one-year anniversary.

A photo of the Stonewall Inn taken a couple months after the June 1969 riots; in the window is written, "We homosexuals plead with our people to please help maintain peaceful and quiet conduct on the streets of the Village."

The idea of an open-and-proud parade for gay people and supporters quickly spread. Today there are Gay Pride Parades held every June in hundreds of locations around the world. In 2016, Stonewall Inn was designated a National Monument.

Who were the New York 21?

The Black Panther Party for Self Defense is primarily associated with Oakland, California, where it was formed in 1966. Black activists in that city who were frustrated with police brutality created a self-defense league that courted controversy by showing up at government buildings and trailing the police while openly carrying firearms. This was legal under California law. But the appearance of armed, self-professed black revolutionaries in their eye-catching militaristic hipster uniform of black leather jackets, black berets, and heavy scowls quickly stoked controversy in political and law enforcement circles. As Black Panther outfits began popping up all over the country, they attracted the attention of federal law enforcement, particularly the FBI's J. Edgar Hoover, who ordered a nationwide campaign to disrupt, discredit, and dismantle the organization.

This campaign came to fruition in New York in 1969, when twenty-one Black Panther leaders in the city were charged with conspiracy to commit murder after they attacked numerous public places, including police stations, department stores, and the Bronx Botanical Gardens. Given the concerted effort to destroy the Black Panthers, and how infiltrated with informers their organization had become, the charges were assumed by most on the political left to be completely without merit. The legal defense fund for the "New York 21" became a cause célèbre. Activist lawyer du jour William Kunstler (1919–1995) involved himself in the case and several liberal celebrities helped to raise funds for the "Panther 21." One of the more famous such parties was an Upper West Side soirée in 1970 hosted by the Maestro himself, Leonard Bernstein (1918–1990). The mix of (white) uptown high society and (black) activists made for one of those snapshot moments that seemed to encapsulate a certain moment in a time of volatile cultural and political conflicts. It was memorably immortalized in a lengthy, savagely satirical report by Tom Wolfe (1930–) that appeared in the June 8, 1970, issue of *New York* and coined the term "radical chic" to mockingly describe the scene of white socialites fawning over leather-jacketed Panthers.

Who were the Young Lords?

Taking their cues from the Black Panther Party, the Young Lords were a politically active Marxist Puerto Rican street gang from Chicago whose New York offshoot announced its formation on July 26, 1969, in Tompkins Square Park. Like the Panthers, the often armed Young Lords focused their activism on addressing issues like police brutality and lower income neighborhoods' lack of access to many city services, believing much of it was motivated by institutional racism. Their actions included occupying hospitals to protest substandard conditions; garbage-dumping campaigns, in which they built street-blocking barricades out of garbage bags that hadn't been collected by the city; and even helping to pass anti-lead poisoning legislation. Also like the Panthers, the Young Lords—

likely because of their support of Puerto Rican independence and revolutionary rhetoric—were aggressively targeted by law enforcement and (perhaps as a result) crumbled during the early 1970s.

What was the "Hard Hat Riot"?

Following the killings of four student protesters at Kent State by National Guardsmen on May 4, 1970, Mayor Lindsay ordered flags lowered in New York. On May 8, several hundred anti-Vietnam War protestors gathered at Federal Hall on Wall Street. To the surprise of just about everybody, a couple hundred construction workers who had left their work sites (including the World Trade Center) appeared carrying American flags and a lot of resentment against the mostly young student protestors. After words were thrown back and forth, some of the construction workers broke through a line of police. Most accounts of the so-called "Hard Hat Riot" note that the police seemed in no hurry to do anything as the workers attacked the protestors. It was one of the most vivid examples of the ways in which the war and accompanying cultural changes were upending traditional alliances, with predominantly white blue-collar workers aligning themselves with the establishment. One construction worker told the *Wall Street Journal* afterward, "I'm doing this because my brother got wounded in Vietnam, and I think this will help our boys over there by pulling this country together."

President Richard Nixon (1913–1994) was said to be very happy about this unexpected development, believing it signaled the existence of a large and angry white working class—the frustrations of whom in the New York area specifically were eloquently and elegiacally encapsulated in Pete Hamill's epoch-defining 1969 article "The Revolt of the White Lower Middle Class"—whose pro-war sentiments would help keep him in office.

What did the fire department call their "War Years"?

Starting in the 1960s, the congruence of multiple negative factors hitting New York simultaneously—from tightening budgets to rapidly rising rates of crime numbers of vacant buildings (from 2,900 in 1965 to 4,344 by 1969)—led to the FDNY having to fight more fires than ever before. The number of fires more than doubled from 61,644 in 1961 to 127,249 in 1970. Arson cases skyrocketed as well, as did the number of false alarms and firefighters who were attacked while riding to and from fighting fires.

Making matters worse for the FDNY was the disastrous reallocation of resources in the 1960s, based on a flawed analysis by the RAND Corporation, and budget cuts in 1975 that dissolved thirty-two fire companies. Politics intervened for the worse, meaning that less-needed firehouses in wealthier neighborhoods stayed open while poorer areas saw their firehouses shuttered at a dangerous rate. All together, these problems fed into a sense that the city was essentially abandoning some areas (like the arson-targeted Bronx). The frantic pace of firefighting during the 1960s and 1970s, with dwindling resources in a city that seemed increasingly hostile to any kind of authority, led to the era being referred to as the "War Years."

What project started in 1970 is not yet completed?

The largest capital construction project in New York history was planned in 1954 and started in 1970, but almost none of its residents will ever see it. Given the prosaic title of City Water Tunnel No. 3, the project is just that: a massive water tunnel that will eventually dramatically increase the city's water capacity and also provide backup in case either of the two earlier, aging tunnels ever failed. The first thirteen-mile (twenty-one-kilometer) stage, from Hillview Reservoir in Yonkers down into Manhattan and then to Queens, didn't open until 1998. Two additional stages opened in 2008 and 2013. The whole project is expected to be finished sometime in the 2020s. So far, the project has cost $6 billion and taken the lives of twenty-four "sandhogs" (the construction workers who specialize in deep underground tunneling).

What did Frank Serpico and David Durk discover?

Frank Serpico (1936–) and David Durk (1935–2012) were New York police officers who, in the 1960s, became disgusted with the endemic spread of graft and venality in their department. Diametrically opposed in style and background—Serpico was a shaggy-haired Korean War veteran, Brooklyn native, and bohemian plainclothes detective who lived in Greenwich Village, while Durk was a clean-cut Amherst graduate—the men shared a belief that corruption and the so-called "blue wall of silence" that stopped police from talking about it were sabotaging everything the department stood for.

Starting in 1967, Serpico and Durk provided detailed complaints to their superiors in the police department, as well as the mayor's office. Nothing happened. Serpico claimed that not only had his on-the-record complaints been ignored, but that he was directly asked to keep things quiet by people from the office of Mayor Lindsay, who was considering running for the presidency at the time. Frustrated with the inaction, the two men ultimately went to the press. Their complaints went public with an explosive front-page story in the *New York Times* on April 23, 1970, which detailed their allegations about just how deeply corrupt the NYPD had become. The two men became instant pariahs in the department for breaking the code of silence. The bestselling book by Peter Maas, *Serpico: The Cop Who Defied the System*, which mostly ignored Durk's role, was turned into a popular and award-winning Sidney Lumet film in 1973 starring Al Pacino in the title role.

Frank Serpico (from a 2013 photo) blew the whistle on corruption in the New York Police Department in the 1960s.

What was "scatter-site housing"?

During the 1960s and 1970s, the lack of both affordable housing and housing for those on assistance in New York had become a serious problem. While that could arguably be said for any time in New York since pigs were still being used for garbage disposal in Five Points, the 1970s saw the issue reach crisis levels in part because of the political, racial, and social fault lines it exposed in the city's fraying municipal alliance. One of the driving factors behind this was the relatively new push for so-called "scatter-site housing." Starting in 1965, the Department of Housing and Urban Development (HUD) enacted a rule stating that cities wanting federal grants had to use part of the money to build housing outside of heavily poor, minority neighborhoods. The idea came in part from the federal government's success in enforcing racial integration in southern institutions like schools. It was believed that the best way to integrate northern cities like New York was to scatter housing for low-income residents (who were believed to be primarily minorities) in white neighborhoods. This caused many racially charged skirmishes throughout the city.

Which politicians came to prominence during the Forest Hills controversy?

One of the most explosive fights over scatter-site housing began in 1971 when the city announced plans to build an 840-unit housing project in Forest Hills, a middle-class Jewish enclave in Queens. Outraged residents—some of whom thought the location had been chosen in the belief that traditionally liberal Jewish residents would welcome the project—furiously protested, even shadowing Mayor Lindsay on his ill-fated presidential campaign swing through Florida. Lawyer Mario Cuomo (1932–2015) was brought in to broker a compromise to the bruising fight, which ultimately constituted several smaller buildings for elderly residents that would ideally be better integrated with the neighborhood.

The controversy grew so heated that it may have caused the Nixon administration to change HUD policy to simple cash subsidies for low-income people so they could find housing wherever they could. Cuomo, whose visibility in the Forest Hills battle helped launch his political career, later wrote that it was a "real tragedy … [that] will not teach, but will only intimidate." Congressman Edward Koch (1924–2013), who had been a staunchly liberal voice in Greenwich Village for years, surprised the Democratic establishment by loudly throwing his support behind the Forest Hills protestors. Bruising as it was, the controversy raised the profile of both Cuomo and Koch, who in the next decade would become prominent New York leaders in almost diametrically opposed ways.

Who was the first famous New York graffiti artist?

The popular imagination of graffiti begins in the 1970s. But the art of marking buildings with spray-painted text or images dates back at least to World War II, when "Kilroy was Here" started popping up in the subway. Modern graffiti is generally believed to have started in Philadelphia during the 1960s. It quickly spread to New York, where messages ranging from a simple signature to a phrase ("Frodo Lives!") began appearing on the sides of buildings or subway trains.

The first star graffiti artist was a Greek-American teenager from Washington Heights named Demetrius (like many of the artists who followed him, he kept his last name secret), who started putting up his tag "TAKI 183" all over town with felt-tip markers. Interviewed by the *New York Times* in 1971, Demetrius noted that he actually got the idea from another artist, JULIO 204, and that he didn't have any particular agenda or theory behind his work.

When did graffiti become ubiquitous in New York?

By around 1973, graffiti—whether from a tag (text and/or image signature), throw-up (two-color outlined text), or piece (those massive full-color murals that cover entire sides of buildings)—was embedded in the city's visual landscape. Subway cars in particular were covered in graffiti and the cash-strapped city was spending over $1 million a year cleaning it up. By the time Norman Mailer (1923–2007) published "The Faith of Graffiti" in the May 1974 *Esquire*, graffiti was solidly associated with urban decay and collapse, leading Mailer to ponder in typically grandiose fashion that perhaps "the unheard echo of graffiti … is the herald of some oncoming apocalypse."

During the mid-to-late 1970s, graffiti became strongly associated with the city's hip-hop music scene. It was a visual cliché of the era in film and TV to signify urban grit or New York simply by showing a graffiti-covered subway car, preferably with hip-hop and police sirens playing in the background. In 1984, a frustrated MTA announced that it was pulling all subway cars with graffiti from service. Increased surveillance pushed most graffiti artists out of the subway by 1990. The argument over whether graffiti was a legitimate art form or sheer vandalism continued for years, even after downtown art galleries began exhibiting and commissioning artists' work.

How long has it taken to build the Second Avenue subway?

In an episode of *Mad Men* set in 1968, a character says "believe me, when they finish the Second Avenue subway, this apartment will quadruple in value." Most New Yorkers watching the show groaned, because they knew exactly what the writers knew: that by the time the show aired in 2013, the Second Avenue subway would be nowhere near completed. A devilish combination of bad timing, budgetary woes, and the challenges of building in one of the most densely populated stretches of the city have turned this plan into an epic saga. Here's a brief timeline:

Artist TAKI 183 (right) at an art exhibition. He became famous in the 1970s for his work.

Year	Event
1929	The city proposes a new subway line to run from downtown up to the Harlem River along Second Avenue. The Great Depression puts that idea on hold.
1942/1955	The Second and Third Avenue elevated lines are torn down. This increases overcrowding on the Lexington Avenue (the 4/5/6) line, today the single most used mass transit line in the country.
1972	Construction begins.
1974	Construction stops because of budget issues.
2007	Construction begins, again, on the four-phase plan.
January 2017	Phase 1 (63rd to 96th streets) opened.
2019	Tunneling to start on Phase 2 (96th to 125th streets).
Uncertain	Completion of Phase 3 (63rd to Houston streets) and Phase 4 (Houston Street to Hanover Square).

Whenever and if it is finally completed, the Second Avenue Subway is supposed to comprise 8.5 miles (13.6 kilometers) of track and sixteen new stations stretching from Lower Manhattan and Chinatown all the way up through the East Village to the Upper East Side and Harlem. Today's riders on the ever-crowded 4/5/6 trains will all agree that that date can't come too soon.

Whose idea was the World Trade Center?

Fittingly, the impetus for the twin colossus that redefined downtown Manhattan for an entire generation originated with David Rockefeller (1915–), whose father, John D. Rockefeller, Jr. (1874–1960), had transformed Midtown with Rockefeller Center. During the 1940s and 1950s, he worked his way up the executive ladder at Chase Manhattan Bank, then one of the most powerful financial institutions in the world. So in 1960, when David led the push to create a world trade and finance center that would revitalize downtown Manhattan, the idea was given serious consideration. The Port Authority of New York and New Jersey agreed to the plan, as did David's son, New York governor Nelson Rockefeller (1908–1979). Construction began in 1966 on a small sixteen-acre site bounded by Vesey, Liberty, and Church streets; its west border, now West Street, which separates the site from the World Financial Center, was the Hudson River.

How big a project was the World Trade Center?

Everything connected to the World Trade Center was massive. To build it, 164 buildings were demolished, annihilating both the neighborhoods of Little Syria and an electronics district known as Radio Row. Excavation down to 70 feet (21 meters) produced over a million cubic feet (28,300 cubic meters) of earth; it was dumped to the west and north as the landfill on which the development of Battery Park City was planted. A seven-story deep "Bathtub" was dug under the Twin Towers' nine-acre footprint and an innovative "slurry wall" created to hold back the river water seeping through lower Manhattan's porous bedrock. Its final cost was a nearly unprecedented $1.5 billion.

In order to maximize office space (the plans called for ten million square feet [929,000 square meters]), architect Minoru Yamasaki (1912–1986) needed multiple tall towers on a small footprint. His imaginative design called for a light and mostly hollow tube-like structure where the strong steel columns forming its walls carried the weight. When the two 110-story buildings were finished in 1973, they were the tallest in the world. The towers, which would eventually be joined by four other buildings, had their own zip code and were said to use enough electricity on their own to power all of Schenectady, New York.

What were the main problems of the World Trade Center?

There were a few. The most immediately obvious one was that its nine million square feet (836,000 square meters) of office space wasn't needed. From the day it opened, the World Trade Center had a difficult time filling its floors. In order to attract more tenants, the Port Authority discounted rental prices. This had the perverse effect of taking tenants away from surrounding buildings, which further depressed the neighborhood that the World Trade Center was supposed to revive.

Also, Yamasaki's design, while groundbreaking, was, to put it mildly, inhuman at first glance. The two towers were certainly awe-inspiring in their size and bulk, but ultimately cold. One wag referred to the style as "General Motors Gothic." Architecture critic Ada Louise Huxtable (1921–2013) wrote that they "could be the start of a new skyscraper age or the biggest tombstones in the world." Eventually, if grudgingly, the city came around to the towers, particularly once the observation deck opened in 1975. Their unmistakable profile on the city skyline soon became an instantly recognizable symbol of New York business might and optimism.

How did a French circus performer walk a tightrope between the World Trade Center towers?

By breaking in. Philippe Petit (1949–) was a puckish French circus trickster who, after seeing a picture of the nearly finished World Trade Center towers, became obsessed with the idea of doing the most impressive high-wire act of all time at 110 stories in the sky. In 1974, Petit, with his girlfriend and a ragtag band of accomplices, began work on what he called his

The iconic twin towers dominated the New York skyline from 1973 until the terrorist attacks of 2001.

"coup." Dressed in disguises, they visited the WTC's construction site dozens of times to plan their caper. Then on August 6, Petit's team snuck into the towers and made their way to the roof, avoiding notice by wandering security guards. They worked in secret overnight to fasten up Petit's heavy walking wire (strung between the two buildings by shooting an arrow over).

At 7 A.M., Petit stepped out into open sky with no safety wire and spent forty-five minutes walking back and forth, even kneeling and lying down on the wire at various points. After finishing his walk, Petit was arrested for criminal trespass and disorderly conduct. The charges were dropped that afternoon in exchange for his agreeing to do a far-less-insane tightrope walk for kids in Central Park. The World Trade Center owners gave Petit a lifetime pass to the observation deck with the expiration date crossed out and replaced with the word "Forever."

How close did New York come to financial collapse?

Less than an hour away. The contributing elements of New York's fiscal crisis had been accruing for years, hidden from notice by ingenious accounting. They all came to the fore with calamitous urgency in 1974, not long after Abraham Beame (1906–2001) was elected mayor. A longtime Brooklyn Democratic operative, Beame had little time to savor his historic role as the city's first Jewish mayor. In the previous decade, expenses had soared and the city had taken on billions in debt to pay for it all. Simply servicing the city's debt was going to swallow billions of dollars it didn't have. The city also found it increasingly difficult to borrow money. By the end of 1974, the city's credit rating was

---

Did the president actually tell New York to "drop dead"?

Not in so many words, no. The front page of the *New York Daily News* on October 30, 1975, was a two-line hammer that would go down in history: "FORD TO CITY: DROP DEAD." The subhead, "Vows He'll Veto Any Bail-Out," tells the real story. Fearing a default, a coalition of city officials and business and labor leaders, joined by many other nervous mayors, vigorously lobbied the federal government for assistance. They worried that a default by the nation's financial capital would be devastating in both real and symbolic terms and set a dangerous precedent for a country already riven with economic anxiety.

The Republican administration of President Gerald Ford (1913–2006) pushed back in the belief that bailing out New York would in effect legitimize what it saw as profligate Democratic spending habits. The *Daily News* headline both encapsulated how embittered New Yorkers were by Ford's refusal and tied him forever to a quote that he never actually uttered. The latter was particularly galling to Ford since he soon reversed his decision and loaned the city $500 million, allowing it to (again) barely escape bankruptcy by the end of the year.

in danger and Beame believed that he would potentially have to lay off thousands of municipal employees.

The following April, a last-minute $400 million state loan was required to keep the city afloat. In the summer of 1975, the city began cutting services and raising transit fees to save money. Police officers protested and sanitation workers let the garbage pile up in the streets in protest. By the fall, the crisis was reaching its climax. On October 17, the city was officially about to run out of cash to meet its debt obligations. Administration officials put together their bankruptcy plan, which included police officers standing by to serve legal papers on the banks who had loaned the city most of its debt. In a film-worthy last-minute escape, an ad-hoc team of private citizens and municipal officials negotiated a loan of about $150 million from the teacher's union pension fund that kept the lights on with just less than an hour to spare. This dramatic rescue was also a troubling harbinger for a city that would be faced with a series of other potentially existential crises over the next few years. Historian George J. Lankevich wrote that in October 1975, "for perhaps the first time in two centuries, the city on the Hudson was clearly an underdog."

Where did the term "Fear City" originate?

In June 1975, several unions representing New York employees were infuriated by Mayor Beame's plans to balance the city's books by laying off many of their members. In response, a group backed by police and fire fighter unions, called the Council for Public Safety, produced and distributed nearly a million copies of a pamphlet titled "Welcome to Fear City: A Survival Guide for Visitors to the City of New York" and emblazoned it with a skull wearing a Grim Reaper-like black shroud. The point of this tongue-in-cheek guidebook ("If you must leave your hotel after 6 P.M., try not to go out alone … ask the doorman to call a taxi while you remain in the hotel lobby") was to strike back at the city leadership by terrifying tourists into staying away, thus depriving the city of badly needed revenue.

Was New York really that dangerous at the time?

Yes, and no. The city wasn't *quite* the wasteland portrayed by "Fear City" (itself a mocking play on a Mayor Lindsay quote about New York being "fun city") and the sub-genre of films about New York going to the dogs and its denizens left to fend for themselves (*The Warriors*, *Death Wish*). But daily life was absolutely more chaotic and crime-filled than it had been for many years. Murders more than doubled in the ten years from 1965 (681) to 1975 (1,690) and less violent crimes like robberies and vandalism skyrocketed as well.

What happened to New York's murder rate in the postwar years?

Murder rates in New York, like in any other city, have had their peaks and valleys throughout history. Killings briefly rose in the middle of the Civil War, then didn't rise again significantly until the early twentieth century's great explosion in population. They spiked during Prohibition for perhaps obvious reasons and then dropped again for several decades. Starting in the 1960s, though, the number of homicides mounted each year as a kind of dark statistical certainty.

The worst year in New York history for murders was 1990. That year, a staggering 2,245 people were murdered. For comparison, that is an average of six murders a day, or nearly as many combat deaths as the American military suffered in the Afghanistan war. After 1990, however, the murder rate steadily declined. The reasons for the decline are multifarious and still being argued about today. But the numbers were as inarguable as they were welcome. Even though the drop in homicides was mirrored around the country, rates had actually fallen faster per capita in New York. On Monday, November 26, 2012, the city saw something not witnessed in living memory: a twenty-four-hour period with not only zero murders but without a single reported violent crime. By 2013, the mayor's office was announcing that New York was officially the safest city in the country. At the end of 2014, the city had seen 334 murders for the entire year, the lowest since the NYPD began keeping track in 1963.

How big was the 1976 Bicentennial in New York?

Landing right in the middle of New York's darkest period, between the 1975 near-bankruptcy and the 1977 blackout riots, the country's Bicentennial celebration in 1976 was a rare moment in that decade during which the city at least appeared to unite in a burst of civic and national pride. One could argue correctly that all the bunting and hoopla merely obscured deep fissures in the body politic. At the same time, one could also argue that in the midst of so much uncertainty and strife, the city just plain needed a break. That doesn't mean it came easy. A private corporation set up to organize the celebration quickly ran out of funds and had to lobby for more from a city that could barely afford it.

But the Bicentennial was seen as a moment for New York to shine once it had been chosen as the national host for the celebrations after both Philadelphia and Washington, D.C.'s plans failed to measure up. The selection of New York "was not illogical," the *New York Daily News* noted later. After all, New York was the nation's first capital and the site of the first major battle of the Revolutionary War. Historic buildings and piers downtown were spruced up in anticipation of the tourists from around the world who were expected to throng the city on July 4.

What was the Bicentennial's main attraction?

The main attraction of the Bicentennial, and its most remembered symbol today, was Operation Sail '76. Five years in the making, this was a massive and dramatic parade of 228 sailing ships (the largest such fleet assembled in modern history), 53 naval ships, and hundreds more assorted small boats that sailed majestically up the Hudson River from the Verrazano Narrows Bridge while hundreds of thousands of onlookers cheered and waved flags on both shores. In a sign of magnanimity from former and then-current rivals, the Queen of England attended and two tall ships from the Soviet Union took part in the naval procession. Everything culminated on July 6, with fireworks downtown and a parade that used so much ticker tape that snowplows were needed to clear it from the streets. The Bicentennial in New York was widely viewed as a bright spot in a tough decade. "I've never seen the city like this," a New Jersey man told the *New York Times*. "Everyone feels so united."

Were there any long-term effects from the Bicentennial?

Besides wall-to-wall media coverage of a spruced-up city and generally problem-free celebrations for the Bicentennial, New York was given another gift in 1976: The Democratic Convention that August. Both events presented a counter-narrative to the standard view of New York as the big, scary city where visitors should tread only warily (see Neil Simon's *The Out-of-Towners* for just one of many examples of that fear). Tourism, which had been in decline since at least 1970, began to inch back up, even with minimal support from a still-strapped city. In 1976, tourism was the city's second-biggest industry, supporting hundreds of thousands of jobs. The following year, the city saw its highest number of visitors since 1969.

What caused the blackout of 1977?

Around 8:30 P.M. on July 13, 1977, lightning struck high-voltage lines in Westchester County. A half-hour later, another lightning strike hit transmission lines in Yonkers. These two events put an enormous strain on the rest of the power grid, which was already taxed by the hundred-degree-plus temperatures. Operators at the utility Con Edison struggled to balance the system, but nothing worked. One after another, the overloaded circuit breakers were overwhelmed. A little after 9:30 P.M., the power went out across all of New York. Power wasn't restored for over twenty-four hours.

Why was the post-blackout looting so extreme?

Many comparisons have been drawn between the two other major blackouts of recent decades in New York: the blackout of 1965 that saw the power go out all across the

---

After the blackout of 1977 began, how long did it take for looting to begin?

Within minutes of the power going out, there were reports of widespread looting from Midtown to uptown Manhattan to the Bronx, Brooklyn, and Queens. Within an hour, the windows of a Pontiac dealership in the Bronx were smashed and fifty cars driven away. Some looters used chains hooked to their cars' bumpers to tear down store security gates. Many stores were then burned. Over the course of the blackout looting, several thousand people were arrested, hundreds of millions of dollars of damage incurred, and the economic spine of several neighborhoods devastated for years to follow. It was the biggest explosion of mayhem in New York during the twentieth century and the largest mass arrest in the city's entire history.

Northeast and the blackout of 2003 which also hit parts of Canada and much of the Eastern seaboard. In both of those events, the response in New York was relatively calm. Many New Yorkers who experienced them tell stories of a laid-back, school's-out atmosphere, with ad-hoc get-togethers by candlelight and a sense of camaraderie. There are stories of average citizens appointing themselves traffic police to direct cars at intersections without traffic lights. By comparison, the speed with which parts of the city plunged into near-anarchy in 1977 stands out.

Many theories have been proffered, the most likely culprit being a mix of factors like the scorching heat and already-high crime rates (in 1976, the city logged seventy-five felonies *every hour*), as well as class and financial issues. In addition, the city was in worse economic shape in 1977. It was deeply in debt, had lost over 350,000 jobs in the previous few years, and had been forced to slash social services and fire and police protection. All of these factors particularly impacted those lower-income neighborhoods where looting was most rampant. An accelerating factor was that when the NYPD issued a call for all off-duty officers to report in that night, they were told not to go to their usual precinct houses, but whatever precinct was closest to them. Since the majority of officers didn't live in the poorer neighborhoods most afflicted by looters, those areas were perversely among the least-policed parts of the city.

When was the Son of Sam caught?

On July 28, 1976, a mentally disturbed man who heard voices that ordered him to commit murder walked up to a parked car in the Bronx and shot the two young women sitting inside, one fatally. Over the next year, David Berkowitz (1953–) terrorized the city with random murders, frequently of young women, committed with a .44 revolver. By the following summer, stoked by letters Berkowitz sent to the police and *Daily News* columnist Jimmy Breslin (1929–), media coverage of "The .44 Killer" and later "The Son of Sam" (how Berkowitz signed his notes) was approaching a frenzy and the city was in panic. Because Berkowitz often targeted women with long brown hair, many women dyed their hair and cut it short. Nightclubs were deserted.

By the time Berkowitz was finally arrested on August 10, 1977, the city—already pushed to the brink by the blackout rioting, the heat wave, and then on August 3, the bombing of two Midtown office buildings by the Puerto Rican terrorist group FALN—was on the verge of a kind of collective nervous collapse. Berkowitz was given six twenty-five-years-to-life sentences, one for each murder he confessed to.

Part of the first Son of Sam letter that was sent to the NYPD.

Did the Bronx actually burn?

One of the most symbolic and enduring moments of late-1970s New York occurred at Yankee Stadium on October 12, 1977. It was game two of the World Series and the Yankees were locked in a grueling struggle with the Los Angeles Dodgers. Before the game began, a fire had started in an abandoned school a few blocks away from the stadium. By nightfall, flames were visible from the broadcast booth. ABC's broadcast of the game cut away to overhead footage from a news helicopter showing the raging fire. Broadcaster Howard Cosell (1918–1995) supposedly immortalized the moment by intoning, "Ladies and gentlemen, the Bronx is burning." The five-alarm fire added to an already-palpable sense of chaos in the stadium; play had to be repeatedly stopped because of debris being thrown from the stands and police chasing errant fans around the field.

It was later argued that Cosell never actually uttered that line; a writer for the *New York Post* called it his "Play It Again, Sam" moment. It still stuck in the public imagination because, in general, the Bronx *was* burning. In the years leading up to that night, an interlocking lattice of poor planning and economic fallout mixed with greed to produce a crisis in the borough. White flight led to slumlords packing poor families into poorly maintained buildings that would sometimes be allowed to deteriorate so radically that owners resorted to arson to collect insurance money. Also, Mayor Lindsay's administration, using new but faulty computer models to determine FDNY resource allocation, had closed many stations around the Bronx. The number of fires quickly exceeded the city's ability to fight them. The number of burnt-out blocks increased year after year, making parts of the South Bronx resemble post-war Berlin and symbolize the nation's worst fears about urban decay.

Where did the biggest cash robbery in New York history take place?

Not at a bank or the Federal Reserve or even the "money train"—the well-guarded subway trains that used to collect cash from token booths at random times and were the occasional target of thieves—but at John F. Kennedy Airport. In July 1978, Henry Hill (1943–2012), a Lucchese crime family member, who was involved in everything from truck hijacking to loan sharking and arson, was released from prison after serving time for extortion. Not long after, he got a tip for a possible score from an airport employee: At the Lufthansa cargo vault, there were often millions of dollars in $50 and $100 bills (a return of currency exchanged by Americans in Europe) left overnight under very light guard before being taken to the bank in the morning. On the morning of December 11, Hill's friend Jimmy "The Gent" Burke (1931–1996) and several associates held six employees at gunpoint before making off with $6.25 million in cash, plus heaps of valuable jewelry; they had only expected about $2 million.

The heist should have ended up making everybody involved rich. But the paranoia it engendered caused a wave of murders that drew law enforcement attention. Hill was arrested and, in exchange for being taken into the Witness Protection Program, agreed in 1980 to testify as a government witness against his former associates; Burke was sentenced to life. The story of the Lufthansa heist was popularized in Nicholas Pileggi's

(1933–) book about Hill, *Wiseguy*, which was adapted by Martin Scorsese (1942–) for the 1990 film *Goodfellas*.

How did Ed Koch become mayor?

In retrospect, nobody would have picked out Edward Koch (1924–2013) as a potential mayor of New York, much less a transformative one who served three terms. A diminutive, media-savvy, and gleefully argumentative iconoclast, Koch was born to Polish Jewish parents in the Bronx in 1924 and raised in Newark. He moved to Greenwich Village in 1956 and spent the rest of his life there except for a few years when he grudgingly agreed to move into the mayoral residence at Gracie Mansion. Koch built his unlikely career by leading the reformist Village Independent Democrats to defeat the last Tammany Hall boss, Carmine DeSapio (1908–2004), for Village district leader in 1961. Koch was elected to the city council in 1966 and represented the wealthy but liberal Upper East Side "Silk Stocking District" in Congress from 1969 to 1977.

Having spent his early career advocating for liberal causes, in the 1970s Koch tacked sharply to the right on a few issues. This wasn't unusual for many white liberals during the decade, after the fraying of the traditional black and Jewish coalition, the fiscal chaos of the Abe Beame administration, and the physical chaos of the 1977 blackout. In his run for mayor that year, Koch broke with his old constituency on law and order issues. Positioning himself as the "liberal with sanity," he called to bring back the death penalty. After a slugfest of a campaign, which included Koch pushing for the death penalty and trawling the city in a Winnebago blaring the song "N.Y.C." from *Annie*, he beat six opponents for the Democratic nomination, including Mario Cuomo and Beame, and demolished the Republican candidate, little-known talk-show host Barry Farber (1930–).

What lost Koch the 1982 race for governor?

Having bested Mario Cuomo in the mayoral campaign, Koch may have thought that he could beat him as well in a run for mayor. Even though both were men of the outer boroughs, Cuomo's more temperate demeanor played better on a state-wide basis. But Koch, who once joked about getting "the bends" whenever he was away from New York for too long, sealed his fate when he groused to *Playboy* magazine about both living in the country ("This rural America thing … it's a joke") or the suburbs ("sterile … it's wasting your life"). His unique personality, memorably described once by Pete Hamill (1935–) as

Ed Koch was mayor of New York City from 1978 to 1989.

"some mad combination of a Lindy's waiter, Coney Island barker, Catskills comedian, irritated school principal and eccentric uncle," was one of many inimitably New York facts of life that just didn't play that well upstate.

What turned New York around in the 1980s?

To hear him tell it, that would be none other than Ed Koch, whose genius for self-promotion was rivaled by no other mayor since LaGuardia and wouldn't be seen again until Giuliani. Inarguably, Koch entered office at a rough time for the city. The blackout crisis had left whole neighborhoods physically scarred and an entire city psychologically battered. Between 1969 and 1977, the city had shed 600,000 jobs, and by 1980 the population would hit a low point of 7.1 million. Whether it was Koch's mix of cheery "How'm I doin'?" showmanship and bureaucracy-rattling or simply good timing is difficult to gauge, but by 1980, there was definitely a sense that the city had turned a corner. Of course, after a year like 1977, almost anything would have been seen as a step up.

Some of these changes needed years to take effect, like the decades-long Times Square revitalization project that Koch spearheaded in 1980. But Koch's shrewd managing of the budget, not to mention a revenue influx from a booming Wall Street, a resurgent tourist business, and his ability to procure aid from the federal government, helped the city pay off its debt and turn the corner on the fiscal crisis by 1985. The city added about 250,000 jobs between 1983 and 1988, a large percentage of those jobs directly or indirectly related to Wall Street.

How important was Wall Street to New York's resurgence in the 1980s?

A long run of bear markets in the 1970s, not to mention the outflux of corporate headquarters from Manhattan, had diminished Wall Street's real and symbolic importance to New York by the time Koch took office. However, that changed starting in the early 1980s. At the same time that President Ronald Reagan (1911–2004) was cutting top tax rates, a combination of easy credit, Congress's deregulation of the savings and loan industry, new financial instruments like the infamous "junk bonds," innovative investment schemes dreamed up by a bright young crop of MBAs, and a rapid increase in business from mergers and acquisitions came together to turbocharge the previously moribund financial sector.

The bond markets also took off in the 1980s, reaping massive windfalls for its traders, who put their bonuses to good work in the nightclubs, high-end clothiers, and nouveau cuisine restaurants that were popping up around the city to take advantage of this brash new-found wealth. Even though Wall Street was responsible for about a quarter of the earnings gain in the city's economy between 1983 and 1988, these gains were mostly at the top of the income bracket. The overt greed of the new breed of Wall Street money-makers, not to mention their often more working-class roots, was a democratic shock to the sector's earlier clubby, blue-blood style. The predatory, flashy, confidently shallow style exemplified in morality tales like the film *Wall Street* (1987) and the satirical novel *American Psycho* (1991) is directly modeled on this period in New York history.

When did the 1980s end on Wall Street?

As with all Wild West-booms, it ended in tears. Hard-charging U.S. Attorney Rudolph Giuliani (1944–) prosecuted a number of high-profile insider-trading cases. On October 19, 1987, the Dow had the greatest single-day loss in its history, ushering in a recession, marking an end to the go-go 1980s, and taking the wind out of Wall Street's sails for a few years.

How important was New York in the fight against AIDS?

Regardless of San Francisco's status as America's unofficial capital of gay culture, New York has been more prominently featured in the hallmarks of American gay politics. As discussed above, key to this were the Stonewall riots, which launched the gay rights movement. As important, though, was New York's leading role in the fight against HIV/AIDS. In 1981, anecdotal reports began to spread in New York's gay community about a strange wasting disease, a combination of pneumonia and sarcoma, infecting gay men. The following year, Gay Men's Health Crisis was founded by a half-dozen volunteers who tried to spread the word about a terrifying new epidemic that they barely understood. The group also gave support to the hundreds of AIDS victims who had been abandoned by friends and family too frightened or homophobic to help them.

In the early days of the epidemic, New York was the hardest hit. In 1985, the leading cause of death for 25-to-44-year-old New Yorkers was AIDS. Four years later, the city was

---

What was ACT UP?

As AIDS continued to spread during the 1980s, efforts to spread safety information about the disease and to coordinate with health professionals were hampered by a mixture of official indifference and public discrimination. As a result, some New York activists chafed at what they saw as the accommodationist tendencies of some in their movement. That frustration metamorphosed into the more radical group ACT UP (AIDS Coalition to Unleash Power).

Founded in 1987, by which time about ten thousand New Yorkers had died of AIDS, ACT UP's more militant approach was indicated in its stark logo: the words "Silence = Death" on a black background and a pink triangle evoked the symbols used by the Nazi regime to identify gays being sent to concentration camps. They specialized in highly photogenic protests designed to generate maximum negative publicity for government and other organizations they believed were hindering the advancement of AIDS research. One of their most famous protests took place on December 10, 1989, when thousands flooded the street outside St. Patrick's Cathedral and dozens more stormed inside to furiously disrupt Mass in protest against Cardinal John O'Connor's statements about gays and AIDS. Not surprisingly, such aggressive tactics won ACT UP many fans, many enemies, and reams of publicity.

home to one out of five known AIDS patients in America. Most of the agitation for research into the disease and changes in public policy grew out of work done by groups like Gay Men's Health Crisis, whose early years were dramatically documented in activist/writer Larry Kramer's (1935–) righteously furious New York-set play *The Normal Heart*. A network of AIDS support groups operated out of the New York Lesbian and Gay Community Center, which opened in 1984 in an old school building on West 13th Street.

How did Bernhard Goetz become famous?

Years after films like *Death Wish* celebrated the lone urban vigilante dishing out semi-automatic justice to street punks became a cinematic staple, Bernhard Goetz (1947–) became an instant celebrity in crime-plagued New York and around the country for taking the law into his own hands, Charles Bronson-style. On December 22, 1984, Goetz, a thirty-seven-year-old white engineer, was surrounded on a subway train by four young black men who asked him for five dollars. Goetz, who carried an unlicensed .38 caliber revolver after having been mugged several times and said later that he thought he was being robbed again, opened fire and wounded all four of the men. Goetz was also reported to have shot one of the men, Darrell Cabey, in the back as he lay wounded on the subway train's floor, paralyzing Cabey. Goetz surrendered to the police several days later.

The story of the "subway vigilante" or "subway shooter" became an instant sensation and yet another wedge in the already polarized racial politics of the city at that time. The onslaught of news coverage muddied the picture thoroughly: on the one hand, Goetz was seen as too troubled and possibly racist to be the pure downtrodden hero, while on the other hand too many of the men he shot had dicey records to come off as pure victims. A jury ultimately acquitted Goetz on charges of attempted murder and assault but found him guilty of criminal possession of a handgun. Cabey sued Goetz in civil court and won a $43 million settlement in 1996.

Were the Westies the last powerful Irish gang in New York?

Once the Gophers were dismembered by law enforcement in 1910, the age of the fierce Irish streetfighting mob had mostly passed. Hell's Kitchen certainly remained a rough neighborhood for decades after, only with less organized criminal activity. In the postwar years, as the neighborhood crumbled, there was less money to be made. In the 1970s, the Hell's Kitchen rackets were controlled by a loan shark named Mickey Spillane (1933–1977)—no relation to the crime novelist—who like many of his Irish brethren had abandoned Manhattan for Queens. He was murdered in 1977 by up-and-coming gangster James Coonan (1946–), whose Hell's Kitchen gang was termed the Westies by the police.

The Westies had a fearsome reputation for violence, which for several years left them essentially impervious to prosecution (nobody would testify against them). But they weren't a gang in the usual sense, like either the Mafia or the narcotics gangs that sprang up in the late 1980s to take advantage of the crack cocaine flooding into the city. Instead, the Westies essentially operated as hired killers for the Gambino crime family, like a latter-day Murder, Inc. The Westies started to fall apart in 1986. That was the year when "Mickey" Featherstone (1949–), a troubled Vietnam veteran who served as the gang's most feared enforcer, gave evidence on his comrades in order to avoid a long sentence for multiple murders. The following year, after several more members were indicted for a laundry list of charges ranging from kidnapping, loan-sharking, and extortion to murder, the Westies were essentially done for.

How did an attempted suicide nearly undo Koch's third term?

In 1985, Koch became just the third mayor since 1898 to win a third term. However, as with most other multi-term mayors, his popularity had peaked before he was done with the job. This truism of New York political life came true in January 1986, when Queens borough president Donald Manes (1934–1986), a Koch ally, was found in a car near Shea Stadium bleeding from knife wounds. Manes claimed he had been attacked but it was soon revealed that the wounds were self-inflicted after Manes realized he was about to be implicated in a massive scandal. Apparently Manes's bagman had been collecting hundreds of thousands of dollars in bribes from companies involved with the Parking Violations Bureau. Manes committed suicide in March 1986.

The resulting investigation toppled a domino chain of officials who had been feeding at the municipal trough for years under Koch's leadership. As investigations and trials followed one after the other—a half-dozen of Koch's appointees ultimately went to jail, while an incredible one-fourth of all city housing inspectors were arrested for graft—the shiny gloss of Koch's first two terms was dulled. He would lose his nomination for a fourth term to David Dinkins in 1989.

What were the Central Park Five accused of?

Early in the morning of April 20, 1989, a twenty-eight-year-old woman was found unconscious in Central Park. Police determined that she had been beaten and raped. The previous night, police had taken into custody several teenagers who had been part of a group of two dozen or more who had been running rampant in the park, throwing rocks and attacking passers-by. The viciousness of the rape, the fact that it took place in Central Park, the racial and class makeup of those supposedly involved (black and Hispanic attackers from poor neighborhoods, white woman who worked in investment banking) fused together in a time of high crime and a yawning socioeconomic gap to create a firestorm of media coverage and visceral public outrage like almost nothing else the city had ever seen.

Day after day, stories about the monstrous "wolfpack" of kids who went "wilding" in the park fueled panic and fury. (Meanwhile, the story of a black woman who was raped and thrown off a building in Brooklyn on the same night was practically ignored.) Channeling the outrage, real-estate magnate and tabloid shouter Donald Trump took out a full-page ad in the *Daily News* demanding to "Bring Back the Death Penalty." Mayor Ed Koch scoffed at having to refer to the suspects as "alleged." The teenagers who would later be called the Central Park Five confessed to the crime after more than fourteen hours of coercion and intimidation by police. They later pled not guilty but in two sensational trials were all convicted for five to thirteen years in prison. In 2002, a confession by Matias Reyes, a serial rapist, and new DNA evidence resulted in the exoneration of all five. They reached a settlement for $40 million with the city in 2014 for their wrongful imprisonment.

Who was Yusef Hawkins?

New York's second media-hyped racially charged crime of 1989 took place on August 23. That was the day that Yusef Hawkins, a black sixteen-year-old from East New York, took the subway with three friends into the mostly Italian Brooklyn neighborhood of Bensonhurst looking for the address listed in a car-for-sale ad. Earlier in the day, ru-

A mural of Yusef Hawkins graces a wall in Brooklyn.

mors had been flying that a local girl had been dating a black teenager. Hawkins and his friends happened to come across a mob of about thirty white teenagers armed with baseball bats and at least one gun. After a confrontation, Hawkins and his friends were chased through the neighborhood. Hawkins was trapped in a doorway and shot dead.

A few days later, Reverend Al Sharpton (1954–) led three hundred mostly black demonstrators in a protest march through Bensonhurst, during which some locals threw watermelon at the protestors and chanted racial epithets and "Central Park." The protest march became almost more controversial than the tragedy of the shooting itself. This was due in large part to the presence of Sharpton, whose ability to vividly express the outrage of the city's black citizens was usually undone by his self-promoting demagoguery. (Case in point being his championing in 1987 of black teenager Tawana Brawley, whose claims of being kidnapped and raped by white police officers were later revealed as a hoax.) Several members of the mob that assaulted Hawkins were convicted, but just one for murder.

Who was New York's first black mayor?

Incredibly, at the end of a decade that appeared to auger worsening racial relations in New York, the close-fought election of 1989 ended with the city electing its first black mayor. David Dinkins (1927–) was a decorous lawyer and former Marine who had been a mainstay of the Harlem Democratic club. He was a member of the influential "Gang of Four" of Harlem politicians, which also included Charlie Rangel (1930–), who represented the district in Congress for forty five years. Unlike the dramatic and fiery Rangel, the quiet Dinkins was well regarded more for his general competence and party loyalty than ability to give electrifying speeches or articulate broad new visions for the city.

Koch had been a popular, if divisive mayor, his reputation scarred by the scandals of 1986 and 1987. Koch's intemperate responses to the Central Park Five and Yusef Hawkins cases had fueled resentment among the city's minorities and white liberals.

That coalition, as well as Dinkins's more measured calls for healing and unity, gave him the Democratic nomination in 1989. It also helped Dinkins defeat the Republican candidate, Rudy Giuliani (who as U.S. attorney had led the investigations that had doomed Koch), by the narrowest margin in a mayoral race since George B. McClellan Jr. beat William Randolph Hearst (1863–1951) in 1905.

What took down the "Teflon Don"?

The Bronx-raised John Gotti (1940–2002) had started out in crime early, running with a gang in East New York and later an organized crime crew through the 1950s and '60s. By the 1970s, he was working his way up in the Gambino crime family, only to reportedly be blocked by the family boss, Paul Castellano (1915–1985), who disap-

David Dinkins, New York's first black mayor, was elected after Ed Koch left office. He served one term from 1990 to 1993.

proved of Gotti's crew dealing heroin. In 1985, Castellano and an aide were gunned down on East 46th Street. After Gotti took control of the Gambino family, his media profile shot up dramatically. Known as both the "Dapper Don" for his flashy suits and chummy way with the local press, and the "Teflon Don" for how charges never seemed to stick (at least one jury foreman was bought off), Gotti was the kind of local celebrity tabloids dream of. In his neighborhood of Howard Beach, Gotti held an annual block party and stoked an image as no-nonsense gangster of honor who looked after his people.

The law finally caught up with Gotti in a dramatic 1992 trial that included the stunning and nearly unprecedented testimony by Salvatore Gravano (1945–), a former Gambino underboss who broke the Mafia code of silence to finger his former associate in the 1985 shooting. Gotti was found guilty on thirteen charges, including racketeering and multiple murders, and sentenced to life. Afterwards, hundreds of flag-waving supporters, who had been bused to the downtown Brooklyn courthouse, rioted in protest. Trials of organized crime figures continued, and the Mafia kept skimming profits from labor unions and contracts ranging from garbage collection to wholesale produce. Still, the Teflon Don's downfall signaled the end of the Mafia as a major power in the city.

What caused the 1991 Crown Heights riots?

The most extensive public disturbance in New York's modern history happened in Crown Heights, a sprawling central Brooklyn neighborhood northeast of Prospect Park shared sometimes tensely by conservative Jews and blacks (a mix of native-born and Caribbean immigrants). It began on a Monday night in August 1991 when a car driven by a Hasidic

Jewish man jumped a sidewalk and crushed two seven-year-olds, one of whom later died. False rumors that the Hasidic ambulance that arrived treated the Jewish driver before one of the black children spread quickly through the gathering crowd. Groups of young black men threw rocks at homes they thought belonged to Jews. The *New York Times* reported "clashes in the surrounding streets, with blacks and Hasidim throwing bottles and rocks at each other, and both sides tussling with the police."

Closer to midnight, a twenty-nine-year-old Hasidic student from Australia was attacked by several black teenagers; he later died from stab wounds. When Mayor Dinkins came to the neighborhood to attempt to restore calm, he was forced to take refuge in a house while a jeering crowd threw rocks and bottles. For four days, Crown Heights was convulsed by street disturbances, fires, looting, and ethnically targeted attacks that the city's official report later determined were exacerbated by the city's poorly coordinated response. During Giuliani's 1993 mayoral campaign, he targeted Dinkins's perceived ineffectualness during the riots, which Giuliani termed a "pogrom."

What happened when the World Trade Center was attacked for the first time?

Just after noon on February 26, 1993, a rented van parked in an underground garage beneath the World Trade Center carrying a 1,200-pound bomb exploded. It created a crater 100 feet (30.5 meters) and several stories deep that killed six people instantly and wounded hundreds of others. Over 50,000 people were evacuated and the towers closed for several weeks. Within days, the FBI connected the bomb to a cell of Islamic fundamentalists and, helped by a lucky break when one of them attempted to retrieve his $400 deposit for the van, began to round them up. The mastermind of the attack, Ramzi Yousef (1968–), was the nephew of Khalid Sheikh Mohammed (1964–), who would later become a key figure in the rise of Al Qaeda and claim to be instrumental in the next attack on the World Trade Center, in 2001.

Just how different a mayor was Rudy Giuliani?

Giuliani became mayor in 1994, beating Dinkins by just 50,000 votes. A well-worn storyline later developed that the former U.S. attorney rode into City Hall like a hero in a Western and within a few years had tamed the city that many Americans had written off as uncontrollable. At the time of Giuliani's election, New York was clearly ready for a change. Crime had been on a generally upward trajectory ever since the 1960s and the city's reputation as a

Mayor Rudy Giuliani was in charge during the September 11, 2001, terrorist attacks on the Twin Towers. His calm, decisive leadership during that time was praised by many.

graffiti-covered gangland persisted. Even though municipal finances were far from the accounting catastrophe that Beame had faced, revenues were far from reassuring and spending on social programs continued to balloon; by one metric, in the early 1990s, one of seven New Yorkers was on welfare. Decades of Democratic rule had resulted in a sclerotic party leadership of generally uninspiring functionaries who came up through the clubhouse system. They were seen (rightly or wrongly) as unwilling to buck powerful interests like city unions and afraid to get tough on crime.

A former federal prosecutor who spent the 1980s busting up the last of the city's organized crime families, Giuliani appeared ready to change all that. Like a latter-day Peter Stuyvesant, Giuliani swept into power declaring a mandate for overhauling the city. He wanted to make New York safer, cleaner, more orderly, and friendlier to big business. He also wanted to undo many of the liberal policies that had been in place since LaGuardia and Lindsay. In his eight years as mayor, Giuliani made many friends and many enemies. An idiosyncratically pro-choice Republican who comedically dressed in drag for special occasions and got into at least as many fights as Koch, Giuliani also transformed New York more than any mayor in living memory.

How did "broken windows" and "zero tolerance" change New York under Giuliani?

One of the most far-reaching changes in crime-fighting tactics that took place under Giuliani's mayorship came about in part because of an influential 1982 magazine article titled "Broken Windows." The tactic, which took its name from that piece, was a variation on zero-tolerance policing that built off the theory that one example of lawlessness leads to others. Thus, a building that has one broken and unrepaired window will soon have all its windows broken. The strategy put into effect in New York by Giuliani and his new police comissioner, Bill Bratton (1947–), proposed that by enforcing the seemingly minor but widespread infractions like fare-beating in the subway or jaywalking, the NYPD could return a general sense of order to the supposedly ungovernable city.

Starting in 1994, the police crackdown resulted in thousands of arrests for petty crimes that had previously been ignored. This aggressive policing infuriated many New Yorkers. But the voices of dissent were muted because of the visible improvements; by 1997 the city's crime rate was already less than half what it was in 1990. Some later ar-

---

What was Compstat?

Another reason proffered for a safer New York was more efficient policing practices like Bratton's introduction of Compstat, a computer database that allowed the NYPD to quickly target high-crime areas. Revolutionary at the time, it later became standard in major police departments around the country. It's widely believed that Bratton was forced out in 1996 by Giuliani, who was reportedly perturbed that his police commissioner was receiving too much of the credit for "saving" New York.

gued that the improvement in safety, which became palpably apparent in many parts of the city, was actually due less to Giuliani's strategy and more to the six thousand new police officers hired by Dinkins and the nationwide drop in crime.

What started to sour New Yorkers on Giuliani?

Populist appeal aside, Giuliani was highly racially divisive and unabashedly favored powerful business and real estate interests over the needs of the poor. He won reelection in 1997 even though unemployment and the number of people living in homeless shelters had risen during his time in office. During his two terms, Giuliani picked many fights that lost him supporters even as his successes piled up. These spats ranged from his controversial and baffling decision in 1999 to withhold funding from the Brooklyn Museum because of an exhibition that included a painting Giuliani believed offensive to Catholics, to his demand that *New York* magazine take down its bus advertisements that touted the publication as "Possibly the only good thing in New York Rudy hasn't taken credit for." Then there was the tabloid matter of the mayor's very public and very dragged-out separation from his wife while he was seen around town with a new girlfriend.

Ultimately, though, Giuliani's legacy was darkened most by the aftershocks of his zero-tolerance approach to all types of offenses (from violent crime to shutting down the city's once vibrant and code-defiant nightlife scene) and his never-apologize defense of the police against all attacks, which many saw as sweeping up in its dragnet many innocent minorities as well as creating a culture of impunity within the NYPD.

Who were Abner Louima and Amadou Diallo?

While previous administrations were faced with police corruption scandals, Giuliani's tenure was marked by a series of incidents where the police were accused of abusing their power and the prosecutor-turned-mayor reflexively fought back against all criticism of the thin blue line. A scathing 1996 report by Amnesty International found evidence of widespread patterns of police brutality and abuse, most particularly in heavily minority neighborhoods.

One of the most vivid episodes of this abuse occurred in August 1997, when a Haitian immigrant named Abner Louima (1966–) was arrested for disorderly conduct outside a nightclub. He was later tortured by police officers, who sodomized him with a toilet plunger handle. Mass protests and wall-to-wall media coverage couldn't budge Giuliani from his staunch support of the NYPD. Another infamous case involved Amadou Diallo, an unarmed twenty-three-year-old West African immigrant who was about to enter his apartment building on a February night in 1999 when he was shot nineteen times by four police officers who thought he was reaching for a gun. Again, Giuliani held firm in the face of outraged protests. When the NYPD shot twenty-six-year-old security guard Patrick M. Dorismond to death in March 2000, he became the fourth unarmed civilian to have been killed by police in thirteen months. The city was perceived as having become safer during Giuliani's time in office. By 2000, though, the mayor's increasingly tone-deaf and callous manner had severely eroded his once-solid support.

Why did New York start shutting down all its nightclubs?

After serious crime rates plummeted through the 1990s, the city under Giuliani turned its attention to smaller infractions. One of these campaigns that raised the most ire was the mayor's particular animus towards nightlife. From the Cotton Club in the 1920s to the Peppermint Lounge in the 1960s, the Mudd Club in the 1970s, and Limelight and Tunnel in the 1980s and '90s, New York's club and music scenes had been one of its signature attractions for a certain kind of nighthawk. But the open nature of drug-dealing and -taking at many clubs, as well as their tendency to disgorge loud patrons into the streets at all hours of the night, was an irritant to some in city government.

Starting in the mid-1990s, the city used the 1926 cabaret law (originally enacted to cut down on race-mixing) to shut down any business that had dancing but no liquor license. The city's Nightclub Enforcement Task Force started vigorously enforcing safety codes as well, resulting in dozens of clubs shutting down. Some eventually reopened. But a less laissez-faire city, ever-rising rents, and changing tastes ensured that new millennium Manhattan would have less "nightlife" in the classic sense than at any time in its recent history.

Was Silicon Alley a place?

When the Internet exploded as a cultural and business phenomenon, most of the companies orbited around the "Silicon Valley" research nexus near California's Stanford University. But the density of capital and the promise of millions to be made ensured that New York would get a piece of the action, too. Starting around 1995, a web of technology companies began to open up well-appointed, airy offices in handsomely refurbished buildings from Chelsea to the Flatiron and SoHo that collectively became known as "Silicon Alley." Skyrocketing stock prices created many overnight millionaires, with lavish parties and questionable business plans following right behind. Many of those capital-rich and revenue-poor outfits evaporated along with the bursting of the Internet bubble in 2000 and 2001.

By 2006, though, a new batch of upstart firms like Gawker, Shutterstock, and Buzzfeed were rebooting the city's online business cred, and more established companies like Google were opening up vast new offices. However, this time around, very few people called this diffuse community Silicon Alley, perhaps to avoid a jinx. Nobody wanted to be seen as another Pseudo.com, the flamboyantly ambitious but never-profitable online streaming video site whose "burn rate" hit about $2 million a month before collapsing in 2000.

What happened on September 11, 2001?

On that morning, nineteen men under the orders of the Islamic terrorist group Al-Qaeda hijacked four commercial airliners to carry out a series of suicide attacks on the East Coast. Two of those airliners, Boeing 767s that had left Boston, headed towards New York. At 8:46 A.M., as workers were still streaming into downtown Manhattan, the hijackers flew United Airlines Flight 11 fast and low down the Hudson River and slammed it into the North Tower between floors 93 and 99, killing everybody on the plane and hundreds in the building. The plane's fuel ignited as planned, shooting a massive fireball into and through the North Tower. As emergency responders poured into the area, speculation spread about whether the crash was accidental. At 9:02 A.M., an evacuation order was broadcast in the South Tower. One minute later, the tower was hit between floors 77 and 85 by United Airlines Flight 175. Incredibly, the thin but deceptively resilient outer steel frame of both towers withstood the impact of the planes. However, the fires their fuel set off inside (fed by the massive amounts of paper in the offices) raged at such high temperatures that the structures couldn't remain intact.

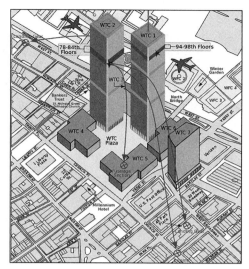

A diagram showing how the two airplanes approached and struck the Twin Towers on September 11, 2001.

The South Tower collapsed first, at 9:59 A.M., sending blinding clouds of smoke and debris through the surrounding streets. Over eight hundred civilians and police and firefighters who had rushed in trying to evacuate the building died in the collapse. After burning for 102 minutes, the North Tower fell at 10:28 A.M., killing over 1,600 people.

How many victims were there in the 9/11 attack??

Due to the catastrophic nature of the attacks, as of 2015 over 1,110 victims remain without positive identification. In the months immediately following 9/11, the *New York Times'* powerful, tragic, and democratic "Portraits of Grief" series crafted individual obituaries for over 2,400 of the dead, giving all of the victims their own full-fledged story, whether a secretary, cop, waiter, or executive.

The majority of the dead were office workers. They hailed from over 100 countries. It was believed that one in five Americans knew somebody hurt or killed in the attacks. Among the fatalities were 23 NYPD officers, 37 Port Authority officers, and 343 firefighters. The day's losses were particularly devastating for the FDNY (it was the department's worst loss of life in a single day since the tragic East 23rd Street fire in 1966 killed twelve firefighters). Many police and firefighters were still dealing with the trauma years later.

How did the attacks affect New York?

Everyone who was living in New York at the time remembers where they were and what they did immediately afterward, whether it was contacting everybody they knew who worked or lived downtown, or walking miles home because the subways were shut down.

Many people working in Manhattan did not even have a way to walk home. An ad-hoc fleet of vessels commandeered by the Coast Guard evacuated over a half-million people from southern Manhattan, still covered in plumes of smoke, to New Jersey and Staten Island. The massive operation was bigger than Dunkirk.

The loss of life and psychological toll was the single most traumatic event in New York history. By one estimate, over 400,000 New Yorkers had post-traumatic stress disorder afterward. Economically, the attack was also devastating. The New York Stock Exchange shut down for an unprecedented six days. About $105 billion evaporated from the local economy in the following month, and over 140,000 jobs were lost as well.

REBUILDING AND MOVING FORWARD

What happened after 9/11 at the World Trade Center site?

Following the collapse of the Twin Towers, as the federal machinery of investigation and war churned, New Yorkers dealt with the attack in ways that were both deeply wounded and highly pragmatic.

After burning for hours, World Trade Center 7 collapsed at 5:20 P.M. on September 11. By nightfall, generators had been set up and the city gotten to work on the other-worldly mountains of debris that became known as "the pile." Construction workers flooded in and got to work. The first order of business was finding survivors and securing the seventeen acres of smoldering wreckage. Following that, the wreckage needed to be cleared and the foundation secured. One of the biggest worries was that the slurry wall would collapse, letting the Hudson River pour through the PATH tunnels before flooding into the main subway system, causing catastrophic damage. To everyone's relief, the slurry wall held. But the greater hope, that more survivors could be found, was almost entirely dashed; only twelve people were discovered alive in the wreckage.

How did Giuliani become "America's mayor"?

In the aftermath of the 9/11 attacks, President George W. Bush (1946–) was frequently absent for security reasons, and Vice President Dick Cheney (1941–) was also often sequestered in an "undisclosed location." By simply being on site, Giuliani filled that void, talking to the press, and conveying a sense of calm but determined resolve amidst the grief. Dubbed "America's Mayor" by none other than Oprah Winfrey and soon bestrewn with honors that included a knighthood, Giuliani was the figure the country looked to for reassurance. Even some of the many New Yorkers who had been growing dissatisfied with their ever-more peevish and authoritarian mayor were willing to give him a second look in a time of crisis.

At the September 29 season premiere of *Saturday Night Live*, Giuliani stood on stage with a grim-faced group of New York first responders as well as the show's producer, Lorne Michaels (1944–). After a tribute to the attack's victims and a performance of "The Boxer" by Paul Simon (1941–), Michaels, playing off the overzealous predictions of some that 9/11 had killed irony, asked Giuliani, "Can we be funny?" Giuliani's quip "Why start now?" may have been the highlight of his late-period renaissance.

How long did that last?

Several years later, after a spectacularly unsuccessful presidential campaign—during which Senator Joe Biden (1942–) joked that all Giuliani needed to make a sentence was "a noun and a verb and 9/11"—and a descent into shrill partisan vitriol and the occasional infomercial, Giuliani had again lost much of the goodwill he briefly regained after the attacks.

Was the 2001 mayoral election delayed after 9/11?

Ten days after the World Trade Center attacks, the candidates vying to be the next mayor of New York swung back into action. Governor George Pataki (1945–) had raised the possibility of postponing the election due to the still-unsettled feeling in the city; much of downtown Manhattan was still sealed off, there was a military presence on the streets, and there was a palpable sense that another attack was just around the corner. Mayor

What happened to all the rubble left over after 9/11?

Rumors abounded of riches to be found in the levels underneath the Twin Towers, but only one true fortune was recovered: Almost two million pounds of gold and silver ingots worth $250 million that belonged to the Bank of Nova Scotia. After nine months of twenty-four-hour labor to clear almost two million tons (1.8 million metric tons) of debris, the pile was declared closed on May 30, 2002. That started the thirteen-year struggle to build not just a memorial to the disaster, but another skyscraper that would stand as a silent rebuke.

The destruction of the Twin Towers on 9/11 resulted in about 200,000 tons (181,000 metric tons) of steel that had to be dealt with in some way. Despite some emotional pushback from relatives of 9/11 victims and concerns about toxins from PCBs and mercury, in 2002 the city decided to sell about 175,000 tons (159,000 metric tons) of the steel as scrap. Most of the steel was sold to American companies. Some of the steel was stored in a massive hanger at JFK airport and doled out by the Port Authority to governmental and nonprofit groups for no charge. Most of these pieces were used in commemorative displays in municipal buildings, town squares, and police and fire departments. About 60,000 tons (54,400 metric tons) was sold overseas and used in everything from appliances to new skyscrapers. *The Atlantic* called it a "strangely appropriate fate for these buildings ... they would eventually find their way into every corner of the world."

Giuliani had suggested extending his time in office by two or three months to make the new mayor's transition easier. But in the end, the election went off as normally as it could, given the sight of a preposterously fractured Democratic field, a billionaire businessman who had switched to the Republican side from the Democrats, and a left-field candidacy from Bernard Goetz (yes, the Subway Shooter himself).

It was a moment of striking symbolism that the office was handily won by Michael Bloomberg (1942–), the billionaire party-switcher. He had made his fortune cornering the market on feeding market data faster than any other service to the information-hungry financial business via the Bloomberg terminals that remain a salient feature of the typical Wall Street office. Not only was the self-funded Bloomberg's victory in some ways a vote of confidence in the wounded financial sector, but the elevation of a mostly nonpartisan technocrat served as a sign of unity in a usually divided city.

How was "Mayor Mike" different than his predecessor?

Bloomberg had received Giuliani's endorsement. But the sitting mayor's tepid announcement came less than two weeks before the election. In the years that followed, Bloomberg kept a generally cool demeanor that set him apart from most other modern mayors. Simultaneously socially liberal and pro-business, he refused to indulge in the same kind of hotheaded divisive assaults that had characterized Koch and Giuliani's time in office.

At the same time, even when dealing with crises like the 2002 budget shortfall or the 2008 financial meltdown, Bloomberg was decisive in ways that the likes of Dinkins and Beame were never able to pull off. He had a couple of advantages that those mayors didn't: An appreciative local media who joked at times about the grand tastes of "Champagne Mike" but were generally on his side; and an ability to throw his own millions at re-election or special programs.

What was Bloomberg like as a mayor?

During his time in office, Bloomberg pushed a wide range of initiatives aimed at making the city more livable. The more visible included the 311 line that residents could call with all non-emergency issues (replacing the baffling tangle of agencies and numbers) and the LED signs that began popping up in subway stations announcing the arrival of the next train (a once-unthinkable modernization that many New Yorkers already can't remember living without). Bloomberg energetically championed causes like the environment and public transit that earned him plaudits. He also tried well-meaning forays into

New York's 108th mayor was Mike Bloomberg, serving from 2002 to 2013.

nanny-state regulations like his widely lampooned attempt to ban giant sodas as a weight-loss and diabetes-prevention tactic. At the same time, his focus on Wall Street and issues like charter schools were seen as overly focused on the upper class at a time when the city's always sizable income gap was becoming even more pronounced.

Bloomberg won reelection twice. His third and last election in 2009 was the most expensive in history (he spent $90 million of his own fortune) but also the most bruising, as it required changing the city's term-limit laws. The latter move was particularly unpopular and almost cost Bloomberg the election.

What was Occupy Wall Street about?

The sudden implosion of the real-estate bubble in 2008 left many New York financial firms grievously exposed due to the size of their investments in risky assets like subprime mortgages. The beginning of the Great Recession was announced by the shockingly swift collapse of storied financial institutions like Bear Stearns, Lehman Brothers, and insurance giant American International Group (AIG), all headquartered in New York. The recession rippled all across the country in the form of cascading defaults and shuttered businesses. But the concentration of high-level failure at the top ranks of New York's financial industry made it a symbol of the short-sighted greed and negligent risk-management that had led to the disaster. The anti-Wall Street resentment was heightened after a swiftly organized government bailout kept massive banks like Goldman Sachs from collapse, even as many homeowners were thrown out of homes they could no longer afford.

Anger about a perceived favoritism towards Wall Street, stoked by the government's inability to hold anybody legally accountable for the disaster, boiled over on September 17, 2011. That day, hundreds of protesters inspired by a call to arms in the satirical magazine *Adbusters* marched through Manhattan and set up camp in Zuccotti Park at Broadway and Liberty Street. The block-sized greenspace became a sprawling open-air protest zone for the leaderless movement, which attracted massive amounts of publicity, celebrity visits, and also spawned related Occupy protests around the world. Even as Occupy's call to redirect government assistance to the "99%" instead of the Wall Street "1%" caught fire, the group was criticized for the fuzziness of its proposals and turning Zuccotti into an eyesore.

What ended the protest?

After Zuccotti was cleared in a late-night police raid in mid-November 2011, the protestors generally faded away. However, the spirit of the movement spawned at least one notable offshoot: when Hurricane Sandy hit the city the following year, a grassroots group of activists called Occupy Sandy sprung up to provide assistance to the many areas around the city where government assistance was lagging or nonexistent.

How much damage did Hurricane Sandy cause?

Like any oceanside community, New York has had its share of false alarms when it comes to storms. One of the more glaring examples was Hurricane Irene, which racked up plenty of scare-mongering headlines in 2011 before petering out. The following year, though, Hurricane Sandy became the first major storm to hit the city since the Long Island Express back in 1938.

By the time Sandy smashed into the Jersey Shore on October 29, 2012—low-lying areas had been evacuated the day before, with all subway and rail service suspended, as was traffic on wind-vulnerable suspension bridges like the Verrazano—it had been downgraded to a Category 1 storm. But the amount of water it had gathered on its way up the coast still made for a substantial wallop. Waves reaching nearly 14 feet (4.25 meters) surged through Manhattan's financial district and poured into train tunnels, some of which would take years to repair. Helicopters had to be used to rescue people from rooftops in Staten Island, and a combination of fire and floodwaters destroyed much of the beach enclave of Breezy Point, Queens. Sandy put about 51 square miles (132 square kilometers) of the city, roughly 17 percent of the total land mass, and was responsible for forty-three deaths in New York.

Who is the public advocate?

After the Board of Estimate was dissolved in 1989 and its authorities divided between the City Council and the mayor, the same charter revision replaced the position of City Council president with a newly created office: the public advocate. An elected position, the public advocate is intended to act as an empowered ombudsman for the city (with the ability to sue other departments and to introduce legislation), watching out for the interests of city residents. The public advocate is also the first in line of succession to replace the mayor during an emergency.

The first public advocate, Mark Green (1945–), who had cut his teeth on consumer advocacy issues with Ralph Nader (1934–), was elected to office in 1993. After tormenting Giuliani for years with probes into charged issues like racial profiling by the police and general police misconduct, Green became the first public advocate to use the office as a political springboard. Winning the Democratic nomination for mayor in 2001, he lost to Bloomberg by one of the narrowest margins in city history.

How did a public advocate become mayor?

In 2013, public advocate Bill de Blasio (1961–) won the race for mayor in a landslide. His Republican opponent, former MTA chairman and Giuliani deputy Joe

Bill de Blasio is the first public advocate to be elected mayor of New York, which happened in 2013.

Lhota (1954–), tried to paint de Blasio as an out-of-touch liberal who would return the city to the bad old days of the 1970s. A progressive who started out in government as a City Hall aide for Dinkins and managed Hillary Clinton's (1947–) 2000 New York Senate campaign before serving on the City Council, de Blasio was the city's most unabashedly liberal mayor since Lindsay. He pledged to fight police abuses, including the controversial "stop and frisk" tactics, and to battle the housing problems and income inequality that had worsened under Bloomberg; he won with the biggest margin since Koch was reelected in 1985.

Why did many police officers literally turn their backs on de Blasio?

In July 2014, an unarmed forty-three-year-old man named Eric Garner, who was illegally selling cigarettes on the street in Staten Island, died while resisting arrest. Protests erupted in December when no charges were filed against the arresting officers, who were charged with using dangerous and banned chokehold tactics on Garner. On December 20, two NYPD officers were gunned down in Bedford-Stuyvesant by a man who had made social media statements about avenging the deaths of Garner and Michael Brown (the unarmed black teenager killed by police that August in Ferguson, Missouri).

The shocking assassination turned into a political firestorm, with the likes of Giuliani blaming protestors. The head of the Patrolmen's Benevolent Association (PBA)—which represents all NYPD officers under the rank of sergeant, and which was at the time fighting over a contract with the city—charged that de Blasio's criticism of police abuses, and statements about cautioning his mixed-race son to be careful around police, meant that his "hands are literally dripping with our blood." A massive crowd of 25,000 people, in-

---

What is stop and frisk?

In the Compstat era, New York police were suddenly expected to regularly show quantitative results. That meant numbers: Arrests, drugs and weapons seized, and so on. One of the tactics used was the so-called "stop and frisk." The original theory was that police in high-crime areas would proactively approach people they thought fit a profile, question them about what they were up to, and frisk them for weapons if it seemed warranted. The tactic had a certain logic.

But the reality was that massive numbers of young minority men were caught up in the sprawling dragnets that ramped up during the Bloomberg administration even as crime in the city fell. Of the nearly 4.5 million stops between 2004 and 2012, over eighty percent involved blacks or Latinos, and nearly ninety percent of those discovered no criminal activity. In 2013 a federal judge ruled that stop-and-frisk tactics violated the constitutional rights of minority city residents. When de Blasio took office, he replaced Bloomberg's pro-stop-and-frisk police commissioner Ray Kelly (1941–) with Bill Bratton, who had spent the years since his dismissal by Giuliani bringing similar reforms to police departments in New Orleans and Los Angeles.

cluding thousands of police officers, attended Ramos's December 27 funeral in Queens. When de Blasio spoke, hundreds of police turned their backs on him in a symbolic protest.

Where is one of the newest subway stations in New York?

Prior to 2015, the last time a new subway station had been opened was 1989. In the intervening time, much of the MTA's new infrastructure capacity was taken up by the seemingly unending project of the Second Avenue Subway line along Manhattan's east side. In September 2015, though, a mile-and-a-half extension was finally built to the Queens-Manhattan 7 train, pushing it from the old terminus at Port Authority on 42nd Street and Eighth Avenue west and then south to 34th Street and Eleventh Avenue. The new station, whose grand appearance and surrounding blocks of new park, gave it a definitely more impressive footprint than most of the older stations, is expected to not just serve the nearby Jacob K. Javits Convention Center but eventually the dense blocks of residential buildings sprouting in the previously derelict and industrial Hudson Yards neighborhood.

Theoretically, the 7 extension is supposed to be just one of a few new transportation changes in the city, such as the decades-in-the-works Second Avenue Subway, extending the Long Island Rail Road into Grand Central, a new East River-hugging streetcar line from Red Hook, Brooklyn, to Astoria, Queens. But every year brings a new budget, and every new budget brings new priorities, of which public transit is just one.

What are New York's plans for dealing with climate change?

Because New York is a coastal city with billions of dollars' worth of infrastructure, from its thousands of miles of easily flooded underground transportation tunnels to massive airports at or near sea level, it faces particular challenges due to rising sea levels. The city's projections assume that as soon as the 2020s, several factors will increase in notable ways: Annual precipitation (up to ten inches), sea levels (four to eight inches), and average temperatures ($2°F–3°F$). By the 2050s, city planners believe that the city will experience more frequent and intense heat waves, downpours, and coastal flooding. The most immediately affected areas would be the shoreline of Manhattan from about Chelsea south to Battery Park, the northwest and southeastern shore of Staten Island, most of Red Hook, a great swath of southern Brooklyn from Coney Island to JFK Airport, and the Rockaways.

Bloomberg launched the city's Climate Change Adaptation Task Force in 2008 to plan for how the city would respond to the effects of climate change over the coming decades. In 2013, recognizing the massive damage created by Hurricane Sandy, the city presented its long-range plan to mitigate the effects of climate change, including the construction of surge barriers, floodwalls, levees, the expansion of beaches and wetlands, and changes to building codes in flood-prone areas.

What is New York going to look like in the future?

Like most great cities, New York has a cyclical history. However, it has generally managed to avoid the lowest swings of the pendulum over the course of its history. In order to ensure that the city is able to keep up that record, in 2007, under the leadership of the ever-technocratic Mayor Bloomberg, the city unveiled PlaNYC. This twenty-five-year blueprint for comprehensive sustainable growth was one of the city's first long-range plans, and it envisioned a city that would continue to add population but simultaneously improve its environment and livability. By 2015, the city had, among other things, planted a million trees, launched a European-style bike-share program, dramatically expanded the recycling system, and cut greenhouse-gas emissions by sixteen percent (the goal is a thirty percent reduction by 2030).

How many security cameras are there in New York?

There is one other factor to keep in mind when thinking about the future of New York and safety: security cameras. Following 9/11, the city became increasingly dense with video surveillance in a plan modeled after London's formidable "Ring of Steel" network. The NYPD can access a rapidly growing network of 6,000 street cameras, plus 4,000 more in the subways, and 7,000 in public housing.

Who will be able to afford New York in the future?

It says something about the new millennium state of real estate anxiety in New York when one of the candidates running for mayor in 2005, Jimmy McMillan (1946–), appeared on behalf of the Rent Is Too Damn High party. This is nothing new. Ever since the first trades were conducted at the Tontine Coffee House on Wall Street, capital has sloshed into the city in waves, continually creating new zones of entitlement where the working- and middle classes could not afford to live. As the city's population and concentrations of wealth have steadily grown over the centuries, save for occasional interruptions like the Great Depression and the decline of the 1960s and '70s, the gap between the very rich and everyone else has only increased. By 2014 it was estimated that about one in every twenty-five New Yorkers was a millionaire.

For the other twenty-four, though, the city's exuberant rebound in population and wealth in the post-9/11 years came with a significant downside. By late 2015, the median rent for a one-bedroom apartment in the city was an eye-popping $3,100, beaten only by the tech-bubble-fueled housing market of San Francisco. In order to afford the median rate, the wage-earner in a one-income family would have to make $38.80 an hour; at the time the minimum wage was $8.75. In response, progressive elements began agitating for both a higher minimum wage and the mayor's office pledged to create 200,000 affordable housing units by 2015.

How did New York become so expensive?

New York is a victim of its own success. If it wasn't simultaneously the most stupefyingly vibrant, diverse, creative, exasperating, and sublime place to live in America, then there wouldn't be so many people wanting a piece of what it has to offer. At the same time, the overabundance of delights for the wealthy classes creates the risk that the city could become a gilded core of millionaires' aeries surrounded by ever-more distant neighborhoods for everybody else.

MANHATTAN

Where did the name "Manhattan" come from?

The Lenape Indians who lived on the island called it "Mannahatta" for "Island of Many Hills." It was an appropriate name, as the island boasted nearly 600 hills of varying heights. This later evolved into today's "Manhattan" and survives only as the title of a particularly exuberant Walt Whitman poem about this place with "the aboriginal name."

What was Manhattan like when the Lenape lived there?

The island was a verdant place and instantly recognized as such. In 1609, Henry Hudson recorded in his journal that "It is as pleasant a land as one can tread upon" and that "The land is the finest for cultivation that I ever in my life set foot upon, and it also abounds in trees of every description." Johan de Laet (1581–1649), a director of the Dutch West India Company, also remarked that the weather was very similar to that of the Netherlands, but "it is a good deal colder there than it ought to be according to the latitude." Besides all the many hills that would be flattened in later centuries (though some would survive in the upper stretches), Manhattan was covered by a thick blanket of forest, including oak, pine, and chestnut, and many stands of old-growth trees. The island was crisscrossed by streams, sometimes dammed by beavers, whose total length reached nearly seventy miles (113 kilometers). The island was thinner than it is today, before landfill began to broaden the contours, particularly towards the south.

Back then, the wooded coastline was still studded with stream outlets, marshes, and sandy beaches perfect for fishing and oystering. In fact, the entire western side of the island from its southern tip up to about 42nd Street was an almost continuous beach. As estuaries are generally very rich in biodiversity, the amount and variety of fish in the Hudson River proved very advantageous to both the Indians and colonials. According to researcher Eric W. Sanderson: "If Mannahatta existed today as it did [in 1609], it would be a national park—it would be the crowning glory of American national parks."

How about today?

Crowded. Very, very crowded. The borough of Manhattan is the single most densely populated county in America. That population also doubles on many days with all the tourists and commuting workers. A surprising number of parks have been hacked out of the street grid, with the largest, Central Park, taking up over 800 acres of prime midtown and uptown real estate. Not surprisingly, the economy is heavily skewed towards finance and business services, with large concentrations of creative jobs as well.

What is Manhattan's population like?

According to a 2016 report by the New York City Economic Development Corporation (NYCEDC), the population of Manhattan is more white and less foreign than almost anywhere else in the city. These are the largest ethnic groups in Manhattan:

- White: 46.9%
- Hispanic or Latino: 25.9%
- Black or African American: 12.6%
- Asian: 11.7%

FINANCIAL DISTRICT/ BATTERY PARK/CIVIC CENTER

Where did Battery Park get its name?

Almost immediately after the Dutch settled on New Amsterdam, they constructed Fort Amsterdam on Manhattan's southwestern corner, with its magnificently commanding and strategically crucial views of the harbor. In 1683, they installed a battery of cannon at the shoreline, thus associating that quadrant of downtown forever after with a military atmosphere that hasn't been present for centuries. Fort George (as the British renamed Fort Amsterdam) was dismantled in 1788, at around the same time that the entire area was landscaped and turned into Battery Park. The park's tree-lined avenues became a beloved strolling destination for the city's most dapper flaneurs.

The Battery's militaristic connotations were briefly extended when the circular West Battery fort was constructed a couple hundred feet offshore in 1811. In the 1940s, Robert Moses faced one of his few defeats here, when he tried to build a massive (and, most thought, unnecessary) bridge between Red Hook, Brooklyn and Battery Park that would have essentially destroyed its usability as a verdant public space at the tip of a very crowded island. In a fit of pique, Moses demolished the popular aquarium that had been built inside the old Castle Garden.

What is Battery Park like today?

Today, the twenty-five-acre Battery Park remains one of the best harbor views in the city, thanks to its long, sweeping promenades. In addition to wandering the park's many wind-

An aerial view of Battery Park as it appears today.

ing paths, visitors can take in the American Merchant Mariners' Memorial, the Irish Hunger Memorial (featuring a roofless cottage and stones from each of Ireland's 32 counties), and the Pier A Harbor House (a 28,000-square-foot Beaux Arts building on a pier that used to house the city's fire boat command post and is now an event space and beer hall).

Where were immigrants arriving in New York Harbor processed before Ellis Island?

From 1855 to 1890, some eight million immigrants were processed through Castle Garden in Battery Park. According to Congressional testimony, this was roughly equal to the entire population of the United States in 1820. The immigrants came from many nations, but overwhelmingly from Europe; over half were from Germany and Ireland. Conditions were reported by some to be quite unsavory at Castle Garden, with charges of everything from sexual misconduct to the financial exploitation of immigrants. A federal government investigation into the station in 1890 caused it to be shut down.

What was Castle Garden's original purpose?

Castle Garden is proudly but modestly situated in the middle of Battery Park on the southeast corner of Manhattan between the Merchant Marines Memorial and the Staten Island ferry terminal. This squat little fortification was originally one of the most important links in the chain of defenses surrounding New York Harbor. Constructed in 1811 as one of four harbor forts (the others were built on Liberty, Governor's, and Ellis islands), it was named first the West Battery and then Castle Clinton for the city's mayor DeWitt Clinton. Its stout circle wall was punctured by twenty-eight cannons, each of which could hurl a shell 1.5 miles (2.4 kilometers).

The fort never saw action. In 1823 it was deeded to the city, which renamed it Castle Garden. Reimagined as a popular entertainment center, the onetime fortress hosted everything from P. T. Barnum-sponsored opera performances to invention showcases and fireworks displays. After its time as an immigration station ended in 1890, Castle Garden spent several decades as the home of the New York Aquarium, which later moved to Coney Island. After barely escaping demolition by Moses (Albany deeded the site back to the federal government in 1950, putting it off-limits), it was eventually restored to its original appearance (except for the surrounding landfill; the fort was originally connected to the mainland by a wooden walkway) and is open to visitors. Most people come to Castle Clinton, as it's now again known, to access the ticket office for the State of Liberty, but its quiet brick enclosure also makes for an interesting spot to break up a stroll through Battery Park.

What was New York's first official park?

Even though Battery Park is lower Manhattan's most prominent greenspace, historically the most important may be the small triangular square just to its northeast at the start of the old Indian path that became Broadway. In the Dutch colonial years, Bowling Green was the site of the city's first public well, as well as a cattle market and parade ground. It was turned into a bowling green in 1733. It was the momentous location of the first public reading of the Declaration of Independence, on July 9, 1776. The park later served as a shared front yard for the many upper-class families who built their homes around it. Starting in the mid-nineteenth century, the area began to change as shipping and other companies built their offices here, the impressive colonnaded facades of which still face onto the green.

Today, compact Bowling Green is notable for its beautiful fountain and a couple sights. On its south side sits the Alexander Hamilton U.S. Customs House, a lavish 1907 Beaux Arts edifice designed by Cass Gilbert (1859–1934) of Woolworth Building fame, which was later refurbished and now houses the National Museum of the American Indian. At the northern point, where Broadway splits into two lanes strides the bronze statue *Charging Bull*; this internationally known symbol of Wall Street was surreptitiously deposited in front of the New York Stock Exchange in 1989 by its sculptor Arturo Di Modica (1941–), who created it at his own expense, and was later moved here by the Parks Department. The fence laced around the park is the same that has been there since 1773.

How new is Battery Park City?

The idea for Battery Park City was first mooted by Governor Nelson Rockefeller in the 1960s as a way to spark new life into the moribund dock area west of the financial district and north of Battery Park. Plans were finalized in the 1970s to build a ninety-two--acre residential and commercial strip from Battery Place north to Chambers Street. Once construction on the World Trade Center began, much of the displaced earth was used as landfill to create this new development. The varied blocks of somewhat generic apartment buildings and office structures don't look like much else in Manhattan, which is either a good or a bad thing, depending on your point of view.

Battery Park City's centerpiece is the World Financial Center, a dense office complex around the north cove's yacht harbor that marks the development's halfway point and serves as a kind of ancillary outgrowth to the financial district just to the east. One of its more interesting features is the Winter Garden, a massive vaulted glass structure that is part shopping mall and part performance space. At the northern end are Rockefeller Park and the elite Stuyvesant High School. The southern end is anchored by the Jewish Heritage Museum and the Skyscraper Museum.

Where was Little Syria located?

In the late 1800s, the waterfront area along the bottom southwest corner of Manhattan was a tightly packed quadrant of tenements and ethnically oriented groceries and other businesses that was not unlike similar districts in Little Italy, or even Yorkville. What set "Little Syria" apart was that it constituted one of America's first Arab-American communities. By World War I, the crowded quarter around Rector and Washington streets was home to many Syrian and Lebanese immigrants fleeing Ottoman oppression, as well as one of the country's first Arabic printing presses and newspapers. Washington Street hosted businesses like Sahadi Bros., which sold "Oriental" groceries, restaurants where customers could smoke hookah, and St. Joseph's Maronite Church (most of the immigrants were Christian).

What happened to Little Syria?

By the 1940s, the neighborhood's Syrian and Lebanese population was nearly 40,000 strong. But today, only a few buildings remain from this era. What wasn't demolished by the construction of the Brooklyn-Battery tunnel in the 1940s was wiped out by the construction of the World Trade Center. The communities scattered like most of New York's twentieth-century ethnic groupings, though a small pocket of Lebanese culture reestablished itself across the river in Brooklyn Heights, where Our Lady of Lebanon Maronite Cathedral opened in 1906 and Atlantic Avenue still boasts a Sahadi's grocery.

Where was the first mosque in New York?

Muslims have been part of the New York population since its very early years. Until quite recently, though, their numbers were quite small. By one account, in the late-nineteenth century there were fewer than a thousand Muslims in the whole city. News reports mention one of the first documented *adhans* (a public call to prayer) being given from a third-story window near Union Square in 1893. There is no clear record as to where the first mosque was built, but there is evidence that one of the earliest was located in Little Syria on Rector Street, between Greenwich and Washington, and was in use from at least 1912 to when it was torn down in the 1950s.

What was the first Catholic church?

Since it was illegal to openly worship as a Catholic in colonial New York, by the time the law banning priests was lifted in 1784, there were only two hundred Catholics in the entire city. St. Peter's, the city's first Catholic church, opened two years later at Barclay and

Church street. It was located just outside city limits, further north than the original site on Broad Street, which was opposed by anti-Catholic city officials. (When protests erupted in 2010 over plans to open a mosque around the corner on Park Street, St. Peter's pastor pointed out the ironic echoes of religious discrimination from centuries earlier in the very same neighborhood.) The original small brick structure was replaced by the current church, a temple-like Greek revival design fronted by Ionic columns, in 1836.

What is the old World Trade Center site used for now?

After the attacks on September 11, 2001, this 16-acre quadrant of the financial district—bordered by West, Fulton, Greenwich, and Liberty streets between Battery Park and Wall Street—spent years in transition, morphing from dust-shrouded mourning space to anxious construction zone. Recently, several new office towers have opened. The 104-story One World Trade Center, originally called the Freedom Tower, stands tall on the northern verge of the old World Trade Center site, an angled rectangle. Its sky-leaping height and gleaming embrasure, along with the 80-story Three World Trade Center and 72-story Four World Trade Center on the site's southeast corner, is meant to impress. (A fourth skyscraper, Two World Trade Center, is still being built as of early 2017.)

The new World Trade Center building was completed in 2011. It replaces the towers that were lost in the September 11, 2001, terrorist attacks.

Recently, the site of the World Trade Center itself (now a museum and memorial) has coalesced into a reflective and surprisingly beautiful addition to a part of town rarely cited for its attractiveness. Finished in 2011, the 9/11 Memorial is composed of elegant rows of swamp white oak trees and two great reflecting pools whose dimensions match the footprints of the north and south Twin Towers. The pools are ringed by a black stone railing inscribed with the names of the attack's victims. Just past the railing, a sheer waterfall drops dozens of feet down to an acre-sized pool, in the middle of which is a square gap into which the water pours as though it were a bottomless cavern. The effect is soothing and disquieting all at once, providing a sense of serenity tinged with unfathomable loss.

What makes the 9/11 Museum different from most other memorials?

Sound and proximity. The entrance to the museum itself, which opened in 2014, is a stark structure near the North Pool that brings visitors down escalators underneath the

Twin Towers site. The clean and stark design is made to contrast painfully with some of the chaotic exhibits from the attack itself, such as a fire engine smashed by falling debris and a piece of structural metal violently distorted as if torn by giant hands. The museum's carefully calibrated approach to storytelling walks visitors through a nearly minute-by-minute recounting of the September 11 attack. An unnerving quiet cacophony of voices pulse through the powerful exhibits: anxious news reports, panicked emergency calls, the sober tales of shell-shocked survivors. It manages to be emotional but not manipulative, creating a full-spectrum portrait of the event that is refreshingly more reliant on oral history than visual show and tell.

What's that thing that looks like a dinosaur's ribcage near One World Trade?

One hit that the city's infrastructure took on 9/11 was the destruction of the World Trade Center PATH station. Given its crucial nature for downtown office workers commuting from New Jersey, restoring service was a top priority in the months that followed. A temporary station reopened in 2003, the first major post-9/11 construction job to be finished at the site. Thirteen years later, the wholly new World Trade Center Transportation Hub was opened to the public and, as with any major new piece of public architecture, came in for its share of applause and disdain.

The station is centered around the eye-catching Oculus designed by international star architect Santiago Calatrava (1951–). The unique, 160-foot-high ridges of glass and white steel spikes have been compared to everything from a cathedral to the ribs of a dead stegosaurus. Oculus aside, the hub's emphasis on consumption over transit (it's essentially a not-particularly bustling PATH station with tunnels to linking subways, surrounded by a shopping mall) was subjected to criticism, though there was general agreement that the station's unusually airy and bright expanse of sparkling white Ital-

---

What is behind the wall at the Virgil Repository at the 9/11 Museum?

Along one wall in the 9/11 Museum that sits between the sites of the North and South towers, there is an eye-catching piece of art. It is covered in hundreds of squares, each a different shade of blue to evoke the sky of the morning of September 11, which was remembered for its piercing morning clarity. The centerpiece, though, is a quote made of 15-inch-high letters crafted out of steel from the towers themselves. It comes from Book 9 of Virgil's *Aeneid*: "No day shall erase you from the memory of time." Whether used wildly out of context (as some classics scholars have argued) or simply as a nod to the indelibility of historical memory, it's a striking and discomfiting line, particularly appropriate given what it conceals. Behind the wall sits a repository for some unidentified victims' remains, a reflection room for victims' family members, and a small work space used by the city's Office of Chief Medical Examiner, which is still working to put names to the remains.

ian marble was astonishing. Other critics pointed out that not only was the whopping $4 billion price tag nearly double the original estimate, but it was also twice as expensive as the just-as-beautiful-but-far-more-necessary Grand Central.

How did Stone Street get its name?

Many street names in lower Manhattan have decidedly prosaic roots. The most obvious of these is Wall Street, or "de Waal Straat," for the place where the (ineffectual) defensive wall was built to keep out the British. There was also Beaver Street, where beaver pelts were loaded onto ships bringing them back to the home country, and the wishfully named Pearl Street, paved with oyster shells. The name for Stone Street, which runs arcs northeast for a couple blocks from Whitehall Street just below Bowling Green towards Hanover Square, came from a similarly obvious source. In the early days it was called Brewer Street for the breweries congregated nearby.

The combination of ever-present mud and brewery effluvium could have caused residents to petition in 1655 that the street had become "unfit for public use" and should be paved. The cobblestones on New York's first paved street, though, were very rough. This was typical of New York streets, which even when later brick sidewalks began to be installed, were so uneven that Benjamin Franklin (1706–1790) once said he could spot New Yorkers in Philadelphia because they were unused to smooth surfaces they walked "like a parrot upon a mahogany table."

Is the South Street Seaport still operational?

The far southeastern corner of Manhattan, from South Ferry up to the Brooklyn Bridge, was once the most bustling part of the city's waterfront. It began in the early Dutch years, when a floating dock was built at what is now Broad Street. Landfill extended the island from Water Street out to its current shape. Spurred by the glut of transported goods available via the Erie Canal, by the 1840s the district had become a dense network of docks, counting houses, sailors' bars, hotels, and warehouses, bristling with ships' masts and teeming with sailors, merchants, and immigrants. The port handled everything from ferry traffic across to Brooklyn to passenger ships from Europe and freight vessels from China. Its business peaked in the 1850s, after which larger passenger and cargo ships shifted to the bigger docks on the Hudson side and later Brooklyn and New Jersey.

In the following decades, many of the buildings no longer needed for the shipping trade were taken over by the Fulton Fish Market, which started with just a cluster of stalls in 1822, was given a permanent building between Beekman and Fulton streets in 1869, and kept sprawling until it occupied many of the blocks nearby. Even with hiccups resulting from increased competition and the occasional federal campaign against the Mafia families that dominated some aspects of the business, the market remained a bustling concern well into the 1990s, with loads of fish being unloaded after midnight and buyers arriving not long after. It was relocated to Hunts Point in the Bronx in 2005. Today the area is gradually being repurposed for lifestyle and tourism, with a somewhat mangy shopping mall, a sprinkling of new restaurants and tourist sites, and a well-preserved block of cobblestone and Georgian-Federal buildings just south of the Brooklyn Bridge that has been so far unblemished by renovation.

What is the oldest continually used building in New York?

St. Paul's Chapel at Broadway and Fulton. Not a standalone church, St. Paul's was built in 1764 as a "chapel-of-ease" for Church of England parishioners of Trinity Church who didn't have time to get there. (That's exactly what George Washington did after his inauguration in 1789, when he ducked in here for a prayer.) Although its parent church was constructed earlier, the chapel stands as the city's longest continuously used building due to it barely surviving the great fire of 1776, when a bucket brigade frantically poured water on the chapel's roof even as almost every nearby building went up in flames.

Built in 1764, St. Paul's Chapel on Broadway and Fulton is still in use today as a place of worship.

Probably no building in downtown Manhattan looks more out of place than this modestly scaled place of worship. Modeled on London's St. Martin-in-the-Field, it is built out of rough-dressed local stone that give it its sturdy and practical, rather than strictly graceful, appearance. The original plan was for it to face the Hudson River. But several years later the larger foot traffic on the opposite Broadway side resulted in the addition of the rear east-facing porch which most people today think of as the church's main entrance. The chapel's surrounding plot of land is marked off by a wrought-iron fence and includes one of the city's oldest cemeteries. For years, an ancient sycamore tree grew in the cemetery; it was large enough that its bulk protected St. Paul's from the collapse of the towers on 9/11. After that day's terrorist attack, St. Paul's served as a sanctuary for responders and mourners, as well as an ad-hoc command center for recovery operations.

When was the first Trinity Church built?

Occupying pride of place at the western edge of Wall Street, the site for Trinity Church has long made it one of the focal points of downtown Manhattan. Overshadowed now by skyscrapers, when first constructed in 1698, it was one of the larger buildings in the city. Situated near the "Land Poort," the gate in Stuyvesant's defensive wall through which Dutch herdsmen brought their cows out to pasture every morning, the first Trinity Church faced the Hudson River instead of east as it does now. The annual rent was set at one peppercorn to be sent to the king. Financing for the building came from many disparate sources, including a government allowance for the church—back then it was much closer to the waterfront—to seize the proceeds of unclaimed shipwrecks, and to also claim any stranded whales for the purpose of selling their oil and other marketable parts. Additional funds were provided by the pirate captain William Kidd; he later owned a pew in the finished church.

What happened to the first two Trinity Churches?

The first church, sizable but fairly ordinary in appearance, burned down along with much of the rest of Manhattan in the fire of 1776. A second church was built in 1790, but a harsh winter in 1836 damaged the roof so severely the entire church was pulled down. The third and current church, a grandly inspiring Gothic Revival beauty that stares down Wall Street like some stern conscience, was finished in 1847. Until the *New York World* building went up in 1890, Trinity's spire was the tallest man-made point in the city. It holds one of the city's most prestigious (if compact) cemeteries, holding the likes of Alexander Hamilton, John Jacob Astor, and George Templeton Strong (1820–1875). The church has another cemetery located far uptown in the 150s by Riverside Drive; they were forced to find more space after the city banned burial south of Canal Street in 1823. Today it's one of the most active Episcopalian parishes in the city and a must-see tourist destination for anyone visiting downtown. When Queen Elizabeth II (1926–) paid a visit in 1976, she was presented with 279 peppercorns as back rent.

Why is there a statue of George Washington at Federal Hall?

Because he took the oath of the presidency on that site at Wall and Nassau streets on April 30, 1789. He swore on a Bible loaned for the occasion by a local Masonic lodge. That same Bible is occasionally on display at Federal Hall, and has been loaned out for the inaugurations of Presidents Warren G. Harding (1865–1923), Dwight D. Eisenhower (1890–1965), Jimmy Carter (1924–), and George H. W. Bush (1924–). The building where Washington took the oath of office—on a balcony so that he could be witnessed by hundreds of cheering onlookers—was at the time the second city hall of New York. Mayor Richard Varick (1753–1831) lent it to the nascent federal government for use as its first capitol; the House of Representatives met in one room, the Senate in the other.

Architect Peter L'Enfant (1754–1825) had remodeled the building in 1788 in what became known as federal style architecture. The current Federal Hall is a handsome Greek Revival structure with a beautiful central rotunda built in 1842 that operated first as a customs house and later as a branch of the Federal Reserve Bank before being turned into the Federal Hall National Monument in 1955. Its foundation was damaged by the shocks of the nearby building collapses on 9/11. The heroic statue of Washington that attracts throngs of tourists on the steps leading down to Wall Street was completed in 1883.

How long have they been trading stocks at the New York Stock Exchange?

The brokers of the New York Stock Exchange have, as a group, been trading stocks in one way or another since twenty-four of them first signed the Buttonwood Agreement on Wall Street in 1792. Since standing under a tree didn't seem like the best long-term solution, they had a variety of short-term offices before finally building themselves a grand edifice on Broad Street just south of Wall in 1903. The New York Stock Exchange

Why are there scars in the outer wall of the J. P. Morgan building on Wall Street?

You wouldn't know it to look at the area's everyday bustle, but the intersection of Wall and Nassau streets isn't just a monument to finance and mercantilism. This is also the street corner where a signature weapon of modern terrorism was given its American debut. On September 16, 1920, just after the noon bells at Trinity Church stopped ringing, a horse-drawn wagon packed with dynamite and hundreds of pounds of iron slugs exploded in front of the headquarters of J. P. Morgan and Co. at 23 Wall Street. The massive explosion ripped into the workday crowd, killing thirty people and shattering windows blocks away. The hooves of a horse were later found in Trinity Cemetery.

The anarchists behind the attack had meant to kill Morgan himself, but the banking tycoon was vacationing in Scotland at the time. It was the most devastating domestic terrorist attack until the 1995 Oklahoma City bombing and proved to be a harbinger of horrors to come. According to author Mike Davis, decades "after that first massacre on Wall Street, car bombs have become almost as generically global as iPods." Even today, you can still see divots punched out of the marble walls of the Morgan Bank's façade, generally ignored by the crowds rushing past.

is an imposing neoclassical church of high finance designed by George B. Post (1837–1913); its great façade of Corinthian columns is overlooked by the watchful statue of George Washington just across Wall Street at Federal Hall.

Were slaves sold on Wall Street?

The story of Wall Street almost always focuses on the buying and selling of futures, stocks, and esoteric financial instruments. However, the story can't be completely told without including at least a mention of a different commerce. On December 13, 1711, the City Council passed a law requiring that all "Negro and Indian slaves" were to be "hired" at a market located where Wall Street met the East River. A 1730 illustration shows a small, high-roofed structure on the waterfront thronged with humanity, both African and possibly Native American, being hired out for the day or bought outright. Slave labor was an important part of the city's early economy. It is believed that slaves cleared land and built many of the city's earliest structures, including the original Wall Street wall in 1653 and Trinity Church. The market was dismantled in 1762. Slavery itself, however, was not abolished in the state until 1827.

How important was slavery to the New York economy?

Even the abolition of slavery didn't sever New York's connection to the "peculiar institution." Up through the Civil War, New York's status as financial hub and shipping port made it a crucial link in the so-called "triangular trade." This was the system by which manufactured goods were shipped to Africa, where they were sold and traded for slaves, who were sent to plantations in the New World. There, sugar was produced for shipment to East Coast ports like New York and Boston, where it was refined into rum, which was then exported to Europe. The great banks and other financial institutions headquartered on or near Wall Street were the only entities wealthy enough to provide credit to many of the South's large plantations.

Slavery was considered so important to the city's fiscal well-being that many business leaders lobbied Lincoln to avoid going to war. Fernando Wood, mayor of New York when war broke out in 1861, even proposed that the city secede from the union. Today, the only permanent legacy of New York's connection to slavery—besides occasional calls for financial institutions with roots in the slave trade to pay reparations—is a small historical marker (one of dozens scattered around the island) placed in a park at Wall and Water streets, about a block from the actual site, in 2015.

How much gold is held at the Federal Reserve Bank of New York?

The largest of the twelve banks in the Federal Reserve System, New York's Federal Reserve Bank actually holds more gold than the more famous repository at Fort Knox in Kentucky and more than any other known gold deposit in the world. An impressively statuesque and blocky fortress of a building at Liberty and Nassau streets just above Wall Street (it's the one whose windows are all laced over with stout iron bars), the bank keeps over half a million gold bars weighing nearly thirty pounds (13.5 kilograms) each in its heavily protected vaults five stories below ground. The massive vault was lowered into the Manhattan bedrock before the building was completed in 1924. Nobody has ever tried to break in. In 2008, the value of the gold in the Federal Reserve's vaults was estimated at around $203 billion.

Where is the Canyon of Heroes?

On certain days in New York, the first dozen or so blocks of Broadway from Battery Park up to the Woolworth Building and City Hall Park turns into the "Canyon of Heroes." Parades have always been a central aspect of the city's social calendar. But in addition to the annual parades like St. Patrick's Day and Gay Pride, there were also many one-off celebrations of individuals or events. The Canyon of Heroes (named for the downtown area's "stone canyons" of office buildings) is one of the most common routes for those fetes, and the only spot in the city where the festivities are heightened by millions of pieces of confetti fluttering through the air like paper snow.

The first so-called ticker-tape parade took place on October 26, 1886, during the ceremonial dedication of the Statue of Liberty. Brokerage workers, who received constant stock-price updates on the still modern-seeming ticker-tape machines invented in 1867, had a plentiful supply of excess paper on hand. They found out that sending the one-inch-wide ticker tape ribbons out the windows made for a pretty effect. Within a few years

A ticker-tape parade at the Canyon of Heroes—a stretch of Broadway in the Financial District—celebrated the return of the *Apollo 11* astronauts in 1969.

this became expected practice and required the pre-parade delivery of tons of confetti (simulating the effect of the old ticker tape ribbons) to office buildings along the route.

What's located in and around City Hall Park?

Another of the triangular-shaped public spaces created by the idiosyncratic sweep of Broadway through Manhattan, City Hall Park, with its graceful fountain, elegantly manicured pathways, and classic wrought-iron fencing, is in many ways the heart of the downtown area north of Wall Street. Its southern edge is a rounded point at Barclay Street, where Park Row splits off from Broadway and loops north where it turns into Lafayette Street, and widens northward up to Chambers Street. Originally a commons area for the Dutch colony (complete with windmill), this not-terribly well-kept land later held a soldiers' barracks and a debtor's prison which held the gallows where British forces executed about 250 prisoners during the Revolutionary War. The grounds were gradually beautified through the nineteenth century and a massive renovation was completed in 1999.

- On the south, City Hall Park is today overlooked from the Broadway side by the beautiful Woolworth Building, which was the tallest building in the world for over two decades after it opened in 1913. F. W. Woolworth's (1852–1919) chain of spectacularly successful five-and-dime stores revolutionized mass merchandising in the late nineteenth century and made him so rich that he paid $13.5 million in cash to

203

build this landmark to his success. Its recently restored lobby is an eye-popping spectacle of gargoyles, marble, and mosaics that easily explains why the skyscraper was known as the "Cathedral of Commerce." Amidst the many medieval-style grotesques is one of Woolworth himself, counting dimes.

- About half way up the park at Murray Street sits the splendid City Hall, still as beautiful a sight in white marble as when it first opened in 1811. At the time of its construction, City Hall was considered to be so far north that marble was only used on the south-facing front and the sides, leaving its north-facing back unadorned because (the argument went) so few people would ever see it.

- Facing onto Chambers Street on the north is the grandiloquent overkill that is the Tweed Courthouse. At one time, this neo-classical building (officially the Old New York County Courthouse) was a byword for civic waste. Construction lasted from 1861 to 1881, during which the budget exploded from $250,000 to over $11 million, at least two-thirds of which was appropriated by Boss Tweed and his confederates, who kept piling on the kickbacks and sweetheart deals, including cost overruns that included a bill of $125,000 for one day of cabinetry work. Today the courthouse (which was nearly demolished in the wrecking ball-happy 1970s) has been fully restored and houses the Department of Education.

- Across from the park's northeast corner is the Manhattan car-and-pedestrian approach to the Brooklyn Bridge. Running on a diagonal slant northeast from there is the Civic Center, an impressive lineup of three soaring colonnaded structures that, if we can imagine City Hall as the head, form the spine of the city's legal and political body: The Manhattan Borough President's Office, the United States District Court, and the New York State Supreme Court.

Where is the African Burial Ground found today?

In 1794 the ravine, and the graves beneath, was filled in and the land divided into housing lots. After that, the cemetery was mostly lost to history until 1991 when workers building the Ted Weiss Federal Building at 290 Broadway between Duane and Reade

Were blacks and whites buried separately in old New York?

In 1697, Trinity Church stopped allowing blacks to be buried in its cemetery. Afterwards, over 20,000 free and enslaved blacks were laid to rest in the Negroes Burial Ground (as it's called in a map from 1755), a seven-acre site in a ravine not far north of the wall that Stuyvesant had ordered the colony's slaves to build decades earlier. In 1788, members of the black community importuned the City Council to stop the medical students who were stealing bodies out of the burial ground; six years later the "Doctors' Riot" resulted when it was discovered that white graves at Trinity were being robbed as well.

streets uncovered human skeletons in coffins. The shroud-wrapped bodies had been buried according to African custom. Construction was stopped so that the bodies could be reburied. Ultimately, 419 bodies were uncovered, almost half of them children, indicating a high level of infant mortality.

The African Burial Ground was proclaimed a national monument in 2006. A small bit of green carved out of the surrounding office complex, the ground level is seven burial mounds containing the reinterred bodies. A visitor's center showcases the history of the slave trade and New York's central role in it. The centerpiece is a hulking black granite monument that's fittingly sober for the subject matter and a reminder that the majority of the cemetery remains underground and undisturbed.

Where was the Collect Pond?

In addition to its many streams, pre- and colonial Manhattan also featured a number of ponds that were given names like Stuyvesant Skating Pond and Buttermilk Pond. At one time, these ponds were part of the fabric of city life. Later, nearly all were filled in. One of the most notable of these was the Collect Pond, a sixty-foot- (eighteen-meter-) deep spring-fed pool located just north of City Hall where Foley Square sits today. The name comes from the Dutch *kolch*, for "small body of water," which English speakers later modified to "collect." Besides being an early source of (relatively) safe drinking water, it was also a popular gathering spot for picnicking in warm weather and ice-skating in cold. Boys would sometimes ice-skate from the Collect Pond through the Lispenard marsh that ran from Broadway to the Hudson, out to the frozen Hudson River, and north up Minetta Stream (which emptied into the river near King Street) and into Greenwich Village.

By the early 1800s, though, the pond had become a polluted affront to the eyes and nose. The city filled in the pond in 1811, covering it with the short-lived community of Paradise Square, which soon began to subside and was suffused with horrible smells. In the 1830s, Paradise Square had acquired a new, more infamous name: Five Points.

What are The Tombs?

The proper, and far less vivid, name for this storied link in downtown Manhattan's archipelago of crime and justice is the Manhattan Detention Center. Situated near the old Collect Pond and conveniently within a few blocks of both the courts at Civic Center and the Five Points neighborhood, the appropriately dark and gloomy edifice was roundly disliked from the day it opened in 1838. Within days, the editor of the *Herald* called for the "loathsome and dreary charnel house" to be torn down. Based for some reason on a picture of an Egyptian mausoleum, the "Halls of Justice" started to be referred to by the public as "the Tombs" and the name stuck even after the original building was torn down and no-cheerier replacements were built around the turn of the century and in 1941.

The current Tombs—a more modernist structure with no Egyptian inspiration—is located at Centre and White streets a block north of Collect Pond Park. During the lifespan of the second Tombs, a steel bridge connected it to the old Criminal Courts Building.

Called the "Bridge of Sighs" because it was crossed by those on their way to execution, it was crossed by about half a million prisoners in its time. Given its long life, the Tombs have featured a rogues' gallery of guests over the years, and even been named for some of them. (From 2007 to 2015, the Tombs was known as the Bernard B. Kerik Complex, after Mayor Giuliani's police commissioner who was later indicted on corruption charges.)

CHINATOWN/LITTLE ITALY/ LOWER EAST SIDE/ TRIBECA/SOHO

What are the current borders of Chinatown?

The Chinatowns one finds in most American cities today are generally little more than a cluster of Chinese restaurants and the occasional scrap of pagoda architecture nodding to its past as a true immigrant enclave. However, New York's Chinatown remains a vibrant, organic neighborhood with some 150,000 residents of Chinese ethnicity, making it the largest Chinese community by population in America. The first Chinese immigrants moved to the city in the mid-nineteenth century. A century later, Chinatown was still relatively small in size, centered around Pell, Doyers, and Mott streets between the Manhattan Bridge and Columbus Park on the Lower East Side.

Chinatown began to expand in the 1960s, moving into blocks that had until then been part of Little Italy. The main cause for this was that after the 1965 immigration

A view of Pell Street in Chinatown.

What is so significant about the playground at Seward Park?

Among the programs undertaken by municipal reformers in the late nineteenth century to improve the lives of New Yorkers was a new idea inspired by John Dewey's advocacy for the importance of play in children's development: playgrounds. America's first playground opened in San Francisco's Golden Gate Park in 1887. But the first permanent, city-built playground opened in 1903 on the Lower East Side at Seward Park on Essex and Canal. It became a model for the playgrounds that spread quickly throughout the city. The Tenement House Commission noted approvingly how important the play available in the park was for the neighborhood's "anemic, underfed, and mentally overdeveloped young people."

quotas were lifted, Chinese immigration increased dramatically at about the same time that Italians, whose immigration to America had peaked earlier in the century, were moving out of the old ethnic neighborhood. Today's Chinatown takes up about three dozen blocks between Broadway and Essex streets, from Worth Street north to around Hester, but concentrated mostly around and below Canal Street.

What was the "Bloody Angle"?

This was the not-exactly salubrious nickname for the bend that Doyers Street takes just south of Pell Street right by one of the oldest restaurants in the city, the Nom Wah Tea Parlor. It was once a favorite spot for members of one tong (Chinatown gangs whose legend always far exceeded their actual numbers, but who still did engage in a fair amount of street skirmishes) to ambush another with revolvers and hatchets. According to the not-always-trustworthy Herbert Asbury, police at around the turn of the century thought that "more men have been murdered at the Bloody Angle" than anywhere else in the world. Apparently, gangsters built tunnels underneath the street to serve as quick escape hatches. Until not too far in the past, the Hip Sing Tong was headquartered just a block away on Pell Street.

Where did Canal Street get its name?

Running through the heart of Chinatown and Little Italy, Canal Street's helter-skelter of merchants and tourists makes it one of the most visible remnants of New York's pre-war hustle and bustle. It originated as a glorified drainage ditch dug to drain water from the filthy Collect Pond into the Hudson. The Collect Pond was filled in by 1811 and Canal Street built in 1820. Today it connects the Hudson Tunnel on the western side of the island with the Manhattan Bridge on the east.

When was the first Feast of San Gennaro Festival held?

An annual religious procession and street fair that takes over Little Italy for eleven days each September was first celebrated in 1926. It was started by new immigrants from

207

Naples who had settled on Mulberry and wanted to continue the tradition of honoring their home city's patron saint on the day of his martyrdom in 305 C.E. For days beforehand, the neighborhood becomes a riot of fried food stands, starry strings of lights, and even carnival rides. The centerpiece of the festival is the September 19 religious procession, during which a statue of St. Gennaro is carried down Mulberry and Mott streets after mass at the Most Precious Blood Church.

Is Little Italy that Italian anymore?

Today, Little Italy is like many other faded ethnic enclaves in major Western cities: a somewhat ersatz collection of restaurants and stores that cater to tourists and the occasional nostalgia-besotted old-timer who wants to see the cold-water flat where grandma and grandpa raised seven kids. In the late nineteenth century, though, this was another tightly packed corner of southeast Manhattan's immigrant processing neighborhoods. Even though the part of East Harlem up around 110th Street actually had more Italian and Italian-American residents, it was always the more densely populated downtown neighborhood that was the community's heart.

Little Italy's borders have shifted over the years with the change of demographics and fading memories. Once it was considered to stretch from City Hall all the way to Houston Street—these days maybe just the few blocks between Canal and Broome. But the center of Little Italy has always been Mulberry Street. That was true back in 1890, when Jacob Riis wrote disapprovingly about the area's "Italian influx" in *How the Other Half Lives*, characterizing it as a "vast human pig-sty."

What's the heart of Little Italy?

Mulberry Street is where you will find all the mainstays of Little Italy. The red-sauce eateries with the aggressive touts flapping menus in tourists' faces, the old guys toddling along smoking cigars, the pastry shops, and all the Italian-flag and mob-movie paraphernalia one could shake a stick at. Most Precious Blood Church is at 109, one of the neighborhood's remaining social hubs. At 176 the Mulberry Street Bar serves as another focal point. Just around the corner from Mulberry at 200 Grand Street is Di Palo's, an Italian food store that opened in 1903 and is still run by fifth-generation family members. Then there's 247 Mulberry, now a boutique but once the location of the Ravenite Social Club, where hundreds of mobsters stopped by in 1985 to pay their respects to the new head of the Gambino crime family just a few days after the old boss Paul Castellano was killed.

Little Italy celebrated in 2006, when Italy won the FIFA World Cup in soccer.

How do you pronounce "Houston Street" like a New Yorker?

Among the many peculiarities of New York pronunciation is the way that locals say the name of the east-west street that divides SoHo and Noho. As newcomers quickly learn, Houston Street is not pronounced the same as one would the Texas city ("HEW-ston") but instead "HOW-ston." The street was built on land owned by Nicholas Bayard III (1644–1707), who named it in honor of his son-in-law, William Houstoun (1755–1813), a Georgia delegate to the Continental Congress. The current spelling, "Houston," is actually a mistake; it was last spelled properly as "Houstoun" in city records in 1811.

The local Mafia isn't what it used to be, though, and there are precious few Italians still living in the old neighborhood. Driven out by a combination of rising rents and the usual postwar immigrant shift to the suburbs, Italian-Americans only accounted for about five percent of the neighborhood's population in the 2000 census. But the ghosts of Mulberry Street's past are stubborn, indeed.

Is there another St. Patrick's Cathedral?

When most people hear "St. Patrick's," they think of the soaring structure up on Fifth Avenue across from Rockefeller Center. But the original St. Patrick's, a Gothic Revival church that looks far bigger inside than out, and which still stands proudly in a historical yet boutique-littered downtown quadrant at Mulberry and Prince streets in Nolita, could be considered the city's true cathedral. Designed by Joseph François Mangin (1758–?), who also crafted City Hall, and opened in 1815, it was the city's second Catholic church (it was built on land purchased by trustees of the first church, St. Peter's, for use as a cemetery) and the diocese's first cathedral. It served as a focal point for the then-heavily Irish neighborhood, which was threatened in 1844 by anti-Catholic rioting. Bishop John Hughes organized protection against the Nativist rioters with the help of armed Irish groups like the Ancient Order of Hibernians, headquartered next door.

Things are quieter these days. It was designated a basilica in 2010 and underwent extensive restoration to be ready for its 206th anniversary in 2015. There is a small aboveground cemetery on the grounds, as well as crypts underneath. In the crypts underneath are a few notable remains, including those of Pierre Toussaint (1766–1853), a Haitian-born slave who became a prominent abolitionist, and Civil War general Thomas Eckert (1825–1910), whose family tomb features ornate black metal grates and is lit by original Thomas Edison bulbs.

How did LOMEX almost destroy SoHo?

This battle of the acronyms took place in the 1960s. Before then, the neighborhood between Houston and Canal streets, Sixth Avenue to about Broadway, was an old industrial district that had fallen on hard times. In the early nineteenth century, after Canal

Street had paved over its polluted namesake, the area had turned into a fashionable residential and shopping area. After the Civil War, factories and offices moved in, many built in the new style of cast-iron architecture, where the functional metal structures were covered up by elaborate Gothic or Italianate facades.

By the 1950s and '60s, many of the buildings had emptied out. Seizing on the opportunity, Robert Moses proposed building the Lower Manhattan Expressway (LOMEX). His ten-lane elevated highway would have demolished much of SoHo and Little Italy so that commuters crossing from New Jersey to Long Island could have a quicker drive. Even though artists had been moving into the neighborhood since the 1950s to take advantage of the large industrial loft spaces and cheap rents, a Moses-friendly group released a report that proclaimed there were "no buildings worth saving" in the "South of Houston Industrial Area" (an abbreviation of which in another planning study from 1963 is where "SoHo" came from).

Who stopped LOMEX?

Moses and Mayor Lindsay pushed hard for LOMEX. But a concentrated campaign by preservationists, including Jane Jacobs—who had scuttled Moses's plans in 1962 to designate Greenwich Village as a slum in order to demolish much of it—fought hard to convince the city of both the uniqueness of the district and lack of need for the expressway. LOMEX was defeated. In 1973, SoHo was officially protected by being designated a historic district.

Not long after, the rightness of Jacobs's cause became clear. Starting in the 1970s, SoHo's artistic ecosystem flowered with galleries, stores, and performance spaces. As SoHo turned into an incubator for the downtown arts scene that transformed the city through the decade and into the 1980s, boutiques, cutting-edge companies, and luxury apartments soon followed. Today, the neighborhood is one of the most expensive and desired retail and residential districts in New York.

What does "Tribeca" mean?

Like most abbreviated New York geographic labels, Tribeca is more prose than poetry. The "Triangle Below Canal" is a smallish area slotted in between the World Trade Center and SoHo, running from about Chambers Street up to Canal, west to the Hudson River and east to Broadway. Originally known as the Lower West Side, it was subdivided into the city's first residential neighborhood in the early nineteenth century. A few decades on, the area became more commercial, centered on the expanding docks on the Hudson and the

A map outlining the boundaries of the Tribeca neighborhood.

Washington Market. The largest such market in the nation, this was a sprawling, cacophonous space built in 1812 at Washington, Vesey, and Fulton streets where most of the city bought its food, much of it brought in thousands of wagons from surrounding farms. The *New York Times* wasn't alone when in 1853 it called the market a "receptacle for filth, a nest of crime, and in every respect a nuisance to the city." The market relocated to Hunts Point in the Bronx in 1967.

Much like SoHo, Tribeca's elegant commercial buildings were seriously decayed and often empty by World War II, but were first reappropriated starting in the 1970s and '80s by artists hunting for creation and performing spaces, then later by cool-hunters and stylish restaurants. The district was economically hard hit by the 9/11 attacks. In 2003, Robert De Niro (1943–) helped start the Tribeca Film Festival as a way of rejuvenating the neighborhood. (One of the world's biggest and most star-studded, the festival continues today, though often at venues so far uptown they make the name something of a joke.) Tribeca today, while just as expensive as SoHo, is more spacious and quiet than its neighbor to the north, which can feel at times like an outdoor shopping mall for millionaires.

GREENWICH VILLAGE/EAST VILLAGE

When was Greenwich Village founded?

In the first century of European habitation on Manhattan, there were almost no settlers living north of Wall Street but for farms that were scattered all the way up to modern-day Harlem. Starting in the 1630s, however, some Dutch had started settling about two miles (three kilometers) north near the Indian fishing village along Minetta Brook. The area was called Noortwyck ("North District"). In the 1670s, Yellis Mandeville (1626–1701) bought land in Noortwyck and called it Greenwijck ("Pine District") for an early Dutch settlement out on Long Island. Mandeville's will recorded the region as Greenwich Village in 1696.

For decades, the Village stood on its own as a quiet suburban hamlet, operating at a different speed from the faster-paced mercantile hustle south of Wall Street. By the time the city's northward sprawl had reached the Village, it had already developed its own unique character, one that the residents fought to preserve over the years. When the 1811 street grid was announced, the Village kept it from remapping their neighborhood. Today, pedestrians crossing west of Sixth Avenue find themselves in a suddenly tilted street plan that has sent more than a few tourists wandering in frustrated circles.

Where did Minetta Street get its name?

Today Minetta Street is one of the city's most charming streets, a block-long, hockey-stick of a lane that bends up from Sixth Avenue and Bleecker like a secret entryway into Greenwich Village. In the seventeenth century, this part of town was known as the Negroes'

211

Farms. The name derived from the freed slaves settled here by Dutch leaders who reportedly wanted a buffer between their small colony downtown and the Native Americans further up the island. A stream named Manetta (Bestavaar's Kill to the Dutch) ran through the settlement and the footpath that followed it was termed "the Negroes' Causeway."

The paths in this area were later renamed Minetta Street and Minetta Lane (which runs across the T at the top end of Minetta Street) after the stream—which ran through the present-day campus of New York University and fed into the swampland that became Washington Square Park—was paved over in the early nineteenth century. Heavily frequented today by camera-wielding tourists and film crews, in the nineteenth century Minetta Street and Lane were the kind of crime-ridden neighborhoods that newspapers loved publishing wild and not necessarily fact-checked stories about.

How come Bank Street got its name when there aren't any banks on it?

About six blocks long, Bank Street runs east through the northern district of Greenwich Village from Greenwich Street to the river. Despite its name, you won't see many banks on this picturesque stretch of low apartment buildings and pocket-sized stores and restaurants. In 1822, a yellow fever epidemic was burning through the city. As in previous outbreaks, people with the means to travel decamped for less populated quarters. This time was no different, with many denizens of lower Manhattan moving up and out of the island's crowded southern quadrant. One of the more popular destinations was the still semi-rural Greenwich Village. So many financial institutions relocated here that this short lane was named Bank Street. Hundreds of houses were built throughout the Village to house the newcomers, many of whom chose to stay after the fever had passed, changing the area's character permanently. The Village's population quadrupled from 1825 to 1840.

Why was part of Greenwich Village called Little Africa?

In 1830, there were around 14,000 freed blacks living in New York, and most of them were concentrated in the part of Greenwich Village near Minetta Street known as Little Africa. A typical view of this part of town was related in an 1896 report by Stephen Crane (1871–1900) in the *New York Herald*, with its lurid tales of crime and mayhem and people with nicknames like "No-Toe Charley" and the "famous bandit" "Black-Cat." The Village at the time was also one of the city's most diverse areas, with newcomers of all kinds drawn by the cheap housing. The 1900 census shows that a small cluster of buildings along Minetta Lane housed Italians, Germans, Russians, Belgians, French, and blacks born in America, Africa, Bermuda, and Barbados, as well as several mixed-race couples. Jacob Riis wrote disapprovingly of the "black-and-tan" saloons that proliferated along "the border land" between Little Africa and the nearby Italian district where black and white customers "meet in common debauch." One of New York's periodic pushes for civic order resulted in the area's tenements being cleared away.

An influx of white immigrants and a desire of many black residents to move to more desirable uptown addresses saw the black population begin to drop after the turn of the century. One of the signs of this move was the shift north, starting in the 1890s, of the

Village's several historic black churches. The Abyssinian Baptist Church on Waverly Street, which had opened its doors in 1808 by First Baptist Church members (including some natives of Ethiopia, then known as Abyssinia) protesting the segregation of blacks into a so-called "slave loft," moved in 1902 to Midtown and eventually Harlem. The name Little Africa was nearly forgotten.

How did the Village get its reputation as America's bohemian capital?

One of the greatest clichés in American culture is the kid from some straight-laced podunk hamlet that they never fit into, moving to New York, finding a cheap place somewhere in Greenwich Village and, after falling in love with its unconventional mélange of cultures and personalities, realizing that they've finally found where they belonged. Certainly the Village's reputation for wildness has long been overblown. But starting in the early twentieth century, the low-slung and jumbled district—bounded by 14th Street on the north, Fourth Avenue on the east, and Houston Street on the south—became an affordable and generally tolerant mecca for political radicals, artistic trailblazers, and generally bohemian free spirits. The low rents, cozy side streets seemingly designed to baffle outsiders, us-against-them insularity, and mix of ethnicities made the Village— particularly its more picturesque West Village quadrant around Bleecker and Hudson streets—a fertile topsoil for creativity and tumult.

The Village nurtured an impressive succession of movements in its narrow confines. In the early twentieth century, activist journalist John Reed (writer of *Ten Days That Shook the World* and basis of Warren Beatty's *Reds*) was the nexus of a cabal of writers that included Eugene O'Neill (1888–1953), Marianne Moore (1887–1972), and Edna St. Vincent Millay (1892–1950). During Prohibition, many of the smaller, more glamorous speakeasies were in the Village. They were followed in the postwar years by clubs promoting jazz, avant-garde theater, and new trends like open-mike poetry readings, stand-up comedy, and the resurgent folk movement. All of this cultural and political energy seemed to turn the neighborhood into America's version of Paris's Left Bank, a sentiment sweetly summed up in the song "Christopher Street" from the 1953 musical

Is the Village still "the Village"?

By any reasonable standard: No. To be fair, that's something people have been saying almost as long as the Village had its own identity. According to Louis Menand (1952–), Floyd Dell (1887–1969) was the first person to say "The Village isn't what it used to be." Dell, a writer from Illinois who'd lived in the Village under three years, reportedly made that declaration back in 1916. There are still great off-Broadway theaters and charming side streets with more character than whole sections of other cities. However, it is safe to say that in an era like today—in 2015 a five-bedroom townhouse on East 10th Street sold for $32 million—the definition of what "the Village" means has perhaps permanently changed.

Wonderful Town: "On your left, Waverly Place / Bit of Paree in Greenwich Village." The Village's status as cultural and social incubator was further cemented by its identification with the Beatnik literary movement in the 1950s and the beginning of the gay rights movement in the 1960s.

What is "the Cage"?

At the intersection of West 4th Street and Sixth Avenue in Greenwich Village, you will find the West 4th Street Courts. This unpresuming court is actually one of the world's most famous sites in basketball lore. The fenced-in court known as "the Cage" is smaller than regulation, which likely enhances the intensity of the pick-up games that frequently draw large appreciative crowds to this corner. The Cage is home to a popular all-star game and slam-dunk contest every summer.

What did Washington Square Park begin as?

Today, Washington Square Park, a crowded but expansive rectangle of greenery, benches, trees, mercenary chess players, buskers, film crews, the occasional drug dealer, skateboarders, and NYU students blowing off classes, is one of the most archetypal and beloved urban parks in the city, if not the country. Sitting at the nexus between Greenwich Village to the west, NYU to the south and east, and to the north the stately grandiosity of Fifth Avenue which begins its march uptown at Washington Square Arch, it incorporates elements of all of those neighborhoods.

As with other now-grand New York public spaces, though, it wasn't always thus. Back in 1797, this was still mostly marshland near the Lenape village of Sapokanikan that had once been farmed by freed slaves and was fed by old Minetta Creek. The city (still located far to the south below today's Canal Street but starting to move north) decided to buy up the area for use as a potter's field for criminals, epidemic victims, or those too poor to pay for a burial. An estimated 20,000 people were buried here in just a few years; the epidemics that burned through the city between 1797 and 1803 carried off many victims. The bodies were never disinterred, so they all remain beneath the park's landscaping. A new potter's field was opened up at what later became Bryant Park; apparently nobody ever wanted to build on top of these grounds. In 1827, the area was declared a free "public space." It was named the Washington Military Parade Ground (shortened to just Washington Square) for the 50th anniversary of the signing of the Declaration of Independence. Over the following decades, the park was transformed by landscaping and surrounded by simple but stately homes. Henry James, who grew up on Washington Place on the park's western verge, remarked in *Washington Square* that circa 1835 it was "the ideal of quiet and of genteel retirement ... [having] a kind of established repose which is not of frequent occurrence in other quarters of the long, shrill city."

Is there actually a "Hanging Tree" in Washington Square Park?

There is an old elm tree on the northwest corner of the park that is called the "Hanging Tree" (or sometimes the "Hangman's Elm"), but it isn't thought that anybody was actually hanged from it. For a time, though, the park was apparently home to active gallows whose customers were in large part drawn from the state's Newgate Prison just west at the Hudson River and 10th Street. The only recorded instance of a person actually being executed at the gallows—supposedly located where the central fountain is today—took place in 1819, when a young black woman named Rose Butler was hanged for arson.

Where's the best place to find somebody to play chess with?

That depends on how good you are, and how much money you have. New York has a deep network of chess stores and clubs that have been turning out championship players for decades. But they can also be found in less rarified settings such as

The Hanging Tree in Washington Square Park probably never got used to hang anyone.

Washington Square Park. The chess hustlers who congregate here are generally pretty sharp at playing an abbreviated game called speed or blitz chess, for money. It's a fairly unforgiving environment but exciting to take part in for everyone from neophytes to pros like Stanley Kubrick (1928–1999), who hung out around the chess tables here in the early 1960s, and even Bobby Fischer (1942–2008). You can also often find willing players in Union Square and other parks around town.

How did the Meatpacking District get its name?

The rough triangle of cobblestone streets and boutiques wedged in south of Chelsea and north of Greenwich Village and facing the Hudson River not so long ago deserved its name, and was almost as famous for its smells as the sights of freshly carved carcasses swaying from metal hooks. The neighborhood developed in the early 1800s with a mix of single-family houses and tenements as well as factories, a not unusual combination in New York at the time. Some of the neighborhood's more elegant townhouses can still be seen in its southern stretches near Gansevoort Street, which follows an old Indian trial to the Hudson, where a never-used fort was constructed to defend the city from the British during the War of 1812. The fort was knocked down in the 1840s to make room for the southern terminus of the Hudson River Railroad.

After the Civil War, following the city's trend of increasing neighborhood segregation, the area began to transition into a more strictly industrial-focused area sandwiched between two primarily residential regions. Instead of fancy homes, the area became known for new wholesale facilities like the Gansevoort Market and West Washington

Market which were built to replace the seedier and more decrepit Washington Market downtown. The latter became one of the biggest neighborhood businesses, with buildings retrofitted with refrigeration and the notable sidewalk-overhanging metal canopies fitted with conveyor-belt hooks to haul carcasses inside for dressing.

When did the Meatpacking District start to change?

For decades, the distinctive low-slung buildings and cobblestoned streets of the Meatpacking District bustled with commerce. When shipping into the west side piers fell off in the 1960s and '70s, the neighborhood also went into decline. But it has roared back in more recent years, with its old signatures (meat packers and transvestite prostitutes) giving way to fancy boutiques, galleries, and restaurants.

When did the Whitney Museum move to the Meatpacking District?

In the 1920s, Gertrude Vanderbilt Whitney (1875–1942) wanted to donate her collection of hundreds of works by new artists to the Metropolitan Museum of Art. However, like most art institutions of the time, the Met wasn't interested in collecting any of the challenging new pieces that were sending shockwaves through the art world. So in 1929 she opened the Whitney Museum of American Art in a row of townhouses on West 8th Street.

The museum later moved uptown, occupying in 1966 the strikingly brutalist purpose-built Breuer Building at 75th Street and Madison Avenue. There, the Whitney es-

Greenwich Village in lower Manhattan is a residential neighborhood with a reputation for being *the* place for bohemian artists and the modern LGBTQ movement.

tablished itself as the preeminent exhibitor of modern American art, with important works ranging from Edward Hopper (1882–1967) to Jasper Johns (1930–) and Georgia O'Keeffe (1887–1986). Starting in the early 1970s, the Whitney Biennial became perhaps the art world's most provocative and attention-grabbing exhibition. After unsuccessfully trying to expand the widely loathed Breuer to accommodate its permanent collection of over 21,000 works, the Whitney finally moved back downtown in 2015 to a brighter and airier building on Gansevoort near the Hudson River.

What does the East Village have to do with Greenwich Village?

Except for a general latitudinal relationship and (at one time, at least) a proliferation of young bar-hoppers, nothing. The so-called East Village runs from 14th down to Houston Street and from the Bowery to the East River. For many years it was considered just a northern offshoot of the Lower East Side. That is, until the 1960s when the artists and writers already getting priced out of Greenwich Village came here looking for cheap housing. Real estate agents got in on the action and thusly the East Village was born. From the 1970s through the '90s, it had a reputation as the rougher hipster neighborhood, where art punks, squatters, and dealers rubbed shoulders in pest-infested apartments and grubby music clubs.

Centered around the blocks-long bazaar of bars, tattoo parlors, and restaurants that is St. Mark's Place and Tompkins Square Park—which the city shut down between 1990 and 1992 after police evictions of a homeless settlement resulted in rioting—the neighborhood's streets are filled with old tenement housing that recalls a past only vaguely

Where was the Old Pear Tree?

One of Peter Stuyvesant's first acts after arriving in New Amsterdam as its new director general in 1647 would end up lasting over two centuries. He planted a pear tree sapling that he had brought from the Netherlands on his farm, which occupied an area north of the city in what became the East Village. The tree flourished and over the years became a symbol of New York's enduring past even as the city blossomed around it. The intersection where the tree stood at 13th Street and Third Avenue eventually became known as "Pear Tree Corner." An 1861 lithograph shows the tree on a busy intersection guarded by a tall metal fence.

The tree lasted as the city's oldest until February 27, 1867, when it was knocked down after two horse carts collided nearby. A mounted cross-section of the original tree can be seen at the New-York Historical Society. In 2003 a new pear tree was planted at the same corner. Also still standing at the same intersection is Kiehl's Pharmacy, which has operated there since 1851 and was originally known as the Pear Tree Pharmacy before expanding into an international concern hawking skin care products that frequently cost more than a meal in a hot new SoHo restaurant.

alluded to in old immigrant clusters like Ukrainian Village. These days the East Village is more known for the gentrifying condos sprouting everywhere and the young crowds of partiers that fill the avenues come the weekend.

What is the only true east–west street in Manhattan?

In order to keep their bearings, New Yorkers tend to think of Manhattan streets as running east to west and avenues north to south. Given the tilt of the island, this is far from true, with both being on a diagonal. But here and there, particularly below 14th Street, small interruptions in the grid plan break that rule. Cutting through the street grid on an apparent slant, Broadway is actually closer to a magnetic north alignment than the other avenues. Also, in the East Village, short Stuyvesant Street, which cuts from Third Avenue just below 9th Street east toward 10th Street, where it dead-ends at St. Mark's Church-in-the-Bowery, is just about the only actual east-west street on the island. This is also one of the only remnants of the old true north street grid laid out on the grounds of Peter Stuyvesant's estate. Incidentally, the Federal-style house at No. 44 was built in 1795, making it probably the oldest building in the entire Village, East or West.

Where's the best church for a poetry slam?

St. Mark's-in-the-Bowery was built in 1799 on top of Peter Stuyvesant's chapel (his family's burial vault sits underneath the church today), making it the oldest site of continuous religious worship in the city. Back then, the Georgian-style church with fieldstone walls was set in the somewhat bucolic surroundings of the Bowery Village, which was so far uptown at the time that it served as a getaway for people escaping epidemics downtown.

In more modern times, while still continuing as an Episcopal place of worship, St. Mark's became a linchpin of the East Village arts scene. Kahlil Gibran (1883–1931) and Edna St. Vincent Millay were involved with the arts committee formed in 1919. Martha Graham (1894–1991) danced here in 1930. Over the following decades, the church became one of the city's most important venues for experimental theater and spoken word events. The Poetry Project has hosted readings at St. Mark's since 1966, including Allen Ginsberg (1926–1997) and Patti Smith (1946–). A fire in 1978 nearly burned the church down; most of the current building was recreated in the years since.

UNION SQUARE/FLATIRON/ MADISON SQUARE/GRAMERCY

What did Union Square start out as?

When the great uniformity of the 1811 street grid was put into place, just about the only irregularity it allowed was the diagonal path of Broadway. Having that street cutting across the city allowed for some unique triangular spaces to break up the grid's rectilinear nature. One of those spaces was Union Place, an old potter's field that the original plan turned into a public square to stretch from 10th (later 14th) to 17th streets and between Broadway and Fourth Avenue. It was renamed Union Square and opened in 1839 as a beautifully landscaped public square focused around a large fountain and meant to evoke the residential squares of London.

One of many such urban spaces designed to keep wealthy Manhattanites from fleeing to the boroughs, it quickly became the nexus of a fashionable neighborhood filled with hotels and close by the city's top-flight shopping district, the Ladies' Mile, and the Academy of Music. After another redesign in 1872 by the then-ubiquitous Frederick Law Olmsted and Calvert Vaux, it also featured a muster ground and reviewing stand. The later part of the nineteenth century saw the square become a frequent gathering spot for marches and labor protests. The first Labor Day march took place here in 1882. That tradition of mass gatherings continued into the next century.

How did Union Square remain vital?

The Union Square neighborhood fell into disrepair in later decades, keeping a kind of vibrancy alive with the presence of bookstores and avant-garde destinations like the music hangout Max's Kansas City on Park Avenue just above the square's northwest corner. Between 1968 and 1973, Andy Warhol's Factory—with its revolving cast of "Su-

Union Square is located where Broadway and 14th Street meet. The name refers to the fact that the park is at the union of these two main streets; it has nothing to do with the Union of the Civil War era, as some might think.

perstars" and hangers-on making art out of themselves in the silvery-walled space while Warhol (1928–1987) recorded and filmed them, when not making his own silkscreen artworks in the midst of all the tumult—operated in the Decker Building on Union Square West. Starting in the 1980s the area began a turnaround, symbolized by the 1985 opening of the iconic Union Square Café. The restaurant took advantage of the square's Greenmarket, which began in 1976, and remains an ever-more-popular destination that started a decades-long trend in casual yet high-end ingredient-focused dining, before succumbing in 2015 to the forces of gentrification that it helped spark.

Today, the square is a luxuriant theater of yuppiedom, walled by stores and restaurants and peopled, particularly in the more wide-open southern stretch, by the college students, musicians, performance artists, protestors, and other performative personalities that make up the modern era's superstars.

Where can you find eighteen miles (twenty-nine kilometers) of books under one roof?

At one point, you could walk south down Fourth Avenue from Union Square and find up to three dozen used bookstores in just a few blocks. The last survivor of what used to be called Book Row is the Strand Bookstore, which started business on Fourth Avenue in 1927 and later moved over to its current location at Broadway and 12th Street. Similar to most of the independent bookstores that have survived in New York, like McNally Jackson on Prince Street, the Strand hits that fine line between cluttered and well-curated selection that brings book lovers from all over. Unlike those other stores, though, the Strand specializes in high-quality used books: about 2.5 million of them on eighteen miles (twenty-nine kilometers) of tightly packed shelves.

How do you get into Gramercy Park?

You don't. One of the defining characteristics of parks in New York (as just about everywhere else) is that they can be enjoyed by anybody. That's part and parcel of their desirability. But as beautiful as Central Park and Prospect Park might be, there's another city park that's almost as gorgeous and nearly impossible for you to see. Why? That's because Gramercy Park, a manicured two-acre greenspace girdled by a thicket of regulations and elegant wrought-iron fencing that covers everything between 18th and 23rd streets, and Third Avenue to Park Avenue South, is the city's only true private park.

The park was built in 1831 as the centerpiece to a London-style planned neighborhood by developer Samuel Ruggles (1800–1881), who drained the swamps and built blocks of elegant townhouses to take advantage of the housing boom that followed the opening of the Erie Canal in 1825. Ruggles, who could have made much more money by partitioning off the park, saw the importance of keeping it as an exclusive, fountain-centered oasis in the clamorous urban environment. The only people who have keys to open the gates are those who live facing the park and pay the fees necessary to keep up the place. The charges are steep and the rules are many (you can't smoke, toss a Frisbee, or take a photograph inside the park). Rumor has it that guests of room-sharing services in certain neighboring buildings get visiting access, but only in the company of their hosts. More simply (if not more affordably), guests at the Gramercy Park Hotel on the north side of the park are given keys inside as well.

Where did Irving Place get its name?

If you look at the city's original 1811 grid plan, there are a few things you won't see on there, such as Central Park. Another is Lexington Avenue, between Park and Third avenues. In the early 1830s, when Ruggles was developing the old Gramercy Farm into his model neighborhood, he lobbied for the right to open up a new avenue running from the southern edge of Gramercy Park at 20th Street down to 14th. His persistence won out; probably because the city was grateful that he spent so much money leveling and draining the swampy, gulley-crossed area. Ruggles was granted the right to add his street to the grid and to name it after his good friend Washington Irving who, contrary to popular opinion, never lived there. There is a rather famous three-story Italianate house at Irving Place and 17th known today as the Washington Irving House even though, again, Irving never lived there. A few years later, the city continued Irving Place to the north of Gramercy Park and called it Lexington Avenue.

How big is Stuyvesant Town?

During the 1940s, in the interest of clearing out slums and creating affordable middle-class housing in the city, the state passed a law encouraging private firms to get involved. One of the most transformative results of that law was the creation of Stuyvesant Town. Built between 1943 and 1947, it displaced eleven thousand people to construct thirty-five buildings with nearly nine thousand apartments in eighteen densely packed but still tree-shaded blocks bounded by First Avenue, 14th and 20th streets, and the East River. Along with the smaller Peter Cooper Village to the north, Stuyvesant Town was a popular and quite affordable housing option for returning veterans. Its success was marred, though, by restrictions that barred anybody but married white couples from living there. More recently the complex has changed owners a few times and the rent increased quite a bit since 1950, when the median rent was $76 a month.

How long was the Ladies' Mile?

It is just about fourteen blocks. Starting in the 1830s and '40s, the neighborhood north of Washington Square became one of the city's most desirable. The side streets were packed with brownstone townhouses, like the one that housed the Roosevelts at 28 East 20th Street. While the avenues featured mansions and, increasingly, shops for the city's growing leisure clas, after the Civil War, the center of the fashionable shopping district shifted more from Broadway north of Union Square over to Sixth Avenue particularly once the elevated Sixth Avenue train station opened in 1878.

From then through the turn of the century, shoppers could start at A. T. Stewart's (1803–1876) new store on 9th Street (his first location, down by City Hall, had been the city's first department store) and proceed north to 23rd Street through the ranks of dry-goods palaces—Brooks Brothers, F. A. O. Schwartz, Lord & Taylor, Macy's, Tiffany's—finding along the way just about everything the fashionable New Yorker could need. Most of the stores catered to the so-called "carriage trade," named for the wealthy women who arrived in horse-drawn carriages. One of the most popular stops was Siegel-Cooper Dry Goods, advertised as "The Big Store—A City in Itself." Built in 1896, this six-story steel frame Beaux-Arts building took up most of a block at 19th Street and Sixth Avenue, featured a huge fountain on its main floor, and reputedly employed eight thousand clerks. As the density of stores increased, boarding houses for their employees began opening on the side streets. After the turn of the century, office buildings began to populate the area, and many of the larger stores started to move further uptown. The Ladies' Mile was designated a historic district in 1989.

What is the Ladies' Mile like today?

The shopping frenzy that once typified the Ladies' Mile area is no more, such densities of consumption having moved north to certain stretches of Midtown or 34th Street west of the Empire State Building. Fifth Avenue and Broadway have regained a certain luster, with more high-end stores and restaurants opening each year in the ever-more-fashionable blocks between Union Square and Madison Square. These days, what the sitcom *Will and Grace* referred to as "that weird part of Sixth Avenue" up to 23rd Street has all the stores that one expects to find in big-box cloverleaf clusters out in the rest of America, not Manhattan: Best Buy; Bed, Bath, and Beyond (in the old Siegel-Cooper building);

The Ladies' Mile is a prime shopping district in Manhattan that established itself as such in the nineteenth century and is still distinguished today.

The Container Store; Burlington Coat Factory; Old Navy; Trader Joe's. There's even an Olive Garden and an Outback Steakhouse for less discriminating diners. The functionality of the old cast-iron architecture, whose lightweight construction allowed for fewer load-bearing pillars and thusly larger and brighter floors, is still attractive to modern retailers. The fact that these chain stores have been retrofitted into the Ladies' Mile's nineteenth-century emporiums, with their brightly spiffed-up facades, makes a certain kind of sense, as those original businesses were the forerunners of all the department stores that would spread the gospel of shopping-'til-you-drop across the country.

What did the Flatiron Building have to do with women's skirts?

Ever since Daniel Burnham's twenty-two-story Beaux-Arts office building went up at Broadway and Fifth Avenues at 23rd Street in 1902, it has retained its status as one of the city's most distinctive and certainly most photographed buildings; framed prints of Alfred Stieglitz (1864–1946) and Edward Steichen's (1879–1973) striking black-and-white shots of the Flatiron adorn many a New York apartment's wall. Technically named the Fuller Building for the Chicago businessman who built it, its north-facing side, squeezed by the intersection of Broadway and Fifth, is an acutely rounded angle resembling a ship's prow that's less than seven feet (two meters) wide. The nickname supposedly came from the triangular shape of the block it sits on, which was said to resemble a pressing iron. The Flatiron's unique shape and design—the *New York Times* fittingly and succinctly termed it a "palazzo-ish wedge"—and location at the intersection of numerous interlocking and overflowing Manhattan regions has given the Flatiron building multitudinous identities over the years. At one point it was considered a symbol of the Ladies' Mile and its northern sentinel. A century later, *New York* magazine called it "the gateway to downtown."

Curiously, the building's construction created powerful wind gusts. These became famous in city lore for blowing up women's skirts at a time when even the sight of a woman's bare ankle was still considered risqué. A 1905 film called *The Flatiron Building on a Windy Day* happily captured the skirt-lifting phenomena, which apparently attracted crowds of gawking men whom the police would frequently have to shoo away. Many sources claim that the policemen's dispersal shouts on 23rd Street gave rise to the catch phrase "Twenty-three skidoo"—meaning, basically: beat it. But the phrase actually predated the Flatiron Building.

After whom is Madison Square Park named?

Unusually, its namesake is a non-New Yorker: Virginian and Founding Father James Madison (1751–1836). This roughly seven-acre park between 23rd and 26th streets, Fifth and Park avenues has been designated as public space since the 1686 City Charter. It was the original site for the potter's field that was moved in 1797 to what became Washington Square, and was later a military parade ground and home for juvenile delinquents. Madison Square officially became a park in 1847. The park has long been a backyard of sorts for the fashionable neighborhood, bracketed by beautiful buildings like the Flatiron on the south side and the Metropolitan Life Insurance Building on the east. Today

223

Madison Square Park is one of the quietest, best designed greenspaces in the city, with frequent public art exhibits and a steady stream of people queuing for burgers or frozen custard at the original Shake Shack stand, when not simply taking the sun.

Where is Bellevue Hospital?

One of Manhattan's largest and most storied institutions is the Bellevue Hospital Center, which occupies the land between First Avenue and the FDR Drive and 26th and 28th streets. The oldest continuously operating hospital in America, it began as a six-bed infirmary on the second floor of the city's first almshouse in 1736 and moved to its current location in 1816. Originally focused on treating epidemic victims, Bellevue continued to expand its remit over the decades. Everything from tuberculosis and dental clinics to schools of midwifery and women's nursing was added on later. Bellevue was a groundbreaker in many ways, including the following firsts:

- Ambulance service (horse-and-buggy)
- American hospital to use hypodermic syringes
- Cesarean section in American hospital
- Maternity ward in American hospital
- Medical facility anywhere in the world to institute an official sanitary code

Today, besides being known for its psychiatric unit and treating many of the city's poorest patients, Bellevue is also the hospital of choice for injured firefighters and police, as well as visiting dignitaries.

CHELSEA/GARMENT DISTRICT/ HUDSON YARDS

What does Chelsea have to do with Christmas?

As discussed elsewhere, it could be said that Christmas was invented in the Chelsea neighborhood. Today, Chelsea runs from Sixth Avenue west to the Hudson, and from 14th Street up to about 28th. Clement Clarke Moore (1779–1863) grew up on the family estate that took up much of this land. His father, a British army captain, had named it Chelsea in honor of London's Royal Chelsea Hospital, which cared for old soldiers. Moore was a professor of literature at the General Theological Seminary, which is still in the neighborhood, on 21st Street between Ninth and Tenth avenues. He became famous for his 1822 children's poem "A Visit from St. Nicholas" which established the cultural origins of America's Father Christmas tradition. Moore was also, not surprisingly, attached to the family estate and was dismayed when the new city street grid began slashing it to pieces. In the 1830s, Moore finally relented and began selling off the estate for private lots at a massive profit. He built a stone wall around the family home between 22nd and 23rd streets to keep out the rapidly encircling city.

What is that tiny cemetery on 21st Street?

Shearith Israel, the city and nation's oldest Jewish congregation, has three historic cemeteries scattered around Manhattan. Their first and oldest cemetery is near Chatham Square downtown and contains the graves of several Revolutionary War veterans. The third cemetery is a tiny lot that was bought in 1829 and operated until 1851 (when the city outlawed burials south of 86th Street), holding about 250 graves. It sits today on West 21st Street between Sixth and Seventh avenues, a small square of green and blurry gravestones sandwiched incongruously between new Chelsea apartment buildings.

Why is the Hotel Chelsea so famous?

The fact that so many books have been written about the Hotel Chelsea—Sherill Tippins's *Inside the Dream Palace*, James Lough's oral history *This Ain't No Holiday Inn*, Dee Dee Ramone's novel *Chelsea Horror Hotel*, to name just a few—and the inspiration for at least two films—Warhol's

Clement Clarke Moore, who is famous for his poem "A Visit from St. Nicholas," lived on a family estate that occupied what is now Chelsea.

225

Chelsea Girls and Ethan Hawke's *Chelsea Walls*—is indicative of the titanic cultural stature held by the twelve-story Victorian apartment building with the distinctive cast-iron balconies with the sunflower designs on 23rd Street between Seventh and Eighth avenues. The Chelsea opened in 1883 as an exclusive co-op, a new trend in a city that had just become used to the idea of apartment dwelling.

It shifted to becoming a hotel after the turn of the century, and it was in that guise that it achieved notoriety. A glittering array of artists and writers called the Chelsea home in the following decades, with some occupying its long-term apartments for years. Arthur Miller (1915–2005) wrote *After the Fall* after his divorce from Marilyn Monroe (1926–62); Bob Dylan (1941–) wrote songs for *Blonde on Blonde*; and Arthur C. Clarke (1917–2008) worked on the screenplay for *2001: A Space Odyssey* while staying there. Other onetime residents included Patti Smith, Sam Shepard (1943–), O. Henry (1862–1910), and Valerie Solanas (1936–1988) before she shot Warhol in 1968. There are ghosts in the hotel as well: Dylan Thomas (1914–1953) died there from alcohol poisoning, as did Nancy Spungen (1958–1978) in a stabbing that her boyfriend, Sex Pistols bass player Sid Vicious (1957–1979), was suspected in. The building, still home to a number of long-term tenants, is being refurbished as a boutique hotel, its patina of drugged bohemia neatly scrubbed away.

Where is the Garment District?

Unlike most American cities, New York has relatively few neighborhoods identified for industries that no longer dominate the area. The most prominent exception to that rule in Manhattan is the Garment District. A thick block of medium-height buildings of mostly undifferentiated architectural styles, it occupies most streets from 35th to 41st streets between Madison and Eighth avenues. Its history is symbolized by a massive, whimsical statue of a 14-foot- (4.25-meter-) wide button and 31-foot- (9.5-meter-) long needle situated at 39th Street and Seventh Avenue. Not far away on the same corner is the statue of a yarmulke-wearing garment worker bent over his sewing machine; it was erected in 1984 in tribute to the many Jews who labored in the neighborhood's "needle trade." Tapping it supposedly brings good luck.

What does FIT stand for?

That would be the somewhat hilariously over-named Fashion Institute of Technology, or just plain FIT. The school was founded in 1944 for the specific purpose of becoming "an MIT for the fashion industries." FIT originally operated in the High School for Needle Trades on 24th Street before moving to its current location in 1959. That siting of that stark and grey eight-building complex on Seventh Avenue between 27th and 28th streets is no accident, situated as it is in the far-southern underbelly of the Garment District. With majors covering almost every aspect of fashion design, FIT currently enrolls over 10,000 students. Frequently featured on cable shows like *Project Runway*, FIT is in part responsible for the recent attempted rebranding of the Garment District as the "Fashion District," given that much of the area's clothing business has moved back towards high-end fashion and couture and away from the mass-scale garment manufacturing that typified the neighborhood during its heyday.

Why is it a bad idea to walk down 28th Street first thing in the morning?

Like the Jewelry District almost twenty blocks north, the Flower District's name is a bit more grandiose than the reality. But the century-old concentration of wholesale and retail flower shops, as well as floral design supply stores, on 28th Street between Sixth and Seventh avenues is still a sight to behold early in the day. Starting as early as 4:00 A.M., the sidewalks become crowded with merchants displaying everything from buckets of flowers to large potted plants while office workers dart through the narrow pathways left for them. The district has dwindled in size, but in a typical year, the stores on this one block still do around $100 million of business.

What did Old Penn Station have to do with the Landmarks Law?

New York's Pennsylvania Station opened for business in 1910. Designed by McKim, Mead, and White, it was a beautifully over-the-top palace of commuting, taking up several acres of land between Seventh and Eighth avenues, from 31st to 33rd streets. The outside was girdled by dozens of Doric columns, while inside grand windows atop the 150-foot (45.7-meter) vaulted ceiling flooded the concourse with light. The architects drew inspiration not just from the Acropolis, but the Brandenburg Gate, St. Peter's Basilica, and (for a final classical grace note) the Roman baths. Visible today only in old photographs, the size and scope of the station is as hard to fathom for modern travelers as the grandeur of some ancient temple.

A photo of the old Pennsylvania Station in 1911, shortly after it opened.

227

In an act of tremendous shortsightedness, the city of New York in 1963 decided to tear the station down. The belief at the time was that since the rest of the nation was throwing all of its transportation eggs into the automotive basket, the same thing would eventually happen in New York. Better to destroy it then, the thinking went, and reuse the land for something else before it became an expensive and useless old hulk, much like Detroit's long-abandoned Central Station. In a prophetic editorial for the *New York Times*, architecture critic Ada Louise Huxtable wrote: "Any city gets what it admires, will pay for, and, ultimately, deserves.... We want and deserve tin-can architecture in a tin-horn culture. And we will probably be judged not by the monuments we build but by those we have destroyed."

What is Penn Station like today?

Today's commuters shuffling through the airless, charmless, and claustrophobic tunnels underneath Madison Square Garden that constitute today's Penn Station would hardly argue with Huxtable's appellation of "tin-can architecture." Architectural historian Vincent Scully (1920–) wrote about the transformation of stations: "One entered the city like a god; one scuttles in now like a rat." But it didn't take long for the city to realize what it had done. Just two years after Penn Station fell to the wrecking ball, Mayor Robert Wagner enacted the New York Landmarks Law. Since then, the New York City Landmarks Preservation Commission has become the bane of fast-cash-hungry developers throughout the region by bestowing landmark status on over 1,300 individual landmarks and over a hundred historic districts. It's very possible that without that law, some of New York's most iconic structures, such as Grand Central Terminal, would no longer be with us.

Is Madison Square Garden the original?

It's nowhere near Madison Avenue and there's nary a speck of greenery to be seen at the bustling Midtown sports and music arena, so it makes perfect sense that Madison Square Garden wasn't always exactly what it looks like today. So far, four buildings have been given the same name, which according to *Harper's Weekly*, conjures up meanings of "hippodrome, theater, ballroom, restaurant, concert hall and summer garden, a sort of pleasure exchange." Everything and everyone from wild west extravaganzas and evangelical preachers to Billy Joel (1949–) and WrestleManias beyond count have filled the seats of this venue over nearly a century and a half.

How many Madison Square Gardens have there been?

- In 1874, P. T. Barnum had opened up his modestly named Great Roman Monster Classical and Geological Hippodrome on the north end of Madison Square Park after Cornelius Vanderbilt shifted his rail operation up to Grand Central Terminal. The open-air arena in what was then a booming entertainment district called the Tenderloin was renamed Madison Square Garden in 1879. No, there still wasn't any garden. That is simply another example of business owners appending "garden" to a location's name to evoke a sense of beauty and grandeur. It hosted everything from circuses to bicycle races to the first-ever Westminster Kennel Club dog show on March 28, 1877.

- Eventually, the first Garden's down-market nature was seen as a limitation. It was demolished and a new Garden designed by Stanford White opened in 1891. This version featured a grander design and a Moorish-themed tower topped by a revolving bronze statue of the Roman goddess Diana (a half-size model of the original is on display at the Met Museum). This incarnation of the Garden has a certain notoriety, as it was in the building's rooftop garden theater that White was fatally shot in the head in 1906. White's building, a beautiful but often money-losing white elephant, was itself torn down in 1925 and replaced by the also beautiful but more sedate Metropolitan Life Building, which still sits on the site today.

- The third Madison Square Garden opened further north at Eighth Avenue and 50th Street in 1926. A less ostentatious structure, it quickly became the city's premier sports venue, hosting storied boxing matches—including Sugar Ray Robinson (1921–1989) and Jake LaMotta's (1922–) first bout in 1942—and also the New York Rangers' first game in 1926. More ignominiously, it was also the location of the 1939 German American Bund rally, where about 20,000 Nazis and Nazi sympathizers proclaimed their solidarity with Hitler's Reich and denounced Roosevelt's New Deal as the "Jew Deal."

- The fourth and current iteration—known to locals, like its previous incarnation, as simply "The Garden"—was built atop the new Penn Station. It opened in 1968 with a gala performance that featured Bob Hope (1903–2003) and Bing Crosby (1903–

The latest incarnation of Madison Square Garden opened in 1968.

1977). After that, the main arena, which seats around 20,000, became synonymous with not just the Rangers but also the New York Knicks basketball team, who made a name for themselves at the Garden in the 1970s with a roster led by Walt "Clyde" Frazier (1945–). The fourth incarnation of the Garden does what it always did: provide entertainment of just about any kind for the city, whether it's the main arena's sporting events and glitzy concerts or touring comics and bands in the 5,600-seat underground theater. There are few New Yorkers today who would agree with the *Harper's* writer from 1889 who called the first Garden a "central palace of pleasure," but its perch above Penn Station and in the throng of Midtown hotels makes it convenient, if nothing else.

How dangerous was the Tenth Avenue Railroad?

In the mid-nineteenth century, before the elevated railway was built along Tenth Avenue, the stretch running through Chelsea was popularly known as Death Avenue. This was due to the number of trains that would hurtle along rails laid in the cobblestone street to and from the Meatpacking District. In order to protect pedestrians, the city actually hired men to ride on horseback in front of the oncoming trains waving red flags (or red lanterns at night). The so-called West Side Cowboys actually operated until 1941.

What is the High Line?

In order to clear some of the street congestion and danger caused by the Tenth Avenue trains, in 1934 the New York Central Railroad built an elevated track from Spring Street north to 34th Street. Unlike many earlier elevated rail lines, the High Line was designed to go through the city blocks instead of over the avenue. The line operated until 1980, when it was shut down due to competition from trucking. Fortunately, the city never quite got around to demolishing the long decomposing rail lines, as many wanted. For over thirty years, the two-story-high viaduct rusted in place until a quixotic campaign finally bore fruit.

In 2012, the High Line reopened as a visionary new kind of park. In short order, the High Line Park, a mile-plus-long ribbon of gentle landscaping, the occasional twee art project, and striking views became one of the city's most innovative and popular attractions. It wasn't long before the park's narrow stretch was almost impassable because of promenading crowds, even on not-so-nice days. Similar projects were soon planned to rehabilitate other abandoned rail lines in Queens, Chicago, and Rotterdam.

What's going on at the Hudson Yards?

One of the least noticed parts of Manhattan is the west side quadrant between the Hudson River and Eighth Avenue, and 28th and 43rd streets. Known as Hudson Yards, it has been dominated since the mid-nineteenth century by railyards, warehouses, and the occasional isolated old tenement. For many years one of the few reasons people might have to venture out this way was to the Jacob K. Javits Convention Center, a glass-lined complex that opened in 1986 at 38th Street and Eleventh Avenue to replace the much-maligned old Coliseum up on Columbus Circle. The great value of the real estate has prompted many plans over the years to better utilize the Hudson Yards (including several never-realized plans for new sports stadiums). After the area was rezoned in 2005 for commercial and residential use, those plans have gone into overdrive.

Current visitors to the Hudson Yards will see soaring cranes and deep foundation pits everywhere. It is evidence of the largest, single real-estate development project in American history, as well as one of the most audacious: the new buildings will be constructed on top of a massive platform over the Yards' tangle of still operational train tracks, much like how Grand Central was built on top of the tracks that once bedeviled the area around Park Avenue and 42nd Street. The plan, expected to be completed around 2024, will utterly transform the area, adding numerous new skyscrapers to the city skyline that will comprise about twenty million square feet (1.86 million square meters) of new office, commercial, and residential space. In preparation for the new residents and workers, the seven-subway line was extended in 2015 to Eleventh Avenue and 34th Street, the MTA's first new station since 1989.

TIMES SQUARE/MIDTOWN WEST/ HELL'S KITCHEN

Where exactly is Times Square?

Until relatively recently in New York history, there was nothing square-like about Times Square. Normally a square implies a large open pedestrian expanse with traffic on its borders and some kind of fountain or monument at its center. Herald Square just a few blocks to the south is much more properly deserving of the name. But for most of its history, Times Square has been the name for the so-called "Bow Tie" where the diagonal run of Broadway intersects with the straight angle of Seventh Avenue between 42nd and 47th streets.

This five-block avenue bounded by luridly over-the-top billboards, with the Theater District just off its western border and the (until the 1990s, at least) proximity of garish movie theaters and street-walkers on 42nd Street, has long been seen

Times Square is located at the juncture of Broadway and Seventh Avenue and is noted for its brightly lit billboards and entertainment venues.

as the virtual heart of New York, at least by non-New Yorkers. Packed with gawkers and shills, promenaders and police, it's the first place many tourists go to when they first arrive in the city, and one of the last places that the average New Yorker wants to be. For many New Yorkers, Times Square, with all its tourists jamming together to take pictures of themselves showing up on the giant video screens that now pass for entertainment there, is the place you sometimes have to fight your way through to get to a Broadway show or sometimes watch on TV on New Year's Eve.

Where was "the Deuce"?

The block of 42nd street between Seventh and Eighth avenues was known to some in the neighborhood, during the seedier decades of the postwar era, as "Forty Deuce" or simply "the Deuce," one of the most infamous blocks in an infamous neighborhood. The street-level peep show offerings on this block were prodigious, even though it was located just west of 42nd and Broadway, still and possibly forever known as the Crossroads of the World. The Deuce was cleaned up along with the rest of the area as part of the organized, multi-decade, private-public process that started as far back as the mid-1970s and wasn't considered a success until well into the 1990s, when chainstores and spiffed-up theaters and masses of sidewalk-choking tourists replaced the derelicts and sex shows.

What part of Times Square was called the Minnesota Strip?

In the mid–1970s, Eighth Avenue from Port Authority at 42nd Street to about 52nd Street was a dense and chaotic conglomeration of street walkers, massage parlors, and topless bars. The general air of disorder led the *New York Times* to call it the city's "sleaziest vice supermarket." Starting around 1975, this stretch of the avenue gained the sobriquet the Minnesota Strip. The name derived from the many young Midwestern women who purportedly came to New York looking for jobs on Broadway and ended up as prostitutes instead, working within sight of the Theater District's glittering marquees.

The less romanticized version of the story was that after Minnesota passed tougher anti-prostitution laws, many of the state's sex workers shifted their operations to New York. In the late 1970s the "Minnesota Pipeline" was considered real enough that Minneapolis detectives actually traveled to New York looking for teenage runaways suborned into the sex trade by pimps. The strip's notoriety gave birth to cultural artifacts on both ends of the morality scale: The heart-tugging 1980 made-for-TV movie *Off the Minnesota Strip* and also a grim song by proto-New York punk band The Dictators ("We like young girls on the Minnesota Strip…").

Where is Hell's Kitchen?

Manhattan's Hell's Kitchen neighborhood covers the densely populated blocks between the theater and garment districts and the Hudson River. The more commonly accepted boundaries are 34th Street (south), Eighth Avenue (east), and 57th Street (north). Its more gentrified eastern boundaries get jumbled up with the less easily defined region of Midtown West, which extends from either Sixth or Seventh to either Eighth, Ninth, or Tenth avenues, depending on who you ask. The true heart of Hell's Kitchen remains in those long, dense blocks of older housing stock in the upper 40s and 50s that haven't yet had their patina of Manhattan grit sandblasted off. However, the now vaguely respectable neighborhood's old nexus used to be 39th Street west of Tenth Avenue, a stretch now mostly stripped of residential buildings but infamous in the late 1800s as Battle Row for all the rioting that happened there.

How did Hell's Kitchen get its name?

Back when this stretch of Manhattan was still forests and manors, it was known as The Great Kill District, for the small stream that flowed into the Hudson River here near the western terminus of 42nd Street. After railroads were built through the area in the 1850s, factories and a surrounding accretion of tenements followed quickly. By the 1860s, the neighborhood was already infamous because of its dense concentration of immigrant workers with a reputation for unruly behavior.

The more colorful version of the neighborhood moniker's origin story, which dates back at least to the late 1800s when it was thickly stocked with slaughterhouses, soap factories, and shanties, has is that one cop (with the fantastic nickname Dutch Fred) says to another, "This place is hell itself," to which the other cop answered, "Hell's a mild climate. This is hell's kitchen." The name could also have come from a particularly brawl-ready West Side Irish immigrant mob from the mid-1800s known as the Hell's Kitchen Gang. These days, after the passing of notorious gangs like the Gophers and the Westies, enterprising real estate agents looking for a less evocative name are likely to refer to the area as Clinton, for DeWitt Clinton, a title whose utter lack of meaning has earned the distinction of being more mocked than the now mostly accepted Nolita (North of Little Italy) or newer and still artificial-sounding NoMad (North of Madison Square).

Why is there an aircraft carrier parked in the Hudson River?

The Essex class aircraft carrier *Intrepid* (CV-11) was launched in April 1943 and saw action in several of the Pacific theater's bigger naval engagements, taking a few direct hits from kamikaze planes and an air-launched torpedo but staying afloat. Later it saw action in the Vietnam War and helped recover space vehicles from the Gemini and Mercury missions. *Intrepid* was decommissioned in 1974, at a time when the Navy was phasing out smaller carriers. Instead of being scrapped, though, the *Intrepid* now floats proudly in the Hudson River alongside Pier 86 at 46th Street, the centerpiece of the best kid-friendly ooh-and-ah collection of awesome American machinery outside of the Smithsonian Air & Space Museum in Washington. Near the entrance, you can duck into the *Growler* for a side excursion before getting to the main attraction. A small-ish Cold War-era submarine armed with four nuclear-tipped cruise missiles, it carried up to one hundred crewmen underwater for two months at a time in impressively claustrophobic conditions.

Back up top, the *Intrepid* offers some interior exhibitions similar to the *Growler*, well-preserved rooms behind glass showcasing the tight and spartan conditions that sailors spent months in. There are a few gun mounts to be clambered over, and nice

233

views from the fo'c'sle. But the main attraction is in the massive hangar level and on the flight deck, where numerous fighters, dive bombers, surveillance craft, and helicopters are lined up for awed inspection. The museum's remit occasionally goes beyond the carrier itself; there's no particular reason to have an Israeli Kfir fighter and Russian MiGs on display other than that they're cool to look at and somebody agreed to loan them. On the back part of the flight deck is perched a giant tent that houses the other reason tourists haul all the way there through Hell's Kitchen: The Space Shuttle *Enterprise*.

Whose idea was it to build Carnegie Hall?

Originally known as the Music Hall, Carnegie Hall is an impressively stately brick neo-Renaissance building at 57th Street and Seventh Avenue whose status as a concert hall is so famous that its name long ago became an imprimatur of top-level performance. One of the few buildings in the world to have inspired its own joke ("How do you get to Carnegie Hall? Practice"), it was first conceived in 1887. Industrialist Andrew Carnegie (1835–1919) and his new bride, Louise Whitfield, were on an ocean liner to Scotland for their honeymoon when they struck up a friendship with new Symphony Space conductor Walter Damrosch (1862–1950), who suggested that the city could use a new concert hall. It opened in 1891 with a five-day music festival that featured Tchaikovsky as guest of honor.

Praised not just for its beauty but the incomparable acoustics, Carnegie Hall quickly became a favorite place for composers to present new works: In the first century, over 1,300 pieces were given their world or U.S. premiere here. The list of performers and composers who have graced Carnegie Hall's stage read like an honor roll of music from Billie Holiday (1915–1959) to Glenn Gould (1932–1982) and Thelonious Monk (1917–1982), and the many speakers who have held forth there include some of the world's most prominent leaders and thinkers, from Theodore Roosevelt to Ernest Hemingway (1899–1961).

Why are there so many unlit apartments in the New York skyline at night?

It's not just because everybody is out sampling the nightlife. At any given time, those multi-million dollar condos that make up the gleaming spires like the Time Warner Center or the Bloomberg Tower are as much as half empty. Why? Many of those dwellings—which can sell for $20 million or more—are owned by foreign million-

Industrialist Andrew Carnegie was behind the music hall that bears his name and was completed in 1891.

234

aires and billionaires who are either staying in one of their other homes or simply using the condo as an investment more than residence. In some instances, the condos are owned by shell companies used to hide the identities of less than salubrious individuals, meaning that crooks could be "living" next door to celebrities on so-called Billionaires' Row.

Where can you find Billionaires' Row?

The farthest north of the extra-wide, east–west streets that cut all the way across Manhattan, West 57th Street between Columbus Circle and Park Avenue has in the last few years gained a new nickname: Billionaires' Row. While the average price for a Manhattan apartment hit nearly $2 million in 2015, that amount would scarcely buy a closet in one of the dwellings on Billionaires' Row, where the clientele barely blinks an eye at paying $15 million and the lists of amenities rival those of the world's finest hotels.

After the new ultra-luxury towers like 432 Park Avenue (at almost 1,400 feet [427 meters] in height, it's the tallest residential building in the Western Hemisphere), Baccarat Hotel and Residences, and the ninety-story One57 tower started opening, it became something of a gossip sport for the city papers to report on who paid how many tens of millions for the newest and biggest penthouse. The spaceship-looking swooping tetrahedron building on West 57th by architect Bjarke Ingels (1974–) looks from the outside like another extension of Billionaires' Row. But about one-fifth of its apartments were set aside as affordably priced. Of course, the definition of "affordable" will most likely be stretched to its furthest possible limit.

When did Columbus Circle become a circle?

The southwest corner of Central Park wasn't particularly defined as anything special, even after the city blocks began to fill up on either side of the park. It transitioned without much fanfare from farmland to warehouses. After the corner was redesigned in 1905 as a traffic circle around a grand statue of Christopher Columbus (1451–1506) atop a seventy-foot (21.3-meter) marble column, the area had a brief fling with being an arts and entertainment center. The Majestic Theatre was here, as well as Reisenweber's, a massively fashionable café that hosted the Original Dixieland Jazz Band starting in 1917, establishing jazz as the hottest thing in town well before the new music craze would spread around the world.

What is Columbus Circle like now?

Today, Columbus Circle is still the place from which all distances to New York are measured, much like distances to London are measured to Trafalgar Square. The statue of Columbus is still there, now in a fully redesigned oasis in the middle of the traffic circle for those pedestrians willing to play Russian Roulette by dashing across the cab-crowded streets to get to it. Watching from the park's southwest corner is the stately memorial to the USS *Maine*, erected in 1913, fifteen years after the battleship exploded in the Havana harbor under mysterious circumstances.

Surrounding the circle today is one of the city's more fascinating architectural menageries. On the south side stands the proud white prow of the Museum of Arts and De-

For all its beautiful and awe-inspiring architecture, there are more unsung disappeared buildings in New York's history than could be listed in a shelf of books. One of the most prominent among them, though, would have to be the New York Coliseum, which makes frequent appearances on lists of the city's least-missed architectural monstrosities. One of Robert Moses's most ungainly buildings, the six-story convention center opened in 1956 on a two-block site on the west side of Columbus Circle after Moses tore down some thirty buildings to create the imperial structure he thought would be his legacy. Like many of the buildings that Moses threw up in his later years, it was architecturally undistinguished, to put it mildly. "It's a great utilitarian achievement," Frank Lloyd Wright (1867–1959) sniffed on opening day, "but architecture is something else again."

The Coliseum lost what luster it had after the much larger Jacob K. Javits Center opened in 1986. The hall and its attendant twenty-six-story office building were demolished in 2000 to make room for the Time Warner Center. The last vestige of the old colossus is a memorably undistinguished bar on West 58th Street that kept the name of The Coliseum. Supposedly this was once a hangout for the Westies, but these days you're more likely to find office workers from the Time Warner Center getting lunch or a happy-hour beer.

sign, an iconoclastic, nine-story oddity originally opened in 1964 as the gleaming, marble-cloaked Huntington Hartford Gallery of Modern Art, built essentially to house the collection of its namesake, an heir to a supermarket fortune. The west side of the circle, once towered over by the featureless white wall of the Coliseum, is now dominated by the sleek curving glass of the Time Warner Center, which encompasses the five-story Shops at Columbus Circle shopping center and two eighty-story skyscrapers containing high-end retail, a luxury hotel, offices, apartments, and Jazz at Lincoln Center in one single ode to upper-class contentment. Another kind of luxury stands tall on the circle's northern border: the old Gulf and Western corporate headquarters, a shining black slab of a forty-four-story skyscraper dating from 1970 that later became Trump International Hotel and Tower.

MIDTOWN EAST

Where is Koreatown located?

Like many other immigrant groups in New York, Koreans established an identifiable neighborhood when they first moved into the city in large numbers. Unlike most of those groups, however, the Korean-identified part of town in Manhattan remains that way today. Korean immigrants to the city in the 1970s gravitated to the streets in the low 30s between Fifth and Sixth avenues east of Herald Square in part due to its proximity to the Garment District. Korean businesses and restaurants began to cluster in the area that quickly became known as Koreatown or K-Town. A stretch of 32nd Street was officially named Korea Way in 1995.

Today, the area is still thick with Korean restaurants and the blocks are dense with Korean signage, Korean-speakers, and locals and tourists trying to figure out which of the dozens of crowded Korean barbecue joints they have a chance of getting into. Even so, the area is almost entirely business-oriented, with very few residents. Most ethnic Koreans live elsewhere in the city, the majority in Queens.

What is New York's most enduring landmark of the Jazz Age?

Possibly the city's most enduring landmark building, the Empire State Building was conceived at the height of the 1920s' stock market and real estate exuberance. Plans were finalized and ground broken (after demolishing the old Waldorf-Astoria) just two months before the stock market crash of 1929. Located at Fifth Avenue between 33rd and 34th streets, the 102-story, Art Deco skyscraper with a limestone and stainless steel facade was completed in record time in early 1931. One reason it was finished so quickly was that each building component was completed off-site and fitted into the structure with no additional work needed. Although it became an instant landmark, not to mention the world's tallest skyscraper, the Empire State Building had difficulty finding tenants at first for its eighty-six floors and over two million square feet (185,800 square meters) of commercial and office space (creating the nickname the "Empty State"). It couldn't turn a profit until after World War II. These days, the two observation decks are the building's best-known attributes, and for good reason: on a good day, you can see for eighty miles (130 kilometers). Some four million people come each year just to admire the view. At night, an LED display installed in 2012 frequently projects complex light shows onto its upper floors for commemorative events ranging from the passing of Frank Sinatra (blue, for Ol' Blue Eyes) to the 2011 legalization of same-sex marriage in New York State (rainbow hues).

Why were the builders of the Chrysler Building and the Empire State Building in a race?

As often happened in the early twentieth century, business rivalries had a way of turning into mammoth ego contests

The Empire State Building, which opened in 1931, remains a symbol of New York City architecture, even though it is no longer the tallest building.

237

waged in the streets and through the skyline of New York. In the late 1920s, Chrysler Corporation founder Walter Chrysler (1875–1940) and former General Motors executive John Raskob (1879–1950) were in a race to erect the world's tallest building. Chrysler got there first, with his 1,046-foot- (319-meter-) high corporate headquarters the Chrysler Building at 42nd Street and Lexington Avenue, just east of Grand Central, built between 1928 and 1930. Raskob's Empire State Building eclipsed the Chrysler at 1,250 feet (381 meters).

The Empire State Building remained the tallest in the world until the World Trade Center opened in 1972. But its iconic status was marred by a couple factors. First, the building was a financial disaster, since the combination of the Great Depression and an oversupply of office space left it largely empty for years. Second, the Chrysler's sleeker art deco design is widely considered a more romantic and elegant icon of this phase of the city's architectural history.

What is the best spot to have lunch in Midtown?

It's actually not a restaurant. The eight-acre Bryant Park between Fifth and Sixth avenues, 40th and 42nd streets, is a welcome splash of green amidst the steel, concrete, and glass skyscraper forest of Midtown and very simply a superb spot to have a sit and a sandwich. In the nineteenth century it was briefly a potter's field before being mostly taken over in 1842 by the Croton Reservoir. The western side of the site was turned into a park first called Reservoir Square. In 1884 it was renamed Bryant Park in honor of *New York Evening Post* editor William Cullen Bryant (1794–1878). The reservoir was torn down and replaced in 1911 with the New York Public Library's stupendous Beaux Arts building on Fifth Avenue, which today holds some fifteen million books (many of them on some seventy-five miles (121 kilometers) of shelving in tunnels underneath the park).

Bryant Park was in rough shape for many years, before successive waves of renovations and private-public partnerships turned it into the meticulously managed public space it is today. Surrounded by elegant walks, nooks with chess and even ping-pong tables, and Parisian-style seating, the main lawn is frequently used for events from free film screenings to the annual Bryant Park Fashion Show.

Why is one corner of Bryan Park named for a Croatian scientist?

Born in Croatia (then the Austrian Empire), Nikola Tesla (1856–1943) immigrated to America in 1884 to work for Thomas Edison. Except for a brief stint in Colorado Springs (which provided more space for many of his more outré experiments), Tesla spent the remainder of his life in New York. Remembered now for his groundbreaking work in the fields of electricity and wireless power transmission, during his lifetime Tesla was something of a fixture on the New York social scene. When not engaged in feuds with the likes of Edison and George Westinghouse (1846–1914), Tesla dined at Delmonico's, ran up a massive tab at the Waldorf Astoria, and hobnobbed with the likes of Mark Twain. His name became attached to the Bryant Park area primarily because he had laboratory space nearby. The legendarily obsessive Tesla also made a point of feeding, and not infrequently talking to, the pigeons in Bryant Park. In 1994, the intersection of 40th street and Sixth Avenue was named Nikola Tesla Corner.

Where is the Diamond District?

Not so much a district per se as it is a block-long bazaar, the fabled Diamond District is essentially just the stretch of 47th Street between Fifth and Sixth avenues. Originally, New York's diamond dealers were concentrated downtown along Maiden Lane. But starting in the 1930s and accelerating with the wartime exodus of Jewish traders from Europe's Low Countries, this street quickly became a center of gravity for the wholesale and retail diamond trade. Today, the nondescript street marked only by a pair of diamond-shape-topped posts and an unusual (for Midtown, at least) density of Orthodox Jews and Hebrew signage, is chockablock with great consumer jewelry emporiums and warrens of offices for buying, selling, stone-cutting, and haggling. One of the vast exchanges on the street is supposedly the world's largest, with about 500 jewelers on site. The street's over two thousand businesses also include the Diamond Dealers' Club and the only Bukharan kosher restaurant in Manhattan.

How did Turtle Bay get its name?

The original Turtle Bay was a small divot in the hilly wooded eastern shore of Manhattan near today's 47th Street where a small stream emptied into the East River. The name likely came not from any particular density of turtles, but the original Dutch name for the cove, Deutal Bay. Originally rolling farmland, it was carved up for residential lots after the Civil War, when the bay itself was filled in. Onetime resident Edgar Allan Poe wrote about his dismay at the area's future development: "I could not look on the magnificent cliffs and stately trees … without a sigh for the inevitable doom." True to his worries, the Turtle Bay area from Lexington Avenue to the river, 43rd up to 53rd Street, soon became a classically ugly nineteenth-century urban patchwork of tenements, factories, and breweries. First Avenue in the 40s was so dense with abattoirs that it was known as "Blood Alley."

More fashionable clusters of townhouses and developments like Turtle Bay Gardens began popping up during the 1920s. Stylish supper clubs, journalist-thronged bars, and famous residents like E. B. White (1899–1985), Kurt Vonnegut (1922–2007), and Katharine Hepburn (1907–2003) followed. In the 1950s, the Third Avenue elevated train line was torn down and the United Nations complex rose on the East River. From that point, Turtle Bay began transforming into the traffic-choked, luxury high-rise district, increasingly similar to Kips Bay and Murray Hill to the south and the Upper East Side to the north, that it is today.

Why was the United Nations headquarters built in New York?

The easy answer is that after World War II, most of the world's leading nations had either been physically devastated by the fighting or were deeply mired in postwar trauma and economic malaise; that or they were authoritarian states like the Soviet Union and China. The exception was the United States, then the undisputed leader of the democratic world. **239**

Philadelphia and San Francisco campaigned to be chosen, as did more quixotic locales like Niagara Falls and the Black Hills, but New York was ultimately chosen as the headquarters of the United Nations. It helped that John D. Rockefeller donated $8.5 million to buy eighteen riverside acres in Turtle Bay to give the organization a home.

The international committee of designers came up with a stark, modernist vision that reflected the views of member Le Corbusier (1887–1965), and was unlike anything yet seen in New York. The complex's centerpiece was the Secretariat Building, a thirty-nine-story sky-stabbing glass slab that opened in 1951. Somewhat less impressive is the low bow-tie swoop of the undistinguished General Assembly building next to it. One of several notable public works of art inside the fence that surrounds the complex is *Good Defeats Evil*, a 1990 allegorical sculpture showing St. George slaying a dragon (partly made up of old American and Soviet ballistic missiles) representing nuclear war. About 20,000 people work at the United Nations headquarters, whose larger meetings like the General Assemblies can bring Midtown traffic to a halt with all the attendant caravans of security-ringed diplomatic vehicles.

Whose idea was Rockefeller Center?

Unlike some developments that are named for donors or in honor of a heroic individual, Midtown's Rockefeller Center is actually named for the man who willed it into ex-

One of the most favored spots in New York City is the ice skating rink at Rockefeller Center. It has often appeared as a setting in movies and television shows over the years.

istence. Around the turn of the century, the highly religious John D. Rockefeller Jr. began working to change the image of Standard Oil and other related companies that his namesake father had turned into a byword for monopolies and corporate heartlessness. After a 1914 strike at a Rockefeller-owned company in Colorado turned violent, Rockefeller redoubled his philanthropic efforts. In the following years, he created or helped create some of the city's most enduring icons, such as Riverside Church and the Cloisters, and donated the money to buy the land that the United Nations headquarters was built on. His greatest physical legacy in the city, however, is the nineteen-building complex between Fifth and Sixth avenues, 49th and 52nd streets that bears his name. Its construction, which employed about 40,000 people, came at a good time for the Depression-wracked city.

When it opened in 1933, Rockefeller Center's sleek grey limestone Art Deco office towers, pedestrian-friendly plazas, and innovative underground shopping arcades linking the buildings to each other and the subway redefined not only Midtown but the entire concept of mixed-use urban planning. Today, the Center's attractions like Radio City Music Hall, the Rainbow Room, NBC studios, and its ice-skating rink are some of the most cherished spots for tourists to visit. A less fortunate part of Rockefeller Center's legacy is that its example was followed poorly in many subsequent projects that tried to mix office buildings with pedestrian plazas. See MetroTech Center in downtown Brooklyn and parts of Battery Park City for examples of cold, alien, corporate complexes that deadened neighborhoods instead of bringing them to life.

What Midtown cathedral was once mocked as "Hughes' Folly"?

The seat of the New York archdiocese and the starting point of the St. Patrick's Day and Easter Parade, St. Patrick's Cathedral is the most well-known place of worship in the city, occupying an almost cross-denominational place of importance almost on par with Trinity Church. Its construction was conceived of by Archbishop "Dagger" John Hughes in the aftermath of the 1844 anti-Irish Nativist riots and after the Vatican made New York an archdiocese in 1850. The fundraising campaign was prolonged, with wealthy Catholics pledging $1,000 each and Irish washerwomen saving up their pennies for what some termed "Hughes' Folly." When the cornerstone was laid in 1858, the city block that the church had purchased on Fifth Avenue between 50th and 51st streets appeared to promise that the cathedral would be marooned in the hinterlands (the block was originally intended as a cemetery).

By the time doors opened in 1879, though, the critics had been silenced. The wealthy were already putting up mansions in the suddenly fashionable area and the Fifth Avenue Presbyterian Church had opened just a few years before. More importantly, though, the grandeur of the cathedral's sparkling white Gothic Revival style announced it as a near-instant landmark not just for the city's Catholics but the city itself. Designed by James Renwick, who was also the architect for Grace Church downtown, St. Patrick's soaring spires and elegant vaulted ceilings combine to create one of Midtown's most awe-inspiring sights.

Where do presidents traditionally stay when they visit New York?

New York streets are frequently thrown into (even worse) gridlock by caravans of SUVs and police escorts taking dignitaries to and from the United Nations. The arrival of an American president is an even greater event these days, given the ever-more elaborate security precautions. One thing that doesn't change, though, is their destination. The Waldorf Astoria hotel has occupied the block between Park and Lexington avenues, 49th and 50th streets since 1931 (the Empire State Building now sits on its original site). It's one of the largest art deco buildings in the world, containing over 1,400 hotel rooms.

Traditionally, American presidents have stayed here whenever they visit New York, particularly when coming to the United Nations General Assembly. Rumors that have long circulated about a secret elevator that ran up to the presidential suite from the railyard directly underneath the hotel (it was built on top of the lines running to Grand Central just to the south) for the usage of President Franklin Delano Roosevelt, who wanted to avoid being seen exiting his car in a wheelchair, have turned out to be just rumors. In late 2015, President Barack Obama (1961–) broke with tradition by staying at the nearby Palace Hotel for his UN visit. This was due to the fact that the Waldorf Astoria had been bought by a Chinese company, which as of 2016 was planning to shut the hotel down and convert it into luxury condos.

What's so important about the Lever House and Seagram Building?

Today, the Lever House at Park Avenue between 53rd and 54th streets appears to be just another Midtown glass tower, its only unique details possibly being the broad two-story base that the comparatively narrow twenty-one-story tower sits on and the stilts that the whole structure rests on. Built in 1952, it was one of the first International Style office buildings in the country and as such was highly influential. It was unusual for the time in not using all of its (quite expensive) space to maximize revenue. The ground-floor courtyard features a sculpture garden by Isamu Noguchi (1904–1988), while the second-floor garden was designed to include shuffleboard courts.

A block to the south and on the eastern side of Park Avenue is the Seagram Building, the other great modern architecture landmark on this stretch of Park Avenue. Imitations of his work flourish around town, but this is the only building in New York actually designed by Ludwig Mies van der Rohe (1886–1969). Depending on your taste, it's a rather awe-inspiring or terrifying thirty-eight-story rectangular block. Many architectural critics believe it to be the finest single still-standing expression of the International Style. The effect these days is dulled by it having been the model for so many knockoffs around the world.

What does MoMA stand for?

From the outside, the Museum of Modern Art (MoMA) on 53rd Street between Fifth and Sixth avenues looks like one of the least architecturally distinguished museums in the city, particularly now that the Whitney has moved to its new Meatpacking District digs. But inside the frequently expanded International-style building from 1939, visitors will find one of the world's best surveys of modern art, set in an airy space that easily accommodates its frequent blockbuster shows. An expansion designed by Philip Johnson (1906–2005) in the 1950s added the Abby Aldrich Rockefeller Sculpture Garden, a quiet and tree-shrouded space studded with a rotating cast of modern sculptures.

The collection of about 150,000 pieces is not the city's biggest but its range is impressive, from Vincent van Gogh's (1853–1890) *Starry Night* to Andy Warhol's Campbell Soup cans and Pablo Picasso's (1881–1973) *Les Demoiselles d'Avignon*. MoMA is also a standout for its focus on cinema, hosting a regular series of retrospective and special screenings, and including prints of classics like *The General* and *Steamboat Willie* in its archives.

Where is the oldest continuously used synagogue in New York?

For decades, the Lower East Side and pockets of Queens and Brooklyn have been, and in many cases still are, home to deeply rooted Jewish communities. But the synagogue that's been worshipped in longer than any other in the city is located on Lexington Avenue and 55th Street. The Central Synagogue was opened in 1872, around the same time that other great palaces of worship were going up in Midtown. Its twin-towered, onion-domed design of sandstone and limestone is based on a Budapest synagogue. The first worshippers were mostly German-speaking immigrants from Bohemia who had originally settled on Ludlow Street downtown but had prospered enough to begin moving uptown. Not one

The Central Synagogue has been open since 1872 and has become a fixture of the city's Jewish community.

243

of the taller buildings in this skyscraper-packed area, it still makes quite an impression when one turns the corner and is confronted by this grand Moorish Revival marvel. It was designated a National Historic Landmark in 1966—the only synagogue in the state to be so labeled—and is currently one of the country's biggest Reform communities.

Is The Plaza still a hotel?

At the time of this writing, yes. But given the vicissitudes of the New York real estate scene and the number of hands that this landmark building has passed through, that could always change. The site on 59th Street and Fifth Avenue at the southeast corner of Central Park just across from Grand Army Plaza has been one of the city's flashiest locales ever since the likes of Cornelius Vanderbilt started building mansions here in the late nineteenth century. The nineteen-story hotel designed by Henry Janeway Hardenbergh (1847–1918), in the same French Chateau style he used for the Dakota, first opened in 1907, standing on the site of an old skating pond and an older demolished hotel. The rooms went for just $2.50 a night.

Within a few years, the Plaza became one of the city's most iconic hotels, its luxurious rooms and institutions like the (now closed) Oak Room Bar holding a status rarely matched in people's imaginations even by the Waldorf Astoria. Various royal persons, celebrities such as the Beatles, and even Frank Lloyd Wright (who lived there for six years) became loyal customers. The hotel's hold on the popular imagination was further cemented in 1955, when Kay Thompson (1902–1998) published *Eloise*, a children's book about a rambunctious six-year-old tomboy who lives at the Plaza and treats it like her own private playground. The Plaza has been something of a real estate hot potato over the last few decades, with everyone from Donald Trump to Saudi Prince Al-Waleed (1955–) and Indian billionaire Subrata Roy (1948–) owning it at one point. These days, the Plaza is part condo tower and part hotel, with a still-splendid position at the top end of Fifth Avenue's luxury shopping corridor.

CENTRAL PARK

Whose idea was it to create Central Park?

As happens with cities that are growing fast but still feel themselves not being accorded the correct amount of respect by their urban peers elsewhere, some of New York's greatest innovations came about at least in part out of jealousy. The city's leading men did not understand why London and Paris could have grand gardens in the midst of their hustle and bustle and not New York. In the 1811 grid, a 260-acre park called the Grand Parade was planned between 23rd and 34th streets, between Third and Seventh avenues; a miniature version of this exists today as Madison Square Park.

Within a few years, though, pressures from landowners had significantly whittled down the plan for the Grand Parade. Later decades, though, saw an increased desire for parks from the upper classes, who wanted well-manicured spaces to promenade in without having to rub elbows so closely with the working classes. There was also a growing belief among reformers during the mid-nineteenth century that if the working classes had better access to green spaces and open air, they wouldn't suffer from so much disease or riot so much. (The suggestion that higher wages, better working conditions, or expensive infrastructure developments like public transportation, hospitals, and clean water supplies could help the situation was still seen as dangerously radical.)

How did the park's construction begin?

In 1848, leading American landscape architect Andrew Jackson Downing (1815–1852) proposed the creation of a huge public park that could double as the "lungs of the city." Eight years later, the city carved a massive rectangle out of the city grid stretching 2.5 miles (4 kilometers) north from 59th to 106th streets between 5th and 8th avenues. At the time, there were a half million people living below 14th Street on chockablock streets where almost no building was taller than six stories. They needed somewhere to go.

How many people had to be moved out of Central Park?

Fortunately for New York, by the time the planning of Central Park began in earnest, its long expanse hadn't been completely surrounded by mansions, factories, and tenements. That luck was in part because of the fact that this central stretch of Manhattan, alternatingly rocky and swampy, was among its least desirable. Maps at the time showed very few habitations there beyond a few farms. Mayor Fernando Wood (1812–1881) had actually claimed that it was "almost uninhabited." That was stretching the truth a bit. There were shantytowns clustered around hog farms and piggeries (the odiferous ad-hoc hog-rendering shops shunted uptown after harassment by the Common Council).

The park also housed to the north Seneca Village, the city's largest community of black landowners. Established in 1825, the polyethnic Seneca Village had some 250

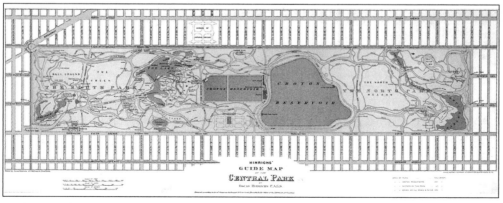

An 1875 map of Central Park. It was officially completed just two years prior. It has undergone several renovations since that time.

black, German, and Irish families, and several churches. The city claimed eminent domain in 1853 and four years later ordered the great expanse of land cleared all of residents. Some five thousand people were ultimately relocated.

What are some of the top sights in Central Park?

Central Park's original Greensward Plan was studded with sights and attractions, from large monuments to small surprises, which have been tweaked and added to over the years. Here are some highlights to watch for:

- Central Park Zoo—Not part of the original park, this small, superbly curated menagerie (the smallest of the city's five zoos) is now one of its top attractions, and not just because of its central role in the *Madagascar* movies. Animals on display range from penguins and grizzlies to sea lions and red pandas. Those entering from the 65th Street Transverse on the north pass underneath the Delacorte Clock, a three-tiered musical clock populated by mechanical animals.

- The Mall—One of the park's grandest sights, this long straight boulevard runs from just above the 65th Street Transverse up to Bethesda Terrace. Perfect for promenading, the Mall is bordered by American elms (some of the only ones to survive the Dutch elm disease outbreak of the early twentieth century) as well as statues of authors like William Shakespeare and Robert Burns (1759–1796) that provide its other name: The Literary Walk.

- Bethesda Terrace—The planned center of the park, this sweeping terrace links the mall to the lake. Its upper deck is meant as a viewing platform for the Ramble just to the north. The fountain with its angel figure celebrates the 1842 opening of the Croton Reservoir.

- The Ramble—A 36-acre thicket of gardens, trees, and streams, Olmsted's "wild garden" is fully artificial, of course, but a delightful sanctuary in the middle of the park. It's generally considered the best spot in the park for birding.

- Belvedere Castle—A pretend castle that doubles as a visitor center, this fanciful structure doubles as a gathering point and viewing platform for the sprawling Great Lawn to the north.

How do you figure out where you are in Central Park?

Just look for the nearest park light. There are over 1,800 of these electric light poles scattered throughout Central Park. Each is stamped with a vertical four-digit number. The top two digits will tell you what the nearest numbered street is, and the next two whether you're closer to the east (even) or west side (odd). As a woman from the Central Park Conservancy told the *New York Times*: "All the odd people live on the West Side."

- Delacorte Theater—One of the latest additions to the park, the open-air Delacorte Theater opened in 1962 and still produces two free plays each summer. The top spire of Belvedere Castle provides a beautiful backdrop.

- Jacqueline Kennedy Onassis Reservoir—The Central Park Reservoir was renamed in 1994 for the former first lady who used to live across the street in a penthouse at 1040 Fifth Avenue. The pathway circumnavigating its expanse is one of the park's most popular running tracks.

- Conservatory Garden—This serene, six-acre formal garden near the iron-wrought Vanderbilt Gate (made in Paris, it originally graced the Vanderbilt Mansion) on Fifth Avenue near 105th Street is divided into three distinct smaller gardens in the Italian, English, and French style.

What is the oldest outdoor manmade object in New York?

Just like London, New York features an ancient Egyptian obelisk. Both of the 69-foot- (21-meter-) tall, 220-ton hieroglyph-scrawled granite obelisks were built in 1450 B.C.E. The Romans later floated the obelisks down the Nile to Alexandria where they acquired their current nickname: Cleopatra's Needles. In 1801, Egypt offered one Needle to England as a thank-you for helping defeat Napoleon. It was finally erected along London's Victoria Embankment in 1878. Egypt later presented one to the United States in thanks for financial assistance.

After a concerted campaign by the editor of the *New York World* and the American consul-general in Cairo, the obelisk was promised for New York. It took 112 days to move the massive Needle from the Hudson River to its current position on a knoll just west of the Metropolitan Museum of Art. Cecil B. DeMille (1881–1959) donated the plaques that translate the hieroglyphics. The time capsule that was buried in 1881 beneath the Needle—now officially known as the Obelisk—contains an 1870 census, the Bible, a Webster's Dictionary, the complete works of Shakespeare, a copy of the Declaration of Independence, and (for good measure) a guide to Egypt.

LINCOLN SQUARE/UPPER WEST SIDE

Why was the Lincoln Square area once called San Juan Hill?

The neighborhood once known as San Juan Hill was nearly as important to New York's black culture in the early twentieth century as Harlem. The area bordered by the Hudson River on the west, 57th Street to the south, 64th Street to the north, and east to Amsterdam Avenue was earlier called Bloomingdale by the British. In the 1850s, it was comprised of small farms and country homes for the wealthy.

By the turn of the century the idyllic countryside had been paved over to make room for blocks and blocks of tenements that together were called San Juan Hill. The possibly idealized etymology has the name being used to honor the 10th Calvary, a black unit that fought with distinction alongside Teddy Roosevelt's Rough Riders at the Battle of San Juan Hill and whose veterans may have settled in the area. Another version proposes instead that the name derived from all the street battles being waged in the area between the district's mainly black residents and the Irish and Italian neighborhoods that surrounded it. However, at the same time, San Juan Hill was also a widely recognized epicenter for the city's nightlife.

What happened to San Juan Hill?

In the postwar years, San Juan Hill kept its reputation for battling gangs, so much so that Leonard Bernstein and Jerome Robbins (1918–1998) set their 1957 musical *West Side Story* amidst its teeming tenements. Not long after, opening scenes of the film adaptation were shot in the neighborhood as it was being readied for demolition. Starting in 1958, thousands of residents were moved out so that Robert Moses's urban-renewal machine could transform it into the performing arts mecca that is today's Lincoln Center.

What did performers and composers like so much about the Hotel Ansonia?

Now just known as the Ansonia, this monumental and yet delicately gorgeous seventeen-story beaux-arts beauty was built as a hotel on Broadway between 73rd and 74th streets in 1904. The incongruously chateau-style building is an attraction in its own right, with its balconies, elaborate ironwork, and corner towers. When the Ansonia first opened, it had a farm with livestock on the roof. For a time, it also featured the world's largest indoor swimming pool. But the building has also been a favored residence for artists ranging from Arturo Toscanini to Igor Stravinsky due to its impeccable soundproofing—some apartments have even been converted to recording studios—and convenient distance from Lincoln Center. Verdi Square sits just across from the Ansonia.

Who built the American Museum of Natural History?

In 1869, Harvard-trained naturalist Albert Smith Bickmore (1839–1914) convinced a number of prominent New Yorkers (including J. P. Morgan) to help him organize a preeminent natural history museum. Originally housed in the old Central Park Arsenal, it moved into a new, purpose-built

American naturalist Albert Smith Bickmore was one of the founders of the American Museum of Natural History.

building in 1877. Designed by Calvert Vaux and his Central Park assistant Jacob Wrey Mould (1825–1886), it's an impressive Victorian Gothic structure that occupies the area between Columbus Avenue and Central Park West, from 77th up to 81st streets. The reason that the museum's siting seems today like an outcropping of Central Park into the dense towers of the Upper West Side is intentional, as it had been planned as one of the two crowning elements of the Central Park plan: The Metropolitan Museum of Art was the other.

Today, the American Museum of Natural History is one of the greatest destinations in the city for children and visitors of any age. The galleries are packed full of a constantly rotating cast of dioramas and displays, including rare animals and an extraordinarily cool dinosaur floor. One of the most popular attractions here is a newer addition, the Hayden Planetarium, which takes up the upper half of the space age-looking glass-enclosed Rose Center for Earth and Space. Also on most visitors' checklists is the Milstein Hall of Ocean Life, which overwhelms people with its massive model of a blue whale that hangs from the ceiling. Also, once each summer the museum holds "ID Day," when anybody can bring in whatever natural object they have so that the staff can try and identify it.

Why is there a building called the Dakota on the Upper West Side?

When Edward Clark (1811–1882), of the Singer Sewing Machine fortune, started building the now-famous Dakota apartment building in 1882 at 72nd Street and Central Park West, there wasn't much else in the area to entice the city's smarter set uptown. It seemed an odd location for a building that claimed to be a luxury dwelling. Then, the fashionable part of town was still located closer to Murray Hill and the mansions of lower Fifth Avenue. What became the Upper West Side seemed then as remote to the city's cognoscenti as the Dakota Territory. A modern parallel might be a tower with $20 million condos going up in Bay Ridge, Brooklyn.

When it opened in October 1884, remote or not (an 1890 photograph shows the building standing tall and alone next to the park, like a scout waiting for the rest of the city to catch up), the Dakota soon became recognized as one of the most beautiful residences in the city; a status it still holds today. The nine-story German Renaissance structure studded with balconies and etched with detailed stonework, and featuring a spacious interior courtyard, was unlike anything the city had seen before. The Dakota redefined full-service apartment living as acceptable for the upper classes who had previously regarded staffed homes as the only proper residences.

Who lives in the Dakota today?

Things are a touch more glamorous at the Dakota these days, with the building's co-op board rejecting even the likes of Billy Joel. Famous residents who have made the cut included Lauren Bacall (1924–2014), Leonard Bernstein, and John Lennon (1940–1980) and Yoko Ono (1933–). The Dakota's apartments regularly sell for $10 million and up. For all the building's beauty—it was accorded National Landmark status in 1976—it is most associated in the public imagination with ugliness. On the imaginary side of things, it was the Satanist-filled location for Mia Farrow's (1945–) apartment in the 1968 horror film *Rosemary's Baby*. Tragically, it was just across the street from the Dakota that Lennon was shot and killed on December 8, 1980. Today, there is a popular memorial to Lennon near that spot in Central Park called Strawberry Fields. The memorial is small and intimate, centered on a mosaic inspired by Lennon's song "Imagine," that was donated by the city of Naples, Italy.

UPPER EAST SIDE

Why do they call part of the Upper East Side the "Silk Stocking District"?

Starting in the late nineteenth century, parts of Manhattan's Upper East Side became known as the "Silk Stocking District" due to all the mansions that were cropping up east of Fifth Avenue. Many prominent families in the area (Vanderbilts, Roosevelts) were also members of the Seventh Regiment of the New York National Guard, which became known as the Silk Stocking Regiment. They raised the money to build their own grand armory on Park Avenue and 66th Street. Fittingly for an armory that seemed better attuned to receptions than military training, it's now known as the Park Avenue Armory and hosts a glittering repertoire of cultural events from art exhibitions to operas. The term "Silk Stocking District" is rarely used these days, except in historical discussions of Mayor John Lindsay, who represented this area in Congress and exemplified a brand of upper-crust liberal Republicanism (pro-civil rights, pro-Great Society) that was somewhat unique to the area and had mostly disappeared by the end of the twentieth century.

What's that castle on Park Avenue and 66th Street?

Back when New York seemed frequently on the verge of armed insurrection, the city fathers decided it made sense to build armories at strategic points around the city. Also,

---

What store gives out the best-known bags in the city?

For the classic New York shopper, there might have been other stops around Madison and Fifth avenues, Bergdorf Goodman and Tiffany's, in particular, not to mention Barney's. But there remains only one Bloomingdale's. Originally directed at the sensible, middle-class shopper, Bloomingdale's first opened in 1872. Its current Art Deco building, which occupies the whole block between 59th and 60th streets, from Lexington and Third avenues, opened in 1931. In the decades since, it began to target a more upscale shopper. Its brown shopping bags, labeled "small," "medium," and "large," with the trademark curved sans-serif typeface, were introduced in the early 1970s and remain iconic today.

What was the Mount Vernon Hotel Museum and Garden originally?

Now a clamorous district of high-rise apartment buildings and heavily trafficked avenues, in the early 1800s this sloping stretch of the Upper East Side was far away from the bustling turmoil of downtown. The tidy little brick structure at 61st Street and First Avenue that looks today like a traveler out of time sits on land that was originally bought by John Adams's daughter, Abigail Adams Smith (1765–1813), who had plans to turn it into a luxurious estate. That didn't work out, and by the 1820s the house was operating as a then-newfangled thing in America: the "day hotel," where men and women of means looking to get away from town could spend the day dining, drinking, fishing, and gossiping and be taken back home by stagecoach come nightfall. These days, the house operates as a historical museum.

some of the wealthy participants in some of the units thought it would be advantageous to have a practice and drilling space that doubled as a cool clubhouse. The Seventh Regiment Armory, also known as the Park Avenue Armory, is a striking brick Gothic Revival building. Its many well-appointed interior rooms, designed by Louis Comfort Tiffany (1848–1933) and Stanford White, among others, surround the central 55,000-square foot drill hall. Built in 1880, the Park Avenue Armory is now used primarily as a performing arts venue, with its drill hall putting on a fascinating mix of opera and theater performances, as well as art shows.

Where is the world's richest apartment building?

By the time you read this, one of the towers on Billionaires' Row may have taken this title. But for decades, the nineteen-story limestone apartment building constructed in 1930 at 740 Park Avenue and 71st Street has been popularly known as having the densest concentration of vertical wealth in the city. The thirty-two lavishly outfitted apartments (duplexes with grand staircases are a common feature) are comparatively vast for the city and devilishly hard to pry out of the hands of the co-op board, even with over $100 million in the bank (that's considered a good place to *start*). Jackie Onassis, whose grandfather built the pile, grew up here. The power of its residents was a fact not to be taken lightly, particularly after a documentary about the building was pulled from the schedule for the local PBS affiliate because of its critical tone.

What museum is technically in Central Park?

Most visitors who come up its great broad staircase on Fifth Avenue don't quite think of the Metropolitan Museum of Art this way. But technically this repository of art and architecture is a resident of Central Park. Sprawling along a particularly tony stretch of the avenue from 80th up to 84th streets, "the Met" is very simply the most formidable and rewarding museum of art or anything else in the entire city.

251

Established in 1870, the Metropolitan Museum of Art is the largest art museum in the United States, containing over two million individual works of art.

Founded in 1870 by a group of fifty city leaders, the Met had a couple of smaller locations before officially opening at its current site. The original Gothic Revival structure has since been completely encircled by additions that started just a few years later. The awesome Beaux-Arts entry hall that dominates the Fifth Avenue side was completed in 1926, serving as a superb anchor point for Museum Mile. Now the leading art museum in America, the Met has a massive collection of some two million pieces of art and draws over six million visitors a year. Note: the voluntary entry fee isn't mandatory but "suggested." That being said, donations are always appreciated.

What are some highlights of the Met's collection?

- American Wing—An awesome section of the museum with a well-rounded collection of domestic artists. Its focal point is the spacious and light-filled Garden Court, whose miscellany includes a Tiffany stained glass window and a complete marble façade from a bank that once stood on Wall Street. Just off to one side of the court you can find an entire living room from a Wisconsin home designed by Frank Lloyd Wright.

- Arms and Armor—The Met is unique in that not only does it hold a surprisingly deep and varied roster of armor and weaponry, including medieval armor and jeweled pistols, it is also probably the only museum in America to keep a full-time master armorer on the payroll.

- Costume Institute—A unique collection of over 35,000 costumes and accessories from the fifteenth century to the present that is frequently represented in sweeping, stylish exhibitions.

- Temple of Dendur—This complete sandstone Nile Delta temple dating from approximately 10 B.C.E. was gifted to the United States from the Egyptian government in 1965 and now has pride of place by the Sackler Wing's sweeping floor-to-ceiling windows.

What is Museum Mile?

This is the name for the particularly art-dense stretch of Fifth Avenue from 82nd up to 105th Street. The selection is richly varied, starting with the Goethe House German Cultural Center and the Met at the southern end. In between, you can find:

- Solomon R. Guggenheim Museum (88th Street)—Never called anything but the Guggenheim, this swirling stack of white rings was the last major project by Frank Lloyd Wright, who died six months before it opened in 1959. Built to house Guggenheim's impressive collection of "non-objective art," the museum features dramatic interior ramp-like walkways that have been accused of overwhelming the art itself, which is no slouch (Léger, Kandinsky, Modigliani, Noguchi, Mapplethorpe).

- Cooper Hewitt Smithsonian Design Museum (91st Street)—Once housed downtown at Cooper Union, this highly targeted museum is dedicated to the study and display of the decorative arts. It has been a part of the Smithsonian Institution since 1969. Fittingly for a design museum, it's a handsome complex housed in the old Andrew Carnegie mansion and featuring a smart little garden.

- Jewish Museum (92nd Street)—The biggest institution of its kind in the world, this museum in Felix Warburg's (1871–1931) French Gothic Revival Gilded Age mansion holds about thirty thousand items (art, religious artifacts, photographs) in its survey of four thousand years of Jewish history.

- Museum of the City of New York (103rd Street)—The best spot to learn everything about the city that you didn't already read about in this book, this museum is housed in a staid early twentieth-century Colonial Revival building filled with historical artifacts and art. Among the 1.5 million items in its collection are photographs by Jacob Riis and a massive classic toy collection. Recent exhibitions have included explorations of graffiti art, Green-Wood Cemetery, Hurricane Sandy, and a history of New York activism.

- El Museo Del Barrio (104th Street)—This museum was founded in 1969 as an expression of cultural pride and independence by a group of Puerto Rican activists. Its current home is a former orphanage dating from the 1920s. The varied collection ranges from pre-Columbian Taino artifacts to modern art, with a particular focus on Puerto Rican and Caribbean art.

Where is Carnegie Hill?

Confusingly, it's nowhere near Carnegie Hall. Occupying a prime section of real estate between 86th and 96th streets, from Central Park to Third Avenue, Carnegie Hill is a beautiful and dignified landmark-protected district of historic mansions and townhouses built mostly between the late 1800s and the 1930s. Its name comes from Andrew Carnegie, who started the Gilded Age land rush here in 1898 when he built his four-story, sixty-four-room mansion facing the park at 91st Street. The swooping lines of the Guggenheim are just about the only interruption of the modern age in this almost Parisian enclave of small shops, quiet restaurants, and old-money luxury.

What is New York's "Little White House"?

That would be the Archibald Gracie Mansion (Gracie Mansion for short, aka "the People's House") is the home of New York's mayor. A two-story Federal-style house with beautiful wraparound porches, it was built in 1799 by Scottish-born merchant Archibald Gracie (1755–1829) on Horn's Hook, a spot on the East River near where 88th Street would eventually run. The mansion passed through the hands of several private owners before

Gracie Mansion—sometimes called the People's House or the Little White House—is home to the mayor of New York.

being bought in 1896 by the Parks Commission, which turned the surrounding grounds running along the river from 84th Street up to 90th into Carl Schurz Park. After restoration and several years as the first location of the Museum of the City of New York, in 1942 it became the official mayoral residence when Fiorello LaGuardia moved in. In 2002, Mayor Mike Bloomberg broke from tradition by announcing that he wouldn't live at Gracie Mansion, preferring instead to stay at his townhouse on East 79th Street.

MORNINGSIDE HEIGHTS/HARLEM

When did Columbia University move uptown?

By 1897, Columbia University (then still Columbia College) had long outgrown its early reputation as a second-tier school that was less an educational institution than an outpost of the Anglican Church. During the nineteenth century, schools of physicians and surgeons, engineering, architecture, nursing, law, and teaching were added, along with graduate programs in political science and philosophy. The school relocated in 1857 from its original site near City Hall to 49th Street and Madison Avenue, but soon outgrew that campus as well.

In 1897, Columbia moved into its current home, an impressive cluster of Italian Renaissance-styled buildings designed by McKim, Mead, and White that forms the heart of the Morningside Heights neighborhood between Broadway and Amsterdam Avenue above 114th Street. Today, Columbia is the most prestigious university in New York and one of the top institutions of higher learning in the country and the world.

How did Columbia University's physics department change the world?

During the mid-1930s, Columbia University physicist John R. Dunning started building a cyclotron out of salvaged material and donations. Colloquially known as an atom smasher, the cyclotron used magnetic fields to spin particles in circles at improbably high speeds before smashing them into other particles. On January 25, 1939, Dunning and several other Columbia physicists working with the cyclotron in the basement of the university's Pupin Hall successfully split a uranium atom. Dunning jotted in his notebook the understatement that he believed "we have observed new phenomenon of far-reaching consequences." Even though Enrico Fermi (1901–1954) had done the same thing a few years earlier in Rome, this repeat of that experiment was in effect the beginning of the Manhattan Project, which operated for the next two years out of Pupin Hall before relocating to the University of Chicago and culminating with the creation of the atomic bomb in 1945. Pupin Hall was later designated a National Historic Landmark.

Where is the largest church in the United States?

The location of St. Patrick's Cathedral in the heart of Midtown has helped make it the city's most well-known place of worship. Still, it's by no means the biggest. The idea for building an immense Episcopalian cathedral was first proposed in 1828. Construction of the Cathedral Church of St. John the Divine, taking up an entire block on Amsterdam Avenue and 112th Street just east of Columbia University, began in 1892. A primarily Gothic structure, its design included elements of French Gothic and Byzantine styles as well. The cathedral's size and scope (its main vault is 124 feet high and over 600 feet long [38 meters high by 183 meters long]) has meant that the construction time is more reminiscent of medieval Europe than modern America. Work stopped completely at the outbreak of World War II and didn't resume until 1979.

The awe-inspiring building is still not complete, but the cathedral has nonetheless operated as a church over the years. Martin Luther King Jr. (1929–1968) preached at a service here in 1956 and in 1974 Duke Ellington's (1899–1974) funeral gathered over 12,500 mourners. The nearby Diocesan House holds the Madeleine L'Engle Library; the author of *A Wrinkle in Time* (1918–2007) worked there as librarian and was a member of the congregation for decades.

How did Harlem get its name?

There are a couple explanations for this, both involving the city of Haarlem in the Netherlands. One story goes that Harlem got its name for being the same distance (11 kilometers) from New Amsterdam as Haarlem was from Amsterdam. The other explanation is a bit more complicated. When New Amsterdam was first founded, it was hoped that upper Manhattan would be able to support great tobacco plantations. That plan failed, but the colony still wanted the region settled in order to stave off Indians or English who might encroach from the north. A 1658 ordinance offered cheap land and a fifteen-year tax exemption for any who would settle in the new village, whose defensive placement and name of Nieuw Haarlem might have evoked memories of that town's staunch resistance to the Spanish in the Eighty Years War. Today, Harlem is used to denote most of northeastern Manhattan from 110th Street up to the Harlem River, west to Morningside Avenue and east to Fifth Avenue.

How has Harlem changed over the years?

In colonial terms, Harlem began with just twenty-five settlers, connected to points south by a road that ran along an old Indian trail: Broadway. For about two centuries, it was occupied by the estates of wealthy families that included Alexander Hamilton. Starting in the 1880s, elevated train lines brought Italian and German immigrants looking for more space and developers eager to accommodate them with new brownstones.

Not long after the turn of the century, the neighborhood's Jewish population burgeoned, making it the second most Jewish district in the city after the Lower East Side. However, the move of black New Yorkers and new arrivals from the South to Harlem, after being dislocated from the Tenderloin and the Village, was even more dramatic. By

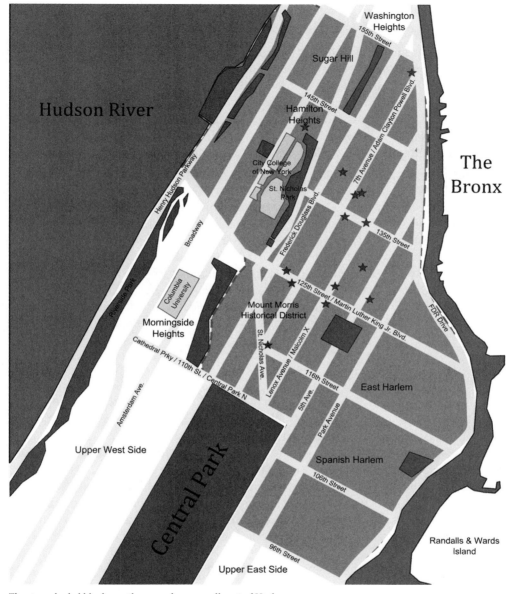

The gray-shaded blocks on the map above are all part of Harlem.

the end of the 1920s, Harlem's black residents numbered over 200,000, with a population density more than twice that of the rest of the city. The neighborhood's fortunes have ebbed and waned over the decades, from the flowering of the Harlem Renaissance in the 1920s and '30s to the current battles over gentrification. Nevertheless, its status as the unofficial "Capital of Black America" has cemented Harlem as an iconic place in the American imagination.

257

Who *is* buried in Grant's Tomb, anyway?

That awe-inspiring granite and marble edifice at the northern end of Riverside Park near 122nd Street seems out of place in more than one way. The largest mausoleum in the United States, it looks like it more rightly belongs on the Mall in Washington, D.C., than Morningside Heights. There is also the fact of the stark imbalance between the grandiosity of its presentation (the closest thing that America has to Napoleon's similarly grandiose tomb in Paris) and the low profile that its occupant ranks in the modern American memory.

After Ulysses S. Grant (1822–1885) served two terms as president, from 1869 to 1877, that were distinguished more by mediocrity and corruption than statesmanship, he moved to New York. At the time of his death in 1885, though, he was still fondly viewed as the savior of the nation for his leadership of the Union Army in the Civil War. The Greek temple-style Grant's Tomb opened to the public in 1897 in a ceremony and parade attended by over a million people. The first part of the answer to the trick question posed by Groucho Marx (1890–1977), "Who's buried in Grant's Tomb?" is: Ulysses S. Grant *and* his wife, Julia Grant (1826–1902). The second part is: neither are actually *buried* there. Their matching sarcophagi of red Wisconsin marble sit side by side underneath the rotunda.

Where is the center of Harlem?

Running river to river, 125th Street has long been the main commercial and entertainment thoroughfare of Harlem. The Apollo Theater and the Studio Museum (which exhibits African and African-American art) are here, with legendary venues like the Lenox Lounge just off it and Marcus Garvey Park a block to the south on Fifth Avenue. In addition, 125th Street was also the site of the big 1935 riots, sparked by rumors that a black boy had been killed at a store known for being happier to serve blacks than to hire them. Today the street is ever-thicker with chain stores, which have a complicated profile here, with some residents nervous about the area losing its uniqueness and others relieved to finally have access to similar goods and services as much of the rest of the city.

Why is the Apollo Theater so important to Harlem history?

The Apollo Theater opened as the Hurtig and Seamon's New (Burlesque) Theater on West 125th Street in Harlem in 1913. It operated as a whites-only burlesque theater and then a movie house until it was bought by new owners in the early 1930s, after the demographics had changed with the dramatic new influx of Caribbean blacks and southern African Americans. In 1934 it reopened as the desegregated Apollo Theater, fortuitously timed with the explosive cultural activity associated with the Harlem Renaissance.

Advertised as "The Only Stage Show in Harlem," the Apollo has been host to a glittering array of performers, from bandleaders like Count Basie (1904–1984) and Duke

Ellington to Bill "Bojangles" Robinson (1878–1949). The theater remained one of the city's premier venues for decades. A critical link in the country's so-called "chitlin circuit" for black touring acts (like the Regal Theater in Chicago), the Apollo has also been a prized venue for many white artists. The roll call of star performers has included Stevie Wonder (1950–) and James Brown (1933–2006), jazz masters Stan Getz (1927–1991) and Buddy Rich (1917–1987), and comedians Richard Pryor (1940–2005) and Redd Foxx (1922–1991). Moms Mabley (1894–1975) and B. B. King (1925–2015) recorded live albums there. The Apollo closed for a couple years in the late-1970s but has remained open ever since as one of the linchpins of Harlem's main commercial and creative thoroughfare. It was accorded landmark status in 1983.

What is the significance of the stump of wood on the Apollo's stage?

The Apollo was special to New York and Harlem in particular not just because of its staggering array of star performers. Amateur Night started in 1933 at the nearby Lafayette Theater and moved to the Apollo the following year. Amateur Night was and remains today a raucous and wildly popular weekly talent show (at one point it was nationally broadcast on radio and was later syndicated nationwide on TV as *Showtime at the Apollo*) where audience reactions range from the lacerating to the rapturous, often with little in-between. The man who escorts losing performers off-stage has used everything over the years from a cap gun to (more recently) a broom.

Among the performers who got their start at Amateur Night were Wilson Pickett (1941–2006), Sarah Vaughan (1924–1990), Luther Vandross (1951–2005), and Ella Fitzgerald (1917–1996), who was only fifteen the night she won for her performance. The outcomes are often wildly unpredictable. There is one constant tradition. All performers who want to win an enthusiastic response rub for good luck the old tree stump sitting on a pedestal at stage right before their performances. Legend has it that good luck would come to performers who walked underneath the elm tree that used to grow a few blocks up Seventh Avenue. When the tree was cut down to make room for a widening road, a foot-and-a-half segment was saved and brought to the Apollo to help future amateurs achieve their dreams.

The legendary Apollo Theater in Harlem started, ironicaly, as a whites-only theater in 1913. It transformed into a venue for black entertainers in the 1930s.

Where was Malcolm X assassinated?

Black nationalist leader Malcolm X (1925–1965) was born in Omaha and relocated to Boston as a teenager. During his early years as a criminal, he was a habitué of Harlem. In the 1940s, as the minor-league dealer and burglar nicknamed "Detroit Red," he worked as a waiter at the famous integrated nightclub Small's Paradise at Seventh Avenue and 135th Street. After spending six years in jail, during which time he converted to the then-small Nation of Islam sect, the newly named Malcolm X returned to New York in 1954 to head up the group's Harlem temple on 116th Street. Malcolm, who lived with his family in a small home in Queens, quickly gained a reputation as a fiery preacher. Like a latter-day Marcus Garvey, the more disciplined and abstemious Malcolm also railed against institutionalized racism while calling on blacks to establish themselves as a separate and self-sufficient community.

Due mostly to Malcolm's efforts, the Nation of Islam gained thousands of followers in Harlem, where they opened a network of black-owned businesses. In 1964, a disenchanted Malcolm split with the Nation of Islam. Afterward, he adopted a more nuanced rhetoric and practiced a more traditional form of Islam. During a rally at the Audubon Ballroom at Broadway and 165th Street on February 21, 1965, Malcolm was assassinated by three members of the Nation of Islam. The Ballroom is now known as the Malcolm X and Dr. Betty Shabazz Memorial and Educational Center.

How did Sugar Hill and Strivers' Row get their names?

Much of north Harlem from 144th to 155th streets between Edgecome and Amsterdam avenues sits on a hill, from where its residents could literally look down on Harlem residents to the south. It likely acquired the name Sugar Hill because residents of its elegant townhouses and apartment buildings were assumed to be living the sweet life. Many wealthy and famous black New Yorkers lived there during the 1930s and '40s, including Thurgood Marshall (1908–1993), W. E. B. Du Bois (1868–1963), Paul Robeson (1898–1976), and Count Basie. Another enclave for professional blacks was Strivers' Row, a well-maintained selection of beautiful townhouses built in the 1890s (originally for white clients, who mostly moved out a few decades later as the neighborhood became increasingly black) by Stanford White and other noted architects that takes up 138th and 139th streets between Seventh and Eighth avenues.

Is there anything left of the Polo Grounds?

A high forested ridge just west of the Harlem River above 155th Street, Coogan's Bluff was the home of the city's first true sports stadium, the Polo Grounds, from 1890 to 1964. After being abandoned by both the Giants and the Mets, the stadium was demolished and replaced by housing projects. Today its only remnant is a staircase that bends steeply down the bluff through Highbridge Park, from Edgecombe Avenue to Harlem River Driveway.

What's the difference between East Harlem, Spanish Harlem, and El Barrio?

Generally, not much besides the name. All three labels generally denote the same stretch of Manhattan from the Upper East Side at 96th Street north and east to the curve of the FDR Drive and the Harlem River, and west to the border of Harlem proper at Fifth Avenue. The city began to expand up this way when the New York and Harlem Railroad, which ran north up Park Avenue from City Hall to the Harlem River, opened in the 1830s.

Tenements swiftly displaced shantytowns in the 1880s with the new Second and Third avenue elevated train lines delivering a dense concentration of southern Italian immigrants, who created Manhattan's other Little Italy. In the 1920s, just as blacks were moving into Harlem, East Harlem became home to a growing number of Hispanics. In the postwar years, the neighborhood gained the "Spanish Harlem" and "El Barrio" monikers as it transitioned to a primarily Puerto Rican population. It was hit particularly hard in the 1950s and '60s by a wave of urban renewal that saw streets of tenements torn down and replaced by ranks of unloved public housing tower.

Where is the first purpose-built mosque in New York?

Planned since the 1960s, the Islamic Cultural Center of New York didn't host its first service until 1991. The 21,000-square-foot structure at the southern verge of East Harlem on 96th Street and Third Avenue is the first such building constructed as a mosque in the entire city. The Mecca-facing building generally referred to as simply the New York Mosque features a 130-foot (39.6-meter) minaret. Several thousand Muslims, both Sunnis and Shias, gather each week for services. The congregation includes members from an incredible seventy different countries.

UPPER MANHATTAN

What is the highest point in Manhattan?

Most of the hills in old Manhattan were not that tall, with most in lower Manhattan topping out below 30 feet (9 meters) high. The point of highest elevation in Manhattan has, since the time of the first European settlements, been Bennett Park in Washington Heights between 183rd and 185th streets. It rises about 265 feet (81 meters) above sea level, or about 40 feet (12 meters) lower than the Flatiron Building. Once a heavily wooded spot called Penadnik by the Lenape, it later served as Fort Washington, headquarters for George Washington during the battles for New York in 1776. The Continental Army had to abandon it in November 1776. Opened to the public in 1929, the small park is named for James Gordon Bennett (1795–1872), the Scottish immigrant who started the *New York Herald* in 1835 and became one of the city's most important and wealthiest media figures before purchasing, in 1871, the land the park now occupies.

What is the High Bridge?

The High Bridge is a 1,450-foot- (442-meter-) long stone-arch pedestrian bridge modeled after ancient Roman aqueducts. It stretches from Highbridge Park in Washington Heights across the Harlem River to the Bronx. The High Bridge was built between 1839 and 1848 as the last stage in the massive project that brought water from the Croton River in Westchester over forty miles (sixty-four kilometers) south to the city's then-main reservoir at 42nd Street; the aqueduct's massive pipes sit below the bridge's walkway. After it opened, the bridge's high vistas (114 feet [34.75 meters] above the water at high tide) and the greenery on either side quickly made it a

Foot and bicycle traffic was allowed back on High Bridge in 2015 after it was renovated to prevent people from dropping objects over the side.

popular spot for perambulating. There were boat races along this stretch of the river and horse-racing along the Harlem River Speedway, a two-mile path that opened in the late 1800s and ran under the High Bridge. A water tower and reservoir were built nearby on the Manhattan side in 1872 to help supply water to upper Manhattan.

The tower is still there today, while the reservoir was rebuilt as a public swimming pool in 1936; still operational now, it's the largest public pool in Manhattan. The aqueduct was shut down in the 1950s and the bridge itself closed to foot traffic in the early 1970s, in part because reportedly people had been dropping objects from the span onto boats passing underneath. After a lengthy renovation, the High Bridge reopened to foot and bicycle traffic in 2015.

Where is the oldest surviving house in Manhattan?

Sitting today in a well-maintained pocket park in Harlem at 160th Street and Edgecombe Avenue, the Morris-Jumel Mansion is a two-story house first built as a summer villa in 1765 by the British Army Colonel Roger Morris (1727–1794) as the centerpiece of his 130-acre estate that stretched from the Hudson to the Harlem rivers. Situated at one of Manhattan's highest points, and offering excellent views of the Harlem valley, it was considered strategically important to be occupied during the Revolutionary War by General Washington (who planned the Battle of Harlem Heights here) as well as British and Hessian troops.

In 1810, the house was purchased by French sugar merchant Stephen Jumel. Years after his death, Jumel's widow Eliza (1775–1865) married Aaron Burr, and the two lived in the mansion until their divorce in 1836. The city of New York bought the mansion in 1903 and it opened as a museum the following year. Nearby at 163rd Street and St. Nicholas Avenue you can find an English elm tree that George Washington was reputed to have stood under on September 21, 1776, while he watched New York burn.

What is the busiest bridge in the world?

Long Island is stitched into the roadways of New York and surrounding regions by a network of bridges across the East River. There is just one bridge connecting New York across the Hudson River to the American mainland by way of the New Jersey Palisades. Called the most beautiful bridge in the world by modernist architect Le Corbusier, the George Washington Bridge was erected in 1931, between Washington Heights in upper Manhattan and Fort Lee. Spanning 3,500 feet (1,067 meters), it was at the time the longest suspension bridge in the world. Today, the George Washington (usually referred to as "the GW" by New Yorkers) is the busiest bridge in the world, with over 100 million cars crossing it annually on one of its two decks; the second was added by the bridge's architect Othmar Ammann (1879–1965) in 1962 to accommodate extra traffic.

Why is there a medieval-style monastery in upper Manhattan?

Beautifully placed in the wooded heights of Fort Tyron Park in far northwestern Manhattan, with a beautiful view over the Hudson River, The Cloisters looks like either an ancient monastery or an estate built by some Gilded Age tycoon before upper Manhattan became too crowded with commoners. But this fascinating oddity, with its quiet courtyards and hushed galleries filled with glittering antiquities, was actually purpose-built to display the Metropolitan Museum's wealth of medieval art. Much of the collection was acquired in the late-nineteenth and early twentieth centuries by George Grey Barnard (1863–1938), a noted sculptor who made a fortune scouring Europe for medieval treasures and selling them to eager American millionaires. As part of his dream of constructing "an intellectual Coney Island" in uptown Manhattan, Barnard later displayed many of his finds at a gallery built next to his house in Washington Heights.

The Met bought Barnard's massive collection of medieval antiquities in the 1920s. During the same period, John D. Rockefeller Jr. (who had given the museum the money for the Barnard purchase) donated the 62 acres of wooded cliffside land he owned just south of Inwood Hill Park to the city. That land became Fort Tyron Park, with 4 acres carved out for a museum in the neo-Gothic-styled grounds designed by Frederick Law

---

Where in New York can you find a shrine to an American saint?

The first American saint is venerated with a beautiful, recently restored mosaic mural in the Saint Frances Xavier Cabrini shrine at the north end of Fort Washington Avenue just below Fort Tyron Park. The Italian-born Cabrini (1850–1917) was asked by Pope Leo XIII to come to America to serve the growing numbers of Italian immigrants. The shrine to her memory contains most of her body molded into a wax figure in a glass coffin. (Her arm is in Chicago, and her heart in Codogno, Italy, where she founded the order that bears her name.) Cabrini was canonized in 1946 and soon after declared the patron saint of immigrants.

Olmsted Jr. (1870–1924); Rockefeller also donated 700 acres he owned in the New Jersey Palisades across the river, in part to preserve the view from the Manhattan side. Designed by Charles Collens (1873–1956), who also planned Riverside Church, The Cloisters opened in 1938.

What can you find at The Cloisters?

The neo-Gothic Cloisters museum building and surrounding gardens were not designed to imitate any one building but to incorporate many different influences as a way of telling the story of medieval art and architecture. Built in part by imitating Roman construction methods, it includes many pieces of actual medieval cloisters (a monastery or convent) and other sites all over Europe. The most eye-catching part of the building is the tower, a replica of one at the Cuxa Cloister in France. Barnard's hundreds of items form the core of the museum's 3,000-piece collection, which include everything from jewelry and statuary to tapestries and a chapel with stonework from a French church dating to the twelfth century. The centerpiece in The Cloisters collection is the series of seven fantastical hangings, woven in wool and silk with silver and gilded threads, known collectively as *The Unicorn Tapestries*. It's highly possible that Barnard's acquisitions saved many pieces of antiquity from looting or destruction during World War II.

Where can you best see what Manhattan looked like in pre-colonial times?

At the far northwestern corner of Manhattan near the Inwood neighborhood, just above Fort Tyron Park and The Cloisters and at the southern terminus of the Henry Hudson Bridge across Spuyten Duyvill Creek to the Bronx, you can find the pocket of ancient woodlands and old salt marsh called Inwood Hill Park. Somehow, as developers marched farther and farther up Manhattan over the centuries, this hilly wooded corner of the is-

A view of The Cloisters from the Hudson River is like getting a glimpse of a historic European site.

land, tangled with ravines and caves, remained untouched. Evidence has been found in the eastern part of the park of Lenape encampments dating from the seventeenth century. The area was called Shorakapok ("the place between the ridges") by the Lenape and then Cox Hill by colonials who farmed and lived there. Briefly home to a Continental Army fort seized by British and Hessian troops in 1776, Cox Hill was the site of several estates for the wealthy, including the Macy's-owning Straus family.

In 1916, the city bought the land, demolished most the buildings on it—one exception was the Dyckman House, the last standing Dutch farmhouse on Manhattan, dating from around 1785—and established Inwood Hill Park. Today, the 196-acre park is the last remaining stand of primeval forest on the entire island. Sadly, its oldest living thing, a tulip tree planted by the Dutch in 1658, came down in 1938.

Where can you find the oldest rocks in New York?

The oldest natural object in the entire New York metropolitan area is the Fordham Gneiss. A roughly 1.1 billion-year-old pre-Cambrian rock formation, the Fordham Gneiss was formed when an unknown landmass smashed into the North American continent and caused sedimentary rock to recrystallize into unique black-and-white-banded metamorphic rock structures. One of the easiest spots to see the Fordham Gneiss aboveground is north from Inwood Hill Park towards the Bronx across the Harlem River (or Spuyten Duyvil Creek at that point) where the tall rocky cliff facing the Columbia University athletic stadium has been consistently painted a giant "C."

THE BRONX, BROOKLYN, QUEENS, AND STATEN ISLAND

THE BRONX

Which borough is not an island?

The Bronx is the only one of New York's five boroughs that is actually situated on the continental mainland. Like the boroughs of Queens and Brooklyn, it transitions from densely urban neighborhoods closer to Manhattan into more spacious residential areas that transition to suburbs further from the city's core. It is the third most densely populated county in the United States, and yet roughly one-fourth of its land is open space.

Separated from Manhattan by only the narrow Harlem River, and home to municipal crown jewels like Yankee Stadium and the New York Botanical Garden, the Bronx is in some ways the most distant of boroughs, due to its separation from the power centers of Midtown and the Financial District. Nevertheless, its population of 1.385 million puts it in the top ten largest cities in the nation. It is growing faster than any other borough except for Staten Island, perhaps not coincidentally, as that is the borough besides the Bronx that is most often considered (fairly or not) a bedroom community for Manhattan.

How diverse is the Bronx's population?

According to the New York City Economic Development Corporation (NYCEDC) in 2013, the Bronx has more residents who spoke Spanish at home (46.3%) than any other borough. Roughly a third of its population is foreign-born, up from about twenty-two percent in 2000.

These are the largest ethnic groups in the Bronx:
- Hispanic or Latino: 53.8%
- Black or African American: 29.9%
- White: 11.1%
- Asian: 3.4%

Who were the first settlers of the Bronx?

When the Europeans first established New Amsterdam, just to the north, the shorelines of Long Island Sound, including Pelham Bay and the southern part of the Bronx, were dotted with small settlements of Lenape Indians known as the Siwanoy. The Siwanoy ("southern people") engaged in fur trade with the Dutch and English, but conflict over the encroachment of colonists soon sparked.

Following a massacre of hundreds of Indians at a village at Pound Ridge in later-day Westchester County, the Siwanoy killed Anne Hutchinson (1591–1643)—a religious dissenter banished from Boston who had settled in the Bronx—and several of her followers in retaliation. After several more years of war and disease, Siwanoy habitation in the area mostly came to an end following the signing of a peace treaty in 1654 at which English settler Thomas Pell (1612–1669) bought the land that later became part of Pelham Bay Park.

Where did the Bronx's name originate?

Jonas Bronck (c. 1600–1643) grew up on a farm in Sweden and later worked as a sea captain in Amsterdam before the economic chaos of tulip-bulb mania sent him to New Amsterdam in 1639. Later he became the first European to settle north of the Harlem River. The Broncks' stone house, called Emmaus, built high up on what would later be Lincoln Avenue and 132nd Street, reportedly held the largest library in the entire colony. Emmaus was also the site in 1642 of the signing of a peace treaty between the Weckquasgeeks and Dutch.

According to lore, people visiting Emmaus would say they were going to "the Broncks." The tradition stuck well after Jonas Bronck had died and his wife remarried and relocated further north. The borough and the Bronx River (called Aquahung by Indians) were named for them. Today, the Bronx is the only borough to always have an article preceding it. Nobody ever says they are going to "the Queens" or "the Brooklyn."

What was Morrisania?

Today, Morrisania is a small-ish quadrant of the South Bronx east of the Grand Concourse. From the 1670s, it was the two-thousand-acre estate of farms and dairies owned by the Morris family, a powerful and aristocratic New York family whose members included a governor, chief justice of the state of New York, and a signer of the Declaration of Independence. After the Revolutionary War, Lewis Morris (1671–1746) offered the family estate to the new nation as its capital. The Morris's generous offer was turned down. Governor Morris was later instrumental in putting together Manhattan's 1811 street grid, whose severe regularity would be replicated in the mid-nineteenth century as Morrisania's farms were rapidly transformed into bustling urban immigrant neighborhoods.

What house did Babe Ruth build?

In 1921, the New York Yankees were still sharing the Polo Grounds in upper Manhattan with the New York Giants. That was the year they bought ten acres across the Harlem

River in the Bronx at 161st Street and River Avenue to build their own new ballpark. The original Yankee Stadium, the first ballpark with a triple deck and the first to be called a stadium, opened two years later with an official seating capacity of 67,224. Its walls featured a special fortified concrete that Thomas Edison developed. The April 18 opening ceremonies were led by John Philip Sousa (1854–1932) and the Seventh Regiment Band, while Governor Al Smith threw out the opening pitch. The Yankees beat the Boston Red Sox 4–1 after a three-run homer by Babe Ruth (1895–1948). It became known as "The House That Ruth Built" in large part due to the ability of the "Sultan of Swat" to deliver the hits (1,971 RBIs as a Yankee)

A photo of Babe Ruth and teammates at the 1923 opening of Yankee Stadium.

and bring in fans to the very expensive facility season after season.

The stadium and the team it hosted for championship after championship would go on to become probably the borough's most treasured icon, even after it was replaced with a new stadium next door to the original site in 2009. In an ironic twist, the last game played in the original Yankee stadium in 2008 was a loss to the Baltimore Orioles, which is what the Yankees were known as before moving to New York in 1903.

What was "The Park Avenue of the Middle Class"?

The Bronx's Grand Concourse stretches about 4.5 miles (7.25 kilometers) from 138th Street in the southwestern corner below Yankee Stadium through the heart of the borough up to Moshulu Parkway in Norwood. It was planned in the pre-highway and pre-subway late-nineteenth century as a way to connect Manhattan to the (still remote, to some) northern Bronx. Part of the popular nineteenth-century City Beautiful urban-revival movement, it was planned as a broad parkway that would be for the Bronx what the Champs-Elysées is for Paris; a planning illustration from 1895 shows elegant roads framed by forested parks and fountains.

When the Grand Concourse opened in 1909 (at the time it extended only to 161st Street), it dovetailed with the influx of New Yorkers looking to escape crowded downtown Manhattan. In its early twentieth-century boom, the roadway was quickly lined with dozens of fashionably designed five- and six-story apartment buildings, including enough Art Deco and Art Moderne architecture to earn comparisons with Miami Beach's Ocean Drive. Apartments in the area were advertised based on how far they were from the Grand Concourse. The Grand Concourse's place as a status symbol to striving second-generation New Yorkers is encapsulated in *The Jazz Singer*, where Al Jolson promises his mother that if he's a success, "we're gonna move up to the Bronx. A lot of nice green grass up there, and a whole lot of people you know." This staunchly bourgeois neighborhood was home to more famous New Yorkers—everyone from E. L. Doctorow (1931–2015) and Babe Ruth to Stanley Kubrick and Milton Berle (1908–2002)—than any area outside of Brooklyn. The area went into decline, as did many other parts of the Bronx, in the 1950s and '60s. But years of preservation, community organizing, and rehabilitation have more recently turned much of it around so that the Grand Concourse has been able to remain the backbone of the borough.

Where is New York's largest zoo?

At 265 acres in size and featuring about 4,000 animals constituting more than 650 different species, the Bronx Zoo is far and away the largest and most diversely populated zoo in the New York area and the largest metropolitan zoo in the country. Situated in the north-central part of the borough between Fordham University and East Bronx, it occupies the southern part of a broad pocket of greenery that also includes the New York Botanical Garden.

The Bronx Zoo opened in 1899 with a number of Beaux Arts structures and 843 animals. It features many beautiful architectural details, including the grandly elaborate buildings in the Astor Court designed by the same firm that designed the Cathedral of St. John the Divine in Morningside Heights, and an elaborately sculpted ornamental gate in the French Arts Decoratifs style. The zoo's size and emphasis on conservation (it's one of the country's largest conservation parks) make it in many ways more of a park than urban zoo. It was also groundbreaking, appointing the first full-time zoo veterinarian in America, opening the country's first animal hospital in 1916, and leading the way in situating its animals in close simulacra of their natural settings. One of its most remarkable sights is the Rocking Stone, a seven-foot- (two-meter-) high, 30-ton cube of pink-hued granite that dates from the Ice Age. About two million people visit the zoo every year.

Why was there a "Fort Apache" in the Bronx?

In the 1970s, the South Bronx was synonymous with street crime. Many NYPD officers stationed in the 41st Precinct, which saw upwards of 120 homicides each year and featured gangs like the Savage Skulls and Ghetto Brothers, viewed the area as a combat zone. Due to the chaos on the streets (and a legendary story about an unknown assailant who reportedly shot arrows at police), the stout stone station house on Simpson Street, which had been built in a Renaissance Revival style in 1914 that later fell out of fashion, gained the nickname "Fort Apache." The term was popularized in a 1976 book and 1981 film of the same name. Once arson had done its work on the neighborhood, some wags gave the station house a new nickname: "Little House on the Prairie."

Where is the largest herbarium in the Western Hemisphere?

An herbarium is a repository of dried plant specimens used for scientific reference. The herbarium at the Bronx Botanical Garden—technically the New York Botanical Garden but almost nobody calls it that—has more than any other in this half of the world, with some 7.3 million plants kept on file for botanists and other researchers. The Garden was conceived in 1888 after a Columbia University professor and his wife (both botanists) took an eye-opening trip to England's Royal Botanic Garden in Kew and decided that New York needed a garden equal in stature to what they had just witnessed. The Garden was incorporated in 1891. Its then-remote, 250-acre site in the Bronx, next to Fordham University, on the north border of the Bronx Zoo, featuring rolling meadows and wide swaths of old-growth forest bisected by the Bronx River, was selected in 1895.

The current layout, with winding forest paths and sculpted gardens, is based on a design by Calvert Vaux. Besides its world-famous research facility, the Garden also has an educational program and a strong year-round selection of exhibitions incorporating themes as varied as orchids and Frida Kahlo (1907–1954) in the Haupt Conservatory. Its 40 acres of virgin forest constitute the largest preserve of its kind in the New York metropolitan area.

What battle took place in Van Cortlandt Park?

One of the New York area's more beautiful outdoor spaces, Van Cortlandt Park is located in the upper stretches of the Bronx near Woodlawn Cemetery and Riverdale. Home to a golf course, skating rink, and equestrian center, it's also where one of the less-remembered battles of the Revolutionary War took place.

On August 31, 1778, Chief Daniel Nimham (1726–1778) and seventeen Stockbridge Mohican Indians from the Massachusetts area, all allied to the American cause, moved into the area to scout on British troop movements. A contingent of British and Hessian troops ambushed the Mohicans, killing all of them. The Mohicans were buried by a wealthy Dutch family who owned the land where the battle took place. A plaque in honor of Chief Nimham and his Mohicans was raised on the site in 1906.

How did a highway kill a Bronx neighborhood?

For decades, the name Robert Moses has been mud to a broad cross-section of New Yorkers. His critics long deplored how his impersonal public works projects transformed the city during the twentieth century. His dictatorial impulses and car-centric planning obsessions were put most vividly on display in his decades-long project to build the seven-mile-long Cross-Bronx Expressway across the borough. It's one of the city's most crowded and hated freeways, and is also seen as a permanent blight on the borough that it loudly bisects. The damage wrought by the construction of the Cross-Bronx, which ultimately displaced a quarter-million people, was laid out by Robert Caro in the "One Mile" chapter of his Moses biography, *The Power Broker*.

Caro describes how one stretch of the otherwise straight freeway inexplicably dipped south through East Tremont, effectively destroying one of the borough's most livable and ethnically mixed neighborhoods. East Tremont's large and reasonably priced apartments, access to Crotona Park, and easy commutes to the Garment District, where many of its Jewish residents worked, gave the neighborhood that hard-to-find balance of convenience and space that many New Yorkers spend years searching for in vain.

Starting in 1952, thousands of residents were told that their buildings were slated for demolition. A frantic campaign to move the Expressway just two blocks south to the north verge of Crotona Park (which would have saved about 1,500 apartments) was brusquely denied. About 15,000 of the neighborhood's 60,000 residents were forced to move. By 1960, after years of earthquake-like demolition blasts and clouds of apocalyptic soot had helped drive away even those who weren't evicted, the freeway was finished. But the neighborhood was effectively dead. Caro writes that by 1965, many of the area's once-cherished buildings "were ravaged hulks" and the garbage-filled streets roamed by criminals and addicts. East Tremont was far from the only once-viable New York neighborhood gutted by development, but it remains a vivid example of the fragility of the ecosystems that bind cities together.

Was Edgar Allan Poe from the Bronx?

You might be forgiven for thinking so, since there's a small restored cottage called the Edgar Allan Poe Cottage on Grand Concourse and Kingsbridge Road just west of Fordham University. But the Boston-born Edgar Allan Poe (1809–1849) only lived here from 1846 to 1849. At the time, the area was called Fordham Village and it was primarily countryside. Poe moved here with his wife Virginia in the hope that the country air would help her tuberculosis. From this 1812-built cottage, Poe had a beautiful view east to Long Island.

While living here, Poe wrote several pieces, including "The Bells" and "The Cask of Amontillado." Some of his writing took inspiration from his surroundings. "I have been roaming far and wide over this island of Mannahatta," Poe recounted in an 1844 dispatch to a Pennsylvania newspaper. "Some portions of its interior have a certain air of rocky sterility which may impress some imaginations as simply dreary—but to me it conveys the sublime."

This was Poe's last home. He died in October 7, 1849, while visiting Baltimore. During his time in New York, Poe and his family also lived in the Financial District, Greenwich Village, and Turtle Bay.

Whatever happened to Freedomland?

Co-op City was built on the marshy grounds of Freedomland. Now mostly forgotten—except by urban historians and fans of the Bronx-born writer Richard

A cottage in the Bronx is named after Edgar Allan Poe, but the poet only lived there for three years in the late 1840s.

> ## What is Co-op City?
>
> Co-op City was opened in 1968 as the biggest cooperative housing project in America. It remains one of the largest housing complexes of any kind. With 15,000 apartments in thirty-five giant towers, and hundreds of two-family townhouses, on about a square mile of the northeastern Bronx near Pelham Bay Park, the somewhat self-sufficient Co-op features several schools, three shopping centers, a thirteen-screen movie theater, and over a dozen places of worship. Despite being remote and architecturally uninspiring, Co-op City's quiet surroundings and extreme affordability have created years-long waiting lists to get apartments here.

Price (1949–), whose novel *Freedomland* was loosely inspired by it—Freedomland was a 205-acre amusement park that was proclaimed in breathless press coverage as "the Disneyland of the East." On opening day in June 1960, 25,000 people eagerly lined up to see what all the fuss was about.

Conceived as an all-American kind of affair and laid out in the shape of the nation, its attractions (as described in its 1960 guidebook) included river rides, historical reenactments, and a ride called the San Francisco Earthquake. They were grouped in a rather idiosyncratic fashion:

- Little Old New York: 1850–1900 (included: "political pep rally, German band, bank hold-up, suffragettes")
- Chicago: 1871
- The Great Plains: 1803–1900
- San Francisco: 1906
- The Old Southwest: 1890
- New Orleans: Mardi Gras
- Satellite City: The Future

Freedomland was never able to keep up with the popularity of parks like the smaller Disneyland (which had been designed by some of the same people who planned Freedomland). It closed for good in 1964.

BROOKLYN

How diverse is Brooklyn's population?

Brooklyn is the largest borough by population, with 2.5 million people. English is the most prominent language, with nearly half of Brooklynites speaking another language at home.

These are the largest ethnic groups in Brooklyn, according to the NYCEDC's 2013 report:

- White—35.6%
- Black or African American—32.1%
- Hispanic or Latino—20%
- Asian—10.6%

When was Brooklyn first settled by Europeans?

Not long after New Amsterdam was established on Manhattan, the Dutch began scattering other settlements around the harbor. In 1624 there were some trading huts on Wallabout Bay (a corruption of "Walloon Bay"), currently the Navy Yard Basin. In 1636, Dutch settlers began buying up land in the forested hills, flatlands, and swamps on the southwestern verge of Brooklyn. Curiously, the first true village in Brooklyn was not situated on the water but inland, in the central area called Flatbush today but originally Vlacke Bos when it was founded in 1634.

Several other settlements followed as the Dutch bought up more parcels of land from the Canarsie Indians, until by 1680 they had purchased everything in what now constitutes Kings County. The Dutch community of Breuckelen (or, Broken Land, named for a town back in the Netherlands), or Brooklyn Village, which occupies present-day Brooklyn Heights and downtown Brooklyn, was incorporated in 1646. Proud Brooklynites can today point to the fact that their borough was granted municipal government four years earlier than those laggards in Manhattan.

What six towns originally made up Brooklyn?

- Brooklyn
- Bushwick
- Flatbush
- Flatlands
- Gravesend
- New Utrecht

When did Brooklyn become a city?

When the village of Brooklyn became a city in 1834, the mostly rural borough had a population of fewer than 25,000 people. Construction of its grand, column-fronted Greek Revival City Hall just east of Brooklyn Heights was completed in 1848. The city grew swiftly, annexing Williamsburg to the north in 1854 and reaching a population of over a million by the end of the century.

What was America's first suburb?

Brooklyn Heights holds pride of place as one of the nation's first commuter suburbs. People had been taking ferries from Brooklyn to Manhattan almost since the start of

New Amsterdam. But the early nineteenth century saw a wave of speculation sweep through the Heights, a raised plateau just across the East River from lower Manhattan that the Lenape called Ihpetonga ("the high sandy bank"). In Dutch times it was divided up into farms. By the 1760s, the busy "Brookland Ferry" was operating almost underneath where the Brooklyn Bridge soars now, while further to the south on today's Joralemon Street was Dutch patroon Philip Livingstone's gin distillery.

In 1776, the area served as a (ultimately unused) line of fortifications for the Continental Army during its disastrous retreat in the Battle of Brooklyn that ended with its daring nighttime escape across the East River from the base of the Heights. After 1800, most of the orchards and fields in between the Ferry and Joralemon were swiftly parceled up and turned into small lots for small businesses and small wood-frame and later handsome brownstones. Once regular steam ferry service to Manhattan began in 1815, the area became very attractive for those who worked in lower Manhattan but wanted to have a family home that was both convenient and yet out of the city's hurly burly. In the yellow fever epidemic of 1822, the Heights was advertised as being a particularly "healthy" place to live.

Did Brooklyn ever have its own naval base?

Officially named the New York Naval Shipyard but known to everybody in the city as the Brooklyn Navy Yard, this massive military complex encompasses most of Wallabout Bay (now the Navy Yard Basin) on the East River between the Manhattan and Williamsburg bridges. In 1801, President John Adams, concerned about the young nation's lack of a strong naval defense, established five naval yards along the East Coast, including the one in Brooklyn. The Yard played a part in just about every one of America's military endeavors, from outfitting ships to combat the Barbary Pirates, outfitting the country's first ironclad, *Monitor*, and building historic battleships like the USS *Maine*, *Arizona*, and *Missouri*. The facility hit its peak during World War II, when it doubled in size to two hundred acres and employed over seventy thousand laborers who worked around the clock to repair over five thousand ships and convert many more for military use.

Following the war, the need for the Yard declined. By the time it closed in 1966, several thousand workers were still employed there. For several decades, the city tried to retrofit the facility as an industrial park. That effort started taking off after 2004, with the opening of the 310,000-square-foot Steiner Studios, the largest film production complex outside of Hollywood. These days, the retitled Wallabout neighborhood is getting the Dumbo

An aerial view of the Brooklyn Navy Yard in 1944.

treatment, with a new park and high-rise apartment buildings (some on the site of the old Navy Yard brig where drunken sailors were once locked up), while many of the site's crumbling nineteenth-century buildings are either being razed or refurbished.

After whom is Fort Greene Park named?

A smallish and hilly thirty-acre site at the center of the Brooklyn neighborhood it's named for, Fort Greene lies just south of the Brooklyn Navy Yard, its slopes offering pleasant views of Manhattan. This strategic position was originally the site of the Continental Army's Fort Putnam, only briefly occupied during the start of the Revolutionary War. The area became a public space, Washington Park, in 1847, due in part to editorial lobbying by Walt Whitman in the pages of the *Brooklyn Daily Eagle*. It was renamed in 1897 for General Nathanael Greene (1742–1786), who supervised the construction of Fort Putnam. The park also features a butterfly garden, where every year monarch butterflies can be spotted on their annual migration south to Mexico.

What does the Prison Ship Martyrs Monument commemorate?

On a high peak at the heart of Fort Greene, a graceful and forcefully simple 149-foot- (45-meter-) high white granite Doric column marks the final resting place of some of the 11,500 men and women who died during the Revolutionary War on foul and pestilential British prison ships anchored in Wallabout Bay on the East River. (In comparison, fewer than 4,500 American soldiers were killed in combat during the entire conflict.) Originally, the dead had been buried somewhat haphazardly along the shore closer to the Brooklyn Navy Yard. But they were moved into a more smartly designed crypt in 1873 after East River tides began exposing the bones. The Monument, designed by Stanford White, was built above the crypt in 1908, its column topped by a ceremonial bronze urn.

Where is the oldest house in New York?

The oldest home still standing in the New York area is the Pieter Claesen Wyckoff House. Surprisingly, it isn't found in areas with a longer history of habitation, but in Brooklyn's pocket-sized Fidler-Wyckoff House Park in between Flatbush and Canarsie. Claesen (1620–1694), a Frisian indentured farm worker, first landed in the area in 1637. After six years of indentured labor, he became a farmer himself, starting a family and building this home in a then-undeveloped region of Brooklyn. Claesen later took the name Wyckoff; after the English took control of New Netherlands in 1664, they enforced a naming system whereby people needed to use the same surname from one generation to the next. The oldest part of this Dutch Colonial house dates back to around 1652, and the existing structure as a whole to 1740. The Wyckoffs eventually expanded the house to six rooms and occupied it for eight generations until 1901.

How did Red Hook get its name?

First settled by the Dutch in 1636, the area around the Atlantic Basin was christened Roode Hoek for the reddish soil and hook-like shape of the land. It remained largely undeveloped marsh land for a couple centuries. But the Atlantic Basin's construction in the 1840s presaged the start of a booming shipping nexus that transformed the peninsula into a bustling row-house district packed with immigrant dockworkers and their families. Many warehouses still dotting the waterfront date back to the Civil War, when ships from here supplied Union forces. Red Hook, also known as South Brooklyn, gained a gritty reputation due in part to how thoroughly entangled the longshoremen's union was with organized crime.

By the 1950s, New York was the busiest port in the world, and Red Hook shouldered a great deal of that work, employing some 31,000 longshoremen. Unfortunately, many of those workers' jobs were dependent on their kicking back a part of their daily earnings to the mob. Part of that reality was captured in bleak works like the 1964 novel *Last Exit to Brooklyn* and the 1954 film *On the Waterfront*, which ironically was mostly shot in New Jersey, where most of the cargo business would eventually move to with the transition to container shipping. The neighborhood hit hard times in the postwar years as shipping jobs dwindled. The Gowanus and Brooklyn-Queens elevated highways built in the 1950s and '60s helped further cut off a neighborhood already very lacking in public transportation. The Red Hook revival that started in the 1990s started attracting artists and others back to the area. An IKEA furniture big-box store that opened in 2008 on the water near the Red Hook Houses provided an unexpected boon to the area, with its free ferry and bus service helping reconnect the cut-off neighborhood to the rest of the city, to the chagrin of some residents who had relished the isolation.

Where is the heart of Brooklyn?

In many ways, the density of Brooklyn Heights and downtown Brooklyn, with their municipal buildings, court houses, and neighborly distance from Manhattan, constitute the borough's head. But its heart is more likely located at the other end of Flatbush Avenue, which cuts southeast from the Manhattan Bridge to the Barclays Center and Fulton Mall bustle at Atlantic Avenue and onward towards Prospect Park. Here is what you'll find there:

- At the northwest corner of the park sits Grand Army Plaza, an oval of greenery that breaks up the surrounding apartment building-packed grid and built by Prospect Park's designer Calvert Vaux as an entrance to the park. It's something of an isolated space, notable mostly for the incredible Soldiers' and Sailors' Arch, with its dramatically clustered sculptures honoring the Union soldiers and sailors of the Civil War.

- A line of monumental institutions follows the broad swath of Eastern Parkway that lances east from Grand Army Plaza along the north border of the park. First is the Brooklyn Public Library's Central Library, a stern and imposing Art Deco building built in 1941 that features forty-foot- (twelve-meter-) tall bronze doors covered with representations of American literary figures from Rip Van Winkle to Tom Sawyer.

- Next along the parkway is the Brooklyn Botanic Garden, which occupies fifty-two sculpted and manicured acres on the northeast corner of the park. The garden opened in 1911, following a plan laid out by the Olmsted brothers. The beautiful Japanese Hill-and-Pond Garden, one of the first in the nation, opened four years later and is now one of the garden's most popular attractions, particularly during the annual cherry blossom festival.

- Facing the parkway on the north is the Brooklyn Museum. A Beaux-Arts beauty built in 1897 in yet another attempt by the borough to prove that it was the equal of Manhattan, its original plan by McKim, Mead & White—a 1.5 million square foot complex that included separate departments for everything from zoology to engineering and mathematics, in addition to art—would have resulted in the largest museum in the world. Consolidation truncated those grandiose plans. Less visited than its Manhattan counterparts, the Brooklyn Museum has a collection of 1.5 million pieces that are especially strong in their Egyptian and African holdings. One of its most celebrated pieces is Judy Chicago's (1939–) enormous, room-filling installation *The Dinner Party*, the centerpiece of the Elizabeth A. Sackler Center for Feminist Art.

What effect did Central Park have on Brooklyn?

Brooklyn's rivalry with and sometimes outright antagonism towards Manhattan has frequently broken down along predictably stereotypical lines that didn't have much connection to reality: working-class grit versus Wall Street polish, multi-ethnic melting pot versus WASP-y snobbery, and so on. One of the more curious manifestations of this rivalry was the me-too-ism that predominated in the nineteenth century, when the borough made a serious attempt to outdo its wealthier neighbor when it came to things like performing arts palaces (The Brooklyn Academy of Music).

In 1865, seeking to outdo the ambitious green rectangle of Central Park that had finished being carved out of Manhattan a few years prior, the (then still independent city of) Brooklyn decided to create a park of its own. Central Park planners Calvert Vaux and Frederick Law Olmsted were hired and the following year they submitted their design. Their work went at a rapid pace; already by 1868 the unfinished park was getting two million visitors a year. Construction was stopped in 1873 because of a financial crisis. Parts of the park were still being worked on decades later.

How does Prospect Park compare with Central Park?

Unlike the crowded plethora of pastoral scenes that made up Central Park, Vaux and Olmsted's Prospect Park design was smaller in space (526 acres to Central Park's 843) but was nevertheless a roomier thing, not imposing its vision on the landscape but incorporating the wide rolling hills of central Brooklyn forest and farmland into its essence. Vaux and Olmsted ended up not including the park's namesake—the borough's second-highest point, Mount Prospect, at Flatbush and Eastern Parkway—and instead worked on integrating the surrounding area into their plan by building grand avenues like Eastern and

The boathouse at the Lullwater of the Lake on the eastern end of Prospect Park.

Ocean Parkways, as well as Grand Army Plaza at its northwest entrance. They even proposed a series of great avenues (never built) to connect Prospect and Central parks.

Among the park's highlights are the Italianate mansion called the Litchfield Villa; the country's first city-based Audubon Center; many beautifully fanciful bridges (including Boulder Bridge, made entirely of glacial deposit rocks); the dark and wild gorge of the Ravine; roller- and ice-skating rinks at the modern and minimalist LeFrak Center; and the broad knobby expanse of its seventy-four-acre centerpiece, the Long Meadow. Sheep grazed in the Long Meadow until they were sent packing by Parks Commissioner Robert Moses in the 1930s. You can still get bridle path horseback rides from Kensington Stables near the park's southwest corner. Prospect Park's less-cluttered space has made it less tourist destination and more of a place for Brooklynites to picnic, play, and relax. More than one lover of the less-famous park has argued that Vaux and Olmsted saved their best work for Brooklyn, and that Central Park was merely the warmup.

How does Ebbets Field still maintain such a strong hold on the Brooklyn imagination?

Nothing, neither an egg cream nor a good round of stickball, can instantly evoke teary nostalgia of old-time Brooklyn with such power as the mere mention of Ebbets Field. If it still stood today, the park would rival Wrigley Field and Fenway Park as a baseball landmark. Charles Ebbets (1859–1925), the owner of the Brooklyn Dodgers, built the stadium in an unprepossessing lot between Montgomery Street, Sullivan Place, Bedford Avenue, and McKeever Place just east of Prospect Park (previously called Pigtown). He began secretly buying up land just after the turn of the century and opened a smaller version of the field in 1912 that could seat eighteen thousand people.

Eventually, Ebbets Field could seat well over thirty thousand and featured a distinctive rounded home-plate entrance constructed in part of Italian marble. The Brooklyn Dodgers played forty-four seasons there, a time firmly encased in amber for many

279

older Brooklynites. The Dodgers era evokes a long-vanished democratic era of sports fandom when entire neighborhoods would go to (affordably priced) games en masse and see players as not just sports heroes but local guys. The field was torn down in 1960, three years after Walter O'Malley (1903–1979) took the Dodgers to Los Angeles and made his name forever mud in the old borough.

How long did it take professional sports to return to Brooklyn?

It wasn't until 2012 that a professional sports team would play again in the long-deprived borough. For many years, the triangle of land at Flatbush and Atlantic avenues, which had once been the site of the bustling Flatbush Avenue Terminal, intersecting the rapidly gentrifying neighborhoods of Fort Green and Prospect Heights, had been in the sights of development company Forest City. The company wanted to build a new sports arena and surround it with office and residential skyscrapers. This didn't sit too well with many locals, who had seen what the company had done with its massive, sterile MetroTech Center in downtown Brooklyn.

After years of protest and delay, a scaled-back version of the Atlantic Yards development finally moved forward. Its centerpiece, the eighteen-thousand-seat Barclays Center arena, opened in 2012 with a performance by Brooklyn's own Jay-Z (1970–), an early booster who had been involved in the development. NBA team Brooklyn Nets, who had until 2012 been the New Jersey Nets, played their first season at Barclays that year. In a move as symbolic as it was curious, an old flagpole from Ebbets Field was stuck in front of Barclays Center, where baseball isn't played and the seats cost far, far more than fifty cents. But just having a professional sports arena back in the borough that people can walk or take the subway to is still enough to evoke comparisons of Brooklyn's great vanished field of dreams.

Why was Green-Wood Cemetery such a popular tourist destination?

One of the first so-called "rural cemeteries," Green-Wood Cemetery opened for business in 1838 on 478 acres of farmland south of (yet unbuilt) Prospect Park and north of today's rapidly growing Sunset Park neighborhood. At this point in America, the vast majority of burials still took place on church grounds. But Brooklyn Heights real estate magnate and erstwhile city planner Henry Evelyn Pierrepont (1808–1888) thought demand would necessitate a larger municipal cemetery. He was proven right about that, as Green-Wood quickly became a popular burial site. Today it contains about 560,000 graves.

Rather unexpectedly, it also became one of the city's most popular sites for excursions. The cemetery's gently rolling hills, ponds, and many tree-shaded nooks provided wonderful picnicking spots, and its location on the highest point in Brooklyn afforded sweeping views of the Upper Bay. The romanticized Victorian notions of death hinted at by one proposed name for the cemetery (Necropolis) are illustrated in the many elaborately carved graves and mausoleums, filled with beautifully somber winged angels. On nice days, particularly in the years before the opening of Central Park, the carriages of well-to-do Manhattanites passed through the cemetery's Gothic Revival archways by the hundreds. At one point, it was estimated that Green-Wood saw a half-million visitors a year, making it the second most popular attraction in the United States after Niagara Falls. Due to the cemetery having been built on the site of one of the many skirmishes of the Battle of Brooklyn in 1776, each year it hosts a gaggle of musket-toting reenactors to recreate the action on its now-manicured grounds. The *New York Times* wrote in 1866 that "it is the ambition of the New Yorker to live upon Fifth Avenue, to take his airings in [Central] Park, and to sleep with his fathers in Green-Wood."

After whom was Brownsville named?

Brownsville is a southeastern Brooklyn neighborhood situated between Crown Heights and East New York. Prior to the 1880s, it was farmland populated by settlers from the British Isles, as well as Jewish immigrants and some black farmers. It was also the site of the city's main waste dump. A developer named Charles Brown bought up most of the land in the area that would later bear his name. He built hundreds of small frame houses that were much more modest than the middle-class brownstones going up in the rest of Brooklyn at the time. The homes were later marketed to Manhattan Jews looking for a little more room. The campaign was successful and soon the neighborhood was primarily Jewish, a development that was not entirely welcomed. In 1890, locals formed a Hebrew Protection League to guard against attacks by other ethnic groups in surrounding neighborhoods. An 1893 story in the *Brooklyn Eagle* sniffed that "the Jews have driven out the Scotch." By 1910 the area was eighty-five percent Jewish.

Public services took several years to follow the new residents, but once they did the neighborhood bustled with large families and businesses, particularly along Pitkin Avenue, the so-called "Fifth Avenue of Brooklyn," where a lavishly ornate Loew's movie palace opened in 1929. Manufacturers started constructing factories and multifamily tenements in Brownsville, which became not only a vibrant working-class neighborhood by the early twentieth century but a magnet for labor activists and radicals as well. The *Brooklyn Eagle* once reported that a riot occurred after some men criticized socialism in a local tavern and a massive melee ensued. Margaret Sanger (1879–1966) opened the nation's first birth control clinic there on Amboy Street in 1916. Some of the more famous recollections of Brownsville life during this time are *A Walker in the City* by Alfred Kazin (1915–1998) and *Call It Sleep* by Henry Roth (1906–1995).

How did Brownsville change after World War II?

Brownsville was for many decades a place that Lower East Side immigrants aspired to escape to. But the crush of low-quality tenements, prevalence of street gangs and organized crime (Murder, Inc. was mostly a Brownsville crew), and lack of recreational spaces made it markedly less attractive in the postwar years once Jews were able to move to new suburbs and the city's manufacturing base started to decline. An all-too-predictable series of events followed. As white residents left and businesses followed, landlords packed poor black residents into already decaying housing stock, and public-housing complexes were built throughout the neighborhood. A cycle of arson and rising crime came after.

The neighborhood attracted many of the Caribbean immigrants who moved to New York in the 1980s. Today it remains one of the city's poorest and highest-crime areas.

Is Jamaica Bay part of Queens or Brooklyn?

Jamaica Bay's eighteen thousand acres of wetland estuary sits on the southern side of Long Island almost evenly divided between Brooklyn on the western shore and Queens on the east and south. The swampy expanse was originally hunting and fishing grounds for Canarsie and Rockaway Indians. Until the end of the nineteenth century it was still mostly unsettled. As bridges were built through the Bay connecting the mainland to the Rockaways on the south, the area became more populated with residences, resorts, and industry.

During Prohibition, the bay's many small islands and inlets made it the perfect spot for rum-runners. At one point, Broad Channel, an island in the middle of the bay connected to Howard Beach on the north and the Rockaways on the south (that is today the only inhabited part of the bay), was briefly home to enough speakeasies and casinos that it was known as Little Cuba. In an effort to stop it from being spoiled by pollution and overuse, Robert Moses made much of the Bay into a park in 1938. Today, most of the bay on the Brooklyn side is part of the Gateway National Recreation Area. The Jamaica Bay Wildlife Refuge on Broad Channel is one of the biggest bird sanctuaries in the country, with over 330 species sighted in recent years.

Where is Crown Heights?

The hilly stretch of land between Prospect Park and East New York was known during the 1800s as Crow Hill. Many of the residents were blacks who were eventually forced

A view of Jamaica Bay at Broad Channel Cross Bay Bridge with Queens in the foreground.

Was there once a separate free-black community in Brooklyn?

Sometime after New York state outlawed slavery in 1827, a onetime dock worker and voting-rights activist named James Weeks led a small movement to found a settlement in Brooklyn for other free blacks. By 1838, Weeks and his compatriots had bought up numerous small parcels of land and started establishing their own community, with independent schools, churches, an orphanage, and one of the first black newspapers in America. They named this town Weeksville.

Most maps from the time do not specify Weeksville as its own suburban community. But its boundaries stretched across what are today the central Brooklyn neighborhoods of Crown Heights and Bedford-Stuyvesant. Many Weeksville residents were tradespeople, and their number included Susan Smith McKinney-Steward (1847–1918), who became the first black female physician in New York. Weeksville was called home by as many as 700 families at its peak. Increasing white immigration into the area after the Civil War eventually resulted in the community's dissolution. Today, a historic center has been carved out of the crowded urban blocks. It includes four original Weeksville homes built between 1840 and 1883.

out by white residents looking for new land to build houses on. Different sources claim the name came from the racial makeup of the area ("crow" possibly being a term used at the time by whites for blacks) or for the large numbers of crows commonly seen there.

Starting in the early twentieth century, the neighborhood became better known as Crown Heights. One of many bedroom communities for Manhattan commuters in the borough, it went through a familiar period of decline in the 1960s and '70s before seeing a wave of revitalization and gentrification in recent years. Its main thoroughfare is Eastern Parkway, which arcs east from Grand Army Plaza, lined on both sides with ranks of trees, impressive apartment buildings, and some of the borough's iconic structures like the Brooklyn Central Library and the Brooklyn Museum. The neighborhood's diversity is best illustrated by its two most visible ethnic groups. Orthodox Jews, particularly of the Lubavitcher sect (who are headquartered there), began to move into Crown Heights after World War II and still today constitute a large percentage of the population. At around the same time, Caribbean immigrants began moving in. Today the West Indian Carnival parade on Eastern Parkway involves at least one million people, making it possibly the city's largest annual celebration.

Why did Coney Island become New York's summer escape?

A long island in southwest Brooklyn just below Gravesend, Coney Island made itself indispensable to New York's sun-seeking masses by being the closest and broadest stretch of beach to the city's most densely populated neighborhoods. Discovered in 1609 by Henry Hudson before he made it to anywhere else in the future metropolis, the island was then known by the Canarsie Indians as "Land Without Shadows." The Dutch later called it Coney Island for all the rabbits ("coneys") populating the area. At first, it was a tame and genteel recreational location, with several high-end hotels on the eastern side of the island where Brighton Beach is today. Starting in the 1840s, the central stretch of beach was where the working-class would gather for sun and surf during the few hours they weren't working. Walt Whitman wrote enthusiastically about the "long, bare, unfrequented shore" of Coney Island "where I liked, after bathing, to race up and down the hard sand and declaim Homer and Shakespeare to the surf and sea gulls by the hour."

After the Civil War, aided by the construction of several railroads connecting the island to the city, Coney Island swiftly became the city's favorite weekend getaway. The crowds grew even faster later in the century as the city's teeming slums filled up with new immigrants who needed an affordable place to get away from their crowded and dark tenements.

What was there to do at Coney Island?

Businesses expanded rapidly to meet demand, with food vendors, saloons, hotels, theaters, and ever-more inventive entertainment springing up all along the beach. Night-swimming under massive lamps, called "electric bathing," became popular. Among the attractions dreamed up first by impresarios here: the hot dog (still called "coneys" by some), the roller coaster, and the carousel. There was the Elephantine Colossus, a seven-story hotel in the shape of an elephant that opened in 1885; visitors entered through a door in the foot of the hind leg. In 1896, like just about every other legendary attraction at Coney Island, it burned down. The Island's growth as an entertainment district coincided perfectly with the beginning of the motion picture industry. Between 1895 and 1905, over fifty films were shot on Coney Island, and many of them then exhibited there.

What kept drawing people to Coney Island?

Around the turn of the century, three massive amusement parks—Steeplechase Park (opened 1897), Luna Park (1903), and Dreamland (1904)—vied for visitors' nickels with a plethora of amazements and freak shows. Steeplechase was the most straightforward type of park (except for the theater where customers' skirts were blown over their heads by a blast of air) and longest lasting, not shutting its doors until 1964. Luna Park and Dreamland were more fantastical creations, covered in hundreds of thousands of lights and featuring exotic mini-worlds festooned with gleeful Orientalism, as well as apocalyptic tableaus; Dreamland's Hell Gate and infant incubators proved especially popular. They were like miniature World Expositions as curated by Tim Burton.

In 1911, Dreamland burned down in a roaring conflagration that could be seen in Manhattan. Panicked wild animals ran along Surf Avenue. Afterward, Coney Island returned to more prosaic entertainment. Even so, the crowds continued to flock to the place called by some "The Poor Man's Riviera" for its ease of access and affordability. Others called it "a Suburb of Sodom" for all the tawdry attractions and its reputation as a great spot for romance, away from all the prying eyes of the old neighborhood. On July 4, 1947, Coney Island had 1.3 million people visitors, roughly one out of every five people in the entire city.

The Thunderbolt coaster ride at Luna Park on Coney Island is among the rides that have helped keep visitors coming in recent years.

What is Coney Island like today?

Coney Island's name stopped being technically accurate during the 1950s, when most of Coney Island Creek was filled in, connecting it permanently to Long Island. The eighty-foot- (twenty-four-meter-) wide boardwalk, "Coney Island's Fifth Avenue" to some, opened in 1923 and is still in use today. The island went through a rough patch in the mid-to-late twentieth century, as more locals were able to afford further flung vacations, and the attractions declined in quality and number. High-rise housing projects took over more of the skyline than rides. The bleak 1978 novel *Requiem for a Dream* by Hubert Selby Jr. (1928–2004), and the 2000 film version by Darren Aronofsky (1969–), captures much of the area's decrepitude during that time.

Recent decades have seen an uptick in activity, with new sideshows, the popular Mermaid Parade, a minor-league ballpark, and the continued operation of several classic rides like the Cyclone roller coaster. Deno's Wonder Wheel has been in almost continuous operation since 1920. For those new to the area, the massive creaking Ferris wheel might be remembered from its iconic placement in the 1979 film *The Warriors*, in which a teenage gang battles its way across a dangerous, rival gang-infested New York to its home in Coney Island.

How has gentrification affected Brooklyn?

Gentrification, while not a New York-only phenomenon, is a term applied to changing demographics in this city more than almost anywhere else. That should be no surprise, given the combination of limited space, frequent periods of extreme income inequality, racialized housing patterns, discriminatory lending and leasing practices, and a real estate market that could reasonably be described as rapacious. Gentrification is happening in each and every borough, but Brooklyn is where the term is most often applied today.

Starting in the 2000s, Brooklyn started to be seen as a destination for artists, trend-hunters, and other upwardly mobile types. Its sprawling neighborhoods were filled with attractive mid-century and earlier housing stock just begging for restoration, not to mention (comparatively) easy subway access to Manhattan and industrial spaces ideal for studios. Soon, waves of artisanal bakeries, fair-trade coffee shops, and yoga studios were dropping into poorer neighborhoods like airborne troops softening the terrain for the invasion to come.

The metaphors are frequently overheated but the anger and frustration felt by the working class and minority residents being forced out by wealthier and heavily white newcomers often made for highly tense situations. On the one hand, the introduction of new businesses and the renovation of sometimes rundown or even vacant buildings were welcomed by the neighborhoods. But the inevitable rent increases and disruption to sometimes very established communities made for a significant downside. Sometimes the attitudes of newcomers didn't help. In 2014, for instance, a new luxury apartment building in gentrifying Bushwick called Colony 1209 advertised for potential residents by calling them "like-minded settlers" and assuring them that the building had "already surveyed the territory for you."

QUEENS

What is the largest borough in New York?

The borough of Queens has more real estate than any of the other New York boroughs. Queens occupies the northwest corner of Long Island from Newtown Creek—the three-and-a-half-mile-long East River tributary that separates Long Island City from Greenpoint and since the mid-nineteenth century has been a focal point of oil and coal refining, with all the heavy ship traffic and pollution that comes along with that—across from Manhattan's 34th Street up to the Astoria neighborhood, across from Randall's Island. It extends east into semi-suburban Long Island and south to John F. Kennedy International Airport, hooking back west beneath Brooklyn's Coney Island with the long narrow spit of the Rockaways.

Queens encompasses nearly every aspect of the other boroughs: dense blocks of tenements like the Bronx, compact neighborhoods of smaller homes like Brooklyn, and quiet suburban enclaves like Staten Island, along with pockets of manufacturing and shipping, salt marsh, a long ridge of moraine left over from the Ice Age, a large prison complex, a major league baseball stadium, two of the city's three major airports, and the city's greatest mix of ethnicities.

How diverse is Queens's population?

These are the largest ethnic groups in Queens, according to the NYCEDC's 2016 report:

- Hispanic or Latino—28%
- White—25.7%
- Asian—24.7%
- Black or African American—17.4%

Who was living in Queens when the Europeans arrived?

Like Brooklyn, the Indians who lived in Queens were mostly small bands loosely connected to the Lenape people. They hunted and fished and also grew small patches of corn and squash. A few locations in the area were named for the Indians who were thought to have lived nearby (though, as with much early history of the area, many of those old stories are hard to prove), such as Jamaica (the Jameco Indians) and Maspeth (Mespat).

When did Europeans start settling in the borough?

In the late 1630s, the Dutch began awarding land grants in Queens, primarily to English settlers. The first settlement was in what is now Long Island City, across the East River from the United Nations headquarters. Over the next two decades, other settlements began sprouting up across the region, from Far Rockaway to Flushing and Jamaica. Periods of peaceful co-existence with the local Indians were interspersed with bouts of armed conflict, including one in 1643 in which an English settlement at the headwaters of the Newtown Creek was destroyed. By the end of the 1650s, the toll taken by the fighting, as well as a smallpox epidemic in 1658, had resulted in most of the surviving Indians abandoning the area to the conquerors. In 1664, Englishman William Hallet bought over two thousand acres from Chief Mattano, which included what became Astoria.

Where did the name Queens come from?

In 1683, the British carved up the province of New York (which they had taken from the Dutch in 1664) into ten counties. Control over the western region of Long Island was given to the Duke of York. In one of the greater moments of historical sycophancy, in 1683 the Duke named the county of Queens for Queen Catherine of Braganza (1638–1705), the Portuguese wife of his brother, King Charles II (1630–1685). Because she was unable to bear the king a son and due to the fact that she was a Roman Catholic in a Protestant country, Queen Catherine was soundly disliked in England. Besides a possibly true claim that she introduced (or more likely helped popularize) tea to England, Queen Catherine is mostly forgotten these days, much like how her stolid namesake borough is often overlooked in favor of its flashier neighbors.

How important was farming to Queens?

Like in the other boroughs, one advantage to being a farmer in Queens was the close proximity to the hungry markets of Manhattan. Queens also featured flat lots and less

287

population pressure than elsewhere. There were Chinese farmers in Astoria who specialized in supplying Chinatown markets and restaurants. Even after the mid-nineteenth century housing boom, by the 1870s, Queens County was still the most productive farming county in the entire country. Smaller farms, so-called truck gardens, remained common into the 1930s. Today, the Queens County Farm Museum occupies the city's only and oldest operating farm (dating back to 1697) and largest remaining tract of farmland, forty-seven acres out in Floral Park not far from where Queens begins to turn into Long Island, where one can still find the occasional farm.

What caused the population in Queens to boom?

For much of its early history, Queens was comparatively underpopulated. Both the Bronx and Brooklyn, while still heavily rural well into the nineteenth century, quickly sprouted easily accessible bedroom neighborhoods for people who worked in Manhattan. By 1790, the population in Queens was only about 5,400, over a thousand of whom were slaves. The farmlands and scattered villages of Queens began to rapidly transform after 1836, however, when the Long Island Rail Road (LIRR) began operating between Jamaica and Brooklyn. Today primarily a commuter rail line for workers coming in from eastern Long Island (which began in earnest in 1900 after tunnels under the East River allowed direct travel to Penn Station), the LIRR and the railroads that followed helped spark a residential development boom. Developers looking to build everything from villages to cemeteries to factories started buying up swaths of farmland. One neighborhood after another sprouted up well into the twentieth century, many of them ethnic

Where do they make Steinway pianos?

The Steinwegs were a family of piano makers from Germany who immigrated to New York, producing their first piano there in 1853. They opened a huge piano factory at 53rd Street and Park Avenue in Manhattan seven years later. In 1866 they changed their name to Steinway and opened the first Steinway Hall, a two-thousand-seat auditorium, on 14th Street. Their pianos soon became the standard in concert-hall quality and a prized acquisition by many upwardly mobile families. In the 1870s, William Steinway (1835–1896) bought four hundred acres in Astoria on the northern shore of Queens, building factories and an attached company town. Steinway Village was a nearly self-sufficient community, with its own post office, library, fire department, church, and trolley line. Steinway collaborated with beer baron George Ehret (1835–1927) to build the nearby North Beach Amusement Park (now the site of LaGuardia Airport) to provide a more wholesome and close-by recreational alternative to Coney Island. The village is no longer there, having been supplanted by Astoria's many low-slung houses and apartment buildings, though there is still a Steinway street. But the factory is still in operation, with hundreds of employees turning out some 2,500 Steinway pianos annually.

clusters of the different immigrant waves looking for new homes after outgrowing downtown Manhattan.

Are there more dead people than alive in Queens?

Probably, yes. That's due in large part to the 1848 opening by the trustees of St. Patrick's Cathedral of Calvary Cemetery, which since then has gone on to become the largest cemetery in the nation, with about three million interred (the current live population of Queens is not much over two million). Originally taking up about 115 acres, the cemetery now totals 365 acres in two segments just north of Newtown Creek, offering what many believe are the city's best views from a gravesite. Among the notables buried here are Lou Costello, Lionel Barrymore, Al Smith, famed "Italian Squad" police officer Joseph Petrosino, and Annie Moore, the first immigrant to come through Ellis Island.

Why is the 7 train also known as the "International Express"?

For many residents of the borough, the 7 train is their primary transportation conduit, running from Flushing through the heart of Queens and into downtown Manhattan, whose skyscrapers can be seen off in the distance from many of the elevated platforms. That route takes the "International Express" through the most diverse succession of neighborhoods in New York. There are Korean and Chinese areas, Indian, Italian, and Irish, as well as Romanian, Filipino, Columbian, West Indian, Mexican, and a host of others. Nearly every one of those neighborhoods has at least a couple of restaurants good enough for non-locals to make an effort to visit.

What is the city's most diverse neighborhood?

Located just south of LaGuardia Airport in northwest Queens, Jackson Heights is referred to as the most diverse part of New York so often that it's become a cliché. Still, it's a cliché that has a ring of truth. This was mostly farmland even up through 1908, when a real estate company bought up most of the land and began developing it at lightning speed, accelerated by the opening of the Queensboro Bridge in 1909. Just four years later, there were already miles of paved streets and sewers; several elevated train stations opened here in 1917. By the late 1920s, the entire area was developed, mostly with low-rise apartment blocks and mixed-use commercial buildings. With its ease of transit to Manhattan, and generally affordable housing, including its prized garden apartments, Jackson Heights has served as a landing spot for successive waves of immigrants.

Today there are over thirty languages spoken in this neighborhood of about 67,000 people, whose ethnic backgrounds range from Tibetan, Dominican, Guyanese, and Indian to all manner of South and Central American heritages (Columbian, Peruvian, and Mexican, to name just a few). Within a few blocks of each other, you can find Nepali cafes serving fiery thalis, Bollywood-styled salons, immigration law offices, halal butchers, Afghan kebab shops with iftar fast-breaking specials during Ramadan, massive sari emporiums, and Korean fried chicken joints. The United Sherpa Association is a mod-

The Unisphere and New York State Pavilion at Flushing Meadows Corona Park.

est Buddhist temple located in a renovated Christian church that now features colorful prayer flags that snap in the wind.

How many World's Fairs have taken place in Flushing?

Flushing, Queens, sits on the eastern side of Flushing Bay across from LaGuardia Airport. One of the longest settled areas in Queens, it was founded in 1654 and features the city's oldest high school (dating to 1875). Originally a commuter suburb, it became much more densely populated after World War II, and today features a broad mix of immigrants, particularly Hispanic and Asian. It is best known, though, for the large park on its southeastern border and its many unique structures. The 1,255-acre Flushing Meadows Corona Park is an oddity in the city, bisected by multiple highways and known less for its quiet, green spaces than its attractions like its tennis stadium complex where the U.S. Open is held, a pitch and putt, Mets games at Citi Field just to the north, and leftover structures from two World's Fairs.

Well into the twentieth century, this was a forgotten and ignored slice of the borough, a marshy tidal expanse polluted by industry and heaps of garbage and miasmic mounds of coal-furnace residue known as the Corona Ash Dump. (Fitzgerald lovers will recognize it as the "valley of ashes" that the characters in *The Great Gatsby* drive through to get

Where is "The Irish Riviera"?

Like "Little Italy" or "Chinatown" for concentrated ethnic neighborhoods in cities around the country, "Irish Riviera" has long been used as a catch-all term for any spot in the Eastern United States where there was any large concentration of Irish-Americans near the water. In the New York area, the Irish Riviera denotes a secluded Queens quadrant of well-kept bungalows along the western end of Rockaway Island called Breezy Point. It was originally built as a summer colony by city workers, most of whom tended to be Irish.

Today, a majority of residents in Breezy Point and the next-door town of Roxbury are still of Irish descent, including many firefighters and police officers. Because the area is regarded as a shining example of immigrants made good, when it was devastated by a fire that broke out after Hurricane Sandy in 2013, aid came flooding in from Ireland to help rebuild the community. This end of the peninsula provides one of the more interesting views in the city—Coney Island is visible to the *north*—and is also famous for its surfing. However, the land in Breezy Point is all owned by a private cooperative that was formed in 1960. It's patrolled by a private security force and the beach is not open to the public. In fact, the community, which has not surprisingly been accused of insularity, refused the city's offer of post-Sandy assistance in rebuilding their dunes for storm protection because it would have resulted in allowing public beach access. For visitors to the Rockaways, you're better off sticking to the eastern part of the island where the ferry and subway let off for Jacob Riis Park.

from West Egg to the city.) One of Robert Moses's great achievements was his rehabilitation of the once benighted wasteland into a manicured greenspace for the 1939 World's Fair. A breathtakingly optimistic endeavor that included exhibits from sixty nations and thirty three states, the fair's "Building the World of Tomorrow" theme took place in the shadow of World War II. Meadow Lake and its boathouse date to that fair, as does the Queens Museums (which served as the headquarters of the United Nations from 1946 to 1950). Moses' more ambitious planning for the 1964 World's Fair can be witnessed today with its central Unisphere monument and the Philip Johnson-designed New York State Pavilion, whose disused towers still hulk over the site today like alien artifacts.

STATEN ISLAND

Where is Staten Island?

The furthest borough, both physically and culturally, from Manhattan, Staten Island is a hilly island of about sixty square miles (155 square kilometers) tucked into a westward curve of the New Jersey shoreline and only separated from the mainland on its western and north sides by narrow estuaries. The third largest borough in terms of size, it's also the smallest and least dense in terms of population. Staten Island is connected to New Jersey by three major bridges (Outerbridge Crossing, Goethals Bridge, and Bayonne Bridge), to Brooklyn by the Verrazano Narrows Bridge, and to Manhattan by a day-and-night ferry that carries about 70,000 people the 6.2 miles (10 kilometers) into the city every weekday.

What is the population of Staten Island like?

The number of foreign-born residents has started to rise in recent years, but it remains the borough with the largest concentration of white and English-speaking residents. Here's the population breakdown from the NYCEDC:

- White—62.5%
- Hispanic or Latino—18.1%
- Black or African American—9.1%
- Asian—7.9%

Who was the first European to settle on Staten Island?

Michael Pauw (1590–1640) was given a patroonship in 1630 that included Staten Island. It took a while for the Europeans to take hold on the island, however. Three conflicts between the Europeans and Indians in rapid succession—the Pig War (1640), the Whiskey War (1644), and the Peach War (1655)—resulted in heavy casualties among the settlers and several settlements being destroyed. The European presence on Staten Island became permanent with the establishment in 1661 of the colony of Old Town near present-day Fort Wadsworth. Governor Francis Lovelace officially purchased the island from the Indians in 1670.

What did the Indians call Staten Island?

Before Henry Hudson sailed into New York Harbor, Staten Island was inhabited off and on by Raritan Indians, also known as the Munsee, who called it Aquehonga Manacknong (which, depending on the translation, meant either "the high and sandy place" or "the place of bad woods"), likely a better moniker than its current nickname: "the forgotten borough." Possibly in part because Staten Island was less quickly developed than many of the other boroughs, it has been a rich source of Indian artifacts. Evidence has been found of what appear to be seasonal camping sites around the island. In the early years of European settlement, Richmondston had been nicknamed "Cocclestown" due to the massive midden mounds nearby.

Where did Staten Island get its name?

Unlike most regions of New York, Staten Island was not named for a person of royalty or other import, or a town back in Europe. Instead, early Dutch settlers called it Staten Island, or Staten Eylandt at the time, for the Staten-General, or States-General, of the Dutch Republic, known today as the Netherlands. In 1683, Staten Island was named the County of Richmond for Charles Lennox (1672–1723), the Duke of Richmond and illegitimate son of King Charles II.

Staten Island was consolidated into Greater New York in 1898 as the borough of Richmond. It was only officially named Staten Island in 1975. One of the reasons cited at the time for changing the name was the irritation of certain islanders when their mail would wind up in Richmond Hill, Queens, or other Richmond towns around the country. That legacy is celebrated today at Historic Richmond Town, a Colonial Williamsburg-like attraction in the center of the island near Latourette Park. Today, though, Staten Island is still technically part of Richmond County.

Why is Staten Island historic for drinking?

Tales of woebegone Manhattanites coming back drunk on the ferry well after midnight aside, Staten Island has a long and storied relationship with alcohol. Lower Manhattan might have been home to the first Dutch settlement, but there was one thing that island did not have for some time: its own distillery. The first distillery for making spirits out of grain in the New York area, and possibly in all of the Americas, was opened by Governor Willem Kieft in 1640 on Staten Island. It most likely produced applejack, a sweet and brandy-like drink that was at the time the most imbibed hard liquor in and around New Netherland.

The first rum distillery in North America opened in 1664, also on Staten Island. That distillery probably used West Indian molasses, which was imported to the New York area in large quantities as part of the "Triangle Trade" of sugar, slaves, and manufactured goods between the Caribbean, America, and Africa. Rum later became one of the most popular liquors in the area, with seventeen rum distilleries operating in New York by 1770.

Are there any buildings left in New York that date from before the Revolutionary War?

The only pre-Revolutionary War building remaining in the New York area, the Conference House is the centerpiece of Conference House Park, a band of greenery that stretches along the water on the southwestern corner of Staten Island. Today a museum, this modest, two-story stone manor was built around 1680 by Christopher Billopp (1738–1827), a captain in England's Royal Navy. The Conference House was the site of a potentially historic meeting on September 11, 1776, between two representatives from the Continental Congress—John Adams and Benjamin Franklin—and British Lord Admiral Richard Howe (1726–1799), whose brother General William Howe had just defeated Washington's forces in Brooklyn. Howe did his best to convince the Americans to surrender but to no avail.

How did Staten Island fare during the Revolutionary War?

Far better than Manhattan and Brooklyn, certainly. Unlike those more contested districts, Staten Island was only the site of a couple minor skirmishes in 1777, when Continental forces attacked from the mainland but were unable to take the island. This was likely just fine with most of the residents. Staten Island, which had been used by General Howe as his staging ground for the successful 1776 campaign that drove Washington's army out of the city, was generally regarded as a Loyalist stronghold. At one point, Washington referred to Staten Islanders as "our most inveterate enemies," while the always more intemperate John Adams called them "an ignorant, cowardly pack of scoundrels." This reputation made Staten Island a place of refuge for Loyalists and also a staging ground for segregated units filled with enslaved or indentured blacks who answered the British promise of freedom in exchange for military service.

Where is the oldest continually manned military post in the United States?

Fort Wadsworth, a stout, impressively maintained three-story coastal fortification, is situated just north of the Verrazano-Narrows Bridge. The site was first fortified by the British in 1664 to control the narrows. After American revolutionaries took it after the

Fort Wadsworth has been a fortified military post since the British first manned it in 1664, although the current fort buildings only date back to 1847.

cessation of hostilities, their jeering at the evacuating British was sufficiently irritating that one of the British ships fired a shot back at them, which might have been the last action of the war. A new fort was built on the site as part of the harbor fortification campaign in 1812; the current fort dates to 1847. Nearly two thousand soldiers were stationed there during World War II. It was later used for a variety of different army facilities and then as a naval base before being decommissioned in 1994. Today it's part of the National Park System.

What was Snug Harbor built for?

The somewhat out-of-place collection of classically inspired buildings set on eighty-three acres of landscaped greenery on the north shore of Staten Island was originally intended for Manhattan. At the time of his death in 1801, one Captain Robert Richard Randall (c. 1750–1801) had stipulated in his will that his twenty acres of land just north of Washington Square Park would become the Sailors Snug Harbor marine hospital for "aged, decrepit and worn-out seamen." However, by the time a legal dispute to the will was solved, the area had become so much more valuable that it was decided to sell the land and use the proceeds to buy a cheaper plot in Staten Island.

Snug Harbor opened in 1833 with thirty-seven residents and eventually encompassed some fifty buildings serving about nine hundred residents from around the world. Financing dwindled during the twentieth century, as did a need for the center, which fell into disrepair. Five of Snug Harbor's Greek Revival buildings were named landmark structures (the city's first) in the 1960s and more were restored in following years. Today, Snug Harbor houses a cultural center, botanical garden, and two museums.

Why is there a museum for an Italian revolutionary on Staten Island?

Some more knowledgeable visitors to Washington Square Park know that the statue on the east side of the park is of Giuseppe Garibaldi (1807–1882), the revolutionary who fought to unite the kingdoms and city states of Italy. After the Roman Republic that Garibaldi fought for was crushed by the French in 1849, he fled to New York. Here, he lived in exile at the Staten Island home of another Italian exile, early telephonic inventor Antonio Meucci (1808–1889)—who discovered how to transmit a human voice over an electrically charged copper wire years before Alexander Graham Bell—before eventually returning to Italy to fight again. After Italy was finally united, President Lincoln offered Garibaldi a Union Army command; Garibaldi refused. The statue was erected in 1888, four years after his death. In 1907, the house that Garibaldi shared with Meucci was turned into a small museum celebrating the achievements of both men, and is still operated as such today by the Order Sons of Italy in America.

Did the Draft Riots extend to Staten Island?

Even though the bulk of the 1863 Draft Riot violence was confined to certain quarters of Manhattan, Staten Island didn't escape unscathed. The island was home to at least a few notable abolitionists in the run-up to the Civil War, as well as a small settlement of

295

free blacks who established the community of Sandy Ground after New York state abolished slavery in 1827. But the white population was staunchly in the pro-slavery camp, a viewpoint that didn't make the billeting of Union troops there or the draft in 1863 particularly popular. While parts of Manhattan burned in July 1863, smaller mobs on Staten Island looted at least one armory and attacked black neighborhoods; afterwards many blacks fled the island. Perhaps in order to ward off more such violence, Staten Island paid the $300 substitution fee so that its residents wouldn't have to join the army in order to fill the federal draft quota. This left the island perhaps more peaceful during the rest of the war but heavily in debt after peace was declared.

Why is Staten Island referred to as the "greenest borough"?

The Greenbelt is relatively unknown to many New Yorkers. Incredibly, the city's largest forest preserve is this beautiful network of parks and wildlife refuges covering almost three thousand acres in Staten Island's hilly middle region. Its centerpiece is High Rock Park, whose ponds, wetlands, and forested glens are laced with a network of walking trails. Not far to the west along the island's shoreline is Fresh Kills Park.

Starting in 1948, this once-beautiful stretch of tidal creeks and coastal marsh was turned into New York's primary garbage landfill. Within a few years it had become the largest landfill in the world, receiving up to 29,000 tons (26,300 metric tons) of trash a day by the 1980s. Growing protest from Staten Islanders ultimately forced the city to shut the landfill down in March 2001, though it was briefly reopened later that year to receive over a million tons (900,000 metric tons) of material from the World Trade Center site. Currently, the site is in the midst of a massive, long-term restoration project. Fresh Kills Park will be nearly three times as large as Central Park on its completion date, tentatively scheduled for 2036.

Is Staten Island the least racially diverse New York borough?

The local stereotype of Staten Island is as a homogeneous island (literally) of white conservative suburbia in a polyglot immigrant liberal metropolis. This is borne out by some fact about the population: it is largely white, with four out of ten islanders claiming either Italian or Irish descent; they depend more on cars than public transportation to get around; there is a higher percentage of home ownership there than anywhere else in the city; and Staten Island regularly votes for Republican leadership in this heavily Democra-

---

What is the New York Wheel?

Recent years have seen a flurry of development on Staten Island's north shore in what's being called the St. George Waterfront. In addition to the borough's only shopping mall, it will feature the New York Wheel: a $500 million, 630-foot- (192-meter-) tall Ferris wheel (America's tallest) that is expected to open in 2017.

tic city. There is even a joke that on Staten Island if you're not a cop or firefighter, you're married to one. But ethnic diversification is increasing, particularly on the north end of the island. The Hispanic population almost tripled between 1990 and 2010, and there are surprisingly dense pockets of immigrant groups such as Liberians and Sri Lankans.

Why does Staten Island keep threatening to secede from New York?

Much has been written over the years about Staten Island's fraught relationship with the rest of New York. A *New Yorker* writer once commented on how surprising it is to consider that the island is three times larger than Manhattan for "those of us who best know New York's southernmost borough as a beige blob tucked into the lower left-hand corner of the M.T.A. subway map, dwarfed by its neighbors." Existing at such a geographical remove, many islanders have often felt ignored by the rest of New York, and been either happy or resentful of that fact. The population grew swiftly in the twentieth century—expanding from just over 67,000 in 1900 to 443,728 in 2000—mostly concentrated in strip-mall and suburban housing developments instead of high-density apartment towers. This has left Staten Island with a less urban sensibility than most of the other boroughs.

Adding to the feeling of remove on "the Rock" is not just the island's out-of-step conservatism (it's the most reliably Republican borough) and the belief that it is underserved compared to other boroughs, but the fact that several times over the years the city has tried to situate various unwelcome facilities there. These intrusions have ranged from the quarantine facility in Tompkinsville that was burned by angry residents in 1858 after a deadly outbreak of yellow fever, to the garbage dump that the city wanted to open at Fresh Kills in 1948. The latter development led to an assemblyman proposing that Staten Island secede from the city. That attempt didn't go anywhere. Neither did other attempts in 1989, 1993, and 2003.

OTHER ISLANDS

What is that long, skinny island in the East River?

The long and skinny wedge of land that sits almost exactly in the middle of the East River, its southern end opposite the United Nations and the north tip visible from Gracie Mansion, has had several names over the years, at least a couple of them non-salutary. In the New Amsterdam years, the Dutch called it Varckens Eylandt, or Hog Island. It was later named Blackwell's Island for the family from Queens who farmed it for many years, and housed American prisoners of war during the Revolutionary War.

The city bought the island from the Blackwells in 1825 and promptly did what they did with most islands: used it to house undesirables. Blackwell's Penitentiary opened in 1829; its more famous residents included Mae West (1893–1980) and Emma Goldman (1869–1940); The Octagon, or Municipal Pauper Lunatic Asylum, opened in 1839; and a Gothic Revival smallpox hospital began accepting patients in 1850. The miserable conditions of the island's institutions became infamous; when Charles Dickens visited the asylum in 1843, he was overwhelmed by the "ugliness and horror" of what he saw. The reputation of Blackwell's prison being particularly horrific, the city renamed it Welfare Island in 1921 and began shutting down all the troubled institutions. (Ironically, in 1937 Riker's Island was opened as a forward-thinking rebuttal to Blackwell's decrepit corruption; but by 2015 there were calls to shut it down for many of the same problems).

What is Roosevelt Island like now?

Mayor LaGuardia opened a modern hospital on Welfare Island in 1939 as part of FDR's Works Progress Administration. But the island remained mostly empty until

The Roosevelt aerial tramway connects the island to Manhattan—and affords wonderful views!

the city and state rechristened it Roosevelt Island and planned a new, unique, car-free residential environment. In an attempt to keep upwardly mobile people from leaving New York, high-rise towers filled with affordable lower- and middle-income apartments began going up, and an aerial tramway was built at 60th Street and Second Avenue to connect the island to Manhattan. With its uniform towers and crumbling Gothic ruins, Roosevelt Island was for years an odd mixture of quasi-suburban utopian planning and haunted house. A subway station opened there in 1989 and gradually more people moved in. In recent years, real estate pressures have reinvigorated the island's development, with million-dollar-plus apartments, a beautiful new park, a planned research campus for Cornell, and around twelve thousand residents. Much of the lower end of the island is still under construction. But its southern terminus features a couple of worthy attractions that provide two very different memories of the past.

First is the Smallpox Memorial Hospital from 1850. The mostly stabilized, fenced-off, vine-covered, and highly photogenic ruins showcase both the beautiful architecture of an earlier era (it was designed by James Renwick Jr., who also designed St. Patrick's Cathedral) and the bitter isolation it must have once caused for its inhabitants. Second is the recently completed Franklin D. Roosevelt Four Freedoms Park, a serene, almost otherworldly monument of sweeping stone walkways and two lines of trees angled diagonally toward an awe-inspiring edifice, featuring on one side a thoughtful bust of Roosevelt himself and on the back a carved quotation of text from his landmark "Four Freedoms" speech. Fittingly, the park features the best viewpoint in the city of the United Nations headquarters, which Roosevelt and later his New York-born wife Eleanor worked so hard to create and maintain.

After whom is Ellis Island named?

Like many of the smaller islands surrounding Manhattan, Ellis Island was originally un-inhabited. Indians would sometimes use Kioshk, or Gull Island, to access the nearby oyster beds and shad runs. Early Dutch settlers, who in fact called the small lump of land near the New Jersey shore Oyster Island, would sometimes picnic there on nice days. From 1765 up through at least 1839, several pirates were hanged at this location, giving it the name Gibbet Island.

In 1774, merchant Samuel Ellis (1733–1794) acquired the three-and-a-half-acre island that would bear his name. It was purchased by the state of New York and then the federal government in 1808. The island housed a small garrison with a few cannon called Fort Gibson up through the 1850s, when it was handed over to the Navy for use as an arsenal. Newspaper articles about the dangerous conditions of the Ellis Island arsenal, combined with a push to replace state control of immigration with federal, prompted Congressional action. In 1890, legislation was passed to shut down the arsenal and replace it with a federal immigration station. Landfill added two more islands, narrowly connected to the original Ellis Island with bays in between, expanding the total size to over 27 acres.

What is Ellis Island used for today?

The United States Immigration Station at Ellis Island operated from 1892 to 1954. During that time, over twelve million immigrants entered the United States after first passing through Ellis Island. For decades afterward, the deserted island's facilities fell into a photogenic type of disrepair that wasn't halted until a $160 million restoration project began in 1984. The main building, where immigrants had been processed, was re-opened to the public as a museum, library, and education center operated by the National Park Service in 1990. About two million visitors come to Ellis Island every year.

What was Liberty Island first called?

The roughly twelve-acre island just south of Ellis Island was called Minnissais, or "Lesser Island," by local Delaware Indians, who visited it as far back as the tenth century to harvest its many oyster beds. Archeologists, who later dug up an oyster-shell midden on the island that also contained pottery fragments and arrow heads, determined that the Indians most likely did not live on the island year-round but came out there several times a year for hunting and gathering. Later the Dutch named the island Great Oyster (there were two other smaller Oyster islands). Dutch merchant Isaac Bedloe (1627–1673) bought the island in 1667 but doesn't appear to have inhabited it.

Bedloe's island changed hands several times over the following century until the city bought it in 1758. In the following years the island was used mostly as a quarantine zone until its strategically useful location in New York Harbor led to the construction of a star-shaped fort there in 1807. Fort Wood was intermittently occupied and used as a depot until 1937. By then, Bedloe's Island had a new name and was better known for the Statue of Liberty than oysters and disease.

How did Governors Island get its name?

Originally, this small, 172-acre island a half-mile from downtown Manhattan and just 400 yards (366 meters) from Brooklyn's Red Hook was known by local Indians as Pagganck, or "Nut Island" for all the chestnut trees that grew there. The Dutch, who gave it their version of the same name ("Nooten Eylandt"), briefly settled here first before decamping for Manhattan and eventually bought the island from the Indians in 1637. After the British took control of what they called "Nutten Island," they decided it should be given to "His Majestie's Royal Governors" for their use, thusly leading to it being called The Governor's Island and eventually just Governors Island.

What role did Governors Island play in the defense of New York Harbor?

The British didn't utilize the island for much, briefly quarantining thousands of German Palatinates here in 1710 and later using it as a game preserve. Despite Governors Island's obvious strategic importance to New York Harbor, it wasn't known to have been fortified until Washington's second-in-command, General Israel Putnam (1718–1790), took the island with one thousand men and built an earthen works fort on the island's highest point in 1776. The cannon mounted by Putnam briefly engaged the British navy in July, keeping them from sailing further up the East River. This control of the waterway provided cover for Washington to retreat across the river from Brooklyn Heights to Manhattan without being detected by British ships. The day after Washington's retreat, the British began bombarding Governors Island and Putnam pulled out as well; British cannonballs were still being dug up on the island as recently as the early twentieth century.

Castle Williams, built in 1811, is on the northwest corner of Governors Island and proved an effective deterrent against the British during the War of 1812.

What happened on Governors Island after the Revolutionary War?

The artillery exchange of 1776 was the only military action that Governors Island would ever see. Its first real fortifications were only constructed there after the war was finished. Starting in 1794, Congress authorized the building of coastal fortifications at strategic points. Fort Jay, the five-point star-shaped fort built where Putnam had placed his cannon, was finished in 1796 and still stands today. Castle Williams, the stout, round four-story fort on the island's northwest corner that bears a passing resemblance to Castle Clinton, was completed in 1811 and is also still there. Supposedly these two defenses were enough to convince the Royal Navy not to bother attacking New York in the War of 1812. They landed in Maryland and burned Washington, D.C., instead. Governors Island had several further stints as a military outpost afterward, hosting training grounds, Confederate prisoners of war, and eventually the country's largest Coast Guard facility.

Starting in the early twentieth century, the island was expanded by more than one hundred acres to the south using landfill generated by the digging of the subway system. It narrowly avoided being turned into the city's first municipal airport by Mayor LaGuardia. In 2003, it was sold back to the city by the federal government. Today, Governors Island is gradually being turned into an arts community, with the carefully preserved barracks and Greek Revival officers' houses providing work spaces for artists, as well as a historic glimpse of those years when this bucolic setting made it one of the most prized military postings in the world. The southern portion of the island is being transformed into a landscaped park. Ferries bring appreciative crowds over during the summer for festivals and concerts.

Where is New York's potter's field?

Potter's field is a generic term that describes any burial ground for unidentified people, criminals, or the indigent. It comes from a line in the gospels, Matthew 27:7, in which the temple priests use the thirty pieces of silver given to Judas Iscariot for betraying Jesus to buy a potter's field "to bury strangers in," including the suicidal Judas. In New York, the potter's field is located on Hart (sometimes Hart's) Island, a long sliver just east of City Island in the western end of Long Island Sound. The city bought the 101-acre island in 1868 and initially used it as the site of a workhouse. It also saw service as an asylum and military prison during the Civil War. Starting a few years later, the city began burying its unclaimed dead there.

Since then, about a million people have been interred on the island, which is operated by the city's Corrections Department. The desolate place with its abandoned buildings (including an insane asylum) and grim history can seem like something out of a Dickens novel. But this isn't a historic site, the burials continue today at a rate of about 1,500 a year. In a manner not much different than how it was photographed by Jacob Riis in 1890, most of the dead—including the homeless and other unclaimed bodies—are placed in simple pine coffins and stacked by inmates from nearby Rikers Island without ceremony, three deep, in 70-foot- (21-meter-) long trenches that are then buried. After a long legal battle, starting in 2015, family members were allowed to visit Hart Island to pay their respects to the departed.

How did Hell's Gate get less hellish?

In various captains' logs dating back to the eighteenth century, there are numerous mentions of troubles navigating the East River confluence between Blackwell and Ward's islands called Hell's Gate. Each year, around one thousand ships ran aground trying to navigate the churning waters of Hell's Gate, whose devilish mix of rapidly changing tides, powerful winds, and rocks more than earned the area its name. The situation became so problematic for marine traffic—ships would often have to waste time idling while waiting for tides to change—that a campaign began in the mid-nineteenth century to clean the channel up. The greatest blockage was Flood Rock, a nine-acre reef across from 93rd Street that was almost entirely underwater. Removing a mostly submerged target of that size required over nine years of labor. At its conclusion, some 300,000 pounds (136,000 kilograms) of explosives were packed in 22 miles (35.4 kilometers) of metal cylinders seeded through the reef.

On October 10, 1885, about fifty thousand people watched what *The American Naturalist* called "the greatest artificial earthquake in history," and was later determined to be the biggest planned explosion before the first atomic bomb blast. It turned Flood Rock into a massive geyser of water and debris. The shock wave was felt in Princeton, New Jersey. Leftover rock from the blast was used to fill in the gap between Great Mill and Little Mill Rock islands. Today, Mill Rock Island is a quiet space across from 96th Street that has been left to nature.

What's on Randall's Island?

Randall's Island is located where the Harlem and East rivers connect and at the near-intersection of Manhattan, the Bronx, and Queens, it also serves as a base for the Triborough Bridge complex that connects all three. It was originally made up of two islands, Randall's and Ward's, which originally held the usual assortment of asylums and quarantine areas. Starting in the 1930s, though, the city turned the islands into a recreational zone. Parks Commissioner Robert Moses connected the two islands and constructed his headquarters here. It's now one 480-acre greenspace packed with dozens of playing fields, a gold center, bike and walking paths, and a track and field facility. Today, Randall's Island is best known for the annual Governors Ball Music Festival, a weekend-long summertime event that strains ferry and bus services to their capacity.

What's on Rikers Island?

Abraham Rycken (1616–1689) was a Dutch immigrant who bought the 87-acre island in the East River between Long Island and the Bronx in the early seventeenth century. In 1884, the family sold Rikers Island to the city, which used it as a prison farm and later for overflow from its overcrowded jails, the Tombs and Blackwell's Island Penitentiary, and began expanding the island with landfill. After the prison on Blackwell's was shut down, Rikers became the city's primary prison. Today, Rikers Island is akin to a 415-acre penal colony, with ten individual jails able to hold up to 17,000 prisoners (during Giuliani's mayorship, the population ballooned to 24,000), all within just a few hundred feet of the runways at LaGuardia Airport. In recent years, a series of scandals exposing horrific conditions and abuses at Rikers have led to numerous calls for reform, or even shutting it down entirely.

What counties make up Long Island?

Long Island has four counties. The easternmost counties are the smallest and also part of New York City: Queens County (also Queens borough) and Kings County (Brooklyn borough).

In the consolidation of 1898, part of the eastern stretch of what was then Queens County was hived off into Nassau County, which today is lumped into that great stretch of land known to New Yorkers as simply "Long Island." Suffolk occupies the great majority of space on the island, taking up everything east of Nassau, including everything from Fire Island barrier island enclosing the Great South Bay and the Hamptons beach communities seeded along the easternmost part of the island.

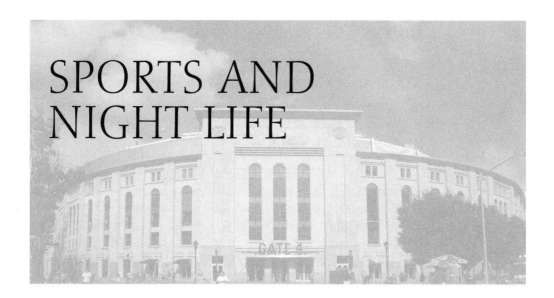

SPORTS AND NIGHT LIFE

SPORTS

What was the first sport likely played by European settlers in New York?

Records held by the Dutch West India Company detailing daily life in New Netherlands don't say much about recreation in general, though they do depict a fairly wanton disposition towards drunkenness. It appears that two of the most common sports played by the settlers were golf and bowling. (There was also apparently a form of recreation called "riding the goose," in which a goose was hung by its feet from a rope stretched across a road and its head thoroughly greased, after which participants would ride their horses underneath and try to grab the goose.)

Golf was frowned upon because of the general chaos it could cause, particularly when combined with the previously mentioned drunkenness. In the upriver settlement of Fort Orange, there were numerous complaints "against the practice of playing golf along the streets, which causes great damage to the windows of the houses, and also exposes people to the danger of being injured and is contrary to the freedom of the public streets." An ordinance was passed that forbade the playing of golf in the street. In 1650, a ferryman in the same area was fined twenty guilders, or two and a half beaver pelts, for striking two people with a golf club. At the time, the Dutch game (called "colf") contained more opportunities for injury than today's more genteel version, as it was played with a ball about 5 inches wide and used four-and-a-half foot-long clubs made of elm or ash with iron or lead club heads.

What is bocce ball?

Bocce ball is another variant of lawn bowling. It was brought to New York by Italian immigrants. Designed more for play on a hard surface instead of a green lawn, bocce is played on a rectangular dirt court where the players stand at one end and try to roll a bocce ball down-court as close as possible to the smaller pallini ball. It's a game made for kibitzing, with large numbers of onlookers (generally male, older) standing off to the sides and offering commentary. The game became particularly widespread in the city in the twentieth century. Photographs of the construction of the United Nations complex in 1948 show the (presumably, though not necessarily, Italian) workers having carved a bocce court out of the land they were excavating. By the 1950s, the city was operating bocce courts at over two dozen parks. The game is still being played in courts in every borough. City-wide tournaments frequently draw dozens of teams.

Where did baseball begin?

According to one myth, baseball was invented at Cooperstown, New York, site of the Baseball Hall of Fame, in 1839. In truth, baseball began in the New York area before the Civil War. Also unlike popular belief, it didn't originate with cricket, but with the British game rounders. For many years, it was believed that the first recorded baseball game took place in 1846 at Elysian Fields in Hoboken, New Jersey. But in all likelihood, groups like the New York Base Ball Club and the Knickerbockers had been playing an early form of baseball for years beforehand in parks like Madison Square.

Where was the first baseball field in New York?

Due to the lack of available spaces in Manhattan, baseball clubs started moving across the river to play at Elysian Fields. The sport started shifting back across the Hudson

River in 1862, when the Union Fields ballpark opened in Williamsburg, Brooklyn. The first of three Polo Grounds stadiums opened for baseball in 1880 with the New York Metropolitans. Starting in 1883, the New York Gothams (later the New York Giants) would also make the Polo Grounds their stadium.

How did the Brooklyn Dodgers get their name?

Like many teams in baseball's early years, the Brooklyn Dodgers didn't really have a set name for a long time. Some of the team's early monikers ranged from the truly terrible, like the Bridgegrooms, to the overly specific, like the Superbas—Hanlon's Superbas were a popular theatrical show at the time and the team's manager was named Ned Hanlon (1857–1937). Starting in the 1910s or thereabouts, the team became known as the Trolley Dodgers for the nimble manner with which Brooklynites dodged the streetcars jamming their crowded streets, and eventually just the Brooklyn Dodgers. Later on, they also picked up nicknames like "the Daffiness Boys" and "Dem Bums," for reasons that should be self-evident.

What barrier was broken on April 15, 1947, in Brooklyn?

Up until this date, professional team sports in America were a strictly white affair. All that changed on the day that Dodger player number 42, Jackie Robinson (1919–1972), took his place in the team's lineup. This was the first time that a black man had played on a Major League Baseball team. He went zero for three in the first game, but ended up hitting .297 that season and stealing more bases than any other player in the National League.

What two baseball calamities befell New York in 1957?

On May 28, 1957, baseball's National League delivered not one, but two pieces of lousy news to the city of New York. Both the New York Giants and the Brooklyn Dodgers were given permission to move to California—Los Angeles and San Francisco, respectively—where both teams still play today. The loss of the Giants stung, to be sure, but their attendance had been dropping for years and uptown fans had easy access to baseball at Yankee Stadium just across the Harlem River.

As in many things, Brooklynites took this day harder, registering a bitterness that in some ways still hasn't dissipated. Dodgers owner Walter O'Malley had been pushing for

The Brooklyn Dodgers famously broke racist hiring practices by bringing Jackie Robinson into their lineup in 1947.

307

a new stadium for years, and in fact wanted to build a domed one just north of the Dodgers' Ebbets Field at Flatbush and Atlantic. But the city's development boss Robert Moses didn't care for that site, and O'Malley turned his nose up at Moses's proposal for a fifty-thousand-seat stadium in Queens near the World Fair site. So at the end of the 1957 season, O'Malley packed up for the West Coast, leaving a heartbroken borough in his rearview mirror.

How long was New York left with only one baseball team?

For five years after the Giants and Dodgers decamped for California, New York's only pro baseball team was the Yankees. Mayor Robert Wagner worked to bring baseball back to the boroughs. In 1961, their work was rewarded when the National League awarded a franchise to the New York Mets. Their name evoked the New York Metropolitans, a short-lived team from the 1880s.

The Mets' logo was a slew of influences, referencing landmarks like the Empire State Building and the Williamsburg Savings Bank, while the colors evoke the Dodgers (blue) and the Giants (orange). The Mets played their first game against the St. Louis Cardinals at the old Polo Grounds in 1962. They moved into a new ballpark in Queens named Shea Stadium in honor of William Shea (1907–1991), the attorney who fought tirelessly to turn Wagner's vision into reality.

How did the Mets become the "Amazin' Mets"?

Their first few years were regarded as an unmitigated disaster. But in the fall of 1969, they shocked a city still glowing from the Jets' Super Bowl win earlier in the year by suddenly amassing one hundred wins, and beating the Atlanta Braves in the playoffs and the Baltimore Orioles to take the World Series. The once sad-sack team became the "Amazin' Mets" (a nickname that's still trotted out from time to time) and ignited an explosion of support in an otherwise downbeat city that is credited by some with helping Mayor Lindsay win reelection.

Needless to say, the Mets didn't stay Amazin'. Over the following years, their good streaks mixed with the miserable, creating a team persona that was far more banged-up and bad luck—poor management was a recurring theme, as was poor fortune, such as when their owners lost fortunes and nearly the team in the Bernie Madoff scandal—than the ever-conquering Yankees. Their lovable loserdom probably helped keep their fans reliably borough-based as opposed to the more Manhattan-centric Yankees. That inter-borough rivalry is stoked each year by the inter-league "Subway Series" of Yankees-Mets games that began in 1997.

Did the Yankees always play in the Bronx?

Like many pro baseball teams, the New York Yankees didn't start out in the location they became famous for. They began, in fact, as the original Baltimore Orioles in 1901. Two years later, a pair of businessmen bought the team for $18,000 and moved them to New York. There, they played at one of the highest points in the city, Hilltop Park at Broadway and 165th Street, which led to their first nickname, the Highlanders.

At a cost of $2.3 billion, the new Yankee Stadium in the Bronx opened in 2009 after three years of construction.

The team's identity began to coalesce in the following years: pinstripes appeared on the uniforms in 1912; they were officially named the Yankees (it had been an unofficial nickname based on their being in the American League) in 1913, the same year that they started sharing the Polo Grounds field with the National League Giants; and they were bought for an incredible $1.25 million in 1915, starting a decades-long connection to big money and big hype. After the Yankees bought Babe "the Bambino" Ruth's contract from the Boston Red Sox in 1919 and opened Yankee Stadium in the South Bronx in 1923, they began turning into the championship dynasty that they (intermittently) remained for decades.

What was the "Curse of the Bambino"?

In an ironic twist, after getting their star attraction from the Red Sox, that team became the Yankees' greatest rival. This irked fans of the perpetually losing Red Sox, who were believed by many to suffer from a supposed "Curse of the Bambino." Hard feelings remained even after the Red Sox finally broke the curse by winning the World Series in 2004. During the building of the luxurious new $1.6 billion palace of a stadium (which opened in 2009 with, remarkably, substantially fewer seats), a construction worker who was also a Red Sox fan buried a team jersey under two feet of cement in the visitors' dugout in hopes of turning the old curse back on the Yankees.

When did they start playing "New York, New York" at Yankee Stadium?

Frank Sinatra (1915–1998) first recorded the brash and instantly iconic "New York, New York" in 1979. It was a cover of the big song from the Martin Scorsese musical of the   **309**

What was the greatest baseball team of all time?

There's no objective way to determine this answer. But according to many baseball experts, it's the Yankees 1927 team. This is due in large part to their fearsome batting lineup. Known as "Murderer's Row," they boasted sixty home runs by Ruth and 175 RBIs by their other great hero, Lou Gehrig (1903–1941).

same name that co-starred Liza Minnelli (1946–). The following year, Yankee Stadium began playing Frank's version of the song after a home-team win and Liza's after a loss. Not surprisingly, she wasn't too happy about this and ultimately the Yankees went with playing Sinatra's after every game, a tradition that continues today.

Who are the *other* New York Giants?

To today's average New Yorker, the New York Giants mean football, not baseball. That isn't surprising, because even though New York is just as much a football as a baseball town, and the early twentieth century is littered with the names of long-gone football franchises (from the Staten Island Stapletons to the Brooklyn Lions and the *other* Brooklyn Dodgers), baseball still manages to loom larger in the collective historical memory.

The New York Giants football team was established in 1925 and played for three decades at the Polo Grounds with the *other* Giants. After that, they shared Yankee Stadium with that baseball team until 1973. They didn't play in their own dedicated stadium until Giants Stadium was constructed in East Rutherford, New Jersey (aka, the "Meadowlands") in 1976. Their early years were unremarkable. Then in the 1950s, the Giants achieved titanic status by having Tom Landry coaching their defense and Vince Lombardi the offense. (They went on to greater fame with the Dallas Cowboys and Green Bay Packers, respectively.) A 1958 championship game against the Baltimore Colts is still spoken of today in NFL circles as "The Greatest Game Ever Played"; the Giants lost in dramatic sudden-death overtime play. The Giants have gone to five Super Bowls and won four.

Are the New York Jets even a New York team?

The New York Jets were founded in 1960 and have been somebody else's guests ever since. Unlike nearly every other team in the New York area, they have never had their own dedicated stadium. For the first three years they shared the Polo Grounds with the Giants, before taking up residence at Shea Stadium from 1964 until 1984, at which point they moved out to Giants Stadium in the Meadowlands. Their image was largely defined in the 1960s by quarterback "Broadway Joe" Namath (1943–), he of the long-flowing hair, fur coats, and late nights at Studio 54. Namath led the Jets to the city's first Super Bowl victory in 1969.

Fittingly for a team that shared space for so long with the Mets, the Jets have long trailed a cloud of trash-talk, problematic off-field behavior, unoriginal fan chants ("J-E-

T-S, JETS! JETS! JETS!"), and general underdog status in their wake. Briefly in the 2000s, there was talk of building a huge new stadium for the Jets at Hudson Yards on the west side of Manhattan. When that plan went nowhere, it reignited discussion over why the team couldn't be called the New *Jersey* Jets. As New Jersey governor Chris Christie (1962–) pointed out in 2011, the team practiced and played in that state. Mayor Mike Bloomberg responded in typically Manhattanite fashion that "We can all root for the Jets, but they don't call him Turnpike Joe." Always runners-up to the Giants, the Jets have won just one Super Bowl in their history.

Why is basketball called "the city game"?

Unlike football, baseball, and hockey, basketball requires almost no equipment, not a lot of space, and can be played by almost any number of people. It isn't even uncommon to see people shooting baskets by themselves. It helps, as well, that as part of Robert Moses's decades-long project to add parks and playgrounds all over the city, basketball courts were frequently included. Even though basketball was technically invented in Springfield, Mass-

Is it true that fantasy baseball was invented at a French restaurant in Midtown?

Yes. Among the many, many casualties of New York's relentless restaurant churn was La Rotisserie Français, an establishment on East 52nd Street. That was the place where, in 1979, writer and editor Daniel Okrent (1948–) and some buddies established the framework for Rotisserie League Baseball. Their idea was simple: Build a league of fake baseball teams in which each participant has his or her own team. Each participant then drafts players for his or her team from a pool of current National or American League players. Over the course of the season, the teams' performances are judged based on how the players delivered in eight categories, including batting averages, home runs, RBIs, and so on. At the end of the season, a winner is declared and takes home the pot of money that all the participants put in at the start of the season. In other words, a glorified, months-long version of statistics-fueled poker.

Readers may know this pastime better as fantasy baseball. As Okrent (best known as the guy providing the drollest commentary in the PBS *Baseball* documentary series) remarked to *USA Today*, he and his co-founders trademarked the Rotisserie name but never put in the kind of time necessary to make any actual money out of it. It was just fun. By 2014, it was estimated that some fifty million Americans spent about $11 billion on various permutations of fantasy sports. Okrent also mused that "Between now and the time I die, if I find a cure for cancer and end the conflicts in Northern Ireland and the Middle East, the obituary will say, 'Okrent dies; invented Rotisserie Baseball'."

311

achusetts, in 1891 and later took root in more rural states like Indiana and Oklahoma, much of what constitutes the sport today was developed on courts in New York.

By the turn of the century, basketball was being played all over the city. One of the first teams to gain traction were the New York Celtics (later the Original Celtics, due to a brouhaha over naming rights), originally a bunch of Irish teenagers from Hell's Kitchen who would go on to become the dominant team in the city. The game also proved particularly popular with young Jewish men, who dominated many teams well into mid-century. Even today, recruiters still keep a close eye on New York's high school teams and the more celebrated basketball courts—like "the Cage" at West 4th Street in the Village or Holcombe Rucker Park near the old Polo Grounds in Harlem, where the likes of Julius Erving (1950–) and Wilt Chamberlain (1936–1999) perfected their game— with their fast, aggressive pick-up games.

Were the Harlem Globetrotters from New York?

From its very early years, basketball was a popular sport with black New Yorkers. However, the sport was not integrated until 1950. For the first half of the twentieth century, a network of local teams like the Washington 12 Streeters and the New York Renaissance (aka, the Rens) were collectively called the Black Fives. Led by the legendary West Indian coach Bob Douglas (1882–1979), the Harlem-based Rens became one of the most popular teams in the country by nature of their dazzling play and frequent barnstorming tours. They also

The New York Knicks (shown here in 2013 in a game against the Wizards) helped establish pro basketball for their city when they were founded in 1946.

became successful due to their long-running rivalry with New York's Original Celtics, a white team, in a series of increasingly close matchups known colloquially as "race games."

Incredibly, years before the sport was integrated, the Rens were invited to the first World Professional Basketball Tournament in Chicago in 1939. There, they beat the champions of the white-only National Basketball League, the Oshkosh All-Stars, and thus became the first pro basketball champions. Incidentally, another black team was invited to the tournament: The Harlem Globetrotters, who were actually based in Chicago and simply used the name for marketing purposes.

When did professional basketball take off in New York?

Even with the above-mentioned teams, during the pre-war years, college basketball was in some ways more popular, with teams from New York University, Fordham University, City College of New York, and St. John's College frequently drawing large crowds. Pro basketball entered the modern era in 1946, when the New York Knickerbockers were established. One of the National Basketball Association's first integrated teams, the Knicks, as they were quickly nicknamed, got off to a strong start, making the playoffs in each of their first ten seasons. They won their first league title in 1969, with a Hall of Fame-heavy lineup that included Walt Frazier and future U.S. Senator Bill Bradley (1943–). The Knicks had a long championship dry spell from the mid-1970s on, even though many of their fifteen seasons with star center Patrick Ewing were winning ones, before returning to prominence in the 1990s under the leadership of Coach Pat Riley (1945–).

The modern era has seen one spectacularly bad season after another for the Knicks, whose most vociferous famous fan, director Spike Lee (1957–), still urges them on from his courtside seat at Madison Square Garden. Since the Knicks have held a virtual monopoly on basketball in the city for decades, it will be interesting to see what effect the introduction to Brooklyn in 2012 of the Brooklyn Nets—previously the New Jersey Nets, now sometimes referred to as the Brooklyn Nyets, for their majority owner, Russian plutocrat Mikhail Prokhorov (1965–)—will have on the Knicks fan base.

Who were the Amerks?

This was the not-precisely original nickname for the New York Americans, New York's first professional hockey team. Like seemingly everything else in the city during Prohibition, the team came with a criminal pedigree. Originally the Hamilton Tigers, they played several uninspiring seasons in Ontario before being bought by New York bootlegger "Big Bill" Dwyer (1883–1946)—who was called "King of the Rum Runners" and known for using armored speedboats to sneak booze across Lake Ontario. The newly christened New York Americans played their first game at Madison Square Garden on December 15, 1925, before a crowd of twenty thousand people eager to see what the fuss was about with this curious new Canadian sport that was sweeping the nation. Dwyer was convicted on racketeering charges the following July.

But the Amerks proved successful, even after the New York Rangers started up in 1926. The team had a good time in the city, living at the Forrest Hotel, whose habitués included many of the raffish Broadway schemers popularized in the stories of Damon Runyon (1884–1946), who lived in the penthouse. They were never nearly as impressive a hockey franchise as the Rangers, however—their motto was reportedly "Join the Americans and laugh yourself to death" and they hobnobbed with the likes of Dutch Schultz (1902–1935) and Legs Diamond (1897–1931). The Amerks, who practiced at the Brooklyn Ice Palace (a skating rink at Bedford and Atlantic that operated as a movie theater in the summer) renamed themselves the Brooklyn Americans and tried to build a new hockey stadium in the borough before folding for good in 1942. Professional hockey was absent from Brooklyn until 2015, when the New York Islanders moved from Nassau County, Long Island, to Barclays Center.

How long have the New York Rangers been playing at Madison Square Garden?

Long enough that they played in the old Madison Square Garden on 26th Street. After the Amerks proved that hockey could draw a good crowd, the Garden's president "Tex" Rickard (1870–1929) decided to get a team for himself. While Rickard's organization scouted for players, New York sportswriters started referring to "Tex's Rangers," which stuck when the team started playing in 1926. Technically an expansion team, the Rangers are one of the "Original Six" teams that constituted the NHL from 1942 until 1967.

The Rangers started off strong, becoming in their second year the first American team to win the Stanley Cup. They won it twice more, in 1933 and 1940. The next couple decades were a drought for the Rangers, who came back to prominence in the late 1960s and '70s and intermittently in the years that followed. The Rangers' biggest rivalry has been with the Islanders, who played in Nassau County, Long Island, from 1972 to 2015, when they relocated to Barclays Center in Brooklyn. Rangers-Islanders games are sometimes referred to as the Battle of New York.

Where is the U.S. Open played?

In Flushing, Queens. The U.S. National Championship began in 1881 as a men's singles and doubles tennis competition. The first matches were played on grass at the Newport Casino complex in Newport, Rhode Island. Women were allowed to play in 1887, and mixed doubles in 1892. In 1915 the organization voted to move the national all-comers annual amateur tournament to the West Side Tennis Club in Forest Hills, Queens. Other tournaments were played in other locations like Philadelphia and Cleveland until 1968 when all the matches were moved to Forest Hills, at which point the entire contest

The U.S. Open is currently held at the USTA Billie Jean King National Tennis Center in Queens.

was renamed the U.S. Open. The increasing popularity of the championship caused it to finally outgrow the 15,000-seat Forest Hills stadium.

The U.S. Open was moved in 1978 to a repurposed outdoor performance space with 16,000 seats built for the 1964 World's Fair close by in Flushing Meadows. One of the biggest changes from this move was actually not the venue but the courts. Starting in 1978, tournaments were played on a hard-court surface, just as they are today. (U.S. Opens were played on grass until 1974, then clay from 1975 to 1977.) Once again, the U.S. Open outgrew its new home. To avoid losing the championship to another city, the tennis-loving Mayor David Dinkins—who controversially had plane traffic from nearby LaGuardia and JFK airports rerouted in order to not disturb play—negotiated the construction of the pricey, new 23,000-seat Arthur Ashe Stadium that opened in 1997. Today, 700,000 fans descend on the park's three stadiums for the U.S. Open, which is held over two weeks in late August and early September every year.

When did Pelé play soccer in New York?

The desire to get Americans to pay attention to soccer has been a decades-long pursuit signified more by failure than success. One of the most-hyped and best-funded campaigns to breach that wall involved the New York Cosmopolitans, a club put together in 1970 in part by music executives Ahmet (1923–2006) and Nesuhi Ertegun (1917–1989). The Cosmos played in the long-struggling North American Soccer League (NASL) and had a tough time getting fans or wins. That changed in 1975, when they signed Brazilian superstar Pelé (1940–) to a three-year, $2.8 million contract that made him the highest paid athlete in the world. The response was instant.

Pelé's first match was unprecedented in two ways: A professional soccer match in America was broadcast live by CBS and watched by ten million people. Home game attendance tripled as Pelé's celebrity swept America and brought more star players onto the roster, forcing the team to move from dowdy Downing Stadium on Randall's Island to Yankee Stadium and then Giants Stadium in New Jersey. They sold out games around the country and counted Henry Kissinger (1923–) and Steven Spielberg (1946–) among their celebrity fans. After Pelé played his last game in 1977, though, the team and sport's balloon-like popularity almost instantly deflated. ABC pulled its crucial broadcast deal and other star players left for Europe. The Cosmos were defunct by 1985.

What soccer teams play in New York today?

Currently, there are two Major League Soccer teams in the New York area: The New York Red Bulls (originally the MetroStars until they were bought by the energy drink company in 2006) play at Red Bull Arena just west of Jersey City; and New York City FC, who played their inaugural season in Yankee Stadium in 2015. A revived New York Cosmos team that plays in the NASL started up in 2013 and plays at Hofstra University's stadium out on Long Island.

FOOD AND DINING

How many restaurants are there in New York today?

Because of New York's density, it can seem like there are restaurants everywhere you look. The number has been growing in recent years. Despite the record number of restaurant closings in the past few years, the city's Department of Health reported that there were 23,705 restaurant permits in the fiscal year 2015, compared to 18,606 in 2006. That includes an incredible diversity of eating establishments, from strip-mall Thai restaurants in Queens to gourmet Manhattan food palaces paying over $20,000 a month in rent. According to a 2012 study, New York has the fourth-highest proportion of restaurants in America, with 25.3 for every 10,000 households. (Third place, at 26.5, was Long Island.)

What was dining out like in early New York?

For most of New York's history, one could always find a meal, as long as it didn't matter that the meal was served in a tavern or rooming house and with a level of inattention to taste or quality that would seem remarkable to even today's most casual and non-fussy diner. The idea of a standalone establishment that did nothing but serve meals was something of a novelty, imported from Paris. At this point in America, dining was still a mostly fraught affair. The traditions of the young nation's British forebears were still baked-in.

The ethnic waves that would transform the country's culinary options in a few short decades had still not made their different tastes known. Eating tended to be a business of quantity and not quality. In 1831, Alexis de Tocqueville (1805–1859), who was otherwise mostly generously inclined toward Americans, could only shake his head at their eating habits: "We are still baffled by their sheer quantity of food that people somehow stuff down their gullets."

What was America's first restaurant?

America's first true restaurant started out as a small shop selling French pastries and delicacies downtown in 1827. After running a smaller French eatery and a hotel, John and Peter Delmonico became full-fledged restaurateurs in 1837, when they opened at the current lower Manhattan location on William Street. The domineering, rounded-front, perspective-skewing building is like a downtown variation on the Flatiron. Originally known as "The Citadel," the space was atypically grand for the pre-Gilded Age, taking up three floors and featuring pillars supposedly imported from Pompeii. But its grandiosity, however unique for the time, is not what cemented Delmonico's place in history.

When Delmonico's opened, it was a revelation to the New Yorkers who could afford to dine there. Before then, fine dining was generally only available in private homes. Now, people could eat out in the classic Parisian tradition, served by professional waiters and sampling grander food than was available anywhere else in the country. Prefiguring the current locavore trend by a century and a half, the restaurant's produce was supplied by their own farm in Brooklyn. Delmonico's success led them to open up multiple locations as far uptown as 44th Street. There were even copycat restaurants bearing the same name with no connection to the original owners. In a way, the name had stopped mattering. Once the idea of the restaurant was introduced to America, the variety of ways it could be modified proved to be nearly infinite.

What dishes were invented at Delmonico's?

Having been in almost continuous operation since 1837, when they had the American fine dining scene almost to themselves, it was almost inevitable that Delmonico's could lay claim to having introduced a thing or two to world cuisine. Among the signature dishes that the restaurant has supposedly invented (several assertions are disputed by culinary historians) are Lobster Newberg, chicken à la Keene (which later morphed into chicken à la king), baked Alaska, and eggs Benedict. Curiously, though, their most famous dish, Delmonico steak, is not always seen on the menu; in part because what exactly constitutes this namesake meal has been lost to time.

What other dishes and foods were invented in New York?

- Chop suey—Debatable. Some sources have it that the chef of a visiting diplomat, Li Hongzhang (1823–1901), was told to throw something together that both the Chinese and their American guests would appreciate. This might have been the first time chop suey was seen on the East Coast at least. The dish—which became a mainstay for playing-it-safe Chinese restaurants throughout the city—was probably based on an old Cantonese standard called *tsap seui*, or "miscellaneous leftovers" and adapted to use ingredients that could be sourced in New York.

- Pasta primavera—In the late 1970s, when Sirio Maccioni's (1932–) Le Cirque was the pinnacle of upscale dining in Manhattan, it was also responsible for a years-long culinary craze: pasta primavera. Maccioni's chef hated the dish (which at first wasn't even listed on the menu) so much that he forced the cooks to make it in the hallway. But this basic concoction of vegetables and spaghetti was for a time the most talked-about dish in the city.

- Thomas' English Muffins—English inventor Samuel Bath Thomas (1855–1919) moved to New York in 1874 with a recipe based on griddle cakes. In 1880, he set up a bakery on Ninth Avenue and 20th Street. His signature

The entrance to Delmonico's on Beaver Street.

item was those uniquely light and fluffy coarse-grained muffins with airy crannies perfect for trapping pockets of butter and jam. Thomas delivered them to hotels and restaurants by horse and wagon (which still appears on their logo today). Thomas' "English Muffins" were soon a popular item. His daughters and nephew took over the rapidly expanding company after his death in 1919.

Pete's Tavern on 18th Street and Irving Place is the oldest continually operating restaurant in New York.

What's the oldest restaurant in New York?

Delmonico's may have gotten started earlier, but because of various interruptions, the record for longest continually operating restaurant probably belongs to Pete's Tavern. A grand old place that's been serving food and drink on the corner of Irving Place and 18th Street since 1864, this is the spot where onetime regular O. Henry supposedly wrote "The Gift of the Magi" in 1904. That may be a positive or a negative for you. But in any case, this remains a charmingly old-fashioned New York eatery, with decent Italian food and a long list of tap beers, on an extremely charming block near Gramercy Park.

When did eating out at restaurants become a common New York activity?

After finer establishments like Delmonico's made it acceptable for wealthier New Yorkers to be seen eating out in public, it was inevitable that this convenient habit would trickle down the socioeconomic ladder. By the 1840s, numerous "eating houses" opened throughout downtown New York to serve the many men working there as well as the high percentage of them who lived in boardinghouses. In the space of a generation, the average New York man switched from eating nearly every meal with his family to dining several times a week in the company of friends or strangers.

Coinciding with the growth of the city's immigrant population, the number of restaurants exploded from perhaps as few as five in 1810 to approximately 5,000 by the 1860s. True to the city's reputation for speed and efficiency (or at least haste at all times), nearly all accounts of eating out in New York during this time emphasize the hurried nature of the typical New York diner, who was barely done swallowing his last bite before paying the bill and getting his coat on.

How many different kinds of restaurants were there in nineteenth-century New York?

Restaurants in nineteenth-century New York could be grouped into several categories, based in part but not entirely on the wealth of their clientele. Historian Cindy R. Lobel broke down the taxonomy of the dining scene thusly:

- Chophouses—Originally a magnet for British expats, these restaurants offering a limited selection of ales and hearty cuts of meat were somewhat quieter, less rushed, and a little pricier than the sixpennies.

- Coffee and cake shops—Starting with Butter-Cake Dick's, a snack bar on Spruce Street popular in the mid-1800s with a late-night crowd of newsies and Bowery Boys, these establishments served up coffee, doughnuts, and the like for a few cents. They eventually branched out into offering regular meals and morphed into today's open-late diners and coffeeshops.

- Delmonican—First-class luxury dining palaces, often based on the French model. Usually the menus were in French, ensuring that the class divide wouldn't be broken. The assumption that the best restaurants were generally always Parisian-style wasn't broken until well into the next century.

- Oyster cellars—Raucous and crowded establishments that served oysters, oysters, and yet more oysters. Generally clustered downtown to be closest to the docks.

- Sixpenny restaurant—Generally seen as the bottom rung on the ladder, these were inexpensive high-volume eateries that charged six pence for main dishes and got their (overwhelmingly male) diners in and out in about a half-hour. Also known as a "Sweeneyorum."

What was the "Canal Plan"?

The easiest way to find a buffet in nineteenth-century New York, outside of the free lunch served at saloons for paying drinkers, was to head down to Canal Street and look for a red-and-white-striped balloon. If illuminated, that balloon signaled that one of the city's many oyster cellars was open for business. Chances are, you could partake of the "Canal Street plan," which allowed customers to eat all the oysters they could for about six cents. (Supposedly proprietors wanting to stop customers eating more than their share would slip a bad oyster onto their plate.)

This wasn't the only place to find oysters in the city, though. For decades, oysters served as the pizza slice of their day, the city's most popular, distinctive, widely available, and affordable food. Every establishment from street carts to high-end eateries like Delmonico's (which popularized serving them raw on the half-shell) made sure to include them on the menu. Oysters were served fried and in stews. But the most popular way to eat oysters was raw, with a few dashes of salt, pepper, and sometimes a little lemon.

When did it become socially acceptable for women to eat at restaurants?

Women could generally always be served at New York restaurants, provided of course that they confined themselves to the women-only dining areas set apart for them by some early taverns. By the mid-nineteenth century, as the number and variety of restaurants in the city began (ever so slowly) to increase, a number of them also made sure to keep separate tables or even dining rooms for women. That way, their respectability would not be questioned if they were seen in a public establishment without a male chaperone.

What dishes did "Oscar of the Waldorf" invent?

Swiss-born Oscar Tschirky (1866–1950) made his name on the burgeoning high-end New York dining scene as maître d'hôtel at Delmonico's in the 1880s, before graduating to running things at the Waldorf-Astoria's restaurant. Among the dishes that Tschirky is reputed to have invented were eggs Benedict, Thousand Island dressing, veal Oscar, and his signature Waldorf salad (apples, grapes, celery, mayonnaise, and walnuts). The salad and eggs Benedict are still given places of honor in restaurants at the Waldorf-Astoria, which moved to its current location on Park Avenue in 1931.

In the 1830s, a number of women's-only establishments began to open. Some of them expressly targeted the upper-class women who liked to frequent the Ladies' Mile and other shopping districts. Increasingly, restaurants, coffee shops, and ice cream parlors began to actively seek out the business of female patrons by offering grander surroundings and the promise of a more respectable atmosphere for women and families than that which proliferated in the city's smoke-heavy chophouses. The quaint cafes still found today in the city's department stores like Macy's and Bloomingdale's are a continuation of this tradition.

Where was the hot dog popularized?

New York can't quite lay claim to having invented the hot dog. However, the city has popularized it more than any other city with the possible exception of the nation's slaughterhouse: Chicago. The highly convenient and portable sausage link wrapped in a soft bun and served either straight or with piles of condiments (onions, relish, mustard, ketchup) was a perfect match for the crowds who thronged out to Coney Island every summer and warm weekend.

Charles Feltman (1841–1910) apparently started the first hot dog stand out on Coney Island in 1871. One of his employees, Nathan Handwerker (1892–1974), broke off to start his own establishment in 1912. It wasn't long before Nathan's Famous became almost synonymous with the New York hot dog. These days, Nathan's Famous is still at Coney Island, serving hot dogs as well as giant beers and piles of their signature crinkle fries that you eat with a tiny fork. Each Fourth of July, they sponsor a hot-dog-eating contest that has become one of the more strangely popular attractions on cable TV. Outside Coney Island, hot dogs can be bought by daring gourmands at any number of street carts around Manhattan.

Was the Automat actually automated?

There was a time in New York when you could walk into a restaurant and have a cup of hot coffee and a slice of fresh pie without ever having to deal with a server. This was the

Automat (from the Greek *automatos*, for "self-acting"), a radically convenient invention that featured solid walls of mirrors and chrome and brass vending machines labeled by category ("Sandwiches," "Pies") and holding individual servings of food visible behind tiny windows and ordered by simply thumbing a few coins into a slot. The idea of fully automated assembly line food was in many ways an illusion. Behind the wall of machines, a large staff hustled to fit fresh-prepared food items into each emptied slot. At a time when dining out was still mostly segregated by class into high-end establishments and low-end cafeterias, the Automats were a hit with people from all across the socioeconomic spectrum. At their peak, the chain was serving 750,000 people a day from their central commissary at 50th Street and 11th Avenue.

A New York City automat is shown here on Broadway around the turn of the twentieth century. The advent of fast food chains in the 1950s brought about the demise of automats by the 1970s.

Where did the term "breadline" come from?

During the 1890s, Fleischmann's Vienna Model Bakery on Broadway and 10th Street near Grace Church began giving away its day-old bread starting at midnight. It quickly became common to see lines of the hungry stretching far away from the bakery's side door. The poignancy of this recurring gathering was immortalized in writing and painting. Theodore Dreiser's (1871–1945) novel of being down and out in urban America, *Sister Carrie*, included a reference to it. Stephen Crane once spent an entire night in the breadline during a blizzard just to research a story.

This breadline itself had ceased operation before the Great Depression. By that time distribution of free food had become such a common sight in American cities, the term "breadline" had entered the lexicon. Today, the oldest continuously operating breadline in America, which started in 1930, can be found at the Church of St. Francis of Assisi on West 31st Street.

What was "The Chinese Delmonico"?

Despite the space it occupied in many Americans' imaginings (usually Orientalist fantasies of opium dens, white slavery, and the like), New York's Chinese population was miniscule until the twentieth century. That meant that if Chinese restaurants were to survive, they needed to attract Occidental customers. In 1897, a vast and luxuriously appointed Chinese restaurant opened on the southeastern verge of the Five Points at 24 Pell

321

Street, in the heart of what was becoming known as Chinatown. To bring in a non-Chinese clientele by way of exploiting a by-then apparently open-source brand, Mon Lay Won (like several other Chinese restaurants that followed) advertised itself as "The Chinese Delmonico," both an authentically foreign experience and a classically New York fine dining emporium. A menu from the period looks mostly similar to what one would find today at many Chinatown restaurants ("Beef Chop Suey," "Chicken Chow main"), along with some dishes that would never be spotted today ("Pigeon with mushroom," "Shark fin").

For what type of Chinese cuisine is Chinatown best known?

You know that know-it-all friend of yours who likes to say things like, "You know, in *China*, they don't eat eggrolls," ignoring the irrelevance of that fact since eggrolls are, well, delicious? They would be the first to roll their eyes at much of what is proffered at restaurants in Chinatown, which have been serving up purposefully Westernized versions of Chinese cuisine to Americans since the nineteenth century. New York's Chinese community before the 1960s hailed primarily from the Cantonese region, and the style of the dishes they made for American tastes (chop suey, moo goo gai pan, egg foo yung, and so on) were adapted from their own cuisine.

Later waves of immigrants from Taiwan and Hong Kong brought a penchant for spicier dishes (known here as "Szechuan" style). Shanghai-style dishes were popularized by chef T. T. Wang (1928–1983), whose high-end Shun Lee Dynasty on 48th Street be-

Where was pizza invented?

What turned into the world-spanning phenomenon called pizza was originally known to most Italian immigrants to America as that catch-as-catch-can dish that their mothers would use to empty out the kitchen, taking whatever was about to go bad, piling it on a crust or bread with some sauce, and throwing it all into the oven. Those from the Neapolitan region knew a more specific kind of meal that was closer to what we would recognize today as pizza: a highly adaptable circular disc of thin and crispy dough covered in tomato sauce, mozzarella cheese, and other vegetable and meat toppings as desired.

There are competing arguments over who created the first "pizza" in America, but the prize is generally awarded to Lombardi's, a still thriving (if tourist-clogged) Nolita establishment on Spring Street. Technically, though, this wasn't where the great invention took place. The story goes that Gennaro Lombardi started selling his Neapolitan-style pies out of a grocery store in Little Italy starting around 1905. The restaurant that carries his name didn't exist until many years later, when it was opened by his grandson. However, many of the city's other great famed pizza makers (like John Sasso of John's Pizzeria in Greenwich Village) are said to have understudied with Lombardi.

New York-style pizza is shown here being served at the Feast of San Gennaro in Manhattan's Little Italy.

came the first Chinese restaurant to be given a four-star review by the *New York Times* in 1967. Most New York neighborhoods today feature at least a couple interchangeable Chinese restaurants which, in the words of Calvin Trillin (1935–), "seem to acquire their food from one gigantic kitchen, presided over in a dictatorial but not terribly inventive way by General Tso."

Why can't you make New York-style pizza elsewhere?

One of the more beloved truisms of old New Yorkers—and they have plenty of them—is that their city has the best-tasting and cleanest water in the country. While difficult to independently verify, this belief is somewhat based in reality, as the city's water, piped in from massive reservoirs upstate, generally tests well for taste. The supremacy of New York water has also been credited for making the city's coal- or stone-oven pizzas and boiled bagels nearly impossible to recreate elsewhere even with all the right culinary technicians and ingredients. Some have even pointed to specific elements in the city's water, like its proportion of calcium and magnesium, as being the cause for these unique doughs.

Do New York Italian restaurants serve Italian food?

This is not as oxymoronic a question as it might seem. When Italian immigrants began arriving in New York during the late 1800s, they brought all of their culinary traditions with them. But a number of factors changed dining habits very fast. First was the fact that many of these immigrants came from desperately poor areas where getting enough

323

to eat was always a struggle. Once given access to New York's abundance of markets with their varied and (comparatively) inexpensive wares, not to mention the proximity to other ethnic groups (particularly immigrants from other parts of Italy with their own micro-regional dishes), the newcomers' cooking habits began to transition.

This new fusion Italian-American cuisine centered on large plates of pasta, layers of cheese, rich red tomato and heavy cream sauces, and meatballs whose proportions would make people back in the old country sick with jealousy. The stereotypical New York Italian restaurant with the "family style" portions of spaghetti and meatballs, glasses of Chianti, and chintzy décor was introduced by Mama Leone's, which Luisa Leone (1873–1944) opened on 34th Street in 1906 on the advice of Enrico Caruso (1873–1921). It was a tourist and celebrity mainstay in the Theater District for more than seven decades thereafter, and is survived in Midtown by numerous red-sauce emporiums like Carmine's and Tony's Di Napoli.

Is there any way to get into Rao's?

One of New York's most venerable Italian restaurants is nowhere near Little Italy. Established in 1896 on 114th Street in what was then the Italian section of East Harlem, Rao's didn't have a large profile in the city at large until Frank Pellegrino (1957–) took it over in the 1970s. Since then, this tiny eatery with just four tables and six booths has been consistently the hardest reservation to get in the city. (It's a scarcity not helped by the fact that many regulars have standing reservations that they're loathe to part with.) The presence of some big-name Mafiosi over the years (Martin Scorsese cast a passel of its regulars in *Goodfellas*), not to mention that shooting at the bar in 2003, has assisted with the mystique more than the so-so reputation of the food. The average New Yorker is content with making pasta at home with the bottled Rao's sauce sold in most city markets.

Is corned beef and cabbage even Irish?

Every St. Patrick's Day, the dozens of Irish bars that continue to proliferate around Manhattan, particularly in Midtown, slap up paper shamrocks and Guinness signs and put out their food offerings. The more recent self-styled "pubs" have stuck with a regular menu that sticks to the Irish-American basics (bangers and mash, fish and chips). But your old-fashioned joints still serve up the classic corned beef and cabbage. Curiously, the whole tradition is a sign of New York's typical mélange of ethnic cuisines.

Irish immigrants arrived in America looking for one of their dietary staples: rashers of bacon. They soon discovered, though, that it was much cheaper to get large quantities of corned beef, or brisket (which was prohibitively expensive and reserved for the upper classes back in the old country), from the city's many kosher butchers and throw it into a pot with cabbage and potatoes. It's possible that this merging of cultural dishes helped inspire the 1912 song, "If It Wasn't for the Irish and the Jews," which noted how, "On St. Patrick's Day, Rosinsky pins a shamrock to his coat." The popularity of this filling, but not precisely flavorful, dish never made it back to Ireland itself.

Often served on St. Patrick's Day, corned beef and cabbage is a dish not from Ireland but, rather, New York City and its Jewish population.

Are there many kosher restaurants left in New York?

You are more likely these days to find "kosher-style," not exactly kosher, eateries in the city. For kosher-style food, it's hard to beat Katz's Delicatessen, the old Lower East Side mainstay on Houston and Ludlow where the wood paneling, brusque service, and piled-high pastrami sandwiches don't seem to have changed much since it opened in 1888. Here's some more strictly kosher places, new and old:

- Ben's Kosher Delicatessen—The 38th Street location in Midtown is loud and pretty jammed on weekdays at lunchtime, but worth it. The matzo ball soup is fantastic, the sandwiches massive, and there's even a selection of kosher beers and wine.

- Taim—Tiny Israeli-style falafel joint (the name means "tasty" in Hebrew) on Waverly Place in the West Village that stands apart from the pack by serving multiple flavors of falafel.

- Yonah Schimmel—Grubby-looking but essential knish bakery (oldest in the city) on Houston and Forsyth streets serving up essentially the same fare as its namesake was flogging from his street cart in 1910.

What is Curry Row?

They might not have dispersed into wider America as quickly and deeply as their Italian and Chinese counterparts, but Indian restaurants have been on the New York dining scene since at least the early twentieth century. News reports note that Indian restaurants on 8th Avenue were serving South Asian laborers as early as 1913. Feeding off the hippie yen for anything seemingly Eastern, a cluster of Indian restaurants serving creamy Bangladeshi dishes and sitar music opened up on a block of 6th Street in the East Village between First and Second avenues that became known as "Curry Row." The stretch has long had a not-so-great reputation for quality (cheap buffets and the like).

More varied options can be found several blocks to the north in the area around Lexington Avenue and 28th Street in Murray Hill known as "Curry Hill." There you can find the standard tikka masalas, but also good dosas, kati rolls, and kebabs.

Where is the city's best steakhouse?

The general consensus is that the best old-fashioned slab-of-meat dining experience involves actually heading out to Williamsburg, Brooklyn. There, you'll find an unprepossessing spot at Broadway and Driggs right by the on-ramp to the Williamsburg Bridge that opened back in 1887 as Carl Luger's Café Billiards and Bowling Alley. Carl's son Peter—who, if a customer complained, insisted on tasting the offending steak—named it for himself after inheriting the business. The famed destination restaurant has carried on his brusque style to this day, not even deigning to print a menu until 1950 and not offering fish until the 1980s. Fortunately, bacon still comes as an appetizer.

Why do those little to-go coffee cups all feature blue-and-white Grecian art?

In just about any movie about New York, you are likely to see somebody walking or running the streets with a tiny, unique little paper cup in their hands. It's small, colored blue and white, with classical Greek imagery and the logo: "We Are Happy to Serve You." It dates back to the 1960s, when a paper cup company was looking for a new product to sell to the hundreds of Greek-operated coffee shops still operating in New York. It was known as the "Anthora" cup, inspired by the Greek word for the jars depicted on the cup: "Amphora." At their peak in 1994 (the same year that Starbucks first opened here), around half a billion of these cups were manufactured each year. These days they are less commonly seen than the starker white designs favored by higher-end barista joints but are still standard-issue at most street coffee-carts.

Who invented chicken and waffles?

According to some, the Pennsylvania Dutch were the first intrepid individuals who brought these two items together, topping their waffles with creamed chicken and gravy. The dish was reintroduced to the modern era (only with crispy fried chicken, which added more of a bite, especially when paired with some hot sauce) by the Wells Supper Club, which opened on Harlem's Adam Clayton Powell Jr. Boulevard in 1938. Wells was apparently a favored late-night haunt for jazz musicians, who would show up too late for dinner and too early for breakfast and settled on a compromise of fried chicken and waffles. According to Harlem chef Marcus Samuelsson (1971–), this also helped the kitchen get rid of the inevitable leftover fried chicken from the dinner service. Wells became a favored spot for certain musicians; Nat King Cole (1919–1965) held his wedding reception there.

It might seem like an odd combination, but chicken and waffles have spread in popularity from New York to restaurants all over the country.

In the following decades, the dish spread across the country, most famously to Los Angeles' Roscoe's House of Chicken and Waffles. These days, Wells is no more, but Harlem restaurants like the venerable soul food spot Sylvia's and Samuelsson's Streetbird on Frederick Douglass Boulevard at 116th Street serve up their variations on the sweet and salty classic.

Can you drink at The Donut Pub?

The sign of the better twenty-four-hour establishment is that it be a place you would be just as happy to walk into at noon as at 3 A.M. That's the case with The Donut Pub, which has served up crullers, jelly donuts, and old fashioneds every hour of the day and night on the corner of 7th Avenue and 14th Street since 1964. They've also got minis and even sprinkled donuts. The offerings aren't as individually delectable as what some of the nouveau-doughnut shops around town (meaning: no Valrhona here, just plain chocolate), but plenty tasty nonetheless. They also serve sandwiches, but determined research has failed to turn up anybody who has ordered one. Note for the thirsty: this is a pub in the sign maker's imagination only; there is no alcohol.

Where can you get a pretzel croissant?

That would be The City Bakery on 18th Street just west of Fifth Avenue. According to some experts on the subject, this is also where you can find not just the greatest chocolate chip cookie in the city, but in the whole world. It's a difficult subject to adjudicate on, though, and settling the matter would require repeat visits to this spacious Flatiron landmark, which opened in 1990. It sells about a thousand cookies a day from the generally packed middle service island, where crowds line up for its many delectable pastries. Among the most popular is the famous pretzel croissant, whose salty/sweet

327

crispy/soft pairing has made it the kind of treat people make special trips to the neighborhood for.

The lofty space adds a sense of theatricality to the whole affair and ensures that even on the busiest days you can usually find a table. The pricey but tasty, small-batch, comfort food, cafeteria-style lunch menu is worth checking out as well. Make sure to stop by in February, because that's when the bakery runs its annual Hot Chocolate Festival, with a different flavor every day (chili pepper, Vietnamese cinnamon, bourbon, salted caramel; the wonders go on).

What desserts and other sweets were invented in New York?

- Black and white cookie—This big and chewy cake-like disc covered with fondant icing divided in half between chocolate and vanilla is a common sight at bigger-is-better bakeries or just wrapped in plastic and stacked on the counter at delis and bodegas. A strange and particularly New York confection (there are upstate variations known as half moon cookies), the black and white cookie has an unclear history but is generally believed to have been created sometime in the late nineteenth century. Immortalized in a *Seinfeld* routine as a dubious metaphor for racial equality.

- Chewing gum—The first piece of modern chewing gum was created by inventor Thomas Adams (1818–1905) in 1856. Curiously, Adams had discovered the rubbery tree gum chicle when visiting the Mexican general Antonio López de Santa Anna (1794–1876) at his home on Staten Island. Santa Anna had wanted to interest somebody in purchasing large amounts of chicle as a substitute to rubber, thus funding his return to power in Mexico. Instead, Adams used chicle as he knew Indians in Mexico did, to chew. Adams added fruit and licorice flavors and within a few years was employing hundreds of workers at a factory near the Brooklyn Bridge to produce tons of chewing gum (including Black Jack) each year.

- Doughnuts—Debatable. Though it is believed that the Dutch introduced some version of the deep-fried treat (sometimes called "crullers," even today) to the continent via New Amsterdam. The first recorded reference to the doughnut is thought to be found in Washington Irving's *History of New York*, where he talks about the foods usually served at parties: "It was always sure to boast an enormous dish of balls of sweetened dough, fried in hog's fat, and called doughnuts, or olykoeks—a delicious kind of cake."

- Egg cream—Unlike some other sweet stuffs that got their start in New York, the egg cream never made it much past the five boroughs—and in some ways never that far past lower Manhattan and Brooklyn. The egg cream, which contains neither eggs nor cream, is a fizzy drink of milk, chocolate syrup (aficionados will only accept Fox's U-Bet brand), and seltzer water. Its origins have been lost to time, but most likely the egg cream was created somewhere on the Lower East Side in the late 1800s or early 1900s. In any case, while an iconic mainstay of old New York, it is these days about as commonly spotted as stickball games or Brooklyn Dodgers gear.

- Häagen-Dazs—In the postwar era, most American ice creams were made with artificial flavors. In the 1960s, Rose (1916–2006) and Reuben Mattus (1912–1994) decided it would be a better idea to start making ice cream with real cream, egg yolks, and more natural ingredients like Belgian chocolate. It was America's first gourmet ice cream, starting a trend that has yet to abate. For all the authenticity of the ice cream's ingredients, though, the name was a fake. The Mattuses made the name up, put a map of Denmark on the carton, and added an umlaut to make their brand seem Danish, and thusly gourmet. The first Häagen-Dazs shop opened in Brooklyn Heights in 1976; it remains in operation today.

- The Oreo—The chocolate wafer and vanilla crème sandwich cookie of many a child's dreams was first constructed in 1912 at the National Biscuit Company (Nabisco) headquarters on Tenth Avenue, currently home to the bustling food emporium the Chelsea Market. Many people today believe that the similar Hydrox cookie is an imitator of the beloved Oreo. Actually, Hydrox was invented in 1908 by the Sunshine Biscuit Company.

Where's the best place to get Viennese coffee in New York?

Tucked away inside the rarified confines of the Neue Galerie—an elegant townhouse on Fifth Avenue and 86th Street that houses a nice collection of German and Austrian art—you can find Café Sabarsky. It's a quietly swank corner spot with dark wood walls and splendid views of the avenue, serving up dark coffee in the Viennese fashion (on a tray with a glass of water on the side) and many decadent tortes.

How about pierogies?

Veselka, a twenty-four-hour refuge for East Village students and night owls at the corner of 9th Street and Second Avenue, has been serving some of the best Ukrainian fare since it first opened its doors in 1954. The varenky (pierogi to the Polish), Eastern European dumplings fried or steamed with a variety of fillings, are just about the best in the city. There's also goulash, kielbasa, and stuffed cabbage on offer, as well as kutya, a traditional pudding made with wheat berries, raisins, walnuts, poppy seeds, and honey. It's worth stopping by between December 24 and January 6, which is when Veselka serves up Sviata Vecheria, a traditional twelve-dish holiday feast.

Does a line outside a New York restaurant mean it's any good?

You can't always trust a big crowd to indicate quality. After all, there's often a wait to be seated at the Times Square Olive Gar-

The popular Oreo cookie originated at the National Biscuit Company on 10th Avenue.

den (yes, there is one, at Broadway and 47th St.) and *Mamma Mia* played to sell-out crowds for *years*. However, sometimes the masses have it right. In New York, that is particularly true in areas with lots of office workers, particularly Midtown and the Financial District. If you walk past a restaurant at noon on a weekday and there is a line out the door, you would be wise to get in that line. Tourists don't eat lunch right at noon and will avoid crowds if they can—unless a TV celebrity chef is involved. But office workers are often planted in the same neighborhood for years and have learned from hard-fought experience what's worth their time and money. Learn from them.

BARS AND NIGHTLIFE

What is the oldest bar in New York?

As with many things in New York, it depends who you ask. If one isn't inclined to go by such metrics as "continuously operating," then Fraunces Tavern downtown at 54 Pearl Street may hold that distinction. First built as a merchant's mansion in 1719, the building later became a tavern before being bought and renamed by Samuel Fraunces in 1762. Fraunces himself was a fascinating character who probably emigrated from the West Indies, was nicknamed "Black Sam" for his presumed biracial heritage, and became one of the central figures in George Washington's New York-based spy apparatus during the Revolutionary War. The tavern, which was briefly a Loyalist tavern during the British occupation, was later a busy crossroads for New York society.

Like so many other historic downtown buildings, the tavern was nearly demolished; unlike many it was saved by preservationists. Over the years it operated as tavern and rooming house before being bought by the Sons of the Revolution in 1904 and restored. These days it's an imposing brick-fronted four-story corner building in a neighborhood that has mostly bulldozed the past. Inside is a warren of dark and dining rooms and cozy drinking nooks with fireplaces, including the Long Room where Washington gave an emotional farewell to his officers on December 4, 1783. There is a visible crack in a wall mural of the city of New York that serves as a reminder of the day in January 1975 when the Puerto Rican terrorist group FALN set off a bomb here that killed four.

What about McSorley's Old Ale House?

The proprietors of McSorley's would say that their establishment holds that honor. A gloriously crusty landmark whose clientele still draws everyone from firemen to tourists and dedicated drinkers—Abraham Lincoln reportedly had a drink there after his famous 1860 speech at Cooper Union just a block away—it first opened in 1854 and for years they served nothing but beer and ale for five cents a glass. As recently as their hundredth anniversary fete in 1954, seven-ounce glasses were going for only ten cents. They still serve only dark and light ales.

The motto was long rendered as "Good Ale, Raw Onions, and No Ladies," since onions have always featured prominently on the simple workingman's menu and women

McSorley's Old Ale House is the oldest, continuously operating such establishment in New York City.

weren't officially allowed inside until a 1970 city ordinance forced the bar to acquiesce (Joseph Mitchell wrote about a "feminist from Greenwich Village" who successfully drank an ale in 1924 by dressing as a man).

What are some other old bars?

More recently, somewhat credible claims to being the oldest bar in New York have been made by places as varied as the Bridge Café down on Water Street (which might have opened seven years before McSorley's) and Neir's Tavern in Woodhaven, Queens (which might have opened in 1829 but which was definitely used for several scenes in *Goodfellas*).

Why were there so many bars in pre-modern New York?

In the early years of urban America, taverns, and their less reputable cousins the unlicensed "grog shops," where the average law-abiding citizen took their life into their own hands upon entering, were not seen as merely places to drink alone or with friends. While alcohol was certainly central to their operation, taverns were much more than watering holes. William Harrison Bayles's *Old Taverns of New York* (1915) called them the central place for city dwellers to socialize and discuss politics or any other issues of the day. According to Bayles, taverns "exercised an influence second only to the church.... There was hardly an event of importance but had its inception in the taverns."

The proliferation of drinking establishments in New York was helped along by the fact that it was originally settled by beer-loving Dutchmen. With occasional interruptions by

331

more abstemious leaders, the production and sale of beer and liquor was never as tightly regulated in New York as it was in the more Puritan regions to the north and east.

What was the first brewery in New York?

The first brewery in America started operations very early in the history of New Amsterdam. Around 1612, just a few years after the colony was founded, a brewery began producing in one of the few buildings then standing at the southern tip of Manhattan. The regional history of brewing is more commonly dated to 1632, when Peter Minuit opened up the Dutch West India Company's brewery on Marckvelt (Market Field, today's Whitehall Street). It operated for just a few years until competition from numerous privately owned breweries put it out of business. When Willem Kieft became governor in 1638, he outlawed the sale of wine and whiskey by tavern keepers. This greatly increased the market for beer, already a popular beverage among colonists as it was safer to drink than the local water.

What were some of the biggest New York breweries?

Two of New York's most successful breweries operated almost right next to each other in the German neighborhood of Yorkville. George Ehret started his Hell Gate Brewery in 1866. Then the largest brewery in the country, the awesome red-brick complex covered several blocks between 2nd and 3rd avenues and 91st and 94th streets. A 1909 newspaper ad proclaimed that Hell Gate brewed a million barrels of beer a year. Jacob Ruppert's (1842–1924) brewery operated nearby on Third Avenue between 91st and 94th streets. Jacob Ruppert Jr. (1867–1939) later took the lead with their popular Knicker-

What did Croton Aqueduct have to do with making beer?

Since New York's water supply was of such dodgy quality, it took a long time for breweries to reach critical mass. Brooklyn was a slight exception to this rule, as it had easier access to fresh water from Long Island. That changed, however, when the Croton Aqueduct started supplying consistently clean water to the entire city in 1842. At the same time, German immigrants began arriving in large numbers. As in the Midwestern cities where they also settled, the Germans began opening dozens of breweries. By 1879, there were over 120 breweries in Manhattan and Brooklyn, including eleven on just one twelve-block strip in Williamsburg. The many beautiful homes lining Bushwick Avenue are testament to the money and status brought to the neighborhood by the owners of its many breweries. The Germans also introduced bottom-fermented and cold-stored lagers that won out over the area's traditional English-style warm-brewed (and warm-served) ales. The lagers were sold in massive quantities at the city's many beer gardens, including one on the Bowery that could hold a thousand people.

bocker brew, becoming an owner of a little sports club called the New York Yankees, and ultimately taking over Ehret's brewery in 1935.

How did New York breweries survive Prohibition?

In some cases, they didn't. Like in the rest of the country, however, some breweries adapted to the new business environment. They retooled to produce goods like ice cream, soft drinks, malt syrup, and medicinal tonics. They also sold a beverage that left few fans: near-beer (no more than 0.5 percent ABV). After Prohibition was repealed in 1933, twenty-three breweries went back into production. As some local beer mavens remember today with some annoyance, the first beer drunk in celebration by Al Smith was in fact not a local brew, but … a Budweiser.

Several decades of relative prosperity followed for New York brewers, but eventually the same forces of consolidation and homogenization that were wiping out smaller breweries around the country came to New York. Ruppert's brewery closed in 1965, at around the same time that the area's brewing industry was entering something of a death spiral. The city's last breweries, Rheingold (sponsors of the legendary Miss Rheingold contest) and Schaefer, closed up shop in 1976. Twenty years later, Brooklyn Brewery started operations, opening the door for a trickle of other microbreweries like Six Point Craft Ales in Brooklyn. Today Brooklyn Brewery, which has a showcase brewhouse in Williamsburg with a fun picnic-table indoor beer garden area, actually makes most of its beer upstate.

What bar was once called "the wickedest place in New York"?

In the 1890s, as until somewhat recently, there were numerous places of ill repute in Greenwich Village, many located on or around Bleecker Street. Even amidst all the dirty groggeries that shocked the city with their racially mixed clientele (like the Black and Tan, where reportedly all the women were white and the men were of any hue), though, there was one establishment that was considered wicker than any of them.

When the *New York Press* called it the "wickedest place in New York" in 1890, the Slide at 157 Bleecker Street was the city's only openly gay drinking establishment. Or it may have simply been a bar that hosted drag shows and possibly had male prostitutes on offer. In any case, it was probably the city's most denounced bar. One account called it "headquarters of a gang of the most depraved and abominable creatures that can be imagined" and one newspaper wrote breathlessly of the "rouged and powdered men and youths" who congregated there. As Luc Sante (1954–) writes in *Low Life*, it was nearly impossible to get a clear idea of what went on at the Slide, because "the loud distaste of contemporary chroniclers made them incapable of turning in an actual description."

If homosexuality was against the law in New York, how did gay bars operate in New York?

Since relations between consenting, same-sex adults were against the law in New York state until 1980, and heterosexual public opinion was strongly opposed to any ac-   333

President Barack Obama declared the Stonewall Inn a national monument in 2016, an event people celebrated there on June 24, 2016.

knowledgement of homosexuality, for most of the city's history, gay New Yorkers were forced into the shadows. Gay-friendly bars or cafes would sometimes be able to operate for a few years—for instance, a Greenwich Village lesbian speakeasy Eve's Hangout had a brief run in the mid-1920s—but police and public pressure generally shut them down quickly. By the 1960s, there were a few more established gay bars like the Stonewall Inn, Julius's, and the 181 Club (also known as "the homosexual Copacabana," featuring lavish drag shows in the late 1940s and early '50s) clustered in the Village, but they were still seen as operating outside the law. Police raids were commonplace and punitive. Arrestees would frequently have their full names and addresses printed in the newspaper and many lost their jobs and families as a result.

What did the Mafia have to do with gay bars?

Since bars that served gay customers were not allowed liquor licenses, Mafiosi like the Genovese family stepped in to run quasi-legal establishments. According to legend they served watered-down booze (often from hijacked trucks) at high prices while bribing the police to give advance warning of raids. The Mafia found that their captive clientele (called *finocchio* or "fairies") made for lucrative business, particularly when they could be blackmailed with the threat of outing. This went on until the Stonewall Uprising of 1969, after which the gay community turned against their extorters. A message was written on the bar's boarded-up windows: "Gay Prohibition Corupt$ Cop$ and Feed$ Mafia." By the 1970s, as a result of the burgeoning gay rights movement, more gay-friendly businesses were allowed to operate in the open without the fear of police harassment or the need for Mafia involvement.

Where did Ray Milland almost drink himself to death in *The Lost Weekend*?

There might be a restaurant there, but the original P. J. Clarke's on 3rd Avenue and 55th Street is and always will be best known as a bar. In addition to serving the martini-swilling ad guys from nearby agencies in the bustling postwar years (*Mad Men* set an early scene here), they catered to a kinetic blend of working stiffs needing a strong pick-me-up and the occasional celebrity (Nat King Cole had a charge account). The blue-collar grit dated back to the late 1800s, when the neighborhood was a rough-and-tumble jumble of Irish tenements and the bar was called Jennings. Even after the white collars started showing up, Clarke's retained its reputation as a place for serious drinkers. Not for nothing was it the setting of Billy Wilder's alcoholic's odyssey *The Lost Weekend* from 1945. It was also known as a place where celebrities could drink mostly unharassed. Liza Minnelli was a regular, along with Frank Sinatra; the Chairman's favorite table was number 20.

The martini was invented at the Knickerbocker Hotel around 1911.

But, times change. The elevated train was moved underground. The rule against unaccompanied women went by the wayside. The tenements came down and luxury towers went up. And so, a few years back, some new owners completely rehabbed the place but did a fantastic job of keeping the scent of living history after scrubbing everything down. They added the upstairs dining room Sidecar, which is where you go if you prefer to eat your bubble and squeak (a specialty) away from the roar of the after-work crowd who still reliably jam the front bar same as in days of yore. Since then, the owners have expanded the brand, opening up carefully curated branch locations around town in Battery Park and near Lincoln Square, as well as far away as Sao Paulo.

What drinks were invented in New York?

- Bloody Mary—This brunch favorite and hangover tonic has a somewhat complicated tale behind it. The story goes that around 1920 Fernand Petiot (1900–1975), a bartender at Harry's New York Bar in Paris, started mixing vodka (courtesy of all the White Russian exiles in town) with canned tomato juice (an American novelty new to Europe) and spices, and called the resulting drink the Bucket of Blood. Petiot introduced it to New York when he was hired to run the King Cole Bar at the St. Regis Hotel in 1933 at Prohibition's end. There, it was called the Red Snapper

What bar did customers have to worry about being "86'd" from?

The best bars don't need to advertise their existence. That was (and maybe still will be) true of Chumley's. It opened in 1928 while Prohibition was still trundling along in its misguided way. A home away from home for a certain brand of Village-centric literati, the bar hosted boldface names like Hemingway and Fitzgerald drinking here, along with more radical types like John Reed and Emma Goldman and the occasional celebrity like Humphrey Bogart (1899–1957). If you came in the unlabeled door at 86 Bedford Street, you had to be careful not to trip down the complicated stairs that owner Leland Chumley (c. 1885–1935) put in to harass Prohibition agents. The address even entered the lingo as a euphemism for being booted from a place, as would happen to those unwanted here: i.e. "86'd." Long after Chumley's stopped needing to be a speakeasy, it left the name off because anybody who needed to know where to find the place was already in the know.

Until 2007, it was a lovely little escape from the world, with a buttery and soft-hued bookish feel to everything, and heavy curtains by the door muffling the sound from the street. Unfortunately, Chumley's had to close in 2007 after part of a wall collapsed. Repairs, complicated by the historic nature of the neighborhood, stretched on. It reopened in late 2016 as a pricey restaurant bearing little resemblance to the cozy old watering hole.

(still what the menu says today), and given more of a kick, with black and cayenne pepper and Worcestershire sauce.

- Manhattan—There are many origin stories for this potent combination of rye whiskey, vermouth, bitters, and a sweet cherry garnish (memories get fuzzy after a few). One of the better and unfortunately false ones pins the invention of the drink on Jennie Jerome (1854–1921), the Brooklyn-born mother of Winston Churchill (1874–1965), who at a November 1874 banquet at the Manhattan Club supposedly asked for rye and vermouth to celebrate Samuel Tilden's (1814–1886) election to the New York governorship. (This turns out to be impossible, as on the date in question Jerome was giving birth to Winston in England.) Another story has it that the Manhattan was invented by the owner of a SoHo saloon in the 1860s. One thing is known about the Manhattan: it originally didn't come with a maraschino cherry; those weren't added in until around 1900.

- Martini—This cool, dry whopper of a cocktail (which H. L. Mencken called "the only American invention as perfect as the sonnet") was invented, according to some, in New York in 1911 or 1912. That was the year when a bartender at the Knickerbocker Hotel named Martini di Arma di Taggia mixed gin and dry vermouth together. It was apparently so salubrious that one of the first to partake of Taggia's invention, one John D. Rockefeller, promptly told all his wealthy buddies about it.

The rest is (pseudo) history. Other stories trace it back to San Francisco in the 1860s. There is also a theory that people simply started calling any cocktail with vermouth a martini, after the Italian brand Martini & Rossi.

THE ARTS

THEATER

What was the first live professional stage play performed in New York?

There are several arguments over the answer to this question. Some sources point to the performance of the comedy, *The Recruiting Officer*, at a place called the New Theatre in 1732. But the consensus has it taking place at the Nassau Street Theatre, a two-story gabled house situated between John Street and Maiden Lane. Like most theaters in the colonies at the time, it was a modest structure befitting the city's still non-cosmopolitan atmosphere. The *Brooklyn Daily Eagle* later wrote that the chandelier was "a barrel hoop, through which were driven half a dozen nails, into which were stuck so many candles," and "the orchestra consisted of a German flute, horn and drum player."

The first play performed at Nassau Street was *Richard III*, on March 5, 1750. *The Beggar's Opera* was also performed that year, making it the first musical produced in New York. Stage plays were still sometimes considered scandalous affairs not worth attending or even discussing in polite company. In fact, through the 1700s some areas had laws banning the professional performance of plays. That didn't stop them from becoming ever-more popular in New York. Several new theaters were constructed soon after that first performance of *Richard III*. Given that the entire population of New York was just around ten thousand people in 1750, the fact that even one theater was open is testament to the colony's desire for entertainment.

What was the response to the stage play of *Uncle Tom's Cabin*?

In 1852, a theatrical adaptation of Harriet Beecher Stowe's (1811–1896) anti-slavery novel *Uncle Tom's Cabin* premiered at the National Theatre near the Five Points slum, where it drew most of its audience from. The play's highly melodramatic and emotional story of suffering and Christian redemption became a staggering hit in the heart of a city whose inhabitants were hardly well disposed to the abolitionist argument. The *New York Herald* noted that the adaptation of this "literary wonder" "draws crowded houses nightly," even though the reviewer huffed about it being "an insult to the South" and an attempt "to poison the minds of our youth with the pestilent principles of abolitionism."

The abolitionist *Liberator* cheered the response by "ragged, coatless men and boys in the pit (the very *material* of which mobs are made) cheering the strongest and sublimest antislavery sentiments." The production was also one of the first times in the North that blacks were allowed to attend a public performance, albeit in highly segregated conditions. The theater's ad specified that only "respectable colored persons," and no women unattended by men, would be allowed in. *Uncle Tom's Cabin* closed after playing fifteen performances a week for a then nearly unheard-of nine months, establishing the precedent for long-running stage plays that help buoy the Broadway community to this day.

Was the American musical invented in New York?

Musical interludes had been a part of live theater ever since antiquity. But the earliest form of what we now think of as the musical was first spotted in New York, of course (you were thinking perhaps Scarsdale?). In 1866, one of the city's most popular so-called "pleasure gardens" was Niblo's Garden at Broadway and Prince. Irish immigrant Billy Niblo (1789–1879) started out as a restaurateur with a theatrical streak (he was famous for wheeling a whole roasted bear into the dining room) and he continued that tendency at Niblo's, which featured not only one of the city's best restaurants at the time but also a hotel, landscaped grounds for strolling, and a 3,000-seat theater.

Dedicated to spectacle above all, Niblo's Garden was the proper venue for *The Black Crook*, a musical born by accident in 1866. Niblo's was about to produce this melodrama when it was contacted by the producers of a European ballet troupe whose theater (the Academy of Music on Irving Place) had just been gutted by fire. So Niblo's enterprising manager William Wheatley decided to throw the two productions together, producing an unwieldy six-hour spectacle that became one of the most unlikely hits in theatrical history. Its array of beautiful and barely clad dancers (the *New York Times* review noted the "Demonese, who wear no clothes to speak of … as to draw forth thunders of applause"), not to mention the devilish subject matter, was excoriated by the press and clergy, which of course helped stoke ticket sales and helped *The Black Crook* run for well over a year. Multiple revivals were mounted well into the 1890s and at least two musicals *about* this apparent parent of the American musical have been produced.

Why was Mae West arrested?

Mae West, the Bushwick-raised winking dispenser of dirty one-liners, was already a star by the time she opened on Broadway. But her play (which she also starred in), helpfully titled *Sex*, was still the surprise hit of the season after it opened in April 1926. It was panned by publications like the *New Yorker*, which called it a "poor balderdash of street sweepings and cabaret sentimentality." But audiences turned out by the hundreds of thousands, much to the chagrin of bluenoses.

In February 1927, West was preparing to open a new, even more controversial play in New York: *The Drag*, which was filled with gay performers playing gay characters. The somewhat stodgy acting mayor Joseph "Holy Joe" McKee (1889–1956) took advantage of Jimmy Walker being on vacation in Havana and sent the police to arrest West and the cast of *Sex* for various morals offenses. She spent the night at the Women's Prison at Jefferson Market. Ultimately the actress spent only eight days imprisoned on Roosevelt Island.

The glamorous singer, actress, and comedienne Mae West (a Brooklyn native) was arrested in 1927 for supposed moral offenses because of her racy play *Sex*.

What was the Federal Theater Project?

The Great Depression hit New York so hard that there wasn't a single sector of jobs that wasn't affected. That included the arts. Unemployment in the theatrical community was so high that the WPA created the Federal Theatre Project (FTP) to keep theaters open and plays being produced. The FTP put people back to work around the country, with about forty thousand theatrical employees on the payroll in states from Alabama to Wisconsin. Not surprisingly, it was most active in New York. Some five thousand theatrical personnel were on the payroll, and by 1935 dozens of plays from drama and vaudeville to amateur, dance, and marionette productions were in the works. The variety of work on offer was dizzying, including: *The Cradle Will Rock*, a 1937 Kurt Weill-inspired agitprop folk opera about a steelworkers' strike; "Living Newspapers," live-action renderings of topical subjects from urban housing to venereal disease and even the generation of electricity (*Power!*); *Voodoo Macbeth*, the unofficial nickname for Orson Welles's headline-grabbing Harlem production with an all-black cast and voodoo theme; and *The Yiddish King Lear*, in which a Jewish businessman in Vilna announces that he will move to Palestine and divide his wealth between his three daughters.

What is the Actors Studio and why were so many actors drawn to it?

In 1947, several members of the famed Group Theatre created the Actors Studio, a nonprofit New York acting school that changed the entire arc of American film and theatrical performance during the postwar years. One of the school's teachers, Lee Strasberg, adapted the theories of Konstantin Stanislavski (1863–1938) into an acting style known as the Method. Strasberg's approach, which trained actors to draw on their own experiences to create more psychologically attuned performances, dovetailed with the advent of the more emotionally complex style of new American playwrights like Tennessee Williams (1911–1983). It was viewed by some as groundbreaking and others as posturing.

341

Who was the "Mayor of Harlem"?

An orphan from Virginia, Bill "Bojangles" Robinson was making a living as a teenager in the 1890s as a "hoofer" (singer and dancer) around New York before he began honing his craft as a tap-dancer. He became a famous vaudeville performer and also made a name for himself performing with Cab Calloway at the Cotton Club. The first nationally famous black performer, he popularized tap dancing with his signature routine the "stair dance" and starred in a number of films with Shirley Temple (1928–2014). Robinson was named the unofficial "mayor of Harlem" by a group of white city leaders in 1934. A larger-than-life character, "Uncle Bo" Robinson had already been made an honorary special deputy sheriff and given a pearl-handled revolver by the NYPD, which he used to foil a mugging in Pittsburgh only to be mistakenly shot by a responding police officer. Robinson went on stage two days later, his wounded arm still in a sling.

When Robinson died in 1949, he left behind one particularly vibrant legend. According to the story, Robinson always made a point of stopping to rub the tall elm called the "Tree of Hope" at Adam Clayton Powell Jr. Boulevard between 131st and 132nd streets for good luck, as did many Harlem entertainers. When the tree died, Robinson paid for a memorial plaque to be left at the site. The tree's stump was moved to the Apollo Theater, where performers rub it for good luck to this day.

The Actors Studio's approach attracted actors like Paul Newman (1925–2008), Robert Duvall (1931–), Dustin Hoffman (1937–), and Marilyn Monroe (1926–1962)—who was eager to be taken seriously as an actress—to its school in a nineteenth-century church on West 44th Street. By far the Method's most famous adherent was Marlon Brando (1924–2004), whose off-kilter, visceral style as exemplified in works like Actors Studio co-founder Eliza Kazan's (1909–2003) *On the Waterfront* inspired an entire generation of actors.

What happened to Broadway in the 1970s?

In the mid-1970s, the Great White Way had seen better days. The drop in the city's older white upper-middle-class population (then and today Broadway's biggest constituency) meant that fewer shows could be mounted. This resulted in many theaters going "dark" for months at a time. The long run of smash postwar musicals like *West Side Story* and *The Sound of Music* trickled to an end. The decade did see a string of adventurous Stephen Sondheim musicals directed by Hal Prince (1928–). But while shows like *Company*, *Follies*, and *A Little Night Music* were rightfully acclaimed, none became the kind of steadily performing year-in, year-out musicals that Broadway needs as an anchor. By 1974, annual Broadway attendance had dropped to 6.6 million.

Which musical is credited with saving Broadway?

In April 1975, the Public Theater opened an odd little show called *A Chorus Line*, with music by Oscar-winning composer Marvin Hamlisch (1944–2012). It didn't tell one story in the manner of most musicals at the time. Instead, *A Chorus Line* was a series of vignettes about Broadway "gypsies," those hard-working chorus dancers hoofing away in anonymity in most of the big musicals, collated from their actual experiences by choreographer Michael Bennett. The show's big-hearted yearning, risqué material, modern rock-inflected score, and ridiculously catchy songs made it an immediate hit.

A Chorus Line transferred in July to Broadway's Shubert Theater, where it would be performed over six thousand times until finally closing in April 1990. Other hit musicals would follow *A Chorus Line*, and Broadway has certainly had other fallow periods. But the runaway success of *A Chorus Line* helped return Broadway to the center of the nation's cultural dialogue decades before *Hamilton* (also produced at the Public before moving uptown) turned into a new millennium cultural phenomenon.

What was the Great Theater Massacre?

By 1982, as many New Yorkers can attest, Times Square had fallen on hard times. Many wax nostalgic in the modern era for a period when the district was still full of peep shows and prostitutes. All that colorful seediness had an impact on the big business in the area: theater. With tourism already in a rocky place for the city, and visitors nervous about all the stories of crime in the area, Broadway shows were taking a hit. Due in part to falling ticket sales, as well as the urge for the kind of bulldoze-happy urban renovation still in vogue, many of the old theaters had to face the wrecking ball.

What is considered the worst Broadway show ever?

It is a certainty that many, many horrendous plays have come and gone from New York stages leaving little to no record of their impeccably bad taste. However, for the twentieth century at least, one play has left a stench in its wake that has stood the test of time. Arthur Bicknell's farcical murder mystery *Moose Murders* opened on February 22, 1983, at the Eugene O'Neill Theatre.

The effect is summed up in a *New York Times* review by Frank Rich, who suggests that in years hence, audience members who had witnessed *Moose Murders* would occasionally gather for reunions "in the noble tradition of survivors of the *Titanic*." Not to be outdone in its disdain, the *New Yorker* said the play "would insult the intelligence of an audience consisting entirely of amoebas," and *New York* wondered whether it had been staged by "a blind director repeatedly kicked in the groin." The show lasted just fourteen performances and became an indelible part of Broadway lore almost immediately.

The low point came in 1982, when five theaters were slated for demolition. A demonstration in March of that year led by many theater impresarios like Joseph Papp (1921–1991) and actors like Jason Robards (1922–2000) and Lauren Bacall protested the knocking down of the Helen Hayes and Morosco theaters; some of the actors performed selections of plays that been mounted at those historic venues dating back to the early twentieth century. Ultimately five theaters on the west side of Broadway between 45th and 46th streets were torn down and replaced in 1985 by the hulking and fortress-like Marriott Marquis. A forty-five-story hotel with a soaring atrium topped by a revolving restaurant, it resembles nothing so much as the looming and fortress-like Renaissance Center in downtown Detroit. The Marquis was sold to the city in part by the fact that it contains a (decent, it must be said, if generic in the classic 1980s style) theater for Broadway shows on the third floor.

What was the Public Theater originally?

Once upon a time, the Public Theater on Lafayette Street just below Astor Place was the Astor Library, and then later the Hebrew Immigrant Aid Society. Threatened with demolition (as with so many places in the city), the grand Victorian structure was saved in 1965 by the Landmarks Preservation Commission and the New York Shakespeare Festival, an audacious company under the tutelage of impresario Joseph Papp that had been reinventing the rules of performance in the city and working to connect the arts with the city's people.

Renaming itself the Public Theater, the company inaugurated the theater with its controversial (what with all that hippie nudity) musical *Hair* in 1967. In the decades that followed, the Public turned into one of the most formidable theatrical institutions in the city, midwifing groundbreaking works like *A Chorus Line, The Normal Heart,*

The Public Theater on Lafayette Street opened in 1967. It was renamed the Joseph Papp Public Theater in 1991 after Papp's death.

and *Hamilton* before sending them up to Broadway while continuing to run a variety of challenging works in its multi-theater venue.

Where can you see Shakespeare for free?

Parks commissioner Robert Moses was originally a fan of Papp, and the well-read Moses thought Papp's New York Shakespeare Festival was top-notch. Once his top aide, an inveterate conservative, took issue with Papp's liberalism, though, Moses began insisting that Papp start charging admission for his productions in Central Park. After a classic Moses campaign of character assassination (which included alleging Papp was a Communist) failed, the commissioner reportedly said, "Let's build the bastard a theater." The open-air Delacorte Theater was inaugurated in 1962 with a production of *The Merchant of Venice* starring James Earl Jones (1931–) and George C. Scott (1927–1999). Each summer, the Public Theater mounts two free plays, usually but not always Shakespearean, at the Delacorte. All the performances are free (tickets are assigned by in-person and online lotteries). The productions are nearly all top-notch, and not-infrequently toplined by surprisingly A-list talent.

Where is the Yiddish Walk of Fame?

One of the earliest live performance communities in New York was the Yiddish theater, which was centered on Second Avenue in the East Village, once known as the Yiddish Broadway. Starting in the mid-to-late nineteenth century, Eastern European Jewish immigrants produced and watched a plethora of old and original musicals, dramas, and comedies all performed in the language of the old country. There were also classic plays translated into Yiddish, from Wilde to Shakespeare.

The first Yiddish-only theater, The Grand on Chrystie and Grand streets, was built in 1902 and run by Jacob Adler (1855–1926), a Russian-born Yiddish theater star (his Skylock and Lear were the stuff of legend) whose daughter Stella Adler became one of the great instructors of Method acting. The Yiddish theatrical community's peak was probably 1925, when some fourteen playhouses from Manhattan to Brooklyn and the Bronx housed Yiddish productions. As the Yiddish-speaking immigrants aged or moved out of the city, and their English-speaking children took in Broadway plays and Hollywood movies, the audience dwindled. One popular venue, the Yiddish Art Theatre at Second Avenue and 12th Street, is now a movie theater, but many of the original Moorish Revival architectural flourishes can still be seen.

Today, on the 10th Street sidewalk just east of Second Avenue near the old 2nd Avenue Deli, can still be seen the Yiddish Walk of Fame, the fifty-odd metal plaques that commemorate stars of the Yiddish theater scene, including some who went on to greater fame, like Paul Muni (1895–1967) and Fyvush Finkel (1922–2016).

What is the oldest surviving Broadway theater?

One of the more striking facades for a Broadway theater is the grey limestone façade, half-dozen Corinthian columns, and distinctive wave-like marquee adorning the Lyceum

Opened in 1866 as the Theatre Français, the Lyceum (c. 1870 at left, and a 2009 photo at right) was renamed in 1871. It is the oldest Broadway theater still in operation.

Theatre on 45th Street. The Lyceum also happens to be probably (there are some varying accounts) the oldest continuously operating theater of any kind in the New York area. Its opening in 1903 was hailed as a boon for theatergoers. Not only was the Beaux Arts design and the foyer's marble staircases impeccably grand, but the auditorium was designed to bring seats closer to the stage and also without pillars that blocked views. The design resulted in an intimate space, one of Broadway's smallest, that's considered ideal for dramas and comedies with smaller casts. The theater was the brainchild of impresario Daniel Frohman (1851–1940), who had a well-appointed penthouse apartment installed at the top of the Lyceum and equipped with a small door through which he could watch performances. Producer David Belasco (1853–1931) was likely influenced by Frohman's penthouse to build his own, many times more lavish, living quarters at the top of the theater that still bears his name.

The theater has housed plays by the likes of Edward Albee (1928-2016), Clifford Odets (1906–1963), Neil LaBute (1963–), Athol Fugard (1932–), and Tom Stoppard (1937–). Charles Laughton (1899–1962) and Burt Lancaster (1913–1994) had their Broadway debuts on the boards here. Over the years, there have been several productions here that ran for hundreds of performances. The record-holder for longevity was the comedy *Born Yesterday*, which premiered in 1946 and ran for 1,642 performances.

What is the longest-running play in New York?

Shows on Broadway are almost by definition held in venues with multiple levels, many hundreds of seats, ushers, and all the other accoutrements of the professional theater—even in the smaller houses on its western verges—but there is the occasional oddity. In a rare second-floor space on Broadway that has not much in common with the nearby theaters except for having a stage and chairs, you can see the longest-running non-musical play in New York.

Perfect Crime by Warren Manzi (1955–2016) opened in Greenwich Village in April 1987 and has been playing somewhere in the city ever since then. A whodunit about a psychiatrist who may or may not have murdered her husband, it's charitably described as a confusing mishmash. The reason for its longevity has long baffled theater fans. One theory: it's a cheap ticket pitched to out-of-towners not too far from the TKTS booth.

What about the longest-running musical?

If you ask the average New Yorker who doesn't spend too much time ruminating on the Great White Way, they might have a couple answers to this question: *Cats*, or maybe *Phantom of the Opera*? *Phantom* comes close (at 11,000 performances and counting, it's the longest-running show on Broadway). The surprising answer, however, is actually a musical that hasn't intruded much into the non-theater consciousness. A magic-suffused musical about a boy and girl and a Romeo and Juliet-like love, *The Fantasticks* opened at the snug Sullivan Street Playhouse in Greenwich Village in 1960 with *Law & Order*'s Jerry Orbach (1935–2004) in the cast. It kept on at the same location night after night until closing in 2002, and reopening in 2006 at an upstairs space in the theater district.

MUSIC

Where was Tin Pan Alley?

At the end of the nineteenth century, a new type of popular music began to emerge in America, much of it written and published in New York. The name "Tin Pan Alley" was given to the geographically shifting cluster of music publishers who concentrated around 28th Street in the 1920s, and then later closer to Broadway, particularly the Brill Building at Broadway and 49th Street. These publishers essentially invented the modern music industry, particularly pioneering how to market a song into a hit, whether it was taking out ads in the newspaper or sending songwriters around to bars and theaters to get their songs performed. The list of Tin Pan Alley composers reads like a who's-who of American music: Irving Berlin (1888–1989), George M. Cohan (1878–1942), Cole Porter (1891–1964), Oscar Hammerstein II (1895–1960), and Fats Waller (1904–1943), to name a few.

Was jazz invented in New York?

If one wants to be technical about it, the date of the birth of jazz can be drawn to New Orleans around the turn of the century. This is when primarily black dance bands began incorporating elements of ragtime, blues, and African rhythms into the fast-paced and often improvised new style of music that would later be called America's true art form.

But just as the blues was born in the Mississippi Delta but needed the industry of Chicago labels to turn it into a phenomenon, jazz needed New York to truly expand itself.

At first in the early 1920s, jazz was centered in Chicago. But after New Orleansian Louis Armstrong (1901–1971) moved to New York in 1924, the center of gravity shifted with him. Armstrong was hired by Fletcher Henderson's Orchestra, one of the city's most popular big bands. By the end of the decade, the city was thronged with swing bands led by such immortals as Duke Ellington, Count Basie, and Cab Calloway, who gained international renown. Further fueling the growth of jazz as an art form wasn't just New York's large concentration of people eager to go out to hear exciting new live music every night, but the city's density of art-amplifying business from radio to music publishing and recording.

How did the Cotton Club become so famous?

The Club Deluxe was a four-hundred-seat nightclub that Jack Johnson—the first black heavyweight boxing champion, considered controversial for his habit of marrying white women—opened in Harlem in 1920 at 142nd Street and Lenox Avenue. It was taken over and reopened by gangster "Owney" Madden (1891–1965) in 1923 as the seven-hundred-seat Cotton Club. The faux-jungle decor played up a kitschy form of Africana for its whites-only clientele while serving up plenty of Madden's bootleg liquor and some of the best music being performed anywhere in the country. The club and its splashy music and dance "Negro Revues" was long a favorite stop for white Manhattan swells coming to Harlem for a night out. Ironically, for a club so central to the cultural history of black New York, blacks wouldn't be allowed in as customers for years, and then only if they were light-skinned.

First opened in 1920, the Cotton Club in Harlem became a hip place for singers, entertainers, poets, and authors. Although the original location closed, in 1977 the club (pictured above) opened at 125th Street in 1977.

But the Cotton Club's true fame dates to about 1927, when Duke Ellington's "Jungle Band" was hired as the house entertainment. Many Ellington classics like "Mood Indigo" were first performed there. His music was helped to reach a broader audience after CBS radio started broadcasting live from the venue. In 1931, Cab Calloway and his band took over music duties. With the help of their hit "Minnie the Moocher," Calloway was soon also launched to national and international fame.

What did many Harlem residents hate about the Cotton Club?

While the Cotton Club became a symbol of the Harlem Renaissance, helping to launch the careers of many other black performers like Lena Horne (1917–2010) and Bill "Bojangles" Robinson, the owners' racial policies (which included requiring the "sepia" chorus girls be lighter-skinned or "copper colored") gave it a more complicated legacy. Langston Hughes (1902–1967) said that he had never gone to the Cotton Club: "Harlem Negroes did not like the Cotton Club and never appreciated its Jim Crow policy in the very heart of their dark community. Nor did ordinary Negroes like the growing influx of whites toward Harlem after sundown … given the best ringside tables to sit and stare at the Negro customers—like amusing animals in a zoo." After the 1935 Harlem riots, the Cotton Club moved downtown to 48th Street and Broadway, where it stayed open until 1940.

How did jazz change in New York after the 1920s?

Once the economics of big bands became problematic, and tastes started to change, jazz began to fracture as a genre. In the 1930s and '40s room was made for smaller combos, and smoky vocalists like Billie Holiday. In the postwar decades, a new kind of raggedy experimentation gave birth to the eclectic bebop scene—Charlie Parker (1920–1955), Dizzy Gillespie (1917–1993)—that would be tied more to an artier, downtown and Greenwich Village scene, as compared to the swinging Midtown and Harlem nightclubs of the Jazz Age.

What role did New York play in rock and roll?

Rock and roll is one of the few great American cultural innovations of the twentieth century that New York didn't have much to do with originating, creatively. A sped-up offshoot of rhythm and blues, rock and roll was originated in the middle of the country by the likes of Chuck Berry (1926-) and Ike Turner (1931-2007) and popularized by DJs like Ohio's Alan Freed (1921–1965). But New York became tuned into the new fad after Freed took a slot at the city's WINS radio station in 1954. Freed's all-star revue shows at Brooklyn's Paramount Theater over the next few years became legendary.

As ever, New York was instrumental in getting the word out about rock and roll. New York-based labels like Atlantic Records helped popularize the music, and it wasn't long before studio musicians and songwriters in Manhattan's Tin Pan Alley were churning out about as many hits as their Southern California counterparts.

Why was folk music so popular in New York?

Politics and intellectuals is the easy answer. In the 1930s, folk music grew up alongside leftist agitators. Performers like Oklahoma's Woody Guthrie (1912–1967), who drew on classics and gave them a contemporary edge, were drawn to New York's progressive climate. This first folk revival, which also produced stars like Lead Belly, was followed in the 1950s and '60s by other performers like Bob Dylan, Pete Seeger (1919–2014), and Odetta (1930–2008), who brought a more introspective style to their songs. It's no surprise that through all these decades, folk music was most commonly performed in Washington Square Park and nearby coffeeshops like Gerde's Folk City, frequented by both the radicals of Greenwich Village and students at New York University.

Shown performing in 2013, Bob Dylan spent much of his early career performing and writing in New York.

Where did Bob Dylan write "Blowin' in the Wind"?

Much of New York cultural history is shrouded in a fog of mystery, promotion, self-aggrandizement, outright lies, the need for mythology, and just plain forgetfulness (there was more than cigarette smoke clouding the clubs). There are many stories repeated over the years that have taken on the patina of truth, whether or not they actually happened. Here's one example: a perennial figure in New York's cultural past, Robert Zimmerman of Hibbing, Minnesota, came to the Village to reinvent himself as Bob Dylan, post-Woody Guthrie troubadour and master of folkish ways. He was supposed to have written one of his most beloved songs, "Blowin' in the Wind," at the original Fat Black Pussycat on Macdougal Street. That has been disputed by Dylanologists, who note that a roster of performers at that club included Mama Cass (1941–1974), Richie Havens (1941–2013), and even Bill Cosby (1937–), but not Dylan. Later, Fat Black Pussycat moved up to its current spot on West 3rd Street across from the Blue Note. The space is currently occupied by a Mexican restaurant that finally painted over the old club's name on the walls just a few years ago.

When did disco start?

Starting in the 1960s, various discotheques like Ondine, Arthur, and Cheetah were following the European trend of nightclubs where instead of live bands, DJs played records for crowds who danced until dawn. In 1970, when rock and roll—whether of the radio-friendly or the fuzzed-up underground variety—was indisputably king, a New York promoter named David Mancuso (1944–) threw a Valentine's Day event called Love Saves the Day in an industrial space on lower Broadway called the Loft. Mancuso's innovative approach involved mixing tracks in such a way to create an active feedback loop between the crowd and the DJ.

Years would pass before there was any new music that could legitimately be called disco. Mancuso's catholic tastes—which included everything from Latin music to acid rock, as long as it could be mixed in a way that was danceable—probably helped to inspire the genre's early sound. The parties at the Loft, which the city frequently threatened to shut down even though it skirted regulation by not serving alcohol or being technically open to the public (thusly all the "invitations" that became de rigeur in dance culture), and other underground dance clubs like 12 West, were particularly popular with a minority and gay crowd. By the middle of the decade, the hedonistic and drug-fueled disco culture proved a popular escape valve for the population of an increasingly tension-filled city.

Why was everyone so intent on getting into Studio 54?

If one is looking for evidence of last-days decadence in New York during the pitfalling 1970s—which had an entirely different feel from the money-first decadence of the 1980s, except that both involved truckloads of cocaine—you wouldn't have to look much further than Studio 54. Still today the most famous nightclub in New York history, it was the unlikely brainchild of a couple of good Jewish boys from Brooklyn. Steve Rubell (1943–1989) was a steakhouse-chain manager before he and his partner Ian Schrager (1946–) got into the disco business. On April 26, 1977, Rubell and Schrager opened Studio 54 in Midtown's old Gallo Theater where Johnny Carson (1925–2005) once broadcast from. Almost instantly, the massive, multi-level club became the hottest ticket in town. No more was disco confined to small gay clubs or outer borough neighborhood discotheques; now it was ground zero for the country's booming celebrity culture.

While inside nubile male attendants poured champagne for visiting dignitaries and fashionably slumming A-listers, out on West 54th Street, the crowds clamored to get past a velvet rope line more zealously guarded than the Berlin Wall. It all provided easy pickings for the paparazzi looking to snap shots of the club's resident celebrities grooving into the wee hours. On the average night at Studio 54, one could find anybody from Mikhail Baryshnikov (1948–) and Andy Warhol to Salvador Dali (1904–1989) and Henry Kissinger bopping to the same disco beat. In 1980, the party came to an end when the owners were sentenced to three and-a-half years in prison for tax evasion. Later, the space was refashioned into a Broadway house for the revival company Roundabout Theatre; fittingly, its first show there was the doom-and-decadence Weimar musical *Cabaret*.

Where did punk get its start?

As in most things cultural, it's hard to make a definitive statement about precisely where or how a particular movement got its start. On the issue of punk, there is a still-unresolved push-and-pull between those pushing the London theory (glam rock, the Sex

Pistols, the Clash) and those favoring the New York school. The public perception of punk favors the flashier London style (full-color mohawks, elaborately studded leather, anarchic politics). New York's grottier mix of stripped-down back-to-basics power chords and snarly performance-art aggression started breaking out in the early mid-1970s, inspiring the British punk explosion that followed in 1976–1977.

One of the first showcases for proto-punk bands was the Mercer Arts Center, a multi-theater performance space that opened in 1971 in the Broadway Central Hotel, which had devolved from grand luxury hotel (the largest in the world when it opened in 1870) to crime- and drug-infested welfare hotel. In addition to off-Broadway plays and cabaret acts, the Mercer booked a groundbreaking slate of performers like glam-rock pioneers the New York Dolls, droning electronic noise-bandit duo Suicide, and punk poetess Patti Smith. After the long-crumbling Broadway Central collapsed in August 1973, killing four, the avant-garde scene that had gathered around the Mercer hived off to other venues like Max's Kansas City and CBGB's, cross-pollinating a fertile underground downtown art/music scene that would set the standard for culture well into the 1980s.

What does CBGB stand for?

Usually just referred to in the shortened possessive ("I was at a Dictators show at CBGB's back in the '70s when Jayne County got into it with this skinhead…"), the full name of the legendarily nasty little warren of a rock-and-roll bar on Bowery just below Spring Street was CBGB's (& OMFUG), which stood for Country, Bluegrass, Blues and Other Music for Uplifting Gourmandizers. The club's owner, Hilly Kristal (1931–2007), might have opened the place in 1973 to showcase the kind of music he liked. But bluegrass and blues were the last things the club would be remembered for. Starting in the mid-1970s, CBGB's started showcasing a disparate collective of sonic explorers ranging from surf rock throwbacks the Ramones, No Wavers Richard Hell and the Voidoids, and world-music devotees the Talking Heads to post prog-rock noodlers Television.

Not one of these bands sounded much like the genre that they gave birth to—Kristal's one dictum was that everybody had to play original material, and not covers.

What happened to CBGB's?

As the Bowery gentrified in the new millennium, the aging Kristal (who made a fortune off licensing the bar's logo to the briefly ubiquitous T-shirts) got bogged down in real estate battles and subpar heavy metal matinee shows. After a series of farewell concerts by bands that had gone on to great critical, if not necessarily popular, acclaim, CBGB's closed in 2006. In a fitting tribute to the mercenary maw of New York, it was replaced by an upscale clothing boutique. Patti Smith, who performed on the club's last night, described it to the *Times* as "a symptom of the empty new prosperity of our city."

Nevertheless, they all became known as the parents of punk rock. CBGB's was their rec room. Generations of musicians and dedicated fans cut their underground musical teeth there. Rarely was a grimy little bar like this remembered so fondly. The location, on a dangerously deserted stretch of Bowery near William S. Burroughs' (1914–1997) bunker, was as much of the appeal as the terrifying bathrooms were not. The Talking Heads immortalized it and another legendary underground music club in their song "Life During Wartime": "This ain't no Mudd Club / or CBGB."

Where did hip-hop begin?

There are almost as many variations on the origin story of hip-hop as there were DJs. Most of the stories, however, converge on one time and rather modest place. In 1973, Clive Campbell, a.k.a. D.J. Kool Herc (1955–), was handling the entertainment for parties at the first-floor community room in his Bronx apartment building at 1520 Sedgwick Avenue. Instead of just playing the right records to make people dance, Herc used two turntables to create a unique sound. He layered songs on top of each other, sometimes playing the same song on both turntables, slowing one down to the breakbeat over and over again. He threw just about any kind of song into his musical stew and also mixed in the Jamaican tradition of toasting, or talking over the beat. Herc thus turned the DJ into more the active style of performer common today than a passive purveyor of hit songs.

Herc's parties became so popular that by 1974 he was hosting larger events in nearby Cedar Park (where the sound systems were often illegally plugged into streetlights) and getting booked into Bronx nightclubs. It would take a few more years for hip-hop culture to truly coalesce in the Bronx but it had become a bonafide organic musical tradition years before anybody had heard of breakdancing or even disco.

What's better: East Coast or West Coast hip-hop?

The East Coast–West Coast rivalry in hip-hop is for the most part a thing of the past, particularly after it played a large role in the shooting deaths of California rapper Tupac Shakur in 1996 and New York's Biggie Smalls in 1997. But disregarding fans' preference of one style over another, the roll-call of great New York rappers is not to be trifled with. Besides inventing the form and fashion with b-boys in the late-1970s and early

The late East Coast rapper Biggie Smalls was a central figure in that region's style of music.

'80s, New York also mainstreamed it with the first group to go gold (Run-D.M.C., from Hollis, Queens) and first hip-hop film (1983's *Wild Style*), then threw graffiti into the mix, added political activism (Public Enemy), and branched out into the more intellectual Afrocentric hip-hop movement Native Tongues in the 1980s and '90s (A Tribe Called Quest, De La Soul, Queen Latifah). West Coast hip-hop briefly gained prominence with the advent of groups like N.W.A. and the Death Row Records label. But in the end, whatever city invented breakdancing probably gets to win that contest. And yes, that would be New York.

FILM AND TV

What was the first film shot on location in New York?

The first film shot on location in New York was most likely Thomas Edison's *Herald Square*. Edison's assistant William Heise (1847–1910) shot the short on May 11, 1896. Just a few seconds long, it shows streetcars and pedestrians bustling through the titular square in much the same fashion they do today.

Where was the first true movie studio built?

Thomas Edison, who started operating his own film company in West Orange, New Jersey, in 1891, did his best to crush the competition by patenting every stage of the film production process. But a number of competitors quickly sprang up. By the turn of the century, there were several film production companies based in the city churning out hundreds of silent films. In the heady rush of New York's early film industry, most shoots took place either on the bustling streets—the city's plethora of varied neighborhoods and natural backdrops in close vicinity making it perfect for shooting a variety of subjects—or in crudely fashioned stages like the one built in 1896 by the Biograph company on top of its 13th Street headquarters. Realizing it needed more room for its booming business, in 1906 the American Vitagraph Company created the country's, and probably the world's, first true standalone studio out in the wilds of Brooklyn's then mostly undeveloped Midwood neighborhood.

Over the next nine years, the complex expanded at a fast pace to keep up with Vitagraph's furious production schedule of up to eight films a week, including the first American feature-length Shakespeare adaptation, 1915's *A Midsummer Night's Dream*. Among the many who were said to have worked for Vitagraph in those early years were Boris Karloff (1887–1969), Fatty Arbuckle (1887–1933), Moe Howard (1897–1975), Oliver Hardy (1892–1957), and even Leon Trotsky (1879–1940)—as an extra, though that's generally believed to be a rumor. Vitagraph, which had for years been the country's largest film studio, opened facilities out in California during the 1920s, and was bought by Warner Bros. in 1925. The studio stayed in use over the years, with everything from *On the Waterfront* to *The Cosby Show* being shot there. The complex, including the iconic Vitagraph smokestack, was torn down in 2015.

What New York landmarks did King Kong climb?

In the 1933 film *King Kong*, when the gigantic ape escapes from the Broadway theater where he's being displayed and tears through Manhattan to find the woman he loves, he eventually climbs up the side of the 102-story Empire State Building. The sight of Kong clinging to the side of the recently completed skyscraper and battling Air Force biplanes before plummeting to his death on the city streets became one of the most arresting and iconic images of Golden Age American cinema. For the 1976 update, the filmmakers updated the premise by having Kong climb not the Empire State Building but the skyscraper that had just overtaken it as the world's tallest building: the World Trade Center. At the film's climax, Kong climbs the South Tower and leaps over to the North Tower before succumbing to gunfire from helicopter gunships and falling to the plaza below. Peter Jackson's 2005 version was a period-specific remake that put Kong back in 1930s New York and had him climbing the Empire State Building again, but this time after an interlude in Central Park that included shots of the Hoovervilles that proliferated there during the Great Depression.

A display case in the Empire State Building contains posters and other memorabilia from the movie *King Kong*.

What other movie monsters have rampaged through New York?

Q, the Winged Serpent (1982)—Giant flying Aztec god-lizard swoops around Manhattan, snatching up unsuspecting sunbathers to the confusion of the NYPD.

Ghostbusters (1984)—After an eruption of cross-dimensional astral spooks terrifies the city, Bill Murray and the gang have to defeat the skyscraper-sized Stay Puft Marshmallow Man.

Mimic (1997)—In one of Guillermo del Toro's less-remembered horror flicks, giant cockroaches emerge from the New York sewers.

Godzilla (1998)—The American remake of the Japanese monster mash series has the undersea dinosaur running around Manhattan and causing havoc.

Cloverfield (2008)—This faux-documentary monster movie has a little-seen Godzilla-like creature devastating the city in particularly offensive ways, such as tearing the head off the Statue of Liberty.

How did New York become such a popular setting for the movies?

After the film industry set up shop in Hollywood, New York was generally represented only in stock footage of street life. All of those grand apartments filled with fabulously dressed swells were created on California soundstages. Until well after the war, filmmakers generally only shot "on location" when they were looking to get some atmosphere on the cheap for a B-grade genre flick. However, notable films like the 1948 noir *The Naked City* (which later spawned a revolutionary TV series that set the template for everything from *Dragnet* to *Law and Order*) organically used the bustle and chaos of New York's streets to great dramatic advantage.

In 1965, Mayor Lindsay (who was frequently referred to as having movie-star looks) signed an executive order that slashed most of the red tape involved with shooting movies on New York streets. This resulted in a great increase in the number of productions that filmed at least in part in the city.

Why was this not always good for New York?

One possible downside of Lindsay's move was that given the state of crime and decrepitude that the city was already then sliding into, this meant that most of the movies shot in New York would be far in tone from the black-and-white comedies of an earlier era. Films like *Little Murders*, *Taxi Driver*, *The French Connection*, *Superfly*, *The Panic in Needle Park*, *Midnight Cowboy*, and *Above 110th Street* refracted a frightening, decayed, and frequently apocalyptic vision of the city around the world that would take years to disperse.

Futuristic films showing the city as a decayed wasteland, like the 1982 sci-fi biker exploitation film *1990: The Bronx Warriors*, shot on location in the borough's more arson-plagued districts, and 1981's *Escape from New York*, in which Manhattan is turned into a giant prison, didn't help matters; though it should be noted that much of the latter film was actually shot in St. Louis.

Where did *The Rocky Horror Picture Show* become a cult classic?

In the mid–1970s, New York featured a number of idiosyncratically programmed movie houses that veered rather far from the standard fare. One of those was the Waverly Theater, in Greenwich Village at 6th Avenue and West 3rd Street. In addition to a solid slate of foreign films and classic retrospectives, the Waverly had been doing a good business showing films like *El Topo* and *Night of the Living Dead* to the midnight-movie crowd. In 1975, 20th Century Fox had released its big-screen adaptation of the underground London cult stage show *The Rocky Horror*

Actor Tim Curry (shown here in 2010) played the cross-dressing alien Dr. Frankenfurter in the cult classic *The Rocky Horror Picture Show,* which debuted in Greenwich Village in 1975.

Picture Show to general bafflement (rock operas about "transsexual" aliens not being to everybody's taste). It soon disappeared from theaters.

The following year, though, the Waverly put the film into its midnight-movie slot. Soon, the same audience members were not only coming back night after night, they were dressing up as some of the film's characters, acting out some scenes (particularly the show-stopping dance number "Time Warp"), and shouting back at the screen. This went on for months and essentially invented the idea of the cult "midnight movie." Incredibly, the phenomenon only spread from there, with similar showings of *The Rocky Horror Picture Show* (just *Rocky* to the initiated) popping up in cities around the country, each one attracting its own core of performers and lip-synchers following variations on the same talk-back script worked out in those first months at the Waverly. The theater currently occupying the old Waverly space, the IFC Center, still shows midnight films as an homage, but not *Rocky*. Nevertheless, four decades-plus on, there is just about always *some* theater somewhere in the city showing it. Bring your own confetti and flashlight.

How prominent was New York in the development of television?

Television didn't begin in New York; America's first television station began broadcasting in Washington, D.C., in 1928. But New York played a crucial in the development of the medium. In the 1930s, the two biggest radio broadcasters, Columbia Broadcasting System (CBS) and the National Broadcasting Company (NBC), started television stations. In 1939, NBC broadcast Franklin Delano Roosevelt's speech from the opening of the 1939 World's Fair in Queens, making him the first president to appear on television. The same year, a Reds-Dodgers doubleheader at Ebbets Field became the first-ever major league baseball game broadcast live on television. Of course, TV sets were still so rare at the time that only about three thousand watched.

That number increased in the postwar years, spiking in the 1950s. Initially a third of the homes with television sets were in New York. This made sense, because TV production was based there, where producers could make use of the city's depth of theater performers for their live broadcasts of variety and comedy shows, as well as theater. Starting with the popularity of the California-shot recorded sitcom *I Love Lucy* after its premiere in 1951, though, the center of gravity began to move west to Hollywood, home to the same film industry that it was in the process of dethroning.

Who hosted the first TV talk show in New York?

One type of television show that New York specialized in was the late-night talk show. NBC's *The Tonight Show* was the gold standard, broadcasting out of New York from 1954 to 1972. Unlike the more manic variety shows or rigidly formulaic Westerns and sitcoms that typified television at the time, the show's first host, Steve Allen (1921–2000), delivered a dry and wry comic tone throughout the monologues and celebrity interviews. Johnny Carson took the reins in 1962 and within a few years began to specialize in gags mocking the New York crime rate: "New York is an exciting town where something is happening all the time … most, unsolved."

357

In 1972, Carson famously broke with tradition by moving the show, which millions of Americans fell asleep to every night, to Burbank, California; but he at least had the decency to continually mock his disappointingly bland new home. In 2014, new host Jimmy Fallon moved *The Tonight Show* back to New York, where onetime Carson protégé David Letterman (1947–) had hosted his more sarcastic, parodic (and some would say, more truly New York, even though both he and Carson were Midwesterners) talk show from 1982 to 2015.

What was the first TV sitcom?

The Rise of the Goldbergs was a long-running fifteen-minute radio drama by Gertrude Berg (1899–1966) about a Jewish family in the Bronx that started broadcasting in 1929. It was one of the few such mainstream shows at the time to deal directly with issues of ethnicity and class. Berg, who wrote and starred in the show, turned it into a situation comedy for CBS in 1949. *The Goldbergs* was far less overt about the family's ethnicity and less topical than the radio version (which wrestled with religious discrimination and Kristallnacht). The first true television sitcom, *The Goldbergs* ran for several years (brief interruptions followed switching of networks and one hiatus due to the Red Scare blacklisting one of the show's leads), eventually moving the family out to the suburbs, much like many New Yorkers were doing. Since the show was mostly shot live, a majority of its episodes no longer exist.

How do you get to Sesame Street?

Ever since it premiered on public television in 1969, the children's show *Sesame Street* has given kids around the country, and later the world, their first real glimpse of what New York is like. The set for the show, with its subway stop, deli, diversity of people, and brownstones is something of an amalgam of different New York neighborhoods from the time. The show's designer used now-demolished San Juan Hill for much of his research for the show's never specifically located generic New York neighborhood.

Who were the Not Ready for Prime Time Players?

In the early 1970s, one of the country's most popular publications was the monthly satire magazine *National Lampoon*. Located in New York, the *Lampoon*, with its edgy anti-establishment vibe and Ivy League-educated staff, became the template for post-Vietnam War humor. When they expanded into radio and live performances, their audience became even bigger.

In 1975, producer Lorne Michaels (1944–) premiered a late-night comedy-sketch show on NBC called *Saturday Night Live* which essentially poached the cream of *Lampoon*'s writers and performers. Ironically, though the opening montage reflected an appropriately gritty view of New York and the show would become iconic for the city, many of its performers came out of the Chicago school of improv comedy. Originally called the Not Ready for Prime Time Players, that first cast of *Saturday Night Live* (still on the air over four decades later) included such immortals as Dan Aykroyd (1952–), John Belushi (1949–1982), Chevy Chase (1943–), and Gilda Radner (1946–1989).

TV producer Lorne Michaels is famous for creating the late-night comedy show *Saturday Night Live*.

How big is the TV industry in New York these days?

Due to a combination of changing tastes, a rapidly evolving new-media landscape, tax incentives, and a broader range of facilities, New York has started to rapidly overtake Southern California as one of the busiest TV production locations in the country. The combined annual contribution of film and TV productions to the city was almost $9 billion, supporting over 100,000 full-time jobs. In 2016, there were nearly fifty episodic TV series being shot in the city, ranging from Marvel superhero shows to sitcoms and HBO series like *Girls*.

ART

Who started the first great American art movement?

The painters of the Hudson River School of the mid-nineteenth century are generally considered the first true artistic movement in the United States. Painters like Frederic E. Church (1826–1900) and Asher B. Durand (1796–1866) became known for their sweeping, panoramic landscape paintings of unspoiled wilderness, particularly inspired by the Hudson River Valley. Ironically, many of the painters were based in the city of New York, a subject they tended not to consider worthy of their time.

Why was the 1913 Armory art show so controversial?

In 1913, the Fighting 69th's Armory at 25th Street and Lexington Avenue hosted the International Exhibition of Modern Art. Unlike the shows that are still held there today, this one caused something more than a few notices in *Art in America*. Among the 1,600-odd pieces of art were pieces from Picasso, van Gogh, Constantin Brancusi (1876–1957), and Edouard Manet (1832–1883), none of whom yet had any profile in America, where realistic representational art was still the standard. The odd-seeming modernist works, with their abstracted and fractured styles, raised eyebrows and hackles, none more so than Marcel Duchamp's (1887–1968) *Nude Descending a Staircase, No. 2*. Visitors gathered in large numbers to gawk at and often ridicule the Cubist painting, which doesn't appear to have either a nude or a staircase. The controversy over Duchamp's painting (which one critic called "an explosion in a shingle factory") and others drew crowds, ironically helping to spread the show's experimental and supposedly threatening ideas.

Who painted *Nighthawks*?

Edward Hopper (1882–1967) was born north of New York in the small town of Nyack but spent most of his life in the city. Influenced by European painters like Edgar Degas (1834–1917) and Manet, Hopper's style tended toward sharp and richly saturated colors, along with sharp lines and a broodingly cinematic mood. He was represented in the 1913 Armory show, but didn't begin to gain attention until years later. The 1942 haunting *Nighthawks* shows four customers and a waiter in a brilliantly illuminated diner spilling light into the dark city streets outside. Some of Hopper's other famous paintings like *House by the Railroad* are more rural in style.

But *Nighthawks* and 1939's *New York Movie* (in which a theater usher stands alone while a crowd watches a movie) captured an iconic sense of isolation and the modern city that has ever since connected Hopper, who kept a studio in Greenwich Village for most of his life, to New York. The Whitney Museum has the deepest selection of Hopper's works, with other pieces on view at MoMA. Unfortunately for Hopper fans in New York, *Nighthawks* itself is in the collection at the Art Institute of Chicago.

Who was the most important New York art critic of the twentieth century?

In the postwar years, the art world in general and in New York in particular was being pulled between the poles of representational and abstract work. Standing firmly in the abstract camp was New York-based Clement Greenberg (1909–1994), who covered the burgeoning art scene for *The Nation*, *Commentary*, and other magazines. At the height of his influence during the 1940s and '50s, Greenberg's championing of artists like Jackson Pollock (1912–1956) helped make their careers. By the time Greenberg's influence began to wane in the 1960s, abstraction had practically become the New York art world's default mode.

Did Andy Warhol actually film the Empire State Building?

A shy kid from Pittsburgh, Andy Warhol worked as a commercial artist in New York in the 1950s before becoming the world's most famous artist. Adopting an assembly-line procedure, Warhol churned out a massive body of work that played with the modern obsession with celebrity and reflected it. Many of his most popular works were silkscreened images of popular celebrities, consumer goods, or photographs from the tabloid media.

Creatively restless, Warhol also branched out into live entertainment (the Exploding Plastic Inevitable multimedia shows of the 1960s on St. Mark's Place), music promotion (the Velvet Underground), publishing (*Interview* magazine, the bible for the downtown art crowd), and film. Using his entourage of "Superstars" like Candy Darling (1944–1974) and Nico (1938–1988), Warhol produced soporific films that played with an audience's expectations, to put it mildly. *Empire* (1965) is one of his most famous and simple: It's

Pop artist Andy Warhol filmed the Empire State Building for eight hours straight in *Empire*.

eight hours of footage of the skyscraper. That's it. Upon its release, the *Village Voice* proclaimed Warhol "the most revolutionary of all filmmakers working today."

Why did Keith Haring paint *Crack Is Wack*?

In the mid-1980s, two very different trends came together in an unexpected way. Keith Haring (1958–1990) was a downtown artist who had started experimenting with graffiti in the subway during the late 1970s and a few years after graduated to gallery and museum shows. His exuberant style was instantly recognizable and poster-ready, with simply drawn cartoon figures dancing or vibrating against bright backgrounds. Even though he was getting hundreds of thousands of dollars for his canvases by the mid-1980s, Haring kept a foot in commerce (selling T-shirts and toys with his work out of his own Pop Shop in SoHo and doing ads for Absolut) and activism, incorporating AIDS awareness and anti-apartheid messages into his work. In 1986, as the crack epidemic was wreaking havoc around New York, Haring painted a large mural titled *Crack Is Wack* on the wall of a handball court in Harlem. The mural is still there, in a playground at 128th Street and Harlem River Drive.

How many art museums are there in New York?

For most of New York's history, the only place to see art was in the homes of the wealthy, or the odd art academy putting on a show of its members' work. Art museums have been a relatively recent, and mostly twentieth-century development. The last century-plus saw an explosion of museums all over the city, particularly where the arts are concerned.

Currently there are at least two dozen museums dedicated at least in part to presenting works of art to the public. They cover a great diversity of interests, from modern (MoMA, Guggenheim) to American (Whitney), classical (The Cloisters), cinema (Museum of the Moving Image), sculpture (Isamu Noguchi Garden Museum), book arts (Morgan Library), photography (International Center of Photography), and also, well, everything (Metropolitan Museum of Art).

How many art galleries are there?

New York isn't just the nation's artistic nerve center, it's also its primary marketplace. All those prospective art buyers need somewhere to check out the new works on offer, and the city's marketplace is willing to oblige. Today there are around six hundred galleries in New York, roughly half of those concentrated in Chelsea. Many are open to the public.

Where are some of New York's greatest paintings found?

One: Number 31 (MoMA)—Jackson Pollock's massive canvas is nine feet by thirteen of beautifully orchestrated chaos. It stands as one of the most dynamic examples of Pollock's "drip painting," whose action-oriented style (Pollock would stand over his canvases and fling and slash paint at it) became one of the most bewitching examples of postwar abstract art popularized in the New York scene.

Portrait of Adele Bloch-Bauer I (Neue Gallerie)—Sometimes known as the "Woman in Gold" painting, Gustav Klimt's (1862–1918) 1907 portrait of the wealthy Austrian patron of the arts, drenched in gold and flecked with bright colors, showcases the painter's sumptuous and sweeping technique. After taking Klimt three years to finish, it was stolen by the Nazis in 1938 and only returned to the Bloch-Bauers in 2006 after a lengthy legal battle, chronicled in the 2015 film *Woman in Gold*.

Les Demoiselles d'Avignon (MoMA)—When Picasso revealed this painting in 1907, it created a furor in multiple ways. First, there was the style, a fractured and splintered approach that pre-figured his turn from representation to Cubism. Second, there was the subject matter of five naked women proudly displaying themselves; the title referred to a Barcelona street known for its brothels. Picasso called the controversial piece "my exorcism painting."

The Subway (Whitney)—This brightly colored yet dark-spirited George Tooker (1920–2011) painting from 1950 shows a coven of commuters hustling through a subway station whose corners, long passageways, and stairways loom like Escher-like traps. An iconic New York work of art, it also captures the paranoia and dislocation of the postwar years throughout America.

Wheat Field with Cypresses (The Met)—While maybe not one of van Gogh's most instantly recognizable works, this 1889 work is by far one of his most exuberant and memorable. The golden wheat field and green cypresses in the foreground are ripe with color and wind-tossed, while the sky above is a swirling, dancing riot of whites, greens, and blues. Oddly, this is just one of three nearly identical paintings Van Gogh made of the same subject.

WRITING

JOURNALISM

What was the first New York newspaper?

The inaugural issue of New York's first newspaper, the *New-York Gazette*, appeared on the streets of Manhattan on November 8, 1725. New York was the third colony with a newspaper, having been beaten to the punch by Massachusetts and Pennsylvania. The *Gazette* was run by publisher William Bradford (1719–1791). Frank Luther Mott's *American Journalism: A History* notes that the paper wasn't much to behold, being merely a "small two-page paper, poorly printed, and containing chiefly foreign news from three to six months old, state papers, lists of ships entered and cleared, and a few advertisements." Bradford's royalist leanings—and, presumably, a hunger for a more substantive publication than the *Gazette*—led to the city's second newspaper, the *New York Weekly Journal*, which was started up eight years later by a former employee of Bradford's, John Peter Zenger (1697–1746). The *Gazette*, considered a mouthpiece for the colonial government, folded in 1744.

Who was the first New York newspaperman to be put on trial?

Today's New York media landscape is hardly as freewheeling as it once was—i.e., no battling brigades of "newsies." Once upon a time, though, the penalties for journalists who ran afoul of powerful interests were far harsher than today. John Peter Zenger was a German Palatine who emigrated at the age of thirteen in 1710. After several years of indentured labor as a printer's apprentice, he set up his own printing business in 1726. In 1733 Zenger began publishing the *New York Weekly Journal*, the territory's first independent political newspaper. Its editorial stance was very critical of colonial governor

---

How did the Zenger trial affect the publishing world?

This decision was a crucial factor in establishing the colonies' tradition of free speech and a free press, and it helped inspire the Constitution's first amendment. The vigorous nature of American, and particularly New York, journalism was soon evident. By 1807 there were over twenty newspapers published in the city. In 1870, ninety newspapers were being published in New York. Incredibly, by 1930, that number would reach 1,000. The nineteenth century definitively established New York as the capital of the nation's media business, a title it has never relinquished.

William Cosby (1690–1736), who was more used to being lionized in the pages of the *Gazette*.

In 1734, Zenger was arrested for libel; even though he hadn't written the offending articles, Zenger as publisher was held legally responsible. Zenger sat in jail for a year before going to court; his wife continued to publish the *New York Weekly Journal* during his incarceration. The highly publicized trial finally began in April 1735 at City Hall (later Federal Hall). Zenger's attorney, Alexander Hamilton, made a stirring argument that "the truth is a defense against libel." The jury determined that the articles in question were based on fact and so found Zenger not guilty.

What was the "penny press"?

In the early nineteenth century, improvements in printing technology increased the possible size of newspapers and the speed with which they could be produced. One of the results of this was the growth of publications for both niche and wider audiences. The 1820s saw the introduction of newspapers aimed at Spanish speakers and also the country's first black newspaper, *Freedom's Journal*. The first of the city's so-called "penny papers" was probably the *New York Sun*, which started in 1833 and carried a heavy dose of human-interest stories. The *Sun* was swiftly followed by dozens of competitors, most importantly the *New York Herald* in 1835.

The intensely competitive penny papers kept introducing new elements to attract readers, from financial and sports coverage to overseas bureaus and larger Sunday editions that soon became a mainstay of the daily city paper. In 1841 the *Herald*'s chief rival, the *New York Tribune*, began operations under the leadership of New York's first true media baron, Horace Greeley (1811–1872).

New York Tribune founder Horace Greeley also pursued politics and was a U.S. congressman for a year and a candidate for the presidency in 1872 on the Liberal Republican Party ticket.

Who was Horace Greeley?

A printer's apprentice who started his career in Vermont and later one of America's most vociferous abolitionists, Horace Greeley left for New York in 1831 and within just a few years fundamentally realigned the city's media environment. After founding a literary paper called *The New-Yorker*, Greeley worked on campaign publications and became heavily involved in Whig party politics. In 1841, Greeley founded the *New York Tribune* as a pro-

Whig paper; he would be its editor for the next thirty one years. His so-called "Gospel according to St. Horace" was based on support for labor and women's rights. Greeley was a diehard proponent of the Homestead Act's potential for giving the chance for land ownership to a larger part of the country's population, and he would later be attributed with the statement, "Go west, young man" (which he at the very least helped popularize in the pages of his paper).

An even-greater passion of Greeley's was abolition, which he vigorously pursued in the pages of *The Trib*. He famously published an open letter addressed to President Lincoln on August 19, 1862, that was called "The Prayer for Twenty Millions" and excoriated Lincoln for not pursuing a more dedicated anti-slavery agenda.

Who started the gossip column?

Surprisingly, given how important it became, the gossip column—in which tidbits of information about high society or celebrities ranging from the quotidian to highly scandalous are bandied about with breathless excitement—came relatively late to the American newspaper business. Benjamin Franklin published some gossipy items under the pseudonym Busy Body. In 1840, James Gordon Bennett Sr.'s (1795–1872) *New York Herald* inaugurated the country's first true gossip column. Before then, journalists focused their coverage on popular subjects like politics, sports, and crime, and all of the biggest figures in those fields. But the new column was the start of the American media's treating the upper classes as newsworthy simply due to their societal status, and taking advantage of the courts' high bar for proving libel. There was a bit of defensiveness to the development, with Bennett announcing that his new column would "prove that American upper-class life was just as dazzling as that of the European aristocracy."

The gossip column proved popular with readers and Bennett used the rest of the paper to more completely cover the city's ever-burgeoning ranks of extremely wealthy residents. In 1848, he went so far as to print the complete text of John Jacob Astor's will on the *Herald*'s front page. The gossip column form was later perfected by New York practitioners like Maury Paul (1890–1914), aka the first of many writers to use the byline "Cholly Knickerbocker," and Walter Winchell (1897–1972), who became nearly as famous as the celebrities whose peccadillos they wrote about so breathlessly. It can still be found today in the *New York Post*'s "Page Six," which continues the style of teasing innuendo.

Which New York newspaper hired Karl Marx as a correspondent?

From 1852 to 1863, the fathers of modern socialism, Karl Marx (1818–1883) and Friedrich Engels (1820–1895), sent dispatches to the *New York Tribune* from London. Published under Marx's name, the articles covered subjects from around the world, though not surprisingly often focusing on issues of class and inequality. The *Tribune* stopped carrying Marx's work at the height of the Civil War, when matters closer to home took precedent at the paper. Before then, Marx wrote about President Lincoln's issuing of the Emancipation Proclamation, one of the acts that would help spark the Draft Riots that gutted the *Tribune*'s offices: "Up to now we have witnessed only the first act of the Civil War—the constitutional waging of war. The second act, the revolutionary waging of war, is at hand."

How did the *New York Times* defend itself from an angry mob during the Draft Riots?

At the zenith of the 1863 Draft Riots, several institutions of power became the target of angry mobs. One of those institutions was the *New York Times*, whose founder and first editor, Henry Jarvis Raymond, had made clear his strong opposition to the rioters' anti-draft stance. Prior to the riots, by not precisely clear means, the pro-Union Raymond obtained three pieces of fearsome modern weaponry: the Gatling gun. Invented by Richard Jordan Gatling (1818–1903) and first put into production earlier that year for the Union army, the guns were large, crank-operated, carriage-mounted multi-barrel machine guns that could churn out up to 3,000 rounds a minute.

Apparently, just the sight of the Gatling guns (one of them manned by Raymond himself) was enough to convince the lightly armed mob that the *Times* building was not going to be worth the effort. They instead turned to attack the nearby offices of the *New York Tribune*, whose founder and editor Horace Greeley was an outspoken abolitionist. The office was gutted by the mob in a matter of minutes, before they were routed by a squad of policemen.

What was America's first comic strip?

Starting in 1895, readers of the *Sunday World* were introduced to something still relatively new in publishing: a weekly illustrated story about the strange and humorous adventures of down-and-out street kids and immigrants called *Hogan's Alley*. Written and drawn by Richard Felton Outcault (1863–1928), who had previously worked as an illustrator for Thomas Edison, the strip featured a curious figure known as the Yellow Kid who would for a time become one of the most popular characters in American popular culture. The strip's surrealistic violence and punchy satire of the upper classes had great appeal to the city's working-class population, particularly its many recent immigrants with little or no command of written English. It soon became one of the paper's most popular features.

Outcault's Yellow Kid was poached by William Randolph Hearst from the *Sunday World* for his *New York Journal* in 1896. Since Outcault's first paper still had the rights to his strip, for a while there were dueling Yellow Kid comic strips. Today, Outcault's Yellow Kid is considered one of the world's first true comic strips, occupy-

A panel from Richard Felton Outcault's *Hogan's Alley,* the first comic strip published regularly in the United States.

> ### Which New York paper confirmed that yes, there is a Santa Claus?
>
> In 1897, an eight-year-old girl named Virginia Hanlon wrote a letter to the *New York Sun* in which she bemoaned the fact that her friends kept telling her that there wasn't a Santa Claus. Trying to get an answer, she threw herself on the mercy of the paper since her father told her, "If you see it in *The Sun*, it's so."
>
> On September 21, the paper published its response. The column excoriated her friends for being victims of "the skepticism of a skeptical age" and expostulated that in the greater cosmos, man's intellect was tiny "as compared with the boundless world about him." This was mere preamble, though, to the column's ringing and only slightly tongue-in-cheek endorsement of a magical view of the universe—"The most real things in the world are those that neither children nor men can see. Did you ever see fairies dancing on the lawn? Of course not, but that's no proof that they are not there"—supported on the broad shoulders of one mythical figure. The *Sun*'s words, "Yes, Virginia, there is a Santa Claus," became one of the building blocks of twentieth-century American Christmas mythology.

ing a revered place in the form's hierarchy, along with *Little Nemo in Slumberland* and *Krazy Kat*.

Was *Newsies* based on a true story?

As usual in these cases, the answer is, sort of. During the Spanish-American War, the fiercely competitive *Evening World* and the *Evening Journal* newspapers, owned by Joseph Pulitzer (1847–1910) and William Randolph Hearst respectively, raised their issues' wholesale prices to cover the expenses of war coverage. By the following year, the prices were still the same but the papers were selling less. This irritated the thousands of "newsies," the sometimes homeless young boys who hawked the papers on the street. They earned at best thirty cents a day and didn't like having to pay more to buy the papers up front, not to mention the no-refund policy for unsold papers. In retaliation, the newsies called a strike that summer, refusing to sell either the Hearst or Pulitzer papers. Ironically, many other newspapers were delighted to run any story that embarrassed their rivals, highlighting the newsies' pluck and showmanship, not to mention fantastic nicknames (Crutchy Morris, Hunch Maddox, Jimmy the Goat). The *New York Tribune* quoted Kid Blink, a newsie who was blind in one eye, riling up a couple thousand fellow strikers: "Dis is a time which tries de hearts of men. Dis is de time when we'se got to stick together like glue…. We know wot we wants and we'll git it even if we is blind."

The striking newsies marched in protest and went after scabs with a street-fighting fervor. After a couple weeks, the publishers compromised by agreeing to give the newsies credit for papers they couldn't sell. The story was mostly lost to history, until historian David Nasaw wrote about it in his 1985 book *Children of the City: At Work and at Play*.

Rather incredibly, that led to an ambitious but unsuccessful 1992 Disney movie musical called *Newsies* (starring future Batman Christian Bale). It developed a cult following and was then recast in 2012 as a Tony-winning Broadway musical.

What is the most famous newspaper headline in New York history?

Some would argue for the hammering headline on the front page of the October 30, 1975, *New York Daily News*. Succinct, dramatic, not entirely true, "Ford to City: Drop Dead" had it all. It achieved immortality not for accurately quoting the president (Ford never said that) but for perfectly encapsulating the bitterness many residents felt toward the federal government at a time when the city was facing bankruptcy. Less remembered than that punchy headline is the fact that Ford soon acquiesced and approved financial aid to help keep New York solvent. But another constituency would push for another headline that has yet to be surpassed for brazen wordplay.

On April 15, 1983, the front page of the *New York Post* screamed: "Headless Body in Topless Bar." The story concerned one Charles Dingle, who had been drinking in a Queens bar before going on a horrific rampage in which he shot bar owner Herbert Cummings dead and took several women hostage. He raped one of the women and forced another to behead Cummings's corpse. Dingle then put Cummings' head in a box labeled "Fine Wines," stole a taxi, and fled with two of his hostages. He was arrested several hours later after falling asleep at the wheel. The resulting headline quickly at-

The headquarters of the *New York Times* are located in Manhattan at 620 8th Ave.

tained cult status, and gave its author, managing editor Vincent Musetto (1941–2015), a cachet few newspaper editors ever receive. (By contrast, the *New York Times* headline for the same incident was "Owner of a Bar Shot to Death; Suspect is Held," proving why they call it the Old Gray Lady.) According to one story, Musetto came up with the headline before it was certain that the bar ever had topless performers. In a rare display of fact-checking for the shoot-from-the-hip publication, the *Post* sent a reporter out to Queens to confirm that detail. Some of Musetto's other *Post* headlines included: "Khadafy Goes Daffy," "500-Pound Sex Maniac Goes Free," and the one he called his personal favorite, "Granny Executed in Her Pink Pajamas."

How many newspapers can New York claim today?

The nation-wide trend of declining circulation due to the drop in classifieds and advertising, not to mention the ever-broader access to news online, has left most big cities, which as recently as the 1980s had at least a couple competing daily papers, with maybe one if they're lucky. New York, however, as the reigning capital of American news media, can yet stake its claim to having more newspapers on hand for people to read than anywhere else in America. Here's a quick rundown:

- *New York Times*—After Alfred Ochs bought the *New York Daily Times* in 1896 he introduced the slogan, "All the News That's Fit to Print." A reputation for stuffiness (P. T. Barnum reportedly bellowed "You forgot to monger ill-founded rumors! You forgot to vilify your political opponents in the most scabrous terms imaginable!") led to nicknames like the "Old Gray Lady." For most of the twentieth century, the *Times* was the leading daily American newspaper. The so-called "paper of record," its unparalleled reporting resources, deep bench of writers, and war chest of Pulitzer prizes and citations (a record 119 by 2016) allowed it to set the pace for what the nation's other journalists felt was worth covering. Recent challenges aside, the *Times* has retained its leading status ahead of brisk competition from the *Wall Street Journal* and the *Washington Post*. As of 2015, its circulation was over 2.1 million, including a swiftly rising number of digital-only subscribers, which dramatically spiked in response to the fake-news glut during the 2016 presidential election.

- *Wall Street Journal*—In 1884, journalist Charles Dow (1851–1902) began hand-delivering a "Customers' Afternoon Letter" containing stock data (just eleven, to start) to customers in Wall Street. Five years later, the Dow Jones & Company news agency launched the *Wall Street Journal*. At first the paper stuck mostly to business and economics news, though the first front page did include a notice about a bare-knuckled prize fight, but later branched out into feature articles and political coverage. The *Journal's* mix of down-the-middle reporting and staunchly free-market editorial page politics made it the preferred upper-class broadsheet through the twentieth century. In a daring acquisition that rattled a newspaper community already hard hit by new media woes, consolidation, and worries over declining quality, Rupert Murdoch (1931–) grabbed it in 2007 for $5.6 billion. The current circulation figure of around 2.4 million is viewed by some as more inflated by bulk purchases than most.

369

- *New York Post*—The oldest, continuously published newspaper in the United States, it was founded by Alexander Hamilton in 1801 as the *New York Evening Post*. For years a passionate and occasionally eloquently liberal tabloid, mixing over-the-top headlines with the gracious moral rectitude of Murray Kempton's (1917–1997) columns, the *Post* was snapped up in 1976 by Rupert Murdoch, when he was still a little-known Aussie tabloid king and not the conservative media hegemon. The paper's politics slammed to the right and news went in large part out the window, replaced by wall-to-wall celebrity coverage on its famous "Page Six" and pulpy, pan-icky, and barely sourced crime stories. Hamilton is no longer to be found on the front page. Currently, print circulation is under a half-million. Like its chief rival, the *Daily News*, the *Post* loses money year in and year out.

- *Daily News*—A newspaper that wins points for being referenced in *Guys and Dolls* ("I'll tell you what's in the *Daily News*"), it is known as the city's other and ever-so-slightly more responsible tabloid besides the *Post*. The *Daily News* came relatively late to the game, launching in 1911 and quickly cornering the market for snappy wiseguy reporting heavy on the sports and gossip. At one point it was the largest daily newspaper in the country, with a circulation of 2.4 million in 1947. Circulation dropped in recent years to about 300,000 as the staunchly liberal paper, long vaunted for pushing stories of hardworking immigrants making it in the big city, fell victim to the same headwinds as other print publications. But in recent years, it's found a more pugnacious spirit: When Sarah Palin (1964–) endorsed Donald Trump for the presidency, the headline read: "I'm With Stupid!"

What other newspapers are based in New York?

A quick perusal of a deeply stocked newsstand in New York will reveal more than these four publications listed above. Among the 175-odd other papers delivering targeted news and opinion to a variety of constituencies are: *Newsday*, a well-regarded daily serving mostly Long Island since 1940; *The Chief*, covering stories for city union employees; *Epoch Times*, a seemingly straight-forward paper that's actually run by followers of the Falun Gong group currently banned in China; the *New York Observer*, a sniffy salmon-colored weekly mostly of interest to high-net-worth uptown types; *Amsterdam News*, a Harlem-based weekly founded in 1909; dozens of niche papers focusing on every immigrant group imaginable, and two daily rags (*AM New York* and *Metro New York*) given out for free in the subway on weekday mornings.

How many magazines are headquartered here?

As for magazines of civic interest, there are again more than can be found in any other major city, but still fewer than there had been a few years ago. One of the most important is the *Village Voice*. Founded as a weekly in 1955 by an intrepid band that included a young Norman Mailer, it doggedly covered local politics and the arts scene with bite and verve. For decades it was the best place to find out who was scamming who down at City Hall, if anything decent was playing at the Angelika, and whether there was a relatively rat-free studio for rent in the East Village. After having set the template for those free alternative weeklies now sported by every American city from Portland, Oregon, to Portland, Maine, the *Voice* still publishes but without the sense of being *the* underground voice of a city that normally has its news dictated from above. On the more fashionable side of things is *New York* magazine, which supplements its (admittedly superb) arts, dining, and entertainment coverage with smart feature writing and snarky cultural reportage that somewhat helps make up for the gap left by the closure of 1980s' sarcasm-magnet *Spy*.

PUBLISHING AND AUTHORS

What was the first book published in New York?

In the summer of 1693, a Quaker printer named William Bradford (1663–1752), who had been charged in Philadelphia with printing a pamphlet that accused Quaker authorities of violating their pacifist principles was named the public printer for the city of New York. Bradford was the first man to hold such a position in America. He opened a print shop on Pearl Street (then Dock) and got to work. The first thing he did was print a book titled *A Journal of the Late Actions of the French at Canada, with the Manner of Their Being Repulsed by His Excellency, Benjamin Fletcher, Their Majesties' Governor of New York*. Individuals of a cynical nature might believe that since Fletcher had presided at the trial in Philadelphia where Bradford was acquitted and later offered him the printing job in New York, it was no surprise that his first job was an encomium for Fletcher. Bradford remained politically astute later in life. When he began printing the city's first newspaper, the *New-York Gazette*, he made sure that its opinions were safely Tory. So it is that the first book most likely published in New York was a token of appreciation for a patronage job.

How did book publishing begin in New York?

One fairly well-substantiated theory explains the early success of New York publishing firms with a simple but surprising anecdote: book piracy. In the eighteenth and nineteenth centuries, the American government wasn't overly concerned with copyright law. In fact, foreign works at the time were simply denied copyright in the United States. Because of that handy little loophole, American publishers could simply send their agents over to London bookstores, buy the most popular titles, bring them back home, run off thousands of their own copies, sell them all across the country, and not pay the original author or publisher a cent.

New York and Philadelphia were the cities with the most printers and booksellers (often those two were the same thing), with New York winning out by the 1850s, likely due at least in part to it having longer established trade routes with London. There was great competition between publishers to get the next hottest book. Charles Dickens and Sir Walter Scott (1771–1832) were among the most in-demand.

How did Charles Dickens react to his first trip to New York?

When he was at the height of his fame, Charles Dickens was, if possible, as popular in New York as back in London. Ever the smart businessman, he stoked that popularity by publishing many of his works by installment. One old story has it that in 1841, bookworms were so inpatient to get the newest cliffhanger chapter of *The Old Curiosity Shop*—and learn whether or not Nell was still alive—that they rioted on the Manhattan dock while waiting for the ship carrying it to arrive.

The following year, Dickens came to New York during his first trip to America. Just thirty years old but already the most famous writer in the world, Dickens was the toast of New York society. But his travels had soured him on a country he found filled with boorish and boastful money-grubbing yokels; "This is not the republic of my imagination," he wrote in a letter.

When famed British author Charles Dickens visited New York City in 1842 he was not impressed by New Yorkers, whom he considered money-grubbing and boorish.

By the time Dickens came to New York, he was ready to let his true feelings show about a subject every writer cares about: royalties. After pointing out that all writers would greatly benefit by copyright law that applied across borders and allowed them to be paid for the books they sold, the press turned on him. The New York *Courier and Enquirer* called Dickens a "low-bred scullion." The writer returned the favor in his cutting *American Notes*, which was singularly unimpressed with New York ("by no means so clean a city as Boston"). But Dickens returned for a popular public reading tour in 1867, by which time the quarrel had been, if not forgotten, at least overlooked.

What did Henry James think when he returned to New York?

Some of Henry James's (1843–1916) books, like *Washington Square,* were set in New York. But the native son spent the greater part of his writing life in Europe. In 1904, after having lived abroad for over a quarter-century, the famous novelist returned to the city of his birth to start a lecture tour. It was a wildly different place than what he remembered. This was the same year that over a million immigrants landed at Ellis Island, and the resulting demographic shift in the city's population did not please James, who characterized the cultural shifts he witnessed akin to seeing a ghost in one's old home. James saw that the old family home at 21 Washington Square was gone and that the quieter city of his youth had been replaced by a hustling metropolis of nouveau riche mansions and skyscrapers where the citizens seemed to think of nothing but earning and spending money. He wrote to his sister Alice (1848–1892), saying, "I could come back to America (could be carried back on a stretcher) to *die*—but never, never to live." James was granted his wish. He died in his London home in 1916 but was buried in the family plot in Cambridge, Massachusetts.

Who were the members of the Algonquin Round Table?

Arguably the most famous literary clique this side of the beatniks—though their published works are far less remembered—the Algonquin Round Table began as simply a group of friends in the literary, journalism, and theater worlds who during the 1920s met regularly for boozy, gossipy lunches at the Algonquin Hotel on 44th Street. Sprightly conversation was the rule, as was slashing scorn for those who didn't make the cut. Edna Ferber (1885–1968) referred to them as the "Poison Squad." *New Yorker* founder Harold Ross (1892–1951) was a regular member, as was Dorothy Parker (1893–1967), Ferber, and *New York Times* drama critic Alexander Woollcott (1883–1943). Many of the stalwarts were urbane wits who filed dashing columns dripping with urbane wit for tony publications like *Vanity Fair* and *Harper's Bazaar*. The group could be as merciless with their criticism as they were steadfast in support of other members; everyone traded quotes in each other's columns.

Like many elements of New York glamour in the halcyon pre-Depression Café Society days, the Round Table's appeal was based in large part on gauzy aspirational desire, which wasn't hurt by their tendency to occasionally allow actors from Harpo Marx (1888–1964) to Tallulah Bankhead (1902–1968) to sit in from time to time. By the time the 1920s came to a close, the Round Table was no more, with its members dispersed to other places of employment or gone to Hollywood in search of even easier money, if less literate conversation.

Which two writers ran for mayor of New York?

New York is a city that deeply respects its home-grown literary culture. Writers deeply love the city for reasons both pragmatic (all the agents, publishers, and magazines based here) and atmospheric (high ratio of citizens to bars and cafes, not needing to own a car). But while the writer-city relationship is a mutually beneficial one in many ways, the city knows where to draw the line. For instance, both William F. Buckley Jr. and Norman Mailer ran for mayor in the 1960s and the city was smart enough to recognize that neither, no matter how entertaining their campaigns, was City Hall material.

When did the Harlem Renaissance take place?

When large numbers of blacks from the American South began moving to New York, particularly Harlem, in the early twentieth century, they arrived in a city already in artistic ferment, with the early stirrings of the avant-garde and modernist movements that would define American cultural life for much of the century. The resulting "Harlem Renaissance," occurring in tandem with the explosion of interest in jazz, was a flowering of black creative talent unlike anything the world had ever seen before. The multidisciplinary outpouring, mostly from people new to Harlem who were forever after associated with it, wrestled with, among other things, the very idea of what it meant to be black in America and finding pride in their frequently denigrated culture.

The Renaissance included exciting work from new voices like the writers Jean Toomer (1894–1967), Langston Hughes, and Zora Neale Hurston (1891–1960). Other highlights of the period included painters, sculptors, and the 1921 all-black music revue *Shuffle Along* on Broadway. The Great Depression put a damper on the movement, which for all its successes wasn't able to alleviate the suffering of people living in overcrowded, exorbitantly priced, and generally neglected Harlem. The neighborhood exploded in rage in March 1935. After a false rumor spread that the police had killed a teenaged boy, the result was two days of rioting that left three people dead and the Harlem Renaissance definitively ended.

Did William F. Buckley Jr. have a shot at becoming mayor?

Ultimately, no. When Buckley, the baroquely verbal editor of the *National Review* and the lead intellectual jouster of the conservative movement, ran for mayor of New York, he was not exactly seen as a shoo-in. After writing a joking column for his magazine teased on the cover as "Buckley for Mayor," the thirty-nine-year-old was convinced to make a real go of it by conservative activists who wanted a corrective to the liberal Republican mayor John Lindsay. Buckley's loose and feisty debate style and anti-government campaign resonated with the conservative, anti-New Deal resurgence of the Barry Goldwater (1909–1998) era. A surprise rise in the polls seemed to make Buckley take the campaign more seriously. But ultimately the outsider took only thirteen percent of the vote, with Lindsay squeaking out a win over Democratic challenger Abe Beame. When Buckley was asked at a news conference what he would have done first if he won the election, his response went down in political history: "Demand a recount."

Did Norman Mailer's mayoral campaign have a better chance?

Everything that one probably needs to know about Mailer's run for the mayor's office in 1969 (with writer Jimmy Breslin on the ticket for City Council), which seemed part protest screed and part performance art, can be summed up by his campaign slogan: "No More Bullshit." Just four years after Buckley's outside-chance run, the pugilistic literary firebrand (of whom Buckley said, "He's a genius and I'm not") who had once stabbed his wife and wrote epoch-defining tomes when not picking physical and written fights, decided to also give John Lindsay some heartburn before Election Day.

Mailer's platform was more gag than serious policy—"We'll have compulsory free love in those neighborhoods that vote for it, and compulsory attendance in church on Sunday in those that vote for that"; "The difference between me and the other candidates is that I'm no good and I can prove it"—but he pushed it with brio and verve. His campaign manager, Joe Flaherty, later called it "a dull campaign in a sad city with a grimace of despair carved into its face" and noted that Mailer and Breslin managed, "for a short season, to turn that grimace into a grin." Mailer finished fourth out of five candidates for the Democratic nomination.

Which superheroes are New Yorkers?

The easy answer would be: just about every one that you can name off the top of your head. Here's a short but impressive list of the superheroes who call New York (or its stand-ins Gotham or Metropolis) their home, even as they frequently destroyed it in the name of fighting evil:

- The Avengers (Frick Collection; the model for the first Avengers headquarters)
- Batman
- Captain America (Brooklyn, Lower East Side)
- Daredevil (Hell's Kitchen)
- Spider-man (grew up in Forest Hills, Queens, to be specific; worked at the *Daily Bugle* building, which was based on the Flatiron Building)
- The Spirit
- Superman

Why are there so many superheroes in New York?

Because the comic-book industry was, for all intents and purposes, created in New York. Comic books are as intrinsically New York as the movies are Los Angeles. Both of the two great comic-book conglomerates whose avatars currently dominate the screens at your local multiplex were started in New York. Detective Comics was one of the early outfits that started publishing original illustrated stories on cheap paper in the 1930s to capitalize on the exploding popularity of newspaper comic strips, reprints of which were being published in standalone volumes. Detective Comics, later known as DC Comics, published the first Superman story in the first issue of *Action Comics* in June 1938. Batman followed in 1939 and Wonder Woman (very definitely *not* a New Yorker) in 1941. Superman's Metropolis and Batman's Gotham were alternately shinier and darker variations on New York (no comics reader ever really bought them as anything else).

But it was DC's rival Marvel Comics that really put their inky stamp on the city. Started in 1939 as Timely Comics and later Atlas, Marvel introduced the Nazi-bashing hero Captain America in March 1941. Marvel didn't begin to achieve parity with DC until the 1960s, when it started rolling out more psychologically complex characters like Spider-man, the Fantastic Four, Incredible Hulk, and the X-Men. Many of these characters were grounded in a New York kind of grit, due to the influence of Marvel's chief writer and editor, New Yorker Stan Lee (1922–), who thought basing the stories in real-life places gave them an extra kick of verisimilitude. Thusly Spider-man's humble Queens home, the Thing's childhood on "Yancey Street" (Delancey on the Lower East Side), Iron Man Tony Stark's Midtown headquarters, and Doctor Strange's townhouse on Bleecker Street. This hometown-boy feeling made it all the more wrenching when these various superheroes were forced to smash the place up.

How did Captain America upset New York Nazi sympathizers?

Not long after his introduction as a Nazi-fighting machine, Captain America went instead after the New York-based German-American Bund. In the fifth issue, "Killers of the Bund," a German-American is threatened by Bund members for refusing to join. This storyline so enraged actual Bund members that they started sending anti-Semitic death threats to Timely Comics's heavily Jewish staff. According to Ronin Ro's *Tales to Astonish*, Mayor LaGuardia sent police to guard the building and called the office to say "You boys over there are doing a good job. The city of New York will see that no harm comes to you."

Who built the Erie Canal, connecting New York to the Midwest's farms?

DeWitt Clinton (1769–1828) held just about every important political office that there was to take in New York. His legacy, though, had less to do with elections than it did with engineering. The idea of building a canal between Lake Erie and the Hudson River that would open up the harbor of New York to a potentially profitable flow of goods from the American heartland had been mooted for years by many people, including George Washington. But it was the dynamic Clinton's position on the Canal Commission that finally turned the canal (initially derided as "Clinton's Ditch") from plan into reality.

The son of Revolutionary War general James Clinton and nephew of longtime New York governor and James Madison's vice president, George Clinton, DeWitt was elected to the New York Assembly from 1797 to 1798, graduating quickly to the New York and then U.S. Senate, before serving as mayor of New York from 1803 to 1815, and later two-term governor of New York state. In his fourteen years as mayor, Clinton created the city's public school system, a monumental task by itself. He also commissioned the 1811 plan that laid out the now recognizably rigid street grid for the rapidly developing area north of Houston Street to 155th Street. The grid of some two thousand mostly uniform 200-foot- (61-meter-) long blocks not only tried to bring flattened order to its sprawl of unplanned settlements and undulating hills but to leave open space for future parks. Clinton's statue at his grave in Green-Wood Cemetery is a suitably Romanesque and heroic pose, staring boldly into the future of a city that he in many ways helped form.

Which New Yorker controlled the railroads?

Unlike many of the robber barons of nineteenth-century New York, Cornelius Vanderbilt (1794–1877) was a home-grown son. Born in Staten Island to poor parents, Vanderbilt started out working at age eleven, which wasn't entirely uncommon for the time. What was less common was that while still a teenager he started his own ferry service for passengers and freight between Staten Island and Manhattan. After securing a lion's share of the business by undercutting his rivals, as well as other more bruising methods, the combative Vanderbilt quickly expanded his steamboat service. By the 1840s, he was a wealthy man living in a Greenwich Village mansion and known as the "Commodore," but still looked down upon by the city elite, who never took to his brusque manners.

Two decades later, Vanderbilt began aggressively buying up and merging railroad companies, quickly dominating the nascent business just as it was reaching maturity. The move increased his wealth many times over. Also, his focus on capital improvements and competitive pricing introduced sorely needed efficiencies and helped create America's first true nationwide transportation system. The ruthless tycoon had amassed a nearly unheard-of fortune by the time of his death. But unlike other business grandees of the time, such as Carnegie or Rockefeller, Vanderbilt left little in the way of a philanthropic or architectural legacy.

Who was the driving force behind Consolidation?

Perhaps the most important New Yorker that most New Yorkers have never heard of: Andrew Haswell Green (1820–1903). Called by some the city's greatest builder next to Robert Moses, Green was a Massachusetts-born lawyer who moved to New York as a teenager and used a series of powerful civic positions to pursue his true passion: the betterment of the city. Green was named comptroller of the Central Park Commission and wrangled the finances and schedule of the sprawling, ambitious project. In 1871, when the collapse of the Tweed Ring left the city's organizational structures in chaos, Green was elected city comptroller and over the next five years whipped municipal finances into shape.

Over the next couple of decades, Green was a perennially losing mayoral candidate and the most vocal proponent of the idea of consolidation. After helping to quiet dissenters (particularly Brooklyn), he ultimately drafted the Consolidation Law of 1895. Green's life ended on a strange and tragic note: While leaving his office near City Hall, Green was fatally shot by a man who mistook Green for the romantic partner of the woman he loved. Over the course of his career, Green was also partially or primarily responsible for the creation of a stunning roll call of beloved civic institutions: The American Museum of Natural History, Riverside Park, Morningside Park, the Metropolitan Museum of Art, the Bronx Zoo, and the New York Public Library. Green's only monument in the city he did so much to improve is a marble bench overlooking a ravine in the northern section of Central Park.

Which school dropout wrote "Rhapsody in Blue"?

A Jewish kid from the Lower East Side, George Gershwin (1898–1937) went to public schools and didn't receive much in the way of music education. That changed when, at age eleven, the family bought a piano for his brother, Ira (1896–1983). George took to the piano first and was soon getting lessons and knocking out popular tunes. At fifteen, George dropped out of school and was soon working on Tin Pan Alley as a "song plugger" (a journeyman musician hired to play and promote a music company's new songs) and writing his own material. After Al Jolson turned "Swanee" into a hit, George's career took off. Through the 1920s and '30s, George composed songs for Broadway and film, with his brother Ira writing the lyrics, that later became standards. "Someone to Watch Over Me," "Let's Call the Whole Thing Off," and "Oh, Lady Be Good" were a few. Many songs were inspired by his life in New York.

A master when it came to quickly knocking out a popular tune—he and Ira had a factory-like process that allowed them to turn around a masterpiece in about a week—George was also a great innovator. His masterpieces, *Rhapsody in Blue* and *An American in Paris*, were somewhat avant-garde attempts to bring

Famed composer George Gershwin was a child of the Lower East Side who went on to write "Rhapsody in Blue."

jazz rhythms and syncopation into an orchestral structure. Of all the Broadway shows to his name, Gershwin's 1935 "folk opera" *Porgy and Bess*, inspired by his first-hand research of the music and living conditions of blacks in the South, is now his most frequently revived. With an influential body of work that sprawled between jazz, classical, Broadway, and popular music, by the time of his sudden death from a brain tumor in 1937, Gershwin was considered one of the greatest figures in American music.

Which New Yorker was the first Catholic to run for president?

Born to Irish parents in a tenement on South Street that would very quickly be in the shadow of the new Brooklyn Bridge, Alfred E. Smith (1873–1944) rose from the grotty streets of the Fourth Ward to the highest office in the state. He went to work at the Fulton Fish Market at the age of twelve, after his father died and left him as the family's sole breadwinner. A witty facility with language (self-taught, as his education likely never advanced beyond the local parochial school) and a nervy ability to grasp the workings of complex power relationships put Smith into a lower-rung position in the Tammany Hall political machine. He was elected to the state assembly in 1903 and put in several uneventful years in Albany. Smith distinguished himself there by being one of the only members to actually read the bills they voted on, and thus his grasp of the minutiae, plus his bonhomie, gained him many powerful allies. His mixture of political canniness and ardent passions (cynical or not) for helping out the lower-class workers he had once been part of came together when he was given the vice chairmanship of the commission investigating the Triangle shirtwaist factory disaster. The wave of labor reforms that Smith shepherded into reality helped secure him the governorship in 1918.

379

Massively popular with the people of New York, Smith was re-elected three times; Will Rogers (1879–1935) once told him: "The man you run against ain't a candidate, he's just a victim." He was less successful seeking higher office, losing decisively to Republican Herbert Hoover (1874–1964) in the 1928 presidential election. Some attributed Smith's defeat to anti-Catholic sentiment, with the Ku Klux Klan warning that Smith would turn control of America over to the Vatican and fliers telling voters that if Smith was elected all Protestant marriages would be instantly annulled. During the administration of Franklin Delano Roosevelt, a onetime friend turned rival, the once fiery reformer Smith turned into an anti-progressive Republican scold, lamenting the New Deal as governmental overreach.

Who was New York's most famous First Lady?

Like many others in her illustrious family, Eleanor Roosevelt (1884–1962) had New York in her veins. Raised on West 37th Street, she lost both her parents before the age of ten. After time at a boarding school outside London, she came back to New York and immersed herself in community service. Eleanor married her cousin Franklin in 1905 and over the next eleven years had six children with him. She took on the duties of a politician's wife with some unease. However, Eleanor's innate curiosity, ambitious drive, and desire for social justice kept her extraordinarily active in that role. She led the women's platform committee at the 1924 Democratic National Convention, and during Franklin's twelve years as president, traveled the country on listening tours, and advocated strenuously against sexism and racism, even when it conflicted with Franklin's policy goals.

Following Franklin's death in 1945, Eleanor moved back to New York. She expanded her profile in the political arena by serving as delegate to the United Nations from 1946 to 1952 and frequently traveling the globe to champion for numerous causes. Eleanor published a syndicated newspaper column, "My Day," from 1935 to 1962, which she also used to advance her causes. By the time of her death, Eleanor's fierce fighting for human rights had not only made her one of the most famous and respected women in America but fundamentally changed the role of First Lady forever.

Who represented Harlem in Congress for twelve terms?

Son of the pastor of Harlem's Abyssinian Baptist Church, Adam Clayton Powell Jr. (1908–1972) was one of the great clergymen-activists of the twentieth century's civil rights movement. Powell graduated from Columbia University and started working for his father at Abyssinian, one of the corner stones of Harlem life, in the 1930s. After becoming pastor in 1937, he became active in local politics, pushing for better treatment of blacks and the poor in the city. He became the first black member of the City Council in 1941. In 1945 he became the first black congressman from the Northeast. Popular with his constituents, he won re-election eleven more times, usually in a landslide.

Unafraid of using the sting of moral reproach in his activism, the grandiloquent Powell was a force to be reckoned with in Congress, pushing through dozens of pieces of legislation to help poor and minority Americans. At the same time, he cut a flamboyant path through the city, with his dashing outfits and frequent appearances at Broadway shows and nightclubs. Powell's taste for the high life, though, had its downsides, particularly his penchant for using every perk a congressman was allowed, and then some. His arrogance also began to work against him. After being convicted of libel for accusing a woman of taking graft, he refused to pay and was removed from his seat in 1967 for contempt of court. He later retired to an island in the Bahamas. Today, Powell's profile as activist and successful legislator looms even larger.

Who was the quintessential New York playwright of the twentieth century?

Even though Tennessee Williams (1911–1983) lived in New York for many years and saw most of his success in the city, there's another frequently revived mid-century playwright who holds a stronger grip on New York's psyche. Arthur Miller (1915–2005) had a well-appointed childhood in Harlem until 1928, when his father's manufacturing business went south and they had to move to Midwood, Brooklyn, then transitioning from partly rural to solidly urban. After graduating from the University of Michigan, Miller returned to New York in 1940, living at several addresses around Brooklyn Heights, then an affordable neighborhood popular with the creative class. After a few years of middling success, Miller hit his stride with landmark plays like *All My Sons* (1947) and *Death of a Salesman* (1949) that not only redefined American theatrical realism but were heavily influenced by his years spent in Brooklyn and the voices of its working classes trying to keep their lives together in the borough's postwar tumult. Miller moved to Manhattan in the 1950s with his second wife, Marilyn Monroe (the two were famous bar crawlers on the nightlife scene), and then later to Connecticut. But Brooklyn remained in his accent and his work.

Who saved much of New York from the bulldozer?

Even though she was born in Scranton, Pennsylvania, and died in Toronto, Jane Jacobs (1916–2006) is as New York as they come. A writer for her hometown paper, she moved to New York in 1934, where she found work as a freelance writer. Living originally in Brooklyn Heights and later Greenwich Village, Jacobs had an early and fierce love for the organic ecosystem of economic, architectural, and ethnic diversity that characterized its most successful and pleasant-to-live-in neighborhoods. While working at *Architectural Forum* in the 1950s, Jacobs began developing her theories of urbanism and city planning.

Playwright Arthur Miller was born in Harlem.

381

These were in stark contrast to the prevailing notions of central planning and sweeping away all "slums" (a catchall used to describe any pre-war low-rise apartments and commercial buildings, particularly if minorities and the poor resided there) to replace them with sterile, gargantuan new towers surrounded by blank green parks.

Jacobs published her manifesto, *The Death and Life of Great American Cities,* in 1961. The book argued that "There is no logic that can be superimposed on the city; people make it, and it is to them, not building, that we must fit our plans." Still used today as a resource and inspiration for activists pushing for vital grassroots community and neighborhood development, it helped marshal the activists who, along with Jacobs, were pushing back against the city's rubber-stamp approval of massive neighborhood demolitions for new apartment towers or freeways. Her nemesis, city planner Robert Moses, had once seemed unstoppable in his towering arrogance (he once furiously described protestors of one of his projects as merely "a bunch of MOTHERS!"). Jacobs helped stop his plans to destroy much of Greenwich Village, SoHo, and other neighborhoods now deemed among the city's most beloved. An anti-war activist, Jacobs moved to Canada in 1967 to keep her sons from the draft. Nevertheless, the legacy of her few decades in New York mark her as one of the city's fiercest and most eloquent champions.

Who started Shakespeare in the Park?

Born Yosl Papirofsky, Joseph Papp (1921–1991) started off very far from the lights of Broadway, and in some ways, always kept his distance. Growing up in a poor Jewish family in Williamsburg, Papp spoke only Yiddish for the first few years of his life. After serving in the Navy during World War II, Papp studied at the Actor's Laboratory Theatre in Hollywood and joined a touring company of *Death of a Salesman.* After that, even though he worked for several years as a television stage manager at CBS, Papp spent the rest of his life immersed in theater. Always looking for new ways to present plays and attract different audiences, Papp started the then-revolutionary New York Shakespeare Festival in a church on the Lower East Side in 1954. The festival's *raison d'être* was not just creating top-flight Shakespearean productions, but putting them on for free. After his legendary battle with Robert Moses, Papp was able to house his previously wandering festival in a purpose-built theater in Central Park in 1962.

Four years later, Papp established the other institution that he would be remembered for: the Public Theater. A multi-theater complex in the old Astor Library on Lafayette Street in SoHo, "the Public" became the city's theatrical laboratory, producing a string of out-of-the-box musical blockbusters from *A Chorus Line* to *Hair* and *Hamilton,* along with striking and politically charged dramas like Larry Kramer's *The Normal Heart.* Over the course of his life, Papp nurtured the careers and up-and-coming playwrights like John Guare (1938–) and actors from James Earl Jones to Meryl Streep (1949–), produced over 350 plays, and fundamentally reshaped the course of modern American theater.

What famous publisher loved being terrible at sports?

George Plimpton (1927–2003) was born in New York as a true American blue blood whose family could trace its history back to the *Mayflower*. His father was a wealthy corporate lawyer and American ambassador to the United Nations. After turns in a roll call of elite schools (Phillips Exeter, Cambridge, Harvard), Plimpton moved to Paris and began a lifelong career as an aesthete. In 1953, he co-founded *The Paris Review*, still one of the most prestigious American literary magazines, having published everybody from Philip Roth (1933–) and Jack Kerouac (1922–1969) to Jay McInerney (1955–)—even though, as Plimpton later noted, it had no reviews and pretty soon wasn't based in Paris. Starting a high/low dichotomy that he kept going the rest of his life, Plimpton then returned to the States, where he started a decades-long career as sports writer. He made his name with a series of bestselling books of what he called "participatory journalism," in which he would throw his gangly amateur body into a series of tough contests (joining the Detroit Lions pro football team, boxing, and golfing very badly) and chronicling the resulting misadventures.

Plimpton's seemingly affected mid-Atlantic William F. Buckley-esque accent, diffident style, and upper-class background marked him as a preppie from the jump. But he used the contrast between that persona and his self-deprecating charm to win subjects over for his many varied projects. A writer of the highest caliber, Plimpton wasn't above taking on TV, commercial, and movie gigs not just because they seemed a lark, but it always helped bring in the money that helped keep *The Paris Review* afloat. A magpie of the city's intellectual scene, he also wrote acclaimed oral biographies of Truman Capote (1924–1984) and Edie Sedgwick (1943–1971), was named New York's unofficial "fireworks commissioner," hung out with the Kennedys, and played piano at Amateur Night at the Apollo (he came in second).

Who was "the Italian Hamlet" and why?

While politics often elevates people who are emblematic of their eras and backgrounds, every so often it hurls into prominence men and women who are so individualistic that it is hard to assign them to any particular time or place. One of New York's most atypical yet iconic leaders was Mario Cuomo (1932–2015). Raised in a classically New York multiethnic Queens neighborhood by Italian immigrant parents who ran a grocery, Cuomo graduated from St. John's University Law School. He made a name for himself in law

The late Mario Cuomo was one of the city's iconic leaders, serving as governor for three terms in the 1980s and 1990s.

advocating for causes, like helping the small Queens neighborhood of Corona fight off condemnation, and the Forest Hills public-housing controversy that he negotiated through a morass of racial and class resentments. Appointed secretary of state in 1975, he rose through state government as an unusually forceful idealist who combined the hard-nosed realism of the born negotiator with the rigorous evidentiary instincts of an investigator and a philosophically Catholic view (he could quote Augustine and Aquinas when the situation called for it) of advancing the public good.

A three-term governor of New York (1983–1994), Cuomo cut a national profile due in large part to his inspirational speeches. His 1984 keynote at the Democratic National Convention starkly contrasted Ronald Reagan's "shining city on a hill" rhetoric with a "tale of two cities" theme about the yawning inequities of the 1980s. Cuomo was perennially courted as a Democratic presidential candidate. But his penchant for prevarication and analysis—in an earlier time, Jimmy Breslin termed him "talent willing to be tortured"—kept Cuomo almost comically unable to commit or decline. In one famous 1991 incident, the "Italian Hamlet" kept a jet idling on the runway while he decided whether or not to seek the nomination. Cuomo died the same day in 2015 that his (more aggressively decisive) son Andrew Cuomo (1957–) was sworn in as New York's governor for the second time.

Who was the first graffiti artist to make it big?

At the time that Jean-Michel Basquiat (1960–1988) was leaving his graffiti tag "SAMO" (same old shit) around the city, seeing the scrawls of spray paint as anything but vandalism was still a minority idea. But unlike most of the other taggers around town, Basquiat had his eyes on bigger things. By 1981, he was selling his graffiti- and politics-inflected paintings in galleries and running with the neo-punk downtown art scene. Charismatic and heavy with mystique, Basquiat was frequently mistaken for an outsider artist on the basis of his race and his wide usage of Afro-Caribbean imagery, notwithstanding that he had been raised in a middle-class Brooklyn household.

By the mid-1980s, he was increasingly proclaimed one of the nation's hottest artists. In 1985, he collaborated in a blockbuster show with one of his heroes and champions, Andy Warhol. Basquiat died of a drug overdose in 1988. Today, his paintings are among the most sought-after for any modern art collection.

What was Joey Ramone's real name?

Like the rest of the members of New York's quintessential punk band the Ramones, lead singer Joey Ramone (1951–2001) had a different name. Born Jeffrey Hyman in middle-class Forest Hills, Queens, he founded the band in 1974 with three other guys with different last names. A tall, gangly, shy-seeming stick of a guy forever shrouded in long hair, sunglasses, and leather jacket, Joey wasn't a likely rock and roll frontman. But from the time they started playing at CBGB's and launched their first album in 1976, his striking presence and unique creative sensibilities helped craft the band's signature image and sound. Mixing a love of 1960s' girl-group bubblegum pop and trashy comics and hor-

President Trump's anti-immigration policies have won him few fans in New York City, a metropolis filled with immigrants.

ror films, Joey's songs like "I Wanna Be Sedated," "Beat on the Brat," and "The KKK Took My Baby Away" hit a sweet spot within the band's blitzkrieg-paced, three-chord loudness and his quirky but sensitive lyrics. Even after the Ramones broke up in 1996 after playing over 2,200 concerts, Joey remained an elder statesman of sorts in the punk community until his death from cancer in 2001.

Who is known occasionally as just "The Donald"?

Right after seltzer and a cheerful disregard for Don't Walk signs, one of the more notable elements of New York life has for some time been the presence of one Donald John Trump (1946–). Raised in Queens, Donald aspired early on to both model himself on the success of his real-estate magnate father Fred Trump. Brash and magnetically drawn to celebrity and notoriety, Donald Trump was tailor-made for the go-go Manhattan scene that he burst into in 1980, when he rehabilitated a shabby old commuter hotel near Grand Central into the glittering new Grand Hyatt. A loudmouthed fixture on the tabloid scene, the thrice-married Trump made headlines as quickly as he made gargantuan real estate deals and erected flashy Manhattan high-rises that were the opposite of his father's stolid legacy. He talked about building the biggest shopping mall on the East Coast and cut deals for everything from the Plaza Hotel to a string of Atlantic City casinos.

Trump's braggadocio, chronicled in braggy bestsellers like *The Art of the Deal*, got ahead of him in the early 1990s, when a number of high-profile deals went south. Afterwards, the ever quicksilver and self-adulatory Trump reimagined himself as a brand, extolling louche luxury with all the subtlety of a claw hammer. He became a reality TV star (on the long-running *The Apprentice*), outsourced much of the actual construction work to other parties, and took a percentage for putting his name on buildings and products from bottled water to steak and a "university" criticized as a scam. By the time he elbowed himself into politics in 2012, the self-described "billionaire" was more of a shadow mogul, with very few real-estate holdings left in New York. In the 2016 election, Trump (a onetime Democrat) reinvented himself as a right-wing bomb-thrower given to outrageous outbursts. Trump was elected president after winning fewer than nineteen percent of the vote in his home town, whose residents turned out by the tens of thousands to protest his inauguration in January 2017.

What director is synonymous with Brooklyn?

Even though Shelton Jackson "Spike" Lee (1957–) was actually born in Atlanta and later moved to Manhattan, his career remains indelibly associated with the borough of Brooklyn, where he was raised. Born into a creative family (his father is a jazz composer), Spike made waves with his first feature film, *She's Gotta Have It*, an edgy and extremely low-budget sex comedy released just four years after his graduation from film school. *Do the Right Thing* (1989) was an incendiary portrait of how racial and economic tensions on one Bedford-Stuyvesant block crumbling under summer heat escalated into a full-blown riot.

Lee is a student of the classics who also excelled at experimental film with a political edge and cultivated a lucrative string of commercial work, particularly his iconic Michael Jordan ads for Nike (co-starring Lee himself). He frequently broke out into other subjects from historical epics (*Malcolm X*) to political farce (*Chi-Raq*), and his often bruisingly

confrontational style seemed most confident when on his home turf, such as in the New York-set dramas *Summer of Sam*, *25th Hour*, and *Inside Man*. Lee's production company, 40 Acres and a Mule, is headquartered in Fort Greene, Brooklyn.

What's Jay-Z's real name and why is he famous?

New York is filled with rags-to-riches stories, and the modern era has few better than that of Shawn Carter (1969–). Before he was the rap star-entrepreneur Jay-Z (or Hova, as he's also sometimes called), Carter grew up in the projects of north Brooklyn's Bedford-Stuyvesant neighborhood. He came up as an MC during the

Rapper Jay-Z is shown here performing in a 2014 concert to end homelessness in Central Park.

late-1980s and '90s, when he was dealing drugs to make a living. He started Roc-a-Fella Records in 1996, a step that would eventually put him in the modern rap-mogul trinity: more artistically accomplished than Sean Combs (1969–) and more business-minded than Kanye West (1977–).

Carter first hit big with 1998's "Hard Knock Life," which sampled the chorus from the *Annie* song. After a string of blockbuster albums, 2003's *Black Album* was meant to be a retirement announcement, but in actuality it just kicked his career into the next level. By the 2010s, Carter was married to pop diva Beyoncé (1981–), running his own fashion label (Rocawear) and Flatiron sports bar-lounge 40/40 Club on 25th Street, and expanding into everything from streaming-music services to sports team-ownership. He was even a part-owner of the Brooklyn Nets for a time, having lobbied publicly to bring the team to the new Barclays Center, walking distance from the projects he was raised in.

QUIRKY NEW YORK

What bar is haunted by George Raft?

According to some, the Landmark Tavern, which first opened for business at 11th Avenue and 46th Street in Hell's Kitchen back in 1868, is haunted by the ghost of Raft (1901–1980), a loyal customer. Other spirits believed to haunt the same establishment are a Confederate veteran who was stabbed in a fight and died in a second-floor bathtub that's still there for inspection by the curious, and an Irish immigrant girl whose ghost inhabits the third floor.

How many places are supposedly haunted by Dylan Thomas?

The New York establishment most famously associated with the poet Dylan Thomas is the White Horse Tavern, a late-nineteenth-century drinking establishment that became a home away from home for writerly drinkers like the frequently inebriated Thomas. The "do not go gentle into that good night" scribe died in 1953 allegedly after proclaiming at the White Horse: "I've had eighteen straight whiskies … I think that's the record."

Since then, the occasional patron at the White Horse, which is more a college hangout today though it still has a pleasant atmosphere on less crowded days, has claimed to see Thomas's ghost. Additionally, his specter has been spotted further uptown at the Hotel Chelsea, where he was living at the time of his demise.

Are there ghosts on Broadway?

This is a difficult question to answer, and not just because of the many people who would argue the foolishness of even asking the question to begin with. Actors and theater folk have been a superstitious lot from the jump, with a dense mental listing of actions and words that can confer good or bad luck. It's rumored that the old saw about never wishing a performer "good luck" but instead to "break a leg" dates back to John Wilkes Booth (1838–1865), originally an actor, breaking his leg after leaping to the stage of Ford's

Theatre after assassinating President Lincoln. The old imprecation against even saying the title of Shakespeare's play *Macbeth*, and instead referring to it as simply "The Scottish Play," dates back even further as it was first performed in 1611. Nobody is ever supposed to say that a theater is closed but that it is "dark," and so on.

One of the most poetic superstitions still to be witnessed—at least by those in the craft, not audience members—is the tradition of the ghost light. Theatrical norms demand that a theater should never be allowed to go completely dark, even if it is utterly unoccupied. A single, uncovered light bulb is left burning onstage all night: The ghost light. The supernatural basis for doing so is supposedly that leaving a light on will disrupt the spirits who might otherwise congregate in the darkness. More practically, it means that the first person entering the theater the next day doesn't have to stumble around in the gloom looking for a light switch … and possibly breaking a leg. Even less poetically, OSHA rules dictate that at least one theater on Broadway—the New Amsterdam on 42nd Street—has to leave more than one light on at all times.

Is Ellis Island haunted?

Given the number of people who passed through it, and the many who died there (everyone from executed pirates to patients in the quarantine wards), many would assume without any further research that the answer was: yes. One story actually predates the island's days as an immigration station. The *New York Times* reported in 1886 that "older residents" of New Jersey told a romantic story about a young woman who tried to help her lover, a young soldier who'd been imprisoned there, escape the island in a small boat. When the boat capsized, both perished. Many later claimed to have seen the pair at night walking hand in hand along the beach near where they drowned.

Who was the "Amiable Child"?

St. Claire Pollock was five years old when he died in 1797, possibly after falling off the cliffs by the Hudson near Claremont Hill, now part of the Columbia University campus in

The abandoned hospital on Ellis Island lends itself well to rumors of ghosts.

Morningside Heights. The boy's father, linen merchant George Pollock, erected a simple monument to his son's memory in the form of an urn on top of a pedestal. Today it sits surrounded by a metal fence not far north of Grant's Tomb on the side of Riverside Drive, one of the only private cemeteries in the city of New York. The urn (originally marble, it's been replaced a couple times in the intervening years) is known as the Amiable Child Monument because of its inscription: "Erected to the Memory of an Amiable Child."

Who was Cropsey?

During the 1980s, the nightmares of many Staten Island children were filled by the terrifying figure of Cropsey. According to rumors—which were replicated in some form at campsite firesides up the Hudson Valley—Cropsey was an escaped mental patient with a hook for an arm. Traumatized by the tragic death of his son, he was purported to kidnap unwary children, particularly those who wandered into the tangled woods that still stood at the island's center. At first, the story seemed merely an urban legend born from tales that swirled around the ruins of the abandoned Seaview Hospital and the infamous Willowbrook State School for mentally disabled children, which was closed down in 1987 following a series of lurid exposés (one by a young Geraldo Rivera).

But the mystery of Cropsey took on a more chilling resonance following the disappearance of several children, and a homeless man who camped by Willowbrook was ultimately convicted of murdering a twelve-year-old girl whose body was found nearby. The mystery of who was responsible for those killings remains. Ghost hunters still nervously hunt the shadows of Seaview and Willowbrook, now operated as the College of Staten Island.

What New Yorker was sworn in as president after being woken up?

Two presidents have been sworn into office in New York. The first and better known of them is George Washington. The oath of office was administered to the former commander of the Continental Army at Federal Hall on Wall Street on April 30, 1789. The less famous presidential swearing-in took place on September 20, 1881, at a brownstone at 123 Lexington Avenue and 28th Street.

At the time this was the residence of Vice President Chester A. Arthur, who was awakened with the news that President James Garfield, who had been shot in July, was dead. The oath making Arthur the twenty-first president of the United States was administered well after midnight in the building's ground-floor parlor. No official landmark status has been awarded to the building, though a number of plaques commemorating the event have been stolen over the years. The address has another kind of distinction: since 1944 it has been home to Kalustyan's, the city's most storied Indian spice market.

Who were "The Hermits of Harlem"?

Homer (1881–1947) and Langley Collyer (1885–1947) were brothers who lived alone but together in their family's brownstone on Fifth Avenue and 128th Street after their parents passed away in the 1920s. Langley had once been a concert pianist and Homer

391

an admiralty lawyer. The brothers were early examples of what would today be called hoarders, as they never threw anything away and essentially cut themselves off from the outside world. The house, which was cut off from utilities like gas, water, and electricity, became increasingly decrepit and filled with junk, particularly after Homer was hit by a stroke in the 1930s. The police tried to carry out an eviction order in 1942 because the Collyers, though wealthy, had stopped making mortgage payments. They were allowed to remain in the house until the tip-off on March 21, 1947.

Responding officers discovered that all the house's windows and doors were barricaded. Finally breaking in through a second-story window, they discovered a trash heap of gothic proportions. Newspapers, books, and random detritus ranging from a partial auto chassis to a horse's jawbone and fourteen grand pianos were piled everywhere to the ceiling. The Collyers had only been able to move around by tunneling through their garbage. Rats were everywhere. Homer's body was discovered; he had apparently died of starvation. Langley, though, was nowhere to be seen. The excavation, eagerly covered by newspapers for a fascinated public, went on for weeks. Finally, on April 8, Langley's body was discovered. It was determined that while bringing food to the blind and paralyzed Homer, the paranoid Langley had died of a heart attack after hundreds of pounds of garbage had fallen on him. Langley had mistakenly triggered one of the booby traps he had made to defend the house from supposed intruders. The brothers, who the tabloids dubbed "The Hermits of Harlem" and "Harlem's Most Fascinating Mystery," died just feet away from each other. Today, the site of their old brownstone is now Collyer Brothers Park, a small "vest-pocket" park.

What is different about the townhouse at 58 Joralemon Street, Brooklyn?

If you turn down Joralemon Street in Brooklyn Heights towards the water, you will find yourself in one of the most beautiful corners of the charming neighborhood known as Willowtown. But the quaintly slanting, tree-lined cobblestone street also hides an odd municipal secret. The townhouse at 58 Joralemon looks at first like any other three-story building on this block. But on second glance, it seems a little … unoccupied. It features none of the greenery and knick-knacks that residents have used to decorate their homes in this neighborhood. And why are the windows all blacked out? That's because in a neighborhood where brownstones regularly sell for north of $10 million, nobody has lived here for over a century.

The house was built in 1847 and bought by the IRT in 1908 and gutted. It is currently operated as a ventilation system and escape route for the Lexington Line (aka the 4 and the 5) that runs underneath. Since it's a sensitive part of the infrastructure, the city doesn't talk about it, but supposedly during the city's occasional post-9/11 terror alerts, the building that's been called "the world's only Greek Revival subway ventilator" is well guarded.

Who was Ota Benga?

The Bronx Zoo started an unusual exhibit starting on September 8, 1906, that displayed not an animal but a man, whose humanity was laughingly doubted by many visitors. Ota Benga (c. 1883–1916) was a Congolese pygmy whose family had been massacred by Belgian soldiers of the infamous Force Publique. Afterwards Benga was sold into slavery. Benga was selected at the slave market by an American missionary who was looking for native people to display at the 1904 World's Fair in St. Louis. Unable to return to his previous life in Africa, Benga later took up residence at the American Museum of Natural History and then the Bronx Zoo, where he was allowed to wander at will.

Eventually Benga was encouraged to take part in a so-called "exhibit" in the Monkey House that involved him dancing with an orangutan for the amusement of a delighted crowd. Protests by white and black ministers led to the cancelling of the exhibit. Benga later went to live in the Howard Colored Orphan Asylum in Brook-

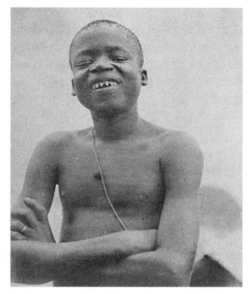

Ota Benga was a pygmy from the Congo who was put on display at the Bronx Zoo in 1906.

lyn's Weeksville (where, a newspaper reported, the four-foot-eleven Benga was about the same size as the orphan children living there), a onetime town of free blacks in Brooklyn, before eventually settling in Lynchburg, Virginia.

Who was Topsy?

For years, one of the top attractions at a touring circus that frequented Coney Island was a six-ton, ten-foot- (three-meter-) tall Indian elephant named Topsy. Her owners were less enamored of her than the adoring crowds. In just three years, Topsy killed three of her trainers, including one who attempted to feed her a lit cigarette. In 1902, her latest trainer overindulged one night and rode Topsy down Surf Avenue; she eventually tried to bust into the police precinct house. The following year, after she was put to work helping to build Luna Park, Topsy's owners selected her for a publicity stunt execution.

After protests scotched their first bizarre idea (a hanging), Thomas Edison volunteered to help out. Eager to prove the superiority of his alternating-current electricity, as part of his long-running feud with West-

An illustration of Topsy, a female Asian elephant that was executed by electrocution for killing her trainers.

393

inghouse's direct current, Edison planned to execute Topsy by electrocution and film the whole thing. On January 4, 1903, in front of over a thousand onlookers, Edison's electricians attached electrodes to her legs and copper sandals to her feet. Topsy was fed cyanide-laced carrots, which didn't kill her. Then the current was turned on, six thousand volts. Ten seconds later, she was dead. Today there is a Topsy memorial at the Coney Island Museum.

Who was the "Chinese Devil Man"?

One of the first documented Chinese-born men to take up permanent residence (though never American citizenship) in New York is believed to be Quimbo Appo. Born Lee Ah Bow in 1825 on an island near Shanghai, Appo came to New York around 1853, after several years in California. In New York, he married Irish-born widow Catherine Fitzpatrick, who bore him a son. Interracial relationships caused much consternation among the city's white population and later led to fevered tabloid scares about Chinese men kidnapping women into opium-induced "white slavery." Given the overwhelmingly male proportion of Chinese immigrants, Asian-European romantic pairings were not uncommon, particularly Chinese-Irish. In 1869 the *New York Tribune* claimed that "Chinamen" had "a peculiar fancy for wives of Celtic origin."

Appo was generally well-known and respected around New York in the years he worked at a tea shop. That changed in 1859 when he was convicted of murdering his landlady. Over the next couple of decades, the increasingly mentally disturbed Appo (dubbed the "Chinese Devil Man" by a pervasively racist press) went back to prison on an assault charge and was eventually committed to a mental hospital after killing a man in an argument over checkers. His son George later became a notorious pickpocket and flimflam man.

Did New York invent Christmas?

For all intents and purposes, the answer is yes. Washington Irving's 1809 origin story for the city, *A History of New York*, contained some fanciful Dutch-inspired fairy tales. One of them concerned a certain Saint Nicholas, the patron saint of New Amsterdam and children who back in the Netherlands had his own feast day on December 6, when he would supposedly leave little gifts for children in their shoes. According to Irving, Santa Claus (the Anglicized version of the Dutch "Sinterklaas") liked to fly through the air in

---

Where is Scrabble Corner?

Sharp-eyed visitors to Jackson Heights, Queens, will notice a curious street sign at the intersection of 81st Street and 35th Avenue: $35T_1H_4 A_1V_4E_1N_1U_1E_1$. This denotes the fact that in this neighborhood in 1938, Alfred Mosher Butts (1899–1993), an architect who had been laid off during the Great Depression, invented the game Scrabble.

How many official New York condoms does the city give out for free?

On Valentine's Day 2007, New York's Department of Health and Mental Hygiene distributed over 150,000 official NYC condoms, the first city-branded male prophylactic in the United States. It was a new approach to a problem the city has long struggled with: driving down rates of teen pregnancy and transmission of HIV and other STDs (something it has succeeded in doing in recent years). In the Bloomberg administration, New York began an aggressive campaign to provide free condoms to social-service organizations, and at one point was distributing a million condoms a month. In 2014, the city distributed 37 million condoms in two sizes: regular and large (or KNYG).

a wagon "wherein he brings his yearly presents to children." The 1821 children's book *The Children's Friend*, published by a New York bookseller, introduced the image of Santa Claus carrying presents in a reindeer-pulled sleigh.

Clement Clarke Moore, whose estate took up most of what is now Chelsea, was so inspired by Irving's story that in 1823 he published the poem "A Visit from Saint Nicholas," which solidified the American myth of Christmas and Santa Claus. Later on, German immigrants in New York popularized the tradition of the Christmas tree, city merchants pushed the idea of Christmas gift-giving, and Thomas Nast's Christmas cartoons for *Harper's Weekly* created the classic visual template for Santa Claus (jolly bearded fat man in a red suit).

What *was* that smell?

Once it would have seemed incredible that New Yorkers would stop on a dime one day and ask of each other in a wrinkled nose, mystified manner, "What *is* that weird smell?" The city has come a long way since the nineteenth century, when sewage was regularly dumped out in the open and horses would often be left on the street where they dropped dead. In 1880 alone, the city removed 15,000 horse carcasses from the streets.

Nevertheless, in 2005, 2006, and 2009, strange waves of pungently sweet smells swept across the city, baffling everyone in their path. These episodes were termed "maple syrup events" and for years nobody had a clue what caused them. The city kept investigating, sending air testers out with canisters to collect air samples once the calls started coming in. Then, in February 2009, a source was discovered, and to the delight of bridge-and-tunnels-haters across the city, it was placed across the river. The cause of the smell were the seeds of fenugreek, a plant used for making fragrances at a factory in North Bergen, New Jersey.

Where is the most popular place in New York to commit suicide?

Since, for obvious reasons, officials are reluctant to release official statistics, this is a difficult question to answer. Folklore, as well as its iconic nature in the popular imagination, points to the Brooklyn Bridge. In the Coen brothers film *Inside Llewyn Davis*, a musician is disappointed to hear about a man who leaped from the George Washington Bridge: "George Washington Bridge?" He harrumphs. "You throw yourself off the Brooklyn Bridge, traditionally."

However, the facts, such as they are, may not bear this out. The pedestrian walkway on the Brooklyn Bridge is set back from the edge, requiring quite a bit of climbing work to get the deed done. The longer and less trafficked (by pedestrians, at least) George Washington Bridge has only a waist-high handrail to stop the people who show up on average every three or four days to try and commit suicide. A 2007 study by the National Institutes of Health found that jumping from a high place was a more common method of suicide in New York than the rest of the country. The study also found that at least 10 percent of suicides in the city were nonresidents, clustered around Midtown skyscrapers and the George Washington Bridge, suggesting a pattern of "suicide tourism" where people travel to the city for the express purpose of killing themselves by jumping from or out of a popular landmark.

How dangerous is walking in New York?

Comedian Denis Leary (1957–), ruminating in an early 1990s routine on the threats posed to city-dwellers by everything from race riots to subway crashes and exploding manhole covers, said in a tone of near-admiration: "There are *so many ways to die* in New York City." The city has become notably safer since then. Still, Leary's observation remains somewhat true. In short, in New York, death comes unexpectedly. If it didn't the city wouldn't have around six thousand different codes to define accidental deaths. To wit:

- 2015—While walking on West 12th Street, a woman died after being struck by a large piece of plywood that blew off a construction site on the former location of St. Vincent's Hospital.

- 2008—A construction crane on East 51st Street suddenly collapsed on a Saturday afternoon, demolishing a townhouse and killing seven people.

- 1993—A police officer died in Washington Heights after a thirty-pound bucket of spackle was dropped on him. Two years later, another officer narrowly missed being hit by a sixty-pound steel trash can hurled from the roof of a project by a teenager being initiated into the Latin Kings gang. NYPD officers refer to such projectile attacks as "airmail."

- Unknown date—According to a story that former New York medical examiner Judy Melinek told in her memoir *Working Stiff*, after an eggroll-making machine exploded in Chinatown, one worker lost his life and the other an arm.

- Never—Urban myth has it that a penny dropped from the top of the Empire State Building could kill an unwary pedestrian below. Not only has that never happened, but scientists believe that even if a person were to be hit by a penny from that height, the impact would be less than lethal.

When does Manhattanenge take place?

One of the Manhattan street grid's unintended but nevertheless poetic results is that on two days each year (usually the end of May and mid-July), the sun aligns in such a way that it beams straight through nearly all of Manhattan's 155 cross-streets. It's a phenomenon that Neil deGrasse Tyson (1958–), positing that future civilizations might imagine that New York's grid was constructed just for this reason in the manner of a massive urban Stonehenge, termed *Manhattanhenge*.

Since the days correspond usually to Memorial Day and Major League Baseball's All-Star Break, Tyson pondered whether "Future anthropologists might conclude that, via the Sun, the people who called themselves Americans worshipped War and Baseball."

Of course, if you believe the state's Department of Health, the leading cause of death among New Yorkers for years running has been heart disease. That is followed by cancer, pneumonia and influenza, and diabetes; none of which rate nearly as many headlines as collapsing cranes.

What are some of New York's odder laws?

Every state and city has its share of curious, or simply rarely enforced laws. For your own safety and education, here are a few of New York's:

- Turn in found money—Since money is considered property, if you find cash or property worth $20 or more, you are obliged to return it to the person or, if that's not possible, to the police.

- Don't wear masks in public gathering—This law dates to 1845, when Hudson Valley tenant farmers disguised as Indians killed landlords.

- Sell wine in a grocery store—This is currently against the law in the city. Grocery stores and bodegas can only sell beer. Wine and all hard liquors can only be sold in dedicated liquor stores.

- Use profanity or obscene hand gestures—Against the law for candidates running for office in the city.

- Tattoos or piercing for pets—This can be punished by up to fifteen days in prison and/or a fine of not more than $250.

- Spitting—Just don't do it.

Has anybody ever figured out what the "sixth borough" is?

No. That is a convenient figure of speech used by New Yorkers to any geographic area that feels connected to the city but not quite officially part of it yet. Nearby communities like Jersey City and Yonkers often get slapped with this descriptor, as have larger cities like Philadelphia which aren't exactly next door but are close enough that people have been known to make the hour-and-a-half train run from there twice a day for work.

The fact that there continues to be disagreement and discussion over this fact ((for example, Mayor Mike Bloomberg's quixotic and unsuccessful attempt to label the local waterways and waterfronts as the town's sixth borough) reveals something about New Yorkers' assumptions about the tractor beam-like pull of the five existing boroughs.

Mayors of
New York City

(* = acting mayor)

Mayor	Years in Office
Thomas Willett	1665
Thomas Delavall	1666
Thomas Willett	1667
Cornelius Van Steenwyck	1668–70
Thomas Delavall	1671
Matthais Nichols	1672
John Lawrence	1673–74
William Dervall	1675
Nicholas De Meyer	1676
Stephanus Van Cortlandt	1677
Thomas Delavall	1678
Francis Rombouts	1679
William Dyre	1680–81
Cornelius Van Steenwyck	1682–83
Gabriel Minvielle	1684
Nicholas Bayard	1685
Stephanus Van Cortlandt	1686–88
Peter Delanoy	1689–90
John Lawrence	1691
Abraham De Peyster	1692–94
Charles Lodwik	1694–95
William Merrett	1695–98
Johannes De Peyster	1698–99
David Provost	1699–1700
Isaac De Reimer	1700–1
Thomas Noell	1701–2
Philip French	1702–3
William Peartree	1703–7
Ebenezer Wilson	1707–10
Jacobus Van Cortlandt	1710–11
Caleb Hearthcote	1711–14
John Johnson	1714–19
Robert Walters	1720–25

Mayor	Years in Office
Johannes Jansen	1725–26
Robert Lurting	1726–35
Paul Richard	1735–39
John Cruger	1739–44
Stephen Bayard	1744–47
Edward Holland	1747–57
John Cruger, Jr.	1757–66
Whitehead Hicks	1766–76
David Matthews	1776–84
James Duane	1784–89
Richard Varick	1789–1801
Edward Livingstone	1801–3
DeWitt Clinton	1803–7
Marinus Willett	1807–8
DeWitt Clinton	1808–10
Jacob Radcliff	1810–11
DeWitt Clinton	1811–15
John Ferguson	1815
Jacob Radcliff	1815–33
Cadwallader D. Colden	1818–21
Stephen Allen	1821–24
William Paulding	1825–26
Walter Browne	1829–33
Gideon Lee	1833–34
Cornelius Van Wyck Lawrence	1834–37
Aaron Clark	1837–39
Isaac L. Varian	1839–41
Robert H. Morris	1841–44
James Harper	1844–45
William F. Havemeyer	1845–46
Andrew H. Mickle	1846–47
William V. Brady	1847–48
William F. Havemeyer	1848–49
Caleb S. Woodhull	1849–51
Ambrose C. Kingsland	1851–53
Jacob A. Westervelt	1853–55
Fernando Wood	1855–58
Daniel F. Tiemann	1858–60
Fernando Wood	1860–62
George Opdyke	1862–64
C. Godfrey Gunther	1864–66
John T. Hoffman	1866–68
*Thomas Coman	1868
A. Oakley Hall	1869–72
William F. Havemeyer	1873–74
*Samuel B. H. Vance	1874

Mayor	Years in Office
William H. Wickham	1875–76
Smith Ely, Jr.	1877–78
Edward Cooper	1879–80
William R. Grace	1881–82
Franklin Edison	1883–84
William R. Grace	1885–86
Abram S. Hewitt	1887–88
Hugh J. Grant	1889–92
Thomas F. Gilroy	1893–94
William L. Strong	1895–97
Robert A. Van Wyck	1898–1901
Seth Low	1902–3
George B. McClellan	1904–9
William J. Gaynor	1910–13
*Ardolph L. Kline	1913
John Purroy Mitchel	1914–17
John F. Hylan	1918–25
James J. Walker	1926–32
*Joseph V. McKee	1932
John P. O'Brien	1933
Fiorello H. LaGuardia	1934–45
William O'Dwyer	1946–50
Vincent R. Impellitteri	1950–53
Robert F. Wagner	1954–65
John V. Lindsay	1966–73
Abraham D. Beame	1974–77
Edward I. Koch	1978–89
David N. Dinkins	1990–93
Rudolph W. Giuliani	1994–2001
Michael R. Bloomberg	2002–13
Bill de Blasio	2014–

Idioms, Slang, and Expressions

(Note that a number of these terms are now extremely outdated and not said by anyone; use with caution or not at all.)

bodega—A local convenience store, frequently located on a street corner, that usually sells a small selection of groceries, along with staples like soda, beer, cigarettes, and newspapers. The term is derived from the Spanish *la bodega* (grocery store), but while they were once found mostly in Spanish-speaking—particularly Puerto Rican—areas, bodegas are now found in most neighborhoods located farther away from major retailers.

bridge-and-tunnel—Not a reference to the powerful Triborough Bridge and Tunnel Authority, which has been responsible for maintaining those structures since the 1920s. It is instead slang for those who live in the suburbs and towns surrounding New York proper, particularly New Jersey, who require bridges and tunnels to get into town and are suspected of still having acid-wash denim somewhere in their closet. Used pejoratively by Manhattanites and occasionally with own-the-insult pride by those it refers to. Example: "I stopped going out in the Village; the crowd is all bridge-and-tunnel on the weekend now."

Bronx cheer—Blowing a raspberry; only a "cheer" in the sarcastic sense.

brownstoner—The urban revivalists who, starting in the early 1960s, pushed back against the middle-class emigration to the suburbs by buying up and renovating some of the city's decaying stock of tall, narrow brownstones, particularly on the Upper West Side.

canner—A person who collects cans and bottles from garbage cans or the recycling bags residents pile on the sidewalk for pickup, and takes them to the centers that pay a few cents for each recyclable item.

cruller—A doughnut, to some.

curb your dog—A reminder to both pick up after one's dog and generally keep it under control. It has been against the law to not pick up your pet dog's droppings from a New York sidewalk since 1978. The old "curb your dog" signs were not always clear to some visitors. In his *American Language*, H. L. Mencken confessed to being baffled by the signs' meaning.

desnuda—The racier alternative to the people dressed up as cartoon characters and superheroes in Times Square and who ask for tips from people who take a picture with them. *Desnudas* are the topless women covered in body paint who also cadge tips for pictures and occasionally arouse the ire of city officials and scandalized passers-by.

dollar van—Small shuttles or minivans that pick up and drop off commuters at pre-arranged spots for a small, flat price (originally a dollar).

fancier—A person who raises pigeons in coops, usually on the top of apartment buildings.

featherbedding—Creating rarely show or no-show (but still fully paid) positions at a job site as favors.

fugazi—Fake, no good. Some believe that this term derived from the Italian (Fugazi is an Italian surname). There is also evidence that it was Vietnam War-era slang for something messed up. Pronounced *fu-GAY-zee*.

glom—To attach yourself to something, usually in an unwelcome manner; as in "He glommed on to us after the party." From the Gaelic *glam*: to grab or snatch.

goo-goo—Derived from "goody-goody" and probably coined by the *New York Sun* in the 1890s, this is the once-popular and mostly disparaging term (now generally just used by political news junkies) to describe the (to some, naïve and elitist) "Good-Government" reform activists who inveighed against the kind of back-room deals that establishment and machine politicos insisted were necessary to keep the city running.

grass eater—Early 1970s slang for a police officer who accepted free meals and other small gifts as part of the job. Also "meat eater," for an officer who didn't just accept freebies and tips but who actively shook people down for money in exchange for not arresting them.

Green Book—The official directory of the city of New York, its name comes from the color of the cover, which has, in fact, not always been green. A massive compilation of data about the sprawling government's various entities (including the names of every single city employee), it's been available online since 2012.

gypsy cab—Hired-car drivers who operate without a medallion or as part of a company. Typically seen hanging around the airport and asking people who have just gotten their luggage if they need a car.

hack—A cab-driver. Believed to derive from the old horse-drawn Hackney carriages.

hooker—Prostitute. While a very common usage elsewhere, included here because it may have originated in New York. *Bartlett's Dictionary of Americanisms* (1856) defines "hooker" as "a strumpet, a sailor's trull," and noted that the term likely derived from Corlears Hook, the bend of the East River just below the Manhattan side of the Williamsburg Bridge that was once thick with bordellos popular with sailors.

The Island—Anywhere on Long Island east of Queens and Brooklyn, as in "it's all the way out on the Island." Almost never used to refer to Staten Island, even by residents of that borough.

livery cab—Also known as "black cars" or "car service" vehicles, these are the cars that one can call to take you from one place to another (usually to or from the airport) for a fixed price. They are different from yellow or green cabs in that you cannot hail them on the street and they don't use meters for payment.

Macy's Day Parade—The Thanksgiving Day Parade sponsored by Macy's department store.

mole people—Not-always-appreciated name for ad-hoc communities of people who live in abandoned tunnels underneath the city; first popularized by a 1993 essay of the same name, as well as the documentary *Dark Days*.

mutzadell—Mozzarella, to some Italian Americans (particularly those of southern Italian descent), whose pronunciations have been known to baffle modern Italian speakers (e.g., "gabagool" for capicola, and "reegot" for ricotta).

no-goodnik—Lowlife, bum.

Nuyorican—A Puerto Rican residing in New York. Best known to non-New Yorkers because of the Nuyorican arts movement, a loosely defined agglomeration of Puerto Rican artists who became active in the 1970s. The Nuyorican Poets Café has hosted poetry slams and other performances in an East Village off and on since 1975.

on line—The average New Yorker tends not to stand "in line" but rather "on line."

on the arm—The (now less common) practice by which restaurants would give police officers a free meal. Even though there is no bill, police were usually expected to leave a tip for the server.

pie—A whole pizza.

Port Authority—Short-hand for the Port Authority Bus Terminal at 8th Avenue and 42nd Street. If someone says they're going to "Port Authority," be assured they mean to catch a bus and not visit the offices of the Port Authority of New York and New Jersey.

Pulling a Crater—In 1930, Joseph Crater (1889–1930), a showgirl-loving Tammany Hall judge, walked out of a Hell's Kitchen restaurant and was never seen again. It was one of the most famous unsolved missing person cases in the city's history. For years afterward, his name was slang for disappearing without a trace.

rat with wings—A pigeon.

red-sauce joint—An old-school restaurant serving hearty portions of Italian-American dishes like spaghetti and meatballs, manicotti, and the like, preferably with Sinatra on heavy rotation.

regular—Coffee, with milk and two sugars.

sandhog—The primarily Irish and Grenadian workers who dig the massive subway and water tunnels underneath New York. An elite and tightly knit corps, they are among the best paid construction laborers in the city and take the highest risks.

Sanka—America's first brand of decaffeinated coffee. Marketed primarily to the elderly, it was first introduced in America in the 1920s and enjoyed decades of popularity before disappearing for being, well, horrible. Curiously, New York remains one of the few places where "I'll have a Sanka" isn't *always* met with a blank stare.

schlep—To haul or carry something; particularly used when the hold is onerous, annoying, and inconvenient. One of many Yiddish or Yiddish-derived words in the New York vernacular. Other such Yiddish-derived words are *fakakta* (broken, terrible, doesn't work); *oy* ("argh"); *putz / schlemiel / schmuck* (idiot, fool); *schmear* (spread for your bagel; i.e., cream cheese); *schtup* (have sex); and many others freely utilized by the city's population, regardless of their ethnicity.

sidewalk shed—According to the city, these are "temporary structures built to protect people or property." According to the average New Yorker, these are the noxious dark tunnels of metal tubing topped by wooden slats that cover sidewalks in front of buildings where construction is being done. The fact that the sheds seem to stay up for years at a time, and often when no work is being done, just adds insult to injury.

skell—Derelict, loser, bum, drunk, punk.

slice—There is generally no need to specify "slice of pizza" when going into a Ray's or other takeout pizza place. Just "a slice" will do. If not otherwise specified (pepperoni, sausage, Sicilian, the mysterious "special slice"), you'll get plain cheese.

Spanglish—The common hybrid that sometimes results when speakers of both English and Spanish freely mix the two in conversation. The less frequently used "Chinglish" refers to a blend of Chinese and English.

stoop—The flight of stairs leading up to the second-story entrance of a townhouse or brownstone. From the Dutch *stoep*, meaning "stone steps at the entrance of a house."

straphanger—A subway commuter; from the straps that once hung from the subway car ceilings.

upstate—A fairly vague term that is supposed to actually refer to the northern part of New York state but is quite commonly used to mean anywhere north of Yonkers.

wilding—When youths go rampaging through a park or other public space, as happens from time to time. Came into wide usage in media coverage of the 1989 Central Park jogger attack. Provenance is unclear, though at least one account points to it coming from a police officer mishearing the arrested teens singing along to the hip-hop song "Wild Thing."

yardbird and strings—Jazz Age slang for fried chicken and spaghetti.

For Further Research

Allen, Irving Lewis. *The City in Slang: New York Life and Popular Speech*. New York: Oxford University Press, 1993.

Anbinder, Tyler. *Five Points: The 19th-Century New York City Neighborhood That Invented Tap Dance, Stole Elections, and Became the World's Most Notorious Slum*. New York: Free Press, 2001.

Asbury, Herbert. *Gangs of New York: An Informal History of the Underworld*. New York: Thunder's Mouth Press, 1990.

Barron, James, ed. *New York Times Book of New York: Stores of the People, the Streets, and the Life of the City Past and Present*. New York: Black Dog & Leventhal, 2009.

"Blackout Looting!" Ford Foundation report, 1979.

Burns, Ken, Sarah Burns, and David McMahon. *The Central Park Five*. Florentine Films, 2012.

Burns, Ric. *New York: A Documentary Film*, New York Historical Society/Steeplechase Films, 1999.

Burrows, Edwin G., and Mike Wallace. *Gotham: A History of New York City to 1898*. New York: Oxford University Press, 1999.

Caro, Robert. *The Power Broker: Robert Moses and the Fall of New York*. New York: Knopf, 1972.

Cohen, Gerald. "Origin of New York City's Nickname "The Big Apple." Monograph, 1991.

Ellis, Edward Robb. *The Epic of New York City*. New York: Basic Books, 2011.

Glaeser, Edward L. "Urban Colossus: Why Is New York America's Largest City?" *Federal Reserve Bank of New York Economic Policy Review*, December 2005: 7–24.

Gratz, Roberta Brandes. *The Battle for Gotham: New York in the Shadow of Robert Moses and Jane Jacobs*. New York: Nation Books, 2010.

Helmreich, William B. *The New York Nobody Knows: Walking 6,000 Miles in the City*. Princeton, NJ: Princeton University Press, 2013.

Homberger, Eric. *The Historical Atlas of New York City*. New York: Holt, 2005.

Jackson, Kenneth T., Lisa Keller, and Nancy Flood, eds. *The Encyclopedia of New York City*, 2nd edition. New Haven, CT: Yale University Press, 2010.

Jacobs, Jane. *The Death and Life of Great American Cities*. New York: Random House, 1961.

Jaffe, Steven H. *New York at War: Four Centuries of Combat, Fear, and Intrigue in Gotham*. New York: Basic Books, 2012.

Kaufman, Herbert, and Wallace S. Sayre. *Governing New York City: Politics in the Metropolis*. New York: Russell Sage Foundation, 1960.

Koeppel, Gerard. *City on a Grid: How New York Became New York*. Boston: Da Capo Press, 2015.

Langwiesche, William. *American Ground: Unbuilding the World Trade Center*. New York: North Point Press, 2002.

Lankevich, George J. *New York City: A Short History*. New York: NYU Press, 2002.

Lepore, Jill. *New York Burning: Liberty, Slavery, and Conspiracy in Eighteenth-Century Manhattan*. New York: Knopf, 2005.

Lobel, Cindy R. *Urban Appetites: Food & Culture in Nineteenth-Century New York*. Chicago: University of Chicago Press, 2014.

Lundrigan, Margaret. *Staten Island: Isle of the Bay*. Charleston, SC: Arcadia Publishing, 2004.

Mahler, Jonathan. *Ladies and Gentlemen, the Bronx is Burning: 1977, Baseball, Politics, and the Battle for the Soul of America*. New York: Macmillan, 2006.

McNeil, Legs, and Gillian McCain. *Please Kill Me: The Uncensored Oral History of Punk*. New York: Grove Press, 2006.

McNeur, Catherine. *Taming Manhattan: Environmental Battles in the Antebellum City*. Cambridge, MA: Harvard University Press, 2014.

Nevius, James, and Michelle Nevius. *Inside the Apple: A Streetwise History of New York City*. New York: Simon & Schuster, 2009.

"The Newest New Yorkers: Characteristics of the City's Foreign-Born Population." Department of Planning, City of New York report 2013.

Reitano, Joanne. *The Restless City: A Short History of New York from Colonial Times to the Present*. New York: Routledge, 2010.

Roberts, Sam. *A History of New York in 101 Objects*. New York: Simon & Schuster, 2014.

Rosenzweig, Roy, and Elizabeth Blackmar. *The Park and the People: A History of Central Park*. Ithaca, NY: Cornell University Press, 1992.

Sanders, James. *Celluloid Skyline: New York and the Movies*. New York: Knopf, 2001.

Sanderson, Eric. *Mannahatta: A Natural History of New York City*. New York: Harry N. Abrams, 2013.

Sante, Luc. *Low Life: Lures and Snares of Old New York*. New York: Vintage Books, 1992.

Taylor, William R. *Inventing Times Square: Commerce and Culture at the Crossroads of the World*. Baltimore: John Hopkins University Press, 1996.

White, E. B. *Here Is New York*. New York: Harper & Bros., 1949.

Winn, Christopher. *I Never Knew That About New York*. New York: Plume, 2013.

Index

Note: (ill.) indicates photos and illustrations.

NUMBERS

2nd Avenue Deli, 345
3rd Street, 143, 350, 356
4 line, 162, 392
4th Street, 214, 312
5 line, 162, 392
5th New York Regiment, 94
6 line, 162
6th Street, 117, 326
7 line, 14, 188, 289
7th Regiment, 97
8th Street, 216
9/11
    the Gilded Age, 118–19
    independence of New York, 82
    Manhattan, 196–97, 199–200,
      211
    quirky New York, 392
    rebuilding and moving forward
      after, 182–89
    the sixties to, 155–82
    World War II and the postwar
      era, 148
9/11 Museum, 196–97
9th Street, 218, 221, 329
10th Cavalry, 248
10th Street, 213, 215, 218–19, 321,
  345
11th New York Regiment, 97
12 West, 351
12th Street, 220, 345, 396
13th Street, 173, 217, 354
14th Street
    food and dining, 327
    Manhattan, 213, 217–19, 221,
      225, 245
    Queens, 288
    transportation, 31
15th New York National Guard Infantry, 130
17th Street, 219, 221
18th Street, 220, 318, 327
19th Street, 222
20th Century Fox, 356

20th Company, 94
20th Street, 86, 221, 317
21, 132
21st Street, 225
22nd Street, 225
23rd Street, 20, 52, 181, 220, 222–
  23, 225–26, 244
24th Street, 226
25th Hour, 386
25th Street, 224, 360, 387
26th Street, 101, 223–24, 314
27th Street, 226
28th Street, 224–27, 230, 326, 347,
  391
29th Street, 97
31st Street, 124, 227, 321
32nd Street, 237
33rd Street, 124, 149, 227, 237
34th Street
    food and dining, 324
    Manhattan, 222, 230–32, 237,
      244
    Queens, 286
    rebuilding and moving forward
      after 9/11, 188
    transportation, 31
    World War II and the postwar
      era, 148
35th Avenue, 394
35th Street, 226
37th Street, 61, 380
38 Witnesses (Rosenthal), 154
38th Street, 230, 325
39th Company, 94
39th Street, 226, 233
40 Acres and a Mule, 386
40/40 Club, 387
40th Street, 84, 238–39
41st Precinct, 270
41st Street, 226
42nd Street
    the Gilded Age, 117, 119, 121–
     22
    independence of New York, 83–
     84

    Manhattan, 191, 231–33, 238,
     262
    quirky New York, 390
    rebuilding and moving forward
     after 9/11, 188
    transportation, 31–32
43rd Street, 230, 239
.44 Killer, 168
44th Street, 96, 117, 317, 342, 373
45th Street, 117, 344, 346
46th Street, 95, 176, 233, 344, 389
47th Street, 231, 239, 330
48th Street, 322, 349
49th Street, 241–42, 255, 347
50th Street, 229, 241–42, 321
51st Street, 122, 241, 396
52nd Street, 232, 241, 311
53rd Street, 239, 242–43, 288
54th Street, 242, 351
55th Street, 243, 335
57th Street, 232, 234–35, 247
58th Street, 236
59th Street, 244–45, 250
60th Street, 250, 298
61st Street, 251
63rd Street, 162
64th Street, 247
65th Street Transverse, 246
66th Street, 250–51
69th Company, 94–95
69th Regiment Armory, 360
70th Street, 46
71st Street, 251
72nd Street, 249
73rd Street, 248
74th Street, 116, 248
75th Street, 216
77th Street, 249
79th Street, 255
80th Street, 251
81st Street, 249, 394
82nd Street, 253
84th Street, 251, 255
86th Street, 225, 254, 329
88th Street, 253–54

409

90th Street, 128, 255
91st Street, 253–54, 332
92nd Street, 253
93rd Division, 130
93rd Street, 302
94th Street, 332
96th Street, 28, 162, 254, 261, 302
103rd Street, 253
104th Street, 253
105th Street, 247, 253
106th Street, 245
110th Street, 28, 208, 256
112th Street, 256
114th Street, 255, 324
116th Street, 61, 260, 327
120th Street, 61
122nd Street, 258
125th Street, 6, 162, 258, 348
128th Street, 361, 391
131st Street, 342
132nd Street, 268, 342
135th Street, 127, 260
138th Street, 260, 269
139th Street, 260
142nd Street, 348
144th Street, 260
145th Street, 118, 130, 132
155th Street, 72, 260, 377
159th Street, 39
160th Street, 262
161st Street, 269
163rd Street, 262
165th Street, 260, 308
181 Club, 334
183rd Street, 261
185th Street, 261
207th Street, 29
218th Street, 39
311 line, 184
369th Infantry Regiment, 130
911 response system, 154
2001: A Space Odyssey, 226
2010 Census, 10–11

A

A line, 29
Abby Aldrich Rockefeller Sculpture
    Garden, 243
ABC, 169, 315
Above 110th Street, 356
Absolut, 361
Abwehr, 146–47
Abyssinia. See Ethiopia
Abyssinian Baptist Church, 213, 380
The Academy of Music, 219, 340
Achkenheshacky Indians, 35
Acropolis, the, 227
ACT UP (AIDS Coalition to Unleash
    Power), 172
Action Comics, 376

Actor's Laboratory Theatre, 382
Actors Studio, 341–42
Adam, 45
Adam Clayton Powell Jr. Boulevard,
    327, 342
Adams, Abigail, 67, 251
Adams, John, 59, 61, 68, 251, 275,
    293–94
Adams, Thomas, 328
Adbusters, 185
Adler, Jacob, 345
Adler, Stella, 345
advantages economically of, 23
Adventure, 51
Aenied (Virgil), 197
affordability of, 189
Afghanistan, 166
Afghanistanis as inhabitants, 14,
    289
Africa, 8, 39, 202, 212, 293, 393
African Americans as inhabitants
    animals, 6
    bars and nightlife, 333
    British colonial era, 53–54
    Bronx, 267
    Brooklyn, 274, 281–83
    ethnicity, 12–13
    the Gilded Age, 126–27, 129–30
    independence of New York, 67,
        69, 75, 79–80, 82, 84–85
    industrialization and immigra-
        tion, 101
    Manhattan, 192, 201, 204, 211–
        13, 215, 245–48, 256–61
    music, 347–49
    notable New Yorkers, 379–80
    police, 17
    Queens, 287
    quirky New York, 393
    rebuilding and moving forward
        after 9/11, 187
    religion, 15
    Revolutionary War, 63–65
    the sixties to 9/11, 157, 170,
        173–77
    slavery and the Civil War, 91, 93,
        95–97
    sports, 307, 312–13
    Staten Island, 292, 294, 296
    theater, 340–42
    World War II and the postwar
        era, 146, 153
    writing, 364, 374
African Burial Ground, 53, 67, 204–
    5
African Communities League, 129
African Free School, 69
Africans as inhabitants, 13, 179
After the Fall (Miller), 226
age of trees, 4–5
Ahmet, 315
AIDS, 172–73, 361

AIDS Coalition to Unleash Power
    (ACT UP), 172
Air Corps, U.S., 148
Air Defense Command, 150
Air Force, U.S., 355
Alabama, 341
Alaska, 52
Albany
    British colonial era, 48, 55
    Dutch colonial era, 39–40, 45
    government, 16
    Great Depression era, 142
    independence of New York, 69–
        70, 87–88
    Manhattan, 194
    notable New Yorkers, 379
Albee, Edward, 346
Alberti, Peter Caesar, 108
Alexander Hamilton U.S. Customs
    House, 194
Alexandria, Egypt, 247
Algerians as inhabitants, 97
Algonquin Hotel, 373
Algonquin Indians, 23, 35, 44
Algonquin Round Table, 373
All My Sons, 381
Allen, Steve, 357
Allen, Woody, 20, 147, 358
Alley Pond Park, 5
All-Star Break, 397
All-Stars, Oshkosh, 313
Almshouse Hospital, 52
Al-Qaeda, 177, 180
Al-Waleed, Prince, 244
AM New York, 370
Amagansett, 147
Amateur Night, 259, 383
"Amazin' Mets," 308
Amboy Street, 281
American Acclimatization Society, 9
American Bowling Congress, 306
American Federation of Labor, 103
American International Group
    (AIG), 185
American Jewish Congress, 147
American Journalism: A History
    (Mott), 363
American League baseball, 309, 311
American Merchant Mariners'
    Memorial, 193
American Museum, 101
American Museum of Natural His-
    tory, 248–49, 378, 393
The American Naturalist, 302
American Notes (Dickens), 5, 372
American Party, 92
American Psycho (Ellis), 171
American Revolution
    British colonial era, 55
    business and economy, 24
    Dutch colonial era, 46, 48

independence of New York, 74–75

Revolutionary War, 55, 57, 63

American Telephone and Telegraph, 137

American Vitagraph Company, 354

American Wing, 252

Americans, Brooklyn, 314

Americans, New York, 313–14

America's Dunkirk, 60

Amerks, the. See Americans, New York

Amherst College, 159

Amiable Child Monument, 390–91

Ammann, Othmar, 263

Amnesty International, 179

Amsterdam, the Netherlands, 39, 42, 44, 256, 268

Amsterdam Avenue, 247, 255–56, 260

Amsterdam News, 370

An American in Paris, 379

Anabaptists as inhabitants, 15

Anastasia, Albert "Chief Executioner," 144

Ancient Order of Hibernians, 209

Andros, Gov. Edmund, 15, 48

Andy Warhol's Factory, 219

Angelika, 370

Anglicans as inhabitants, 15, 54, 78, 255

animals, 5–10

Annapolis, Maryland, 67

Annie, 170, 387

Annie Hall, 20

Ansonia, the, (Hotel), 248

Anthora cups, 326

Anti-Saloon League, 131

anti-Semitism, 45–46, 84, 106–8, 111, 146, 376

apartment building, richest, 251

apartments, empty Manhattan, 234–35

Apollo 11, 203

Apollo Theater, 258–59, 259 (ill.), 342, 383

Appo, George, 394

Appo, Quimbo, 394

The Apprentice, 385

Aquahonga Manacknong, 292

Aquahung, 268

Aquinas, Thomas, 384

Arabs as inhabitants, 195

Arbuckle, Fatty, 354

Archangel, 50

Archibald Gracie Mansion. See Gracie Mansion

Architectural Forum, 381

Arizona, 10, 140

Arms and Armor, 253

Arms of Amsterdam, 42

Armstrong, Louis, 348

Army, British, 262

Army, Confederate, 93, 301, 389

Army, Continental
  Brooklyn, 275–76
  independence of New York, 66
  Manhattan, 261, 265
  quirky New York, 391
  Revolutionary War, 59, 61, 63
  Staten Island, 294

Army, Union, 258, 277, 295–96, 366

Army, U.S., 95, 128, 130, 148, 150

Aronofsky, Darren, 285

art, 359–63

Art Deco style, 237–38, 241–42, 250, 269, 277

Art in America, 360

art in the subway, 31–32

Art Institute of Chicago, 360

Art Moderne style, 269

The Art of the Deal (Trump and Schwartz), 385

Arthur, 350

Arthur, Chester, 85, 106, 391

Arthur Ashe Stadium, 315

"The Artichoke King," 142

Articles of Capitulation, 47

Articles of Confederation, 67

arts, the
  art, 359–63
  film and TV, 354–59
  music, 347–54
  Revolutionary War, 55
  theater, 339–47
  writing, 363–76

Arts for Transit, 31

Asbury, Herbert, 115, 207

Asch Building, 125–26

Asia, 37, 133

Asians as inhabitants
  Bronx, 267
  Brooklyn, 274
  ethnicity, 12–13
  food and dining, 326
  independence of New York, 79
  Manhattan, 192
  Queens, 287, 290
  quirky New York, 393–94
  Staten Island, 292

assassinations, 58, 96, 120, 124, 128, 260

Astley Belt, 101

Astor, Caroline Schermerhorn, 104

Astor, John Jacob, 23, 72, 116, 200, 365

Astor Court, 270

Astor Library, 344, 382

Astor Place, 344

Astoria, 7, 188, 286–88

Atlanta, Georgia, 308, 386

The Atlantic, 183

Atlantic Avenue, 195, 277, 280, 308, 314

Atlantic Basin, 277

Atlantic City, New Jersey, 385

Atlantic Coast, 11, 48, 56

Atlantic Flyway, 6

Atlantic Highlands, 150

Atlantic Ocean
  Dutch colonial era, 36, 40
  the Gilded Age, 127, 131
  Great Depression era, 144
  independence of New York, 75
  landscape, 1
  storms, 4

Atlantic Records, 349

Atlantic Seaboard, 58

Atlantic Yards, 280

Atlas Comics, 376

attitude toward the Civil War, 93

Audubon Ballroom, 260

Audubon Center, 279

Augustine of Hippo, 384

Auschwitz, 224

Australia, 8, 177

Australians as inhabitants, 370

Austria, 89, 140

Austrian Empire, 238

Austrians as inhabitants, 329

authors and publishing, 371–76

auto fatality, first, 116

Automat, 320–21, 321 (ill.)

The Avengers, 375

Avenue A, 143

Aykroyd, Dan, 359

Aztecs, 355

B

Bacall, Lauren, 249, 344

Bacarat Hotel and Residences, 235

bags, best shopping, 250

Baha'is as inhabitants, 15

Bahamas, 381

bald eagles, 8–9

Baldwin, James, 146

Bale, Christian, 368

Baltimore, Maryland, 67, 269, 272, 308, 310

Bangladeshis as inhabitants, 13, 29, 326

Bank of New York, 68–69

Bank of Nova Scotia, 183

Bank of the Manhattan Company, 68

Bank of the United States, 77

Bank Street, 212

Bankhead, Tallulah, 373

Baptists as inhabitants, 15

Barbados, 212

Barbary Pirates, 275

Barcelona, Spain, 362

Barclay Street, 195, 203

Barclays Center, 277, 280, 314, 387

Barnard, George Grey, 263–64

Barney's, 250
Barnum, Phineas Taylor, 101–2, 194, 228, 369
Barnum & Bailey Greatest Show on Earth, 102
Barrymore, Lionel, 289
bars and nightlife, 330–37
Bartholdi, Auguste, 102
Baryshnikov, Mikhail, 351
baseball
    Bronx, 268–69
    Brooklyn, 279–80
    early history, 306
    Manhattan, 260
    Queens, 286, 290
    quirky New York, 397
    the sixties to 9/11, 169
    sports, 306–11
Baseball [TV show], 311
Baseball Hall of Fame, 306
basic information, 1–32
Basie, Count, 258, 260, 348
basketball, 214, 230, 280, 311–13
Basquiat, Jean-Michel, 384
Baths of Carcalla, 124
Batman, 74, 368, 375–76
Battery, the, 66, 74, 192
Battery Park
    all about, 192–206
    bars and nightlife, 335
    Dutch colonial era, 42
    independence of New York, 74
    industrialization and immigration, 113
    photo, 193 (ill.)
    rebuilding and moving forward after 9/11, 188
    Revolutionary War, 65
Battery Park City, 5, 162, 194–95, 241
Battery Place, 194
Battle, Samuel Jesse, 126–27
Battle Annie, 115
Battle of Brooklyn, 60–62, 275, 281
Battle of Bunker Hill, 59
Battle of Central Park, 151–52
Battle of Gettysburg, 86, 96
Battle of Golden Hill, 57–58, 58 (ill.)
Battle of Harlem Heights, 61, 63, 262
Battle of Lexington and Concord, 63
Battle of Long Island, 60
Battle of New York, 314
Battle of San Juan Hill, 248
Battle of White Plains, 63
Battle Row, 115, 233
Battle Row Ladies' Social and Athletic Club, 115
Battles of Bull Run, 94
Bay Ridge, 249
Bayard III, Nicholas, 209
Bayard Street, 88
Bayles, William Harrison, 331

Bayonne Bridge, 292
Beach, Alfred Ely, 100–101
Beach Haven, 10
Beame, Abraham, 164–65, 170, 178, 184, 375
Bear Stearns, 185
bears, black, 5
"Beat on the Brat," 385
Beatles, the, 154–55, 244
Beatniks, 214
Beatty, Warren, 213
The Beautiful and the Damned (Fitzgerald), 145
Beaux Arts style
    Bronx, 270
    Brooklyn, 278
    the Gilded Age, 117, 119, 122
    industrialization and immigration, 113
    Manhattan, 193–94, 222–23, 238, 248, 252
    theater, 346
    transportation, 31
Beaver Street, 198, 317
beavers, 3, 5, 9, 21, 23, 41–43, 198
Bed, Bath and Beyond, 222
Bedford Avenue [Brooklyn], 279, 314
Bedford Street [Manhattan], 336
Bedford-Stuyvesant, 187, 283, 386
Bedloe, Isaac, 299
Bedloe's Island, 102, 299
Beekman Street, 198
The Beggar's Opera, 339
Belasco, David, 346
Belgians as inhabitants, 212
Bell, Alexander Graham, 295
Belleau Wood, 130
Bellevue Establishment, 52
Bellevue Hospital Center, 224
"The Bells," 272
Belushi, John, 359
Belvedere Castle, 83, 246–47
Benchley, Peter, 10
Benga, Ota, 392–93, 393 (ill.)
Bennett, James Gordon, 261
Bennett, Michael, 343
Bennett Park, 261
Bennett Sr., James Gordon, 365
Ben's Kosher Delicatessen, 325
Bensonhurst, 14, 175
Berg, Gertrude, 358
Bergdorf Goodman, 250
Berkowitz, David "Son of Sam," 168
Berle, Milton, 270
Berlin, Germany, 124, 131, 169
Berlin, Irving, 347
Berlin Wall, 351
Bermuda, 212
Bernard B. Kerik Complex, 206
Bernstein, Leonard, 153, 157, 248–49

Berry, Chuck, 349
Best Buy, 222
Bestavaar's Kill, 212
Bethesda Terrace, 246
Beyoncé, 387
Bible, the, 247
Bible Belt, 15
Bicentennial, 1976, 166–67
Bickmore, Albert Smith, 248, 248 (ill.)
Bicknell, Arthur, 343
Biden, Joe, 183
"The Big Apple," 2–3
"Big Board," 68
The Big Oyster (Kurlansky), 9
Bill the Butcher, 92
Billionaires' Row, 235, 251
Billopp, Christopher, 293
Biograph, 354
birds, 6–9, 31, 246, 282
The Birth of a Nation, 134
Black Album, 387
Black and Tan, 333
black bears, 5
Black Brigade, 64
black cars, 28
The Black Crook, 340
Black Fives, 312
Black Hand, the, 120, 138, 142
Black Hills, 240
Black Jack, 328
Black Joke Engine Company, 19, 95
Black Monday, 137
Black Nationalism, 260
Black Panther Party for Self-Defense, 130, 157
Black Thursday, 137
Black Tom Island, 127, 146
Black-Cat, 212
blackout of 1977, 167–68, 170
Blackwell family, 297
Blackwell's Island, 297–98, 302
Blackwell's Penitentiary, 297–98, 302
Bleecker Street, 211, 213, 333, 376
Bliss, Henry, 116
Blonde on Blonde, 226
Blood Alley, 239
Bloody Angle, 207
Bloomberg, Michael
    Manhattan, 255
    police, 18
    politics, 21
    quirky New York, 395, 398
    rebuilding and moving forward after 9/11, 184 (ill.), 184–89
    sports, 311
Bloomberg Tower, 234
Bloomingdale [neighborhood], 247
Bloomingdale's, 250, 320
"Blowin' in the Wind," 350
Blue Note, 350

BMT (Brooklyn-Manhattan Transit Co.), 119, 149
Board of Education, 70, 153
Board of Estimate, 186
boating, 262
bocce ball, 305–6
bodegas, 26
Body, Busy, 365
Boess, Gustav, 131
Bogart, Humphrey, 336
Bohemianism, 213–14, 216
Bohemians as inhabitants, 41, 243
Bollywood, 289
Bolshevik Revolution, 20
Bolting Act, 48–49
Bonanno family, 139
The Book of New York Verse, 37
Book Row, 220
BookCourt, 220
Booth, John Wilkes, 389
Born Yesterday, 346
boroughs, the five
    business and economy, 26
    firefighting, 19
    furthest, 291–92
    government, 16
    greenest, 296
    largest, 273, 286
    location, 1
    map, 2 (ill.)
    names, 1
    only mainland, 267
    police, 17
    population, 11–12
    reason for number, 16
    sixth borough, 397–98
    sizes, 2
    smallest, 292
    transportation, 31
Boston, Massachusetts
    British colonial era, 51, 54
    Bronx, 268–69, 272
    business and economy, 21, 23
    the Gilded Age, 118
    independence of New York, 82
    Manhattan, 202, 260
    population, 12
    Revolutionary War, 57–58
    the sixties to 9/11, 180
    sports, 309
    storms, 4
    writing, 372
Boston Massacre, 57–58
Boston Tea Party, 57
Boulder Bridge, 279
Bowery, the, 65, 81, 85, 116, 217, 332, 352–53
Bowery Boys, 81, 88, 92, 319
Bowery G'hals, 81
Bowery Road, 219
Bowery Street, 41, 80, 147, 352
Bowery Theater, 80

Bowery Village, 72, 218
bowling, 194, 305–6
Bowling Green, 43, 59, 194, 198, 306
"The Boxer," 183
Boy Mayor, 127–28
Bradford, William, 363, 371
Bradley, Bill, 313
Brancusi, Constantin, 360
Brand, Bill, 32
Brandenburg Gate, 124, 227
Brando, Marlon, 342
Bratton, Bill, 178, 187
Braves, Atlanta, 308
Brawley, Tawana, 175
Brazil, 26, 46, 335
Brazilians as inhabitants, 46, 315
Breezy Point, 186, 291
Breslin, Jimmy, 168, 375, 384
Breuckelen, 274
Breuer Building, 216–17
Brewer Street, 198
bridge, busiest, 263
Bridge Café, 331
Bridge of Sighs, 206
Bridgegrooms, the, 307
bridges, 29
A Brief Description of New York: Formerly Called New Netherlands (Denton), 373
Brighton Beach, 284
Brill Building, 347
Britain. See Great Britain
British Army, 262
British as inhabitants
    bars and nightlife, 330
    Bronx, 268, 271
    Brooklyn, 276
    Dutch colonial era, 37–38, 41, 43–48
    food and dining, 316–17, 319
    independence of New York, 74, 87
    industrialization and immigration, 101–2
    Manhattan, 192, 198, 203, 215, 225, 247, 256, 262, 265
    music, 352
    origins of inhabitants, 11
    other islands around the boroughs, 300
    Queens, 287
    religion, 15
    Revolutionary War, 55–66
    seal, 3
    sports, 306
    Staten Island, 294–95
    writing, 372–73
British colonial era, 47–55
British East India Company, 50, 57
British Empire, 22, 54–55
British Isles, 66, 281

Broad Channel, 282
Broad Channel Cross Bay Bridge, 282
Broad Street, 41, 52, 196, 198, 200
Broadway
    British colonial era, 52
    Dutch colonial era, 39, 41
    film and TV, 355
    food and dining, 321, 326, 330
    the Gilded Age, 117, 119, 128, 134
    government, 16
    independence of New York, 67, 72, 78
    industrialization and immigration, 100–101, 108
    Manhattan, 194, 199, 202–5, 207, 209–10, 213, 218–23, 231–32, 248, 255–56, 260
    music, 347, 349, 351–52
    notable New Yorkers, 379, 381–82
    quirky New York, 389–90
    rebuilding and moving forward after 9/11, 185
    Revolutionary War, 61–62, 65
    slavery and the Civil War, 96
    sports, 308, 314
    theater, 340, 342–47
    World War II and the postwar era, 147
    writing, 368, 374
Broadway Central Hotel, 352
Broken Land, 274
broken-window policy, 178–79
Bronck, Jonas, 268
Bronson, Charles, 173
Bronx
    all about the, 267–73
    animals, 5, 7
    early history, 268
    ethnicity, 14
    film and TV, 358
    the Gilded Age, 119, 127
    Great Depression era, 141, 143
    independence of New York, 83
    industrialization and immigration, 104
    location, 1
    Manhattan, 198, 211, 262, 264–65
    music, 353
    other islands around the boroughs, 302
    population, 10–11, 267
    Queens, 286, 288
    Revolutionary War, 63
    the sixties to 9/11, 158, 167–70, 176
    size, 2
    sports, 308–9
    the five boroughs, 1, 2 (ill.)

413

theater, 345
World War II and the postwar
  era, 151
Bronx Botanical Garden, 157, 267,
  270–71
Bronx River, 268, 271
Bronx Terminal Market, 142
The Bronx Warriors, 356
Bronx Zoo, 270–71, 378, 392–93
Brookland Ferry, 275
Brooklyn
  all about, 273–86
  bars and nightlife, 332–33, 336
  British colonial era, 52–53
  Bronx, 267–68, 270
  Dutch colonial era, 36, 38, 40
  early history, 35, 274
  ethnicity, 14, 274
  film and TV, 354
  food and dining, 317, 326, 328
  geology, 33
  the Gilded Age, 119, 134
  Great Depression era, 144
  independence of New York, 74,
    79
  industrialization and immigra-
    tion, 101, 104, 106, 108, 116
  Manhattan, 192, 198, 220, 241,
    243, 249
  music, 349, 351
  notable New Yorkers, 378, 381,
    384, 386–87
  other islands around the bor-
    oughs, 300, 303
  population, 10–12, 273
  Queens, 286–88
  quirky New York, 390, 392–93
  rebuilding and moving forward
    after 9/11, 188
  religion, 15
  Revolutionary War, 60
  the sixties to 9/11, 159, 164,
    167, 174–76
  size, 2
  slavery and the Civil War, 92
  sports, 169, 307–8, 310, 313–14
  Staten Island, 292–94
  the five boroughs, 1, 2 (ill.)
  theater, 341, 345
  transportation, 29, 31
  World War II and the postwar
    era, 146, 150, 153–54
  writing, 375
The Brooklyn Academy of Music,
  278
Brooklyn Botanic Garden, 278
Brooklyn Brewery, 333
Brooklyn Bridge
  animals, 8
  British colonial era, 54
  Brooklyn, 275
  food and dining, 328

the Gilded Age, 117
industrialization and immigra-
  tion, 104–6, 105 (ill.), 109–10
Manhattan, 198–99, 204
notable New Yorkers, 379
quirky New York, 396
Brooklyn Daily Eagle, 276, 339
Brooklyn Eagle, 281
Brooklyn Heights
  Brooklyn, 274–75, 277, 280
  food and dining, 329
  industrialization and immigra-
    tion, 105–6
  Manhattan, 195
  notable New Yorkers, 381
  other islands around the bor-
    oughs, 300
  quirky New York, 392
  Revolutionary War, 59–61
Brooklyn Historical Society, 84
Brooklyn Ice Palace, 314
Brooklyn Museum, 179, 278, 283
Brooklyn Navy Yard, 275 (ill.), 275–
  76
Brooklyn Public Library, 277, 283
Brooklyn Village, 274
Brooklyn-Battery Tunnel, 195
Brooklyn-Manhattan Transit Co.
  (BMT), 119, 149
Brooklyn-Queens Expressway, 277
Brooks, Mel, 358
Brooks Brothers, 222
Broome Street, 152, 208
Brother Island, 118, 124
Brown, Charles, 281
Brown, James, 259
Brown, Michael, 187
Brown Building, 126
Browne, Arthur, 127
Brownsville, 144, 281
Bruder, Charles, 10
Bryan, William Jennings, 131
Bryant, William Cullen, 238
Bryant Park, 85, 214, 238–39
Bryant Park Fashion Show, 238
Buckley Jr., William F., 20, 374–75,
  383
Budapest, Hungary, 140, 243
Buddhists as inhabitants, 15, 290
Budweiser beer, 333
Buffalo, 74–75
building, oldest, 199
Bukharians as inhabitants, 239
Bulloch, Martha "Mittie," 93
Bull's Head Tavern, 65
Bund, the, 146, 146 (ill.), 229, 376
Burbank, California, 358
burials, segregated, 204
Burke, Jimmy "The Gent," 169
Burlington Coat Factory, 223
Burnham, Daniel, 223
Burns, Robert, 246

Burr, Aaron, 68–69, 75, 83, 262
Burroughs, William S., 353
Burton, Mary, 54
Burton, Tim, 284
buses, 27, 29, 32
Bush, George H. W., 200
Bush, George W., 182
Bushnell, David, 61–62
Bushwick, 274, 286, 340
Bushwick Avenue, 332
busiest bridge, 263
busiest subway stations, 31
business, 21–26, 55
Butler, Rose, 215
Butter-Cake Dick's, 319
Buttermilk Pond, 205
Buttonwood Agreement, 21, 67–68,
  200
Butts, Alfred Mosher, 394
Buzzfeed, 180
Byzantine, 256

C

cab drivers, ethncities of, 28–29
Cabaret, 351
Cabey, Darrell, 173
Cabrini, Saint Frances Xavier, 263
cabs, green, 28
cabs, yellow, 27
Caesar, Sid, 358
Café Sabarsky, 329
Café Society, 145–46, 373
Cage, the, 214, 312
Cairo, Egypt, 247
Calatrava, Santiago, 197
California
  bars and nightlife, 337
  Bronx, 273
  Brooklyn, 280
  business and economy, 22
  film and TV, 354, 356–59
  food and dining, 327
  Great Depression era, 142
  independence of New York, 70
  industrialization and immigra-
    tion, 114
  Manhattan, 207, 240
  music, 349, 353
  number of Native Americans, 11
  population, 10–11
  quirky New York, 394
  rebuilding and moving forward
    after 9/11, 187, 189
  the sixties to 9/11, 157, 172, 180
  sports, 307–8
  writing, 375
Call It Sleep (Roth), 281
Callery pear, 4
Calloway, Cab, 152, 342, 348–49
Calvary Cemetery, 289

414

Calvinism, 39
Calvinists as inhabitants, 15
Cambridge, Massachusetts, 373
cameras, security, 189
Camorra, the, 120
Campbell, Clive, 353
Campbell Soup, 243
Canaan, 373
Canada
    animals, 9
    British colonial era, 50, 55
    business and economy, 26
    Dutch colonial era, 38
    early history, 35
    geology, 33
    ironworkers, 11
    notable New Yorkers, 381–82
    Revolutionary War, 57, 64–65
    the sixties to 9/11, 168
    slavery and the Civil War, 92
    sports, 313
Canal Commission, 377
Canal Plan, 319
Canal Street, 31, 80, 200, 207–10,
    214, 319
Canarsie, 33, 276
Canarsie Indians, 35–36, 274, 282,
    284
Cantonese as inhabitants, 114
Canyon of Heroes, 202–3, 203 (ill.)
Cape Verde, 144
capital, as national, 67
"Capital of Black America," 257
Capote, Truman, 383
Captain America, 375–76
"Captain Kidd in New York Harbor,"
    51 (ill.)
Cardinals, St. Louis, 308
Caribbean, the, 23, 39, 44, 176, 293
Caribbeans as inhabitants, 13, 254,
    258, 282–83
Carl Luger's Café Billiards and
    Bowling Alley, 326
Carl Schurz Park, 255
Carmine's, 324
Carnegie, Andrew, 234, 253–54, 378
Carnegie Hall, 234, 234 (ill.), 254
Carnegie Hill, 254
Caro, Robert, 151, 271–72
Carr, Caleb, 87
cars, black, 28
cars, livery, 28–29
Carson, Johnny, 351, 357–58
Carter, Jimmy, 200
Carter, Shawn. See Jay-Z
Caruso, Enrico, 324
Casino, 135
"The Cask of Amontillado," 272
Cass, Mama, 350
Castellano, Paul, 176, 208
Castle Clinton, 74, 193–94, 301
Castle Garden, 113, 192–94

Castle Williams, 300 (ill.), 301
Cathedral Church of St. John the
    Divine, 256, 270
Cathedral of Commerce, 204
Catherine of Braganza, Queen, 287
Catholic Church, 69, 155
Catholic Spanish Empire, 39
Catholicism, 287
Catholics as inhabitants
    British colonial era, 50, 54
    Dutch colonial era, 46
    education, 20
    the Gilded Age, 134
    independence of New York, 70,
        78–80
    industrialization and immigra-
        tion, 99, 107
    Manhattan, 195–96, 209, 241
    notable New Yorkers, 379–80,
        384
    religion, 15
    the sixties to 9/11, 179
    slavery and the Civil War, 95
    World War II and the postwar
        era, 153, 155
Cats, 347
Catskills, the, 171
CBGB's, 352–53, 384
CBS, 315, 349, 357–58, 382
Cedar Park, 353
Celtics, New York, 312
cemeteries
    animals, 5
    Bronx, 271
    Brooklyn, 280–81
    geology, 33
    independence of New York, 67
    Manhattan, 199–201, 204–5,
        209, 225, 241, 253
    notable New Yorkers, 377
    Queens, 288–89
    quirky New York, 391
    slavery and the Civil War, 92
Census Bureau, U.S., 11–12, 92
Central Americans as inhabitants,
    14, 289
Central Europe, 106
Central Library, 277, 283
Central Park
    all about, 244–47
    animals, 5, 7, 9
    Brooklyn, 278–81
    film and TV, 355
    the Gilded Age, 135
    independence of New York, 72,
        74, 83, 86–87
    industrialization and immigra-
        tion, 101
    Manhattan, 192, 220–21, 235,
        244, 249–52, 254
    map, 245 (ill.)

notable New Yorkers, 378, 382,
    386
the sixties to 9/11, 156, 164, 174
sports, 306
Staten Island, 296
theater, 345
weather, 3–4
World War II and the postwar
    era, 151
Central Park Arsenal, 248
Central Park Commission, 378
Central Park Conservancy, 246
Central Park Five, 174–75
Central Park Reservoir. See Jacque-
    line Kennedy Onassis Reservoir
Central Park West, 46, 116, 151, 249
Central Park Zoo, 86, 132, 141, 246
Central Station, 228
The Central Synagogue, 243, 243
    (ill.)
Centre Street, 80, 97, 205
century, a new, 137–89
Chamber of Commerce and Indus-
    try, 21–22
Chamber of Horrors, 147
Chamberlain, Wilt, 312
Chambers Street, 194, 203–4, 210
Champs-Elysees, 269
change in population, 12
Charging Bull, 194
Charles I, King, 37
Charles II, King, 47, 287, 293
Charleston, South Carolina, 53, 106
Charter of 1686, 49
Chase, Chevy, 359
Chase Manhattan Bank, 162
Chateau-Thierry, 130
Chatham Square, 225
Chatham Street, 80
Cheetah, 350
Chelsea, 180, 188, 215, 225–31, 362,
    395
Chelsea Girls, 226
Chelsea Horror Hotel (Ramone),
    225
Chelsea Market, 329
Chelsea Walls, 226
Cheney, Dick, 69, 182
chess players, 215
Chicago, Illinois
    Bronx, 273
    business and economy, 22
    film and TV, 359
    food and dining, 320
    independence of New York, 70,
        77
    industrialization and immigra-
        tion, 108
    Manhattan, 223, 230, 259, 263
    music, 348
    population, 10, 12
    the sixties to 9/11, 157

415

sports, 313
transportation, 27–29
Chicago, Judy, 278
The Chief, 370
Children of the City: At Work and at Play (Nasaw), 367
The Children's Friend, 395
China
  business and economy, 26
  Dutch colonial era, 36–37
  food and dining, 322
  Manhattan, 198, 239
  quirky New York, 394
  transportation, 31
  writing, 370
Chinatown
  all about, 206–11
  food and dining, 322–23
  independence of New York, 80
  industrialization and immigration, 110, 114
  Manhattan, 206 (ill.)
  Queens, 288, 291
  quirky New York, 396
  the sixties to 9/11, 162
  World War II and the postwar era, 152
Chinese as inhabitants
  ethnicity, 13
  food and dining, 317, 321–23, 325
  independence of New York, 80
  industrialization and immigration, 114
  Manhattan, 206–7
  Queens, 288–89
  quirky New York, 394
  World War II and the postwar era, 146, 152
Chinese Devil Man, 394
Chi-Raq, 386
cholera, 82–83
A Chorus Line, 343–44, 382
Christianity, 339
Christians as inhabitants, 46, 80, 107, 195, 290
Christie, Chris, 311
Christmas, 132, 225, 367, 394–95
Christodora House, 110
Christopher Street, 156
"Christopher Street" [song], 213
Christopher Street Liberation Day, 156
Chrysler, Walter, 238
Chrysler Building, 237–38
Chrysler Corporation, 238
Chrystie Street, 345
Chumley, Leland, 336
Chumley's, 336
church, first Catholic, 195–96
Church, Frederic E., 359
church, largest, 256

Church of England, 199
Church of Jesus Christ of Latter-Day Saints, 15
Church of St. Francis of Assisi, 321
Church Street, 162, 196
Churchill, Winston, 54, 336
The Citadel, 316
Citi Field, 290
city, becoming a, 49, 51, 274
The City Bakery, 327
City Beautiful, 269
City Charter, 141, 223
City College of New York, 84, 313
City Council
  British colonial era, 49
  government, 15
  independence of New York, 67, 72, 89
  Manhattan, 201, 204
  notable New Yorkers, 380
  rebuilding and moving forward after 9/11, 186–87
  writing, 375
City Hall
  British colonial era, 52, 54
  Brooklyn, 274
  business and economy, 26
  Dutch colonial era, 46
  the Gilded Age, 116, 118, 128
  government, 16 (ill.)
  Great Depression era, 139
  independence of New York, 67, 78, 80, 83, 88–89
  industrialization and immigration, 109
  Manhattan, 204–5, 208–9, 221, 255, 261
  notable New Yorkers, 378
  rebuilding and moving forward after 9/11, 187
  Revolutionary War, 56, 59, 63
  the sixties to 9/11, 177
  writing, 364, 370, 374
City Hall Park, 16, 57, 202–4
City Island, 301
"City of Churches," 15
City University of New York, 84
City Water Tunnel No. 3, 159
Civic Center, 192–206
civil rights, 129, 156, 250, 380
Civil War
  Brooklyn, 277, 283–84
  independence of New York, 79, 81
  industrialization and immigration, 104–5, 110–11, 114
  Manhattan, 201, 209–10, 215, 219, 221, 239, 258
  other islands around the boroughs, 301
  the sixties to 9/11, 165
  slavery and the, 91–97

sports, 306
Staten Island, 295
writing, 365–66
Civil Works Administration (CWA), 138
Claesen (Wyckoff), Pieter, 276
Claremont Hill, 390
Clark, Aaron, 78
Clark, Edward, 249
Clarke, Arthur C., 226
The Clash, 352
Cleopatra's Needles, 247
Clermont, 70
Cleveland, Grover, 103, 106
Cleveland, Ohio, 314
climate, 3–4, 188
Climate Change Adaptation Task Force, 188
Clinton, 233
Clinton, DeWitt, 19, 69, 74–75, 78, 193, 233, 377
Clinton, George, 66–67, 74, 377
Clinton, Henry, 64
Clinton, Hillary, 187
Clinton, James, 377
Clinton's Ditch, 74, 377
The Cloisters, 362
Cloisters, the, 241, 263–64, 264 (ill.)
clothing, importance of to business, 25
Cloverfield, 355
Club Deluxe, 348
Coast Guard, 182, 301
Cobble Hill, 220
Cobh, Ireland, 113
Codogno, Italy, 263
Coen brothers, 396
Cogswell, Henry D., 130
Cohan, George M., 347
Coimbra, 148
Cold War, 150, 233
Colden, Gov. Cadwallader, 56
Cole, Nat King, 327, 335
colf, 305
Coliseum, 231, 236
Collect Pond, 205, 207
Collect Pond Park, 205
College of Staten Island, 391
colleges, 54, 84
Collens, Charles, 264
Collyer, Homer, 391–92
Collyer, Langley, 391–92
Collyer Brothers Park, 392
Colman, John, 38
Colombians as inhabitants, 254, 289
Colombo family, 139
colonial era, 36–55
Colonial Revival, 253
Colonial Williamsburg, Virginia, 293
Colony 1209, 286
Colorado, 238, 241

Colorado Springs, Colorado, 238
Colored Orphan Asylum, 96
Colts, Baltimore, 310
Columbia (College) University
    British colonial era, 54
    Bronx, 271
    independence of New York, 66, 84
    Manhattan, 255–56, 265
    notable New Yorkers, 380
    quirky New York, 390
    Revolutionary War, 61
Columbian Order, 75
Columbus, Christopher, 235
Columbus Avenue, 249
Columbus Circle, 151, 231, 235–36
Columbus Park, 206
Combs, Sean, 386
comic strips, 366 (ill.), 366–67
Commentary, 20, 153, 360
Commission, the, 139
Commissioners' Plan, 72
Committee of 51, 57
Common Council, 6, 49, 52, 77–78, 93, 99, 245
commonality of trees, 4
Commons, the, 56–58
Communism, 20, 345
Communist Party USA (CPUSA), 20
Company, 342
Compstat, 178, 187
ConEd, 104, 145, 167
Coney Island
    Brooklyn, 283–85, 285 (ill.)
    Dutch colonial era, 47
    food and dining, 320
    the Gilded Age, 131
    Great Depression era, 141, 144
    Manhattan, 194, 263
    Queens, 286, 288, 291
    quirky New York, 393
    rebuilding and moving forward after 9/11, 188
    Revolutionary War, 60
    the sixties to 9/11, 171
    World War II and the postwar era, 147, 153
Coney Island Creek, 285
Coney Island Museum, 394
Confederacy, the, 96
Confederate Army, 93, 301, 389
Confederate Navy, 94
Conference House, 293
Conference House Park, 293
Congo, the, 393
Congolese as inhabitants, 392
Congregationalists as inhabitants, 54
Congress, Continental, 56–57, 59, 61–62, 66–67, 209, 293
Congress, U.S.
    business and economy, 23

the Gilded Age, 123
government, 16
independence of New York, 67, 77
industrialization and immigration, 99, 108
Manhattan, 250
notable New Yorkers, 380–81
other islands around the boroughs, 301
the sixties to 9/11, 170–71, 175
slavery and the Civil War, 91
Connecticut
    British colonial era, 54
    Dutch colonial era, 44
    early history, 35
    Great Depression era, 144–45
    industrialization and immigration, 101, 105
    notable New Yorkers, 381
    Revolutionary War, 61–63
Connecticut River, 47
Conscription Act, 95
Conservatory Garden, 247
Consolidated Edison (ConEd), 104, 145, 167
Consolidation, 16
Consolidation Law of 1895, 378
Constitution, 78
Constitution, U.S., 45, 67, 78, 363
The Container Store, 223
Continental Army
    Brooklyn, 275–76
    independence of New York, 66
    Manhattan, 261, 265
    quirky New York, 391
    Revolutionary War, 59, 61, 63
    Staten Island, 294
Continental Congress, 56–57, 59, 61–62, 66–67, 209, 293
Coogan's Bluff, 260
Coonan, James, 173
Co-op City, 272–73
Cooper Hewitt Smithsonian Design Museum, 253
Cooper Union, 96, 253, 330
Cooperstown, 306
Copacabana, 334
Copperheads, 93, 95
Corinthian style, 345
Corlears Hook, 44
Cornell University, 298
Corona, 384
Corona Ash Dump, 290
Corsair Fleet, 148
Cosby, Bill, 350
Cosby, William, 364
The Cosby Show, 354
Cosell, Howard, 169
Cosmopolitans ("Cosmos"), New York, 315
cost of a subway ride, 31

cost of a taxi medallion, 27–28
Costello, Frank, 144, 150
Costello, Lou, 289
Costume Institute, 253
Cotton Club, 115, 132, 180, 342, 348 (ill.), 348–49
Council for Public Safety, 165
counterterrorism, 17–18
County, Jayne, 352
County Cork, Ireland, 113
Courier and Enquirer, 372
Cowboys, Dallas, 310
Cox Hill, 265
coyotes, 5
CPUSA (Communist Party USA), 20
Crack Is Wack, 361
The Cradle Will Rock, 341
Crane, Stephen, 212, 321
creation of Central Park, 86
creation of New York, 33
crime
    British colonial era, 54
    Bronx, 270, 272
    Brooklyn, 277, 281–82
    business and economy, 21
    Dutch colonial era, 46
    film and TV, 356–57
    the Gilded Age, 120, 132
    Great Depression era, 138–39, 144
    independence of New York, 67, 80, 88
    industrialization and immigration, 109–10, 115
    Manhattan, 205, 208, 211–12, 214, 260
    music, 352
    notable New Yorkers, 386
    other islands around the boroughs, 301
    police, 18
    rebuilding and moving forward after 9/11, 187
    the sixties to 9/11, 158, 164–66, 168–70, 173–80
    sports, 313
    theater, 343
    World War II and the postwar era, 150, 153–54
    writing, 365, 370
Criminal Courts Building, 205
Cripplebush, 35
Croatia, 140, 238
Croatians as inhabitants, 14, 238–39
Croix de Guerre medal, 130
Cropsey, 391
Crosby, Bing, 229
Cross Island Parkway, 5
Cross-Bronx Expressway, 271–72
"Crossing Brooklyn Ferry," 105
Crossroads of the World, 232
Croton Aqueduct, 82–84, 332

"Croton Ode," 83
Croton Reservoir, 83–85, 238, 262
Croton Reservoir Tavern, 84
Croton River, 83, 262
Crotona Park, 272
Crow, Jim, 349
Crow Hill, 282
Crown Heights, 154, 176–77, 281–83
Crown Heights Maccabees, 154
Crutchy Morris, 367
Cruz, Ted, 21
Crystal Palace, 85–86
Cuba, 100, 114, 235, 341
Cubism, 360, 362
Cullullo Telawana, 36
Cummings, Herbert, 368
Cuomo, Andrew, 384
Cuomo, Mario, 160, 170, 383 (ill.), 383–84
Curran, "One Lung," 115
Currency Act, 56
Curry, Tim, 356 (ill.)
Curry Hill, 326
Curry Row, 325–26
"Curse of the Bambino," 309
Customs House, 42
Cuxa Cloister, 264
CWA (Civil Works Administration), 138
Cyclone, 285
Cypress Hills Cemetery, 33

D

"The Daffiness Boys," 307
Daily Bugle, 375
The Dakota, 244, 249–50
Dakota Territory, 249
Dali, Salvador, 351
Dallas, Texas, 310
Damrosch, Walter, 234
danger factor, 165, 396–97
"Dangerous Stretch," 116
Danish as inhabitants, 109
Dapper Don, 176
Daredevil, 375
Darkness and Daylight: A Woman's Story of Gospel, Temperance, Mission, and Rescue Work (Campbell et al.), 112
Darling, Candy, 361
Dauphine, 36–37
Davis, Mike, 201
DC (Detective) Comics, 376
de Blasio, Bill, 186 (ill.), 186–88
De La Soul, 354
de Laet, Johan, 191
De Niro, Robert, 211
dead, city to drop, 164

The Death and Life of Great American Cities (Jacobs), 382
Death Avenue, 230
Death of a Salesman, 381–82
Death Row Records, 354
Death Wish, 165, 173
Decker Building, 220
Declaration of Independence, 59, 194, 214, 247, 268
decline of manufacturing, 25
Degas, Edgar, 360
DeKalb Avenue, 32
del Toro, Guillermo, 355
Delacorte Clock, 246
Delacorte Theater, 247, 345
Delancey Street, 117, 147, 376
Delanoy, Peter, 49, 77
Delaware, 35, 40
Delaware Indians, 10, 35, 299
Delaware River, 11, 40, 47
Delaware Valley, 45
Dell, Floyd, 213
Delmonico, John, 316
Delmonico, Peter, 316
Delmonico's, 81, 238, 316–22, 317 (ill.)
"Dem Bums," 307
Demetrius, 161, 161 (ill.)
DeMille, Cecil B., 247
Democratic Convention, 167
Democratic National Convention, 380, 384
Democratic Party
    Great Depression era, 143
    independence of New York, 76–79, 87
    industrialization and immigration, 99
    notable New Yorkers, 384
    rebuilding and moving forward after 9/11, 184, 186
    the sixties to 9/11, 160, 164, 170, 176, 178
    slavery and the Civil War, 93, 95–96
    Staten Island, 296–97
    writing, 375
Denmark, 109, 329
Deno's Wonder Wheel, 285
dens, opium, 152, 152 (ill.), 321
Denton, Daniel, 373
Department of Corrections, 301
Department of Cultural Affairs, 17
Department of Education, 17, 19, 26, 204
Department of Environmental Protection, 8
Department of Fire. See FDNY (Fire Department of the City of New York)
Department of Health, 17, 316, 395, 397

Department of Housing and Urban Development (HUD), 160
Department of Information Services, 17
Department of Justice, 130
Department of Parks, 143, 194, 345
Department of Police. See NYPD (New York Police Department)
Department of Records, 17
Department of Street Cleaning, 110
Department of Transportation, 29
Depression. See Great Depression
DeSapio, Carmine, 170
destructive events, 81–82
Detective (DC) Comics, 376
Detroit, Michigan, 228, 344, 383
Detroit Red, 260
the Deuce, 232
Deutal Bay, 239
Dewey, John, 207
DeWitt, Simeon, 72
Dey Street, 97
Di Modica, Arturo, 194
Di Palo's, 208
Diallo, Amadou, 179
Diamond, Legs, 314
Diamond Dealers' Club, 239
Diamond District, 239
Diana, 229
Dickens, Charles, 5, 80, 298, 301, 371–72, 372 (ill.)
The Dictators, 232, 352
Dingle, Charles, 368
dining, food and, 316–30
Dinkins, David, 174–77, 176 (ill.), 179, 184, 187, 315
The Dinner Party, 278
Diocesan House, 256
discrimination
    Brooklyn, 286
    Dutch colonial era, 45–46
    film and TV, 358
    the Gilded Age, 129–30
    independence of New York, 76, 79–80, 84
    industrialization and immigration, 106–8, 111, 114
    Manhattan, 196
    the sixties to 9/11, 172
    World War II and the postwar era, 146, 151
Disney, 368
Disneyland, 273
District Court, U.S., 204
District of Columbia, 67
diversity
    affordability, 189
    animals, 7, 270
    art, 362
    Bronx, 267
    Brooklyn, 273–74
    early history, 11, 41

ethnicity, 12–13, 289–90
film and TV, 358
firefighting, 19
food and dining, 316
languages, 14
Manhattan, 212
police, 79
Queens, 287, 289–90
religion, 15
Staten Island, 296–97
DJ Kool Herc, 353
"Do not go gentle into that good night," 389
Do the Right Thing, 386
Dock Street, 371
Doctor Strange, 376
Doctorow, E. L., 270
Doctors' Riot, 204
Dodgers, Brooklyn [baseball], 169, 279–80, 307–8, 328, 357
Dodgers, Brooklyn [football], 310
Dodgers, Los Angeles, 280
dogs, 5–6
Dominican Republic, 39
Dominicans as inhabitants, 13, 29, 39, 151, 289
Domino Sugar Refinery, 24
"The Donald," 385–86
Dongan, Gov. Earl Thomas, 49 (ill.)
The Donut Pub, 327
Dorismond, Patrick M., 179
Douglas, Bob, 312
Douglas Plaza Mall, 5
Dow, Charles, 369
Dow Jones & Company, 369
Dow Jones Industrial Average, 137–38, 172
Downing, Andrew Jackson, 245
Downing Stadium, 315
Doyers Street, 206–7
Draft Riots, 19, 94–96, 96 (ill.), 101, 126, 295–96, 365–66
The Drag, 341
Dragnet, 356
Dreamland, 284
Dreiser, Theodore, 321
Driggs Street, 326
drivers, ethnicities of cab, 28–29
drivers, percentage of, 29
Duane, James, 78
Duane Street, 78, 204
DuBois, W. E. B., 260
Duchamp, Marcel, 360
Dumbo, 275
Dunkirk evacuation, 60, 182
Dunning, John R., 255
Durand, Asher B., 359
Durk, David, 159
Dutch as inhabitants
   bars and nightlife, 331
   British colonial era, 49
   Bronx, 268, 271

Brooklyn, 274–75, 277, 284
business and economy, 21, 23
early history, 35–36
food and dining, 326, 327 (ill.), 328
the Gilded Age, 131
independence of New York, 73, 78
industrialization and immigration, 105
Manhattan, 192, 194, 198–99, 203, 211–12, 265
origins of inhabitants, 11
other islands around the boroughs, 297, 299–300, 302
police, 17
Queens, 287
quirky New York, 394
seal, 3
sports, 306
Staten Island, 293
the five boroughs, 16
Dutch colonial era, 36–48
Dutch Colonial style, 276
Dutch East India Company, 39
Dutch Fred, 233
Dutch Reformed Church, 45–46, 69
Dutch Republic, 293
Dutch West India Company
   bars and nightlife, 332
   Dutch colonial era, 37, 39–40, 42, 44, 46, 48
   Manhattan, 191
   origins of inhabitants, 11
   sports, 305
Dutchess County, 83
Duvall, Robert, 342
Dwyer, "Big Bill," 313
Dyckman House, 265
Dylan, Bob, 226, 350, 350 (ill.)

E

Eagle, 62
eagles, 3, 8–9
early days of New Amsterdam, 41
early history
   all about, 33–89
   bars and nightlife, 330–32
   Bronx, 268
   Brooklyn, 274
   food and dining, 316–17
   Manhattan, 191
   Queens, 287
   sports, 305–6
   Staten Island, 292
   theater, 339–40
ease of business, 21–22
East 10th Street, 213
East 20th Street, 221
East 23rd Street, 181

East 37th Street, 61
East 46th Street, 176
East 51st Street, 396
East 52nd Street, 311
East 79th Street, 255
East Bronx, 270
East Coast, 180, 202, 275, 317, 353–54, 385
East Harlem, 108, 142, 208, 261, 324
East New York, 175–76, 281–82
East River
   British colonial era, 51–52
   Brooklyn, 275–76
   business and economy, 23
   Dutch colonial era, 40–42
   geology, 33
   the Gilded Age, 117, 124
   Great Depression era, 144
   independence of New York, 73
   industrialization and immigration, 104–5
   landscape, 1
   Manhattan, 201, 217, 221, 239, 254, 263
   other islands around the boroughs, 297–98, 300, 302
   Queens, 286–88
   rebuilding and moving forward after 9/11, 188
   Revolutionary War, 60–61
East River Bridge. See Brooklyn Bridge
East Rutherford, New Jersey, 310
East Side Story, 153
East St. Louis, Illinois, 129
East Third Street, 117
East Tremont, 271–72
East Village
   all about, 211–18
   food and dining, 326, 329
   independence of New York, 72
   industrialization and immigration, 110
   the sixties to 9/11, 162
   theater, 345
   trees, 4
   writing, 371
Easter Parade, 241
Eastern Europe, 107, 119, 133, 329, 345
Eastern Parkway, 277–79, 283
Eastern Seaboard, 21, 23, 43, 75, 168
Ebbets, Charles, 279
Ebbets Field, 279–80, 308, 357
Eckert, Thomas, 209
economy, 21–26, 201–2
Ecuadorians as inhabitants, 13
Edgar Allan Poe Cottage, 272
Edgecombe Avenue, 260, 262
Edison, Thomas

419

Bronx, 269
  film and TV, 354
  the Gilded Age, 123
  industrialization and immigra-
    tion, 104, 111
  Manhattan, 209, 238
  quirky New York, 393–94
  writing, 366
Edison Electric Illuminating Company of New York, 104
education, 19–20, 69–70, 84
Edwards, William H., 124
effect of 9/11 on, 181–82
effect of Central Park on, 87, 278
effect of the Civil War on, 94
Egypt, 224, 247, 306
Egyptians as inhabitants, 45
Ehret, George, 288, 332–33
Eiffel Tower, 119
Eight Men, 44
Eighteenth Amendment, 130–31
Eighth Avenue
  food and dining, 326
  the Gilded Age, 120, 124
  Manhattan, 226–27, 229–30,
    232, 245, 260
  rebuilding and moving forward
    after 9/11, 188
  transportation, 31
  writing, 368
Eighty Years' War, 256
Eisenhower, Dwight D., 200
El Barrio, 261
El Museo Del Barrio, 253–54
El Topo, 356
Election Day, 375
electricity, 104
Elephantine Colossus, 284
elevated railways, 97–98
Eleventh Avenue, 188, 230–31, 321,
  389
Eleventh Ward, 77
Elizabeth A. Sackler Center for
  Feminist Art, 278
Elizabeth II, Queen, 166, 200
Elizabeth Street, 88
Ellington, Duke, 256, 258–59, 348–
  49
Ellis, Edward, 64, 105
Ellis, Samuel, 299
Ellis Island
  the Gilded Age, 119, 127, 133–34
  Great Depression era, 140
  industrialization and immigra-
    tion, 103, 108, 112 (ill.), 112–
    14
  Manhattan, 193
  other islands around the bor-
    oughs, 299
  Queens, 289
  quirky New York, 390
  writing, 372

Ellis Island Museum, 113
Elmhurst, 14
Eloise (Thompson), 244
Elysian Fields, 306
Emancipation Proclamation, 95,
  365
Emergency Medical Services (EMS),
  19
Emergency Quota Act, 133
Emmaus, 268
Empire, 361
Empire State Building
  animals, 8
  art, 360–61
  film and TV, 355
  Great Depression era, 144
  Manhattan, 222, 237 (ill.), 237–
    38, 242
  quirky New York, 396
  sports, 308
  World War II and the postwar
    era, 148–49, 149 (ill.)
employment, 16–17, 26
empty Manhattan apartments, 234–
  35
Empty State, the, 237
EMS (Emergency Medical Services),
  19
Engels, Friedrich, 365
Engine Company Number 1, 97
Engineers' Gate, 128
England
  bars and nightlife, 336
  British colonial era, 49–50, 52,
    55
  Bronx, 271
  Dutch colonial era, 47–48
  film and TV, 356
  independence of New York, 70,
    74, 80–81, 85, 89
  industrialization and immigra-
    tion, 110
  Manhattan, 199, 219–20, 225,
    235, 244, 247
  music, 351–52
  notable New Yorkers, 380
  Queens, 287
  rebuilding and moving forward
    after 9/11, 189
  Revolutionary War, 56–57
  seal, 3
  the sixties to 9/11, 166
  Staten Island, 293
  trees, 4
  writing, 365, 371–73
Englishmen as inhabitants. See
  British as inhabitants
Enterprise, 234
Episcopalians as inhabitants, 200,
  218, 256
Epoch Times, 370
equestrian, 262, 271

Equitable Building, 128
Erie Canal, 74–75, 198, 220, 377
Ertegun, Nesuhi, 315
Erving, Julius, 312
Escape from New York, 356
Escher, M. C., 362
Esquire, 161
Essex Street, 207
Ethiopia, 146, 213
Ethiopian Regiment, 63–64
ethnicity
  all about, 12–14
  Bronx, 267
  Brooklyn, 274
  Manhattan, 192
  Queens, 287
  Staten Island, 292
  transportation, 28–29
  World War II and the postwar
    era, 146
Eugene O'Neill Theatre, 343
Eurasia, 8
Europe
  bars and nightlife, 335
  business and economy, 24
  Dutch colonial era, 39, 41–42,
    46
  the Gilded Age, 122, 124, 133
  independence of New York, 74
  industrialization and immigra-
    tion, 103
  Manhattan, 193, 198, 202, 256,
    263–64
  religion, 15
  the sixties to 9/11, 169
  sports, 306, 315
  Staten Island, 293
  writing, 372
Europeans as inhabitants
  animals, 7
  Bronx, 268
  Brooklyn, 274
  business and economy, 23
  Dutch colonial era, 36–39, 41–
    43, 45–46
  early history, 34–36
  ethnicity, 13
  food and dining, 329
  the Gilded Age, 119
  industrialization and immigra-
    tion, 106–7
  landscape, 1
  Manhattan, 211, 239, 261
  origins of inhabitants, 11
  Queens, 287
  quirky New York, 394
  Revolutionary War, 59
  sports, 305
  Staten Island, 292
  theater, 340, 345
  trees, 4
Evacuation Day, 64–66

"Evacuation Day and Washington's Triumphal Entry in New York City, November 25, 1783," 65 (ill.)
Evangelicals as inhabitants, 15
Evening Journal, 367
Evening World, 367
Eve's Hangout, 334
Ewing, Patrick, 313
Exchange Place, 108
Exchange Street, 81
Exhibition of the Industry of All Nations, 85
Exploding Plastic Inevitable, 361
Exxon, 39

F

F. & M. Schaefer Brewing Company, 333
falcons, 8 (ill.), 8–9
Fallon, Jimmy, 358
FALN, 168, 330
Falun Gong, 370
Fantastic Four, 376
The Fantasticks, 347
fantasy baseball, 311
F.A.O. Schwarz, 222
Far Rockaway, 29, 287
Farber, Barry, 170
farming in Queens, 45, 287–88
Farrow, Mia, 250
Fascisti, 134
Fashion District, 226
Fashion Institute of Technology (FIT), 226–27
The Fashionable Adventures of Joshua Craig (Phillips), 125
Fat Black Pussycat, 350
fatality, first auto, 116
Father Christmas, 225
Father Knickerbocker, 73
fauna, 5–10
FBI (Federal Bureau of Investigation), 130, 147, 157, 177
FC (Football Club), New York City, 315
FDNY (Fire Department of the City of New York), 18 (ill.), 97, 158, 169, 181
FDR Drive, 224, 261
"Fear City," 165
Feast of San Gennaro Festival, 207–8, 323 (ill.)
Featherstone, "Mickey," 174
Federal Bureau of Investigation (FBI), 130, 147, 157, 177
Federal Hall, 67, 158, 200–201, 364, 391
Federal Hall National Monument, 200
Federal Reserve, 169, 202

Federal Reserve Bank of New York, 200, 202
Federal style, 200, 218, 254
Federal Theatre Project (FTP), 341
Federal Tort Claims Act, 149
Federalist Party, 68–69
Feigenbaum, Harriet, 224
Felix the Cat, 132
Feltman, Charles, 320
Fenway Park, 279
Ferber, Edna, 373
Ferguson, Missouri, 187
Fermi, Enrico, 255
Ferris, Jean Leon Gerome, 51
Fidler-Wyckoff House Park, 276
FIFA World Cup, 208
Fifth Avenue
    animals, 9
    Brooklyn, 281, 285
    food and dining, 327, 329
    the Gilded Age, 128–30
    independence of New York, 84
    industrialization and immigration, 99, 103
    Manhattan, 209, 214, 222–23, 237–39, 241, 243–45, 247, 249–53, 256, 258, 261
    quirky New York, 391
    World War II and the postwar era, 151
Fifth Avenue Presbyterian Church, 241
Fighting Cocks, 62
Filipinos as inhabitants, 289
film and TV, 354–59
filth as image of, 110–11
finance, 25
financial collapse, near, 164–65
Financial District, 8, 186, 192–206, 267, 272, 330
Finkel, Fyvush, 345
fire, Bronx, 169
Fire Department of the City of New York (FDNY), 18 (ill.), 97, 158, 169, 181
Fire Island, 303
fire of 1776, 62–64, 73, 199–200
fire of 1835, 81–82, 82 (ill.)
firefighting
    beginning of, 18–19
    British colonial era, 52
    the Gilded Age, 125–26
    independence of New York, 76, 80–81
    industrialization and immigration, 97, 99
    Manhattan, 224
    Queens, 291
    the sixties, 9/11, 158, 165, 168–69, 181
    slavery and the Civil War, 95
    Staten Island, 297

fires of 1741, 53–54, 54 (ill.)
First Avenue, 221, 224, 239, 251, 326
First Bank of the United States, 23
First Baptist Church, 213
First Battle of Bull Run, 94
First Houses, 143–44
Fischer, Bobby, 215
Fisher, Watson Stanley, 10
FIT (Fashion Institute of Technology), 226–27
Fitzgerald, Ella, 259
Fitzgerald, F. Scott, 145–46, 290, 336
Fitzgerald, Zelda, 145
Fitzpatrick, Catherine, 394
Fiume, Hungary, 140
Five Families, 139
Five Nations Indians, 35
Five Points, 78–80, 108, 114–15, 160, 205, 321, 339
Five Towns, 36
Flagg, Ernest, 128
Flaherty, Joe, 375
Flatbush, 33, 274, 276
Flatbush Avenue, 60, 277–78, 280, 308
Flatbush Avenue Terminal, 280
Flatiron, 180, 218–24, 316, 327, 387
Flatiron Building, 223, 261, 375
The Flatiron Building on a Windy Day, 223
Flatlands, 274
Fleischmann's, 321
Fletcher, Benjamin, 22, 50, 371
Fletcher Henderson's Orchestra, 348
Flood Rock, 302
flora, 4–5
Floral Park, 288
Florida, 12, 144, 160, 269
Flour Riot, 82
Flower District, 227
Flushing, 14, 45, 77, 287, 289–91, 314
Flushing Bay, 290
Flushing Meadows Corona Park, 290, 290 (ill.), 315
Flushing Remonstrance, 45
Foley Square, 205
Follies, 342
Foner, Eric, 92
food and dining, 316–30
football, 260, 268, 310–11, 383
Force Publique, 393
Ford, Gerald, 164, 368
Fordham Gneiss, 265
Fordham University, 80, 270–72, 313
Fordham Village, 272
Ford's Theatre, 389–90

foreign-born people as inhabitants, 13–14
Forest City, 280
Forest Hills, 160, 314–15, 375, 384
Forest Park, 33
Forest Service, U.S., 4
Forrest Hotel, 313
Forsyth Street, 325
Fort Amsterdam, 40, 42, 192
Fort Apache, 270
Fort George, 53, 65–66, 192
Fort Gibson, 299
Fort Greene, 276, 280, 386
Fort Greene Park, 276
Fort Hancock, 150
Fort James, 50
Fort Jay, 301
Fort Knox, Kentucky, 202
Fort Lee, 263
Fort Monmouth, 7
Fort Orange, 39–40, 305
Fort Putnam, 276
Fort Sumter, 93
Fort Tilden, 150
Fort Tyron Park, 263–64
Fort Wadsworth, 292, 294, 294 (ill.)
Fort Washington, 63, 261
Fort Washington Avenue, 263
Fort Wood, 299
Forty Deuce, 232
Forty Thieves, 99
Foster, George, 81
founding of New Amsterdam, 40
"Four Freedoms," 298
Four Hundred, 104
Fourth Avenue, 119, 213, 219–20
Fourth Ward, 379
Fox's U-Bet, 328
Foxx, Redd, 259
France
    bars and nightlife, 335
    British colonial era, 50
    Bronx, 269
    business and economy, 22, 24, 26
    Dutch colonial era, 36
    food and dining, 316
    the Gilded Age, 130
    independence of New York, 89
    industrialization and immigration, 102, 104, 110
    Manhattan, 213–14, 244, 247, 258, 264
    notable New Yorkers, 383
    Revolutionary War, 66
    sports, 306
Francis, Pope, 242
Francis I, King, 36
Franco-American Union, 102
Frank N. Furter, Dr., 356
Franklin, Benjamin, 61, 198, 293, 365

Franklin D. Roosevelt Four Freedoms Park, 298
Fraunces, Phoebe, 58
Fraunces, Samuel "Black Sam," 330
Fraunces Tavern, 22, 58, 66–67, 330
Frazier, Walt "Clyde," 230, 313
Frederick Douglass Boulevard, 327
Fredericks, Alfred, 42
Free Academy of the City of New York, 84
Free School Society, 19, 70
Freed, Alan, 349
Freedom Tower, 196, 196 (ill.)
Freedom Trail, 57
Freedomland, 272–73
Freedomland (Price), 273
Freedom's Journal, 364
French and Indian War, 54–55, 66
French Arts Decoratifs, 270
French as inhabitants
    British colonial era, 50, 55
    food and dining, 316, 319
    industrialization and immigration, 102
    Manhattan, 212
    Revolutionary War, 57
    the sixties to 9/11, 163
    slavery and the Civil War, 94, 97
French Calvinists as inhabitants, 15
French Chateau style, 244
The French Connection, 356
French Empire, 54
French Gothic Revival style, 253
French Gothic style, 256
French Jesuits as inhabitants, 41
French Renaissance Revival, 16
Fresh Kills Park, 296–97
Frick Collection, 375
Frohman, Daniel, 346
FTP (Federal Theatre Project), 341
Fugard, Athol, 346
Fugitive Slave Law of 1850, 91
Fuller Building, 223
Fulton, Robert, 70, 105
Fulton Fish Market, 198, 379
Fulton Mall, 277
Fulton Street, 196, 198–99, 211
funnies, reading the, 141
future of, 188–89

G

Gallagher, John J., 124
Gallo Theater, 351
Gambino family, 139, 173, 176, 208
Gang of Four, 175
gangs
    bars and nightlife, 333
    Bronx, 270
    Brooklyn, 281, 285
    the Gilded Age, 132

Great Depression era, 139, 142, 144
    independence of New York, 76, 78, 81, 88
    industrialization and immigration, 114–15
    Manhattan, 207, 233, 248
    music, 348
    quirky New York, 396
    the sixties to 9/11, 157, 173–74, 176, 178
    World War II and the postwar era, 150–53
Gangs of New York, 92
Gansevoort Market, 215
Gansevoort Street, 215, 217
Garden Court, 252
Gardiners Island, 51
Garfield, James, 391
Garibaldi, Giuseppe, 295
Garibaldi Guard, 94
Garment District, 24 (ill.), 25, 225–32, 237, 272
Garner, Eric, 187
Garvey, Marcus, 129 (ill.), 129–30, 260
Gates of Hell, 224
Gateway National Recreation Area, 282
A Gathering, 31
Gatling, Richard Jordan, 366
Gawker, 180
Gay Men's Health Crisis, 172–73
Gay Pride Parade, 157, 202
Gaynor, William Jay, 124, 128
Gehrig, Lou, 310
Gelbart, Larry, 358
Gemini mission, 233
The General, 243
General Assembly, 240, 242
General Electric, 137
General Motors, 238
General Slocum, 117–18, 118 (ill.)
General Theological Seminary, 225
General's Guard, 58
Genovese, Kitty, 154
Genovese family, 139, 334
gentrification, 285–86
geographic location, 1
geology, 33
George II, King, 54
George III, King, 58
George Washington Bridge, 8, 63, 263, 396
Georgia, 209, 308, 386
Gerde's Folk City, 350
German Lutherans as inhabitants, 15
German Renaissance, 249
Germans as inhabitants
    bars and nightlife, 332
    food and dining, 329
    the Gilded Age, 117–18, 127

Great Depression era, 143
independence of New York, 79–80, 86, 88
industrialization and immigration, 99, 107, 110
Manhattan, 212, 229, 246, 256
origins of inhabitants, 11
other islands around the boroughs, 300
Queens, 288
quirky New York, 395
Revolutionary War, 59
slavery and the Civil War, 94
World War II and the postwar era, 146–47
writing, 363, 376
Germany
the Gilded Age, 124, 127, 131
independence of New York, 79
industrialization and immigration, 111
Manhattan, 193
the sixties to 9/11, 169
World War II and the postwar era, 146
Gershwin, George, 378, 379 (ill.)
Gershwin, Ira, 84, 378–79
Getz, Stan, 259
Ghetto Brothers, 270
Ghostbusters, 18, 355
Ghostbusters 2, 18
ghosts, 389–91
Giants, New York [baseball], 260, 268, 307–10
Giants, New York [football], 310–11
Giants Stadium, 310, 315
Gibbet Island, 299
Gibran, Kahlil, 218
"The Gift of the Magi" (Henry), 318
Gilbert, Bradford Lee, 108–9
Gilbert, Cass, 194
Gilded Age, 116–35, 253–54, 263, 316
Gillespie, Dizzy, 349
Gilmore's Garden, 101
Gimbel Brothers, 132
Ginsberg, Allen, 22, 218
Girls, 359
Giuliani, Rudolph
Manhattan, 206
other islands around the boroughs, 303
politics, 21
rebuilding and moving forward after 9/11, 182–84, 186–87
the sixties to 9/11, 171–72, 176–80, 177 (ill.)
Glaeser, Edward L., 24
Glazer, Nathan, 153
Globetrotters, Harlem, 312–13
Glorious Revolution, 49
Goat's Town, 74

"God Save the Queen," 60
Godzilla [character], 355
Godzilla [movie], 355
Goering, Hermann, 147
Goethals Bridge, 292
Goethe House German Cultural Center, 253
Goetz, Bernhard, 173, 184
Goldberger, Paul, 125
The Goldbergs, 358
Golden Age, 355
Golden Gate Park, 207
Goldman, Emma, 20, 297, 336
Goldman Sachs, 185
Goldsborough, Fitzhugh Coyle, 125
Goldwater, Barry, 374
golf, 149, 271, 305
Gomez, Esteban, 37
Good Defeats Evil, 240
Goodfellas, 170, 324, 331
Google, 180
Gophers, 115, 173, 233
gossip columns, 365
Gotham (Wallace), 39
Gotham [city], 375–76
Gotham [magazine], 14
"Gotham" [nickname], 73–74
Gotham Jewelers, 74
Gothams, New York, 307
Gothic Revival style, 200, 209, 241, 251–52, 280, 297
Gothic style, 163, 210, 256, 298
Gotti, John "Teflon Don," 176
Gould, Glenn, 234
government of, 15–20
Government Workforce, 16
Governors Ball Music Festival, 302
Governors Island, 40, 193, 300–301
Gowanus Canal, 61
Gowanus Expressway, 277
Grace Church, 241, 321
Gracie, Archibald, 254
Gracie Mansion, 170, 254 (ill.), 254–55, 297
graffiti, 160–61, 178, 253, 354, 361, 384
Graham, Martha, 218
Gramercy, 218–24
Gramercy Farm, 221
Gramercy Park, 125, 220–21, 318
Gramercy Park Hotel, 221
The Grand, 345
Grand Army Plaza, 244, 277, 279, 283
Grand Central [Station] Terminal
animals, 10
the Gilded Age, 118–22, 121 (ill.), 124, 126
Great Depression era, 145
Manhattan, 198, 228, 231, 238, 242
notable New Yorkers, 385

rebuilding and moving forward after 9/11, 188
transportation, 31
Grand Central Depot, 119
Grand Central Parkway, 5
Grand Concourse, 141, 268–70, 272
Grand Hyatt, 385
Grand Parade, 244
Grand Street, 208, 345
Grange, the, 61
Grant, Julia, 258
Grant, Ulysses S., 102, 258
Grant's Tomb, 258, 391
Gravano, Salvatore, 176
Gravesend, 274, 283
Gravesend Bay, 47, 60
Great Britain, 23–24, 70
Great Crash of 1929, 137–38, 146, 237
Great Depression
film and TV, 355
food and dining, 321
the Gilded Age, 135
Manhattan, 238, 241
quirky New York, 394
rebuilding and moving forward after 9/11, 189
the sixties to 9/11, 162
theater, 341
to a new century, 137–38, 140
writing, 373–74
Great Exhibition, 85
Great Famine, 79
Great Fire of 1776. See fire of 1776
Great Fire of 1835. See fire of 1835
The Great Gatsby (Fitzgerald), 134, 145, 290
Great Hall, 113
The Great Kill District, 233
Great Lakes, 33, 74
Great Lawn, 83, 246
Great Migration, 126, 151
Great Mill Island, 302
Great New England Hurricane of 1938. See Long Island Express
Great Oyster, 299
The Great Plains, 273
Great Recession, 185
Great Roman Monster Classical and Geological Hippodrome, 228
Great Society, 250
Great South Bay, 303
Great Theater Massacre, 343–44
Great White Way, 342, 347
"The Greatest Show on Earth," 101–2
Greek Revival style, 274, 295, 301, 392
Greek Temple, 258
Greeks as inhabitants, 161, 326
Greeley, Horace, 364 (ill.), 364–66
Green, Andrew Haswell, 378
Green, Mark, 186
Green Bay, Wisconsin, 310

423

green cabs, 28
Greenbelt, 296
Greenberg, Clement, 360
Greene, Nathanael, 276
Greenland, 37
Greenmarket, 220
Greenpoint, 286
Greensward Plan, 86–87, 246
Greenwich Street, 97, 195–96, 212
Greenwich Village. See also East Village; West Village
    all about, 211–18
    art, 360
    bars and nightlife, 331, 333–34, 336
    Bronx, 272
    film and TV, 356
    food and dining, 322
    the Gilded Age, 134
    independence of New York, 72, 80
    industrialization and immigration, 108
    Manhattan, 205, 210, 216 (ill.), 256
    music, 349–50
    notable New Yorkers, 378, 381–82
    the sixties to 9/11, 156, 159–60, 170
    sports, 312
    theater, 347
    World War II and the postwar era, 153
Greenwijck, 211
Green-Wood Cemetery, 33, 92, 253, 280–81, 377
grid of Manhattan's streets, 70, 71 (ill.), 72–74, 218
Griffith, D. W., 134
Grim Reaper, 165
Gross, Harry, 150
Groton, Connecticut, 62
Group Theatre, 341
Growler, 233
growth of New Amsterdam, 41
Guam, 115
Guangzhou, China, 31
Guare, John, 382
The Guggenheim, 253–54, 362
Guggenheim, Solomon R., 253
Guiness, 324
Gulf and Western, 236
Gull Island, 299
Guthrie, Woody, 350
Guyanans as inhabitants, 13, 289
Guys and Dolls, 370
GW, the. See George Washington Bridge

H

Häagen-Dazs, 329
Haarlem, the Netherlands, 256
Haas Act, 27
Hackensack, New Jersey, 54
Hackensack Indians, 35
Hackensack River Valley, 35
Hair, 344, 382
Haitians as inhabitants, 13, 179, 209
Hale, Nathan, 63, 63 (ill.)
Hale, Samuel, 63
Hall of Fame, 313
Hallet, William, 287
Halls of Justice, 205
Halve Maene (Half Moon), 37, 39
Hamill, Pete, 116, 158, 170
Hamilton, 343, 345, 382
Hamilton, Alexander
    British colonial era, 54
    business and economy, 21
    independence of New York, 67–69
    Manhattan, 200, 256
    Revolutionary War, 61
    writing, 364, 370
Hamilton, Canada, 313
Hamilton, Jeremiah "Prince of Darkness," 82
Hamlisch, Marvin, 343
Hammerstein II, Oscar, 347
Hammett, Dashiell, 146
Hamptons, the, 303
handguns, outlaw of, 125, 128
Handwerker, Nathan, 320
Hanging Tree, 214–15, 215 (ill.)
Hangman's Elm, 214
Hanlon, Ned, 307
Hanlon, Virginia, 367
Hanlon's Superbas, 307
Hanover Square, 162, 198
Hanover Street, 50
Hard Hat Riot, 158
"Hard Knock Life," 386
Hardegan, Reinhard, 148
Hardenbergh, Henry Janeway, 244
Harding, Warren G., 200
Hardy, Oliver, 354
Haring, Keith, 361
Harlem. See also East Harlem
    all about, 255–61
    animals, 6
    art, 361
    food and dining, 327
    the Gilded Age, 119, 126–27, 129–30, 132
    independence of New York, 80, 84
    industrialization and immigration, 98, 115
    Manhattan, 211, 213, 247, 262
    map, 257 (ill.)
    music, 348–49
    notable New Yorkers, 380–81
    quirky New York, 391–92
    the sixties to 9/11, 162, 175
    sports, 312–13
    theater, 341–42
    World War II and the postwar era, 146, 151
    writing, 370, 374
Harlem Democratic Club, 175
Harlem Flat, 72
Harlem Heights, 61
Harlem Hellfighters, 130
Harlem Line, 122
Harlem Railroad, 261
Harlem Renaissance, 257–58, 349, 374
Harlem River, 162, 256, 260–62, 265, 267–69, 302, 307
Harlem River Drive, 361
Harlem River Driveway, 260
Harlem River Speedway, 262
Harmonie Club, 107
Harper, James, 87
Harper's Bazaar, 373
Harper's Police, 87
Harper's Weekly, 96, 99, 228, 230, 395
Harry's New York Bar, 335
Hart Island, 150, 301–2
Harvard University, 54, 248, 383
Hasidic Judaism, 176–77
haunted New York, 389–91
Haupt Conservatory, 271
Havana, Cuba, 235, 341
Havemeyer family, 24
Havens, Richie, 350
Hawaii, 115
Hawke, Ethan, 226
Hawkins, Yusef, 175, 175 (ill.)
hawks, 9
Hayden Planetarium, 249
HBO, 359
headlines, famous newspaper, 368–69
Hearst, William Randolph, 176, 366–67
heart of Brooklyn, 277–78
Hebrew Immigrant Aid Society, 344
Hebrew Protection League, 281
Heise, William, 354
Helen Hayes Theater, 344
Hell, Richard, 352
Hell Cat Maggie, 115
Hell Gate, 74, 117, 284, 302
Hell Gate Brewery, 332
Hell's Kitchen, 115, 115 (ill.), 173, 231–36, 312, 375, 389
Hell's Kitchen Gang, 233
Hemingway, Ernest, 234, 336
Henry, O., 226, 318
Henry Hudson Bridge, 264

Henry IV, Part I, 9
Henry Street Settlement, 110
Hepburn, Katharine, 239
Herald Square, 31, 117, 132, 231, 237
Herald Square [film], 354
herbarium, largest, 271
Hermits of Harlem, 391–92
Herod, King, 131
Hertz, 27
Hertz, John, 27
Hessians, 59–60, 63, 262, 265, 271
Hester Street, 207
Heth, Joice, 101
Hibbing, Minnesota, 350
Hickey, Sgt. Thomas, 58
High Bridge, 104, 262, 262 (ill.)
High Line, 230
High Line Park, 230
High Rock Park, 296
High School for Needle Trades, 226
Highbridge Park, 260, 262
highest point in Manhattan, 261
Highlanders, New York, 308
Highlanders, Scottish, 59
Hill, Henry, 169–70
Hilltop Park, 308
Hillview Reservoir, 159
Hindus as inhabitants, 15
Hip Sings, 115, 207
Hippodrome, 101
Hispanics as inhabitants
    Bronx, 267
    Brooklyn, 274
    ethnicity, 12
    independence of New York, 79
    Manhattan, 192, 261
    police, 17
    Queens, 287, 290
    the sixties to 9/11, 174
    Staten Island, 292, 297
    World War II and the postwar era, 151
Historic Richmond Town, 293
history, early
    all about, 33–89
    bars and nightlife, 330–32
    Bronx, 268
    Brooklyn, 274
    food and dining, 316–17
    Manhattan, 191
    Queens, 287
    sports, 305–6
    Staten Island, 292
    theater, 339–40
A History of New York from the Beginning of the World to the End of the Dutch Dynasty, by Diedrich Knickerbocker (Irving), 45, 73, 328, 394
History of the English-Speaking Peoples (Churchill), 54

Hitler, Adolf, 141, 147, 229
Hitler Youth, 146
HIV/AIDS, 172–73, 395
Hoboken, New Jersey, 105, 124, 306
hockey, 229–30, 311, 313–14
Hoffman, Dustin, 342
Hofstra University, 315
Hog Island, 297–98
Hogan's Alley, 366, 366 (ill.)
Hogarth, William, 57
Hogtown, 6
Holcombe Rucker Park, 312
Holiday, Billie, 234
Holland, 39, 48
Holland Tunnel, 141
Holliday, Billie, 349
Hollis, 354
Hollywood, 146, 275, 345, 355, 357, 373, 382
Holocaust, 224
Home Insurance Building, 108
Homer, 284
Homestead Act, 365
Homophile Youth Movement, 156
homosexuality
    bars and nightlife, 333–35
    Manhattan, 214, 216, 237
    music, 351
    politics, 20
    the sixties to 9/11, 155–57, 172–73
    theater, 341
    World War II and the postwar era, 153
Hone, Philip, 81
Hong Kong, 31
Hong Kongers as inhabitants, 322
Hooligan Navy, 148
Hoover, Herbert, 380
Hoover, J. Edgar, 130, 157
Hooverville, 138, 355
Hope, Bob, 229
Hopper, Edward, 217, 360
Horne, Lena, 349
Horn's Hook, 254
Horsmanden, Daniel, 53–54
hospitals, 52
Hot Chocolate Festival, 328
Hotel Astor, 117
Hotel Chelsea, 20, 225–26, 389
house, oldest, 262, 276
House by the Railroad, 360
House of Representatives, 16, 87, 200
"The House That Ruth Built," 268–69
houses, settlement, 110
housing, public, 143–44
housing, scatter-site, 160
Houston, Texas, 10, 12, 22, 209
Houston Street, 70, 162, 208–9, 213, 217, 325, 377

Houstoun, William, 209
Hova. See Jay-Z
How the Other Half Lives (Riis), 109–10, 112, 208
Howard, Moe, 354
Howard Beach, 176, 282
Howard Colored Orphan Asylum, 393
Howe, Richard, 293
Howe, William, 59–61, 63, 293–94
HUD (Department of Housing and Urban Development), 160
Hudson, Henry, 37–38, 191, 283, 292
Hudson Bay, 38
Hudson River
    animals, 8–9
    business and economy, 21, 23
    Dutch colonial era, 37–40, 42
    early history, 35
    the Gilded Age, 120, 124
    independence of New York, 69–70, 74
    industrialization and immigration, 115
    location, 1
    Manhattan, 191, 198–99, 205, 207, 210, 215, 217, 225, 230, 232–34, 247, 262–64
    notable New Yorkers, 377
    origins of inhabitants, 11
    quirky New York, 390
    rebuilding and moving forward after 9/11, 182
    Revolutionary War, 59, 62–63
    the sixties to 9/11, 162, 165–66, 180
    slavery and the Civil War, 92
    sports, 306–7
Hudson River Railroad, 215
Hudson River School, 359
Hudson River Valley, 33, 359
Hudson Street, 213
Hudson Tunnel, 207
Hudson Valley, 55, 391, 397
Hudson Yards, 188, 225–31, 311
Hughes, John, 70, 80, 95, 209, 241
Hughes, Langston, 127, 349, 374
"Hughes' Folly," 241
Huguenots as inhabitants, 11
Hull, Cordell, 147
Hunch Maddox, 367
Hungarians as inhabitants, 94
Hungary, 140, 243
Huntington, 63
Huntington Hartford Gallery of Modern Art, 236
Hunts Point, 198, 211
Hurricane Irene, 185
Hurricane Sandy, 4, 4 (ill.), 185–86, 188, 253, 291
Hurston, Zora Neale, 374

Hurtig and Seamon's New (Burlesque) Theater, 258
Hutchinson, Anne, 268
Huxtable, Ada Louise, 163, 228
Hydrox, 329
Hylan, John, 134, 149
Hyman, Jeffrey. See Ramone, Joey

I

I Love Lucy, 357
"I Wanna Be Sedated," 385
Ice Age, 270, 286
ID Day, 249
Idlewild Airport, 141
"If It Wasn't for the Irish and the Jews," 325
IFC Center, 357
Ihpetonga, 275
IKEA, 277
Illinois
    Bronx, 273
    business and economy, 22
    film and TV, 359
    food and dining, 320
    the Gilded Age, 129
    independence of New York, 70, 77
    industrialization and immigration, 108
    Manhattan, 213, 223, 230, 259, 263
    music, 348
    population, 10, 12
    the sixties to 9/11, 157
    slavery and the Civil War, 97
    sports, 313
    transportation, 27–29
"Imagine," 250
immigration
    Brooklyn, 283
    ethnicity, 13–14
    the Gilded Age, 119, 133–34
    Great Depression era, 138
    independence of New York, 72
    industrialization and, 97–116
    Manhattan, 193–94, 206–7
    other islands around the boroughs, 299
    population, 12
    Queens, 289
    quirky New York, 390
Immigration Station, U.S., 299
importance of to early economy, 22
Inauguration Day, 141
Incredible Hulk, 376
Independence Day, 65, 88, 166, 320
independence of, 66–89
Indian Ocean, 50
Indiana, 12, 312
Indianapolis, Indiana, 12

Indians as inhabitants, 13, 29, 244, 289, 325–26, 391, 393
Indonesia, 224
Industrial Revolution, 98
industrialization and immigration, 97–116
industries, important early, 23–24
Ingels, Bjarke, 235
Ingoldsbody, Lt. Gov. Richard, 50
Inquisition, 46
Inside Llewyn Davis, 396
Inside Man, 386
Inside the Dream Palace (Tippins), 225
Interborough Rapid Transit (IRT), 118–19, 149, 392
International Center of Photography, 362
International Exhibition of Modern Art, 360
International Express, 289
International Style, 242–43
Internet, 57, 180
Interview, 361
Intolerable Acts, 57
Intrepid, 233
Invalid Corps, 95
invasions of the British, 47–48, 59, 61
Inwood, 5, 39, 264
Inwood Hill Park, 43, 263–65
iPods, 201
Iranians as inhabitants, 14
Ireland, 79, 113, 123, 193, 291, 311, 325
Irish as inhabitants
    animals, 6
    bars and nightlife, 335
    Dutch colonial era, 41
    food and dining, 324–25, 325 (ill.)
    the Gilded Age, 120, 123–24, 128, 134
    Great Depression era, 139
    independence of New York, 75, 78–81, 86, 88
    industrialization and immigration, 99, 101, 107–8, 113, 115
    Manhattan, 209, 233, 241, 246, 248
    notable New Yorkers, 379
    Queens, 289, 291
    quirky New York, 389, 394
    seal, 3
    the sixties to 9/11, 173–74
    slavery and the Civil War, 94–96
    sports, 312
    Staten Island, 296
    theater, 340
    transportation, 29
    World War II and the postwar era, 149, 153

Irish Brigade, 95
Irish Dead Rabbits, 88
Irish Hunger Memorial, 193
"The Irish Riviera," 291
Iron Man, 376
ironworkers, 11
Iroquois Indians, 35, 44
IRT (Interborough Rapid Transit), 118–19, 149, 392
Irving, Washington, 45, 73 (ill.), 73–74, 221, 328, 394–95
Irving Place, 221, 318, 340
Isamu Noguchi Garden Museum, 362
Islamic Cultural Center of New York, 261
Islanders, New York, 314
islands around the boroughs, other, 297–303
Israel, 15, 154
Italian Renaissance, 255
Italian Squad, 120, 289
Italianate style, 210, 279
Italians as inhabitants
    Dutch colonial era, 41
    food and dining, 318, 322–25
    the Gilded Age, 120, 125, 134
    Great Depression era, 138–43
    independence of New York, 80
    industrialization and immigration, 108, 114
    Manhattan, 207–9, 212, 248, 256, 261, 263
    notable New Yorkers, 383–84
    Queens, 289
    the sixties to 9/11, 175
    slavery and the Civil War, 94
    sports, 305–6
    Staten Island, 295–96
    transportation, 29
    World War II and the postwar era, 146–47, 153
Italy
    animals, 7
    food and dining, 316, 324
    the Gilded Age, 119–20, 124
    Great Depression era, 140
    Manhattan, 208, 250, 255, 263
    sports, 306
    Staten Island, 295
    World War II and the postwar era, 146
Ivy League, 84, 359

J

J. P. Morgan and Co., 201
Jackson, Andrew, 77
Jackson, Peter, 355
Jackson Heights, 14, 289–90, 394
Jacksonville, Florida, 12

Jacob K. Javits Convention Center, 188, 230, 236
Jacob Riis Park, 291
Jacobs, Jane, 143, 210, 381–82
Jacqueline Kennedy Onassis Reservoir, 128, 247
Jaffe, Steven H., 22
Jamaica [country], 37, 129
Jamaica [neighborhood in Queens], 134, 287–88
Jamaica Bay, 35, 282, 282 (ill.)
Jamaica Bay Wildlife Refuge, 282
Jamaica Pass, 60
Jamaicans as inhabitants, 13
Jameco Indians, 287
James, Alice, 373
James, Henry, 214, 372–73
James II, King, 47 (ill.), 49
Jamestown, 52
Japan, 146
Japanese as inhabitants, 146
Japanese Hill-and-Pond Garden, 278
Jaws (Benchley), 10
Jay, John, 67
Jay-Z, 280, 386 (ill.), 386–87
Jazz Age, 134–35, 145, 237, 349
Jazz at Lincoln Center, 236
The Jazz Singer, 269
Jefferson, Thomas, 66–67, 69, 75
Jefferson Market, 341
Jehovah's Witnesses as inhabitants, 15
Jenney, William Le Baron, 108
Jennings, 335
Jennings, Elizabeth, 84–85
Jennings v. Third Avenue Railroad, 85
Jerome, Jennie, 336
Jerome Park Reservoir, 83
Jersey City, New Jersey, 120, 127, 315, 397
Jersey Shore, 7, 10, 186
Jesuits as inhabitants, 41
Jesus Christ, 130, 301
Jet Stream, 4
Jets, New York [football], 308, 310–11
Jets, the [gang], 153
Jewelry District, 227
Jewish Heritage Museum, 195
Jewish Museum, 253
Jews as inhabitants
    Bronx, 272
    Brooklyn, 281, 283
    Dutch colonial era, 45–46
    education, 20
    film and TV, 358
    food and dining, 325 (ill.), 325–26
    the Gilded Age, 117, 125
    Great Depression era, 139–40, 143

    independence of New York, 80, 84
    industrialization and immigration, 106–8, 110–11
    Manhattan, 225–26, 229, 239, 243–44, 253, 256
    music, 351
    notable New Yorkers, 378, 382
    religion, 15
    the sixties to 9/11, 160, 164, 170, 176–77
    sports, 312
    theater, 341, 345
    transportation, 29
    World War II and the postwar era, 146–47, 153–54
    writing, 376
JFK Airport, 28, 36, 169, 183, 188, 286, 315
Jim Crow Laws, 126
Jimmy the Goat, 367
Joel, Billy, 228, 249
Jogues, Isaac, 41
John, King, 74
John F. Kennedy Airport, 28, 36, 169, 183, 188, 286, 315
John Paul II, Pope, 242
John Street, 339
Johns, Jasper, 217
John's Pizzeria, 322
Johnson, Jack, 348
Johnson, Lyndon, 155
Johnson, Philip, 243, 291
Jolson, Al, 269, 379
Jones, James Earl, 345, 382
Jonge Tobias, 39
Joralemon Street, 275, 392
Jordan, Michael, 386
Joseph Papp Public Theater, 344
A Journal of the Late Actions of the French at Canada, with the Manner of Their Being Repulsed by His Excellency, Benjamin Fletcher, Their Majesties' Governor of New York, 371
journalism, 363–71
JPMorgan Chase, 68
Juan Rodriguez Way, 39
Judaism, 20, 107
Judas Iscariot, 301
Juet, Robert, 37
Julius's, 334
Jumel, Eliza, 262
Jumel, Stephen, 262
Jungle Band, 349

K

Kaczynski, Ted "The Unabomber," 145
Kael, Pauline, 152

Kahlo, Frida, 271
Kaiser Wilhelm der Grosse, 124
Kalustyan's, 391
Kandinsky, Vasily, 253
Kansas, 130
Karloff, Boris, 354
Katz's Delicatessen, 325
Kazan, Eliza, 342
Kazin, Alfred, 281
Kefauver, Carey Estes, 150
Kelly, James Edward, 61
Kelly, Ray, 187
Kempton, Murray, 370
Kennedy family, 383
Kensington Stables, 279
Kent State University, 158
Kentucky, 202
Kerouac, Jack, 383
Kew, England, 271
Kew Gardens, 154
Kfir fighter, 234
Kid Blink, 367
Kidd, William, 50–51, 51 (ill.), 200
Kieft, Willem, 35, 43–44, 293, 332
Kieft's War, 36, 43
Kiehl's Pharmacy, 217
King, B. B., 259
King Cole Bar, 335
King Jr., Martin Luther, 256
King Kong [character], 355
King Kong [movie], 355, 355 (ill.)
King Street, 205
King's Bridge, 104
King's College, 54, 84
Kings County, 53, 274, 303
Kingsbridge Road, 272
Kioshk, 299
Kips Bay, 61, 239
Kissinger, Henry, 315, 351
"The KKK Took My Baby Away," 385
Kleindeutschland, 118
Klimt, Gustav, 362
The Knick, 152
"Knickerbocker," 73–74
Knickerbocker, Cholly, 365
Knickerbocker beer, 332–33
Knickerbocker Hotel, 335–36
Knickerbockers, New York [baseball], 306
Knicks, New York [basketball], 230, 312 (ill.), 313
Know-Nothing Party, 78, 81, 92
Koch, Ed
    independence of New York, 84
    rebuilding and moving forward after 9/11, 184, 187
    the sixties to 9/11, 160, 170 (ill.), 170–71, 174–76, 178
Koeppel, Gerald, 41
Korea Way, 237
Korean War, 159

Koreans as inhabitants, 26, 236–37, 289
Koreatown, 236–37
Kramer, Larry, 173, 382
Krazy Kat, 367
Kristal, Hilly, 352
Kristallnacht, 358
K-Town, 236–37
Ku Klux Klan, 134, 380
Kubrick, Stanley, 215, 270
Kunstler, William, 157
Kurlansky, Mark, 9

L

LaMotta, Jake, 229
La Rotisserie Francais, 311
labor, division in the police department, 17–18
Labor Day parade, 103, 219
Laboulaye, Édouard de, 102, 102 (ill.)
LaBute, Neil, 346
Ladies' Mile, 219, 221–23, 222 (ill.), 320
Lady Gophers, 115
Lafayette Street, 203, 344, 382
Lafayette Theater, 259
LaGuardia, Fiorello
    Great Depression era, 138, 140 (ill.), 140–44
    Manhattan, 255
    other islands around the boroughs, 298, 301
    the sixties to 9/11, 171, 178
    World War II and the postwar era, 147
    writing, 376
LaGuardia Airport, 141, 148, 288–90, 303, 315
Lake Erie, 74
Lake Ontario, 313
Lancaster, Burt, 346
Lancaster, Pennsylvania, 67
Land Poort, 199
"Land Without Shadows," 284
Landmark Tavern, 389
Landmarks Law, 227–28
Landmarks Preservation Commission, 344
Landry, Tom, 310
landscape, 1
languages, 14, 20
Lankevich, George J., 165
Lansky, Meyer, 139, 144
largest city by population, as, 11–12
Last Exit to Brooklyn (Selby), 277
Latin Kings gang, 396
Latinos as inhabitants, 26, 187, 192, 267, 274, 287, 292
Latourette Park, 293

Laughter on the 23rd Floor, 358
Laughton, Charles, 346
Laurentide Ice Sheet, 33
Law & Order, 347, 356
"Law Concerning Dogs," 6
Lawrence, Cornelius Van Wyck, 49, 77–78
laws of, odd, 397
Lazarus, Emma, 103
Le Cirque, 317
Le Corbusier, 240, 263
Lead Belly, 350
Leary, Denis, 396
Lebanese as inhabitants, 195
LeBrun, George, 125
Lee, Robert E., 96
Lee, Spike, 313, 386
Lee, Stan, 376
Lee Ah Bow, 394
LeFrak Center, 279
Left Bank, 213
Léger, Fernand, 253
Lehman Brothers, 185
Leisler, Jacob, 50
Leisler Rebellion, 49–50
Lenape Indians
    animals, 9
    Bronx, 268
    Brooklyn, 275
    Dutch colonial era, 39, 41, 43
    early history, 34–35
    Manhattan, 191, 214, 261, 265
    origins of inhabitants, 10–11
    Queens, 287
Lenapehoking, 10
L'Enfant, Peter, 200
Lennai Lenape Indians, 10
Lennon, John, 249–50
Lennox, Charles, 293
Lenox Avenue, 127, 130, 348
Lenox Lounge, 258
Leo XIII, Pope, 263
Leone, Luisa, 324
Lepore, Jill, 82
Les Demoiselles d'Avignon, 243, 362
"Let's Call the Whole Thing Off," 379
letter, Son of Sam, 168 (ill.)
Letterman, David, 358
Lever House, 242–43
Lexington Avenue
    art, 360
    food and dining, 326
    Manhattan, 221, 238–39, 242–43, 250
    quirky New York, 391
    the sixties to 9/11, 162
Lexington Line, 392
Lhota, Joe, 186–87
Li Hongzhang, 317
Liberal Republican Party, 364
liberalism, 20–21

liberation of New York, 64–66
Liberator, 340
Liberians as inhabitants, 297
Liberty Boys, 56
Liberty Island, 74, 193, 299
liberty poles, 57–58
Liberty State Park, 127
Liberty Street, 162, 185, 196, 202
Lichtenstein, Roy, 32
Lichtfield Villa, 279
Life, 25
"Life During Wartime," 353
Life Guards, 58
Life Underground, 31
Limelight, 180
Limerick, Earl of, 49 (ill.)
Lincoln, Abraham, 93–97, 202, 295, 330, 365, 390
Lincoln Avenue, 268
Lincoln Center, 248
Lincoln Square, 247–50, 335
Lincoln Tunnel, 141
Lindsay, John
    film and TV, 356
    Manhattan, 210, 250
    rebuilding and moving forward after 9/11, 187
    the sixties to 9/11, 156, 158–60, 165, 169, 178
    sports, 308
    writing, 374–75
Lindy's, 171
Lions, Brooklyn, 310
Lions, Detroit, 383
LIRR (Long Island Rail Road), 124, 188, 288
Lispenard Marsh, 205
The Literary Walk, 246
Lithuania, 341
Lithuanians as inhabitants, 145
Little Africa, 212–13
Little Cuba, 282
"Little Flower," 141
Little Germany, 118
"Little House on the Prairie," 270
Little Italy
    all about, 206–11
    food and dining, 322–24
    independence of New York, 80
    Manhattan, 195, 208 (ill.), 233, 261
    Queens, 291
Little Mill Rock Island, 302
Little Murders, 356
Little Nemo in Slumberland, 367
A Little Night Music, 342
Little Old New York, 273
Little Syria, 162, 195
Little White House. See Gracie Mansion
livery cars, 28–29
"Living Newspapers," 341

Livingston, Robert, 70
Livingstone, Philip, 275
Lobel, Cindy, 318
location, geographic, 1
location of immigrants, 14
Loew's, 281
Loft, the, 351
Lombardi, Gennaro, 322
Lombardi, Vince, 310
Lombardi's, 322
LOMEX (Lower Manhattan Express-
way), 209–10
London, England
   British colonial era, 50, 52
   film and TV, 356
   independence of New York, 70,
      80–81, 85, 89
   industrialization and immigra-
      tion, 110
   Manhattan, 199, 219–20, 225,
      235, 244, 247
   music, 351–52
   notable New Yorkers, 380
   rebuilding and moving forward
      after 9/11, 189
   trees, 4
   writing, 365, 371–73
London planetree, 4
London Underground, 118
Long Island
   animals, 7
   bars and nightlife, 332
   British colonial era, 51
   Bronx, 272
   Brooklyn, 282, 285
   Dutch colonial era, 47
   early history, 35–36
   food and dining, 316, 324
   geology, 33
   the Gilded Age, 117
   Great Depression era, 142, 144
   industrialization and immigra-
      tion, 104–5
   landscape, 1
   Manhattan, 210–11, 263
   other islands around the bor-
      oughs, 302–3
   Queens, 286–88
   Revolutionary War, 63
   sports, 314–15
   World War II and the postwar
      era, 147–48
   writing, 370
Long Island City, 286–87
Long Island Express, 4, 144, 186
Long Island Expressway, 5
Long Island Rail Road (LIRR), 124,
   188, 288
Long Island Sound, 142, 268, 301
Long Island State Park Commis-
   sion, 142
Long Meadow, 279

Long Room, 330
Longacre Square, 116–17
looting, blackout, 167–68
Lopez, Charles Albert, 224
Lord & Taylor, 222
Los Angeles, California
   Brooklyn, 280
   business and economy, 22
   food and dining, 327
   independence of New York, 70
   number of Native Americans, 11
   population, 10–11
   rebuilding and moving forward
      after 9/11, 187
   sports, 307
   writing, 375
loss in population, 12
loss of by the Dutch, 48
The Lost Weekend, 335
Lough, James, 225
Louima, Abner, 179
Louisiana, 3, 128, 187, 273, 347
Love Saves the Day, 351
Lovelace, Francis, 292
Low Countries, 239
Low Life (Sante), 333
Lower Bay, 35–37
Lower East Side
   all about, 206–11
   Brooklyn, 281
   Dutch colonial era, 44
   ethnicity, 14
   food and dining, 325, 328
   the Gilded Age, 117–18, 125,
      130–31
   Great Depression era, 138
   industrialization and immigra-
      tion, 107–8, 110, 113
   Manhattan, 217, 243, 256
   notable New Yorkers, 378–79,
      382
   writing, 375–76
Lower Manhattan
   Brooklyn, 275
   business and economy, 23
   Dutch colonial era, 40
   ethnicity, 14
   food and dining, 316, 328
   independence of New York, 81,
      89
   industrialization and immigra-
      tion, 105, 114
   Manhattan, 194, 198, 212, 217,
      261
   the sixties to 9/11, 162–63
   Staten Island, 293
Lower Manhattan Expressway
   (LOMEX), 209–10
Lower West Side. See Tribeca
Loyalists, 63, 294, 330
Lubavitch Judaism, 154, 283
Lucchese family, 139, 169

Luciano, Charles "Lucky," 139, 139
   (ill.), 142, 144
Ludlow Street, 243, 325
Lufthansa, 169
Luger, Carl, 326
Luger, Peter, 326
Lullwater of the Lake, 279 (ill.)
Lumet, Sidney, 159
Luna Park, 284, 285 (ill.), 393
Lutherans as inhabitants, 15
Lyceum Theatre, 345–46, 346 (ill.)
Lynchburg, Virginia, 393

M

M&Ms, 133
Maas, Peter, 159
Mabley, Moms, 259
Macbeth, 390
Maccioni, Sirio, 317
Macdougal Street, 350
Maclay Bill, 80
Macy's, 132–33, 222, 265, 320
Macy's Christmas Parade, 132
Macy's Day Parade. See Thanksgiv-
   ing Day Parade
"Mad Bomber," 145
Mad Men, 161, 335
Madagascar, 246
Madden, Owney, 115, 348
Madeleine L'Engle Library, 256
Madison, James, 66–67, 223, 377
Madison Avenue, 101, 216, 224, 226,
   228, 250, 255
Madison House, 110
Madison Square, 101, 119, 218–24,
   233, 306
Madison Square Garden, 102, 122,
   146, 228–30, 229 (ill.), 313–14
Madison Square Park, 223–24, 228,
   244
Madoff, Bernie, 308
Mafia, the
   bars and nightlife, 334–35
   food and dining, 324
   Great Depression era, 138–39,
      141–42
   Manhattan, 198, 209
   the sixties to 9/11, 156, 173, 176
Mahican Indians, 35
Mahoney, Michael P., 128
Maiden Lane, 5, 53, 239, 339
Mailer, Norman, 161, 370, 374–75
Main Building, 113
Main Concourse, 122
Maine, 47, 66, 371
Majestic Theatre, 235
"Major," 5
Major Deegan Expressway, 5
Major League Baseball (MLB), 397
Major League Soccer (MLS), 315

Malcolm X [movie], 386
Malcolm X [person], 260
Malcolm X and Dr. Betty Shabazz
    Memorial and Educational Center,
    260
The Mall [Manhattan], 246
The Mall [Washington, D.C.], 258
Mallon, "Typhoid" Mary, 123 (ill.),
    123–24
Mama Leone's, 324
Mamma Mia, 330
Mamzelle Champagne, 122
Manchuria, 146
Mancuso, David, 351
Mandeville, Yellis, 211
Manes, Donald, 174
Manet, Edouard, 360
Mangin, Joseph Francois, 209
Manhattan
    animals, 5–7
    bars and nightlife, 332
    Battery Park, 192–206
    British colonial era, 49
    Bronx, 267–69, 272
    Brooklyn, 274–78, 280–81, 283–
        84, 286
    business and economy, 22–23,
        26
    Central Park, 244–47
    Chelsea, 225–31
    Chinatown, 206–11
    Civic Center, 192–206
    Dutch colonial era, 37, 39–44
    early history, 35, 191
    East Village, 211–18
    ethnicity, 14, 192
    film and TV, 355–56
    Financial District, 192–206
    Flatiron, 218–24
    food and dining, 316–17, 320,
        323–24, 328
    Garment District, 225–31
    the Gilded Age, 118, 121, 123–
        24, 127–28, 134
    Gramercy, 218–24
    Great Depression era, 143
    Greenwich Village, 211–18
    Harlem, 255–61
    Hell's Kitchen, 231–36
    Hudson Yards, 225–31
    independence of New York, 68,
        70–74, 79, 81–85, 89
    industrialization and immigra-
        tion, 98, 101, 104–5, 113–14,
        116
    Lincoln Square, 247–50
    Little Italy, 206–11
    Lower East Side, 206–11
    Madison Square, 218–24
    Midtown East, 236–44
    Midtown West, 231–36
    Morningside Heights, 255–61

music, 348–49
    notable New Yorkers, 378, 381,
        385–86
    origins of inhabitants, 10–11
    other islands around the bor-
        oughs, 298–300, 302
    population, 10–11, 192
    Queens, 286–89
    quirky New York, 397
    rebuilding and moving forward
        after 9/11, 183, 185–86, 188
    Revolutionary War, 58–64
    the sixties to 9/11, 159, 162–63,
        167, 171, 173, 180, 182
    size, 2
    slavery and the Civil War, 93, 97
    SoHo, 206–11
    sports, 306, 308, 311
    Staten Island, 291–97
    the five boroughs, 1, 2 (ill.), 16
    theater, 345
    Times Square, 231–36
    transportation, 28–29, 32
    trees, 4
    Tribeca, 206–11
    Union Square, 218–24
    Upper East Side, 250–55
    Upper Manhattan, 261–65
    Upper West Side, 247–50
    World War II and the postwar
        era, 148, 151
    writing, 363, 368, 372
Manhattan Appellate Courthouse,
    224
Manhattan Borough President's Of-
    fice, 204
Manhattan Bridge, 206–7, 277
Manhattan Club, 336
Manhattan Detention Center, 205
Manhattan Ladder Company 8, 18
    (ill.)
Manhattan Project, 255
Manhattanenge, 397
manmade object, oldest outdoor,
    247
manufacturing, 24–25
Manzi, Warren, 347
Mapplethorpe, Robert, 253
Maranzano, Salvatore, 139
Marckvelt Street, 332
Marcus Garvey Park, 258
Marcy Avenue, 117
Mardi Gras, 273
Mariott Marquis, 344
Market Field, 332
Marshall, Thurgood, 260
Martha's Vineyard, 37
Martin, Walter, 31
Martini & Rossi, 337
Marvel, 359
Marvel Comics, 376
Marx, Groucho, 258

Marx, Harpo, 373
Marx, Karl, 365–66
Marxism, 107, 157
Maryland, 61, 67, 269, 272, 301,
    308, 310
Masonic Hall, 78
Maspeth, 287
Mass, 172, 208, 242
Massachusetts
    British colonial era, 51, 54
    Bronx, 268–69, 271–72
    business and economy, 21, 23
    the Gilded Age, 118
    independence of New York, 82
    Manhattan, 202, 260
    notable New Yorkers, 378
    population, 12
    Revolutionary War, 57–58
    the sixties to 9/11, 180
    sports, 309, 311–12
    storms, 4
    World War II and the postwar
        era, 148
    writing, 363, 372–73
Massachusetts Institute of Technol-
    ogy (MIT), 226
Masseria, Joe, 139
Masstransiscope, 32
Matawan Creek, 10
Mattachine Society, 156
Mattano, Chief, 287
Mattus, Reuben, 329
Mattus, Rose, 329
Max's Kansas City, 219, 352
Mayflower, 48, 383
mayors, first, 48–49, 77
McClellan Jr., George B., 118, 176
McCullough, David, 60
McDougall, Alexander, 56, 56 (ill.)
McGuire, Peter J., 103
McInerney, Jay, 383
McKee, Joseph "Holy Joe," 341
McKeever Place, 279
McKim, Charles, 124
McKim, Mead, and White, 227, 255,
    278
McKinley, William, 120
McKinney-Steward, Susan Smith,
    283
McMillan, Jimmy, 189
McNally Jackson, 220
McSorley's Old Ale House, 330–31,
    331 (ill.)
Meadow Lake, 291
Meadowlands, the, 310
Meatpacking District, 215–17, 230,
    243
Mecca, Saudi Arabia, 261
medallions, taxi, 27–28
Melinek, Judy, 396
Memorial Day, 134, 397
Menand, Louis, 213

Mencken, H. L., 132, 336
Mercer Arts Center, 352
The Merchant of Venice, 345
Mercury mission, 233
Mermaid Parade, 285
Merrimack, 94
Mespat Indians, 287
Met, the. See Metropolitan Museum of Art ("the Met")
Met Museum, 229
Metesky, George "Mad Bomber," 145
Method, the, 341–42, 345
Metro New York, 370
MetroCard, 31
Metropolis, 375–76
Metropolitan Fire Department, 19, 97
Metropolitan Life (MetLife) Insurance Building, 8, 122, 223, 229
Metropolitan Life (MetLife) Tower, 119
Metropolitan Museum of Art ("the Met")
    art, 362–63
    Great Depression era, 138
    independence of New York, 86
    Manhattan, 216, 247, 249, 251–53, 252 (ill.), 263
    notable New Yorkers, 378
Metropolitan Transit Authority (MTA)
    animals, 8
    business and economy, 26
    Manhattan, 231
    map, 30 (ill.)
    rebuilding and moving forward after 9/11, 186, 188
    the sixties to 9/11, 161
    Staten Island, 297
    transportation, 29, 31
    World War II and the postwar era, 149
Metropolitans, New York, 307–8
MetroStars, New York, 315
MetroTech Center, 241, 280
Mets, New York, 260, 290, 308, 310
Meucci, Antonio, 295
Mexicans as inhabitants, 13, 289, 328, 350
Mexico, 9, 149–50, 276, 328
Miami, Florida, 144
Miami Beach, Florida, 269
Michaels, Lorne, 183, 359, 359 (ill.)
Michigan, 100, 228, 344, 383
Middle East, 7, 311
Midnight Cowboy, 356
A Midsummer Night's Dream, 354
Midtown
    all about, 231–44
    Bronx, 267
    food and dining, 324–25, 330
    the Gilded Age, 116, 128

Manhattan, 213, 222, 228, 230, 256
music, 349, 351
    notable New Yorkers, 386
    quirky New York, 396
    the sixties to 9/11, 162, 167–68
    sports, 311
    transportation, 27–28
    writing, 376
Midtown East, 236–44
Midtown West, 231–36
Midwood, 354, 381
MiG, 234
military post, oldest manned, 294–95
Mill Rock Island, 74, 302
Milland, Ray, 335
Millay, Edna St. Vincent, 213, 218
Miller, Arthur, 226, 381, 381 (ill.)
Milstein Hall of Ocean Life, 249
Mimic, 355
Minelli, Liza, 310, 335
Minetta Brook/Creek/Stream, 205, 211–12, 214
Minetta Lane, 212
Minetta Street, 211–12
Minneapolis, Minnesota, 232
Minnesota, 145, 232, 350
Minnesota Pipeline, 232
Minnesota Strip, 232
"Minnie the Moocher," 349
Minnissais, 299
Minuit, Peter, 43, 332
Miss Rhinegold, 333
Mississippi Delta, 348
Missouri, 187, 308, 356, 393
Mistake of '98, 115–16
MIT (Massachusetts Institute of Technology), 226
Mitchel, John Purroy, 127–28
Mitchell, Joseph, 331
MLB (Major League Baseball), 397
MLS (Major League Soccer), 315
Moderation Society, 130
modern fire department, 19
Modigliani, Amedeo, 253
Mohammed, Khalid Sheikh, 177
Mohawk Indians, 11
Mohican Indians, 271
MoMA (Museum of Modern Art), 243, 360, 362
Mon Lay Won, 322
monastery in, 263–64
Monitor, 94, 275
Monk, Thelonious, 234
Monkey House, 393
Monroe, Marilyn, 226, 342, 381
Montauk Indians, 35
Montgomery Street, 279
Montreal, Canada, 11
"Mood Indigo," 349
Mooney, William, 75

Moore, Annie, 113, 289
Moore, Clement Clarke, 225, 225 (ill.), 395
Moore, Marianne, 213
Moore, Sir Henry, 56
Moorish Revival style, 244, 345
Moose Murders, 343
Morgan, J. P., 118, 201, 248
Morgan Bank, 201
Morgan Library, 362
Morning Telegraph, 3
Morningside Avenue, 256
Morningside Drive, 72
Morningside Heights, 14, 255–61, 270, 391
Morningside Park, 378
Morosco Theater, 344
Morris, Gouverneur, 72, 268
Morris, Lewis, 268
Morris, Roger, 262
Morris family, 268
Morrisania, 268
Morris-Jumel Mansion, 262
Moscow, Russia, 80
Moses, Robert
    Bronx, 271
    Brooklyn, 279, 282
    Great Depression era, 138, 142–43, 143 (ill.)
    Manhattan, 192, 194, 210, 236, 248
    notable New Yorkers, 378, 382
    other islands around the boroughs, 302
    Queens, 291
    sports, 308, 311
    theater, 345
    World War II and the postwar era, 151–52
Moshulu Parkway, 269
mosque, first, 195, 261
Most Precious Blood Church, 208
Mott, Frank Luther, 363
Mott Street, 114, 152, 206, 208
Mould, Jacob Wrey, 249
Mount Prospect, 278
Mount Vernon Hotel Museum and Garden, 251
Moustache Petes, 139
moving forward and rebuilding after 9/11, 182–89
MTA (Metropolitan Transit Authority). See Metropolitan Transit Authority (MTA)
Mudd Club, 180, 353
Muhammad, 224
Mulberry Bend, 108
Mulberry Street, 80, 88, 208–9
Mulberry Street Bar, 208
Mumford, Lewis, 73
Muni, Paul, 345
Municipal Lodging Houses, 138

Municipal Pauper Lunatic Asylum, 297

Muñoz, Paloma, 31

Munsee Indians. See Raritan Indians

Murder, Inc., 139, 144, 150, 173, 281

"murder of the century," 122–23

murder rate, 165–66

"Murderer's Row," 310

Murdoch, Rupert, 369–70

Murphy, "Mallet," 115

Murray, Bill, 355

Murray, Robert, 61

Murray Hill, 61, 239, 249, 326

Murray Street, 100, 204

Musetto, Vincent, 369

Museum Mile, 252–54

Museum of Arts and Design, 235–36

Museum of Modern Art (MoMA), 243, 360, 362

Museum of Natural History, 86

Museum of the City of New York, 253, 255

Museum of the Moving Image, 362

music, 347–54

Music Hall, 234

Muslims as inhabitants, 15, 177, 180, 195, 260–61

Mussolini, Benito, 134, 146–47

"My Day," 380

Myrtle Avenue, 32

N

N line, 14

Nabisco (National Biscuit Company), 329

Nader, Ralph, 186

The Naked City, 356

Namath, "Broadway" Joe, 310–11, 311

naming parts of New York
    Bank Street, 212
    Battery Park, 192
    Bronx, 268
    Brooklyn Dodgers, 307
    Brownsville, 281
    Canal Street, 207
    Ellis Island, 299
    from New Amsterdam to New York, 47
    Governors Island, 300
    Harlem, 256
    Hell's Kitchen, 233
    Hudson River, 37–38
    Irving Place, 221
    Liberty Island, 299
    Little Africa, 212–13
    Manhattan, 191
    Meatpacking District, 215–16
    Minetta Street, 211–12

Queens, 287

Red Hook, 277

Staten Island, 293

Stone Street, 198

Strivers' Row, 260

Sugar Hill, 260

the five boroughs, 1

Tribeca, 210–11

Turtle Bay, 239

Naples, Italy, 208, 250

Napoleon, 74, 80, 247, 258

Napoleonic wars, 24

Narrows, the, 38, 74, 94, 148

Nasaw, David, 367

NASL (North American Soccer League), 315

Nassau County, 303, 314

Nassau Street, 200–202

Nassau Street Theatre, 339

Nast, Thomas, 98–100, 395

Nathan's Famous, 320

The Nation, 360

Nation, Carry, 130–31

Nation of Islam as inhabitants, 15, 260

National Basketball Association (NBA), 280, 313

National Basketball League (NBL), 313

National Biscuit Company (Nabisco), 329

National Championship, U.S., 314

National Football League (NFL), 310

National Guard, 82, 158, 250

National Historic Landmarks, 244, 249, 255, 259

National Hockey League (NHL), 314

National Institutes of Health, 396

National Lampoon, 358–59

National League baseball, 307–9, 311

National Museum of the American Indian, 194

National Museum, Smithsonian, 11

National Origins Act, 133

National Park Service, 113, 299

National Park System, 295

National Review, 20, 374

National Theatre, 339

Native Americans as inhabitants
    animals, 9
    Bronx, 268, 271
    Brooklyn, 274–75, 282, 284
    business and economy, 23
    Dutch colonial era, 37–39, 41–45
    early history, 34–36
    ethnicity, 13
    food and dining, 328
    ironworkers, 11
    landscape, 1

Manhattan, 191, 194, 201, 211–12, 214–15, 254, 256, 261, 265
    number of Native Americans, 11
    origins of inhabitants, 10
    other islands around the boroughs, 299–300
    police, 17
    Queens, 287
    quirky New York, 397
    seal, 3
    slavery and the Civil War, 91
    Staten Island, 292

Native Tongues, 354

navigation within Central Park, 246

Navy, Confederate, 94

Navy, Royal, 293, 300–301

Navy, U.S., 74, 233, 299, 382

Navy Submarine Force Museum and Library, U.S., 62

Navy Yard Basin, 274–76

Nazism, 146–47, 172, 229, 362, 376

NBA (National Basketball Association), 280, 313

NBC Studios, 241, 357, 359

NBL (National Basketball League), 313

Nebraska, 260

Necropolis, 280

Needle, the, 247

Negro Moses, 130

Negroes Burial Ground, 204

Negroes' Causeway, 212

Negroes' Farms, 211–12

Neir's Tavern, 331

neo-Gothic, 84, 263–64

Nepalis as inhabitants, 289

Nesbit, Evelyn, 122

Netherlands, the
    Bronx, 268
    Brooklyn, 274
    Dutch colonial era, 39, 41–42, 44, 46–48
    Manhattan, 191, 217, 230, 256
    quirky New York, 394
    Staten Island, 293

Nets, Brooklyn, 280, 313, 387

Nets, New Jersey, 280, 313

Neue Galerie, 329, 362

New Amsterdam [place]
    animals, 5
    bars and nightlife, 332
    British colonial era, 48, 51–52
    Bronx, 268
    Brooklyn, 274–75
    business and economy, 21, 23
    Dutch colonial era, 39–48, 40 (ill.)
    early history, 34
    food and dining, 328
    Manhattan, 192, 217, 256
    origins of inhabitants, 11

other islands around the boroughs, 297
quirky New York, 394
writing, 373
New Amsterdam [theater], 390
"The New Colossus," 103
New Croton Aqueduct, 83
New Deal, 141, 229, 374, 380
New England, 144
New Haven, Connecticut, 54
New Jersey
animals, 8, 10
British colonial era, 51, 54
Brooklyn, 277
Dutch colonial era, 40, 45
early history, 35
film and TV, 354
the Gilded Age, 120, 123–24, 127, 134
independence of New York, 67, 69, 74
industrialization and immigration, 104–5
Manhattan, 197–98, 210
notable New Yorkers, 385
other islands around the boroughs, 299, 302
quirky New York, 390, 395, 397
Revolutionary War, 63–64
the sixties to 9/11, 167, 170, 182
slavery and the Civil War, 91
sports, 306, 310–11, 315
Staten Island, 292
World War II and the postwar era, 150
New Jersey Palisades, 263–64
New Netherland, 39–40, 43–44, 276, 293, 305
New Orange, 48
New Orleans, Louisiana, 3, 187, 273, 347
New Sweden, 40
New Theatre, 339
New Utrecht, 274
New World, 36–37, 42, 47–48, 55, 103, 202
New Year's Eve, 117, 232
New York, 157
New York 21, 157
New York American, 123
New York Aquarium, 194
New York Assembly, 377
New York Base Ball Club, 306
New York Botanical Garden. See Bronx Botanical Garden
New York Bridge. See Brooklyn Bridge
New York Bridge Company, 105
New York Burning (Lepore), 82
New York Central Railroad, 115, 120, 124, 230

New York City Economic Development Corporation (NYCEDC), 192, 267, 274, 287, 292
New York City FC (Football Club), 315
New York City Landmarks Preservation Commission, 228
New York City Transit Authority, 149
New York Coliseum, 151
New York Daily News
the sixties to 9/11, 156, 164, 166, 168, 174
slavery and the Civil War, 93
World War II and the postwar era, 151
writing, 368, 370
New York Daily Times, 369
New York Dolls, 352
New York Elevated Railroad Company, 97
New York Evening Post, 238, 370
New York Harbor
animals, 10
business and economy, 22
Dutch colonial era, 36–37, 39–41, 48
the Gilded Age, 127
industrialization and immigration, 108
Manhattan, 193
other islands around the boroughs, 299–300
Revolutionary War, 61
slavery and the Civil War, 94
Staten Island, 292
World War II and the postwar era, 147–48
New York Herald, 93, 117, 205, 212, 261, 340, 364–65
New York Historical Society, 217
New York Hospital, 66–67
New York Insurance Company, 68
New York Journal, 366
New York Law School, 134
New York Lesbian and Gay Community Center, 173
New York magazine, 179, 223, 343, 371
New York Metropolitan Police Force, 88–89
New York Mosque, 261
New York Movie, 360
New York Municipal Police Force, 17, 87–89
New York Naval Shipyard. See Brooklyn Navy Yard
"New York, New York," 309–10
New York Observer, 370
New York Police Department (NYPD). See NYPD (New York Police Department)

New York Post, 169, 365, 368–70
New York Press, 333
New York Public Library, 83–84, 145, 238, 378
New York Renaissance, 312–13
New York Shakespeare Festival, 344–45, 382
New York State Pavilion, 290 (ill.), 291
New York State Supreme Court, 204
New York Stock Exchange
Great Depression era, 137
independence of New York, 68, 68 (ill.), 81, 84
Manhattan, 194, 200–201
the sixties to 9/11, 182
New York Sun, 79, 120, 364, 367
New York Times
Brooklyn, 281
food and dining, 323
the Gilded Age, 117, 128, 134
independence of New York, 76, 79 (ill.)
industrialization and immigration, 99, 104, 106, 115
Manhattan, 211, 223, 228, 232, 246
music, 352
quirky New York, 390
the sixties to 9/11, 159, 161, 167, 177, 181
theater, 340, 343
World War II and the postwar era, 154–55
writing, 366, 368 (ill.), 369, 373
New York Tribune, 76, 85, 93, 109, 130, 364–67, 394
New York University, 84, 126, 140, 212, 214, 313, 350
New York Weekly Journal, 363–64
New York Wheel, 296
New York World, 109, 200, 247
New Yorker, 297, 340, 343, 373
Newark, New Jersey, 170
"The Newest New Yorkers," 13
Newgate Prison, 215
Newman, Paul, 342
Newport, Rhode Island, 314
Newport Casino, 314
Newsboys' Lodging, 112
Newsday, 370
Newsies, 367–68
Newtown Creek, 286–87, 289
New-York Gazette, 363–64, 371
The New-Yorker, 364
NFL (National Football League), 310
NHL (National Hockey League), 314
Niagara Falls, 240, 281
Niblo, Billy, 340
Niblo's Garden, 340
nicknames for, 2–3, 73–74
Nico, 361

Nicoll, Gov. Richard, 48
Nieu Nederlandt, 40
Nieuw Haarlem, 256
Night of the Living Dead, 356
Nightclub Enforcement Task Force, 180
Nighthawks, 360
nightlife, bars and, 330–37
Nike, 386
Nikola Tesla Corner, 239
Nile Delta, 253
Nile River, 247
Nimham, Chief Daniel, 271
Ninth Avenue, 97, 225, 232, 317
Nixon, Richard, 158, 160
No Wavers, 352
Noguchi, Isamu, 242, 253
NoHo, 209
Nolita, 209, 233, 322
Nom Wah Tea Parlor, 207
NoMad, 233
Noortwyck, 211
Nooten Eylandt, 300
Norden bombsight, 147
The Normal Heart, 173, 344–45, 382
North America, 8, 39, 46, 48, 52, 114, 293
North American Soccer League (NASL), 315
North Beach Amusement Park, 288
North Bergen, New Jersey, 395
North Brother Island, 118, 124
North Carolina, 126
North District, 211
North Pool, 196
North Street, 70, 72
North Tower, 181, 197, 355
Northern Europe, 119
Northern Ireland, 311
Northwest Passage, 36–37, 41
Norway maple, 4
Norwegians as inhabitants, 41
Norwood, 269
Not Ready for Prime Time Players, 358–59
notable New Yorkers, 377–87
No-Toe Charley, 212
Nottinghamshire, England, 74
Nova Scotia, Canada, 65
Nude Descending a Staircase, No. 2, 360
number of art museums and galleries, 361–62
number of boroughs, 16
number of bridges, 29
number of calls answered by the FDNY, 19
number of casualties on 9/11, 181
number of city employees, 16–17
number of dead people in Queens, 289

number of fire houses in the FDNY, 19
number of foreign-born people, 13
number of free condoms, 395
number of Madison Square Gardens, 228–29
number of MTA users, 29
number of Native Americans, 11
number of newspapers, 369–70
number of people displaced by Central Park, 245–46
number of people in each borough, 11
number of pets, 7
number of pigeons, 7
number of restaurants, 316
number of schools, 19
number of security cameras, 189
number of slaves, 53
number of trees, 4
Nut Island, 40, 193, 300
Nutten Island, 300
N.W.A., 354
Nyack, 360
"N.Y.C.," 170
NYCEDC (New York City Economic Development Corporation), 192, 267, 274, 287, 292
NYPD (New York Police Department)
   Bronx, 270
   duties of the, 17–18
   film and TV, 355
   the Gilded Age, 120, 126–27, 134
   photo, 17 (ill.)
   quirky New York, 396
   rebuilding and moving forward after 9/11, 187, 189
   the sixties to 9/11, 156, 159, 166, 168, 178–79, 181
   theater, 342
   World War II and the postwar era, 147, 154

O

Oak Room Bar, 244
Oakland, California, 157
Obama, Barack, 242, 334
Obelisk, the, 247
O'Brien, John, 139
Occupational Safety and Health Administration (OSHA), 390
Occupy Sandy, 185
Occupy Wall Street, 20, 185
Ocean Drive, 269
Ocean Parkway, 279
Ochs, Alfred, 369
O'Connell, Daniel, 113
O'Connor, John, 172

The Octagon, 297
odd laws of, 397
Odets, Clifford, 146, 346
Odetta, 350
O'Dwyer, Paul, 3
O'Dwyer, William "Bill-O," 149–50
Off the Minnesota Strip, 232
Office of Chief Medical Examiner, 197
"Oh, Lady Be Good," 379
Ohio, 314, 349
O'Keefe, Georgia, 217
Oklahoma, 35, 201, 312, 350
Oklahoma City, Oklahoma, 201
Okrent, Daniel, 311
The Old Curiosity Shop (Dickens), 372
Old Gray Lady, 369
Old Navy, 223
Old New York County Courthouse, 204
Old Pear Tree, 217
Old Penn Station, 227 (ill.), 227–28
The Old Southwest, 273
Old Taverns of New York (Bayles), 331
Old Testament, 154
Old Town, 292
O'Leary, Daniel, 101
Olive Garden, 223, 329–30
Olmsted, Frederick Law, 86–87, 219, 246, 278–79
Olmsted Brothers, 278
Olmsted Jr., Frederick Law, 263–64
Omaha, Nebraska, 260
O'Malley, Walter, 280, 307–8
On the Waterfront, 277, 342, 354
Onassis, Jackie, 251
Once Upon a Time in America, 152
Ondine, 350
One: Number 31, 362
One Police Plaza, 17 (ill.)
One Righteous Man (Browne), 127
One Times Square, 117
One57, 235
O'Neill, Eugene, 213
Ono, Yoko, 249
Ontario, Canada, 35, 313
Operation Sail '76, 166
opium dens, 152, 152 (ill.), 321
Orange, Prince of, 48
Orange Riot, 99
Orbach, Jerry, 347
Order Sons of Italy, 295
Oregon, 371
Oreos, 329, 329 (ill.)
Orientalism, 284
Original Celtics, New York, 312–13
Original Dixieland Jazz Band, 235
Original Six, 314
origins of business, 21
origins of education, 19

origins of Greenwich Village, 211
origins of inhabitants, 10–11
origins of New Amsterdam, 40
origins of the fire department, 18
origins of the police department, 17
Orioles, Baltimore, 269, 308
Orthodox Judaism, 107, 283
Oscar of the Waldorf, 320
Oscars, 343
OSHA (Occupational Safety and
    Health Administration), 390
Oshkosh, Wisconsin, 313
"the other half," 109–10
Otis, Elisha, 86
Otterness, Tom, 31
Ottoman Empire, 195
Our Lady of Lebanon Maronite
    Cathedral, 195
Outback Steakhouse, 223
Outcault, Richard Felton, 366
Outerbridge Crossing, 292
outlaw of slavery, 91
The Out-of-Towners (Simon), 167
Oyster Bar, 10, 122
Oyster Bay, 123
Oyster Island, 299
oysters, 3, 9–10, 198, 299, 319

P

P. J. Clarke's, 335
Pacific Islanders as inhabitants, 13
Pacino, Al, 159
Packers, Green Bay, 310
Paganck, 300
Page Six, 365, 370
Pakistan, 224
Pakistanis as inhabitants, 14, 29
Palace Hotel, 242
Palatinates as inhabitants, 300, 363
Pale Male, 9
Pale of Settlement, 107
Palermo, Italy, 120
Palestine, 341
Palin, Sarah, 370
Pan-Africanism, 129
The Panic in Needle Park, 356
Panic of 1857, 88 (ill.), 89
Panther 21, 157
Papirofsky, Yosl. See Papp, Joseph
Papp, Joseph, 344–45, 382
parade, Labor Day, 103, 219
Paradise Square, 205
Paramount Theater, 349
Paris, France
    bars and nightlife, 335
    Bronx, 269
    food and dining, 316
    independence of New York, 89
    industrialization and immigra-
        tion, 102, 104, 110

Manhattan, 213–14, 244, 247,
    258
notable New Yorkers, 383
The Paris Review, 383
park, first, 194
Park Avenue
    food and dining, 320
    the Gilded Age, 120–22, 131
    Great Depression era, 137
    Manhattan, 219, 221, 223, 231,
        235, 242, 250–51, 261
    Queens, 288
    Revolutionary War, 61
Park Avenue Armory, 250–51
"The Park Avenue of the Middle
    Class," 269–70
Park Avenue South, 220
Park Row, 16, 109, 116–17, 203
Park Slope, 21, 61
Park Street, 196
Parker, Charlie, 349
Parker, Dorothy, 373
Parking Violations Bureau, 174
Parks, Rosa, 84–85, 156
Parks Commission, 255
Parliament, 55–57
Pataki, George, 183
PATH. See Port Authority of New
    York and New Jersey
Patriots, 57–58
Patrolmen's Benevolent Association
    (PBA), 187
Paul, Mary, 365
Paul VI, Pope, 155 (ill.), 242
Pauw, Michael, 292
Pavonia Massacre, 44
PBA (Patrolmen's Benevolent Asso-
    ciation), 187
PBS, 251, 311
Peach War, 45, 292
Pear Tree Corner, 217
Pear Tree Pharmacy, 217
Pearl Street, 9, 50, 80–81, 104, 198,
    330, 371
Peg Leg Peter. See Stuyvesant, Peter
Pelé, 315
Pelham Bay, 268
Pelham Bay Park, 268, 273
Pell, Thomas, 268
Pell Street, 206 (ill.), 206–7, 321–22
Pellegrino, Frank, 324
Penadnik, 261
Pennsylvania
    art, 360
    British colonial era, 51
    Bronx, 272
    business and economy, 21, 23
    Dutch colonial era, 40–41
    food and dining, 326
    the Gilded Age, 122, 132
    independence of New York, 67,
        70, 80–81

industrialization and immigra-
    tion, 105
Manhattan, 198, 240
notable New Yorkers, 381
population, 12
quirky New York, 398
Revolutionary War, 57
the sixties to 9/11, 160, 166
slavery and the Civil War, 92
sports, 314
theater, 342
writing, 363, 371
Pennsylvania "Penn" Station, 31,
    120, 145, 227 (ill.), 227–30, 288
Pennsylvania Railroad, 120, 124
penny presses, 364
people of, 10–15
The People's House. See Gracie
    Mansion
Peppermint Lounge, 180
Perfect Crime, 347
Perkins, Frances, 126
Peruvians as inhabitants, 289
Peter Cooper Village, 221
Pete's Tavern, 318, 318 (ill.)
Petiot, Fernand, 335
Petit, Philippe, 163–64
Petrosino, Guiseppe "Joe," 120, 289
pets, 7
Phantom of the Opera, 347
Philadelphia, Pennsylvania
    British colonial era, 51
    business and economy, 21, 23
    Dutch colonial era, 41
    the Gilded Age, 132
    independence of New York, 67,
        80–81
    industrialization and immigra-
        tion, 105
    Manhattan, 198, 240
    population, 12
    quirky New York, 398
    Revolutionary War, 57
    the sixties to 9/11, 160, 166
    slavery and the Civil War, 92
    sports, 314
    writing, 371
Philippines, the, 115
Phillips, David Graham, 125
Phillips Exeter Academy, 383
Phoenix, Arizona, 10
Picasso, Pablo, 243, 360, 362
Pickett, Wilson, 259
Pier 86, 233
Pier A Harbor House, 193
Pierrepont, Henry Evelyn, 280
Pieter Claesen Wyckoff House, 276
Pig Alley, 6
Pig War, 292
pigeons, 7–9
pigs, 5–6
Pigtown, 279

435

Pileggi, Nicholas, 169
Pine District, 211
pirates, 50–51
Pitkin Avenue, 281
Pittsburgh, Pennsylvania, 122, 342, 360
Pizza Connection, 32
PlaNYC, 189
Playboy, 170
playgrounds, 111, 207
The Plaza, 244
Plaza Hotel, 385
Pleistocene Era, 33
Plimpton, George, 383
Poe, Edgar Allan, 239, 272, 272 (ill.)
Poe, Virginia, 272
The Poetry Project, 218
poetry slams, 218
Poison Squad, 373
Poland, 108
Poles as inhabitants, 110, 170, 329
police
    bars and nightlife, 334–35
    beginning of, 17–18
    Bronx, 270
    the Gilded Age, 120, 125–29, 131–32, 134
    Great Depression era, 140, 144–45
    independence of New York, 78–79, 85–89
    industrialization and immigration, 97, 100–101, 108–11
    Manhattan, 206–7, 217, 223–24, 232, 242
    Queens, 289, 291
    quirky New York, 392–93, 396–97
    rebuilding and moving forward after 9/11, 183, 185–88
    the sixties to 9/11, 165, 168, 173–75, 177–79, 181
    Staten Island, 297
    theater, 341–42
    World War II and the postwar era, 149–50, 152–61
    writing, 366, 374, 376
police department. See NYPD (New York Police Department)
political demographics of, 20–21
Polk, Frank, 128
Pollock, George, 391
Pollock, Jackson, 360, 362
Pollock, St. Claire, 390
Polo Grounds, 260, 268, 307–10, 312
Pompeii, Italy, 316
Pontiac, 167
Poole, William, 92
poor, the
    animals, 6
    Brooklyn, 281–82, 286

Dutch colonial era, 46
    food and dining, 323
    geology, 33
    Great Depression era, 141
    independence of New York, 70, 84
    industrialization and immigration, 109–11, 115
    Manhattan, 214, 224
    notable New Yorkers, 377, 380, 382
    the sixties to 9/11, 158, 160, 168–69, 174, 179
    slavery and the Civil War, 95
    World War II and the postwar era, 151
"The Poor Man's Riviera," 284
Pop Shop, 361
Pope, the, 78
population
    Bronx, 267
    Brooklyn, 273
    general, 10–12
    Manhattan, 192
    Queens, 287–89
    slavery and the Civil War, 92–93
    Staten Island, 292
Porgy and Bess, 379
Port Authority of New York and New Jersey, 162–63, 181–83, 188, 197, 232
Porter, Cole, 347
Portland, Maine, 371
Portland, Oregon, 371
Portrait of Adele Bloch-Bauer I, 362
"Portraits of Grief," 181
Portuguese as inhabitants, 37
Post, George, 84, 201
Post Office, 81
postwar era, World War II and the, 146–55
Potato Famine, 107
potter's fields, 150, 214, 219, 223, 238, 301–2
Pound Ridge, 268
Powell, Colin, 84
Powell Jr., Adam Clayton, 380–81
Power! 341
The Power Broker (Caro), 271
"The Prayer for Twenty Millions," 365
pre-Cambrian era, 265
pre-colonial era, 33–36, 264–65
Presbyterian College, 54
Presbyterians as inhabitants, 241
president born in, 86
presidents' visits to, 242
prey, birds of, 8–9
Price, Richard, 272–73
Prince, Hal, 342
Prince Street, 101, 209, 220, 340
Princeton, New Jersey, 67, 302

Princeton Club, 125
Princeton University, 54
Prison Ship Martyrs Monument, 276
Prohibition
    bars and nightlife, 333, 335–36
    Brooklyn, 282
    the Gilded Age, 130–32, 134
    Great Depression era, 138–39
    Manhattan, 213
    the sixties to 9/11, 165
    sports, 313
    World War II and the postwar era, 148
Project Runway, 226
Prokhorov, Mikhail, 313
pronunciation of "Houston Street," 209
Prospect Heights, 280
Prospect Park, 33, 176, 220, 277–80, 279 (ill.), 282
prosperity of business, 24 (ill.), 24–25
Protestantism, 49, 287
Protestants as inhabitants
    British colonial era, 54
    Dutch colonial era, 40, 45–46
    the Gilded Age, 131
    independence of New York, 70, 78–80
    industrialization and immigration, 107
    notable New Yorkers, 380
    religion, 15
    slavery and the Civil War, 95
Pryor, Richard, 259
Pseudo.com, 180
public advocates, 186–87
Public Enemy, 354
public housing, 143–44
Public School Society, 70
Public Theater, 343–45, 344 (ill.), 382
publishing and authors, 371–76
Puerto Rican Day Parade, 151
Puerto Ricans as inhabitants
    bars and nightlife, 330
    business and economy, 26
    independence of New York, 80
    Manhattan, 253–54, 261
    the sixties to 9/11, 157–58, 168
    World War II and the postwar era, 151, 153
Puerto Rico, 12, 115, 151
Pulitzer, Joseph, 102, 109, 367
Pulitzer Prize, 369
Pupin Hall, 255
Pure Food and Drug Act, 123
Puritanism, 48, 332
Putnam, Israel, 300–301

Q

Q, the Winged Serpent, 355
Quakers as inhabitants, 15, 45, 91, 371
Quartering Act, 56
Queen Latifah, 354
Queens
  all about, 286–91
  animals, 5, 7
  bars and nightlife, 331
  British colonial era, 53
  Bronx, 267–68
  Brooklyn, 282
  Dutch colonial era, 45
  ethnicity, 14, 287
  film and TV, 357
  food and dining, 316
  geology, 33
  the Gilded Age, 119, 134
  Great Depression era, 143
  industrialization and immigra-
    tion, 98, 104, 116
  languages, 14
  Manhattan, 230, 237, 243, 260
  music, 354
  notable New Yorkers, 383–85
  other islands around the bor-
    oughs, 297, 302–3
  population, 10–11, 287–89
  quirky New York, 394
  rebuilding and moving forward
    after 9/11, 186, 188
  the sixties to 9/11, 159–60, 167,
    173–74
  size, 2
  sports, 308, 314
  Staten Island, 293
  the five boroughs, 1, 2 (ill.)
  transportation, 29
  trees, 4–5
  weather, 4
  World War II and the postwar
    era, 153–54
  writing, 368–69, 373, 375–76
Queens County, 288, 303
Queens County Farm Museum, 288
Queens Giant, 4–5
Queens Museum, 291
Queensboro Bridge, 289
Queenstown, Ireland, 113
quirky New York, 389–98

R

Radical Whigs, 57
Radio City Music Hall, 145, 241
Radio Days, 147
Radio Row, 162
Radner, Gilda, 359
Raft, George, 389

railways, elevated, 97–98
Rainbow Room, the, 241
Ramadan, 289
The Ramble, 246
Ramone, Dee Dee, 225
Ramone, Joey, 384–85
Ramones, the, 352, 384–85
Ramos, Rafael, 188
RAND Corporation, 158
Randall, Robert Richard, 295
Randall's Island, 286, 302, 315
Rangel, Charlie, 175
Rangers, New York, 229–30, 313–14
Rao's, 324
Raritan Bay, 10
Raritan Indians, 35–36, 43, 292
Raritan River, 35
Raskob, John, 238
rats, 9
Ravenite Social Club, 208
The Ravine, 279
Raymond, Henry Jarvis, 366
reaction to Lincoln's death, 96–97
Reade Street, 204
Reagan, Ronald, 171, 384
rebellion against the British, 57
Rebels, 59, 62–64, 94
rebuilding and moving forward after
  9/11, 182–89
Receiving Reservoir, 83
Recife, Brazil, 46
Reckouwacky Indians, 36
The Recruiting Officer, 339
Rector Street, 195
Red Bull Arena, 315
Red Bulls, New York, 315
Red Cap, 126
Red Hook, 188, 192, 277, 300
Red Hook Houses, 277
Red Scare, 134, 358
Red Sox, Boston, 269, 309
Redcoats, 58, 63
Reds, 213
Reds, Cincinnati, 357
red-tailed hawks, 9
Reed, John, 213, 336
Reform Judaism, 107, 244
Regal Theater, 259
Reich, 229
Reiner, Carl, 358
Reisenweber's, 235
relationship between Europeans and
  Indians, 38–39
Reles, Abe "Kid Twist," 144
religion, demographics of, 14–15
Renaissance Center, 344
Renaissance Revival, 270
Rens, the, 312–13
rent control, 148
Rent Is Too Damn High Party, 189
Renwick Jr., James, 241, 298
replacement of manufacturing, 25

Republican Party
  Great Depression era, 141, 143
  independence of New York, 68
  industrialization and immigra-
    tion, 111
  Manhattan, 250
  notable New Yorkers, 380, 385
  politics, 21
  rebuilding and moving forward
    after 9/11, 184, 186
  the sixties to 9/11, 164, 170,
    176, 178
  slavery and the Civil War, 95
  Staten Island, 296–97
  writing, 374
Requiem for a Dream (Selby), 285
Reservoir Square, 238
restaurants, oldest, 316–18
Restein, Ludwig, 65
Resurrection Men, 66
Revolutionary War
  bars and nightlife, 330
  British colonial era, 52, 54
  Bronx, 268, 271
  Brooklyn, 276
  business and economy, 23–24
  Dutch colonial era, 41
  early history, 55–66
  firefighting, 18
  independence of New York, 68
  industrialization and immigra-
    tion, 106
  Manhattan, 203, 225, 262
  notable New Yorkers, 377
  other islands around the bor-
    oughs, 297, 301
  the sixties to 9/11, 166
  Staten Island, 293–94
Reyes, Matias, 175
Rhapsody in Blue, 378–79
Rheingold Brewery, 333
Rhode Island, 37, 314
Rich, Buddy, 259
Rich, Frank, 343
Richard III, 339
richest apartment building, 251
Richmond, Duke of, 293
Richmond County, 293
Richmond Hill, 293
Richmondston, 292
Richter scale, 127
Rickard, "Tex," 314
Riis, Jacob, 109–12, 208, 212, 253,
  301
Riker's Island, 298, 301–3
Riley, Pat, 313
Ring of Steel, 189
Ringling Bros. and Barnum & Bai-
  ley Combined Shows, the Greatest
  Show on Earth, 102
riot, medical student, 66–67
riot, walking, 101

riots, Crown Heights, 176–77
riots of 1844, 80
riots of 1935, 258, 349, 374
The Rise of the Goldbergs, 358
River Avenue, 269
Rivera, Geraldo, 391
Riverdale, 271
Riverside Church, 8, 241, 264
Riverside Drive, 72, 200, 391
Riverside Park, 5, 258, 378
Ro, Ronin, 376
Robards, Jason, 344
robbery. See crime
Robbins, Jerome, 153, 248
Robert F. Kennedy Bridge, 143
Roberts, Archibald, 59
Robeson, Paul, 260
Robinson, Bill "Bojangles," 259, 342, 349
Robinson, Jackie, 307, 307 (ill.)
Robinson, Sugar Ray, 229
Roc-a-Fella Records, 387
Rocawear, 387
Rockaway Indians, 36, 282
Rockaway Islands, 36, 150, 188, 282, 286, 291
Rockefeller, David, 162
Rockefeller, John D., 240
Rockefeller, Nelson, 162, 194
Rockefeller Center, 162, 209, 240 (ill.), 240–41
Rockefeller Jr., John D., 162, 241, 263–64, 336, 378
Rockefeller Park, 195
Rocking Stone, 270
rocks, oldest, 265
The Rocky Horror Picture Show, 356–57
Rodriguez, Juan, 39
Roebling, Emily, 106
Roebling, John Augustus, 105–6
Roebling, Washington, 106
Rogers, Will, 380
Roman Catholicism, 287
Roman Catholics as inhabitants, 20, 134
Roman Republic, 295
Romanesque style, 377
Romanians as inhabitants, 289
Rome, Italy, 124, 255
Romeo and Juliet, 153, 347
Roode Hoek, 277
Rooftop Murder, 123
Roosevelt, Eleanor, 144, 298, 380
Roosevelt, Franklin D.
    film and TV, 357
    the Gilded Age, 135
    Great Depression era, 138, 140 (ill.), 141
    Manhattan, 242
    notable New Yorkers, 380

other islands around the boroughs, 298
Roosevelt, Theodore, 86, 93, 110–11, 120, 229, 234, 248
Roosevelt family, 250
Roosevelt Island, 297–98, 298 (ill.), 341
Roscoe's House of Chicken and Waffles, 327
Rose Center for Earth and Space, 249
Rosemary's Baby, 250
Rosenthal, A. M., 154
Rosh Hashanah, 46
Ross, Harold, 373
Roth, Henry, 281
Roth, Philip, 383
Rotisserie League Baseball, 311
Rotterdam, the Netherlands, 230
Rough Riders, 248
Roundabout Theatre, 351
rounders, 306
routes, Hudson's, 38 (ill.)
Rowell, Charles, 101
Roxbury, 291
Roy, Subrata, 244
Royal Botanic Garden, 271
Royal Chelsea Hospital, 225
Royal Navy, 293, 300–301
Royalists, 65
Rubell, Steve, 351
Ruggles, Samuel, 220–21
Run-D.M.C., 354
Runyon, Damon, 146, 314
Ruppert Jr., Jacob, 332–33
Ruppert Sr., Jacob, 332
Russia, 41, 80, 108
Russian Roulette, 235
Russians as inhabitants, 13, 110, 212, 313, 335, 345
Ruth, Babe, 268–70, 269 (ill.), 309–10
Rutherfurd, John, 72
Rycken, Abraham, 302

S

Sackler Wing, 253
Sadie the Goat, 115
Sahadi Bros., 195
Sailors Snug Harbor, 295
Saint Martin, 44
Saint Nicholas, 394
sale of Manhattan, 42 (ill.), 42–43
Salem Witch Trials, 54
Salmagundi Papers, 74
SALT (Strategic Arms Limitation Treaty), 150
Samuel J. Battle Plaza, 127
Samuelsson, Marcus, 327
San Antonio River, 37–38

San Francisco, California, 172, 189, 207, 240, 273, 307, 337
San Francisco Earthquake, 273
San Francisco Mint, 89
San Juan Hill, 247–48, 358
San Marco Bell Tower, 119
Sanders, James, 146
Sanderson, Eric W., 191
Sandy Ground, 296
Sandy Hook, New Jersey, 51, 74, 150
Sanger, Margaret, 281
Santa Anna, 328
Santa Claus, 133, 367, 394–95
Sante, Luc, 333
Santo Domingo, Dominican Republic, 39
Sao Paulo, Brazil, 335
Sapokanikan, 214
Sartre, Jean-Paul, 73
Sasso, John, 322
Satanism, 250
Satellite City, 273
Saturday Night Live, 182, 359
Saudi Arabia, 261
Savage Skulls, 270
Sawyer, Tom, 277
Scarsdale, 122
scatter-site housing, 160
Schagen, Peter, 42
Schenectady, 163
Schieffelin, Eugene, 9
schools, primary, 19–20, 69–70, 111
Schrager, Ian, 351
Schultz, Dutch, 314
Scientific American, 100
Scorsese, Martin, 92, 170, 309, 324
Scotland, 50, 57, 201, 234
Scots as inhabitants, 59, 254, 261, 281
Scott, George C., 345
Scott, Sir Walter, 371
Scrabble, 394
Scrabble Corner, 394
Scranton, Pennsylvania, 381
Scully, Vincent, 228
Seagram Building, 242–43
seal, city, 3, 9, 42, 49
Seamen's Savings Bank, 88 (ill.)
Sears, Isaac, 56
Seaview Hospital, 391
secession from, Staten Island's threats of, 297
secession from the Union, possibility of, 93–94
Second Anglo-Dutch War, 47
Second Avenue
    bars and nightlife, 332
    British colonial era, 52
    food and dining, 326, 329
    Manhattan, 261
    other islands around the boroughs, 298

rebuilding and moving forward after 9/11, 188
the sixties to 9/11, 161–62
theater, 345
Second Battle of Bull Run, 94
Secretariat Building, 240
secrets of the Grand Central Terminal, 122
security cameras, 189
Sedgwick, Edie, 383
Seeger, Pete, 350
segregation
food and dining, 321
the Gilded Age, 129
independence of New York, 84–85
Manhattan, 213, 215, 258
Staten Island, 294
theater, 340
Segwick Avenue, 353
Seinfeld, 328
Selby Jr., Hubert, 285
Senate, New York, 187, 377
Senate, U.S., 134, 187, 200, 377
Seneca Chief, 75
Seneca Village, 245
Sephardic Judaism, 46
Serpico, Frank, 159, 159 (ill.)
Serpico: The Cop Who Defied the System (Maas), 159
Sesame Street, 358–59
Sesame Street [TV show], 116, 358
settlement houses, 110
settlers, earliest, 34 (ill.), 34–35
Seven Years' War, 54
Seventh Avenue
animals, 6
food and dining, 327
the Gilded Age, 120, 124
Manhattan, 225–27, 231–32, 234, 244, 259–60
Seventh Regiment, 88, 250
Seventh Regiment Armory. See Park Avenue Armory
Seventh Regiment Band, 269
Seward Park, 207
Sex, 340–41
Sex Pistols, 226, 351–52
Seymour, Horatio, 95
Shake Shack, 224
Shakespeare, William, 9, 246–47, 284, 345, 354, 390
Shakespeare in the Park, 345, 382
Shakur, Tupac, 353
Shaler, Gen. Alexander T., 19
Shanghai, China, 322, 394
sharks, 10
Sharks, the, 153
Sharpton, Al, 175
Shea, William, 308
Shea Stadium, 154, 174, 308, 310
Shearith Israel, 46, 225

Shepard, Sam, 226
She's Gotta Have It, 386
Shia Islam, 261
Shmira, the, 154
Shomrim, the, 154
shopping bags, best, 250
Shops at Columbus Circle, 236
Shorakapok, 265
Showtime at the Apollo, 259
Shubert Theater, 343
Shuffle Along, 374
Shun Lee Dynasty, 322
Shutterstock, 180
Sicily, Italy, 120
Sidecar, 335
Siege of Boston, 59
Siegel-Cooper Dry Goods, 222
Sierra Leone, 65
Silent Parade, 129
Silicon Alley, 180
Silicon Valley, 180
Silk Stocking District, 170, 250
Silk Stocking Regiment, 250
Simon, Neil, 167, 358
Simon, Paul, 183
Simpson Street, 270
Sinatra, Frank, 237, 309–10, 335
Sinclair, Upton, 84
Singer Building, 119, 128
Singer Sewing Machine Corporation, 119, 249
Sister Carrie (Dreiser), 321
Siwanoy Indians, 268
Six Point Craft Ales, 333
Sixth Avenue
animals, 6
film and TV, 356
independence of New York, 85
Manhattan, 209, 211, 214, 221–22, 225, 227, 232, 237–39, 241, 243
sixth borough of, 397–98
Sixth Ward, 78, 80
sixties to 9/11, the, 155–82
size of MTA, 29
size of the police department, 17
sizes of the boroughs, 2
skating, 205, 240–41, 244, 271, 279, 314
Skyscraper Museum, 195
skyscrapers, 108–9, 109 (ill.), 119, 128
slavery
and the Civil War, 91–97
British colonial era, 51–54
Brooklyn, 283
business and economy, 24
early history, 36
food and dining, 321
the Gilded Age, 126
independence of New York, 69

industrialization and immigration, 102
Manhattan, 201–2, 204–5, 209, 212–14
Queens, 288
quirky New York, 393–94
Revolutionary War, 63–64
Staten Island, 293–94, 296
theater, 339–40
writing, 365
The Slide, 333
Sloughter, Gov. Henry, 50
slums, 111
Smallpox Memorial Hospital, 298
Smalls, Biggie, 353, 353 (ill.)
Small's Paradise, 260
smell of, 395
Smith, Abigail Adams. See Adams, Abigail
Smith, Alfred "Al" E., 106, 134, 142, 269, 289, 333, 379–80
Smith, Arthur, 116
Smith, Patti, 218, 226, 352
Smith, William F., 148–49
Smithsonian, 11
Smithsonian Air & Space Museum, 233
Smithsonian Institution, 253
Snug Harbor, 295
soccer, 208, 315
Society of St. Tammany, 75
SoHo, 180, 206–11, 217, 336, 361, 382
Solanas, Valerie, 226
Soldiers' and Sailors' Arch, 277
Solomon R. Guggenheim Museum. See The Guggenheim
"Someone to Watch Over Me," 379
Son of Sam, 168
Sondheim, Stephen, 342
Sons of Liberty, 56–58
Sons of the Revolution, 330
The Sound of Music, 342
Sousa, John Philip, 269
South America, 8, 39
South Americans as inhabitants, 289
South Bronx, 169, 268, 270, 309
South Brooklyn, 277
South Carolina, 53, 106
South Ferry, 198
South of Houston Industrial Area. See SoHo
South Street, 379
South Street Seaport, 198–99
South Tower, 181, 197, 355
South William Street, 46
Southern Europe, 119, 133
Soviet Bear, 150
Soviet Union, 150, 166, 239
Spain, 22, 37, 100, 362
Spanish Armada, 59

439

Spanish as inhabitants, 256, 364
Spanish Harlem, 261
Spanish-American War, 115–16, 151, 367
speakeasies, origins of, 132
Spider-man, 375–76
Spielberg, Steven, 315
Spillane, Mickey, 173
The Spirit, 375
sports
    all about, 305–15
    Bronx, 268–69, 271
    Brooklyn, 279–80
    early history, 305
    Manhattan, 194, 205, 208, 214, 229–30, 240–41, 244, 260, 262
    notable New Yorkers, 383
    Queens, 286, 290
    quirky New York, 397
    the sixties to 9/11, 169
    World War II and the postwar era, 149
Spring Lake, 10
Spring Street, 230, 322, 352
Springfield, Illinois, 97
Springfield, Massachusetts, 311–12
Springsteen, Bruce, 155
Spruce Street, 319
Spungen, Nancy, 226
Spuyten Duyvil Creek, 1, 104, 264–65
Spy, 371
squirrels, 9
Sri Lankans as inhabitants, 297
St. Anthony's Day, 37
St. Bartholomew's Church, 122
St. Gennaro, 208
St. George, 240
St. George Waterfront, 296
St. John's College, 313
St. John's University Law School, 383
St. Joseph's Maronite Church, 195
St. Louis, Missouri, 308, 356, 393
St. Mark's Church-in-the-Bowery, 218
St. Mark's Evangelical Lutheran Church, 117
St. Mark's Place, 217, 361
St. Martin-in-the-Field, 199
St. Nicholas Avenue, 262
St. Nicholas Terrace, 72
St. Patrick's Cathedral
    Manhattan, 209, 241–42, 256
    other islands around the boroughs, 298
    Queens, 289
    the sixties to 9/11, 172
    slavery and the Civil War, 95
    World War II and the postwar era, 155
St. Patrick's Day, 324–25

St. Patrick's Day Parade, 202, 241
St. Paul's Chapel, 62, 101, 199, 199 (ill.)
St. Peter's Basilica, 195–96, 209, 227
St. Regis Hotel, 335
St. Vincent's Hospital, 396
Stalin, Joseph, 147
Stamp Act, 55–58
Stamp Act Congress, 56
Standard Oil, 241
Stanford University, 180
Stanislavski, Konstantin, 341
Stanley Cup, 314
Stapletons, Staten Island, 310
Starbucks, 326
Stark, Tony, 376
starlings, 9
Starry Night, 243
Staten Island
    all about, 291–97
    animals, 7, 9–10
    Bronx, 267
    Dutch colonial era, 36–38, 43, 45
    early history, 35–36
    ethnicity, 292
    food and dining, 328
    independence of New York, 74
    industrialization and immigration, 105, 110
    notable New Yorkers, 377–78
    population, 11–12, 292
    Queens, 286
    quirky New York, 391
    rebuilding and moving forward after 9/11, 186–88
    Revolutionary War, 59, 64
    seal, 3
    the sixties to 9/11, 182
    size, 2
    sports, 310
    the five boroughs, 1, 2 (ill.)
    transportation, 29
    weather, 4
Staten Island Ferry, 29, 193, 292
Statue of Liberty, 102–3, 103 (ill.), 127, 194, 202, 299, 355
statues, 6
Stay Puft Marshmallow Man, 355
Steamboat Willie, 243
steamboats, 70
Steeplechase Park, 284
Steichen, Edward, 223
Steiner Studios, 275
Steinway, William, 288
Steinway Hall, 288
Steinway Street, 288
Steinway Village, 288
Steinweg family, 288
Stewart, A. T., 221
Stieglitz, Alfred, 223

Stillwell, Leslie, 10
stock market crash. See Great Crash of 1929
Stockbridge Mohican Indians, 271
Stone Street, 198
Stonehenge, 397
Stonewall Inn, 156, 156 (ill.), 334, 334 (ill.)
Stonewall Uprising, 155–56, 172, 334
stop and frisk, 187
Stoppard, Tom, 346
storms, 4
Stowe, Harriet Beecher, 339
Strand Bookstore, 220
Strasberg, Lee, 341
Strategic Arms Limitation Treaty (SALT), 150
Straus family, 265
Stravinsky, Igor, 248
Strawberry Fields, 250
Streep, Meryl, 382
"A Street Arab," 111
Street Arabs, 111–12
Streetbird, 327
streets, grid of Manhattan's, 70, 71 (ill.), 72–74, 218
Strivers' Row, 260
Strong, George Templeton, 79, 200
Strong, William, 110–11
Stuart, James, 47 (ill.)
Studio 54, 310, 351
Studio Museum, 258
Stuyvesant, Peter
    animals, 5
    British colonial era, 48
    Dutch colonial era, 40, 44–47, 45 (ill.)
    independence of New York, 72
    Manhattan, 199, 204, 217–18
    police, 17
    the sixties to 9/11, 178
    trees, 4
Stuyvesant High School, 195
Stuyvesant Skating Pond, 205
Stuyvesant Street, 72, 218
Stuyvesant Town, 221
suburb, first, 274–75
"Suburb of Sodom," 284
The Subway, 362
Subway Series, 308
subways
    art, 361–62
    Bronx, 269
    Brooklyn, 280, 286
    ethnicity, 14
    film and TV, 358
    the Gilded Age, 116–19
    industrialization and immigration, 98, 100 (ill.), 100–101
    Manhattan, 197, 231, 241

other islands around the boroughs, 298, 301
quirky New York, 392, 396
rebuilding and moving forward
after 9/11, 182, 184, 186, 188–
89
the sixties to 9/11, 160–62, 169,
173, 175, 178, 181
Staten Island, 297
transportation, 29–32
World War II and the postwar
era, 149
writing, 370
Suez Canal, 102
Suffolk County, 303
suffrage, 75
Sugar Act, 56
Sugar Hill, 260
Suicide, 352
suicide, most popular spots for,
395–96
Sullivan, Tim "Big Feller," 125
Sullivan Law, 125, 128
Sullivan Place, 279
Sullivan Street, 140
Sullivan Street Playhouse, 347
Sultan of Swat, 269
Summer of Sam, 386
Sun Belt, 12
Sunday, Billy, 129
Sunday World, 366
Sunni Islam, 261
Sunset Park, 14, 60, 280
Sunshine Biscuit Company, 329
Super Bowl, 308, 310–11
Superbas, the, 307
Superfly, 356
superheroes, 375–76
Superman, 375–76
support under Dutch rule, 41–42
Supreme Court, New York State,
204
Surf Avenue, 284, 393
Sviata Vecheria, 329
"Swanee," 379
sweatshops, 98, 107, 114
Swedes as inhabitants, 45, 268
Swiss as inhabitants, 14
Sylvia's, 327
Symphony Space, 234
synagogue, oldest, 243–44
Syrians as inhabitants, 14, 195

T

Tactical Patrol Force, 156
Taggia, Martini di Arma di, 336
Taim, 325
Taino as inhabitants, 254
Taiwanese as inhabitants, 322
Tajikistanis as inhabitants, 14

Tales to Astonish (Ro), 376
Talking Heads, the, 352–53
Tammany Hall
the Gilded Age, 124–25, 127
Great Depression era, 139–41
independence of New York, 75–
77, 76 (ill.), 87
industrialization and immigra-
tion, 98–99, 108
notable New Yorkers, 379
the sixties to 9/11, 170
Tavern on the Green, 151
Taxi Driver, 356
taxis, 27–28
Tchaikovsky, Pyotr, 234
Ted Weiss Federal Building, 204
Teddy Boys, 81
Teflon Don, 176
Television, 352
Temple, Shirley, 342
Temple of Dendur, 253
Ten Days That Shook the World
(Reed), 213
Tenderloin, the, 101, 123, 228, 256
Tenement House Commission, 207
tennis, 314–15
Tenth Avenue, 225, 230, 233, 329
Tenth Avenue Railroad, 230
Terranova, Ciro "The Artichoke
King," 142
Tesla, Nikola, 238
Texas, 10, 12, 22, 113, 209, 310
Thai as inhabitants, 316
Thanksgiving, 66, 132
Thanksgiving Day Parade, 132–33,
133 (ill.)
Thaw, Harry, 122–23
theater, 55, 339–47
Theater District, 115, 231–32, 324
Theatre FranÁais, 346 (ill.)
Thing, the, 376
Third Avenue
bars and nightlife, 332, 335
Manhattan, 217–18, 220–21,
239, 244, 250, 254, 261
quirky New York, 390
the sixties to 9/11, 162
slavery and the Civil War, 95
Third Reich, 147
Third Street, 117
This Ain't No Holiday Inn (Lough),
225
This Side of Paradise (Fitzgerald),
145
Thomas, Dylan, 226, 389
Thomas, Samuel Bath, 317–18
Thompson, Kay, 244
Throgs Neck Bridge, 8
Thunderbolt, 285 (ill.)
Tibetans as inhabitants, 289
Tiffany, Louis Comfort, 46, 251
Tiffany's, 222, 250, 252

Tigers, Hamilton, 313
Tilden, Samuel, 336
Time Warner Center, 234, 236
"Time Warp," 357
Timely Comics, 376
Times Square
all about, 231–36
food and dining, 329
the Gilded Age, 116–18, 117
(ill.)
Great Depression era, 138
Manhattan, 231 (ill.)
the sixties to 9/11, 171
theater, 343
transportation, 31–32
Times Square Mural, 32
Tin Pan Alley, 134, 347, 349, 378
Tippins, Sherill, 225
Titanic, 343
TKTS, 347
Tobagoans as inhabitants, 13
Tocqueville, Alexis de, 316
Tombs, the, 205–6, 302
Tompkins Square Park, 118, 130,
157, 217
Tompkinsville, 297
tong wars, 114–15
The Tonight Show, 357–58
Tontine Coffee House, 68, 189
Tony Awards, 368
Tony's Di Napoli, 324
Tooker, George, 362
Toomer, Jean, 374
Topsy, 393 (ill.), 393–94
Tories, 59, 63–64
Toronto, Canada, 381
Toscanini, Arturo, 248
tourism, 26
Toussaint, Pierre, 209
Tower Building, 108–9, 109 (ill.)
Trader Joe's, 223
Trafalgar Square, 235
trains
animals, 5
bars and nightlife, 335
the Gilded Age, 118–22
industrialization and immigration, 97–98, 101, 115
Manhattan, 221, 230–31, 239,
256, 261
Queens, 289
quirky New York, 398
rebuilding and moving forward
after 9/11, 184, 186, 188
the sixties to 9/11, 160, 162,
169, 173
transportation, 29, 31–32
Transit Museum, 31
transportation
the Gilded Age, 118–19
in New York, 27–32
independence of New York, 70, 85

441

industrialization and immigration, 97–98, 100–101, 116
slavery and the Civil War, 91–92
trash as fame of, 110–11, 296, 395
Treaty of Paris, 64
Treaty of Westminster, 48
Tree of Hope, 342
trees, 4–5
Tremont, 271–72
Trenton, New Jersey, 67
Triangle Below Canal. See Tribeca
Triangle Shirtwaist Factory, 125
Triangle Shirtwaist Fire, 125 (ill.), 125–26, 379
A Tribe Called Quest, 354
Tribeca, 206–11, 210 (ill.)
Tribeca Film Festival, 211
Triborough Bridge, 143, 302
Trieste, Italy, 140
Trillin, Calvin, 323
Trinidadians as inhabitants, 13
Trinity Cemetery, 201
Trinity Church, 45, 62, 109, 199–201, 204, 241
Trolley Dodgers, the, 307
Trotsky, Leon, 354
Troy, 74
Truman, Harry, 150
Trump, Donald, 134, 154, 174, 244, 370, 385 (ill.), 385–86
Trump, Fred, 134, 153, 385
Trump International Hotel and Tower, 236
Trump Village, 153
Tschirky, Oscar, 320
Tso, General, 323
Tuckahoe, 121
Tunnel, 180
Turks as inhabitants, 45
Turner, Ike, 349
Turtle, 61–62, 62 (ill.)
Turtle Bay, 239–40, 272
Turtle Bay Gardens, 239
TV and film, 354–59
Twain, Mark, 238
Tweed, William M. "Boss," 98 (ill.), 98–101, 105–6, 204
Tweed Courthouse, 204
Tweed Ring, 99–100, 378
Twelve Men, 43–44
Twin Towers, 162–63, 163 (ill.), 177, 181 (ill.), 181–83, 196–97
Tye, Col., 64
Typhoid Mary, 123 (ill.), 123–24
Tyson, Neil deGrasse, 397

U

U-123, 147–48
Uber, 28
U-Boats, 147–48

Ukrainian Village, 218
Ukrainians as inhabitants, 110, 329
Uncle Tom's Cabin [play], 339–40
Uncle Tom's Cabin (Stowe), 339
Underground Railroad, 91–92
UNIA (Universal Negro Improvement Association), 129
The Unicorn Tapestries, 264
Union, the, 93–96, 202, 219, 258, 366
Union Army, 258, 277, 295–96, 366
Union Fields, 307
Union Jack, 65–66
Union Place, 219
Union Square, 20, 31, 94, 195, 215, 218–24, 219 (ill.)
Union Square Café, 220
Union Square West, 220
Unisphere, 290 (ill.), 291
United Airlines, 180–81
United Kingdom, 26
United Nations
    Manhattan, 239–42
    notable New Yorkers, 380, 383
    other islands around the boroughs, 297–98
    Queens, 287, 291
    sports, 306
    World War II and the postwar era, 150, 155
United Sherpa Association, 289
Universal Negro Improvement Association (UNIA), 129
University of Cambridge, 383
University of Chicago, 255
University of Michigan, 381
Upper Bay, 37, 280
Upper East Side
    all about, 250–55
    animals, 7, 9
    the Gilded Age, 118
    Manhattan, 239, 261
    the sixties to 9/11, 162, 170
    World War II and the postwar era, 147
Upper Manhattan, 261–65
Upper West Side, 7, 21, 157, 247–50
uprisings, slave, 53
U.S. Open, 290, 314–15
USA Today, 311
USS *Arizona*, 275
USS *Maine*, 235, 275
USS *Missouri*, 275
Uzbekistanis as inhabitants, 14

V

Valentine's Day, 351, 395
Van Cortlandt Park, 5, 271
van der Rohe, Ludwig Mies, 243
van Gogh, Vincent, 243, 360, 362–63
Van Sant, Charles, 10

Van Schaick, William, 117–18
Van Winkle, Rip, 277
Vanderbilt, Cornelius, 105, 119–21, 124, 228, 244, 377–78
Vanderbilt family, 250
Vanderbilt Gate, 247
Vanderbilt Mansion, 247
Vandross, Luther, 259
Vanity Fair, 373
Varckens Eylandt, 297–98
Varick, Richard, 200
Vatican, the, 78, 241, 380
Vaudeville, 117
Vaughan, Sarah, 259
Vaux, Calvert, 86–87, 219, 249, 271, 277–79
Velvet Underground, 361
Venice, Italy, 7, 119
Verdi Square, 248
Vermont, 364
Verplanck, Gulian, 77
Verrazano, Giovanni di, 36–37
Verrazano Narrows Bridge, 8, 38, 166, 186, 292, 294
Veselka, 329
Vesey Street, 162, 211
Vespers, 242
Vicious, Sid, 226
Victoria Embankment, 247
Victorian, 344
Victorian Gothic, 249
Viele, Egbert, 246
Vienna, Austria, 89
Vienna Model Bakery, 321
Vietnam, 158, 174
Vietnam War, 158, 233, 359
Village, the. See Greenwich Village
Village Independent Democrats, 170
Village Voice, 361, 370–71
Vilna, Lithuania, 341
Vinegar Hill, 79
Virgil, 197
Virgil Repository, 197
Virginia, 64, 67, 293, 342, 393
"A Visit from St. Nicholas," 225, 395
Vitagraph, 354
Vlacke Bos, 274
Voidoids, the, 352
Vonnegut, Kurt, 239
Voodoo Macbeth, 341

W

Wagner, Robert, 228, 308
Waldorf Astoria, 155, 237–38, 242, 244, 320
Walker, James "Jimmy," 131, 134–35, 135 (ill.), 139, 341
Walker, Polly, 131
A Walker in the City (Kazin), 281
walking, danger of, 396–97

walking riot, 101
Wall Street
    British colonial era, 48
    Brooklyn, 278
    business and economy, 21, 23
    Dutch colonial era, 41, 44
    the Gilded Age, 116
    independence of New York, 68,
        82, 89
    Manhattan, 194, 196, 198–203,
        211, 252
    notable New Yorkers, 386
    quirky New York, 391
    rebuilding and moving forward
        after 9/11, 184–85, 189
    the sixties to 9/11, 158, 171–72
    slavery and the Civil War, 96
    World War II and the postwar
        era, 149
    writing, 369
Wall Street [movie], 171
Wall Street Journal, 158, 369
Wallabout Bay, 40, 274–76
Wallace, Mike, 39
Waller, Fats, 347
Walloon Bay, 274
Walloons as inhabitants, 11, 40
Wang, T. T., 322
War of 1812, 23, 74, 105, 215, 300–
    301
War Years, FDNY, 158
Warburg, Felix, 253
Ward's Island, 302
warfare, role of in business, 22–23
Warhol, Andy, 220, 225–26, 243,
    351, 360–61, 361 (ill.), 384
Waring, George, 111
Warner Bros., 354
Warren Street, 100
The Warriors, 165, 285
wars, tong, 114–15
Washington, D.C.
    business and economy, 23
    film and TV, 357
    independence of New York, 67, 74
    Manhattan, 233, 258
    other islands around the bor-
        oughs, 301
    the sixties to 9/11, 166
    sports, 312
    storms, 4
    World War II and the postwar
        era, 147
Washington, George
    bars and nightlife, 330
    industrialization and immigra-
        tion, 101
    Manhattan, 199–201, 261–62
    notable New Yorkers, 377
    other islands around the bor-
        oughs, 300
    quirky New York, 391

Revolutionary War, 58–66
Staten Island, 293–94
Washington 12 Streeters, 312
Washington Heights, 39, 161, 261–
    63, 396
Washington Irving House, 221
Washington Market, 92, 211, 216
Washington Military Parade
    Ground, 214
Washington Park, 276
Washington Place, 214
Washington Post, 369
Washington Square, 214, 221, 223,
    372
Washington Square Arch, 214
Washington Square (James), 214,
    372
Washington Square Park, 125, 212,
    214–15, 215 (ill.), 295, 350
Washington Street, 195, 211
Water Street, 8, 68, 198, 202, 331
water supply, 82–84, 159
Waverly Place, 214, 325
Waverly Street, 213
Waverly Theater, 356–57
WCTU (Women's Christian Temper-
    ance Union), 130–31
weather, 3–4
Webster's Dictionary, 247
Weckquaesgeek Indians, 43, 268
Weehawken, New Jersey, 69
Weeks, James, 283
Weeksville, 283, 393
Weill, Kurt, 341
Weimar, 351
Welfare Island, 297–98
Welles, Orson, 341
Wells Supper Club, 327
West, Kanye, 387
West, Mae, 115, 297, 340–41, 341 (ill.)
West 3rd Street, 350, 356
West 4th Street, 214
West 4th Street Courts, 214, 312
West 8th Street, 216
West 12th Street, 396
West 13th Street, 173
West 20th Street, 86
West 21st Street, 225
West 31st Street, 321
West 37th Street, 380
West 44th Street, 342
West 54th Street, 351
West 57th Street, 235
West 58th Street, 236
West 125th Street, 258
West Battery, 193
West Battery Fort, 192
West Coast, 308, 353–54
West Egg, 291
West Indian Carnival, 283
West Indians as inhabitants, 68,
    289, 330

West Indies, 24, 46, 51, 293, 312
West Orange, New Jersey, 354
West Side, 233, 246
West Side Cowboys, 230
West Side Story, 152–53, 248, 342
West Side Tennis Club, 314, 314
    (ill.)
West Street, 162, 196
West Village, 213, 325
West Washington Market, 215–16
Westchester County, 63, 167, 262,
    268
Western Hemisphere, 39, 53, 94,
    155, 235, 271
Westies, 173–74, 233, 236
Westinghouse, George, 238, 393–94
Westminster Kennel Club, 229
Wheat Field with Cypresses, 362–63
Wheatley, William, 340
Whig Party, 57, 77–78, 92, 364–65
Whiskey War, 292
White, E. B., 239
White, Stanford, 122–23, 229, 251,
    260, 276
White Horse Tavern, 389
White Russia, 335
White Street, 205
Whitehall Slip, 62
Whitehall Street, 48, 198, 332
Whitfield, Louise, 234
Whitman, Walt, 79, 96, 105, 191,
    276, 284
Whitney, Gertrude Vanderbilt, 216
Whitney Biennial, 217
Whitney Museum of American Art,
    216–17, 243, 360, 362
Wild Style, 354
Wild West, 172
Wilde, Oscar, 345
Wilder, Billy, 335
Wilgus, William, 120–21
Wilkes, John, 57
Will and Grace, 222
"Will You Love Me in December (As
    You Do in May)?" 134
Willett, Mayor Thomas, 48
William of Orange, 49
William Street, 46, 316
Williams, Alexander "Clubber," 101
Williams, Tennessee, 341, 381
Williamsburg, Virginia, 293
Williamsburg [neighborhood in
    Brooklyn]
    animals, 7
    bars and nightlife, 332–33
    Brooklyn, 274–75
    business and economy, 24
    early history, 35
    food and dining, 326
    the Gilded Age, 117
    notable New Yorkers, 382
    sports, 307

Williamsburg Bridge, 117, 326
Williamsburg Savings Bank, 308
Williamson, John, 396
Willowbrook State School, 391
Willowtown, 392
Wilmington, Delaware, 40
Wilson, Woodrow, 127, 129
Winchell, Walter, 365
windmills, 3, 41–42, 48–49
Winfrey, Oprah, 182
WINS, 349
Winter Garden, 195
Wisconsin, 252, 258, 310, 341
Wisconsin Glacial Stage, 1
Wisconsin Ice Sheet, 33
Wiseguy (Pileggi), 170
Witness Protection Program, 169
Wizards, Washington, 312
WNYC, 141, 147
Wolfe, Tom, 121, 157
wolves, 5
Woman in Gold, 362
Women's Christian Temperance
  Union (WCTU), 130–31
Women's Prison, 341
Wonder, Stevie, 155, 259
Wonder Wheel, 147
Wonder Woman, 376
Wonderful Town, 214
Wood, Fernando, 87–89, 93, 94
  (ill.), 95, 202, 245
Woodhaven, 331
Woodlawn Cemetery, 5, 271
Woolcott, Alexander, 373
Woolworth, F. W., 203–4
Woolworth Building, 119, 194, 202–
  3
Working Stiff (Melinek), 396
Works Progress Administration
  (WPA), 138, 141, 143, 298, 341
World Exposition, 284
World Financial Center, 162, 195
World Professional Basketball Tour-
  nament, 313
World Series, 169, 308–9
World Trade Center

film and TV, 355
the Gilded Age, 119
Manhattan, 194–98, 196 (ill.),
  210, 238
rebuilding and moving forward
  after 9/11, 182–83
the sixties to 9/11, 158, 162–64,
  177, 181 (ill.)
Staten Island, 296
World Trade Center Transportation
  Hub, 197
World War I, 7, 126–27, 130, 133,
  137, 146, 195
World War II
  and the postwar era, 146–55
  animals, 7
  Brooklyn, 275, 281–83
  business and economy, 25
  the Gilded Age, 119, 128, 134
  Manhattan, 211, 237, 239, 256,
    264
  notable New Yorkers, 382
  population, 12
  Queens, 290–91
  the sixties to 9/11, 160
  Staten Island, 295
World's Fair
  film and TV, 357
  independence of New York, 85
    (ill.), 85–86
  Queens, 290–91
  quirky New York, 393
  sports, 308, 315
  World War II and the postwar
    era, 147
Worth Street, 207
WPA (Works Progress Administra-
  tion), 138, 141, 143, 298, 341
WrestleMania, 228
Wright, Frank Lloyd, 236, 244, 252–
  53
Wrigley Field, 279
A Wrinkle in Time (L'Engle), 256
writing, 363–76
Wyckoff, Pieter Claesen, 276

X, Y, Z

X-Men, 376
Yale Club, 131
Yale University, 54, 62–63, 143
Yamasaki, Minoru, 163
Yancey Street, 376
Yankee Clipper. See Long Island Ex-
  press
Yankee Stadium
  Bronx, 267, 269, 269 (ill.)
  the sixties to 9/11, 169
  sports, 307, 309 (ill.), 309–10, 315
  World War II and the postwar
    era, 155
Yankees, New York, 169, 268–69,
  308–10, 333
"Year of the Blood," 44
Yellow Cab Company, 27
yellow cabs, 27
Yellow Kid, 366
Yemenis as inhabitants, 26
Yiddish Art Theatre, 345
Yiddish Broadway, 345
The Yiddish King Lear, 341
Yiddish Walk of Fame, 345
Yippies, 20
Yonah Schimmel, 325
Yonkers, 159, 167, 397
York, Duke of, 47, 287
Yorkshire, England, 373
Yorkville, 118, 147, 195, 332
Young Lords, 157–58
Your Show of Shows, 358
Yousef, Ramzi, 177
Zenger, John Peter, 363–64
zero-tolerance policy, 178–79
Zimmerman, Bob. See Dylan, Bob
Zionism, 107
Zoning Resolution of 1916, 128
zoo, largest, 270
Zuccotti Park, 185